The Backbone of History

For the same reasons that explorers of the early twentieth century strove to reach the poles and the highest peaks, and their modern counterparts journey to outer space or deep into the oceans, most people want to visualize the contours of the human experience – the peaks of adaptive success that led to human growth, expansion, and flowering of civilization, and the valleys of despair in which human presence ebbed and retreated. *The Backbone of History* defines the emerging field of macrobioarchaeology by gathering skeletal evidence on seven basic indicators of health to assess chronic conditions that affected individuals who lived in the Western Hemisphere from 5000 BC to the late nineteenth century. Signs of biological stress in childhood and of degeneration in joints and in teeth increased in the several millennia before the arrival of Columbus as populations moved into less healthy ecological environments. Thus pre-Columbian Native Americans were among both the healthiest and the least healthy groups to live in the Western Hemisphere before the twentieth century.

Richard H. Steckel is Professor of Economics and Anthropology at Ohio State University. His most recent publications include *Health and Welfare during Industrializaion,* which he coedited with Roderick Floud, and *A Population History of the United States,* coedited with Michael Haines.

Jerome C. Rose is Professor of Anthropology at the University of Arkansas. He has conducted bioarchaeological excavations in Illinois, Arkansas, Texas, Egypt, and Jordan.

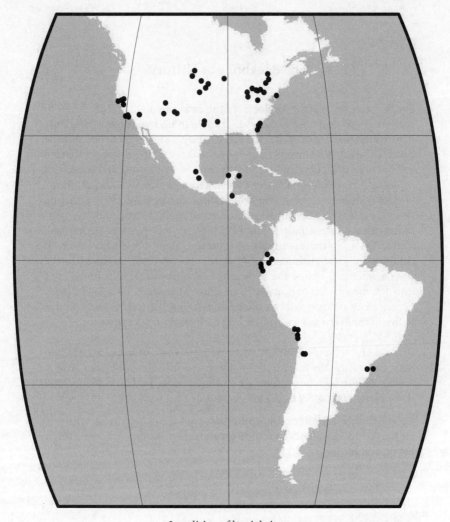

Localities of burial sites.

The Backbone of History

Health and Nutrition in the Western Hemisphere

Edited by

RICHARD H. STECKEL

Ohio State University

JEROME C. ROSE

University of Arkansas

CAMBRIDGE UNIVERSITY PRESS
Cambridge, New York, Melbourne, Madrid, Cape Town, Singapore, São Paulo

Cambridge University Press
40 West 20th Street, New York, NY 10011-4211, USA

www.cambridge.org
Information on this title: www.cambridge.org/9780521801676

First published 2002
Reprinted 2003
First paperback edition 2005

Printed in the United States of America

A catalog record for this book is available from the British Library.

Library of Congress Cataloging in Publication Data
Steckel, Richard H. (Richard Hall), 1944–
The backbone of history : health and nutrition in the Western Hemisphere / Richard H.
Steckel, Jerome C. Rose.
p. cm.
Revised papers from a second conference sponsored by the National Science
Foundation (SBR-9423435) and held March 7–10, 1996 at Ohio State University, Columbus.
Includes bibliographical references and index.
ISBN 0-521-80167-2 (hardback)
1. Indians – Food – History – Congresses. 2. Indians – Health and
hygiene – History – Congresses. 3. European Americans – Health and hygiene –
History – Congresses. 4. African Americans – Health and hygiene – History – Congresses.
5. Human remains (Archaeology) – America – Congresses.
6. America – Antiquities – Congresses. I. Rose, Jerome Carl. II. Title.
E59.F63 S74 2002
614.4'27 – dc21 2001037965

ISBN-13 978-0-521-80167-6 hardback
ISBN-10 0-521-80167-2 hardback

ISBN-13 978-0-521-61744-4 paperback
ISBN-10 0-521-61744-8 paperback

To Barbara

Contents

Preface

From a practical point of view, this project stems from the 1988 Economic History Association meetings held in Detroit, for which Winifred Rothenberg organized a session on the Neolithic Revolution featuring papers by anthropologists George Armelagos, Alan Goodman, Debra Martin, and Jerome Rose. Familiar with the research on stature by economic historians, Jerome had contacted Richard Steckel prior to the meetings to arrange for discussion of common interests in the health and nutrition of the black population. Over coffee, they agreed that the fields of economic history and physical anthropology had much to learn from each other, but they also lamented the impediments to communication. Although using data of interest to historians, physical anthropology journals published rather technical articles, which often focused on skeletons from narrow geographic sites of excavation and which assumed considerable training in human biology. Ordinary historians could not read, much less contribute to, this vehicle of publication. Similarly, physical anthropologists were largely untrained in issues and methods of interest to historians and were unfamiliar with the conventions of publication in that field.

Nevertheless, Steckel and Rose sensed that an important research opportunity was available. The quincentennial of 1492 was just around the corner, which would help focus research interests in both fields. The issue was how to bring the groups together for interdisciplinary research. They organized a small planning conference, funded by Ohio State University and by the Wenner-Gren Foundation, at Ohio State University in the fall of 1990. The historians and physical anthropologists who came all agreed that a truly comparative project would require: (1) introductory training of historians in methods of physical anthropology, focusing on the meaning of skeletal lesions; (2) pooling of skeletal data from numerous physical anthropologists to obtain sample sizes of sufficient analytical interest; (3) a common data-reporting format, because while working for an entire career on, at most, a score of skeletal collections, physical anthropologists often devised their own, sometimes idiosyncratic reporting schemes, which hindered true comparability of results across time, space, and ethnic groups; (4) a methodology for integrating information and assessing health using skeletal data; (5) interdisciplinary research teams, each headed by an historian and a physical anthropologist, that would reinterpret the prehistory/history of a particular region, time period, and ethnic group based on the new skeletal database (and other relevant sources); (6) a publication vehicle, such as a conference volume, which defined and illustrated concepts in ways that made results accessible to a larger audience.

This approach to studying the past coalesced in the form of grant proposals by Steckel, Rose, and Paul Sciulli. The National Science Foundation (SBR-9223781) and Ohio State University (through the L. Edwin Smart Lecture Series in Economics, the College of Social and Behavioral Sciences, and the Anthropology Department) together sponsored a much larger second meeting of nearly 40 participants at Columbus, Ohio, in September of 1993. The conference featured training for historians in methods of physical anthropology; a session devoted to a common data-reporting format; a session on methodology in interpreting skeletal data; organization of research teams; and time devoted to administrative matters. The grants also paid for assistance in coding data in the format devised at the conference.

After the assembling and cleaning of the data sent to Ohio State University by 16 physical anthropologists and additional co-workers, the combined database of 12,520 individuals was ready for analysis in the late summer of 1995. This development was an essential prelude to the second major conference sponsored by the National Science Foundation (SBR-9423435) and held March 7–10, 1996, in Columbus, Ohio. This gathering featured presentation and discussion of papers on topics as diverse as nineteenth-century poorhouse populations of the Northeast and the transition to settled agriculture in the Mississippi Valley. The skeletal materials underlying these papers provide not only age at death and stature, but also numerous aspects of chronic conditions such as arthritis, dental health, and infections. Moreover, skeletal evidence is widely available for "historic" periods from cemetery excavations, which enables scholars to compare and contrast health as seen through skeletons with data from written sources. Pooling the evidence collected in numerous local studies allowed investigators to compare skeletal health not only within but also across widely disparate populations. This volume consists of the revised papers from the second conference.

We are indebted to numerous scholars for their advice and encouragement. From the project's early stages, George Armelagos, Jane Buikstra, Philip Curtin, Herbert Klein, Kenneth Kiple, and William Pollitzer made numerous valuable suggestions. Lois Carr, David Feeny, Anne Grauer, Kenneth Kiple, George Milner, Susan Pfeiffer, Mary Lucas Powell, William McNeill, Larry Neal, Cecilia Andrea Rabell, Carole Shammas, Daniel Scott Smith, Alan Swedlund, and Dennis Van Gerven ably served as discussants or session chairs at the conferences, or in other ways contributed their thoughts on aspects of the project. Nancy Tatarek and Christopher Barrett provided valuable research assistance. Several conference presentations helped sharpen ideas and refine the analysis, including those at the National Bureau of Economic Research, the Economic History Association meetings, the Social Science History Association meetings, the meetings of the American Association of Physical Anthropologists, and the Twelfth Congress of the International Economic History

Association. Seminars at numerous universities were also quite helpful in developing thoughts presented in the book, including those at Harvard University, University of Michigan, University of Kansas, University of Arkansas, University of Illinois, Indiana University, the Stanford-Berkeley Economic History workshop, Ohio State University, University of Colorado, University of Toledo, Colby College, and the University of Munich Preconference for the Twelfth Congress of the International Economic History Association.

Richard H. Steckel and Jerome C. Rose

Contributors

George J. Armelagos
Anthropology Department
Emory University
Decatur, GA 30322

Gerry Boyce
173 Bridge Street
Belleville, Ontario
Canada K8N 1N3

Peter J. Brown
Anthropology Department
Emory University
Decatur, GA 30322

Cindy Condon
12264 SW 105th Lane
Miami, FL 33186

Keith Condon
12264 SW 105th Lane
Miami, FL 33186

Alfred W. Crosby
67 North Centre Street
Nantucket Island, MA 02554

Philip D. Curtin
42 Windermere Way
Kennett Square, PA 10348

James M. Davidson
Department of Anthropology
University of Texas at Austin
Austin, TX 78712

Andres Del Angel
Instituto de Investigaciones Antropológicas
Universidad
Nacional Autonóma de México, Circuito Interior
México, D. F., México

Alan H. Goodman
Social Sciences
Hamsphire College
Amherst, MA 01002

Mark C. Griffin
Anthropology Department
San Francisco State University
San Francisco, CA 94132

Myron P. Gutmann
ICPSR
Institute for Social Research
University of Michigan
Ann Arbor, MI 48106

Michael R. Haines
Economics Department
Colgate University
Hamilton, NY 13346

Ann Herring
Department of Anthropology
McMaster University
Hamilton, Ontario
Canada L8S 4L9

Rosanne L. Higgins
Health Sciences Department
Cleveland State University
Cleveland, OH 44115

Rob Hoppa
Department of Anthropology
University of Manitoba
Winnipeg, Manitoba
Canada R3T 2N

Dale L. Hutchinson
Anthropology Department
East Carolina University
Greenville, NC 27858

S. Ryan Johansson
Cambridge Group for the History of Population and Social Structure
27 Trumpington Street
Cambridge CB2 1QA
United Kingdom

Susan Klepp
History Department
Temple University
Philadelphia, PA 19122

Clark Spencer Larsen
Anthropology Department
Ohio State University
Columbus, OH 43210

Lourdes Marquez Morfin
Escuela Nacional de Antropología e Historía, México
Périferico Sur y Zapote s/n. Col. Isidro Fabela
14030 México, D. F., México

Debra L. Martin
Social Sciences
Hampshire College
Amherst, MA 01002

Robert McCaa
History Department
University of Minnesota
Minneapolis, MN 55455

Walter Alves Neves
Laboratório de Estudos Evolutivos Humanos
Departamento de Biologia
Instituto de Biociências
Universidade de São Paulo
São Paulo, Brazil

Linda A. Newson
Geography Department
King's College London
Strand
London WC2R 2LS
United Kingdom

James Oberly
History Department
University of Wisconsin
Eau Claire, WI 54701

Douglas Owsley
Anthropology Department
National Museum of Natural History
Smithsonian Institution
Washington, DC 20560

Ted A. Rathbun
Anthropology Department
University of South Carolina
Columbia, SC 29208

Daniel T. Reff
Division of Comparative Studies
Ohio State University
Columbus, OH 43210

Jerome C. Rose
Anthropology Department
University of Arkansas
Fayetteville, AK 72701

Christopher B. Ruff
Department of Cell Biology and Anatomy
Johns Hopkins University Medical School
725 North Wolfe Street
Baltimore, MD 21205

Katherine F. Russell
Department of Biology
University of Massachusetts, Dartmouth
Dartmouth, MA 24740

Lars G. Sandberg
Economics Department
Ohio State University
Columbus, OH 43210

Shelley R. Saunders
Anthropology Department
McMaster University
Hamilton, Ontario
Canada L8S 4L9

Larry Sawchuk
Department of Anthropology
Scarborough College
University of Toronto
Scarborough, Ontario
Canada M1C 1A4

Margaret J. Schoeninger
Anthropology Department
University of California
San Diego, CA 92093

Paul W. Sciulli
Anthropology Department
Ohio State University
Columbus, OH 43210

Leslie E. Sering
Museum of Anthropology
University of Michigan
Ann Arbor, MI 48109

Scott W. Simpson
Department of Anatomy
Case Western Reserve University
Cleveland, OH 44106

Joyce E. Sirianni
Anthropology Department
University of Buffalo
Buffalo, NY 14261

Paul S. Sledzik
National Museum of Health and Medicine
Armed Forces Institute of Pathology
Washington, DC 20306

Vernon Smith
Interdisciplinary Center for Economic Science
George Mason University
Fairfax, VA 22030

Richard H. Steckel
Economics & Anthropology Departments
Ohio State University
Columbus, OH 43210

Ann L. W. Stodder
Department of Anthropology
The Field Museum
1400 S. Lake Shore Drive
Chicago, IL 60605

Rebecca Storey
Anthropology Department
University of Houston
Houston, TX 77204

Jeffry L. Takács
Anthropology Department
University of North Carolina
Chapel Hill, NC 27599

Mark F. Teaford
Department of Cell Biology and Anatomy
Johns Hopkins University Medical School
Baltimore, MD 21205

Russell Thornton
Anthropology Department
University of California, Los Angeles
Los Angeles CA 90095

Douglas H. Ubelaker
Anthropology Department
National Museum of Natural History
Smithsonian Institution
Washington, DC 20560

Phillip L. Walker
Anthropology Department
University of California, Santa Barbara
Santa Barbara, CA 93106

Lorena Walsh
Colonial Williamsburg Foundation
Williamsburg, VA 23187

Verônica Wesolowski
Laboratório de Estudos Evolutivos Humanos
Departamento de Biologia
Instituto de Biociências
Universidade de São Paulo
São Paulo, Brazil

PART I

CHAPTER ONE

Introduction

Richard H. Steckel and Jerome C. Rose

Human biologists, historians, and other social scientists have expressed enduring interest in the evolution of human health over the past several millennia. The search for knowledge is propelled in part by intellectual curiosity. For the same reasons that explorers of the early twentieth century strove to reach the poles and the highest peaks, and their modern counterparts journey to outer space or deep into the oceans, most humans are inquisitive about their past. They want to understand how they evolved and how they shaped and adapted to their environments. They want to visualize or imagine the contours of the human experience – the peaks of adaptive success that led to human growth, expansion, and flowering of civilization, and the valleys of despair in which human presence ebbed and retreated.

But more practical considerations also lead the quest for knowledge. Not only a basic ingredient in the quality of life, health is intertwined with demographic, social, economic, and political change and with the outcomes of wars and other conflicts. Length of life and other aspects of health affect work capacity and the incentives to invest in skills that contribute to economic growth. Basic indicators of the standard of living, such as the human development index proposed by the United Nations, have a substantial health component (UNDP, 1990). Historians and political scientists have identified inequality, not only in income or wealth, but also in the form of disparities in health and nutrition, as a driving force in social, political, and economic change. Thus, health has played a central role in human history, both as an agent of change and as an outcome measure indicating the quality of life. Skeletal measures of health, which are the central focus of this book, furnish the best and, in many cases, the only picture available of human health over the millennia.

Study of skeletal remains for insights into health in the past creates valuable long-term perspective on several modern social problems. Virtually all researchers are aware, at some level, of the significant processes of evolution that gave rise to modern societies over the past several millennia. They understand that many modern problems have roots reaching very deep into the human past, and that current conditions were often created by complex interdependent processes that unfolded over very long periods of time. In evaluating the results of their research, most social and medical scientists would like to have access to very long-term historical studies that would, for example, place in perspective the prevalence of trauma and violence, urbanization and health, child health, aging and health, and biological inequality.

Research on prehistoric and historic skeletons will also contribute to understanding the evolution of modern medical problems. Numerous modern diseases evolved with humans adapting to humans living in proximity to one another and to animals in a wide variety of ecological environments. Recent advances in the extraction of DNA from pathogens found on skeletons now make it possible to study the coevolution of humans with many diseases. Important first steps in the research agenda are to describe the evolution of human health and to understand its change in response to varying ecological environments.

Despite widespread interest and the general importance of health to human change over the past several thousand years, relatively little is known about the subject. Raw data on population size by age and on deaths by age are virtually unavailable prior to the nineteenth century, and thus, investigators cannot tabulate traditional measures of health, such as life expectancy at birth. Average height, a measure of health long known to human biologists and now familiar to some social scientists, is available in quantity from military muster rolls and other sources as far back as the eighteenth century, but height data are very sparse for earlier eras (Steckel, 1995). Thus, the story of very long-term trends in health cannot be told with traditional evidence, or even with newly developed sources of information, such as average height.

In the 1980s, the fields of history, economics, and physical anthropology began to develop some common interests and methodologies. Since the mid-1970s, economic historians have been applying average human stature, which measures a population's history of net nutrition, to issues in slavery, mortality, inequality, and health during industrialization (Steckel, 1998). They have used a measure familiar to physical anthropologists, but applied it to a broad range of well-established historical problems.

Similarly, by the early 1980s, physical anthropologists were mounting substantial efforts to study long-term trends (in health), the traditional domain of historians. *Paleopathology at the Origins of Agriculture*, edited by Mark Cohen and George Armelagos, was the first significant publication of this type. Contributors to the book assembled skeletal evidence of disease patterns that compared the health of hunter-gatherer societies with that of settled agriculturalists. This transition has been long celebrated by social scientists as a major advance in civilization, but to the surprise of those outside physical anthropology, the book reported that health deteriorated during the changeover.

This book brings together 18 essays that study long-term trends in health in the Western Hemisphere using evidence of chronic disease or biological stress measurable from skeletal remains. Basic information on the geographic, ethnic, and temporal distribution of the database for the project is listed in Table 1.1. Nearly 80 percent of the 12,520 individuals were Native Americans, with the remainder almost evenly split between Euro-Americans and African-Americans. About two-thirds of the

Table 1.1: Distribution of Skeletons in the Database

| | Native American | | | | |
Period	North America	Middle America	South America	Euro-American	African-American
1750+	627	0	0	1201	1380
1500–1749	2580	0	39	113	0
1000–1499	888	236	1095	0	0
1 AD–999	1642	594	382	0	0
1000 BC–AD 0	250	0	247	0	0
Before 1000 BC	485	343	418	0	0
TOTAL	6472	1173	2181	1314	1380

Grand total = 12,520.

Native Americans resided in what is now the United States (noted as North America in the table and in parts of the text), as opposed to Middle America (11.9 percent) or South America (22.2 percent). Slightly more than one-half (52.6 percent) lived in the Western Hemisphere prior to the arrival of Columbus, and nearly 14 percent lived prior to the birth of Christ (ages of individual sites are reported in years BP, that is, before present, taken as 1950).

Developed in recent decades by physical anthropologists, these data are unfamiliar to most social scientists, but they are likely to be the best single source available to scholars for measuring and analyzing very long-term trends in health. Therefore, the first section of the book formulates the methodology, and remaining sections examine applications to Native Americans, Euro-Americans, and African-American populations in North America, Mesoamerica, and South America.

The essays are the culmination of over a decade of intense interdisciplinary activity inspired by these two movements – the acceptance and use by economists and historians of measures traditional in human biology and physical anthropology (especially average height), and the study of long-term trends in health by physical anthropologists. Our efforts depart from and contribute to these movements, and draw attention to the advantages of collaboration. Historians, economists, and other social scientists gain by acquiring measures of health available to study long-term trends and differences in health. Similarly, physical anthropologists acquire a fresh reservoir of research questions and methodologies that are found beyond their traditional, localized spheres of interest. It is our hope that all groups go forward in this collaboration with renewed energy and purpose.

The essays take Cohen and Armelagos as their starting point, but go beyond their book in several important respects. First, the data assembled in *Paleopathology at the Origins of Agriculture* were not truly comparable because contributors utilized varying coding schemes for individual records. Researchers included the frequency of common variables, such as degenerative joint disease, skeletal infections, and linear enamel hypoplasias, but the specific measures were not reported using the same scale, which complicated comparisons. The essays herein utilize a common data-reporting format. Second, the size and diversity in our data resources by region, time period, and ethnic group exceed that studied in Cohen and Armelagos. We assemble over 12,500 observations on individuals who lived in the Western Hemisphere from over 4000 BC to the early 1900s, which is by far the largest comparable data set of this type ever created. Third, this project explicitly and extensively incorporates interdisciplinary perspectives. We do not claim this is necessarily desirable in itself, but the book is innovative in its collaborative strategy of using physical anthropologists, historians, and economists, who jointly headed most research teams producing essays. This approach broadens the range of questions typically asked of skeletal data to include widespread comparative study and brings new methodologies to their analysis. Prominent among the latter are the concept of a health index and measures of assessing inequality in health. Fourth, the range of questions asked of the data exceeds that in Cohen and Armelagos. *Paleopathology at the Origins of Agriculture* focused mainly on health during the transition, whereas this project considers issues over a broader time span, including the dynamics of pre-Columbian health, the consequences of contact, and the fates of Euro-Americans and African-Americans up to the early twentieth century.

The first chapter in the methodology section discusses something fundamental to the remaining chapters – indicators of skeletal disease. Bones are living tissue that respond or adapt to biological stress, which may be caused by numerous persistent conditions, such as a deficient diet, various infections that penetrate soft tissue, and arduous work or physical effort. With the help of a few necessary photographs, Alan Goodman and Debra Martin articulate these indicators of stress and disease and explain what they mean and show how they may be interpreted.

The chapter on the health index by Richard Steckel, Paul Sciulli, and Jerome Rose brings several innovations to the measurement of health using skeletal data. First, attributes of health, such as stature, infections, and degenerative joint disease, are scored by severity on a scale of 0 (lowest) to 100 (highest, indicating no visible impairment). Second, the scores of each attribute are pooled by site, converted to age-specific rates, and adjusted by the distribution of person-years lived by age in a reference population. Third, the resulting indexes for each attribute are averaged to create an overall health index that is comparable across sites. Sites are then ranked, and their placement within the rankings, by the index and its components, become an object of comparative study.

Robert McCaa's chapter tackles the difficult and thorny question of estimating life tables from skeletal data on deaths by age. Demographers learned long ago that the age distribution of deaths is more sensitive to variations in fertility rates than variations in mortality rates. Yet, useful information about life expectancy is recoverable from the age distribution of deaths if proper allowance is made for possible fluctuations or differences in fertility rates and for possible biases caused by selective migration, that is, if the age distribution of deaths is studied in context.

The remaining chapters are organized by sections of ethnic and regional groupings. Each section is introduced by a brief discussion of results on the health index that raise questions for readers to consider in perusing individual essays. The health of Euro-Americans and of African-Americans in North America is considered first because many readers are familiar with issues in their health and authors can readily attach more familiar measures of health to the discussion, all of which helps newcomers to this work to calibrate the meaning of skeletal data. The groups under study are diverse with respect to socioeconomic conditions, ranging at the top from the middle and upper class in Belleville, Ontario, to southern plantation slaves. In between lie the free blacks in the urban East and in the frontier West, soldiers, and those who died in Rochester's poorhouse. The health rankings that emerge confirm several findings based on other approaches and sources, but they also challenge our methodology and preconceptions of health in relation to social status.

The remaining chapters, which comprise about one-half of this volume, consider the health of Native Americans in Central America, South America, and North America. The chapters on Central America examine the biological stresses endured by the declining Maya and the pre-Hispanic populations of central Mexico. The older prehistoric populations examined in Ecuador and Brazil lived in ecological environments that led to better health. The North American groups under study were extraordinarily diverse, living under hunter-gatherer or agricultural conditions and in the pre- and postcontact periods. Thus, some of both the healthiest and least healthy populations in our database were found among natives in North America.

Considerable scholarly energy has been devoted to formulating models or explanations of long-term changes in health. Although a comprehensive explanation has been beyond anyone's reach, various factors thought to have been important, at least in some contexts, have been identified. Subsistence shifts, climate, population growth, technological change, and political evolution have all been suggested as active ingredients contributing to changes in health. Although it would be interesting to investigate all such hypotheses with the data at our command, our ambitions are more limited. We have acquired evidence and developed new methodologies that help elucidate a series of microstories, which are enhanced by our comparative perspective using comparable data and the health index. Despite our large database, we feel that considerably more diverse evidence would be required for adequate evaluation of broad explanations. Eventually, we hope to acquire considerably more data and a global perspective for this purpose. Nevertheless, the chapter on "Patterns of Health in the Western Hemisphere" and the "Conclusions" appraise some hypotheses and draw attention to various patterns in the skeletal evidence.

In the "Epilogue," prominent physical anthropologists and an historian who are familiar with the project comment on our methods and results from the perspective of their disciplines. Although these short essays might be considered the first reviews of the book, our objective is to initiate a dialogue from which all scholars interested in very long-term health trends may advance this fascinating and important research agenda.

For decades, bioarchaeologists have intensively studied skeletons in their microenvironments as learned from burial artifacts and various features of burial sites. While this type of work is essential for the objectives of this volume, we anticipate this book will also stimulate greater comparative study of skeletal remains in their historical, economic, ecological, and cultural contexts. In short, we hope our collective efforts lead to the flowering of macrobioarchaeology.

REFERENCES

Cohen, Mark N., and George J. Armelagos, eds. *Paleopathology at the Origins of Agriculture.* New York: Academic Press, 1984.

Steckel, Richard H. "Stature and the Standard of Living." *Journal of Economic Literature* 33 (1995): 1903–1940.

"Strategic Ideas in the Rise of the New Anthropometric History and Their Implications for Interdisciplinary Research." *Journal of Economic History* 58 (1998): 803–821.

UNDP. *Human Development Report.* New York: United Nations Development Programme, 1990.

PART II

METHODOLOGY

CHAPTER TWO

Reconstructing Health Profiles from Skeletal Remains

Alan H. Goodman and Debra L. Martin

ABSTRACT

This chapter provides a selective review of nine skeletal and dental lesions that have been used to construct the skeletal database employed in the development of the health index. These lesions are described within a biosocial framework. Change in length of subadult long bones can identify differences in nutrition and health. Linear enamel hypoplasias provide information on the severity and temporal pattern of stress during infancy and childhood. Porotic hyperostosis is a lesion of the skull associated with iron deficiency. Bony responses to bacterial infections are associated with differences in contact with bacteria and the levels of resistance. Patterns of healed fractures indicate activities that include living on difficult terrain, hazardous occupations, and the extent of warfare and interpersonal violence. Osteoarthritis indicates the degree of regular strenuous activity and quality of life. Dental decay and tooth loss have functional significance for nutritional status.

INTRODUCTION AND PURPOSE

Analyses of skeletal remains are providing a unique window onto patterns of health in past human populations. Until very recently the surviving human tissues, most often bones and teeth (and less often skin, hair, and fluids, such as blood), have usually been ignored in historical and prehistoric research, or at best, their analysis was relegated to appendixes of archaeological site reports (Buikstra, 1991).[1] However,

---

The ideas developed in this chapter have had a long gestation. For help in the development of these ideas we especially wish to acknowledge George Armelagos and Jerome Rose. Jerome Rose and Paul Sciulli also helped to develop the organization of this chapter. This most recent reincarnation of our ideas about the measurement of stress and adaptation in skeletal remains represents an evolving synthesis of our prior work with new ideas and new developments in the field.
[1] On the surface it may seem ironic that scientific recognition of the importance of human remains has come at a time when in the United States and elsewhere, laws such as the Native American Graves Protection and Repatriation Act (NAGPRA, U.S. Public Law 101-601) have been passed to provide a mechanism for the possible repatriation of the skeletal remains of indigenous peoples. However, a benefit of NAGPRA is that

archaeologists and historians have begun to realize that human remains are the most direct means for assessment of past biologies – and how these biologies interacted with social, political, and economic processes. The question remains: "How can we read past lives from bones and teeth?"

The first purpose of this chapter is to provide a brief overview of the history of study of skeletal and dental lesions to reconstruct prehistoric health. Second, we outline the principles behind a "general stress perspective." It may seem unusual to be studying stress in skeletal remains; however, by stress we mean a measurable physiological disruption or perturbation that has consequence for individuals and populations. A general stress perspective applied to the past suggests that the specific "stressor" (the cause of physiological disruption) is seldom known and the physiological response is no longer directly observable. However, in most cases, multiple interacting stressors are involved, and fortunately the outcome of the *individuals' interactions with these stressors* often leaves recognizable scars in skeletal tissues.[2]

The main body of this chapter is devoted to a selective review of skeletal and dental lesions for reconstructing patterns of health and nutrition that are used throughout this volume and especially in the development of the health index for skeletal remains (see Steckel, Sciulli, and Rose, this volume): growth/stature, linear enamel hypoplasias, porotic hyperostosis/anemia, periosteal reactions/infectious disease, trauma, degenerative disease, and caries, dental abscesses, and tooth loss.[3] Specific attention is paid to the state of the art: what has been established for each indicator, and what research is most essential from epidemiological and anthropological perspectives. At present, there are but a handful of formal studies of such key constructs as validity (generally defined as how well an indicator measures an underlying construct, the "true" situation (MacMahon and Pugh, 1970)) and comparability (generally defined as the ability to obtain the same result from different observers at different times). We consider how well measures conform to epidemiological principles. Where possible, we focus on the possible adaptive and functional implications of indicators. These inferences come mostly from the study in contemporary contexts.

This review of paleoepidemiology, the study of disease in past human populations, is intended for those social scientists who are not directly engaged in the work of reconstructing health from skeletal lesions. For more detailed discussions of method and theory, a variety of references should be perused: Larsen (1987,

---

it led to efforts to "standardize" data collection from human skeletal remains (Buikstra and Ubelaker, eds., 1994). As well, the pressure to show the relevance of such studies might also be seen as a positive movement.

[2] As with all paleontological studies, one can only directly observe what remains to be studied. The rest needs to be inferred. Taphonomic processes, the loss of information through time, eliminate a great deal – thoughts, voice, soft tissues, and physiological reactions – from direct observation. As well, not everything that might be considered stressful leaves identifiable scars on osteological remains. A key challenge, therefore, is to understand what does leave scars (versus what does not) and the validity of this partly obscured window into the past.

[3] The utility of the Steckel, Sciulli, and Rose index is that it is highly repeatable. We focus on these indicators, and do not mean to suggest that others would not be of value. Also, in order to provide some greater sense of process, we sometimes present a more complex discussion of indicators, such as the process of distinguishing active lesions.

1997), Goodman et al. (1984b), Huss-Ashmore et al. (1982), Buikstra and Cook (1980), and Roberts and Machester (1995). This chapter, in fact, is an abstract and interpretation of these reviews. Edited general methods and theory volumes include Katzenberg and Saunders (2000), Iscan and Kennedy (1989), and Gilbert and Mielke (1985). Ortner and Putschar (1981) have provided an essential reference for identification of bone pathologies, with updated and expanded information available in Aufderheide and Rodríguez-Martín (1998). Tyson (1997) has recently edited an extensive international bibliography of human paleopathology that has been regularly updated. Excellent compilations of examples of research in paleopathology can be found in edited volumes by Cohen and Armelagos (1984), Grauer (1995), Ortner and Aufderheide (1991), Powell (1991), Verano and Ubelaker (1992), Owsley and Jantz (1994), Larsen and Milner (1994), Sobolik (1994), Poirier and Bellantoni (1997), and Lambert (2000).

We leave the study of mortality to McCaa (this volume), although the skeletal lesions reviewed below are frequently discussed, by necessity, in relationship to age-specific disease risks. In fact, the question of age-specific risk is related to a broader question of variation in individual frailty within populations (Wood et al., 1992). Wood and co-workers (1992) further suggest that individuals with evidence for disease may actually be "healthy survivors" (also see Milner et al., 2000). They propose that frail individuals would have died without evidence of a bony response. We contend, in response, that such a condition should be seen in differing mortality profiles. Further, use of multiple indicators should help to discern patterns of health and function. As these issues raised by Wood and colleagues have neither been resolved nor tested with skeletal analysis, we look upon the health index presented in this volume as one method to test these propositions.

Finally, we wish also to emphasize the importance of a biocultural or biosocial perspective. Bones and biologies come alive when they are seen as a part of interacting processes: biological, ecological, sociocultural and political-economic.

HISTORICAL OVERVIEW

The study of diseases in prehistoric skeletal materials is a rather old hobby. Since at least the 1700s, physicians and naturalists have shown great interest in how individuals looked and how they lived and died (Ubelaker, 1982). Following prior historians of paleopathology, the study of disease in prehistoric skeletal remains, Ubelaker (1982: 337) divides the history of the discipline into four phases, all beginning well before the 1960s (also see Armelagos et al., 1982; Roney, 1959).

1. 1774–1870   Focus on Quaternary fauna
2. 1870–1900   Focus on human trauma and syphilis
3. 1900–1930   Focus on infection and medical interventions
4. 1930–   Focus on disease in ecological context

As Ubelaker (1982) suggests, evidence for an epidemiological/ecological approach is apparent as far back as the work of Hooton (1930) on Pecos Pueblo, New Mexico. In an oft-cited effort to study disease on the level of the population,

Hooton estimated the prevalence of different morbid conditions in the Pecos human remains and tried to relate epidemiological patterns to culture and ecology. Hooton's work, however, was not the norm for its time. Research before the 1960s was not dominated by anthropologists or by anthropological concerns. In fact, until the last quarter of a century, most research in prehistoric disease was not epidemiological, had little concern for the role of culture, and seems to have been practiced more as an avocation of medical scientists than as a field of anthropological inquiry. The focus of most studies was on understanding first occurrences and the geographic and historical limits of a disease (Armelagos et al., 1982; Ubelaker, 1982). A tangible reminder of this period is found in skeletal collections, including Pecos Pueblo, which are biased toward the inclusion of crania and the best-preserved individuals.[4]

If the study of prehistoric health as an anthropological enterprise could be said to have been born in a single year, then 1968 is an apt choice. In the late 1960s an interdisciplinary field was born with a coherent theoretical underpinning and questions to be answered, such as the relationship between agricultural intensification and population development. By the end of the 1960s, Don Brothwell in London (Brothwell and Sandison, 1967) and Calvin Wells in Bradford (Wells, 1964) had begun to explore a number of issues in the health of past populations. Especially in Brothwell's work, one may see the clear formulation of the ecological perspective in bioarchaeology and the origins of paleodemography, paleopathology, and paleonutrition (Brothwell, 1967). In the United States, Lawrence Angel and George Armelagos were soon to be joined by Jane Buikstra and a host of colleagues and students in formulation of the active bioarchaeology/paleopathology programs at the Smithsonian Institution, Northwestern University, and Universities of Massachusetts, Kansas, Wisconsin, and Colorado, to name just a few. The field was further trumpeted by the publication of two edited volumes, Brothwell and Sandison's (1967) monumental *Disease in Antiquity* and Jarcho's (1966) *Human Paleopathology*, in addition to such key articles as Angel's (1966) "Porotic Hyperostosis, Anemias, Malarias, and Marshes in the Prehistoric Eastern Mediterranean," Armelagos's (1969) "Disease in Ancient Nubia," and Kerley and Bass's (1967) "Paleopathology: Meeting Ground of Many Disciplines," all significant for having been published in *Science*, the world's most widely circulated scientific periodical.

The literature at the birth of paleopathology clearly exhibits the tensions between the dual goals of focusing on diagnosis and history of conditions versus understanding disease and other maladies in cultural and ecological contexts. Jarcho's (1966) volume was dominated by a focus on first occurrences and specific diagnosis; while these are important concerns, they are a carryover of the "old paleopathology," whereas Brothwell and Sandison (1967) contains some well-developed ecological papers. These tensions notwithstanding, by the end of the 1960s there was a clear and growing literature in anthropological bioarchaeology and paleopathology. This new (ecological) perspective on the field was soon to further develop in programs such as Buikstra's in North American Bioarchaeology at Northwestern and such similar

---

[4] The Pecos Pueblo human remains were repatriated in May 1999.

programs as those mentioned above at Universities of Kansas, Massachusetts, and Tennessee and the Smithsonian Institution. A generation of bioarchaeologists and skeletal biologists emerged mainly in the United States and largely focused on North American skeletal remains (Lovejoy et al., 1982).

What prompted the development of paleopathology/bioarchaeology in the late 1960s? The two obvious parent fields were the "new archaeology" and human adaptability. The recently formulated new (or processual) archaeology provided a set of scientific principles and focused on ecological explanation (see Binford and Binford, 1968). Human adaptability developed as a means of combining interests in evolutionary change with concern for the various adaptive problems faced by humans today, especially those living on political and ecological margins. With questions focusing on how humans, the most adaptive of species, managed to survive and adapt (behaviorally, physiologically, developmentally, or genetically) to environmental constraints and stressors, human adaptability clearly shared an ecological perspective with the new archaeology (Baker, 1962; 1966; Lasker, 1969).

The ecological perspective – so evident in the new archaeology, human adaptability, and bioarchaeology – also did not arise by chance. The 1960s witnessed the development of ecological approaches throughout the social and biological sciences. Growing awareness of environmental destruction, the angst of the Vietnam War, concerns with the consequences of population growth, and civil rights were some of the popular issues that influenced the direction of the sciences. Within anthropology, this ecological perspective is attested to in such publications as Rappoport's (1967) *Pigs for the Ancestors* and Bennett's (1966) *Northern Plainsmen.* In sum, paleopathology fit comfortably into the development of scientific and ecological approaches in anthropology.

Paleopathology since 1984

A reevaluation of the adaptiveness of gathering-hunting, the basic mode of production of humans, was a key event in paleopathology. In Lee and DeVore's *Man the Hunter* (eds., 1968), Lee (1968) and Sahlins (1968), among others, presented a view of contemporary gatherer-hunters as materially satisfied, if not well-off (Sahlins's Buddhist economics). Furthermore, Dunn (1968) suggested that gatherer-hunters might actually be healthier and better nourished than their agricultural neighbors.

A direct result of these issues was a conference on "Paleopathology at the Origins of Agriculture" and the resultant volume edited by Cohen and Armelagos (1984). The volume is the first to provide comparative paleopathological information focused on a specific question. To this end, 19 case studies documented the health changes associated with agricultural intensification in different populations from around the globe. Second, there was a pioneering effort to focus on similar indicators of health and even to collect the data in a similar fashion, what Cohen (1984) refers to as an effort at controlled comparison (also see Cohen and Armelagos, 1984; Goodman et al., 1984a).

Since the publication of *Paleopathology at the Origins of Agriculture,* the science of paleoepidemiology has continued at a rapid pace. A number of new methodologies, such as dental microwear (Teaford, 1991) and isotopic and trace elemental analysis of bones and teeth (Price, 1989; Sandford, 1993), have emerged. Research continues into better understanding how to interpret various lesions, such as porotic hyperostosis (Mensforth, 1991; Stuart-Macadam, 1989), periosteal reactions (Ortner, 1991), and enamel developmental defects (Goodman and Rose, 1990, 1991), as well as the pattern of mortality (see Storey, 1992: 1–26 for an excellent review of paleodemographic issues). Perhaps most importantly, the "lens" of the skeleton has been applied to a number of new research questions, such as the evidence for disease and death at the time of European colonization of the Americas (see Larsen and Milner, 1994; Verano, and Ubelaker, 1992), the consequences of life as a prehistoric farmer in the American Southeast (Lambert, 2000), inferences about warfare and interpersonal violence from pattern of bone trauma (Martin and Frayer, 1997), and the influence of sex and gender on health in the past (Grauer and Stuart-Macadam, 1998).

THE SYSTEMIC STRESS PERSPECTIVE

There are a number of implied goals and reasons for studying skeletal lesions. Perhaps the oldest of these is to understand the precise etiological agent responsible for the lesion: what infectious agent caused a particular form of bone modification, what nutrient deficiency led to a skeletal condition, and what instrument caused a trauma? We share an appreciation from the potential anthropological insights that may be gained by focusing on the "trees of specific etiology," and especially on the implied need to understand the biological processes leading to the observed skeletal lesions. However, we also do not wish to lose focus on the "forest of context." Excessive focus on specific etiology may be unproductive because infirmities are usually the result of multiplicative and interactive forces, and the skeleton typically responds in nonspecific ways. Fortunately, what may be of greatest anthropological interest is not the specific agent that caused infirmity, but the severity, duration, and temporal course of physiological perturbation. These characteristics, as they may be read and deciphered from skeletal lesions, provide a means for assessment of health status and functional impairment.

Goodman and co-workers (1984a) have developed a stress model to apply to studies of health in the past. This model, which focuses on the etiology and skeletal manifestations of stress, was later revised to consider feedbacks and the functional implications of stress (Goodman et al., 1988; Goodman and Armelagos, 1988; Larsen, 1997; Martin et al., 1991). The purpose of this model is to provide a mechanism for systematically examining and reflecting on the adaptive process and the centrality of health to this process.

From left to right, the model starts with environmental constraints to adaptation (Figure 2.1). These are typically divided between limiting resources and stressors. The most important limiting resources are likely to be basic ones: food, water, shelter. Stressors may be related to climatic extremes, such as excesses of heat and cold, or low partial pressure of oxygen. All of these climatic and physical stressors are important because they may have an effect on resistance to disease. Other environmental stressors, such as parasites and predators, have more direct effects on health and longevity.

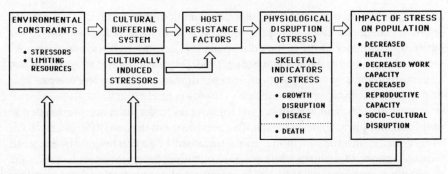

Figure 2.1. Stress model adapted for use in skeletal series. Although stress, as a physiological disruption, cannot be directly measured, a variety of skeletal changes may be used to infer stress and its impact on individual and population adaptation (from Goodman and Armelagos, 1989: 226).

There are numerous general means to adjust to environmentally initiated constraints and stressors. Culture, through its technological, social, and ideological systems, mediates the process of extracting resources from the environment. Cultural systems are generally effective in buffering environmental constraints and stressors, or removing the individuals from contact with the stressor. There are numerous examples of effective cultural buffering of stressors and limiting resources. Shelter and clothing are generally well suited as buffers against extremes of cold and heat. May (1960), for example, relates how peasants in the hilly region of North Vietnam have customarily built their houses on stilts, about 8 to 10 feet above the ground. This is just above the flight ceiling of *Anopheles minimus,* a very fierce malaria vector.

The adoption of agriculture is an economic adjustment that brings about a number of changes in the ability of a culture to buffer stress. The energetic efficiency of agriculture and the amount of food produced per unit area is greater than that of hunting and gathering. Thus, agriculture would seem to provide a buffer against malnutrition. However, a nearly invariable demographic covariate of agricultural intensification is greater population density. Unfortunately, the increased population density, as well as other ecological and demographic changes associated with agricultural intensification, have unforeseen consequences for health, such as increasing conditions for the spread of infectious diseases (Cohen and Armelagos, eds., 1984).

The important point is that cultural systems operate as both a buffering system and a producer of new stressors and constraints. As cultures change, the nature of environmental adaptation changes. Improved adjustment to one environmental condition is frequently only made by increasing exposure to another condition. Compromised adaptations are the rule. Cultures can also vary in how well different segments of the population are buffered from stressors (Goodman and Armelagos, 1989).

The environmental constraints that are not well buffered by the cultural system, along with the newly produced cultural stressors, reach the individual members of the culture. From this point on, adaptation depends on the individual's level of host resistance, a function of one's genetic, developmental, and physiological status. If a stressor is persistent and life threatening over millennia, then a genetic resistance might develop, such as appears to have been the case in West Africa, where the frequency of the hemoglobin S allele (i.e., sickle-cell anemia) increased genetic resistance to malaria (Livingstone, 1958). More commonly, stressors are not so persistent and a genetic "solution" is never developed. Rather, a developmental or physiological change may come first (Thomas et al., 1979).

Unfortunately, chronic stressors and limiting resources often overburden developmental and physiological systems. The persistence of the condition often results in decreased health and nutritional status, which will be further lowered by exposure to new stressors. Individuals who have poor nutrition, for example, are less resistant to infectious diseases, and infectious disease further lowers nutritional status (Allen, 1984; Martorell, 1980; Mata et al., 1971).

The severity and duration of the stress response may be viewed as a function of the degree of cultural and environmental constraints and stressors, balanced against the adequacy of the cultural buffering system and individual resistance resources. Fortunately for the paleoepidemiologist, the stress response, a stereotypic physiological change resulting from the struggle to adjust, is frequently manifest in relatively permanent skeletal changes. While some stressors, such as virulent infections, may not leave any evidence of a skeletal response because of the rapidity of the disease process (Ortner, 1991), many stressors do leave scars on skeletal elements. Because bone and teeth are limited in their response repertoire, one finds evidence that a struggle to adapt has occurred, but we may not be able to identify the specific stressor.

Health and adaptation have significance that extends beyond the individual to the population and society. Undernutrition, for example, has a negative effect on work capacity, fertility, morbidity, and other mortality that often disrupts the social, political, and economic structure of communities (Allen, 1984). In turn, these cultural and population level changes cycle back to cause further changes in the environment and cultural system.

It is a challenge to historians and prehistorians to go beyond the individual to examine how patterns of disease and disruption have significance for families, larger social groups, and cultures. Similarly, it is a challenge to go beyond concerns with proximate causes of illness to examination of the broader and underlying social, economic, and political factors that determine patterns of nutrition, health, and mortality.

THE EVIDENCE OF STRESS IN SKELETAL TISSUES

The following section provides information on seven classes of indicators of health status. The important point to be made at the outset is that these indicators need to be examined in relationship to each other. As well, many conditions are age-dependent; that is, risk changes with age, perhaps representing a cumulative risk or age-specific risk. Thus, accurate aging and sexing of skeletal remains is key to analysis and comparison of populations (See McCaa, this volume).

Subadult Growth and Adult Stature

INTRODUCTION: CONTEMPORARY STUDIES
AND FUNCTIONAL INTERPRETATIONS

The size and shape of humans, the subject matter of anthropometry, has always fascinated anthropologists and human biologists. Anthropometry came into prominence as a readily apparent method for categorizing and differentiating among human varieties. However, for earlier typologists, human morphology was found to be a poor choice for such a task (Boas, 1892). Size and shape, while having strong genetic components, are also clearly influenced by the environment in which individuals develop (Tanner, 1981).

Precisely because of their sensitivity to the environment, anthropometric measures have become central to the study of human adaptation. A wide variety of studies have shown that anthropometric variations are due to environmental limitations (Eveleth and Tanner, 1976, 1990). Growth in parameters, such as height, weight, and arm circumference, is a sensitive indicator of nutritional status (Eveleth and Tanner, 1990; Sutphen, 1985), defined as "the state resulting from the balance between the supply of nutrients on the one hand and the expenditure of the organism on the other" (McLaren, 1976:3). In fact, the assessment of growth is nearly synonymous with the assessment of nutritional status (Bogin, 1988; Sinclair, 1985; Tanner, 1978).

The most important distinction to be made in paleoepidemiology is between studies of subadults or adults (see Johnston and Zimmer, 1989; Saunders, 2000). Studies of adult size and shape (completed growth) versus subadult growth and development yield different kinds of information. The main advantage of studies of subadults is that they provide the most sensitive measures of changes in nutritional status because older subadults may undergo *catch-up* growth, the increase in growth rate following recovery from growth-dampening conditions (Bogin, 1988). Furthermore, variation in subadults is likely due to immediate conditions, whereas size variation in adults is more likely to reflect chronic conditions.

Height (stature, supine length) and weight are the most basic and established techniques for measurement of anthropometric status (Sutphen, 1985). Other common techniques include measurement of skinfold thickness (such as triceps, subscapular), circumferences (upper arm, head, trunk), and computation of ratios, such as height to sitting height or height-to-weight. Among these measures, head circumference is generally considered to be least affected by undernutrition, while measures which involve fat stores (such as skinfold thickness and weight) are considered to be the most sensitive to undernutrition (especially of calories). Taken together, these measures illustrate a *hierarchy* of the consequences of environments: some aspects of growth are more readily disrupted by environmental deprivation than are others. This hierarchy of sensitivity also helps to explain why severely malnourished children characteristically have thin bodies (growth in trunk and arm circumference has stopped) and relatively normal-size heads.

The pattern of relative growth disruption can also provide insights into the timing and type of disruption. As a case in point, head circumference is of particular interest because the head grows rapidly during infancy and early childhood. Therefore, variation in head circumference in older individuals may reflect conditions during the time of rapid cranial development (Tanner, 1978). Clarke and co-workers (1986) suggest a similar interpretation for the size of the vertebral canal. In general, however, growth is a cumulative phenomenon. Length and width measures, which are mainly dependent on skeletal dimensions, reflect this cumulative pattern (Huss-Ashmore et al., 1982).

Some nutrients, such as total calories, protein, zinc, and vitamin A, have been shown to be especially important in maintaining growth (Allen, 1984); however, it is usually impossible to isolate specific nutrient effects in living humans, and this task becomes even more difficult in studies of the past (Huss-Ashmore et al., 1982). Finally, a variety of other factors intervene between diet and nutritional status, including work and disease loads (Allen, 1984).

While growth is a sensitive indicator of environment, it is also a highly nonspecific and cumulative indicator. Tanner (1986), in fact, has proposed that growth can be used to measure the degree of classlessness. He suggests that when variation in growth between groups disappears, one may conclude that there exists a truly classless society, or one in which all individuals have equal access to resources.

Interest in anthropometric studies has been roused by increased understanding of the relationship between anthropometric measures and functional capacities, such as resistance to illness and work capacity (Allen, 1984). Chavez and Martinez (1982) have found that mild-to-moderate malnutrition in Mexican peasant children has a profound effect on their activity levels, social behavior, learning patterns, and disease resistance. For example, the most malnourished children (who show the greatest deficiencies in growth) tend to be far less exploratory, cry more often, are less interactive with their parents, and are ill for longer periods of time (Chavez and Martinez, 1982).

A number of studies have begun to demonstrate the long-term effects of poor nutrition. For example, Chen (1980), Bhargava and co-workers (1985), Briend and co-workers (1986, 1987), and Smedman and co-workers (1987) have shown that deficient anthropometric status, in particular low height-for-age and arm circumference, is a powerful predictor of future mortality probabilities (also see Henry and Ulijaszek, eds., 1996). In summary, the anthropometric status of living individuals and groups provides insight into their general quality of life.

ANTHROPOMETRIC STUDIES OF SKELETAL POPULATIONS

Subadult Growth. A number of practical factors have limited the interpretation of subadult growth variations in prehistoric populations (see Hoppa and Fitzgerald 1999; Johnston and Zimmer, 1989; and Saunders, 2000 for detailed reviews).

1. Prehistoric skeletal series are frequently plagued by small sample size, particularly between 5 and 16 years of age when mortality is lowest and thus skeletons in cemeteries the fewest. This is the primary reason for the paucity of comparative studies of growth of prehistoric subadults.

2. There is a technical problem of measuring long bones with and without epiphyses (the unattached growing ends of long bones), which are frequently unattached and lost during excavation. This irregularity has the potential of adding considerable measurement error.

3. Because the archaeological sample is cross-sectional (in fact, a death assemblage), the results can be used to infer periods of peak stress only when conditions are relatively stable over time. Furthermore, cemetery-based studies represent not the healthy or even the "average" child, but those who died (Milner et al. 2000; Wood et al., 1992).

4. Dental age is the best-known proxy for chronological age. This can be considered a potential source of error by providing a bias toward a more conservative estimation of growth, as dental age (based on calcification and eruption times) is also likely to be somewhat affected by environment (Garn et al., 1963). Unfortunately, the differential effects of environment on growth in long bones versus dental age is not precisely known.

5. Similarly, inability to distinguish the sex of subadults disallows comparisons between boys and girls.

6. We have only limited ability to compare growth in prehistory directly to that of contemporary groups. The only sample from which longitudinal growth of long bones is well established is from the childhood growth study conducted in Denver, Colorado (Maresh, 1955).

In spite of these limitations, a number of useful paleoepidemiological studies have focused on subadult growth (e.g., Armelagos et al., 1972; Cook, 1971; Jantz and Owsley, 1984; Johnston, 1962; Lallo, 1973; Mensforth, 1985; Merchant and Ubelaker, 1977; Sundick, 1978; Walker, 1969; Y'Edynak, 1976). For example, Hummert and Van Gerven (1983) examined growth changes over time in Sudanese Nubia and found that changes in growth velocities correspond to changes in political centralization. Others have found some evidence for growth dampening, especially around the ages of two to five years. This appears to be a period of increased vulnerability for the growing child, and diet, nutrition, health, and activity patterns all may be contributing to the poor growth of children (Goodman and Armelagos, 1989).

Steckel, Sciulli, and Rose (this volume) offer a novel solution to the problem of comparison. They compare achieved growth of long bones to the age-specific standards of Maresh (1955) and present a method for assessing the degree of malnutrition for each individual. Thus, groups can be compared by the percents of individuals within different classifications of undernutrition.

Anthropometry of Adults. Studies of adults are not as much constrained by problems of assignment of age and sex or small sample sizes. Because of the relative stability of height by age in early adulthood, age is of little consequence, and whereas sex is difficult to determine in subadults, it is rather easily determined in adults.

Unfortunately, the largely technical advantages of studying adults are offset by disadvantages. As in studies of adult anthropometry of living populations, the main drawback to studies in prehistory revolves around the loss of sensitivity for clarifying underlying processes affecting growth and ultimate size at adulthood. The loss of the most stressed segment of the population (subadults) due to death before adulthood, coupled with the ability to catch up in growth, renders adult morphology less sensitive to environmental variation when compared to subadult growth and development.

Nonetheless, comparisons of adult stature can be very informative, and a wide variety of studies of adult anthropometry have been performed. In a review of stature (derived from long bone lengths) in prehistoric populations from Mesoamerica, Genoves (1967:76, also Bass, 1971; Brothwell, 1981; Ubelaker, 1981) finds that female stature decreases from a mean of around 62 inches in northern Mesoamerica and the American Southwest to about 58 inches in southern Mesoamerica. Male stature also declines from around 66 inches in the North to around 62 inches in the South. Genoves suggests that subsistence differences may be responsible for the differences in height between the two regions (also see Nickens, 1976). Other researchers have looked at variability within single populations. For example, Haviland (1967) suggests that intragroup variation in stature at Tikal (a large prehistoric Mayan center in Guatemala) may be related to social class differences.

SUMMARY

Anthropometric studies of living populations have profoundly influenced similar studies of prehistoric populations. Studies of adult stature and subadult long bone lengths are best thought of as nonspecific indicators of stress. Because the consequence of growth faulting looks the same regardless of specific stressor or limiting resources, it is necessary to have contextual information if one is to interpret the cause of the growth faltering. Some sense of the severity and temporal pattern of stress may be inferred from the pattern of disruption. As with studies of mortality, studies of subadult growth are frequently hampered by imprecision in estimation of age and small sample sizes. Despite these limitations, anthropometric studies of past populations continue to yield valuable information, and this is perhaps a testament to the vitality of the indicator. Our ability to assess subadult growth and adult morphology from skeletal remains provides a powerful tool for the assessment of nutritional status in prehistoric humans. Stature and growth also provide a means for linking the study of archaeological skeletons with the analysis of heights recorded during the past three centuries and employed by historians and economists to study changes in nutrition and health during the recent past (Steckel and Floud, 1997).

Linear Enamel Hypoplasias

PATHOPHYSIOLOGY AND ETIOLOGY

Linear enamel hypoplasias (LEH) are a class of developmental enamel defects (DED). They are recognizable as transverse or linear deficiencies in enamel thickness caused by a disruption during the enamel secretion stage of tooth crown development (Goodman and Rose, 1990; Schultz et al., 1998; Suckling, 1989). The importance of these defects rests in the fact that they provide an indelible indicator

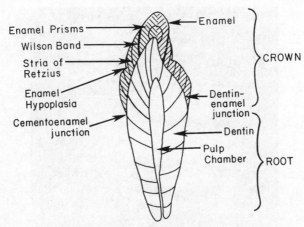

Figure 2.2. Diagrammatic representation of a longitudinal section through a human mandibular canine. Enamel hypoplasia is shown as an area of reduced thickness (from Rose et al., 1985).

of periods of stress during tooth crown development (prenatally to 12 months for deciduous teeth, and birth to 7 years for permanent teeth).

The general mechanism by which enamel develops (and disruptions occur) is well understood (Jenkins, 1978). Through an inductive process, ameloblasts (cells that form enamel) begin to line up at what will eventually become the dentin-enamel junction (Figure 2.2). Dentin formation begins at the occlusal (crown tip) border between ameloblasts and odontoblasts (the dentin-forming cells) (Slavkin et al., 1984). The ameloblasts follow in secreting enamel proteins that form the enamel matrix. As the process continues, more cervically located ameloblasts and odontoblasts are recruited to secrete protein and make enamel and dentin matrix, respectively (Shawashy and Yaeger, 1986).

As these secretory ameloblasts complete their function of forming the enamel matrix, they begin to undergo changes in both shape and ultrastructure consistent with their change in function from secretion (tall secretory cells) to resorption and transport (short, ruffle-bordered resorptive cells) (Reith and Cotty, 1967). Influenced by the functionally changed ameloblasts, the enamel matrix loses protein and water and becomes more completely calcified; mature enamel consists of approximately 97% calcified salt by weight and volume. If during the process of matrix secretion a group of ameloblasts are disrupted to a degree that they lose their functional capacities, then less matrix will be formed and the resulting enamel will be thinner, producing what is called a linear enamel hypoplasia (LEH).

Enamel hypoplasias, which can be identified visually as linear areas of thin enamel, vary from light multiple and single pits to lines of increased enamel thickness and thick bands of missing enamel (Figure 2.3). Based on the pattern of defects within and among teeth, hypoplasias can reliably be distinguished as to whether they result from one of three conditions: (1) an hereditary anomaly, (2) a localized trauma, or (3) a systemic metabolic stress (Shawashy and Yaeger, 1986).

Although enamel hypoplasias due to systemic stresses are common and easily discerned from defects due to nonsystemic factors, it is difficult to attribute a more

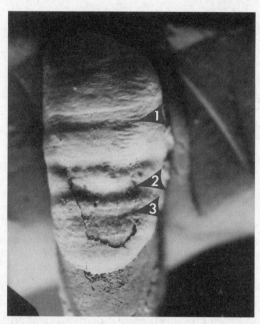

Figure 2.3. Left mandibular canine with three of its linear enamel hypoplasias labeled and numbered (from Goodman and Rose, 1990). This tooth begins crown formation at around 6 months
and ends formation around 6.5 years. Thus, the first LEH formed around 2.5–3.0 years developmental age and the second and third around 4.0–4.5 and 4.5–5.0 years developmental age,
respectively.

exact cause to these defects (Pindborg, 1982). This is true in the clinical setting
(Cutress and Suckling, 1982; Pindborg, 1982) as well as in archaeological series
(Rose et al., 1985). Cutress and Suckling (1982) have compiled nearly 100 factors
considered to be possible causes of enamel defects. The list of potential causes,
which includes nutritional imbalances, drug toxicities, and almost any disease which
severely stresses metabolism, gives credence to the view that enamel defects are
highly sensitive to physiological and metabolic changes and are best considered to
be indicators of nonspecific stress.

Perhaps the most important characteristic of LEH is that from its location it is
possible to estimate the developmental age of the individual at the time of LEH
formation. For example, permanent maxillary central incisors begin enamel formation around birth and end formation around four years. Matrix formation
follows a clear progression from the most superior point of the dentin-enamel
junction, to the occlusal point of outer enamel, and then progressively down the
sides of the tooth. A number of issues affect the accurate estimation of age at
development of a defect (Fitzgerald and Rose, 2000; Goodman and Rose, 1991), and
it therefore should be kept in mind that developmental age is not exactly equal to
chronological age.

Nonetheless, this methodology provides a chronological record of physiological
stress experienced by individuals (Kreshover, 1960; Sarnat and Schour, 1941). For

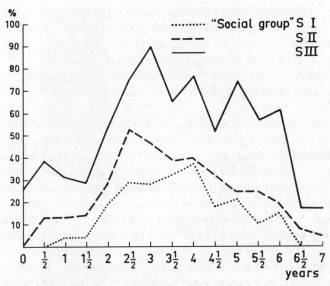

Figure 2.4. Comparison of the chronological distribution of linear enamel hypoplasias by social group from Westerhus, Sweden (from Swardstedt, 1966). Social group S I are landowners, group S II are peasants, and group S III are slaves. Note the increase in defects from group I to III at all developmental ages.

example, Swärdstedt (1966) capitalized on this quality to derive a chronological comparison of the prevalence of enamel defects by half-year developmental periods in "social groups" at Westerhus, medieval Sweden (Figure 2.4). This method enables us to study the pattern of infant and childhood stress of those who lived to be adolescents and adults.

While the index of health used in this volume focuses on LEH on permanent teeth, it should be mentioned that there are other developmental enamel defects, most notably defects in enamel calcification/coloration, commonly called dental opacities or hypocalcification. These defects have an entirely different etiology and should not be confused with LEHs. Defective enamel can also be observed histologically. While this more detailed level of analysis can provide important additional and confirmational data (Rose et al., 1985), histological studies are destructive and less commonly conducted during the analysis of skeletons.

ENAMEL HYPOPLASIAS IN CONTEMPORARY
AND PREHISTORIC POPULATIONS

Epidemiological studies of the frequency of enamel hypoplasias in contemporary populations support a general association between the prevalence of enamel hypoplasias and general living conditions. While direct comparison is difficult due to differences in method of diagnosis and sampling of individuals and teeth (Goodman and Armelagos, 1985a, 1985b), individuals in developed countries tend to have lower rates of enamel defects when compared to individuals from underdeveloped areas. The frequency of individuals with one or more hypoplasias on permanent teeth is generally less than 10% in most populations from developed, industrialized countries (see Cutress and Suckling, 1982, for a review) and is usually over 50% in developing countries (Goodman and Rose, 1990, 1991; also see Anderson and Stevenson, 1930; Baume and Meyer, 1966; Enwonwu, 1973; Jelliffe and Jelliffe, 1971; Moller et al., 1972; Sawyer and Nwoku, 1985; Schamschula et al., 1980).

The pioneering works of Sweeney (Sweeney and Guzman, 1966; Sweeney et al., 1969, 1971) established a general association between enamel hypoplasias and socioeconomic status. Sweeney and co-workers (1971) found an association between enamel hypoplasias of the deciduous upper central incisors (teeth whose crowns develop from about 6 months prenatally to about 3 months postnatally) and the degree of malnutrition in Guatemalan children. Forty-three percent of the children ages two to seven years with second-degree malnutrition (61% to 75% weight-for-age) had hypoplasias, whereas 73% of children with the more severe third-degree malnutrition (60% or less weight-for-age) had enamel hypoplasias.

Goodman and colleagues (1987) studied the frequency and chronological distribution of enamel hypoplasias in Mexican children from five rural communities, selected because of the presence of endemic mild-to-moderate malnutrition (children at 60% to 95% weight-for-age). They found one or more hypoplasias on 46.7% of 300 children examined. For the permanent teeth, there is a clear central tendency toward hypoplasia occurrence at between 18 and 36 months developmental age. As weaning generally takes place in the second year in these Mexican communities, they suggest that the increased frequency of hypoplasias may result from stresses associated with weaning. Further analysis revealed that LEHs are inversely associated with growth and socioeconomic status at around seven years of age (Goodman et al., 1992). A prospective study in another town in highland Mexico has confirmed that LEHs are about half as frequent in children who were provided nutrient supplements (Goodman et al., 1991). Because the multinutrient supplement also reduced the incidence and severity of respiratory and diarrheal diseases, the reduction in LEH frequency cannot be attributed to a single nutrient (Goodman et al., 1991).

LEHs have frequently been used to compare stress levels among different prehistoric populations. For examples, numerous authors, including Cassidy (1980, 1984), Goodman and co-workers (1980, 1984b), Perzigian and co-workers (1984), and Smith and co-workers (1984), have noted an increased frequency of defects in agriculturalists versus hunting and gathering groups. Goodman and colleagues (1984c) also note that the peak period of stress tends to be earlier in the agriculturalists versus gatherer-hunters. Hutchinson and Larsen (1988) found a greater frequency of hypoplasias in individuals from the Georgia coast post–European contact as compared with precontact individuals. Corruccini and co-workers (1985) evaluated the chronological distribution of enamel defects in slaves from Barbados. They found a relatively late peak age at development of defects (around 3.5 to 4.0 years) and attribute this peak to a historically documented late age at weaning and postweaning stress.

SUMMARY

Linear enamel hypoplasias are one of the most frequently studied skeletal mani-festations of stress. In comparison to measures of completed growth, which tend to signify chronic stress, these measures of growth disruption are time specific and may indicate more acute and short-term periods of stress. As with growth status, they are best thought of as nonspecific (general) indicators of stress. However, when combined with measures of achieved growth, they can help to provide information on the severity and temporal pattern of stress during childhood.

Enamel hypoplasias have been subject to tests of reliability and their etiology has been studied through ecological, case-control and prospective designs (Goodman and Rose, 1991). These studies have helped sharpen our understanding of the utility of these defects, but they have not answered all questions. Among a few concerns that need further attention are the best means of estimating an individual's age at devel-opment of defects, the best set of teeth for evaluation of stress in survey studies, and how best to characterize the size and shape of defects (see Fizgerald and Rose, 2000).

Porotic Hyperostosis and Anemia

BACKGROUND: PATHOPHYSIOLOGY, ETIOLOGY, AND FUNCTIONAL INFERENCES

Porotic hyperostosis is a commonly studied condition of cranial and flat bones that is associated with anemia. Anemias can potentially affect any bone of the skeleton that is involved in the production of red blood cells. The extent of the involvement of postcranial as well as cranial bones usually indicates how severe an anemia is and whether it is associated with a hemoglobin variant or is nutritionally induced (Stuart-Macadam, 1987, 1989, 1998). The possible etiologies for anemia include a discrete genetic trait (Mensforth et al., 1978), a hereditary hemolytic anemia (Angel, 1964, 1966, 1967; Zaino, 1967), or some form of nutritional disorder (Moseley, 1965; Nathan and Haas, 1966). However, of all of these potential causes, nutritional anemia has been suggested to be the primary factor in the etiology of porotic hyperostosis for the vast majority of the documented cases in prehistory (Carlson et al., 1974; El-Najjar et al., 1975; Hengen, 1971; Mensforth et al., 1978; Mensforth, 1991; Palkovich, 1987; Stuart-Macadam, 1987; Walker, 1985).

Porotic hyperostosis is a descriptive term for lesions on the cranium, the roof of the eye orbits, and the ends of long bones. These lesions are produced by bone mar-row proliferation that is diagnostic of anemia. The lesion, as the name implies, has a very porous (coral-like) appearance that develops when the diploe (the trabecular portion of the cranial bone that separates the inner and outer surfaces) expands (Figure 2.5). With the expansion of the diploe, the outer layer of bone becomes thinner and may eventually disappear, exposing the porous trabecular bone.

The expansion of the diploe can be caused by any anemia that stimulates red blood cell production and bone marrow proliferation. Differential diagnosis is aided in part by understanding the degree and severity of involvement. Whereas hereditary

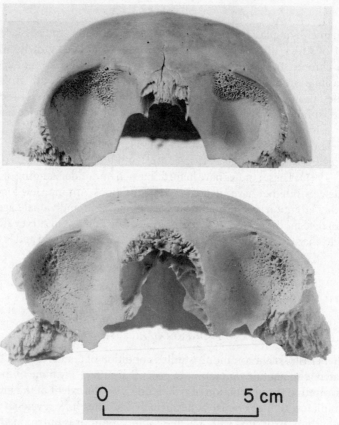

Figure 2.5 (*top*). Porotic hyperostosis (also referred to as cribra orbitalia) in the orbital regions of a subadult from prehistoric Sudanese Nubia. In the active state, there is marked porosity due to the thickened diploe which revealed the trabecular bone usually found between the inner and outer bone tables. Figure 2.6 (*bottom*). Remodeled porotic hyperostosis in the orbital regions of a subadult from prehistoric Sudanese Nubia. When the underlying condition of anemia is no longer creating rapid expansion of the diploe, the process of bone remodeling (replacement of old bone tissue with new well-mineralized tissue) begins to replace the porous tissue with normal tissue.

anemias such as sickle-cell anemia and thalassemia can result in dramatic skeletal responses, nutritional anemias usually result in relatively minor responses, typically restricted to the crania (Hershkovits et al., 1997; Mensforth et al., 1978; Palkovich, 1980).

Porotic hyperostosis is usually symmetrically distributed and presents as a tight cluster of small porous openings that are visible to the naked eye. The bones of the cranial (frontal, temporals, parietals, occipital) and the superior border of the eye orbits typically exhibit the lesion. Many researchers have given the expression of the disease as it appears in the orbits the label of "cribra orbitalia," because for many years it was not clear that the two locations (vault and orbit) had the same etiological definition. Currently, however, there is overwhelming evidence that both types of lesions are part of the same disease process (see Stuart-Macadam 1987, 1989, 1998) and should be referred to as porotic hyperostosis. In a review of the literature on clinical evidence of bone changes in anemic individuals, Stuart-Macadam (1987) provides compelling evidence that bony lesions are a product of iron-deficiency anemia in the living. In addition to finding a thickening of the diploe of cranial and orbital bones in anemia patients, the lesion is usually distributed in a symmetrical pattern on the cranium.

Porotic hyperostosis in the New World is most likely related to iron-deficiency anemia (Carlson et al., 1974; El-Najjar et al., 1975; Hengen, 1971; Lallo et al., 1977; Mensforth et al., 1978). This view, according to Mensforth and co-workers (1978:7), developed from three lines of evidence. First, iron-deficiency anemia and porotic hyperostosis are widespread throughout the New and the Old Worlds. Second, the distribution of porotic hyperostosis corresponds to the distribution of dietary staples that are low in utilizable iron. Finally, there is no pre-Columbian evidence to support the occurrence of skeletal changes that are characteristically found in the hemolytic anemias associated with hemoglobin variants.

Researchers need to interpret rates of porotic hyperostosis with caution, for even though the underlying etiology may include iron-deficiency anemia, several other important factors, such as infectious diseases and parasitism, can affect the occurrence of anemia (Lambert and Walker, 1991; Larsen and Sering, 2000; Mensforth et al., 1978). In fact, it is this same high degree of covariance between iron deficiency, other nutrient deficiencies, and infectious disease and parasitism that makes it difficult to isolate the functional consequences of iron deficiency.

Iron-deficiency anemia is a common health problem in both industrialized and nonindustrialized nations (Dallman et al., 1984; Simmons and Gurney, 1982). It is particularly pronounced in children, adolescents, and women during child-bearing years (Dallman et al., 1980; Jackson and Latham, 1982; Meyers et al., 1983; Simmons et al., 1982). In surveying the prevalence of iron-deficiency anemia worldwide, Witts (1966) suggests that it is so pervasive a health problem that it could be regarded as an index of the overall nutritional health of a population.

The functional consequences of mild anemia are well understood and have been shown to be profound (Scrimshaw, 1991). Iron deficiency, even where hemoglobin and hematocrits levels are normal, that is, iron deficiency without anemia, can lead to a suite of functional costs. A variety of organs and systems show structural changes with borderline iron deficiency. Vyas and Chandra (1984:45) note that the multiple consequences of iron deficiency are not surprising because iron is "an essential cofactor of several enzyme systems that play an important role in metabolic processes and cell proliferation. . . ." Many of these enzymes are involved in vital functions, such as DNA synthesis, mitochondrial electron transport, and catecholamine metabolism.

The organismal-level consequences of iron deficiency are typically divided into three areas: (1) disease resistance, (2) activity/work capacity, and (3) cognition and behavior. Pollitt has shown that mild iron deficiency, without low hemoglobin, is associated with learning deficiencies (1987). Of particular note are changes in attention- and memory-control processes. In separate reports, Howell (1971) showed that three- to five-year-old anemic children had decreased attention spans, and Sulzer et al. (1973) illustrated that anemic children of the same age had lower IQ measures and impaired associative reactions. These results suggest that iron is a critical element for the normal functioning of the nervous system and that cognitive functions can be disrupted by relatively mild iron deficiency.

Work capacity has frequently been shown to be proportional to hemoglobin concentration (Scrimshaw, 1991). Anemic subjects cannot maintain the same pace and duration of work as can nonanemic subjects, and they reach a lower mean maximal workload. Anemic Guatemalan laborers performed much more poorly on the Harvard Step Test than their nonanemic peers, and the work output and pay of Indonesian rubber tappers correlates almost perfectly with their hemoglobin levels (Scrimshaw, 1991). Decreased oxygen affinity and increased cardiac output are the "adaptive" responses to anemia (Vyas and Chandra, 1984). However, these adaptations can only cover for deficiency when the organism is sedentary or at rest.

Iron deficiency has a variety of effects on immunocompetence and infection. Especially noteworthy is anemia's effect on cell-mediated immunity (Dallman, 1987). Experimentally induced iron deficiency results in a reduction in lymphocyte proliferation, the production of rosette-forming T cells, and the microbicidal capacity of neutrophils (Dallman, 1987; Vyas and Chandra, 1984). In humans, iron supplements have led to a decreased prevalence of diarrhea and upper- and lower-respiratory infections. Interestingly, a few studies have shown that iron supplementation may lead to an increase in infection, perhaps because the anemic condition was "starving" pathogens which needed iron to multiply in their host. This possibility suggests that anemia is "adaptive" (Stuart-Macadam, 1992). However, we doubt this situation was typical of past populations because the increase in microbial growth appears to occur only in situations of rather heroic medical and/or nutritional interventions (Goodman, 1993).

PALEOEPIDEMIOLOGY

Several examples from the archaeological record serve to highlight issues in interpreting rates of porotic hyperostosis. Research groups led by Lallo (Lallo et al., 1977) and Mensforth (Mensforth et al., 1978) examined the frequency and distribution of the lesion within refined age categories. The study by Lallo and colleagues demonstrated through use of very small age-group categories that the cluster of lesions in younger children reflected an increased need for iron metabolism during growth and development in a prehistoric population from Dickson Mounds, Illinois. An analysis of the relationship between porotic hyperostosis and infectious diseases strongly suggested that the two occurred together and acted in a synergistic fashion, with porotic hyperostosis increasing the potential for infectious disease. Porotic hyperostosis had an earlier age of onset than infection, and the diseases co-occur in high frequencies in subsequent ages. Thus, Lallo and colleagues (1977) were able to document their claim that iron deficiency predisposed children to infectious disease, possibly by lowering their resistance.

On the other hand, Mensforth and colleagues (1978) were able to document the reverse process for a prehistoric population from Libben, Ohio: infectious diseases predisposed children to iron-deficiency anemia. Using refined age categories and making distinctions between healed and unhealed lesions, they showed a synergistic relationship whereby in this population, infectious disease acted as the initial stress that predisposed individuals to iron deficiency.

Palkovich (1987) added a new dimension to the analysis of porotic hyperostosis using subadult skeletal material from Arroyo Hondo, New Mexico. Palkovich demonstrated that in different situations, weaning might not be the major cause of porotic hyperostosis. For Arroyo Hondo, the early age of onset of porotic hyperostosis is coincident with active periostitis in infants ages newborn to one year. Her interpretation of this finding is that a chronically poor diet was affecting the pregnant females and their fetuses, "acting synergistically with immediately acquired infections, not weaning diets" to produce the pattern of porotic hyperostosis seen for Arroyo Hondo (1987:527).

The importance of these two studies is that in each archaeological population, there were different ecological and cultural conditions causing the same lesion (porotic hyperostosis). They show clearly the importance of looking at pathologies within a populational as well as a cultural, ecological, and biological context.

Scoring systems for porotic hyperostosis have been established that distinguish lesions by severity, location, and amount of remodeling that had occurred. Remodeling in this case means the amount of new bone that has formed in response to the lesion (almost all bone destruction triggers new bone formation). If the disease persists, the effect of remodeling will not be seen because bone will be destroyed as quickly as it is formed. If the disease ceases or lessens, however, there will be a visible replacement of formerly diseased bone with newly mineralized bone (Figure 2.6). Thus, the amount of healing is subject to the length of time that the disease has been acting on bone, the severity of the disease response, the speed of new bone formation, and the overall health status of the individual.

The amount of remodeling provides some measure, in and of itself, of an individual's and a population's ability to respond and essentially "adapt" to the anemic condition. Although destruction of bone tissue is the result of the anemic condition, it does not necessarily imply cause of death. Illness can result from the inability of the body to circulate iron, and therefore oxygen, to supporting tissues from the medullary cavities of the bone where red blood cell production takes place. It has been clinically established that most individuals can live for a very long time even with a chronic iron deficiency (Finch and Cook, 1984). Nonetheless, iron deficiency can have consequence for mortality via its relationship to immunocompetence and other functions.

Thus, either active or healed porotic hyperostosis does not demonstrate that the individual died from iron-deficiency anemia. Conversely, it does suggest that iron deficiency, in combination with other factors, may have contributed significantly to poor health and to functionally compromised individuals. The state of the lesion is critical for providing information on the capacity of the individual's and, by extension, the population's competence to respond to stressors in their immediate environment.

The evaluation of porotic hyperostosis provides one more valuable tool to reconstruct health profiles of past individuals and populations. Because of the likely role of iron, some specific inferences become apparent, such as the role of maize (with low iron bioavailability) in the etiology of porotic hyperostosis. Perhaps most fascinating, however, are the clear functional implications. With a sense of the functional significance of iron status in contemporary populations and the severity of porotic hyperostosis in some past populations, one can begin to get a sense of how infirmity may have affected the lives and livelihoods of past peoples.

Infectious Disease

BACKGROUND: PATHOPHYSIOLOGY AND CAUSAL INFERENCES

Infectious diseases have been key selective forces in human evolution (Armelagos and Dewey, 1978; Haldane, 1949) and, in combination with undernutrition, continue to be the largest contributor to morbidity and mortality worldwide (Keusch and Farthing, 1986). Infants and children are usually the most severely affected by infectious diseases, and the rate of subadult infection is often used as indicators of community health and population fitness (Gordon et al., 1967). With the spread of AIDS and cholera and the reemergence of tuberculosis, it is all the more clear how pervasive and persistent infectious diseases are, and how significant they remain and have always been as forces in human history and determinants of well-being.

Perhaps the most perplexing problem in the study of infectious disease via skeletal remains is the fact that only some infectious episodes leave diagnostic markers on the skeletal system. In general, acute (short-term) infections do not affect the skeleton because microbial attack and physiological response run their course, with individuals either recovering or dying, before profound bone involvement takes place (Ortner, 1979, 1991). Conversely, it is fortunate for paleopathologists that the more common, "garden variety" and highly prevalent microorganisms that cause infection also affect bone.

The continuum of chronic to acute infectious processes yields different kinds of information. Virulent epidemics reveal information on population responses to relatively short-term crises and high death rates. Chronic (and typically nonlethal) conditions are important to track at the community level because they may shed light on everyday occurrences of nutritional adequacy, diet, the level of transmissible diseases, the state of waste disposal, and hygiene. In other words, low-level, lingering, but nonlethal bouts of infection can reveal something about lifestyle and group living that the more virulent and epidemic infections do not.

The general inflammatory response always begins vascularly (Ortner and Putschar, 1981:104). Dilated capillary walls burst and cells normally retained in the circulatory system are released. These cells, which include albumins, globulins, and leukocytes, travel to the site where there are bacteria. Leukocytes can engulf and destroy bacteria, or the bacteria, if numerous or virulent, can disintegrate the

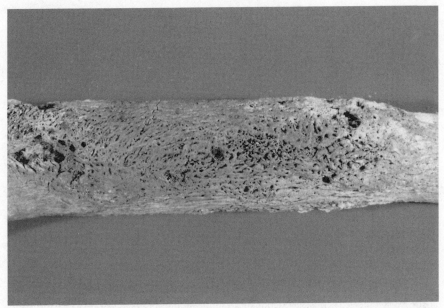

Figure 2.7. Active periosteal reaction on an adult tibia from a prehistoric Anasazi female from Black Mesa, Arizona. Periosteal reactions are largely bone-producing responses; the outer surface of the bone begins to rapidly produce new bone cells in response to the hypervascularized state, and this production of bone results in a raised, irregular appearance.

leukocytes and continue to proliferate. Pus is produced when leukocytes (along with proteins and fibrin) are at the site of the bacterial invasion.

Many kinds of infections or inflammatory conditions (including osteomyelitis and periostitis) cause the same skeletal response: an elevation of the fibrous outer periosteal layer of the bone (Figure 2.7). This stems from the compression and stretching of minute blood vessels surrounding the bone, as well as the vascular network within the bone. Subperiosteal hemorrhage occurs when the vessels stretch, compress, and tear, and this in turn reduces blood supply to the bone.

Most examples of infectious disease found on prehistoric skeletal remains are nonspecific in nature. That is, the lesions can be caused by a number of pathological conditions, and differential diagnosis concerning exact etiology is often difficult. The most common causes of infectious disease are microorganisms, such as *Staphylococcus* and *Streptococcus*, making up nearly 90% of cases (Ortner and Putschar, 1981:106).

If the physiological disruption is severe and long-term, the periosteal bone tissue will die; however, bone constantly remodels (resorption of old bone, apposition of new bone). The rate of remodeling is dependent on a number of physiological factors and varies from individual to individual. Through remodeling, some bone remains intact, while other parts are destroyed and die (become necrotic). If the infection subsides, remodeling will eventually replace all the necrotic bone with new healthy tissue. In addition to evaluating the extent and severity of osseous

Figure 2.8. Remodeled periosteal reaction on an adult femur from a prehistoric Anasazi male from Black Mesa, Arizona. If the agent causing infection is not persistent or if the immune response is strong enough to overcome the infectious disease, through the remodeling process, necrotic bone will be removed and new, healthy bone tissue will replace it. The newly remodeled bone appears smooth where new tissue is, but pitted and irregular where there are remnants of the periosteal reaction.

involvement, it is also possible to evaluate whether a periosteal reaction was active at the time of death. Nonremodeled (active) lesions appear as smooth, irregular, lattice-like layers of new bone formed over the existing bone. In advanced cases, they exhibit a hypervascularized scablike appearance of variable thickness. But even in mild cases, discernible patterns are evident. The amount of necrotic (dead), raised bone gives a relative indication of the severity and longevity of the infection. Once the periosteum begins to heal, the raised lattice-like layers begin to recede, and while still irregular and pitted, bone that is healing will eventually return to normal texture through the remodeling process (Figure 2.8).

As with porotic hyperostosis, the status of the lesion (active or healed) provides an important distinction for paleoepidemiological inferences. Active, unremodeled lesions generally display a very fibrous and vascularized irregular new layer of bone. Healed or remodeled lesions show resorption and redistribution of new bone as the bone is incorporated into the normal cortex. It appears as dense, smooth bone with some small but patterned irregularities.

Ortner and Putschar (1981) point out that trauma-induced periosteal reactions tend to be small, localized, and nondestructive, whereas infectious diseases tend to be generalized and destructive, and they usually affect multiple long bones. Periosteal reactions due to infectious diseases are usually systemic in nature, in most cases bilaterally affecting multiple long bones. When scoring tibias (the most sensitive bone, probably due to the bone's closeness to the skin and frequency of cuts and scrapes) for periosteal reactions, as an example, other long bones should be evaluated. If other bones are involved, then the tibia is scored as having a systemic infectious disease reaction. If only the tibia shows infectious involvement, then it could be considered a localized response to trauma and should be scored as such.

PALEOEPIDEMIOLOGICAL CONSIDERATIONS

Bony signs of infectious lesions are easily identified. A key to their study is to evaluate the pattern of involvement within and between groups. One example of this paleoepidemiological approach is Lallo and co-workers' (1978) study of periosteal lesions in 595 burials from Dickson Mounds, Illinois. They demonstrated that the prevalence and severity of periosteal reactions increased dramatically as the population changed from a relatively isolated and seminomadic hunting and gathering group (Late Woodland) to one with increased trade, greater population density and sedentism, and greater reliance on maize agriculture (Middle Mississippian). In addition, they were able to show that infectious lesions were slightly greater in Middle Mississippian–period females versus males, and individuals with infections died at an earlier age, thus demonstrating the impact that infectious disease can have on the population structure. A paleoepidemiological and demographic approach to the analysis of infections in prehistoric contexts concentrates on delineating the number of individuals by age and sex who have skeletal lesions. Such an analysis may reveal effects on subgroups at risk, on population structure, on age and sex differences in distribution, and ultimately on ecological and cultural factors predisposing some individuals to infection while protecting others.

Perhaps no single endeavor has entertained (and perhaps frustrated) paleoepidemiologists more than efforts to determine the specific infectious agents responsible for osseous lesions. At present, these efforts have been most successful in evaluation of bone responses due to tuberculosis and treponemal disease. Tuberculosis is usually contracted via the respiratory tract; it is a chronic infectious disease that has come to be associated with crowded living conditions (Aufderheide and Rodríguez-Martín, 1998; Ortner and Putschar, 1981). The bony response usually is detected in the vertebral column, although tuberculosis can affect virtually any skeletal joint system and the cranium as well.

Treponemal infections include a number of different diseases, including venereal syphilis, yaws, pinta, and nonvenereal (or endemic) syphilis. As with tuberculosis, differential diagnosis is difficult but possible (Ortner and Putschar, 1981). Key diagnostic traits of advanced syphilis include saber shins, polydactylitis, and osteolytic lesions of the external nasal vault and nasopalatal region (Ortner and Putschar, 1981; Powell, 1991).

SUMMARY

It is relatively easy to identify systemic periosteal reactions and signs of chronic infectious disease. However, as with most other paleopathological indicators, there is little comparability across studies. In fact, in our experience, the range of periosteal involvement can shift radically from group to group. Therefore, without published standards for comparison, what might be considered moderate to severe periostitis in one study may be considered mild to normal in another.

Perhaps the biggest issue facing studies of infection in past populations is better estimation of what fraction of the total burden of infection is represented in skeletal lesions. A key to solving this riddle is to pay attention to the pattern of other indicators of morbidity, the pattern of mortality, and the archaeological contexts. For example, high mortality and low infectious morbidity could suggest an epidemic-type infection in certain cultural contexts.

Ortner (1991) has also argued that periosteal reactions might be interpreted as signs of an individual's responding and adapting to infectious disease. Indeed, periosteal reactions are as much due to the physiological response of an individual as they are due to the actions of an invading organism. We suggest that the adaptiveness of the response can be evaluated if a multiple indicator approach is used. If, for sake of argument, periosteal reactions are associated with long life, then they might be considered to be adaptive, at least in the sense that they have a minimal effect on mortality (although it remains of interest to know why some and not all individuals might be exposed to infection). Conversely, if individuals with periosteal reactions suffer from increased mortality and also appear to be nutritionally compromised, then it is difficult to consider these lesions to be anything but signs of physiological disruption. Wood and colleagues (1992) in their presentation of the "osteological paradox" suggest otherwise and, in particular, that it is not possible to know if the absence of infectious bony reactions is because the people were robust enough to resist the disease or so frail that they simply died before there could be any bony response. As they have not yet provided a statistical solution to this problem or any actual testing of this proposition with skeletal samples, both the health index and the case studies presented in this volume interpret the frequency of infectious reactions only within the context of all other indicators of disease and nutrition.

Trauma

BACKGROUND: PATHOPHYSIOLOGY AND CAUSAL INFERENCES

Traumatic lesions caused by physical force encompass a broad range of clinical classifications that include fractures, crushing injuries, wounds caused by weapons and other devices, dislocations, and an assortment of biomechanically induced pathologies, such as exostoses, osteochondritis dissecans and spondylolysis (Aufderheide and Rodríguez-Martín, 1998; Merbs, 1989; Ortner and Putschar, 1981; Steinbock, 1976). The process and timing of the trauma can often be determined by analyzing the intensity and direction of the force. Interpretations concerning trauma are generally more transparent than other kinds of pathologies. For example, if the traumatic lesion occurs with periosteal reactions, then both the bone and soft tissue were involved. Conversely, simple fractures that do not break through the soft tissue and skin rarely become infected (Steinbock, 1976). Also, the degree to

Figure 2.9. An unaligned, healed fracture of the tibia (lower leg) on a prehistoric Anasazi adult male from Black Mesa, Arizona. After fracturing, the lower (distal) part of the tibia was never properly set or realigned. The healing process continued until the two unaligned portions of the bone were awkwardly conjoined. The distal tibia in the normal state tapers to a slender shape; however, this healed fracture has left the distal tibia a large bulbous shape.

which a trauma has healed provides a clue to the relationship between the traumatic event and the possible contribution of the trauma to morbidity and mortality.

Fractures in long bones, ribs, and vertebrae are the most frequently reported of the traumatic lesions (Merbs, 1989), and also are the most easily assessed. Fractures can be classified into a number of categories ranging from micro stress fractures to greenstick breaks to comminuted and complete breaks (Figure 2.9). The response of bone to any kind of fracture is the same. New bone formation begins within a few days after the break occurs. Calcium salts are released from bone and are used in calcifying the callous matrix that forms a binding and connecting sheath around the two fractured ends. Within two weeks calcification is underway and the internal remodeling and reorganization of the bone callus begins. The healing process can last for months or years, depending on the age and health of the individual and the severity of the break (Ortner and Putschar, 1981). Even a poorly aligned bone will eventually mend itself if infection does not interfere with the healing process. The healing process occurs much more quickly in children than in adults. Union of two bone ends can be complete in four to six weeks in children, while in adults this process can typically persist for over four months (Merbs, 1989).

Depression fractures occur most frequently on the flat bones of the crania and have been reported for many prehistoric individuals (Ortner and Putschar, 1981). Merbs (1989) defines a depression fracture as one produced by a force applied to just one side of a bone, whereas compression fractures are produced when there is force

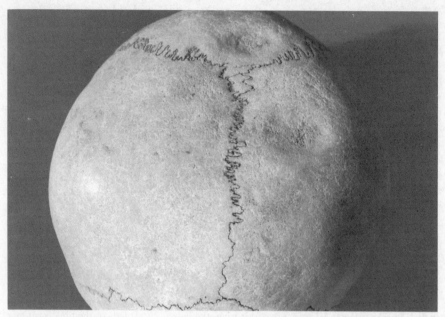

Figure 2.10. Two healed depression fractures on an eighteen-year-old female Anasazi from Black Mesa, Arizona. Although these fractures are completely healed, bone damage and compression have left telltale concavities that suggest severe blows to the back of the head.

from two sides; however, these distinctions can be difficult to make in archaeological specimens. These fractures usually result from a blow to the head by a blunt object. On the cranium, this results in a depression in the outer bony table, and if the skin is broken, there will be some infectious response as well. The pathophysiological responses are similar in cranial fractures: there is a coagulation of blood at the site with resultant formation of new bone at the fracture site. After the site has completely remodeled and healed, a telltale depression in the cranium usually remains (Figure 2.10).

In archaeological specimens, fractures and traumatic lesions in the process of healing or with complete healing are fairly easily identified and counted. However, when traumatic events occur around the time of death, it can be difficult to distinguish the perimortem bone damage from postmortem changes. Although numerous researchers have attempted to isolate the differences between perimortem and postmortem trauma, it is almost impossible to make firm diagnostic interpretations without other information regarding the context of the burial (White, 1992). For example, although bone crushed from the blow of a blunt object will shatter differently when it is fresh versus later when it is dry, recovery of all of the pieces of bone is necessary for distinguishing the timing of the breaks (Mann and Murphy, 1990). The amount of bone beveling and the type of fracturing (spiral versus straight) are important indicators of when the trauma occurred and therefore whether it is significant in the reconstruction of health. Another factor potentially hampering diagnosis is incomplete recovery of broken elements. For example, if the distal end is not recovered, then the nonunion of the proximal end of a fracture could be misinterpreted as an amputation.

Careful observation of the entire skeleton of individuals with trauma can aid in understanding the timing of the event and subsequent health problems. For example, a fractured and healed femoral neck may contribute significantly to osteoporosis and osteoarthritis in adjacent bones (Merbs, 1989). Asymmetry in body proportions may occur when unaligned bones heal, making compensatory biomechanical changes necessary. These kinds of secondary changes are important to note because they could contribute significantly to our understanding of the quality of life and changes in health that may accompany a traumatic event.

The extent to which fractures disable and deform individuals can sometimes be assessed, and this information can be very important in understanding functional capacities and community health dynamics. Adults crippled by unaligned fractures could be less productive in subsistence activities. Furthermore, lifelong accumulated adjustments in the form of limping and inefficient gait would also enhance osteoarthritic changes in joints and other health problems. The medical intervention aspects of trauma in prehistoric groups are largely speculative, although Merbs (1989) has reviewed a number of cases where "bonesetting" was clearly a skill that some groups practiced.

In a special issue of the *International Journal of Osteoarchaeology* (Eisenberg and Hutchinson, eds., 1996), a wide range of paleopathological studies are presented; they represent culturally, temporally, and geographically diverse examples of trauma, ranging from axe and blade injuries to fractures and cut marks, and decapitation is also presented. Authors go beyond simple wound identification to consider the basics of bone fracture physics and the wider behavioral implications of trauma, "using the presence, patterning and distribution of traumatic lesions as powerful tools for interpreting lifestyle from the skeleton" (Eisenberg and Hutchinson, 1996:1).

PALEOEPIDEMIOLOGY

Reconstruction and interpretation of trauma in prehistoric societies is a challenging task, complicated by the fact that the only direct evidence comes from the osteological and archaeological record (although on occasion there may be mummified soft tissue or artwork that provides more conclusive evidence regarding the nature of the traumatic event). Some studies on trauma in past societies have focused on warfare (Bamforth, 1994; Blakely and Mathews, 1990; Hutchinson, 1996; Milner et al., 1991). Others have looked at nonwar violence (see edited volumes by Eisenberg and Hutchinson, 1996; Martin and Frayer, 1997) where the resulting trauma is related to behaviors such as homicide, ritualized nonlethal combat, hand-to-hand fighting, scalping, sacrifice, cannibalism, domestic violence, and other acts that are part of conflict and strife, show of power, or conflict resolution.

Analyses of the specific types of trauma can provide a direct inference about behavioral patterns; specific activities predispose individuals to recognizable types of accidental or intentional trauma. Moreover, various forms of interpersonal violence (warfare, scalping, mutilation, lacerations, cannibalism) and of surgical intervention (trephination, amputation) can sometimes be identified (Merbs, 1989; White, 1992). Fractures of the forearm (radius and ulna) can reveal information about the activities of the group. A common fracture referred to as a Colles fracture occurs near the wrist and typically results when an individual who is falling extends the arms in order to break or soften the fall. Fractures that occur farther up along the forearm may result from the raising of the arm in front of the face to ward off a blow (these are called parry fractures, as in "to parry a blow"). In a sense, the frequency of parry fractures could begin to provide an index of violence, whereas the frequency of Colles fractures provides some insight into activity patterns (such as walking rapidly over rough terrain). The patterning of the trauma within a population can be very enlightening as to environments conducive to accidents, as well as inter- and intragroup strife. The occurrence of multiple injuries, injuries from artifacts and weapons, and the demographic pattern by age and sex can provide insights into the use of force or violence in a society or the potential problems in lifestyle and subsistence activities that lead to accidents.

Trinkaus and Zimmerman (1982) have provided a thorough account of trauma in the Shanidar Neanderthals. In one individual, fractures in the humerus appeared to damage some nerves, which in turn affected other bones as well. Because of the severe fracture to the humerus, disuse atrophy significantly reduced the size of the right humerus, clavicle, and scapula. The detailed analysis of this one individual has provided a wealth of insights into Neanderthal lifestyles.

One of the most thorough analyses of long bone fractures at the population level is presented by Lovejoy and Heiple (1981) for the Libben skeletal collection. A quantitative approach to the analysis of long bone fractures was demonstrated to be valuable in interpreting various behavioral aspects of the population. These researchers report that: (1) most fractures occurred as a consequence of accidents, (2) the fracture rate was highest in the 10–25 and 45+ age groups, (3) care of patients by group members was skillful, particularly in the setting of bones, and (4) the chance of acquiring a fracture was largely determined by accumulated years of risk in the population.

An analysis of the patterning of cranial wounds can begin to aid in the understanding of violence in prehistoric groups (Stewart and Quade, 1969). Walker (1989) presents convincing evidence that the prehistoric inhabitants of the Channel Islands and the California coast were practicing ritualized fights during which nonlethal blows to the head were regularly inflicted upon both adult males and females. Here, numerous healed cranial lesions were found primarily on adult females, on the front and sides of the skulls. Another example showing how the patterning of cranial lesions was used to interpret group behavior comes from the La Plata River Valley in New Mexico (Martin, 1997). Some (but not all) adult women demonstrated numerous healed cranial lesions primarily found on the front, sides, and back of the head. Females with cranial lesions were found buried with no grave goods and little burial preparation. The combined osteological and archaeological analysis suggested that a group of "targeted" women were either captive slaves or part of an underclass of immigrant women.

SUMMARY: EPIDEMIOLOGICAL ISSUES AND FUNCTIONAL IMPLICATIONS

Patterns of trauma from cranial and postcranial remains can be very instructive about a range of group activities that link morbidity with behaviors. Trauma is represented in the archaeological record in a variety of forms, from healed, broken ribs that may have been little more than an annoyance to the victims, to severe, nonunited long bone fractures that resulted in lifelong disability and possibly severe pain and discomfort. Patterns of violence and aggression can be tracked when there is evidence of multiple lesions in varying degrees of healing.

Fractures represent the most easily identified of all the traumatic lesions, and a complete description of the location and status aids in making interpretive assessments of the impact on the individual and in populations. Unlike other diseases in the paleopathology repertoire, trauma is not directly caused by external factors such as nutrition or microbes. It is the direct result of "hostile encounters with the environment and other humans" and as such, provides unique insights into prehistoric health status (Merbs, 1989:187).

Osteoarthritis and Degenerative Joint Disease

BACKGROUND: PATHOPHYSIOLOGY

Osteoarthritis is one of the oldest and most common ailments. Yet, evaluating the severity of arthritic involvement is difficult because of the potentially large number of areas to be assessed (each vertebra and all joint systems) and the range of variation in bony response among individuals. While many factors may contribute to the breakdown of skeletal tissue, the primary cause of osteoarthritis is related to biomechanical wear and tear and functional stress (Aegerter and Kirkpatrick, 1968; Duncan, 1979; Jurmain, 1977; Ortner and Putschar, 1981). Although osteoarthritis is ubiquitous in both contemporary and past populations, focused analyses on functional significance suggests that there is great variation from individual to individual in how much movement impairment or pain is associated with any specific degree of osteoarthritis, thus hampering our ability to make general statements about its severity and meaning at the population level (1993 Paleopathology Association Seminar).

Osteoarthritis is most apparent at the articular surfaces of long bone joint systems and is referred to as degenerative joint disease (DJD) (Figure 2.11). DJD has been linked to activity patterns that habitually put strain on joint systems (Bridges, 1991; Kennedy, 1989). There may also be an association between DJD and other health problems. At Dickson Mounds, individuals with multiple joint involvement demonstrated a statistically higher percentage of periosteal reactions. Both infectious lesions and DJD appear to be a function of age in this population. Furthermore, females demonstrated higher frequencies of DJD in the shoulder and elbows than age-matched males, suggesting that subsistence activities such as corn grinding may have been "women's work" (Martin et al., 1979).

Degenerative joint disease is generally defined by breakdown of bone at the articular surface areas of joints. Following the exposure of subchondral bone, the bone

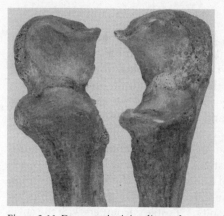 

Figure 2.11. Degenerative joint disease from a prehistoric adult from Dickson Mound, Illinois. The lipping at the margins of the joint system (elbow on left, shoulder on right) show degeneration and macroporosity and would likely cause some stiffness and possibly disability (from Martin et al., 1979).

contact points become pitted, with marginal lipping and erosion (see Figure 2.11). Eventually eburnation, the formation of a hard, shiny bone callus, takes place. DJD is not an inflammatory disease but develops on the basis of age-related changes and breakdown of the cartilage and lubricating systems. The condition is slowly progressive but is not found to occur in all older adults in the same form. Thus, the condition probably represents the accumulation of years of alterations of the articular cartilage and breakdown of the joint.

PALEOPATHOLOGY

The analysis of DJD typically considers the severity of the condition, distinguishing slight involvement from severe. There are numerous sets of criteria published to devise a graded scale of severity of involvement (Aegerter and Kirkpatrick, 1968; Ortner, 1968; Steinbock, 1976). In addition, degenerative joint diseases are rarely confined to a single joint complex. The weight-bearing joints, such as the lower back, hip, and knees, and those exposed to chronic trauma, such as the shoulder and elbow, are most frequently affected (Jurmain, 1978). The pattern, distribution, severity, and onset by age, class, and sex in adults can be used to interpret the role of cultural activity, as well as in the overall understanding of quality of life for individuals within the community.

Vertebral osteophytosis is a specific form of degeneration that is characterized by lipping (extra bony growths, usually in long spikes) on the vertebral bodies. It has been associated with changes in the intervertebral discs (Chapman, 1973; Stewart, 1932). Commonly found in prehistoric and modern populations, this degeneration typically begins at 30 years of age and affects almost all individuals by the age of 60 (Steinbock, 1976). The lipping may range from a slight sharpness to complete fusion of contiguous vertebral bodies (Figure 2.12).

Figure 2.12. Osteophytosis along the lumbar vertebrae from a 40-year-old Anasazi male from Black Mesa, Arizona. The osteophytosis is not an advanced case; there is lipping along the borders of the vertebral bodies, and there is some degeneration in body height. Normal vertebral bodies are smooth and rounded with no extended bone spicules.

Ortner's (1968) revealing study of DJD in prehistoric Alaskan Eskimos and Peruvian Indians focused on degenerative changes in the distal humerus. His research design included using the patterning of DJD to assess handedness, sexual division of labor, and cultural practices which influence type and degree of elbow use. Alaskans had significantly higher frequencies of elbow DJD than the Peruvians, and this was related to spear throwing and other hunting activities regularly engaged in by Eskimos.

A second in-depth analysis of osteoarthritic changes related to activity patterns is Merbs's (1983) study of a prehistoric population from the Canadian Arctic. He found that there were significant differences between male and female vertebral osteophytosis, with females demonstrating more thoracic involvement, and males, more lumbar involvement. This resulted from males' hunting and females' habitual domestic activities. Females also displayed a greater loss of mandibular anterior teeth and temporomandibular DJD due to the long periods of time spent chewing and softening leather.

Kennedy (1989) has provided a detailed listing of degenerative bone changes that appear to be related to occupations. For examples, Angel (1966) and Bridges (1987) show relationships between spear throwing and DJD of the humerus. Merbs (1983) found a connection between kayak paddling and high rates of osteoarthritis of the scapula, and "seamstress fingers" with DJD of the thumbs and index finger joints. Bridges (1991) showed an increase in DJD with intensification of agriculture in precontact Alabama groups, while Williamson (2000) documents differences in DJD between upland and lowland agriculturalists along the Georgia coast, showing the influence of the environment. Walker and Hollimon (1989) demonstrated an increase in DJD in prehistoric California coast groups that shifted toward intensive exploitation of marine resources.

The bony response to biomechanical wear and tear on both joint systems and vertebrae includes two basic morphological characteristics: growth of osteophytes (hypertrophic osteogenesis) and the destruction of the joint surface (macroporosity and bone breakdown). On both joint systems and vertebral elements, the degenerative changes occur on the joint surface (where two bones articulate), the areas that are contiguous with but peripheral to the joint, and on various parts of the bone that come indirectly into contact with other bones in the movement of joint systems (such as vertebral spines and processes and various fossa and landmarks on long bones).

The pattern of degenerative joint disease within individuals and groups provides a further set of clues about the life of past individuals. Similar to traumatic pathologies, there is no need to invoke an environmental agent. Rather, DJD is related to how humans act upon the environment. Unlike trauma, which represents sudden, acute interactions, DJD is reflective of cumulative and repetitive motions. The systematic assessment of DJD and vertebral osteophytosis can provide an indicator of lifestyle and work habits in prehistoric populations. However, clinicians working in the area of gerontology and arthritis caution against the direct correlation of osteoarthritic changes with pain and dysfunction (Aegerter and Kirkpatrick, 1968). Any morphological changes less than total fusion of vertebral bodies or joint systems cannot be directly linked to immobility, and physicians suggest that there is little correlation between severity of osteoarthritis and an individual's level of pain. Thus, although levels of pain and dysfunction in prehistoric groups may not be ascertained, the presence and status of osteoarthritis can be used as an indicator of biomechanical stress which reflects the accumulative stresses and strains of habitual use of the musculoskeletal system. In this sense, it is also related to quality of life in terms of how intense workloads might have been and how division of labor may have affected males or females preferentially.

SUMMARY

In summary, osteoarthritis is a common and easily discerned condition that is cumulative with age. Although the relationship between bony change and disability is not easily predicted, osteoarthritis has consequences for mobility and quality of life.

Dental Caries and Tooth Loss

The dentition may well provide a direct record of conditions under which the individual lived. The state of his health, his diet, age, and certain aspects of his material culture are indicated by the appearance of the teeth and the supporting bone. The problem is how to read this record. (Molnar, 1971:188)

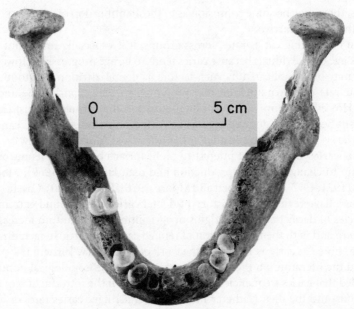

Figure 2.13. An adult mandible from Black Mesa, Arizona. This individual, whose dental health is typical for this group, displays dental decay (right molar), severe attrition of the anterior teeth, and antemortem tooth loss. Antemortem loss is easily distinguished from postmortem loss due to the resorption of root sockets. Loss of posterior teeth (resorbed sockets, compared to anterior unresorbed root sockets) as in this example, may very well be related to caries.

Teeth are among the most frequently recovered skeletal elements and, as Molnar (1971) suggests, they provide critical information on diet and other behaviors. Our purpose in this section is to consider two key aspects of dental health, caries and tooth loss, in light of their potential implications for reconstructing diet and overall health status. Alt et al. (1998), Kelley and Larsen (1991), and Lukacs (1992) have edited sets of articles that focus on dental anthropology with a focus on dental health.

DENTAL CARIES: ETIOLOGY AND PALEOEPIDEMIOLOGY

Dental caries is a disease process characterized by areas of demineralization due to the action of acidogenic bacteria, such as *Streptococcus mutans*, which grow in plaque on tooth surfaces (Larsen, 1997). Caries is a multifactorial disease. The extent of decay depends on a variety of interacting variables, including factors of host resistance and hygiene, the pathogenic agent, and the environment, including what is eaten (Lukacs, 1989; Powell, 1985).

Caries data are often collected by location on the tooth. The most common site of decay is the occlusal surface of multicusped teeth; decay tends to develop in areas where plaque can adhere to a tooth surface (Figure 2.13). Caries rates, therefore, tend to vary by tooth position, with the highest rates found on posterior and maxillary teeth. Although decay is frequently and easily observed in teeth from archaeological contexts, there may be some confusion as to the identification of "arrested" lesions, that is, they are not active.

When comparing caries rates across groups, it is especially important to consider the age of individuals because caries tends to be age progressive. However, this pattern may be complicated by such factors as dental attrition and tooth loss. A moderate rate of crown attrition may promote caries by exposing the underlying dentin. However, a more vigorous rate of attrition may protect against caries development because the decayed enamel is worn away before the lesion can spread. Similarly, it is important to consider antemortem loss (discussed below).

Dental caries is of greatest interest to prehistorians because of its historical relationship to changes in food production and diet. Hardwick (1960), Moore and Corbett (1971, 1973, 1975; Corbett and Moore, 1976), Keene (1980), Caselitz (1998), and others have reviewed the history of dental caries. They found extremely low frequencies of decay before the origins of agriculture and quantum increases after agriculture and with the introduction of refined carbohydrates. In fact, this association was noted as early as 1869 with the work of Mummery. Turner (1979), having reviewed the literature on the frequency of caries in anthropological populations, concluded that caries frequencies may be diagnostic of the introduction of agricultural foods into the diet. Gatherer-hunters generally have caries rates of less than 2% of permanent teeth, mixed economies have more variable rates with a mean around 5%, and agricultural economies have higher and also more variable rates, from 2% to over 25%, with a central tendency around 10%.

These data have been confirmed by numerous studies in *Paleopathology of the Origins of Agriculture* (Cohen and Armelagos, eds., 1984). Thirteen of 19 case studies report caries data. The majority of these show dramatic increases in carious teeth, frequently on the order of a tenfold or greater increase, after agriculture (see Larsen, 1984; Martin et al., 1984; Perzigian et al., 1984). From these studies it can be assumed that the increased production of maize in prehistoric North America contributed to a rise in caries frequencies. However, Rose and co-workers (1984) and Allison (1984) caution that less is known about the relationship between food preparation techniques and caries. Caselitz (1998) documents a 12,000-year worldwide increase in carious lesions using data from 518 skeletal collections where the peaks of increase are associated with major subsistence changes.

PREMORTEM TOOTH LOSS: ETIOLOGY, PALEOEPIDEMIOLOGY, AND FUNCTIONAL CONSEQUENCES

Pre- or antemortem tooth loss is also of interest both as a reflection of dental health and because it may entail functional impairment. Premortem loss is frequently associated with a variety of dental conditions, including abscessing, extreme alveolar resorption, excess attrition, and caries (Figure 2.13). Premortem loss may, in fact, be due to any one or combination of these factors.

Because tooth loss is assumed to be due to caries, oral epidemiologists working with modern populations by convention express caries rates as percent or number per mouth of teeth that are either decayed, missing, or filled (DMF rates). This convention, while very useful for comparative purposes, is somewhat problematic for those working with anthropological populations. Teeth and the surrounding alveolar bone are frequently missing; thus, it is difficult to extrapolate a DMF (or DM) rate per mouth. Furthermore, teeth are frequently lost premortem for reasons other than invasive decay.

Regardless of cause, tooth loss has important functional implications. In a sense, premortem tooth loss represents the ultimate diminution of functional, masticatory capacity. Rampant tooth loss may have a strong effect on the health and nutritional status of the individual (Geissler and Bates, 1984; Nagao, 1992; Palmer and Pappas, 1989). With endemic tooth loss, foods become increasingly more difficult to chew, thus limiting the range of dietary options. Palmer and Pappas (1989) have calculated a 20% loss of nutrient intake in people who have lost all of their teeth.

Based on the belief that most dental pathologies increase with agriculture, one might assume that tooth loss will also increase as a secondary effect of this dietary shift. In fact, Cook (1984) and Smith et al. (1984) found increases in tooth loss with agricultural intensification. However, Cassidy (1984) and Meiklejohn and co-workers (1984) have found the opposite trend. These contradictory results may be due to the effects of high gatherer-hunter attrition rates, which also can cause tooth loss.

SUMMARY: THE USES OF DENTAL PATHOLOGIES

Dental caries and tooth loss information can provide information that is useful in a variety of serendipitous and circuitous ways. They provide an index of the carbohydrate composition of the diet, they have functional significance for dietary intake and nutritional status, and they may reflect in complex ways the immunological and host-resistance status of the individual.

As with many indicators already noted, dental caries and antemortem tooth loss are relatively easily identified. However, we have reached a period of scientific development in which identification is not enough – data need to be collected in reliable and comparable fashion. And, as with many of the indicators, the hard part is not the collection of the data, but their interpretation.

CONCLUSIONS

Many of the most exciting developments in anthropology have come in the overlapping fields of paleonutrition, paleopathology, and paleodemography. These fields, which respectively focus on the nutrition, health, and demography of past populations, have all enjoyed promising advancements in methodology. Even more consequential, improved understanding of the context, causes, and consequences of morbidity and mortality for individuals and groups has led to new inferences and research directions. The human skeleton found in archaeological context is now widely understood to provide key historical and human ecological information.

This chapter has provided an assessment of the abbreviated tool kit for measurement and analysis of health, nutrition, and overall biological well-being from

Table 2.1: Summary of Indicators of Stress Used in Rose and Co-workers' "Nutrition & Health Index" and Discussed in This Chapter

Indicator	Requirements	Groups at risk of	Severity and timing stress/disruption	General comments and functional implications
Life tables (mortality)	Well-represented skeletal population	All	Chronic, severe	General indicator w/group production and reproduction effect
Adult stature	Adult long bones	Subadults	Cumulative of preadult factors	Reflect undernutrition, host of functional consequences
Subadult size	Subadults with dentitions and long bones	Subadults	Cumulative and acute	Can indicate time of greatest stress; host of functions affected
Linear enamel hypoplasia	Any tooth	0.5 in utero to age 7	Temporally known and relatively acute	General, sensitive and chronological record w/functional implication
Porotic hyperostosis	Cranium	Subadults, females	Acute to severe	Fe and associated pathology; immune, cognitive, and work-functional consequences
Periosteal reaction	Long bones	All	Chronic	Generalized infection; potential activity and social consequences
Trauma	All bones	All	Acute	Accidents, activity, and interpersonal violence
Osteoarthritis and osteophytosis	Vertebrae and joints	Adults	Chronic	Habitual activity; pain and immobility?
Dental caries	Any tooth	All	Chronic; low	Multifactorial: diet-related tooth loss and pain; possible results
Antemortem tooth	Any tooth	All/adult	Chronic, cumulative	Diet and dental health; lower dietary intake

48

skeletal remains employed in the health index presented in this volume, as well as employed by most of the individual authors in their case studies. In addition to briefly reviewing the historical development of paleoepidemiology, a subfield of bioarchaeology that focuses broadly on evidence for disease and infirmity, we advocate for a general stress perspective and its compatibility with anthropological concerns. An anthropological approach incorporates the notions that a multiplicity of interacting factors pattern the microenvironment, humans help in shaping their environments, and individuals and groups simultaneously adjust and lose adaptive flexibility due to repeated episodes of stress, disease, and death.

We have focused on indicators adopted for use in the health index (see Steckel, Sciulli, and Rose, this volume) (Table 2.1), which were selected because of common use (and a large available comparative database), ease of study, relatively sound understanding, and potential functional implications. All indicators provide unique information. Some indicators, such as growth and linear enamel hypoplasia, are very nonspecific, while others such as trauma key in to a particular form of stress. What is important is studying indicators within a demographic context and understanding the health profile that develops from using multiple indicators.

In general, tremendous advancements have been made in our ability to make diagnoses and causal inferences. However, many indicators still suffer from poor understanding of the biological processes leading to their formation, and comparability can be hampered by lack of standardized procedures. Because of the inherently imperfect nature of the measures (they are neither perfectly reliable nor perfectly indicative of underlying concepts) and the fact that each measure provides related but different information, we advocate for the importance of multiple measures of stress.

The development of an index of health and nutrition, and efforts to translate this index to estimates of functional impairment, as outlined by Steckel, Sciulli, and Rose (this volume), is an exciting development because it offers great potential for improved understanding of the distribution of infirmities within and between populations, and especially the consequences of ill health. Such an approach is a logical and bold extension of recent trends toward understanding the consequences of health conditions in past populations and provides a series of key challenges for theory and method.

REFERENCES

Aegerter, E.; Kirkpatric, J. A. Jr. *Orthopedic Diseases*. 3d Ed. Philadelphia: W. B. Saunders Co., 1968.

Allen, L. H. Functional indicators of nutritional status of the whole individual or the community. *Clinical Nutrition*; 1984; 3(5): 169–175.

Allison, M. J. Paleopathology in Peruvian and Chilean populations. In: Cohen, M. N.; Armelagos, G. J., eds. *Paleopathology at the Origins of Agriculture*. New York: Academic Press, 1984: 515–530.

Alt, K. W.; Rösing, F. W.; Teschler-Nicola, M., eds. *Dental Anthropology: Fundamentals, Limits, and Prospects*. New York: Springer-Verlag, 1998.

Anderson, B. G.; Stevenson, P. H. The occurrence of mottled enamel among the Chinese. *Journal of Dental Research*; 1930; 10: 233–238.

Angel, J. L. Osteoporosis: thalassemia? *American Journal of Physical Anthropology*, 1964; 22: 369–374.

Porotic hyperostosis, anemias, malarias, and marshes in prehistoric eastern Mediterranean. *Science*, 1966; 153: 760–763.

Porotic hyperostosis or osteoporosis symmetrica. In: Brothwell, D. R.; Sandison, A. T., eds. *Diseases in Antiquity*. Springfield, Ill.: Charles C. Thomas, 1967: 378–389.

Armelagos, G. J. Disease in ancient Nubia. *Science*, 1969; 163: 255–259.

Armelagos, G. J.; Carlson, D. S.; Van Gerven, D. P. The theoretical foundations and development of skeletal biology. In: Spenser, F., ed. *A History of American Physical Anthropology, 1930–1980*. New York: Liss, 1982: 305–327.

Armelagos, G. J.; Dewey, J. R. Evolutionary response to human infectious disease. In: Logan, M. H.; Hunt, E. E., eds. *Health and the Human Condition*. North Scituate, Mass.: Duxbury Press, 1978: 101–106.

Armelagos, G. J.; Mahler, P. E.; Owen, K.; Dewey, J. R.; Mielke, J. Bone growth and development in prehistoric populations from Sudanese Nubia. *Journal of Human Evolution*, 1972; 1: 89–119.

Aufderheide, A. C.; Rodríguez-Martín, C. *The Cambridge Encyclopedia of Human Paleopthology*. Cambridge: Cambridge University Press, 1998.

Baker, P. T. The application of ecological theory in anthropology. *American Anthropologist*, 1966; 64: 15–22.

Human biological variation as an adaptive response to the environment. *Eugenics Quarterly*, 1962; 13: 81–91.

Bamforth, D. G. Indigenous people, indigenous violence: Precontact warfare on the North American Plains. *Man*, 1994; 29: 95–115.

Bass, W. M. *Human Osteology: A Laboratory and Field Manual of the Human Skeleton*. Columbia, Mo.: University of Missouri Archaeological Museum Society, 1971.

Baume, L. J.; Meyer, J. Dental dysplasia related to malnutrition, with special reference to melanodontia and odontoclasia. *Journal of Dental Research*, 1966; 45: 726–741.

Bennett, J. W. *Northern Plainsmen: Adaptive Strategies and Agrarian Life*. Chicago: Aldine, 1966.

Bhargava, S. K.; Ramji, S.; Kumar, A.; Mohan, M.; Marway, J.; Sachdev, H. P. S. Mid-arm and chest circumferences at birth as predictors of low birth weight and neonatal mortality in the community. *British Medical Journal*, 1985; 291: 1617–1625.

Blakely, R. L.; Mathews, D. S. Bioarchaeological evidence for a Spanish–Native American conflict in the sixteenth-century Southeast. *American Antiquity*, 1990; 55: 718–744.

Binford, S. R.; Binford, L. R., eds. *New Perspectives in Archaeology*. Chicago: Aldine, 1968.

Boas, F. The growth of children. *Science*, 1892; 19: 256–257.

Bogin, B. *Patterns of Human Growth*. Cambridge: Cambridge University Press, 1988.

Bridges, P. S. Osteological correlates of weapon use. Paper presented at the 86th Annual Meeting of the American Anthropological Association, Chicago: 1987.

Degenerative joint disease in hunter-gatherers and agriculturalists from the southeastern United States. *American Journal of Physical Anthropology*, 1991; 85: 379–391.

Briend, A.; Dykewicz, C.; Graven, K.; Maxumder, R. N.; Wojtyniak, B.; Bennish, M. Usefulness of nutritional indices and classifications in predicting death of malnourished children. *British Medical Journal*, 1986; 293: 373–380.

Briend, A.; Wojtyniak, B.; Rowland, M. G. M. Arm circumference and other factors in children at high risk of death in rural Bangladesh. *The Lancet*, 1987; Sept. 26: 725–727.

Brothwell, D. R. The bio-cultural background to disease. In: Brothwell, D.; Sandison, A., eds. *Disease in Antiquity*. Springfield, Ill.: C. C. Thomas, 1967: 56–68.

Digging Up Bones. Ithaca, N.Y.: Cornell University Press, 1981.

Brothwell, D. R.; Sandison, A. T., eds. *Disease in Antiquity*. Springfield, Ill.: C. C. Thomas, 1967.

Buikstra, J. E. Out of the appendix and into the dirt: Comments on thirteen years of bioarchaeological research. In: Powell, M. L.; Bridges, P. S.; Mires, A. M. W., eds. *What Mean These Bones?* Tuscaloosa Ala.: University of Alabama Press, 1991: 172–188.

Buikstra, J. E.; Cook, D. C. Paleopathology: An American account. *Annual Reviews of Anthropology*; 1980; 9: 433–470.

Carlson, D.; Armelagos, G. J.; Van Gerven, D. Factors influencing the etiology of cribra orbitalia in prehistoric Nubia. *Journal of Human Evolution*; 1974; 3: 405–410.

Caselitz, P. Caries – ancient plague of humankind. In: Alt, K. W.; Rösing, F. W.; Teschler-Nicola, M., eds. *Dental Anthropology: Fundamentals, Limits, and Prospects*. New York: Springer-Verlag, 1998: 203–226.

Cassidy, C. M. Nutrition and health in agriculturalists and hunters-gatherers: A case study of two prehistoric populations. In: Jerome, N. W.; Kendel, R. F.; Pelto, G. H., eds. *Nutritional Anthropology*. Pleasantville, N.Y.: Redgrave, 1980: 117–145.

  Skeletal evidence for prehistoric subsistence adaptation in the central Ohio River Valley. In: Cohen, M. N.; Armelagos, G. J., eds. *Paleopathology at the Origins of Agriculture*. New York: Academic Press, 1984: 307–346.

Chapman, F. H. Comparison of osteoarthritis in three aboriginal populations. *Proceedings of the Indiana Academy of Science for 1973*; 1965; 74: 84–86.

Chavez, A.; Martinez, C. *Growing Up in a Developing Community*. Mexico City: Instituto Nacional de la Nutricion, 1982.

Chen, L. C.; Chowdhury, A. K. M. A.; Huffman, S. L. Anthropometric assessment of energy-protein malnutrition and subsequent risk of mortality among preschool aged children. *American Journal of Clinical Nutrition*; 1980; 33: 1836–1845.

Clarke, N. G.; Carey, S. E.; Srikandi, W.; Hirsch, R. S.; Leppard, P. I. Periodontal disease in ancient populations. *American Journal of Physical Anthropology*; 1986; 71: 173–183.

Cohen, M. N. An introduction to the symposium. In: Cohen, M. N.; Armelagos, G. J., eds. *Paleopathology at the Origins of Agriculture*. New York: Academic Press, 1984: 1–11.

Cohen, M. N.; Armelagos, G. J., eds. *Paleopathology at the Origins of Agriculture*. New York: Academic Press, 1984.

Cook, D. C. Patterns of nutritional stress in some Illinois woodland populations. Unpublished thesis, Department of Anthropology, University of Illinois, 1971.

  Subsistence and health in the Lower Illinois Valley: Osteological evidence. In: Cohen, M. N.; Armelagos, G. J., eds. *Paleopathology at the Origins of Agriculture*. New York: Academic Press, 1984: 235–269.

Corbett, M. E.; Moore, W. J. The distribution of dental caries in ancient British populations IV: The 19th century. *Caries Research*; 1976; 10: 401–414.

Corruccini, R. S.; Handler, J. S.; Jacobi, K. P. Chronological distribution of enamel hypoplasias and weaning in a Caribbean slave population. *Human Biology*; 1985; 57: 699–711.

Cutress, T. W.; Suckling, G. W. The assessment of non-carious defects of enamel. *International Dental Journal*; 1982; 32: 117–122.

Dallman, P. Iron deficiency and the immune response. *American Journal of Clinical Nutrition*; 1987; 46: 329–334.

Dallman, P.; Simes, R.; Stekel, A. Iron deficiency in infancy and childhood. *American Journal Clinical Nutrition*; 1980; 33: 86–118.

Dallman, P. R.; Yip, R.; Johnson, C. Prevalence and causes of anemia in the United States, 1976 to 1980. *American Journal of Clinical Nutrition*; 1984; 39: 437–445.

Duncan, H. Osteoarthritis. *Henry Ford Hospital Medical Journal*; 1979; 27: 1–9.

Dunn, F. L. Epidemiological factors: Health and disease of hunters-gatherers, In: Lee, R.; DeVore, I., eds. *Man the Hunter*. Chicago: Aldine, 1968: 221–228.

Eisenberg, L.; Hutchinson, D., eds. *International Journal of Osteoarchaeology*; 1996; 6: 1–118.

El-Najjar, M.; Lozoff, B.; Ryan, D. The paleoepidemiology of porotic hyperostosis in the American Southwest: Radiological and ecological considerations. *American Journal of Roentgenology, Radium and Thermal Nuclear Medicine*; 1975; 125: 918–924.

Enwonwu, C. O. Influence of socio-economic conditions on dental development in Nigerian children. *Archives of Oral Biology*; 1973; 18: 95–107.

Eveleth, P. B.; Tanner, J. M. *Worldwide variation in human growth*. Cambridge: Cambridge University Press, 1976.

   Worldwide variation in human growth. 2d Ed. Cambridge: Cambridge University Press, 1990.

Finch, C. A.; Cook, J. D. Iron deficiency. *American Journal of Clinical Nutrition*; 1984; 39: 471–477.

FitzGerald, C. M.; Rose, J. C. Reading between the lines: Dental development and subadult age assessment using the microstructural growth markers of teeth. In: Katzenberg, M. A.; Saunders, S. R., eds. *Biological Anthropology of the Human Skeleton*. New York: Wiley-Liss, 2000: 163–186.

Garn, S. M.; Rohmann, C. G.; Guzman, M. A. Genetic, nutritional and maturational correlates of dental development. *Journal of Dental Research*; 1963; 44: 228–242.

Geissler, C. A.; Bates, J. F. The nutritional effects of tooth loss. *American Journal of Clinical Nutrition*; 1984; 39: 478–89.

Genoves, S. Proportionality of the long bones and their relation to stature among Mesoamericans. *American Journal of Physical Anthropology*; 1967; 26: 67–78.

Gilbert, R.; Mielke, J. *The Analysis of Prehistoric Diets*. New York: Academic Press, 1985.

Goodman, A. H. On the interpretation of health from skeletal remains. *Current Anthropology*; 1993; 34 (3): 281–288.

Goodman, A. H.; Allen, L. H.; Hernandez, G. P.; Amador, A.; Arriola, L. V.; Chavez, A.; Pelto, G. H. Prevalence and age at development of enamel hypoplasias in Mexican children. *American Journal of Physical Anthropology*; 1987; 72: 7–19.

Goodman, A. H.; Armelagos, G. J. Factors affecting the distribution of enamel hypoplasias within the human permanent dentition. *American Journal of Physical Anthropology*; 1985a; 68: 479–493.

   The chronological distribution of enamel hypoplasia in human permanent incisor and canine teeth. *Archives of Oral Biology*; 1985b; 30: 503–507.

   Childhood stress and decreased longevity in a prehistoric population. *American Anthropologist*; 1988; 90 (4): 936–944.

   Infant and childhood morbidity and mortality risks in archaeological populations. *World Archaeology*; 1989; 21 (2): 225–243.

Goodman, A. H.; Armelagos, G. J.; Rose, J. C. Enamel hypoplasias as indicators of stress in three prehistoric populations from Illinois. *Human Biology*; 1980; 52: 515–528.

Goodman, A. H.; Lallo, J.; Armelagos, G. J.; Rose, J. C. Health changes at Dickson Mounds, Illinois (AD 950–1300). In: Cohen, M. N.; Armelagos, G. J., eds. *Paleopathology at the Origins of Agriculture*. New York: Academic Press, 1984b: 271–306.

Goodman, A. H.; Martin, D. L.; Armelagos, G. J.; Clark, G. Indications of stress from bones and teeth. In: Cohen, M. N.; Armelagos, G. J., eds. *Paleopathology at the Origins of Agriculture*. New York: Academic Press, 1984a: 13–49.

Goodman, A. H.; Martinez, C.; Chavez, A. Nutritional supplementation and the development of linear enamel hypoplasias in children from Tezonteopan, Mexico. *American Journal of Clinical Nutrition*; 1991; 53: 773–781.

Goodman, A. H.; Pelto, G. H.; Allen, L. H.; Chavez, A. Socioeconomic and anthropometric correlates of linear enamel hypoplasia in children from Solis, Mexico. In: Goodman, A. H.; Capasso, L. L., eds. *Recent Contributions to the Study of Enamel Developmental Defects*. (Monographic Publication #2 of *Journal of Paleopathology*.) Termano, Italy: Edigrafital, 1992: 373–380.

Goodman, A. H.; Rose, J. C. Assessment of systemic physiological perturbations from dental enamel hypoplasias and associated histological structures. *Yearbook of Physical Anthropology*; 1990; 33: 59–110.

Dental enamel hypoplasias as indicators of nutritional status. In: Kelley, M.; Larsen, C., eds. *Advances in Dental Anthropology*. New York: Wiley-Liss, 1991: 279–293.

Gordon, J. E.; Wyon, J. B.; Ascoli, W. The second year death rate in less developed countries. *American Journal of Medical Sciences*; 1967; September: 121–144.

Grauer, A. L. *Bodies of Evidence: Reconstructing History Through Skeletal Analysis*. New York: Wiley-Liss, 1995.

Grauer, A. L.; Stuart-Macadam, P., eds. *Sex and Gender in Paleopathological Perspective*. Cambridge: Cambridge University Press, 1998.

Haldane, J. B. S. Disease and evolution. *La Ricerca Scientifica*; 1949; 19: 68–76.

Hardwick, J. L. The incidence and distribution of caries throughout the ages in relation to the Englishman's diet. *British Dental Journal*; 1960; 108: 9–17.

Haviland, W. A. Stature at Tikal, Guatemala: Implications for ancient Maya demography and social organization. *American Antiquity*; 1967; 32: 316–325.

Hengen, O. P. Cribra orbitalia: pathogenesis and probable etiology. *Homo*; 1971; 22: 57–75.

Henry, C. J. K.; Ulijaszek, S. J. eds. *Long-term Consequences of Early Environment: Growth, Development and the Lifespan Developmental Perspective*. New York: Cambridge University Press, 1996.

Hershkovits, I.; Rothschild, B. M.; Latimer, B.; Dutour, O.; Leonetti, G.; Greenwald, C. M.; Rothschild, C.; Jellema, L. M. Recognition of sickle-cell anemia in skeletal remains of children. *American Journal of Physical Anthropology*; 1997; 104: 213–226.

Hooton, E. A. *The Indians of Pecos Pueblo: A Study of Their Skeletal Remains*. (Papers of the Southwestern Expedition 4.) New Haven, Conn.: Yale University Press, 1930.

Hoppa, R. D.; Fitzgerald, C. M., eds. *Human Growth in the Past: Studies from Bones and Teeth*. Cambridge: Cambridge University Press: 1999.

Howell, D. *Significance of iron deficiencies. Consequence of mild deficiency in children. Extent and meaning of iron deficiency in the United States*. Washington, D.C.: National Academy of Sciences, 1971.

Hummert, J. R.; Van Gerven, D. P. Skeletal growth in a medieval population from Sudanese Nubia. *American Journal of Physical Anthropology*; 1983; 60: 471–478.

Huss-Ashmore, R.; Goodman, A. H.; Armelagos, G. J. Nutritional inference from paleopathology. *Advances in Archaeological Method and Theory*; 1982; 5: 395–474.

Hutchinson, D. Brief encounters: Tatham Mound and the evidence for Spanish and Native American confrontation. *International Journal of Osteoarchaeology*; 1996; 6: 51–65.

Hutchinson, D. L.; Larsen, C. S. Determination of stress episode duration from linear enamel hypoplasias: A case study from St. Catherine's Island, Georgia. *Human Biology*; 1988; 60: 93–110.

Iscan, M. Y.; Kennedy, K. A. R., eds. *Reconstruction of Life from the Skeleton*. New York: Alan R. Liss, 1989.

Jackson, R. T.; Latham, M. C. Anemia of pregnancy in Liberia, West Africa: A therapeutic trial. *American Journal of Clinical Nutrition*; 1982; 35: 710–714.

Jantz, R. L.; Owsley, D. W. Temporal changes in limb proportionality among skeletal samples of Arikara Indians. *Annals of Human Biology*; 1984; 11 (2): 157–163.

Jarcho, S. The development and present condition of human paleopathology in the United States. In: Jarcho, S., ed. *Human Palaeopathology*. New Haven, Conn.: Yale University Press, 1966: 3–30.

Jelliffe, D. B.; Jelliffe, E. F. P. Linear enamel hypoplasia of deciduous incisor teeth of malnourished children. *American Journal of Clinical Nutrition*; 1971; 24: 893.

Jenkins, G. N. *The Physiology and Biochemistry of the Mouth*. 2d Ed. Oxford: Blackwell, 1978.

Johnston, F. E. Growth of the long bones of infants and young children at Indian Knoll. *American Journal of Physical Anthropology*; 1962; 20: 249–254.

Johnston, F. E.; Zimmer, L. O. Assessment of growth and age in the immature skeleton. In: Iscan, M. Y.; Kennedy, K. A. R., eds. *Reconstruction of Life from the Skeleton*. New York: Alan R. Liss, 1989: 11–22.

Jurmain, R. D. Stress and the etiology of osteoarthritis. *American Journal of Physical Anthropology*; 1977; 46: 353–366.

Katzenberg, M. A.; Saunders, S. R., eds. *Biological Anthropology of the Human Skeleton*. New York: Wiley-Liss, 2000.

Keene, H. J. History of dental caries in human populations: The first million years. In: Tanzer, J. M., ed. *Animal Models in Cariology*. Washington, D.C.: Information Retrieval Inc., 1980: 23–40.

Kelley, M. A.; Larsen, C. S., eds. *Advances in Dental Anthropology*. New York: Alan Liss, 1991.

Kennedy, K. A. R. Skeletal markers of occupational stress. In: Iscan, M. Y.; Kennedy, K. A. R., eds. *Reconstruction of Life from the Skeleton*. New York: Alan R. Liss, 1989: 129–160.

Kerley, E. R.; Bass, W. Paleopathology: Meeting ground for many disciplines. *Science*; 1967; 157: 638–644.

Keusch, G. T.; Farthing, M. J. Nutrition and infection. *Annual Reviews in Nutrition*; 1986; 6: 131–154.

Kreshover, S. Metabolic disturbances in tooth formation. *Annals of the New York Academy of Science*; 1960; 85: 161–167.

Lallo, J. *The Skeletal Biology of Three Prehistoric Amerindian Populations from Dickson Mounds*. Diss., Department of Anthropology, University of Massachusetts, 1973.

Lallo, J.; Armelagos, G. J.; Mensforth, R. P. The role of diet, diseases and physiology in the origin of porotic hyperostosis. *Human Biology*; 1977; 49: 471–483.

Lallo, J.; Armelagos, G. J.; Rose, J. C. Paleoepidemiology of infectious disease in the Dickson Mounds population. *Medical College of Virginia Quarterly*; 1978; 14: 17–23.

Lambert, P. M., ed. *Bioarchaeological Studies of Life in the Age of Agriculture: A View from the Southeast*. Tuscaloosa, Ala.: University of Alabama Press, 2000.

Lambert, P. M.; Walker, P. L. Physical anthropological evidence for the evolution of social complexity in coastal Southern California. *Antiquity*; 1991; 65: 963–973.

Larsen, C. S. Health and disease in prehistoric Georgia: The transition to agriculture. In: Cohen, M. N.; Armelagos, G. J., eds. *Paleopathology at the Origins of Agriculture*. New York: Academic Press, 1984: 367–392.

Bioarchaeological interpretations of subsistence economy and behavior from human skeletal remains. *Advances in Archaeological Method and Theory*; 1987; 10: 339–445.

Bioarchaeology: Interpreting Behavior from the Human Skeleton. Cambridge: Cambridge University Press, 1997.

Larsen, C. S.; Milner, G., eds. *In the Wake of Contact: Biological Responses to Conquest.* New York: Wiley, 1994.

Larsen, C. S.; Sering, L. E. Inferring iron-deficiency anemia from human skeletal remains: The case of the Georgia bight. In: Lambert, P. M., ed. *Bioarchaeological Studies of Life in the Age of Agriculture: A View from the Southeast.* Tuscaloosa, Ala.: University of Alabama Press, 2000; 116–133.

Lasker, G. Human biological adaptability. *Science;* 166: 1969; 1480–1486.

Lee, R. B. What hunters do for a living, or, how to make out on scarce resources. In: Lee, R. B.; DeVore, I., eds. *Man the Hunter.* Chicago: Aldine, 1968: 30–47.

Lee, R.; DeVore, I., eds. *Man the Hunter.* Chicago: Aldine, 1968.

Livingstone, F. Anthropological implications of sickle-cell gene distribution in West Africa. *American Anthropologist;* 1958; 60: 533–562.

Lovejoy, C. O.; Heiple, K. G. The analysis of fractures in skeletal populations with an example from the Libben site, Ottawa County, Ohio. *American Journal of Physical Anthropology;* 1981; 55: 529–541.

Lovejoy, C. O.; Mensforth, R. P.; Armelagos, G. J. Five decades of skeletal biology as reflected in the *American Journal of Physical Anthropology.* In: Spenser, F., ed. *A History of American Physical Anthropology, 1930–1980.* New York: Academic Press, 1982: 329–336.

Lukacs, J. R. Dental paleopathology: Methods for reconstructing dietary patterns. In: Iscan, M. Y.; Kennedy, K. A. R., eds. *Reconstruction of Life from the Skeleton.* New York: Alan R. Liss, 1989: 261–288.

Lukacs, J. R., ed. *Culture, Ecology and Dental Anthropology.* Delhi, India: Kamla-Raj Enterprises, 1992.

MacMahon, B.; Pugh, T. F. *Epidemiology: Principles and Methods.* Boston: Little, Brown and Company, 1970.

Mann, R. W.; Murphy, S. P. *Regional Atlas of Bone Disease.* Springfield, Ill.: C. C. Thomas, 1990.

Maresh, M. M. Linear growth of long bones of extremities from infancy through adolescence. *A.M.A. American Journal of Diseases of Children;* 1955; 89: 725–742.

Martin, D. L. Violence against women in the La Plata River Valley (AD 1000–1300). In: *Troubled Times: Evidence for Violence and Warfare in the Past.* New York: Gordon and Breach, 1997: 44–74.

Martin, D. L.; Armelagos, G. J.; Goodman, A. H.; Van Gerven, D. P. The effects of socioeconomic change in prehistoric Africa: Sudanese Nubia as a case study. In: Cohen, M. N.; Armelagos, G. J., eds. *Paleopathology at the Origins of Agriculture.* New York: Academic Press, 1984: 193–214.

Martin, D. L.; Armelagos, G. J.; King, J. Degenerative joint disease of the long bones from Dickson Mound. *Henry Ford Hospital Medical Journal;* 1979; 27: 60–64.

Martin, D. L.; Frayer, D., eds. *Troubled Times: Evidence for Violence and Warfare in the Past.* New York: Gordon and Breach, 1997.

Martin, D. L.; Goodman, A. H.; Armelagos, G. J.; Magennis, A. L. *Black Mesa Anasazi Health: Reconstructing Life from Patterns of Death and Disease.* Carbondale: Southern Illinois University Press, 1991.

Martorell, R. Interrelationships between diet, infectious disease, and nutritional status. In: Greene, L., ed. *Social and Biological Predictors of Nutritional Status, Physical Growth, and Neurological Development.* New York: Academic Press, 1980: 81–106.

Mata, L.; Urrutia, J.; Lechtig, A. Infection and nutrition of children of a low socioeconomic rural community. *American Journal of Clinical Nutrition*; 1971; 24: 249–259.

May, J. The ecology of human disease. *Annals of the New York Academy of Science*; 1960; 84: 789–794.

McLaren, D. Concepts and context of nutrition. In: McLaren, D., ed. *Nutrition in the community*. London: John Wiley and Sons, 1976: 3–12.

Meiklejohn, C.; Schentag, C.; Venema, A.; Key, P. Socioeconomic change and patterns of pathology and variation in the Mesolithic and Neolithic of Western Europe: Some suggestions. In: Cohen, M. N.; Armelagos, G. J., eds. *Paleopathology at the Origins of Agriculture*. New York: Academic Press, 1984: 75–100.

Mensforth, R. P. Relative tibia long bone growth in the Libben and BT-5 prehistoric skeletal populations. *American Journal of Physical Anthropology*; 1985; 68: 247–262.

Paleoepidemiology of porotic hyperostosis in the Libben and BT-5 skeletal populations. *Kirtlandia*; 1991; 46: 1–47.

Mensforth, R. P.; Lovejoy, C. O.; Lallo, J. W.; Armelagos, G. J. The role of constitutional factors, diet and infectious disease on the etiology of porotic hyperostosis and periosteal reactions in prehistoric infants and children. *Medical Anthropology*; 1978; 2 (1): 1–59.

Merbs, C. F. *Patterns of Activity-Induced Pathology in a Canadian Inuit Population*. Ottawa, Canada: National Museum of Man Mercury Series Paper No. 119, 1983.

Trauma. In: Iscan, M. Y.; Kennedy, K. A. R., eds. *Reconstruction of Life from the Skeleton*. New York: Alan R. Liss, 1989: 161–199.

Merchant, V. A.; Ubelaker, D. H. Skeletal growth of the protohistoric Arikara. *American Journal of Physical Anthropology*; 1977; 46: 61–72.

Meyers, L. D.; Habicht, J.; Johnson, C. L.; Brownie, C. Prevalences of anemia and iron deficiency anemia in black and white women in the United States estimated by two methods. *American Journal of Public Health*; 1983; 73: 1042–1049.

Milner, G. R.; Anderson, E.; Smith, V. G. Warfare in late prehistoric West-Central Illinois. *American Antiquity*; 1991; 56: 581–603.

Milner, G. R.; Wood, J. W.; Boldsen, J. L. Paleodemography. In: Katzenberg, M. A.; Saunders, S. R., eds. *Biological Anthropology of the Human Skeleton*. New York: Wiley-Liss, 2000: 467–497.

Moller, I. J.; Pindborg, J. J.; Roed-Petersen, B. Prevalence of dental caries, enamel opacities, and enamel hypoplasia in Ugandans. *Archives of Oral Biology*; 1972; 17: 9–22.

Molnar, S. Human tooth wear, tooth function, and cultural variability. *American Journal of Physical Anthropology*; 1971; 34: 175–189.

Moore, W. J.; Corbett, M. E. The distribution of dental caries in ancient British populations 1: Anglo-Saxon period. *Caries Research*; 1971; 5: 151–168.

The distribution of dental caries in ancient British populations II: Iron Age, Romano-British and medieval periods. *Caries Research*; 1973; 7: 139–153.

The distribution of dental caries in ancient British populations III: The 17th century. *Caries Research*; 1975; 9: 163–175.

Moseley, J. E. The paleopathologic riddle of "symmetrical osteoporosis." *American Journal of Roentgenology*; 1965; 95: 135–142.

Mummery, J. R. On the relations which dental caries, as discovered among the ancient inhabitants of Britain and amongst existing aboriginal races, may be supposed to hold to their food and social conditions. *Transactions, Odontological Society of Great Britain*; 1869; 2: 7–24, 27–80.

Nagao, M. The effects of aging on mastication. *Nutrition Reviews*; 1992; 50 (12): 434–437.

Nathan, H.; Haas, N. "Cribra orbitalia": A bone condition of the orbit of unknown nature. *Israel Journal of Medical Sciences*; 1966; 2: 171–191.

Nickens, P. R. Stature reduction as an adaptive response to food production in Mesoamerica. *Journal of Archaeological Science*; 1976; 3: 31–41.

Ortner, D. J. Description and classification of degenerative bone changes in the distal joint surfaces of the humerus. *American Journal of Physical Anthropology*; 1968; 28: 139–156.

Disease and mortality in the early Bronze Age people of Bab edh-Dhra, Jordan. *American Journal of Physical Anthropology*; 1979; 51: 589–597.

Theoretical and methodological issues in paleopathology. In: Ortner, D.; Aufterheide, A., eds. *Human Paleopathology: Current Syntheses and Future Options*. Washington, D.C.: Smithsonian Institution Press, 1991: 5–11.

Ortner, D. J.; Aufterheide, A., eds. *Human Paleopathology: Current Syntheses and Future Options*. Washington, D.C.: Smithsonian Institution, 1991.

Ortner, D. J.; Putschar, W. G. J. *Identification of Pathological Conditions in Human Skeletal Remains*. Washington, D.C.: Smithsonian Institution Press, 1981.

Owsley, D. W.; Jantz, R. L., eds. *Skeletal Biology in the Great Plains: Migration, Warfare, Health, and Subsistence*. Washington, D.C.: Smithsonian Institution Press, 1994.

Palkovich, A. M. *The Arroyo Hondo Skeletal and Mortuary Remains*. Santa Fe, N.Mex.: School of American Research Press, 1980.

Endemic disease patterns in paleopathology: Porotic hyperostosis. *American Journal of Physical Anthropology*; 1987; 74: 527–537.

Palmer, C. A.; Pappas, A. S. Nutrition and the oral health of the elderly. In Bourne, G. H., ed. Impact of Nutrition on Health and Disease. *World Review of Nutrition and Dietetics*; 1989; 59: 71–94.

Perzigian, A. J.; Tench, P. A.; Braun, D. J. Prehistoric health in the Ohio River Valley. In: Cohen, M. N.; Armelagos, G. J., eds. *Paleopathology at the Origins of Agriculture*. New York: Academic Press, 1984: 347–366.

Pindborg, J. J. Aetiology of developmental enamel defects not related to fluorosis. *International Dental Journal*; 1982; 32: 123–134.

Poirier, D. A.; Bellantoni, N. F., eds. *In Remembrance: Archaeology and Death*. Westport, Conn.: Bergin and Garvey, 1997.

Pollitt, E. Effects of iron deficiency on mental development: Methodological considerations and substantive findings. In F. Johnston, ed. *Nutritional Anthropology*. New York: Alan R. Liss, 1987: 225–254.

Powell, M. L. The analysis of dental wear and caries for dietary reconstruction. In: Gilbert, R. I.; Mielke, J., eds. *The Analysis of Prehistoric Diets*. Orlando, Fl.: Academic Press, 1985: 307–338.

Endemic treponematosis and tuberculosis in the prehistoric southeastern United States: Biological costs of endemic disease. In Ortner, D. J.; Aufderheide, A. C., eds. *Human Paleopathology: Current Syntheses and Future Options*. Washington, D. C.: Smithsonian Institution, 1991: 173–180.

Price, T. D., ed. *Bone Chemistry of Past Populations*. Cambridge: Cambridge University Press, 1989.

Rappaport, R. A. *Pigs for the Ancestors*. New Haven, Conn.: Yale University Press, 1967.

Reith, E. J.; Cotty, E. The absorptive activity of ameloblasts during maturation of enamel. *Anatomy Record*; 1967; 157: 577.

Roberts, C.; Machester, K. *The Archaeology of Death*. 2d Ed., Ithaca, N.Y.: Cornell University Press, 1995.

Rose, J. C.; Burnett, B. A.; Nassaney, M. S.; Blaeuer, M. W. Paleopathology and the origins of maize agriculture in the Lower Mississippi Valley and Caddoan culture areas. In: Cohen, M. N.; Armelagos, G. J., eds. *Paleopathology at the Origins of Agriculture.* New York: Academic Press, 1984: 393–424.

Rose, J. C.; Condon, K; Goodman, A. H. Diet and dentition: Developmental disturbances. In: Gilbert, R. I.; Mielke, J. H., eds. *The Analysis of Prehistoric Diets.* New York: Academic Press, 1985: 281–306.

Sahlins, M. In: Lee, R.; DeVore, I., eds. *Man the Hunter.* Chicago: Aldine, 1968.

Sandford, M. K., ed. *Investigations of Ancient Human Tissues: Chemical Analyses in Anthropology.* New York: Gordon and Breach, 1993.

Sarnat, B. G.; Schour, I. Enamel hypoplasias (chronic enamel aplasia) in relationship to systemic diseases: A chronological, morphological and etiological classification. *Journal of the American Dental Association;* 1941; 28: 1989–2000.

Saunders, S. R. Subadult skeletons and growth related studies. In: Katzenberg, M. A.; Saunders, S. R., eds. *Biological Anthropology of the Human Skeleton.* New York: Wiley-Liss, 2000: 135–161.

Sawyer, D. R.; Nwoku, A. L. Malnutrition and the oral health of children in Ogbomosho, Nigeria. *Journal Dentition for Children;* 1985; March: 141–145.

Schamschula, R. G.; Cooper, M. H.; Wright, M. C.; Agus, H. M.; Un, P. S. H. Oral health of adolescent and adult Australian aborigines. *Community Dentition and Oral Epidemiology;* 1980; 8: 370–374.

Schultz, M.; Carli-Thiele, P.; Schmidt-Schultz, T.; Kerdorf, U.; Keirdorf, H.; Teegen, W.-R.; Kreutz, K. Enamel hypoplasias in archaeological skeletal remains. In: Alt, K. W.; R.ösing, F. W.; Teschler-Nicola, M., eds. *Dental Anthropology: Fundamentals, Limits, and Prospects.* New York: Springer-Verlag, 1998: 293–311.

Scrimshaw, N. Iron deficiency. *Scientific American;* 1991; October: 46–52.

Shawashy, M.; Yaeger, J.: Enamel. In: Behaskar, S. N., ed. *Orban's Oral Histology and Embryology.* St. Louis, Mo.: C. V. Mosby, 1986: 45–100.

Simmons, W. K.; Gurney, J. M. Nutritional anemia in the English-speaking Caribbean and Suriname. *American Journal of Clinical Nutrition;* 1982; 35: 327–337.

Simmons, W. K.; Jutsum, P. J.; Fox, K.; Spence, M.; Gueri, M.; Paradis, R.; Gurney, J. M. A survey of the anemia status of preschool age children and pregnant and lactating women in Jamaica. *American Journal of Clinical Nutrition;* 1982; 35: 319–326.

Sinclair, D. *Human Growth after Birth.* 2d Ed. Oxford: Oxford Medical Publishers, 1985.

Slavkin, H. C.; Zeichner-David, M.; Snead, M. L.; Samuel, N. Genetic and phylogenetic aspects of enamel. *INSERM;* 1984; 125: 341–354.

Smedman, L.; Sterky, G.; Mellander, L.; Stig, W. Anthropometry and subsequent mortality in groups of children aged 6–59 months in Guinnea-Bissau. *American Journal of Clinical Nutrition;* 1987; 46: 369–373.

Smith, P.; Bar-Yosef, O.; Sillen, A. Archaeological and skeletal evidence for dietary change during the late Pleistocene/Early Holocene in the Levant. In: Cohen, M. N.; Armelagos, G. J., eds. *Paleopathology at the Origins of Agriculture.* New York: Academic Press; 1984: 101–127.

Sobolik, K. D. *Paleonutrition: The Diet and Health of Prehistoric Americans.* (Center for Archaeological Investigations Occasional Paper No 22.) Carbondale: Southern Illinois University, 1994.

Steckel, R. H.; Floud, R., eds. *Health and Welfare During Industrialization.* Chicago: University of Chicago Press, 1997.

Steinbock, R. T. *Paleopathological Diagnosis and Interpretation: Bone Diseases in Ancient Human Populations.* Springfield, Ill.: Charles C. Thomas, 1976.

Stewart, T. D. The vertebral column of the Eskimo. *American Journal of Physical Anthropology*; 1932; 17: 123–136.

Stewart, T. D. and Quade, L. G. Lesions of the frontal bone in American Indians. *American Journal of Physical Anthropology*; 1969; 30: 89–110.

Storey, R. *Life and Death in the Ancient City of Teotihuacan*. Tuscaloosa: University of Alabama Press, 1992.

Stuart-Macadam, P. Porotic hyperostosis: New evidence to support the anemia theory. *American Journal of Physical Anthropology*; 1987; 74 (4): 521–526.

Nutritional deficiency disease: A survey of scurvy, rickets and iron deficiency anemia. In: Iscan, M. Y.; Kennedy, K. A. R., eds. *Reconstruction of Life From the Skeleton*. New York: Alan R. Liss, 1989: 201–222.

Porotic hyperostosis: A new perspective. *American Journal of Physical Anthropology*, 1992; 87: 39–47.

Iron deficiency anemia: exploring the difference. In: Grauer, A. L.; Stuart-Macadam, P., eds. *Sex and Gender in Paleopathological Perspective*. Cambridge: Cambridge University Press, 1998: 45–63.

Suckling, G. Developmental defects of enamel – historical and present-day perspectives on their pathogenesis. *Advances in Dental Anthropology*; 1989; 3 (2): 87–94.

Sulzer, J. L.; Wesley, H. H.; Leonig, F. Nutrition and behavior in Head Start children: Results from the Tulane study. In: Kallen, D. J., ed. *Nutrition, Development and Social Behavior*. Washington, D. C.: DHEW publication no. NIH, 1973: 73–242.

Sundick, R. I. Human skeletal growth and age determination. *Homo*; 1978; 29: 228–249.

Sutphen, J. L. Growth as a measure of nutritional stress. *Journal of Pediatric Gastroenterology and Nutrition*; 1985; 4: 169–181.

Swardstedt, T. *Odontological aspects of a medieval population from the province of Jamtland/ Mid-Sweden*. Stockholm: Tiden Barnangen, AB, 1966.

Sweeney, E. A.; Cabrera, J.; Urritia, J.; Mata, L. Factors associated with linear hypoplasia of human deciduous incisors. *Journal of Dental Research*; 1969; 48: 1275–1279.

Sweeney, E. A.; Guzman, M. Oral conditions in children from three highland villages in Guatemala. *Archives of Oral Biology*; 1966; 11: 687–698.

Sweeney, E. A.; Saffir, J. A.; de Leon, R. Linear enamel hypoplasias of deciduous incisor teeth in malnourished children. *American Journal of Clinical Nutrition*; 1971; 24: 29–31.

Tanner, J. M. *Foetus into Man. Physical Growth from Conception to Maturity*. Cambridge, Mass.: Harvard University Press, 1978.

A History of the Study of Human Growth. Cambridge: Cambridge University Press, 1981.

Growth as a mirror of the condition of society: Secular trends and class distinctions. In: Demirjian, A., ed. *Human Growth: A Multidisciplinary Review*. London: Taylor and Francis, 1986: 3–34.

Teaford, M. Dental microwear: What can it tell us about diet and dental function? In Kelley, M.; Larsen, C. S., eds. *Advances in Dental Anthropology*. New York: Alan Liss, 1991: 341–356.

Thomas, R. B.; Winterhalder, B.; McRae, S. D. An anthropological approach to human ecology and adaptive dynamics. *Yearbook of Physical Anthropology*; 1979; 22: 1–46.

Trinkaus, E.; Zimmerman, M. R. Trauma among the Shanidar Neanderthals. *American Journal of Physical Anthropology*; 1982; 57: 61–76.

Turner, C. G. Dental anthropological indications of agriculture among the Jomon people of central Japan X.: Peopling of the Pacific. *American Journal of Physical Anthropology*; 1979; 51: 619–636.

Tyson, R. A. *Human Paleopathology and Related Subjects: An International Bibliography*. San Diego: San Diego Museum of Man, 1997.

Ubelaker, D. H. The development of American paleopathology. In Spenser, F., ed. *A History of American Physical Anthropology, 1930–1980*. New York: Academic Press, 1982: 337–356.

     Human Skeletal Remains: Excavation, Analysis, Interpretation. Chicago: Aldine, 1981.

Verano, J.; Ubelaker, D. H. *Disease and Demography in the Americas: Changing Patterns before and after 1492*. Washington, D.C.: Smithsonian Institution Press, 1992.

Vyas, D., Chandra, R. K. Functional implications of iron deficiency. In: Stekel, A., ed. *Iron Nutrition in Infancy and Childhood*. New York: Raven Press, 1984: 45–59.

Walker, P. L. The linear growth of long bones in Late Woodland Indian children. *Proceedings of the Indiana Academy of Science*; 1969; 78: 83–87.

     Anemia among prehistoric Indians of the American Southwest. In: Merbs, C. F.; Miller, R. J., eds. *Health and Disease in the Prehistoric Southwest*. Tempe, Ariz.: Anthropological Research Papers No. 34, 1985: 139–163.

     Cranial injuries as evidence of violence in prehistoric Southern California. *American Journal of Physical Anthropology*; 1989: 313–324.

Walker, P. L.; Hollimon, S. E. Changes in osteoarthritis associated with the development of a maritime economy among Southern California Indians. *International Journal of Anthropology*; 1989; 4: 171–183.

Wells, C. *Bones, Bodies and Disease*. New York: Praeger, 1964.

White, T. D. *Prehistoric Cannibalism at Mancos 5MTUMR-2346*. Princeton, N.J.: Princeton University Press, 1992.

Wilkinson, R. G.; Van Wagenen, K. W. Prehistoric cranial trauma: Skeletal evidence from the Riviere aux Vase site, Michigan. *Midcontinental Journal of Archaeology*; 1993; 18: 190–216.

Williamson, M. A. A comparison of degenerative joint disease between upland and coastal prehistoric agriculturalists from Georgia. In: Lambert, P. M., ed. *Bioarchaeological Studies of Life in the Age of Agriculture: A View from the Southeast*. Tuscaloosa, Ala.: University of Alabama Press, 2000: 134–147.

Witts, L. J. Anemia as a world health problem. *International Society of Hematology, 11th Congress of the University of Sydney*; 1966; Plenary Session: 85–102.

Wood, J. W.; Milner, G. R.; Harpending, H. C.; Weiss, K. M. The osteological paradox: Problems of inferring prehistoric health from skeletal samples. *Current Anthropology*; 1992; 33: 343–358.

Y'Edynak, G. Long bone growth in Western Eskimo and Aleut skeletons. *American Journal of Physical Anthropology*; 1976; 45: 569–574.

Zaino, E. Symmetrical osteoporosis, a sign of severe anemia in the prehistoric Pueblo Indians of the Southwest. In: Wade, W., ed. *Miscellaneous Papers in Paleopathology: I*. Flagstaff, Ariz.: Museum of Northern Arizona Technical Series No. 7, 1967: 40–47.

CHAPTER THREE

A Health Index from Skeletal Remains

Richard H. Steckel, Paul W. Sciulli, and Jerome C. Rose

ABSTRACT

This chapter describes the data used for the Western Hemisphere project, discusses the format in which the information was coded, and explains the health index, which is a method for measuring and comparing health status using skeletal remains. Skeletal lesions measure primarily chronic health conditions, but they can reflect acute infections to the extent that they affect physical growth, the formation of linear enamel hypoplasias, and other conditions that register on bones. The database contains measurements of seven basic health indicators from 12,520 skeletons of people who lived in North, Central, or South America over the past 7 millennia. For purposes of analysis, many of the 218 sites where people lived were combined into 65 sites based on ecological and chronological similarity. The health index adjusts for the age distribution of the population and incorporates the severity of lesions indicating biological stress. The current (Mark I) version of the index gives equal weight to the health indicators, but this assumption and others explained in the chapter could be modified based on additional research. The Mark I health index could also be readily adapted to incorporate length of life. The index rankings reveal considerable diversity in health status, with Native Americans being among the most but also among the least healthy groups who lived in the Western Hemisphere prior to the end of the nineteenth century.

Social scientists have devised many approaches to measuring the standard of living. Economists use national income accounts and related measures, such as gross national product per capita, to depict material aspects of the quality of life. Demographers emphasize the length of life as an important aspect of well-being, and historians employ various devices, such as real wages, wealth, grain output, and hearths per person.

Unfortunately, these traditional measures cannot be used for studying trends over extended periods of time. The raw data simply do not exist for computing income, life expectancy, or other frequently used measures over the millennia. Moreover, even if the data were available, problems of comparability would arise in some instances. Income and wages, for example, have no clear meaning in a hunter-gatherer society.

Biological measures are the most comparable type of indicator across diverse societies because they assess the quality of life from the point of view of a living organism, which is common to all humans. Views on the afterlife aside, length of life and human growth mean about the same thing to modern Americans as they did to ancient Egyptians. Regrettably, lack of evidence on two widely used measures of this type – life expectancy and average height – forces us to look elsewhere for information on very long-term trends.

Skeletons are possibly unique in furnishing reasonably abundant evidence on the standard of living that is comparable over very long periods of time. Recent methodological developments in physical anthropology and bioarchaeology provide investigators with a rich array of information from skeletal remains, including estimates of the length of a person's life and knowledge of chronic pathological conditions while the person was living. The validity of this information on health has been corroborated by evidence from modern populations. Artifacts collected from burial sites also provide additional important information on living conditions.

Here we quantify health status from skeletons using a method that incorporates three key features sometimes lacking in other approaches: multiple indicators, age adjustment, and severity of skeletal lesions. In principle, the method can measure both the duration and the quality of life at a site, but for reasons explained below, the present effort incorporates only quality while living. Our skeletal measures of health include three attributes that reflect primarily conditions in childhood but also affect the adult quality of life – linear enamel hypoplasias, stature, and signs of anemia; two that apply primarily to adults – dental deficiencies and degenerative joint disease; and two that are relevant at any age – trauma and infections. We begin by describing quality-adjusted life-years, a concept used to depict health status in modern populations. This idea is adapted to skeletal remains with the help of several simplifying assumptions about the character of skeletal evidence. The result is a crude health index, but one capable of refinement and testing for the sensitivity of results to the assumptions.

The attributes of the health index are scored at the individual level, and the index could be estimated for an individual or for groups of individuals. If estimated for individuals, it could be used to assess not only average health but inequality of health within groups. Difficulties in using an individual-level index lead us to consider only those estimates for groups at this time. Findings are reported for Native Americans, Euro-Americans, and African-Americans at 65 sites in North America, Mesoamerica, and South America.

I. METHODOLOGY

The health index incorporates the length of life and physical health while living, an approach inspired by the work of medical examiners and physicians who assigned pensions to Civil War veterans based on an individual's degree of disability.[1]

---

[1] The Consolidation Act of 1873 specified that disability payments for former Union Army soldiers were to be based upon medical examinations that determined the degree of disability for performing manual labor, with scores ranging from 6/18 to 17/18 disability (Glasson, 1918, p. 137).

Various disability systems, such as workers' compensation and Social Security, as well as courts involved in tort litigation, use similar principles to estimate the loss of a person's functional capacity following accidents or injury (Rondinelli, 2000). In addition, researchers in health economics have devised various indexes for appraising the health of patients and for evaluating health-care policies (see Drummond et al., 1987; Lohr, 1989; and Erickson et al., 1989). Indexes that weigh various dimensions of health to obtain a single measure fit the needs of our project. Two of these, the quality of well-being scale and the health utility index, score functional capacity on a scale of 0 to 1, which is the scale we propose.[2]

We can define a health index for individual j as follows:

$$I^j = \sum_{i=1}^{100} Q_i^j \quad \text{where } Q_i^j = Q_i(x_1^j, x_2^j, \ldots, x_k^j).$$

In these equations i denotes the year of life and Q_i is a function whose arguments are measures of the biological quality of life. The functions Q_i, which take on values from 0.0 to 1.0, measure the quality of health in year of life i. Excellent health is indicated by a function value of 1.0, moderate health by a function value near 0.5, and death by a function value of 0.0.

Some simple examples illustrate the meaning of the index. A person who had excellent health throughout life and died at exactly age 100 would have an index value of 100. Age 100 is an upper limit to the life span, at least in the populations under study, and it provides a convenient maximum numerical value for the index. (Obviously, the index could be scaled to accommodate alternative upper limits to the life span.) Similarly, an individual who lived 40 years in moderate health ($Q_i = 0.5$ for all ages from birth to death) would have an index value of 20. Someone who died at birth would have an index value of zero.

Figure 3.1 illustrates a varied age pattern of health. The graph shows the case of a person who had poor health in early childhood (as indicated, for example, by enamel hypoplasias), but was reasonably healthy during adolescence and early adulthood (attaining height, say, only one standard deviation below modern standards). He or she then declined during the late 30s (evident from infections, degenerative joint disease, and declining dental health) and died at age 40. In this formulation, the index value is interpreted as the area under the curve Q that depicts the biological quality of life at each age.

The ideal information to estimate the biological quality of life would be longitudinal data on a person's state of health from birth to death. A sequence of annual physical examinations would achieve this purpose, but more frequent measurements, such as monthly, weekly, daily, or even continuous observations on health, would be desirable. Unfortunately, such data are rare or nonexistent, even in modern populations. Instead, we approximate an individual's record of health using information contained in skeletal remains. Although the skeletal record provides an incomplete picture of health, emphasizing chronic in contrast to acute conditions,

---

[2] For the quality of well-being scale, see Kaplan and Bush (1982). For the health utility index, see Torrance and Feeney (1989); and Feeney, Labelle, and Torrance (1990).

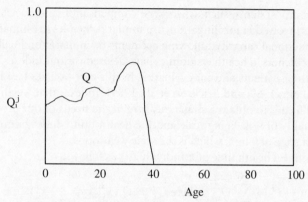

Figure 3.1. An example of the biological quality of life by age.

it nonetheless provides a useful and consistent way of measuring important aspects of the standard of living across diverse populations. Even acute conditions may indirectly affect skeletons, insofar as they affect physical growth, the formation of linear enamel hypoplasias, and other chronic pathological conditions that we do observe.

Any health index tabulated from skeletal remains would be imprecise for several reasons. Age-at-death can be reliably determined for children and young adults, but the accuracy of estimates deteriorates for older individuals. Some physical anthropologists think that older adults are systematically underaged. For this reason, we adjust estimated adult ages upward, and we lump older adults (aged 45+) into one age category.

Our objectives are tempered by the reality that skeletal evidence gives an incomplete chronological record of health. The age at which an insult occurred may be known with little precision. The time window of some insults, such as hypoplasias, is reasonably well defined, but may be vague in others, such as infectious lesions or degenerative joint disease. Opportunities for remodeling of bone tissue from many types of insults increases with the time since healing began. Since estimates based on current methods cannot be precise about the timing of many insults, appraisals of health status could be grouped into two broad age categories: adults and subadults. The boundary between childhood and adulthood is placed at 18 years, though a slightly lower age is defensible. One might infer the duration of stress by applying averages from cases where the duration is known, say, from medical studies of biologically stressed populations found in developing countries. The severity of the lesions may also be related to their duration.

The functional impairment may differ across individuals who had similar skeletal lesions. For example, two individuals who had visually similar evidence of arthritis may have had substantially different levels of pain or loss of use. There may be no way to solve this problem, but we are interested primarily in average levels of health across populations, rather than the health of particular individuals (although this would be interesting to know). It is hoped that errors made in judging the health of particular individuals will approximately cancel in tabulating averages.

Measures of health status using skeletal data may exaggerate the quality of health, in part because acute conditions are unlikely to register directly in bone material. The skeletal measures proposed will not identify whether an individual had yellow fever, small pox, measles, or several other diseases (but these diseases could stunt physical growth or otherwise contribute to the formation of skeletal conditions we do measure). However, the upward bias imposed by this feature is made smaller by the fact that acute conditions did not last long: the individual recovered quickly or died. If recovery is rapid, the loss in quality-adjusted life-years is minimal, and death registers immediately in the attribute system (assuming we incorporate length of life into the health index). The bias is larger, however, if individuals often faced a succession of acute illnesses. In addition, skeletons tell us little about some aspects of health, such as vision or hearing, and in the absence of information, our scoring scheme rates these attributes as unimpaired. Obviously, an individual could be blind in ways that fail to show on the skeleton, and some forms of trauma to the skull that result in blindness, but not death, are identifiable. To the extent that individuals were severely limited in one of these attributes – in an era when people made do without eyeglasses, hearing aids, seeing eye dogs or voice enhancers – it is likely the person was at greater risk of death, which is captured by the system of measuring health status. Skeletal materials are unable to detect emotional states and, to a lesser extent, cognition. Anemia and chronic malnutrition, however, may impair cognitive function, and severe emotional stress or cognitive impairment may weaken the immune system or compromise diet, clothing, and shelter in ways that led to death. Even though estimated health quality is biased upward by these shortcomings, relative to what would be measured in interviews of modern populations, the approach provides a reasonably consistent way of measuring health status over time and across space.

Up to this point, the discussion has assumed that the index would be tabulated for particular individuals.[3] In this method, the health of a group would be measured by averaging or otherwise pooling the health states of its members. However, difficulties with individual-level data lead us to favor an aggregate technique. A limitation of the individual approach stems from the fact that the index is sensitive to the age-at-death. This sensitivity is unavoidable – indeed, it is essential – because quality-adjusted life-years are designed to reflect the length of life. As Chapter 2 on demography has shown, however, the distribution of ages-at-death at a particular site is influenced by the birth rate. The average age-at-death declines as the birth rate increases. Because age-specific death rates are U-shaped by age (the highest death rates apply to young children and to old adults), populations in which there were numerous births also had many deaths at young ages. Therefore, variations in quality-adjusted life-years tabulated from individuals could be caused purely by differences in fertility.

---

[3] The precise details of a procedure are not specified here because the method is impracticable given the data constraints and other difficulties noted below. But several specific approaches are plausible. For instance, scores for stature, anemia, hypoplasias, dental, and DJD (perhaps assuming no functional impairments for the latter two attributes during the subadult years) could be used to depict the subadult health experience for those who lived to adulthood. All seven attributes might be used to depict adult health (and the health of those who did not survive to adulthood). Possible ways of extending or refining the approach, including linear (or nonlinear) deterioration in health among adults, are noted in the section on "Suggestions for Research."

If the birth rate was known (or could be estimated from evidence available at the site), appropriate adjustments to the age distribution of deaths could be made, but unfortunately, such reliable knowledge is lacking for many sites.

Fertility is not the only potential contaminant of a health index constructed from individual-level data. Selective or seasonal migration may also distort the observed or measured age distribution of deaths at a particular site. If young or old individuals systematically entered or left the population under study, the age distribution of deaths and, therefore, the health index is changed for the site. Seasonal migration, such as movements from summer to winter living places, may produce these effects if the age distribution of deaths varied by season of the year. These potential biases might be compounded by incomplete excavation of burial sites or by destruction of skeletal materials. Field researchers are carefully trained to recover skeletons and related artifacts, but the soft bones of infants and of very young children, and sometimes those of adults, may be poorly preserved, particularly in acidic soils. Moreover, at a particular site, some of the young or the very old might have been buried apart from the location excavated. Therefore, the measured age distribution of deaths may contain several potential biases that distort the health of the population under study.

A practical difficulty with individual-level data also leads us to an aggregate approach: incomplete skeletons. Roughly one-half of the skeletons coded for the project contain enough parts to measure a majority of the stress indicators used in the project. Even though the total sample size is huge (more than 12,500 individuals) by standards of work in the area, the effect on the analysis of deleting the incomplete skeletons is substantial because several sites would not have enough complete individuals to make reliable inferences about health. An approach based on individuals sacrifices a great deal of temporal and geographic diversity in the database.

Instead, we employ an aggregate or site-specific method that incorporates every scrap of information recorded for skeletons in which age-at-death is available. This method also overcomes problems associated with biases in the age distribution of death, but at a cost of losing desirable properties of an overall index tabulated from the index scores of each individual. Following details presented in the next section, the technique relies on age-specific measures of the incidence of each component or attribute in the index (hypoplasias, anemia, degenerative joint disease, etc.). Then, to estimate quality-adjusted life-years, the age-specific rates are multiplied by the age distribution of person-years lived in a standard or reference population, in much the same way that demographers would calculate an age-adjusted crude death rate. The reference population chosen roughly approximates mortality conditions in the societies under study.

The technique purges the health index of intrusions caused by biases in the age distribution of deaths as a measure of the underlying mortality schedule, but the index no longer incorporates health differences that could have been caused by genuine variations in the length of life. Because the index is founded purely on the incidence of pathological lesions, it understates the range of health experience in the Western Hemisphere. We know that quality-adjusted life-years are sensitive to the length of life, and it was almost certainly the case that the past several millennia witnessed significant fluctuations or differences in life expectancy. By assuming that the same life expectancy applied to every site, the index no longer captures a component of health that could have differed across time, space, or ethnic group.

Although the limitation is regrettable, the loss may not be as important as one might think for ranking health across the societies under study. It is likely that the incidence of lesions and average length of life were negatively related because many conditions that affected one also affected the other. If correct, these components of health had a similar effect on quality-adjusted life-years. Hard work, poor nutrition, and communicable diseases lowered the life span but also gave rise to anemia, deficiencies in stature, infections, and other pathological conditions measured in the project.

A devil's advocate might argue that the correlation would be weak or, conceivably, positive. It is possible, for example, that rich societies had enough resources to support those with significant disabilities through family connections, networks, or other means. If these resources substantially increased the average length of life, then under some circumstances, the lesions could have been a sign of lower mortality rates. It is known, however, that the measures of biological stress used in this project were unpleasant. Skeletal infections, trauma, anemia, and other components of the health index were painful and limited activity. Thus, an increased incidence of pathological lesions alone in no way indicates better health or improved quality of life.

The questions are whether additional pathologies somehow signified more plentiful resources, and whether the additional resources were capable of generating a longer life span, which more than offset the unpleasant effects of the pathologies, that is, that quality-adjusted life-years improved. While it might be true that rich societies allocated a portion of their additional wealth to care of the sick or the infirm, this care, if effective, would tend to blunt the progression of the pathologies in question, delaying their onset and possibly reducing their severity. The end result would be a greater number of person-years lived with lower pathology scores, thereby increasing the health index. Degenerative joint disease, for example, reflects wear and tear on the body that could be alleviated, slowed, or possibly arrested with help from others. Moreover, rich societies may have allocated resources to the prevention of chronic disease by improving nutrition or reducing work, which would act to create a negative association between resources and pathologies.

If rich societies had more pathological lesions, then poor ones must have had fewer. In contradiction to this line of thought, we know that some societies whose standard of living deteriorated showed a high incidence of skeletal maladies. The pre-Columbian populations of the American Southwest (Anasazi) and of southern Mexico (Mayans) were heavily stressed and registered the highest rates of pathology among all sites in our sample (see discussion and tables below).

Did additional resources significantly lengthen life? Although a strong gradient between income or wealth and health has been widely reported for industrialized countries in the past half century, the modest evidence available on their relationship in the nineteenth century suggests that the connection was loose, or at least that the wealthy and the poor died at similar rates (see, for example, Steckel, 1988, and Preston and Haines, 1991). If the link was weak a century and a half ago, one might venture to suppose that it was also weak in earlier centuries. While the point cannot be proven, the available evidence suggests that access to resources was somewhat related to length of life in the societies under study.

We are reasonably confident that the estimated health index typically moved in the same direction as quality-adjusted life-years. Consistent with this pattern, tentative statistical analysis presented in the "Conclusions" to the book show a positive correlation between the health index and estimated life expectancy at birth.

II. APPLICATION

The health index is constructed using a modified form of a multiattribute system, an approach developed in the 1970s to assess health aspects of the quality of life.[4] In this method, health has attributes or dimensions, such as vision, pain, mobility, dexterity, hearing, and cognition. Several capacity levels are usually specified for each attribute, varying from severely compromised to normal, and health status is given by the level of the individual on each attribute.

Health status – the scores on various attributes of health – can be converted into a single index number reflecting health-related quality of life by using a scoring or utility function, which expresses weights or preferences to be given to various combinations of health states.[5] For example, a system that had 6 attributes and 3 levels of health for each attribute would have $3^6 = 729$ possible health states, each of which could be given a quality score. Preferences are often elicited through questionnaires or surveys that ask individuals to choose or rank various hypothetical alternative health states. Assuming the comparability of preferences, this in turn allows one to make comparisons of health-related quality of life across time, space, and ethnic groups.

Using skeletal materials, we construct a crude approximation to the quality-adjusted life-year. Although it is based only on chronic conditions that register in bones, the vision of a more complete index used in medical economics serves as a guide and inspiration for further research. The index is defined as the sum of the quality-adjusted life-years lived by a synthetic cohort of individuals whose mortality experience was specified by a Model West level 4 life table (Coale and Demeny, 1983).[6] The assumptions or procedures of the first (Mark I) version of the

---

[4] Frank, Gold, and Erickson (1992). For a sense of the evolution of these systems, see Bush et al. (1972); Torrance, Boyle, and Horwood (1982); Cadman et al. (1986); and Feeney et al. (1992).

[5] A utility function is a concept in economics used to describe preferences, or in this context, the satisfaction of various health states or health outcomes. The utility function reflects both the ordinal ranking of health states (the most preferred, next most preferred, . . . , least preferred) and the intensity of preference for each health state.

[6] The index is an example of an additive scoring or utility function. Multiattribute utility theory recognizes three main types of utility functions: additive, multiplicative, and multilinear (Keeney and Raiffa, 1976). Which is appropriate depends upon the type of utility independence that exists. Additive utility independence means that there are no interactions in preferences among attributes. For instance, the evaluation or ranking of hearing would not depend on the level the person was at for mobility or dexterity. In contrast, mutual utility independence, expressed by the multiplicative model, allows for simple interactions

Table 3.1: Scoring Pathologies

Variable	Type
Stature	Continuous
Hypoplasias	3 categories
Anemia	3 categories
Dental Health	
Teeth (75%)	Continuous
Abscesses (25%)	3 categories
Infections	4 categories
Degenerative joint disease	2, 4, or 5 categories, depending on joint
Trauma	2 categories

index are given below, but in view of the tentative nature of some ingredients, we anticipate an ongoing process of experimentation and refinement.

1. The attributes of this system are categories of skeletal lesions or physical characteristics. A detailed technical concept underlies each measure (see Goodman and Martin, this volume), but for convenience in discussing them we use various shorthand terms, including (a) stature; (b) enamel hypoplasias; (c) dental defects; (d) anemia as indicated by porotic hyperostosis or cribra orbitalia;[7] (e) infections as indicated by periosteal reactions; (f) degenerative joint disease; and (g) trauma. These attributes, which are readily recorded by most physical anthropologists, are included in the consolidated database of the project. We minimized the potential problem of interobserver variation in scoring by using slides and physical examples to illustrate the system of coding (see Appendix for details).

2. All attributes of health are weighted equally in the index. While it may be difficult to justify this assumption, given the present state of knowledge it is also difficult to justify any particular set of alternative weights. There is a need for research on the functional consequences of these lesions that could serve as a guide to alternative weights.

3. For each individual, every observable attribute of the health index is scored on a scale of 0 to 100 percent.[8] The scoring is continuous or discrete, depending on the attribute as shown in Table 3.1. For example, stature is scored continuously, and hypoplasias are grouped into three categories: none (score of 100 percent), moderate (score of 50 percent), and severe (score of 0 percent). Scoring is similar for other discrete categories discussed below, that is, if there are 4 categories, the possibilities are 100, 67, 33, and 0.

---

among preferences across attributes. For example, the ranking of vision depends upon the level of hearing. Because the multilinear form is quite complex and would require many measurements for its estimation, practical work in this area has relied upon the additive and multiplicative forms. Interviews and surveys usually reject the additive model, which is a limitation of this application to skeletal remains.

[7] We recognize that some researchers dispute the association between porotic hyperostosis and anemia. For a discussion of issues and recent research, see Hershkovitz et al. (1997) and Schultz (1993).

[8] It is assumed that an individual's health was not correlated with the bones available for study. If the skeleton was incomplete, we posit that parts were missing at random in relation to the health attributes.

4. The health index takes on a value of 0 at death, which is a standard assumption in multiattribute models. An individual who exhibited the most severe deficiency on each attribute, but lived through a particular year of age, receives a quality score of 0 for that year of age. A health status consisting of the worst case of every attribute is equivalent to death.

5. Stature is inferred from long bone (femur) length. Individuals receive a score of 100 percent if they attained or exceeded modern femur standards for their age, as provided by Marion Maresh (1955). Individuals who fall below the third standard deviation of modern standards receive a score of 0, and intermediate results are linearly prorated. Difficulties in determining stature from femur lengths in adolescence lead us to exclude this category from the list of attributes at ages of death from 11.75 to 17.75 years.

6. Dental health has two components: (a) completeness (weight of 75 percent) and (b) abscesses (weight of 25 percent). Completeness is defined by one minus the ratio of the sum of premortem loss and cavities to the sum of teeth and premortem loss. The sum of teeth and premortem loss must be eight or more; otherwise data in this category are deemed incomplete and are not used. Abscesses are scored in three categories: none, moderate, and severe (two or more).

7. The score for degenerative joint disease is determined by the lowest of the scores estimated for the following joints: shoulder and elbow (five categories); hip and knee (five categories); cervical (four categories); thoracic (four categories); lumbar (four categories); temporomandibular (two categories).

8. Trauma or bone fracture is assessed for the following parts of the skeleton: arm (humerus, radius, and ulna); leg (femur, tibia, and fibula); nasal and nasal process; face other than nasal; skull vault; hand; and weapon wounds to any part of the body or head. An individual receives a score of 100 percent if trauma is absent on all parts observed, and the score is 0 if any part of the skeleton shows trauma. This system does not recognize or otherwise incorporate multiple trauma.

9. Skeletal characteristics formed in childhood (stature, anemia, and hypoplasias) are assumed to have functional consequences from birth to death. Though stature is heavily influenced by environmental circumstances in childhood, the effects of impaired growth are often realized throughout life. Several studies of labor markets in developing countries show that wages or productivity increase with stature, and longitudinal studies have established the importance of childhood nutrition for mental development and the acquisition of human capital (Haddad and Bouis, 1991, and Pollit et al., 1995). If anemia is observed in an adult, ordinarily it persisted from childhood. Hypoplasias signify substantial nutritional stress in early childhood, which we assume has consequences in addition to those measured by stature. This procedure gives high weight in the index to childhood health and nutrition.

10. Bones were living tissue that may have changed or remodeled. Therefore, the skeleton provides a limited window on health. The exact length of time that an individual may have endured a pathological condition, such as degenerative joint disease, can only be approximated. Because a condition of this type is often chronic, it is reasonable to venture that it could have existed for many years. Here we assume that conditions observed at death persisted for 10 years prior to death

for dental health, infections, degenerative joint disease, and trauma. This is clearly a simplifying assumption, but one that can easily be changed in the calculation of the index. In reality, it is likely that the window on health varies by the type and severity of the skeletal lesion, the age and nutritional status of the individual, and so on. We await evidence and research that will clarify these issues.

11. Dental defects and degenerative joint disease are assumed to be absent during childhood (up to age 18). Exceptions can be found, particularly for dental health, but the assumption is reasonably accurate for working purposes.

12. In view of evidence that estimated ages-at-death are too low, the reported ages are adjusted according to the method of C. Owen Lovejoy et al. (1985). Specifically, 1.4 years is subtracted from estimated ages of 18 to 29 years, while the following were added at older reported ages: 0.8 at 30–39; 7.4 at 40–49; 6.8 at 50–59; and 13.6 at 60+.

Calculation of the index for a particular site begins with the construction of age-specific rates of attribute scores.[9] The age-specific scores at particular ages are simply averages of the attribute scores for individuals (at the site) whose health was assessed at those ages. It is assumed that the consequences of stature, anemia, and hypoplasias persisted from birth to death. Thus, someone who had a stature score of 50 percent when he or she died at age 40, for example, would contribute one person year lived at each age from birth to age 40 and a score of 50 percent in each year of life. The age-specific scores are essentially ratios, in which the denominators equal the sum of person-years of health assessed at those ages, and the numerators equal the sum of the assessed scores at those ages.

The rates for the remaining attributes, which have 10-year windows, are constructed in a similar fashion, except that person-years lived (and the scores) apply only to the 10-year interval prior to death. Figure 3.2 illustrates these assumptions for an individual who died at age 40, in which the dark lines show the person-years for which the scores apply. If the dental score, for example, was 65 percent at death, we assume the person lived with that score from age 30 to age 40. We make no assumption about (do not calculate) dental scores prior to age 30 (and above age 18 – see next paragraph). Of course, more complicated (and likely more realistic) assumptions about the typical decline in dental health prior to age 40 are possible, with linear (or even nonlinear) declines and windows other than 10 years being examples. But these assumptions also involve more complex computations, which may be justified if additional research reveals what the actual patterns were likely to have been.

Recall that we assume that dental defects and degenerative joint disease did not exist below age 18 (essentially, scores for these attributes equaled 100 at these ages). Someone who died at age 26, for example, would contribute the scores observed only from age 18 to age 26.

The FORTRAN computer program calculated the age-specific attribute scores for single years of age, but partly to compensate for some tendencies of age heaping, and also to smooth the scores at sites with few individuals, we grouped the attribute scores by age categories. We used categories of 0–4, 5–14, 15–24, 25–34, 35–44, and

---

[9] These are not true age-specific rates because the number of individuals alive (at risk) is not known from age-at-death information. Biases could arise if the pathologies hastened the chances of death. However, the problem for ranking health is mitigated if the bias is the same, or at least similar, across populations.

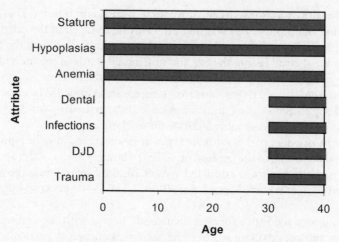

Figure 3.2. Person-years of attribute scores, death at age 40.

45+ years. The last category reflects the fact that the reliability of age estimates declines at older adult ages. In addition, at most sites, relatively few individuals lived beyond age 45.

Next, we calculated an average score for each attribute by first multiplying each age-specific rate by person-years lived in each age category within the reference population. The sum of these numbers divided by life expectancy at birth in the reference population (26.38 years) gives the attribute score as a percent of the maximum attainable. The average of these scores across attributes gives an overall quality score as a percent of the maximum, and this multiplied by 26.38 estimates average quality-adjusted life-years lived at a particular site.[10] The maximum of 26.38 would be attained if pathological lesions or skeletal defects were absent for each individual at every age, that is, if each age-specific attribute rate was 100 percent. Comparisons across sites are facilitated by expressing the result at each site as a percent of the maximum.

If reliable information was available on life expectancy, it could be incorporated into the rankings by multiplying the quality scores by the ratio of the life expectancies at particular sites to life expectancy in the reference population (26.38 years). In turn, these results could be converted to percentage terms by dividing by the highest such score in the sample.

III. RESULTS

The findings for 65 sites are presented in Table 3.2, arranged in descending order of health as measured by quality-adjusted life-years. Perhaps the most striking pattern is that health levels varied enormously in the Western Hemisphere, with quality-adjusted life-years ranging from 53.5 to 91.9 as a percent of the maximum attainable.

---

[10] At a few sites, some attributes were not measured, or the age distribution of deaths was such that gaps were left in the age-specific attribute rates. In these instances, the average was taken across the available rates.

Table 3.2: Health Index by Site

Abbrev.	Site no.	Group	QALY	% of Max.	Investigator	Age	Description
LNC	20	N	24.22	91.8	Neves	1200	Coastal Brazil
111	27	N	23.54	89.2	Larsen	1350	Coastal South Carolina
LNP	21	N	22.97	87.1	Neves	3000	Shell mounds, southern Brazil
ESB	58	N	22.41	85.0	Buikstra	0700	Estuquina, Peru
301	29	N	22.10	83.8	Larsen	0325	Coastal South Carolina
osg	12	N	22.00	83.4	Ubelaker	7425	Sta. Elena, Ecuador
WO7	61	N	21.75	82.4	Walker	1075	Coastal Southern California
cot	13	N	21.52	81.6	Ubelaker	2160	Highland Ecuador
BFT	54	N	21.50	81.5	Owsley	0075	Equestrian Nomad, Blackfoot
201	28	N	21.34	80.9	Larsen	0600	Coastal South Carolina
BU2	50	N	21.20	80.4	Owsley	0200	Plains village, Pawnee
101	26	N	21.19	80.3	Larsen	1350	Coastal South Carolina
W42	65	N	21.10	80.0	Walker	5250	Coastal Southern California
W38	64	N	20.85	79.0	Walker	3834	Coastal Southern California
Dk2	46	N	20.82	78.9	Owsley	0155	Plains village, Omaha
KIT	31	N	20.55	77.9	Sciulli	2600	Archaic, Great Lakes region
rea	11	N	20.39	77.3	Ubelaker	4663	Realto, Ecuador
BUF	35	N	20.40	77.3	Sciulli	0350	Buffalo, Great Lakes region
Sfa	18	E	20.29	76.9	Ubelaker	0190	San Francisco church, Ecuador
KX1	47	N	20.16	76.4	Owsley	0155	Plains village, Ponca
W13	63	N	20.14	76.3	Walker	1625	Coastal Southern California
CRW	48	N	20.01	75.9	Owsley	0075	Equestrian Nomad, Crow
W28	60	N	19.96	75.7	Walker	0434	Coastal Southern California
Lib	16	N	19.81	75.1	Ubelaker	1760	South coast, Ecuador
DW2	49	N	19.82	75.1	Owsley	0170	Plains village, Arikara
3AM	52	N	19.65	74.5	Owsley	0475	Plains Arikara & Oneota
WW7	51	N	19.62	74.4	Owsley	0240	Plains village, Arikara
FAB	1	A	19.48	73.8	Rathbun	0105	Baptist Church, Philadelphia
PEA	32	N	19.44	73.7	Sciulli	0900	Pearson, Great Lakes region
303	30	N	19.41	73.6	Larsen	0325	Coastal South Carolina
MON	34	N	19.22	72.9	Sciulli	0650	Monongahela, Great Lakes region
CHY	53	N	19.24	72.9	Owsley	0071	Equestrian Nomad, Cheyenne
WLE	59	E	19.20	72.8	Walker	0075	Northern California
Lat	14	N	19.18	72.7	Ubelaker	2050	North coast, Ecuador
HPK	10	E	19.08	72.3	Sirianni	0108	Rochester NY poorhouse
SF1	19	E	19.04	72.2	Ubelaker	0090	San Francisco church, Ecuador
SUN	33	N	18.90	71.6	Sciulli	0750	Sun Watch, Great Lakes region
cry	2	E	18.82	71.3	Rathbun	0100	Eastern U.S.
Snt	15	N	18.74	71.0	Ubelaker	0395	Quito convent, Ecuador
Sfc	17	E	18.70	70.9	Ubelaker	0300	San Francisco church, Ecuador
Ftl	7	E	18.58	70.4	Sledzik	0150	Military, East
AZ1	44	N	18.40	69.8	Arriaza	1175	Maitas Chirb., Chile
W43	62	N	18.41	69.8	Walker	1359	Coastal Southern California
41D	6	A	18.35	69.5	Condon	0062	Texas frontier
Y1B	57	N	18.32	69.4	Buikstra	0700	Yaral, Peru
Stt	9	E	18.28	69.3	Saunders	0102	Belleville, Ontario, Canada
MR1	45	N	18.09	68.6	Arriaza	6015	Coastal Chile
3C9	3	A	18.06	68.5	Rathbun	0097	Folly Island Union troops
TL2	41	N	18.04	68.4	Marquez	3100	Tlatilco, Mexico

(continued)

Table 3.2 (*continued*)

Abbrev.	Site no.	Group	QALY	% of Max.	Investigator	Age	Description
SGB	56	N	17.89	67.8	Buikstra	0700	San Geron., Peru
XCA	43	N	17.87	67.7	Marquez	0990	Xcaret, Mexico
CHB	55	N	17.79	67.5	Buikstra	0700	Chiribaya, Peru
GPS	8	E	17.45	66.2	Sledzik	0080	Military, West
CUI	42	N	17.44	66.1	Marquez	1850	Cuicuilo, Mexico
CO1	39	N	17.42	66.0	Marquez	0790	Cholula, Mexico
3La	5	A	17.28	65.5	Rose	0042	Cedar Grove, Arkansas
J73	40	N	17.01	64.5	Marquez	1350	Jaina, Mexico
Teo	25	N	16.28	61.7	Storey	1625	Tlatinga, Mayan
dol	36	N	15.76	59.8	Stodder	1050	Dolores, Colorado
QUI	22	N	15.60	59.1	Neves	1175	Northern Chile
Co9	23	N	15.56	59.0	Storey	1125	Copán, Rural, Mayan
cop	24	N	15.40	58.4	Storey	1125	Copán, Mayan
3C7	4	A	15.42	58.4	Rathbun	0095	Plantation slaves, SC
la8	38	N	15.11	57.3	Stodder	0448	San Cristobal Pueblo, New Mexico
haw	37	N	14.12	53.5	Stodder	0398	Hawikku, New Mexico

Notes: The abbreviations and site numbers are codes internal to the project and may not agree with those assigned by the original investigators. Group refers to Native American (N), Euro-American (E), or African-American (A). The maximum quality-adjusted life-years (QALY) is 26.38, which corresponds to a complete lack of pathological lesions or deficiencies. Only the lead investigator's in data collection is mentioned in the table (for additional information, see the chapters). The ages, given here in "years before the present" (years BP – before 1950), are roughly approximate for prehistoric sites. As a rule of thumb, the older the site, the less is known about its age.

This conclusion is reinforced by the fact that the health index does not incorporate systematic differences in length of life across sites. If life expectancy rose and fell with the index, then actual variation in health was greater than reported.

Notably, Native Americans were both the healthiest and the least healthy in the entire sample. They occupied the top 14 slots and 26 out of the top 27, but they also held 8 of the last 9 positions. Euro-Americans and African-Americans, who occupied 14 sites in total, overwhelmingly were situated in the middle and lower rungs on this scale. Only 3 out of these 14 sites (two Euro-American and one African-American) were situated above the median. Surprisingly, the health index at the Rochester, New York, poorhouse exceeded that for middle- and upper-class Euro-Americans at Belleville, Ontario. As discussed in the "Conclusions" to the book, this site illustrates an "osteological paradox," or a condition in which the depiction of health by several skeletal indicators diverges substantially from other important health measures, such as mortality rates or life expectancy at birth. The poorhouse was quite unhealthy as measured by longevity, and death rates were so high for the newly admitted that many types of skeletal lesions did not have time to form prior to death.

It is interesting to note that African-Americans had among the best and the worst of health outside Native Americans. The poor health of slaves, particularly children, has been observed in small stature and high mortality rates (Steckel, 1986a, 1986b). That the slaves of the South Carolina plantation ranked lowest among African-Americans is not surprising, but it is remarkable that the slaves were near the bottom in the overall rankings (58.4 percent of the maximum), comparable in health to pre-Columbian Native American populations threatened with extinction. It is also surprising that the antebellum blacks who were buried at Philadelphia's First African Church scored 73.8 percent – second highest of all non–Native American populations and superior to small-town, middle-class whites. These data indicate that it was possible for a socially disadvantaged group to carve out a life with reasonably good health in an early-nineteenth-century city.

Health varied considerably by region and time period.[11] Although a more systematic study of determinants of health appears elsewhere in this volume, a superficial glance at Table 3.2 suggests that the American Southwest and Mesoamerica were often tough on health at the sites in the sample. Good health existed on both continents and was often situated on or near coastal areas. There was a tendency for the health of Native Americans to decline over time. The healthiest sites were often quite old, substantially predating the arrival of Columbus, but the equestrian plains nomads were a nineteenth-century exception.

The attribute scores presented in Table 3.3 are useful for diagnosing or explaining differences in the health index.[12] Sites with poor health typically scored low on most attributes, but sites with good health, on average, may not have had uniformly good attribute scores. Some of the healthier populations had relatively low scores on stature. Because stature scores were low in general (average value of 20.7), the lack of information on stature no doubt elevates the index at three of the top four sites. If data were not collected on a particular attribute, the available attributes were weighted equally to form the index. For example, if the missing stature score at the healthiest site (LNC) is replaced by the average score at the top five sites that had stature scores, the index (as a percent of the maximum) falls from 91.8 to 81.5. The top score at a site for which all attributes were observed was 83.4 (Sta. Elena, Ecuador).

The strengths of association among the attributes and between the attribute scores and the health index are specified more formally in Table 3.4. The correlations across sites show that hypoplasias, anemia, and degenerative joint disease were the better

[11] Site age is highly approximate in many cases. Most burials, with the exception of some that apply to the military, occurred over many years, and as a rule of thumb, the older the site, the less is known about its age.

[12] Table 3.3 also presents a measure of sample size. The number of individuals studied at a particular site is only a rough indicator of the volume of information available because many skeletons were incomplete and the age distribution of deaths may have varied across locations. The last column of the table gives total person-years of information acquired for estimation of the index. Its meaning is illustrated by a couple of examples. Someone who died at age 30 and left a complete skeleton for study would provide 166 person-years of information for the index: 30 years each for stature, hypoplasias, and anemia; 10 years for each of the remaining attributes in the 10 years prior to death; and 36 years for dental and degenerative joint disease, which are assumed to be absent up to age 18. A child who died at age 8 and left a complete skeleton would provide 56 person-years of information (8 years for each of seven attributes). A complete skeleton that typified the reference population (died at age 26) would provide 150 person-years. Dividing the last column of the table by this number gives a rough sense of the whole skeleton equivalents, but we caution that this procedure does not take into account the distribution of ages-at-death. Moreover, because many skeletons were incomplete, the number of individuals studied is greater than the result would suggest. Nevertheless, any site with fewer than 2,000 to 3,000 person-years is small, and the results should be regarded with caution.

Table 3.3: Health Index as a Percent of Maximum, Attribute Scores, and Person-Years Observed by Site

Abbrev.	Site no.	Description	% of max.	Stature	Hyp.	Anemia	Dental	Inf.	DJD	Trauma	Person-yrs.
LNC	20	Coastal Brazil	91.8	*	88.4	100.0	82.9	*	93.4	94.4	1713
111	27	Coastal South Carolina	89.2	59.8	*	98.6	99.9	92.9	91.1	93.2	3764
LNP	21	Shell mounds, southern Brazil	87.1	*	75.4	83.6	87.3	*	98.0	91.2	9301
ESB	58	Estuquina, Peru	85.0	*	60.3	92.7	100.0	78.1	86.1	92.6	13019
301	29	Coastal South Carolina	83.8	31.7	92.4	92.6	93.7	92.2	100.0	*	6179
osg	12	Sta. Elena, Ecuador	83.4	8.7	99.7	100.0	91.1	98.7	94.8	90.8	4643
WO7	61	Coastal Southern California	82.4	42.8	85.0	96.1	97.4	83.8	78.6	93.4	30154
cot	13	Highland Ecuador	81.6	7.4	99.7	97.1	94.0	93.5	85.1	94.4	7991
BFT	54	Equestrian Nomad, Blackfoot	81.5	*	*	95.2	86.6	52.5	87.8	85.5	3948
201	28	Coastal South Carolina	80.9	24.3	*	98.4	94.5	83.3	88.2	96.8	18297
BU2	50	Plains village, Pawnee	80.4	21.0	*	99.2	89.0	89.9	90.6	92.5	7435
101	26	Coastal South Carolina	80.3	9.3	*	100.0	99.7	96.6	90.4	86.0	2630
W42	65	Coastal Southern California	80.0	18.6	81.6	95.5	84.5	92.0	100.0	87.7	16028
W38	64	Coastal Southern California	79.0	12.6	89.4	*	95.0	*	100.0	98.1	2055
dk2	46	Plains village, Omaha	78.9	27.2	*	99.8	91.0	86.3	82.4	86.8	3938
KIT	31	Archaic, Great Lakes region	77.9	48.2	92.2	94.5	75.2	83.1	67.8	84.2	11288
rea	11	Realto, Ecuador	77.3	1.2	96.4	99.3	79.4	95.8	80.5	88.4	4786
BUF	35	Buffalo, Great Lakes region	77.3	36.5	88.3	91.9	64.4	86.2	79.3	94.9	8828
sfa	18	San Francisco church, Ecuador	76.9	16.9	99.4	99.6	62.1	98.3	89.8	72.2	1536
KX1	47	Plains village, Ponca	76.4	2.7	*	100.0	92.5	78.8	89.1	95.5	1718
W13	63	Coastal Southern California	76.3	20.4	82.7	87.6	80.7	89.5	91.8	81.6	23596
CRW	48	Equestrian Nomad, Crow	75.9	49.9	*	93.0	90.6	49.3	82.3	90.2	4350
W28	60	Coastal Southern California	75.7	12.2	87.2	90.5	83.9	84.6	85.2	85.8	34194
lib	16	South coast, Ecuador	75.1	2.7	89.1	93.1	81.8	94.1	77.3	87.6	9730
DW2	49	Plains village, Arikara	75.1	16.8	*	99.3	83.1	87.1	72.6	92.0	3573
3AM	52	Plains Arikara & Oneota	74.5	23.7	*	94.0	78.7	67.4	90.6	92.7	2206
WW7	51	Plains village, Arikara	74.4	17.2	*	97.4	84.3	87.0	76.8	83.6	7215

76

FAB	1	Baptist Church, Philadelphia	73.8	49.3	66.4	96.9	64.9	81.5	69.1	88.6	8069
PEA	32	Pearson, Great Lakes region	73.7	33.9	70.5	97.1	67.3	79.7	76.4	90.9	8552
303	30	Coastal South Carolina	73.6	22.4	*	92.9	90.7	53.8	82.2	99.5	10591
MON	34	Monongahela, Great Lakes region	72.9	24.5	93.5	92.0	62.8	81.0	73.1	83.2	11007
CHY	53	Equestrian Nomad, Cheyenne	72.9	47.8	*	99.2	89.5	76.3	81.4	43.4	2591
WLE	59	Northern California	72.8	36.1	60.4	97.2	81.3	89.0	68.5	77.1	11674
lat	14	North coast, Ecuador	72.7	6.8	94.2	100.0	89.7	58.1	71.4	88.7	3306
HPK	10	Rochester NY poorhouse	72.3	33.0	80.1	96.1	71.7	54.0	79.3	92.1	31641
SF1	19	San Francisco church, Ecuador	72.2	12.8	91.0	99.7	67.9	95.2	78.9	59.8	3563
SUN	33	Sun Watch, Great Lakes region	71.6	31.6	83.3	89.3	68.9	66.7	75.2	86.5	10557
cry	2	Eastern U.S.	71.3	28.2	43.3	96.9	73.6	68.6	88.7	100.0	2664
snt	15	Quito convent, Ecuador	71.0	4.8	89.1	95.7	69.3	84.8	94.6	58.8	849
sfc	17	San Francisco church, Ecuador	70.9	3.7	98.6	94.6	71.8	72.8	79.8	75.0	3482
ftl	7	Military, East	70.4	31.7	98.6	94.8	74.0	84.1	85.1	24.8	3888
AZ1	44	Maitas Chirb., Chile	69.8	1.1	*	99.8	73.5	98.2	76.2	*	8127
W43	62	Coastal Southern California	69.8	20.2	97.4	*	87.2	54.5	69.9	89.6	7627
41D	6	Texas frontier	69.5	42.8	53.9	94.5	85.9	46.6	74.0	89.0	71159
Y1B	57	Yaral, Peru	69.4	1.2	*	87.1	100.0	71.5	56.8	100.0	4159
stt	9	Belleville, Ontario, Canada	69.3	36.0	71.8	93.9	71.2	81.5	41.6	89.2	44180
MR1	45	Coastal Chile	68.6	0.4	*	88.4	86.4	86.1	81.5	*	5097
3C9	3	Folly Island Union troops	68.5	41.6	39.0	100.0	74.9	46.9	82.5	94.3	918
TL2	41	Tlatilco, Mexico	68.4	13.2	75.1	86.6	76.5	54.2	80.1	93.0	33758
SGB	56	San Geron, Peru	67.8	4.0	*	79.6	89.3	72.7	61.3	100.0	5590
XCA	43	Xcaret, Mexico	67.7	28.4	67.3	70.3	81.8	50.5	79.1	96.8	3237
CHB	55	Chiribaya, Peru	67.5	3.2	48.4	87.5	86.4	80.1	67.7	98.8	13122
GPS	8	Military, West	66.2	40.6	70.8	96.4	74.3	92.1	78.1	10.8	3602
CO1	42	Cuicuilo, Mexico	66.1	7.9	80.5	90.5	84.1	45.2	69.3	85.1	17858

(continued)

Table 3.3 *(continued)*

Abbrev.	Site no.	Description	% of max.	Stature	Hyp.	Anemia	Dental	Inf.	DJD	Trauma	Person-yrs.
CUI	39	Cholula, Mexico	66.0	7.6	70.7	76.1	80.2	55.5	79.9	92.1	11881
3La	5	Cedar Grove, Arkansas	65.5	67.8	9.8	87.2	77.6	55.0	85.6	75.6	7008
J73	40	Jaina, Mexico	64.5	3.1	54.4	75.7	89.6	58.2	74.2	96.1	5232
teo	25	Tlatinga, Mayan	61.7	12.5	20.3	89.2	88.5	59.7	72.5	89.1	4397
dol	36	Dolores, Colorado	59.8	7.9	34.8	55.0	79.1	91.0	66.8	83.8	2841
QUI	22	Northern Chile	59.1	1.9	71.2	90.0	55.3	64.1	51.4	80.2	20557
co9	23	Copán, Rural, Mayan	59.0	6.0	18.7	82.1	85.1	46.9	81.9	92.2	22168
cop	24	Copán, Mayan	58.4	28.4	35.6	74.3	67.9	44.1	64.0	94.2	4651
3C7	4	Plantation slaves, SC	58.4	3.2	42.7	57.1	81.3	49.5	77.0	98.3	6958
la8	38	San Cristobal Pueblo, NM	57.3	1.7	46.5	53.2	78.5	88.1	52.8	80.2	21118
haw	37	Hawikku, NM	53.5	4.0	26.9	55.8	73.6	80.0	50.0	84.3	13751
Mean			72.6	20.7	71.1	90.5	81.8	75.1	78.9	85.7	
s.d.			7.98	16.86	24.59	11.53	10.39	16.97	12.26	16.12	
Median			72.8	17.2	77.8	94.5	82.9	80.6	79.8	89.4	
Min.			53.5	0.4	9.8	53.2	55.3	44.1	41.6	10.8	
Max.			91.8	67.8	99.7	100.0	100.0	98.7	100.0	100.0	

Note: *denotes data are missing or were not collected for the attribute at that site.

Table 3.4: Correlation Matrix of the Health Index and Its Components

	% of max.	Stature	Hyp.	Anemia	Dental	Inf.	DJD	Trauma
% of Max.	1.000							
Stature	0.304	1.000						
Hypoplasias	0.662	−0.111	1.000					
Anemia	0.668	0.300	0.555	1.000				
Dental	0.412	−0.078	−0.013	0.087	1.000			
Infections	0.461	−0.117	0.471	0.277	0.024	1.000		
DJD	0.664	0.133	0.331	0.438	0.323	0.185	1.000	
Trauma	0.132	−0.202	−0.187	−0.149	0.304	−0.288	−0.033	1.000

Source: Calculated from Table 3.3.

indicators of general health. It is interesting that trauma was weakly associated with the overall index, a finding that holds even if the three military sites are removed from the database. Trauma was surprisingly egalitarian: The individuals at both the healthy and the unhealthy sites were subject to injury that left broken bones. Fractures and expressions of violence were mildly and negatively correlated with several other health attributes. Note, too, that the correlations between the attribute scores were generally low (only one – that between signs of anemia and hypoplasias – exceeds 0.50, amounting to only 0.55), which points to the importance of relying on multiple indicators of health. In short, no single attribute of health substitutes well for others.

IV. SOME IMPLICATIONS

In recent years, a small industry of researchers has emerged to interpret the experience of Native Americans in the Western Hemisphere. While the neglect of Native American history by serious scholars is regrettable, the recent contributions to the literature by historians are, as a whole, idiosyncratic. There has been little exchange of views or cross-fertilization of ideas between historians and physical anthropologists. In their isolation, historians have focused heavily, if not obsessively, on population size in 1492 and on the decimation of Native Americans in the aftermath of contact (see, for example, Cook, 1981; Dobyns, 1983; and Stannard, 1989). Criticism can also be directed at physical anthropologists for failure to tailor their publications and shift their research energies in the direction of questions of interest to the large audience of historians and other social scientists.

While population size in 1492 and the aftermath of contact are certainly interesting questions that are important for Native American history, our results suggest that a richer, more diverse experience is worth exploring. Moreover, population size is, at best, a crude measure of health or the quality of life, and there is a pressing need to place conditions in 1492 and thereafter in long-term perspective. The huge variations in health witnessed by Native Americans prior to 1492 call for explanations and interpretations. The Western Hemisphere before the arrival of Europeans was so diverse that parts of it, at certain times, were like a Garden of Eden or an impoverished wasteland of health by standards of world history prior to the twentieth century. For this reason, it is highly misleading to speak of the health or quality of life of Native Americans as if it was relatively homogeneous, or as if conditions in 1492 were typical.

Euro-Americans and African-Americans tended to occupy the middle and lower portion of the distribution, an intriguing niche in the rankings of health. Comparisons of stature and mortality rates in the eighteenth and nineteenth centuries suggest that Euro-Americans were better off than Europeans. Therefore, skeletal data for the latter might place them very low in the rankings. One might suppose that Europeans in Europe, and especially in the Americas, would have done better given their notable technology, their access to resources, and their institutions of commerce, law, and politics that were placed in the service of global colonization. If these aspects of European or Euro-American life were advantageous, then there must have been significant disadvantages, as least for health, to their way of life.

It may be tempting to argue that most Europeans were victims of inequality. Perhaps their societies were rich and prosperous on average, but only a few lived well while the vast majority accumulated pathological lesions. While Europe in the eighteenth and nineteenth centuries is notable for its inequality, Euro-Americans had no such burden. Occupational differences in stature, for example, were virtually nil on the eve of the American Revolution (Sokoloff and Villaflor, 1982). It has been argued that inequality increased in nineteenth-century America, but it seems hard to believe that a major transformation could have occurred by the middle of the 1800s. The skeletons studied at the Belleville, Ontario, site represented middle- and upper-class Euro-Americans who were not oppressed by inequality, yet they attained only 65.5 percent of maximum quality-adjusted life-years – below the median for the Western Hemisphere sites as a whole.

In searching for explanations, it is useful to consider the advantages that Native Americans may have enjoyed. In the early stages of settling the Western Hemisphere, prime sites were available, resources were remarkably abundant, and population density was very low. In a diverse and resource-abundant environment, there may have been little need for trade, and moreover, low-population density and frequent moves related to local resource depletion probably inhibited commercial relationships and the spread of communicable diseases. Rates of exposure to infectious diseases were very low and food was abundant, resulting in few skeletal signs of chronic conditions.

Increasing population density and depletion of the resource base, including the decline of megafauna, may have been dynamic factors contributing to a long-term deterioration in health. Climatic change was likely a factor in the biological stress noted at some sites, including those in the Southwest. Social scientists often associate technological change with progress and higher living standards, but new methods or devices need not improve health if they were accompanied by repetitive movements that led to DJD, injuries, or the spread of communicable diseases. The cycles in height found in the United States and in the United Kingdom during industrialization are cases in point (Steckel and Floud, 1997).

More relevant to the situation at hand, the development of corn, beans, and other crops associated with the rise of settled agriculture may have led to a decline in dietary diversity and the spread of communicable disease. Political upheavals and warfare no doubt played some role in overall patterns of health among Native Americans.

V. SUGGESTIONS FOR RESEARCH

The health index is capable of refinement, and we hope that these preliminary efforts inspire research to clarify the meaning and enhance the consistency of comparisons across sites. Several assumptions that underlie the Mark I version, while perhaps reasonable, are not easily justified in the face of plausible alternatives. We plan sensitivity tests on several assumptions, examining the outcomes for important changes in rankings. For example, the window of time on health provided by skeletons might be changed in light of research on the rate at which various pathologies are remodeled. As an experiment, the window of time might be changed from 10 to 8 or 12 years for dental, infections, degenerative joint disease, and trauma. Alternatively, we could allow dental health and degenerative joint disease to decline linearly (or even nonlinearly) from age 18 to death (for those who died after age 18). It would be desirable to undertake research that could establish the length of time that lesions had existed, which would clarify the longitudinal picture of functional impairment.

The methods for calibrating DJD scores could be made more extensive and realistic, using likely functional impairments at various joints as a guide. Indeed, the functional implications of DJD, as well as other components of the health index, clearly depend upon culture, lifestyle, and technology in use. Severe DJD, for example, is much more disabling among hunter-gatherers constantly on the move and requiring considerable physical labor than in a society assisted by a variety of mechanical devices and pain medications. Similarly, loss of teeth becomes less consequential if mechanical devices and methods of preparation are available to soften food, and even less so if techniques of modern dentistry are available.

The method of tabulating stature scores uses average stature (femur length) as a standard, but sometime in the distant future, research might make it possible to use genetic material, in its place, to assess individual potential for growth. This step would be particularly useful in comparing the health of numerically small populations, where genetic differences may not approximately cancel.

It is reasonable to think about adding other attributes to the index. We chose the seven based on widespread availability, low cost of collecting, and general acceptance as reflecting important aspects of health. Components such as stature, dental health, and degenerative joint disease speak to general aspects of health during childhood and in the aging process. But these measures give an incomplete picture of health as might be learned from skeletons (and of course, an even less complete picture of health in general). As more components are added, though, especially those that are less general indicators of health, then weighting them according to functional significance becomes even more important.

Research should be done on the implications of weighting the age-specific quality scores by person-years lived in a Model West level 4 life table. Ideally, all populations compared by using the health index (the present, Mark I version) should have about the same life expectancy, and one close to this level. At this point, we do not know (with any reasonable confidence) the actual levels at most of the sites (see McCaa's chapter in this volume), but we impose this assumption in the belief that most of the populations (with the exception of the Rochester poorhouse) fell into a premodern range of roughly the low 20s to the middle 30s, where distortions would not be so great as to lose most of their comparative value. It is clear from the methodology expressed in Figure 3.1 that departures from approximate equality in life expectancies will distort comparisons of health, defined as reflecting both length of life and health quality of life while living. Hence, it is important to improve the reliability of life expectancy estimates, and to modify the health index to incorporate length of life, that is, to better estimate the area under the curve in Figure 3.1 (adapted to a group).

It would be interesting to know more about the possible effect of incomplete skeletons, that is, whether the assumption that bones are missing at random has any important impact on the health index. We will have greater confidence in our procedures if the results are highly correlated under alternative assumptions.

Inequality of health may be studied using the index in the same way that inequality of income or wealth is studied for insights into access to resources. We would like to know, for example, how men and women fared and the extent to which there were differences across classes within societies. The sample sizes are sufficiently large at some sites for this type of analysis.

This chapter merely scratches the surface of the possible causes and consequences of the social, economic, and historical implications of these new measures of health. Investigations of the data are still in the exploratory stage. In the chapter on "Patterns of Health in the Western Hemisphere," we link variations in the health index and its components with such site characteristics as settlement size, topography, plants and animals available for use, and climate. We seek explanations for the long-term decline in health among Native Americans before the arrival of Columbus and for geographic and ethnic patterns of health.

We caution that the health index tabulations should not be viewed as the end product of research, the last things to be done in a research agenda. In an important sense, they should be only the beginning. The index and its components should be objects of study, to be explained by various environmental or ecological variables. It is also important to probe whether the assumptions of the index approximately fit the sites under comparative study with respect to life expectancy, functional implications of impairments, the relevance of skeletal aspects of health not captured by the index, and so forth. Thus, the index should not be taken mechanically at face value, but explored for its weaknesses and for explanations of the patterns observed.

In sum, we have proposed what should be regarded as only an important first step – a work in progress – toward measuring health from skeletal remains. Thorny questions remain and much research lies ahead. But the concept of the health index is a flexible one that can be adapted to incorporate changes that research may bring.

And where empirical evidence may be lacking for its assumptions, sensitivity analysis will provide a range of plausible outcomes that can be compared.

APPENDIX: DATA CODING SCHEME

Introduction

The goal is to develop a numerical index of well-being (adaptation) from skeletal data. Knowledge of both economic indicators (such as gross national product) and health status assessments suggests that useful indexes can be developed from imperfect data. Our collection of skeletal data comes from a large array of genetic, geographic, and temporal groups, which permit us to measure levels of health and to investigate their possible environmental causes.

Inevitably, projects such as this face a trade-off between number of observations and the detail collected per observation. We emphasize number of observations (large number of individuals at a variety of sites) over detail (a complex coding scheme that records numerous features for each observation). We prefer this strategy (a cast of thousands) because diverse sites enhance our comparative perspective. Moreover, even simple coding schemes, such as the one adopted here, can be very effective in representing important aspects of health. For our purposes, the value of additional observations in a variety of ecological settings outweighs extraordinary detail on health for a smaller number of individuals at fewer sites.

Site/Collection Identification

The given skeletal collection is identified by eight (8) alpha/numeric characters. These could be a site number (e.g., 23CG0234) or an abbreviated name (Cedargro).

Individual Identification

Each individual is identified with a unique series of five (5) alpha/numeric characters (e.g., 00345 or 0956B).

Inventory

Any statistical study of lesions must provide information about observable skeletal components. Thus, the coding scheme contains a category indicating that the appropriate skeletal components were available for observation. Any data available for a skeleton was recorded.

Demography

The age and sex distributions of a population reflect mortality and fertility, which are the ultimate measures of adaptive success in past human groups. Moreover, these distributions are useful for delineating differential effects of disease, nutrition, and stress generally by specific age, sex, and status groups.

Sex. It is assumed that the methods employed in the determination of sex are those used in standard analysis. A definite designation is one in which criteria from the pelvis, especially the pubis, is clear and used in conjunction with additional features. The pelvis can, at times, produce ambiguous sex information and thus result in an unknown or probable designation. A probable designation is employed when the pelvis cannot be used but cranial and postcranial attributes predominately indicate one sex or the other. Any designation using fewer than four nonpelvic criteria must remain in the unknown category.

The sex of the individual is designated with the single numeric code as follows: 1) Female, definite designation, the sex is certain; 2) Probable Female, possible designation, but the investigator is uncertain; 3) Male, definite designation, the sex is certain; 4) Probable Male, possible designation, but the investigator is uncertain; 5) Sex is undetermined because the individual is less than 15 years of age and sex determination would be uncertain; 6) Unknown, the sex of the individual cannot be determined with any degree of reliability.

Age. There are a number of aging techniques and many investigators use one technique more effectively than others. Dental development is considered the best for the youngest ages, while epiphyseal closure is used for the later growing years. Adult ages determined from the pubic symphysis and auricular surface of the pelvis are considered the most reliable. There are three columns for recording age: 1) summary age; 2) dental age for children; and 3) age range.

Summary age: The investigator is asked to designate a single year (i.e., 37) as the age-at-death. This is the best estimate that the investigator can make. In its simplest form without additional information, this age is nothing more than the midpoint of the designated age range. Age is given in years using decimals to designate tenths of years (conversion of months). Individuals aged greater than 60 years, and for whom no further estimate is possible, are coded as 99. Summary age is recorded as a four (4) digit numeric field with one decimal place (e.g., 00.6 or 35.5).

Dental age: A dental age for children is required for the growth analysis. In many cases the dental age and the summary age are the same; however, this category uses only dental development, whereas the summary age may stem from other sources of information. Dental age is recorded as a four (4) digit numeric field with one decimal place (e.g., 03.4).

Age range: It is preferable to use standardized age ranges (i.e., 50–54 years), but the data to be coded were already collected and age ranges differ between investigators. On this variable we could not expect true concordance after the fact. The investigator provided the age range in years for that individual. For categories such as subadult or old adult, the investigator defined this category by providing an age range in years. If such ranges are being determined for this project, then standard five-year intervals (i.e., 30–34 years) are employed. Age range is recorded as two numeric fields with two characters in each. The first represents the minimum age (e.g., 30) and the second the maximum age (e.g., 45).

Date of birth: Where known, the date of birth or decade (by using the midpoint, i.e., 1915) is recorded. Date of birth is a single field with four (4) numeric characters.

Continental Ancestry

Each skeleton is assigned to one of these populations of origin: 1) Native American; 2) European; 3) African; 4) Asian; 5) Mixed, any mixture of the above. This code is based on the site context or from the historic literature. Although there are various degrees of mixture in some of the groups, we cannot reliably estimate the mixture for an individual skeleton; 6) Unknown. Continental ancestry is a single character numeric field.

Social Status

An individual's position in a social hierarchy (i.e., social status) can influence access to both luxury items and / or necessities of life (e.g., adequate housing, nutrition, etc.). Thus, social status can have considerable influence on such biological characteristics as height, as well as determining resistance to disease (e.g., impairment of the immune system), physical work load (e.g., seen as increase in degenerative joint disease), and so on.

For some of the skeletal populations, there is clear evidence of social/economic distinctions evident from either the historical records or grave goods (i.e., differential access to luxury or scarce items). Each individual receives a three digit code. The first designates the stratification category of the society, the second indicates the number of strata, while the third indicates that person's place within the society.

Social Stratification Codes. 1) Denotes undifferentiated societies, reflecting the lack of significant differences in social stratification observable in the grave goods, and in archaeological or historical evidence. If there is any doubt whether the presence of grave goods had any status meaning, these individuals or groups are placed here; 2) A ranked society is one in which there are social differences with groups or individuals having clear differential access to luxury or exotic goods. Membership in this category may be determined from either grave goods or historical records, including archaeological interpretation; 3) A class stratified society is one in which there are social differences with groups or individuals having clear differential access to wealth and / or subsistence resources. Assignment to this category may be determined from either grave goods or historical records, including archaeological interpretation.

Number of Social Stratification Code. The number of distinct social strata in the culture is designated by number. An undifferentiated society is coded as 1, a three strata society as 3, and so on.

Individual Position Codes. 1) The person occupies the highest rank in a ranked society or is a member of an undifferentiated society; 2) The person occupies the second from the highest rank in a stratified society; 3) The person occupies the third from the highest rank in a stratified society; 4) The person occupies the fourth from the highest rank in a stratified society; and so on.

Social Stratification Coding. The coding of social stratification uses a three digit numeric code with the first designating the presence or kind of stratification in the society, the second the number of social strata, and the third the position of the individual in the social ranking. For example, a person in an undifferentiated society is coded as 111. A person in an historic class society could be coded as 331 (a class society, three classes, person belongs to highest class). If all that can be determined is that the society is ranked with only tendencies for high or low social status, then the code might be 222 for a ranked society, two levels, with the person belonging to the lower social status.

Growth and Heights

Maximum Diaphyseal Length. Height for dental age is an excellent indicator of nutrition and overall health of children. Maximum diaphyseal lengths of the femora (left is first, then right, if left is unavailable) are used to calculate growth statuses of juveniles using ages determined from dental development. Only the diaphyseal length (no epiphyses) is recorded here. This field contains three numeric characters for the measurement in millimeters.

Femur Length. Adult height is an excellent indicator of nutrition and health during childhood. The variable recorded is the maximum length of the left femur (right if left is unavailable). If necessary, femur length was estimated from other bones using regression formulae. The field contains three numeric characters and the lengths are recorded in millimeters.

Adult Height. The various formulae for calculating stature from the maximum length of the femora or other bones are available in Krogman and Iscan (1986; American Whites and Blacks page 308, Mongoloids page 310, and Indigenes of Central Mexico pages 319–320) and Sciulli et al. (1990: 275–280, Native Americans). The recorder calculated the heights. Heights are recorded in a four character numeric field in millimeters.

Robusticity

Femur. Robusticity provides information on body weight, past diet, current physiological health, work and activity patterns, and degree of mobility. The total subperiosteal area (TA) of the adult femur is most responsive to the combined effects of mechanical demand/physical activity and body weight, but activity is likely most important in behavioral interpretation. The anteroposterior (AP) and mediolateral

(ML) diameters of the adult left femoral midshaft (right if the left is unavailable) is recorded in order to calculate TA. The formula for this calculation is (from Fresia et al. 1990):

$$TA = pi \ (Tap/2)(Tml/2)$$

where

Tap = anteroposterior diameter at midshaft, and

Tml = mediolateral diameter at midshaft.

Human populations vary widely in body size and, consequently, in femoral size. Therefore, it is absolutely essential that the measurement of TA be standardized when comparing populations. This can be done easily by dividing TA by femoral length to the third power in the following manner (Ruff et al. 1993):

$$TAstandardized = [pi \ (Tap/2)(Tml/2)]/\text{max. length cubed.}$$

The anteroposterior (AP) and mediolateral (ML) diameters of the femur midshaft are recorded in millimeters in two fields each of two numeric characters.

Humerus. Robusticity data for the adult humerus is provided by the maximum length and the circumference of the midshaft. These two measurements in millimeters are entered into two fields, the length with three numeric characters and the circumference with two numeric characters.

Enamel Hypoplasias

Enamel hypoplasias are excellent measures of childhood nutritional and morbidity stress, which complement growth rates and adult stature for reconstructing past health. Although they cannot be remodeled, they can be removed by wear and caries. Hypoplasias are reported only on the maxillary incisors and either the mandibular or maxillary canines for both deciduous and permanent teeth. The hypoplasias recorded are only linear grooves that can be clearly seen with the unaided eye under good illumination.

Hypoplasias are recorded for 1) deciduous maxillary central incisor; 2) deciduous canine (maxillary or mandibular); 3) permanent maxillary central incisor; and 4) permanent canine (either maxillary or mandibular). There is one column for each of these teeth. Only systemic hypoplasias are recorded, and the left teeth are used, but rights are reported if lefts are not available. The four teeth are scored as follows: 0 Not observable (no suitable teeth, incomplete development, or too worn, etc.); 1 No hypoplasia; 2 One hypoplasia; 3 Two or more hypoplasias.

Dental Disease

Dental Caries. Caries results from a disease process, and without intervention it results in complete destruction and loss of the affected tooth. In most groups, dental caries is the primary cause of abscessing and loss of teeth. However, there are some groups where rapid wear leads to abscessing and tooth loss, while in others, periodontal disease is the primary cause. The data are recorded for the permanent dentition only, as follows: 1) The total number of permanent teeth observed; 2) The total number of permanent teeth lost before death (antemortem); 3) The total number of teeth with lesions or restorations (i.e., fillings).

The data reported here are used to calculate individual (percent of carious teeth per mouth) and population (percent of total carious teeth per group) statistics on caries prevalence. There are three fields, each with two numeric characters.

Abscess. Abscesses can result from progressive caries or from tooth wear rapid enough to exceed the dentin's ability to fill the pulp chamber. In some cases the cause is not obvious (the loss is spontaneous). There is evidence that abscesses can be life threatening or, at the very least, diminish resistance to disease and, even more than caries, affect dietary intake. Abscesses are recognized by a clear drainage passage leading from the tooth root(s) to the external surface of either maxilla or mandible. The data are recorded in two fields: 1) two numeric characters for the total number of sockets examined; and 2) one numeric character for the total number of abscesses.

Anemia

Anemia (as indicated by cribra orbitalia and porotic hyperostosis) can be caused by a variety of factors, including an iron-deficient diet, disease, and parasites. Scoring these conditions can be very complicated, but the information contained in the various skeletal expressions can be obtained by a simple scoring system. Cribra orbitalia and porotic hyperostosis are scored separately. To score as present or absent, at least one parietal and one orbit must be observable. Scattered fine pitting of parietals and occipital, sometimes called porotic pitting, is not scored as positive. There are two fields, each with one numeric character.

Cribra Orbitalia is scored as: 0 No orbits to be observed; 1 Absent on at least one observable orbit; 2 Presence of a lesion; 3 Gross lesions with excessive expansion and large area of exposed diploe, which is the form associated with sickle-cell disease and other severe forms of anemia.

Porotic Hyperostosis is scored as: 0 No parietals to be observed; 1 Absent on at least one observable parietal; 2 Presence of a lesion; 3 Gross lesions with excessive cranial expansion and huge areas of exposed diploe, which is the form associated with sickle-cell disease and other severe forms of anemia.

Auditory Exostosis

It has been demonstrated that auditory exostoses (i.e., growth of extra bone occluding the ear canal) are associated with swimming in cold water. These growths do impair hearing and are recorded as follows: 0 At least one auditory meatus not present for observation; 1 Auditory meatus exhibits no exostosis; 2 Exostosis present in one or both ears.

Infection/Periosteal Reactions

Infections of the bone (primarily by ubiquitous *Staphylococcus* or *Streptococcus* organisms) can be quite serious and debilitating because they are very difficult for the body's defense mechanisms to combat. All such infections result in pain and swelling (with possible disfigurement), and interfere with normal activities. In addition, the infections are a burden on the individual's defense mechanism, which can result in reduced resistance to other disease processes.

Infectious lesions are complex to score because they can be isolated and minor, localized but chronic and debilitating, or the result of systemic disease. The skeletal sequelae of infection can exhibit the characteristics of active ongoing infection or the healing scars of past disease. Some periosteal reactions can result from trauma (bruising of the bone's periosteum), and these may be difficult to distinguish from infection. However, as most periosteal reactions are due to infection, they are scored as such unless the recorder has some reason to think otherwise. In order to ensure consistency of reporting, only major lesions of the major long bones are employed in the development of the index. Active and healed lesions are not differentiated. We focus almost exclusively on the tibia, which is the most common site for infectious lesions. There are two sets of scores, with the first being for the tibiae and the second for the remainder of the skeleton. Each of the fields contain one (1) numeric character.

Tibial Scores: 0 No tibia(e) present for scoring; 1 No infectious lesions of the tibia(e) with at least one tibia available for observation; 2 Slight, small discrete patch(es) of periosteal reaction involving less than one-quarter of the tibia(e) surface on one or both tibiae; 3 Moderate periosteal reaction involving less than one-half of the tibia(e) surface on one or both tibiae; 4 Severe periosteal reaction involving more than one-half of the tibia(e) surface (osteomyelitis is scored here).

Remaining Skeleton: 0 No periosteal reaction on any other bone than the tibiae; 1 Periosteal reaction on any other bone(s) than the tibiae not caused by trauma; 2 Evidence of systemic infection involving any of the bones (including the tibiae) of the skeleton. This would include specific diseases, such as (but not limited to) tuberculosis and syphilis.

Degenerative Joint Disease

Degenerative joint disease provides considerable information concerning activity patterns because chronic stress on the joints eventually damages the cartilaginous surfaces and, when sufficiently advanced, also the bone surface beneath. Within a given population, those individuals engaged in regularly occurring activities that produce chronic joint stress (e.g., rowing, running, etc.) will develop patterns (i.e., specific joints affected, such as knees or elbows) of degenerative joint disease differing from that in the general population. In addition to differences in the pattern of joints affected, variation in the age at which the damage appears can be informative.

Degenerative diseases can be difficult to score consistently and yet can be very informative even when recorded with great simplicity. There are eight (8) fields, each with one numeric character: 1) shoulder and elbow; 2) hip and knee; 3) cervical; 4) thoracic; 5) lumbar vertebrae; 6) temporomandibular joint; 7) wrist; and 8) hand. The most severe manifestation from either the right or left side is scored.

Shoulder and Elbow are scored as one unit, and if either joint is affected (score the most severely affected joint), it is scored as follows: 0 Joints not available for observation; 1 Joints show no sign of degenerative disease; 2 Initial osteophyte or deterioration of the joint surfaces; 3 Major osteophyte formation and / or destruction of the joint surface, such as eburnation; 4 Immobilization of the joint due only to degenerative disease; 5 Systemic degenerative disease (e.g., rheumatoid arthritis, alkaptonuria, etc.).

Hip and Knee are scored as one unit, and if either joint is affected (score the most severely affected joint), it is scored as follows: 0 Joints not available for observation; 1 Joints show no sign of degenerative disease; 2 Initial osteophyte or deterioration of the joint surfaces; 3 Major osteophyte formation and / or destruction of the joint surface, such as eburnation; 4 Immobilization of the joint; 5 Systemic degenerative disease.

Vertebrae are scored by type: cervical, thoracic, and lumbar. If four or more thoracic vertebrae are present, they are scored, and if two or more cervical or lumbar are present, they are scored. Only the bodies of the vertebrae are scored for the most severe expression:

Cervical: 0 Not observable; 1 No lesions on at least two observable vertebrae; 2 Initial osteophyte formation along rim of the vertebral body(-ies); 3 Extensive osteophyte formation along rim of the vertebrae; 4 Two or more vertebrae fused together.

Thoracic: 0 Not observable; 1 No lesions on at least four observable vertebrae; 2 Initial osteophyte formation along rim of the vertebral body(-ies); 3 Extensive osteophyte formation along rim of the vertebrae; 4 Two or more vertebrae fused together (keeping in mind that kyphosis from tuberculosis would be scored under infectious disease and not here).

Lumbar: 0 Not observable; 1 No lesions on at least two observable vertebrae; 2 Initial osteophyte formation along rim of the vertebral body(-ies); 3 Extensive osteophyte formation along rim of the vertebrae; 4 Two or more vertebrae fused together.

Temporomandibular Joint. Deterioration of the temporomandibular joint (TMJ) can lead to difficulties in chewing, intense pain, and a large, poorly understood array of psychosomatic diseases. Only extreme deterioration is recorded. This is recognized at the level that degenerative disease would be recorded on any other joint, including osteophytes, eburnation, and joint surface deterioration: 0 TMJ not observable; 1 No deterioration; 2 Joint deterioration.

Wrist. Radio-ulnar joint: 0 Bones not observable or not recorded; 1 No degenerative disease of the joint; 2 Degenerative disease of the joint.

Bones of the hand. 0 Bones not observable or not recorded; 1 No degenerative disease of the joint; 2 Degenerative disease of the joint.

Trauma

Trauma provides information about many aspects of society and the relationship of the people to the environment. Different activity patterns and terrains produce different patterns of trauma. For example, walking on rocks tends to produce higher frequencies of fractured ankles, while in less rugged terrain, lower arm fractures tend to predominate. In addition, both intra- and interpopulational violence can be documented by specific types and patterns of trauma, such as parry fractures of the lower arm or depressed fractures of the cranium. The scoring of trauma focuses on the major bones of the limbs and the skull: humerus, radius, ulna, femur, tibia, fibula, and skull. Unless there can be shown to be premortem or perimortem traumata (e.g., saw marks of an amputation or axe wound), they are scored only when there is some evidence of healing. Any form of surgery would be recorded as trauma. It is critical that postmortem modifications or damage not be recorded.

There are seven (7) fields, each with one numeric character: 1) arm; 2) leg; 3) nasal bones; 4) face; 5) skull vault; 6) hands; 7) weapon wounds.

Arm: humerus, radius and ulna. If any bone shows trauma, it is scored as follows: 0 No long bones observable (must have humerus and at least one bone of the forearm to be scored); 1 Not fractured; 2 Healed fracture with acceptable alignment; 3 Healed and poorly aligned; 4 Healed with fusion of the joint; 5 Healed fracture with alignment unknown.

Leg: femur, tibia, and fibula. If any bone shows trauma it is scored as follows: 0 No long bones observable (must have femur and tibia or fibula); 1 No fracture or other trauma; 2 Healed fracture with acceptable alignment; 3 Healed and poorly aligned with some loss of locomotion; 4 Healed with extreme loss of locomotion, such as loss of limb or complete fusion of the joint in the lower limb; 5 Healed with alignment unknown.

Nasal and Nasal Process: 0 No bones to be observed; 1 No fracture; 2 Healed fracture.

Face Other Than Nasal: 0 No bones to be observed; 1 No fracture; 2 Healed fracture.

Skull Vault: 0 No bones to be observed; 1 No fracture; 2 Healed fracture.

Hand Fractures: 0 No bones to be observed or not recorded; 1 No fracture; 2 Healed fracture(s).

Weapon Wounds to Any Part of the Body and Head: 1 No weapon wounds; 2 Weapon wound(s).

REFERENCES

Bush, J. W., M. M. Chen, and D. L. Patrick. "Social Indicators for Health Based on Function Status and Prognosis," *Proceedings American Statistical Association* Soc.Stats.Section (1972): 71.

Cadman, David, Charles Goldsmith, George W. Torrance, et al. "Development of a Health Status Index for Ontario Children. Final Report to Ontario Ministry of Health." Research Grant DM648 (1986): (00633).

Coale, Ansley J., and Paul Demeny. *Regional Model Life Tables and Stable Populations.* New York: Academic Press, 1983.

Cook, Noble David. *Demographic Collapse: Indian Peru, 1520–1620.* Cambridge: Cambridge University Press, 1981.

Dobyns, Henry F. *Their Numbers Became Thinned: Native American Population Dynamics in Eastern North America.* Knoxville: University of Tennessee Press, 1983.

Drummond, Michael F., Greg L. Stoddart, and George W. Torrance. *Methods for the Economic Evaluation of Health Care Programmes.* New York: Oxford University Press, 1987.

Erickson, Pennifer, E. Allen Kendall, John P. Anderson, et al. "Using Composite Health Status Measures to Assess the Nation's Health." *Medical Care* 27 Supplement (1989): 66–76.

Feeney, David, William Furlong, George W. Torrance, et al. "A Comprehensive Multi-Attribute System for Classifying the Health Status of Survivors of Childhood Cancer." *Journal of Clinical Oncology* 10 (1992): 923–928.

Feeney, David, Roberta Labelle, and George W. Torrance. "Integrating Economic Evaluations and Quality of Life Assessments." In *Quality of Life Assessments in Clinical Trials,* ed. B. Spilker, 71–83. New York: Raven Press, 1990.

Frank, Peter, Marthe Gold, and Pennifer Erickson. "Do Utility-Based Measures of Health-Related Quality of Life Predict Future Health Status? Longitudinal Evidence from a Nationally Representative Cohort." 1992 (Unpub).

Fresia, Anne, C. B. Ruff, and Larsen, C. S. "Temporal Decline in Bilateral Asymmetry of the Upper Limb on the Georgia Coast." In *The Archaeology of Santa Catalina de Guale: 2. Biocultural Interpretations of a Population in Transition,* ed. C. S. Larson. Anthropological Papers of the American Museum of Natural History No. 68, pp. 121–132. Washington, D. C.: 1990.

Glasson, William H. *Federal Military Pensions in the United States.* New York: Oxford University Press, 1918.

Haddad, Lawrence J., and Howarth E. Bouis. "The Impact of Nutritional Status on Agricultural Productivity: Wage Evidence from the Philippines." *Oxford Bulletin of Economics and Statistics* 53 (1991): 45–68.

Hershcovitz, Israel, Bruce M. Rothschild, Bruce Latimer, Oliver Dutour, Georges Leonetti, Charles M. Greenwald, Christine Rothschild, and Lyman M. Jellema. "Recognition of Sickle Cell Anemia in Skeletal Remains of Children." *American Journal of Physical Anthropology* 104 (1997): 213–226.

Kaplan, Robert M., and James W. Bush. "Health-Related Quality of Life Measurement for Evaluation Research and Policy Analysis." *Health Psychology* 1 (1982): 61–80.

Keeney, R. L., and H. Raiffa. *Decisions with Multiple Objectives: Preferences and Value Tradeoffs.* New York: J. Wiley & Sons, 1976.

Krogman, Wilton M., and Mehmet Y. Iscan. *The Human Skeleton in Forensic Medicine.* Springfield, Ill.: Charles C. Thomas, 1986.

Lohr, Kathleen N. "Advances in Health Status Assessment: Overview of the Conference." *Medical Care* 27 Supplement (1989): 1–11.

Lovejoy, C. Owen, Richard S. Meindl, Robert P. Mensforth, et al. "Multifactorial Determination of Skeletal Age at Death: A Method and Blind Tests of Its Accuracy." *American Journal of Physical Anthropology* 68 (1985): 1–14.

Maresh, M. M. "Linear Growth of Long Bones of Extremities from Infancy Through Adolescence." *A.M.A. American Journal of Diseases of Children* 89 (1955): 725–742.

Pollit, E., K. Gorman, P. L. Engle, et al. "Nutrition in Early Life and the Fulfillment of Intellectual Potential." *Journal of Nutrition* 125 Supplement 4S (1995): 1111S–1118S.

Preston, Samuel H., and Michael R. Haines. *Fatal Years: Child Mortality in Late Nineteenth-Century America.* Princeton N.J.: Princeton University Press, 1991.

Rondinelli, Robert D. "Practical Aspects of Impairment Rating and Disability Determination." In *Physical Medicine and Rehabilitation,* ed. Randall L. Braddom, 109–124. Philadelphia: Saunders, 2000.

Ruff, Christopher B., E. Trinkaus, A. Walker, and C. S. Larsen. "Postcranial Robusticity in *Homo.* I: Temporal Trends and Mechanical Interpretation." *American Journal of Physical Anthropology* 91 (1990): 21–53.

Schultz, M. "The Initial Stages of Systematic Bone Disease." In *Histology of Ancient Human Bone,* ed. G. Grupe and A. N. Garland, 185–203. Berlin: Springer Verlag, 1993.

Sciulli, Paul W., K. N. Schneider, and M. C. Mahaney. "Stature Estimation in Prehistoric Native Americans of Ohio." *American Journal of Physical Anthropology* 83 (1990): 275–280.

Sokoloff, Kenneth L., and Georgia C. Villaflor. "The Early Achievement of Modern Stature in America." *Social Science History* 6 (Fall 1982): 453–481.

Stannard, David E. *Before the Horror.* Honolulu: University of Hawaii Press, 1989.

Steckel, Richard H. "A Dreadful Childhood: The Excess Mortality of American Slaves." *Social Science History* 10 (1986a): 427–465.

"A Peculiar Population: The Nutrition, Health, and Mortality of American Slaves from Childhood to Maturity." *Journal of Economic History* 46 (1986b): 721–741.

"The Health and Mortality of Women and Children, 1850–1860." *Journal of Economic History* 48 (1988): 333–345.

Steckel, Richard H., and Roderick Floud, eds. *Health and Welfare during Industrialization.* Chicago: University of Chicago Press, 1997.

Torrance, George W., M. H. Boyle, and S. P. Horwood. "Application of Multi-Attribute Utility Theory to Measure Social Preferences for Health States." *Operations Research* 30 (1982): 1043–1069.

Torrance, George W., and David Feeney. "Utilities and Quality-Adjusted Life Year." *International Journal of Technology Assessment in Health Care* 5 (1989): 559–575.

CHAPTER FOUR

Paleodemography of the Americas

From Ancient Times to Colonialism and Beyond

Robert McCaa

ABSTRACT

Great variations in fertility constitute one of the major findings of this project to our
knowledge of the demography of the past. In the Ancient Americas (that is, more than
1,500 years ago), fertility seems to have been surprisingly low (gross reproduction
ratio, GRR, = 2.3), and the brake on explosive population growth was fertility rather
than mortality (life expectancy at birth, e_0, = 34 years). Consequently, the ancient demographic regime was a relatively low-pressure system. A high-pressure system of high
fertility and high mortality dates from the middle period, 1500 BP–500 BP (before the
present). Characteristic of only simple horticulturists in ancient times, a high-pressure
demographic regime seems to have become more general during the middle period,
intrinsic to both complex agrarian systems as well as foragers and fishers (GRR = 3.0
and 2.8, respectively). Agriculture was not the engine of demographic transformation
in prehistoric America because nonhorticulturists also experienced a substantial rise
in fertility. A second great demographic transformation began 500 years ago with
the intrusion of Old World populations and technologies. While these changes were
sweeping, indeed many peoples were thrust to the verge of extinction, the fundamental
demography of the survivors did not change greatly. The old demographic regime persisted into the nineteenth century, if the picture developed here from the osteological
evidence is trustworthy. Likewise, African-American demographic systems seem to
have been under high pressure: very high fertility and high mortality, with the highest pressures characteristic of the free. European-American demographic systems, as
measured here, were decidedly low pressure, with relatively moderate mortality and
moderately higher fertility.

INTRODUCTION

Life chances in ancient times were not as short as commonly thought, if the Health
and Nutrition in the Western Hemisphere database is a reliable guide. This osteological collection, one of the largest, most diverse ever assembled, with more than
12,000 skeletal samples from some 65 sites stretching over a period of four millennia,

94

reveals substantial variation in fertility, as well as life expectancy. From a millennial perspective, three great demographic regimes emerge from these data: a low-pressure system in earliest times (7,000–1,500 years ago), a high-pressure system in the classic era (1500–500 BP), and finally, over the past 500 years, ethno-culturally diverse systems with the merging of Old and New World biospheres. The Health and Nutrition in the Western Hemisphere database is also useful for addressing the impact of the emergence of agriculture on population, as well as illuminating the continuities and change between high- and low-pressure demographic systems. Finally, the vast scope of the Health and Nutrition data encourage the researcher to take into account fertility, an important subject bioarchaeologists have only recently begun to explore. Fertility, presumed to be unchanging and unfathomable, emerges from these data as the clearest window for viewing the demography of archaeological populations, as well as a surprisingly dynamic component of demographic equations, ancient and modern alike.

FERTILITY-CENTERED PALEODEMOGRAPHY

The most important breakthrough in paleodemography in recent years is the recognition that fertility influences the age distribution of deaths much more than mortality. Reading ages from skeletal data reveals much about fertility but little about mortality, or what paleodemographers once called "life expectancy" (i.e., average age at death; for critiques, see Sattenspiel and Harpending 1983; Johansson and Horowitz 1986; Milner, Humpf, and Harpending 1989; Paine 1989; Wood, Milner, Harpending, and Weiss 1992; Johansson 1994; Buikstra 1997). This notion is so counterintuitive that some specialists tenaciously resist the idea that age distributions of human populations, including osteological ones, tell more about fertility than mortality.

The reasoning of fertility-centered archaeological demography is more biological than demographic. Imagine a conventional population pyramid with the eldest at the peak, and the youngest at the base. In mammalian populations, the rate of dying is greatest at the base and peak of the pyramid, killing the young and the elderly in greater proportions than other ages. In contrast, fertility strikes solely at the base of the pyramid, at the instant of birth. Since deaths may occur at any age and births occur only at a single instant, the force of fertility is concentrated at a single point, whereas the force of mortality is dissipated over many ages. High fertility leads to "young" populations, which take the shape of a broad-based, steeply peaked pyramid. Low fertility produces "old" populations, with the age "pyramid" nearly rectangular. Thus, if the paleodemographer is to compare age distributions, fertility offers a larger target than mortality.

This elementary demographic fact, which continues to confound old-fashioned paleodemography, can be readily demonstrated by means of an illustration. Compare mortality effects on age structure in Figure 4.1 with those of fertility in Figure 4.2. In Figure 4.1, mortality is allowed to vary with life expectancy at birth ranging from 20 to 50 years, but fertility is held constant. In the left panel, fertility is fixed at a gross reproduction rate of three female children and in the right at four (average

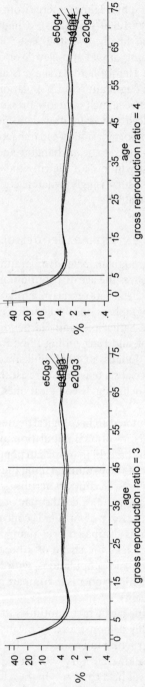

Figure 4.1. Mortality has little impact on age: Labels and lines overlap because mortality effects are minimal where paleodemographic evidence is best (constant fertility; varying mortality ($e_o = 20$–50)).

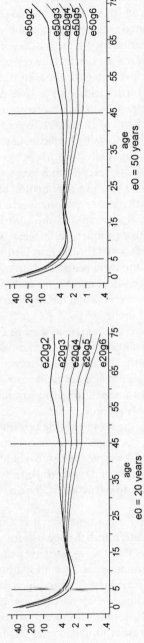

Figure 4 2. Fertility has big impact on age: Fertility effects on age structures are substantial even where paleodemographic evidence is good (ages 5—45) (constant mortality; varying fertility (GRR = 2–6)).

completed family size of six and eight children, respectively). The differences in age structure in each panel are small. Indeed, they are scarcely perceptible between 5 years and 50. This poses an obstacle for conventional paleodemography because these are precisely the ages at which the bioarchaeological evidence is best. This same point may be demonstrated with percentages for a single age group. Model life tables show that when life expectancy at birth is 20 years and fertility is constant (GRR = 3 female children), 12.1% of deaths between age 5 and 49 occur at ages 35–39. When e_0 is 50 years, the percentage declines to 10.5. In other words, a 150% increase in life expectancy at birth yields only a 15% decline in the proportion of deaths at age 35–39. In contrast, with a gross reproduction ratio of 2 (female) children and life expectancy at birth of 20 years, 13.6% of all deaths between ages 5 and 49 occur at ages 35–39. With mortality held constant and the fertility ratio at 3 (an increase of 50%), the percentage of deaths shrinks by one-third to 9.0. Typically, fertility effects on age structure are several times greater than those of mortality. Often age-structure effects of a 30-year improvement in life expectancy amounts to less than a shift of one child in the gross reproduction ratio.

This example for a specific age group and those in Figures 4.1 and 4.2 for a range of ages show that the force of mortality is weak, with little discrimination between age distributions. The fact that the labels in Figure 4.1 blot one another out illustrates how nearly identical the various distributions are – at the ages of greatest interest to paleodemographers, 5–49 years. Within each panel of Figure 4.1 there is little variation in age structure, even though life expectancy varies from extremely low to moderately high.

In contrast, fertility effects are substantial, as seen in Figure 4.2. Here mortality is held constant, and fertility is allowed to vary from moderately low (GRR = 2) to extremely high (GRR = 6). In the first panel, life expectancy at birth (e_0) is fixed at only 20 years, while in the second, e_0 is set at 50 years (moderately high). These panels show that high fertility increases the proportion of deaths at young ages, while low fertility increases the fraction at older ages. Comparing Figures 4.1 and 4.2 confirms that fertility offers the more alluring target to the paleodemographer, while mortality offers almost no target at all. It is also important to note that fertility-centered paleodemography is possible even where skeletal data for children are biased or wholly absent. Because of its powerful effects, fertility may be inferred even where only a portion of the age structure is known, such as that for adults, as shown by Figure 4.2.

However counterintuitive the notion may be, it is a demographic truism that fertility rather than mortality determines the age pattern of deaths in a stable population. Common sense tells us that the age structure of deaths is completely determined by mortality, but common sense is wrong. Although paleodemographers have taken advantage of this elementary demographic truth at least since the mid-1980s (Sattenspiel and Harpending 1983; Johansson and Horowitz 1986; Horowitz, Armelagos, and Wachter 1988), some continue to use the now-discredited average age at death statistic. The rule is simple: higher fertility reduces the mean age of human populations; lower fertility increases it. Age structures obtained from osteological populations may be made to reveal much about fertility in the past, but rather little about mortality, at least directly. For the paleodemographer interested in mortality, not all is lost. On the contrary, much is gained. In addition to learning a great deal about fertility, the paleodemographer can still deduce mortality and life expectancy, although it must be done indirectly.

LIFE EXPECTANCY BY INDIRECTION

While fertility can be estimated directly from the age distribution of a collection of skeletons, mortality requires an additional bit of evidence, unobtainable from the age data: an estimate of the population growth rate. With fertility estimated from the age structure and growth rates obtained from settlement data, mortality can be readily deduced by subtraction (Johansson and Horowitz 1986; Horowitz, Armelagos, and Wachter 1988; Paine 1997a). In this chapter, growth rates provided by the osteoarchaeologists for the Health and Nutrition in the Western Hemisphere database are used to estimate mortality levels and life expectancy. Note that the reported range of growth rates in the database is surprisingly narrow. Few exceed 0.5% per year. How these rates were determined is not indicated in the database, but they are used here to derive estimates of crude death rates. Note, too, that when the population growth rate is zero, life expectancy at birth may be readily approximated by the reciprocal of the crude birth rate. When this is not the case, a proportional adjustment is required. Table 4.1 offers a guide for deriving life expectancy from the crude birth and growth rates. With Table 4.1 the reader can consider a range of mortality levels, different from those proposed here, by simply hypothesizing alternative rates of population change, including negative rates as well as no change at all.

Table 4.1 suggests a way of using the most reliable paleodemographic indicator available, an estimate of fertility, and deriving other demographic statistics from it. The approach is crude, but it is appropriate for the quality of the data and the suppositions required. The first step is to identify fertility levels from the osteological age distribution and use these to derive crude birth rates (upper panel). Then, in the lower panel, birth and growth rates are combined to derive life expectancies. For example, if an age distribution of skeletal material points to a gross reproduction ratio of roughly 3.4 children, the upper panel of Table 4.1 yields a crude birth rate of 50. Then if other archaeological data suggest that the rate of population change was zero, this is a stationary population and life expectancy at birth is approximately the reciprocal of the crude birth rate, here 1/.050, or 20 years. In cases where the inferred growth rate is not zero, the lower panel in Table 4.1 offers a chart for inferring life expectancy at birth (crude death rates are derived by subtracting the rate of natural increase from the birth rate). Thus, if the estimated GRR is roughly 3.0 and the presumed annual rate of natural increase 1%, then the table points to a crude birth rate of 40 (a death rate of 30 is obtained by subtraction), and a life expectancy at birth of 33 years.

The table offers a wide range of combinations for deriving coherent estimates. An even wider range of combinations may be obtained from model life tables. Here, I follow the lead of Johansson and Horowitz (1986:235, 238 note 1) in using Coale and

Table 4.1: Calibrating the Demography of Skeletal Data Using Model Life Table Data and the Whopper Assumption

	−20	−10	0	b,f_{10}	20
Crude birth rate	Gross reproduction ratio (female children)				
90	4.3	4.8	5.5	—	—
80	3.8	4.6	5.4	6.5	—
70	[a]3.2	3.9	4.7	5.7	7.0
60	2.6	3.2	4.0	5.0	6.1
50	—	2.4	3.2	4.2	5.5
[d]40	—	1.9	2.5	[c]3.4	4.4
30	—	1.4	2.0	2.6	3.5
20	—	1.0	1.4	1.8	2.4
	Life expectancy at birth (e_0 in years)				
90	—	—	11	14	17
80	—	10	12	16	20
70	9	11	14	18	23
60	10	13	17	21	28
50	12	15	20	26	34
[e]40	14	19	25	[g]33	45
30	19	25	33	46	—
20	26	35	50	—	—

How to read this table:

[a] In the upper panel, locate the gross reproduction ratio derived from skeletal data.

[b] Estimate the growth rate from analysis of settlement data.

[c] Pinpoint the gross reproduction ratio.

[d] Derive the crude birth rate from the row stub on the left.

[e] In the lower panel, locate the birth rate again.

[f] Find the growth rate column used in the upper panel.

[g] Life expectancy at birth is found at the intersection of these rates.

Crude death rate is obtained by subtracting growth rate from birth rate.

Whopper assumption: empirical age profiles of skeletal populations are representative, valid, and comparable to model population death profiles.

Source: Computed from Coale and Demeny (1983): Females, Model West, mean age at maternity = 29 years using the inverse projection program, Populate (McCaa 1989).

Demeny's female models for region West. Region West model tables offer the "best case" scenario, with greater proportions of deaths at mature adult ages than found in tables for East, North, or South regions. Alternatives to the Coale and Demeny models exist (see Preston, McDaniel, and Grushka 1994; Paine and Harpending 1996; Bocquet-Appel and Bacro 1997), but differences between the various systems are slight, indeed, much less than the effects of mortality, which, as we have seen in Figure 4.1, are virtually imperceptible. Note that using female tables, instead of the technically correct average of male and female model death distributions, inflates fertility estimates by a small fraction (5%–10% for the gross reproduction ratio).

THE UNIFORMITARIAN CHALLENGE

Whatever system of stable population parameters is used, the uniformitarian hypothesis, that historical and paleopopulations experienced broadly similar demographic regimes, is assumed (Howell 1976; see also Hammel 1996). If one accepts this hypothesis, then model life tables derived from modern populations are appropriate for calibrating ancient osteological series.

Nevertheless, some researchers argue that skeletal age patterns depart substantially from model data (Weiss 1973; Lovejoy et al. 1985; Mensforth 1990; Bocquet-Appel and Bacro 1997; Meindl and Russell 1998). In this view, the "survival curve" peculiar to paleodemography contrasts starkly with curves for "technologically and economically advanced societies" (Mensforth 1990). Others see a lack of "immunological competence" in paleopopulations as a possible explanation for such peculiarities (Howell 1982; Lovejoy et al. 1985). Still others argue that models based on a world without smallpox ("post-Jennerian mortality") could not possibly describe pre-Jennerian populations (Bocquet-Appel and Bacro 1997), although it seems unlikely that paleopopulations ever experienced the ravages of density-dependent contagions such as smallpox.

Those who question the uniformitarian thesis invariably describe mortality as the sole determinant of age structures. Inasmuch as we have seen that it is fertility that fixes the age structure of a stable population, the uniformitarian challenge is misdirected. Fertility curves for Homo sapiens have probably not varied greatly over the millennia. Biology determines that childbearing will begin around age 15 for human females, peak at middle age, and end around age 45 or 50. Fertility patterns vary greatly from society to society, but there are probably none where fertility peaks before the age of 20 or after 35. Fertility *rates* may vary enormously from year to year, particularly for small populations, but stable populations, large or small, do not vary – by definition.

Demography offers alternatives to stable population analysis from quasi-stable to chaos theory (Keckler 1997; Bonneuil and McCaa, unpub. MS). Population systems are dynamic, yet age structures are remarkably sensitive to fertility. A quasi-stable system, where fertility remains constant for as little as a quarter of a century even with substantial year-to-year variation, will mimic stability. Paleodemographers are only just now beginning to consider nonstable possibilities, and so these methods are too untried to be considered here.

Other researchers maintain that the peculiar age distributions of osteological populations could be due to errors in the aging of specimens (Howell 1982; Gage 1988; Jackes 1992, 2000; Paine 1997b). Aging of skeletal material continues to be a contentious issue (Meindl and Russell 1998; Jackes 2000). For this study, investigators developed dental ages, minima, maxima, and summary ages. Then, for the construction of the health index, these ages were adjusted for each site, adding 7 years to individuals originally scored as 40 years and older, and 7 additional years at 60 and above. Although I did not make this adjustment for the paleodemographic analysis, their effects are easily visualized. Stretching the age distribution to older ages, as proposed, reduces fertility. The actual magnitude of this adjustment on estimated gross reproduction ratios as derived below is a 10% to 15% reduction in fertility, a rather small adjustment given the orders of magnitude of our results.

HAZARD MODELS AND "FAUX" HAZARD RATES

Proportional hazard modeling is widely recognized among paleodemographers as an important methodological breakthrough for the discipline (Gage and Dyke 1986; Gage 1988; Konigsberg and Frankenberg 1992; Meindl and Russell 1998). Proportional hazard modeling is the method of choice for paleodemographic analysis because of its wide use in the biological and social sciences (*STATA* 1995). Hazard rates are much less volatile than simple, and commonly used, proportions of deaths at specific ages. Computed from successive cumulative totals at each age, hazard rates offer a partial solution to the problem of small frequencies for single-year ages. Hazard rates also smooth digit preferences often apparent in skeletal collections (osteologists favor even ages over odd, and ages ending in five and zero above all). Hazard rates are comparable to statistics derived from model life tables, if the stationarity assumption is accepted. Gage (1988) notes that the hazard rate is nothing more than the life table function m_x, or central death rate (the average annual number of deaths from age x to age $x + n$ divided by the average population alive during the interval defined by x and n).

"Faux" hazard rates might be a more accurate characterization because they are derived solely from the cumulation of deaths, rather than true rates computed from deaths in a population at risk of dying and with a known age structure. We do not know the age structure of osteological populations. If paleodemographers are to exploit hazard analysis, they must first accept what I have dubbed the "whopper" assumption: that empirical age profiles of skeletal populations are representative, valid, and comparable to model population death profiles (d_x). The whopper assumption provides the basis for computing hazard rates. By accepting the whopper assumption, paleodemographers suppose that the skeletal population studied is in fact not only stable, but stationary. The same assumption must be made for model populations, if the comparison between observed and model data is to be fair. If my reading of the recent paleodemographic hazard rate literature is correct, researchers compare observed data transformed by the whopper assumption against untransformed mortality quotients from model populations. It must be noted that criticism directed against the use of the mortality quotient (q_x) by paleodemographers is equally applicable to the central death rate (m_x), or faux hazard rates. In this paper, faux hazard rates are computed for deaths ascribed to ages 5, 15, 25, 35, and 45 and above. Deaths at other ages are ignored to reduce bias due to deposition, recovery, and misclassification.

Hazard rates, whether real or faux, are not the research objective of the paleodemographer. Instead, the goal is to compare the observed pattern of hazard rates with those from model stable populations. If a good fit between the two can be found, or as some would have it, if the observed data can be "shoehorned" into a model pattern (Paine 1997b; Meindl and Russell 1998), then the demographic parameters from the model population are presumed to apply to the empirical population. I computed proportional hazard functions from the age distribution of skeletons for each site in the database (limited to ages 5, 15, 25, 35, and 45, as noted above) and compared those against 120 stable population models. Gross reproduction ratios of 2, 3, 4, and 5, at 0.1 intervals, were tested along with life expectancies at birth of 20, 30, 40, and 50 years, at 10-year intervals. The fact that 10 times as many birth as death scenarios were considered simply reflects the more powerful effects of fertility over mortality. For the 65 grouped sites, 8,060 fittings were assessed, not counting experimental fittings for other model life table regions, smaller increments, extended ranges, alternative groupings, two-sex death distributions (instead of female only), or standard datasets, such as those for ancient Athens, the Pearson complex, the Ward Site, and so on.

Too Many Good-Fitting Models

Good-fitting models were found for each of the 65 grouped sites. In fact, anyone seeking a single best fit will be disappointed because there are too many good-fitting models. At the conventional .05 level, almost 24% (1,888 models) fit. This figure is exaggerated by the fact that if there is a good fit for one level of mortality, there is probably a good fit for one or two others. Dividing the number of good fits by four (the number of mortality levels) still leaves an average of 10 pretty-good-fitting models per site. If our standard is raised to the 0.5 level, the total number of good-fittings contracts to 675. At the 0.95 level, 68 model populations fit the osteological data for 65 grouped sites. All sites yield at least three pretty-good-fitting models. Two-thirds of these are at the 0.8 level or higher. For almost all sites, there are at least three fits at the 0.6 level and higher. The average goodness of fit of the best model exceeds 0.9 for the 65 grouped sites, 0.8 for the second best, and 0.7 for the third.

The plethora of good-fitting models is not a problem. The three best-fitting models for each site tend to cluster in an exceedingly narrow range. Indeed, mapping the fittings with mortality running north–south (life expectancies of 20–50 years), fertility ranging east–west (gross reproduction ratios of 5–2 female children), and p-values flowing over the surface (0–1) produces an image that closely resembles the plains and peaks of South America, with its expansive Atlantic coastal plateau, broader Andean *atliplano* and narrow Pacific shelf. The eastern lowlands are made up of thousands of zero or near-zero p-values of poorly fitting models. The western peaks correspond to the hundreds of high p-values. The eastern flatland of zero p-values is about twice as large as the western highlands. Most of the peaks fall nearer the Pacific, because gross reproduction ratios of 2–3 children characterize most of the better-fitting models. For only three sites do gross reproduction ratios exceed 3.5. None fall below 2. Mountains, made up of p-values of 0.9 or higher, cover less than 2% of the surface. The range of peaks does not run true north–south, because mortality effects on age structure are curvilinear.

P-values do not form a single peak for any site. In every instance the effects of mortality are too slight to force the emergence of a single, dominant peak, even where the site yields several hundred well-preserved specimens, such as nineteenth-century Belleville, Ontario.

The Case of Belleville, Ontario

Belleville exemplifies the nature of the paleodemographic puzzle. This site provides one of the largest osteological collections in the Health and Nutrition in the Western Hemisphere database. Fortunately, the principal investigators, Saunders, Herring, Sawchuk, and Boyce, went beyond the skeletal evidence to consider historical sources, including high-quality parish books and manuscript censuses.

The conventional paleodemographic method, computing the average age of death for the skeletal collection, yields a "life expectancy at birth" of 19.4 years for Belleville. The answer favored by Saunders and her colleagues is 36.5 years, obtained using historical demographic methods. Their historical life table is constructed from authentic age-specific death rates, computed by means of ages at death from parish burial books and the age structure of the population from a population census (Saunders et al, 1995: 104–110).

Proportional hazard models of the Belleville osteological data confirm these findings and also contradict conventional paleodemography. Figure 4.3 and those that follow are designed to allow the reader to assess the range of good-fitting models. Goodness of fit is measured on the vertical axis, and fertility on the horizontal. Instead of an abstract symbol to pinpoint each good-fitting model, life expectancy at birth in years is used to emphasize the seemingly random effects of mortality on the fittings. Zero p-value models and those less than .05 are omitted, but the reader may mentally insert them by imagining "20"-"30"-"40"-"50" overprinted at intervals of 0.1 along the base of each graph, except where a nonzero p-value is already plotted for that level of fertility. As in Figure 4.3, it will be seen that life expectancy points scatter over the surface of the graph in a chaotic pattern, while good-fitting fertility constraints cluster within a narrow band. For Belleville, the three best-fitting models $(P > .95, .93,$ and $.82)$ point to a narrow range of fertility (gross reproduction ratios of 3.0, 3.1, and 3.4, respectively). In contrast, life expectancy spans 30 years (20, 40, and 50 years, with 30 a close fourth at $P > .74$). Figure 4.3 shows that 18 models fit at the conventional level of $p \geq .05$ and 106 do not fit. Two-thirds of the good-fitting models are defined by gross reproduction ratios of 3.0–3.3. The mean is 3.16. Differences in goodness of fit are not statistically significant. Choosing one good fit over another is arbitrary, unless other demographic evidence is taken into account.

A more precise mortality estimate for the Belleville skeletal data is possible but it requires additional information, specifically the rate of natural increase. If the conventional paleodemographic assumption that the annual growth rate (r) was zero is accepted, the crude birth rate is readily derived from the gross reproduction ratio (see Table 4.1 above). A gross reproduction ratio of 3.0 is equivalent to a birth rate of about 48 per thousand. When r is zero, life expectancy at birth is the reciprocal of the crude death rate, here $1/.048$ or 20.8 years, a figure that closely approximates the mean age at death in the skeletal collection.

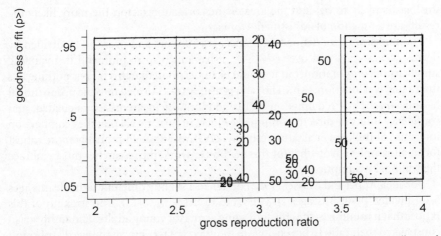

Figure 4.3. Belleville: Many good-fitting models. Better fertility models fit within a small spread (GRR = 2.9–3.5 daughters); mortality models range too widely (e_0 = 20–50 years).

Belleville's growth rate was not zero. Belleville was a fast-developing frontier community, although the precise rate is unknown, as Saunders and her coauthors point out in a subsequent chapter in this volume. If we accept the finding from historical demography that life expectancy at birth was truly 36.5 years, and from paleodemography that the gross reproduction ratio was approximately three, then the annual rate of natural increase was 2.0% or 2.1% and the crude death rate was 28 or 27 per thousand. From Table 4.1, we find that a crude birthrate of 50 and an annual growth rate of 2% are associated with a life expectancy at birth of 34 years. Since the crude birthrate is estimated at 48, we may interpolate a figure of 36 years for life expectancy at birth. What the Belleville data show is that where the age at death data are of good quality and the growth rate is known, both historical and paleodemographic methods lead to the same answer (e_0 = 36 years in this example). Such precision is possible when a population growth rate can be estimated, even approximately. For Belleville, we may conclude that fertility was high, and since the rate of natural increase was high, then mortality was only moderately high, in historical terms. Therefore, life expectancy was moderately low. For paleopopulations, this may be the best that one should hope for.

AGE RATIOS

A summary measure, such as age ratios, may yield more convincing estimates than methods requiring detailed age data, such as proportional hazard analysis (Buikstra, Konigsberg, and Bullington 1986). Paine and Harpending (1996) calibrated age ratios with stable populations and concluded that they were less robust than life table fittings. However, their simulations considered only very low fertility populations (crude birthrates ranging from 16 to 33) and left the problem of bias in the recovery of skeletal material at the youngest and oldest ages for a separate essay (Paine and Harpending 1998). Unfortunately, the smaller the skeletal population, the greater this bias is likely to be, and the greater the correction factor, the more likely the results are a function of adjustments for error.

The Buikstra ratio, defined as deaths ages 30 years and over (30+) divided by deaths ages 5 years and over (d_{30+}/d_{5+}), has much to recommend it, including simplicity of computation, but it should be understood that this ratio is nothing less than a survival function, $_{25}p_5$. The ratio is readily transformed into the proportional hazard $_{25}m_5$. Thus redefined, tests for goodness of fit are easily calculated, and confidence intervals directly computed (which, in turn, reveal that the "comparison intervals" of Buikstra et al. are overly conservative, although probably more robust for small samples). Note that for this method to work, the researcher must embrace the whopper assumption.

Bocquet-Appel and Masset (1982) designed a slightly different ratio, deaths ages 5–14 divided by deaths ages 20 years and over (d_{5-14}/d_{20+}). The strength of this ratio is that it minimizes the effects of aging errors for young adults. The authors also constructed their ratio to be sensitive to the effects of fertility on the age distribution of deaths, apparent in stable populations. Indeed, theirs is much more sensitive to different levels of fertility than Buikstra's. Unfortunately, confidence intervals are not as readily estimated.

The strength of age-ratios methods – only two bits of data need to be reliably measured – is also their principal weaknesses: other bits of data are ignored. Here, proportional hazard models are used instead of age ratios in an attempt to elicit as much information as possible from the skeletal data. It seems to me that multiple points of reference, even though they are only five (5+, 15+, 25+, 35+, and 45+) as in fitting hazard models, are preferable to two points of comparison provided by age ratios. As a matter of methodological curiosity I have posted my analysis of age ratios at: *http://www.hist.umn.edu/~rmccaa/paleodem/index.htm.*

PALEODEMOGRAPHY OF THE AMERICAS

Paleodemographic estimates for 65 sites are summarized in Table 4.2. Gross reproduction ratios and p-values of the three best-fitting models provide the basis for deducing crude birthrates, which, in turn, are coupled with crude growth rates reported by investigators, to derive crude death rates and life expectancies at birth. In the tables, figures, and analysis that follow, data are divided chronologically into three periods: ancient (−1500 BP), classic (1500 BP–500 BP), and historical (1500 AD–). The first two periods are analyzed by settlement type – foragers, villagers, and townsfolk – and the historical period by ethnicity: Native American, European-American, and African-American.

Table 4.2 reports three fertility constraints for each site to emphasize the arbitrariness of selecting a single, best-fitting model. Life expectancies from any other than the best-fitting models are deliberately excluded from the table to foil attempts to "read" mortality from osteological age distributions. The traditional "mean age at death" pseudostatistic is omitted for the same reason. The "best" estimate of life expectancy at birth, derived from the best-fitting fertility model and the best guesstimate of the population growth rate, is found in the last column of the table.

Table 4.2: Paleodemography of the Americas: Sites, Cases, Fertility Estimates, Goodness of Fit, and Indirect Results (Crude Rates and Life Expectancy at Birth in Years)

Year BP/AD	Site: Code	investigator place	Cases Total	Age 5+	Gross reproduction ratio Best	2d	3d	Goodness of fit (p>) Best	2d	3d	Crude rates Birth	Growth	Death	Best life expectancy
ANCIENT (BF)														
Foragers														
7425	osg	Ubelaker Sta. Elena	75	68	2.1	2.2	2.1	0.9	0.9	0.9	32	5	27	37
3000	LNP	Neves Pre-ceramico	126	125	2.1	2.0	2.0	0.8	0.7	0.5	32	0	32	31
2564	KIT	Sciulli Late Archaic	134	101	3.2	3.2	3.1	1.0	0.9	0.8	52	.	.	.
Villagers														
6015	MR1	Arriaza Pre-Ceramic	166	118	2.6	2.5	2.5	0.9	0.9	0.8	42	.	.	.
4663	rea	Ubelaker Realto	51	45	2.1	2.2	2.0	1.0	0.9	0.8	32	5	27	37
3100	TL2	Marquez Tlatilco	343	306	2.1	2.0	2.0	0.9	0.7	0.6	32	5	27	37
2278	cot	Ubelaker Highland	164	161	2.5	2.4	2.4	1.0	0.9	0.9	40	5	35	29
2050	lat	Ubelaker N. Coast	47	45	2.0	2.0	2.0	0.9	0.8	0.7	30	5	25	40
1835	lib	Ubelaker S. Coast	155	129	2.3	2.4	2.2	1.0	0.8	0.7	36	5	31	32
Townsfolk														
1850	CUI	Marquez Cuicuilco	119	108	2.0	2.1	2.1	0.9	0.6	0.6	30	5	25	40
1625	teo	Storey Tlatinja	50	33	2.6	2.5	2.5	1.0	0.9	0.9	42	−5	47	21
CLASSIC (BP)														
Foragers														
1350	101	Larsen 101–110	151	75	2.7	2.6	2.5	0.9	0.9	0.8	43	5	38	26
1350	111	Larsen 111–121	179	78	3.0	3.1	3.0	0.9	0.9	0.8	48	5	43	23
Villagers														
1200	LNC	Neves Ceramico	22	22	2.0	2.1	2.0	0.7	0.6	0.4	30	5	25	40
1200	QUI	Neves Tiwanaku	253	182	2.7	2.7	2.8	0.8	0.8	0.8	43	0	43	23

(continued)

107

Table 4.2 (continued)

Year BP/AD	Code	Site: investigator place	Cases Total	Cases Age 5+	GRR Best	GRR 2d	GRR 3d	Fit Best	Fit 2d	Fit 3d	Birth	Growth	Death	Best life expectancy
1175	AZ1	Arriaza Maitas Chribaya	118	96	2.6	2.6	2.7	0.9	0.9	0.8	42	·	·	·
1125	co9	Storey Copan Rural	239	144	2.7	2.7	2.6	0.8	0.7	0.7	43	−5	48	21
1050	dol	Martin Dolores	43	36	2.7	2.8	2.8	1.0	0.8	0.8	43	5	38	26
900	PEA	Sciulli Pearson	96	73	3.3	3.2	3.3	1.0	0.9	0.9	53	·	·	·
750	SUN	Sciulli Sunwatch	138	70	3.8	3.7	3.8	1.0	0.9	0.7	62	·	·	·
700	CHB	Buikstra Chiribaya	363	249	3.2	3.1	3.2	0.9	0.9	0.7	52	·	·	·
700	ESB	Buikstra Estuquina	426	319	3.0	3.1	3.0	0.8	0.8	0.7	48	·	·	·
700	SGB	Buikstra San Geronimo	99	69	2.8	2.8	2.7	0.8	0.8	0.8	45	·	·	·
700	Y1B	Buikstra Yaral	77	50	3.1	3.2	3.1	1.0	0.9	0.9	50	·	·	·
650	MON	Sciulli Monongahela	122	90	3.1	3.1	3.0	0.9	0.8	0.8	50	·	·	·
600	201	Larsen 201–223	517	280	2.9	2.9	2.9	0.9	0.7	0.6	47	5	42	24
Townsfolk														
1350	J73	Marquez Jaina	106	53	3.4	3.5	3.4	1.0	0.9	0.8	55	0	55	18
1125	cop	Storey Copan Urban	45	37	2.0	2.1	2.0	0.4	0.3	0.1	30	−5	35	29
990	XCA	Marquez Xcaret	35	33	2.0	2.1	2.0	0.9	0.9	0.6	30	−5	35	29
790	CO1	Marquez Cholula	236	178	2.8	2.7	2.7	0.9	0.9	0.9	45	−5	50	20
HISTORICAL (AD)														
Native Americans														
448	la8	Martin San Cristobal	267	193	3.0	2.9	2.9	1.0	0.8	0.7	48	−5	53	19
418	3AM	Owsley Oneota, Arikara	32	31	2.1	2.1	2.0	1.0	0.9	0.9	32	5	27	37
401	snt	Ubelaker Historic	39	38	2.3	2.3	2.4	1.0	0.9	0.9	36	−5	41	24
398	haw	Martin Hawikku	187	146	3.0	3.0	3.0	0.9	0.8	0.7	48	−5	53	19
350	BUF	Sciulli Buffalo	101	72	3.2	3.1	3.2	1.0	0.9	0.9	52	·	·	·
325	301	Larsen 301–302	444	294	3.0	3.1	3.0	0.9	0.8	0.7	48	−5	53	19
325	303	Larsen 303	122	95	2.2	2.2	2.3	1.0	0.9	0.9	34	−5	39	26
247	WW7	Owsley Plains-Arikara	173	125	3.0	2.9	2.9	1.0	0.8	0.7	48	15	33	30
179	DW2	Owsley Plains-Arikara+C19	94	45	4.6	4.5	4.5	1.0	0.9	0.9	75	0	75	13
167	BU2	Owsley Plains-Pawnee	160	98	3.0	2.9	2.9	1.0	0.9	0.8	48	10	38	27

	Code	Group												
155	dk2	Owsley Plains-Omaha	106	55	3.9	3.9	3.9	0.9	0.9	0.8	63	15	48	21
155	KX1	Owsley Plains-Ponca	59	34	3.5	3.6	3.5	1.0	1.0	0.9	57	15	42	24
75	BFT	Owsley Nomad-Blackfeet	67	61	2.0	2.0	2.1	1.0	0.9	0.9	30	−5	35	29
75	CRW	Owsley Nomad-Crow	73	66	2.0	2.1	2.1	0.9	0.7	0.6	30	−5	35	29
71	CHY	Owsley Nomad-Cheyenne	42	41	2.0	2.1	2.0	1.0	0.9	0.9	30	−5	35	29

European-Americans

	Code	Group												
290	sfc	Ubelaker Eur. 1595–1690	104	91	2.0	2.1	2.0	0.9	0.8	0.6	30	5	25	40
179	sfa	Ubelaker Eur. 1690–1800	36	31	2.5	2.4	2.4	1.0	0.9	0.9	40	−5	45	22
150	ftl	Sledzik Ft Laur., Sn.	44	44	2.7	2.8	2.8	1.0	0.8	0.8	43	·	·	·
128	cry	Rathbun Crypt	35	29	2.0	2.0	2.1	1.0	0.9	0.8	30	5	25	40
108	HPK	Sirianni Highland Park	296	220	2.0	2.1	2.0	0.8	0.7	0.5	30	·	·	·
102	stt	Saunders Belleville	604	284	3.0	3.1	3.4	1.0	0.9	0.8	48	20	28	36
97	SF1	Ubelaker Eur. 1800+	54	53	2.0	2.1	2.0	0.3	0.2	0.1	30	10	20	50
84	GPS	Sledzik Glor. Pass	39	39	2.7	2.7	2.6	1.0	1.0	0.8	43	10	33	30

African-Americans

Enslaved

	Code	Group												
95	3C7	Rathbun Remeley	35	31	2.0	2.1	2.1	0.9	0.9	0.8	30			·

Free

	Code	Group												
105	FAB	Rathbun 1st. Afr. Bapt.	90	59	2.5	2.5	2.6	0.9	0.8	0.8	40	5	35	29
97	3C9	Rathbun Folly	18	16	2.7	2.6	2.8	1.0	0.9	0.8	43	·	·	·
62	41D	Condon Dallas City	1157	613	3.4	3.3	3.3	1.0	0.9	0.8	55	15	40	25
42	3La	Rose Cedar Grove	80	46	3.1	3.2	3.2	1.0	0.9	0.9	50	10	40	25

NOT ANALYZED

	Code	Group												
5250	W42	Walker 8 sites	309	307	2.1	2.0	2.0	0.7	0.5	0.3	32	5	27	37
3852	W38	Walker 18 sites	176	175	2.0	2.1	2.0	1.0	0.6	0.2	30	5	25	40
1625	W13	Walker 17 sites	436	430	2.0	2.1	2.0	0.8	0.6	0.4	30	5	25	40
1359	W43	Walker 13 sites	293	270	2.1	2.0	2.0	0.9	0.5	0.4	32	5	27	37
1075	WO7	Walker WO7 & WVO	540	504	2.1	2.0	2.0	1.0	0.7	0.5	32	5	27	37
428	W28	Walker 16 sites	1411	1384	2.1	2.0	2.0	0.6	0.1	0.1	32	5	27	37
78	WLE	Walker Euro-Americans	102	93	2.0	2.1	2.0	0.9	0.8	0.7	30	10	20	50

Where no growth rate estimate is given, no life expectancy is computed. To aid the reader in gauging the strength of the estimates, both the total number of cases and the number of those ages five years and over are reported in Table 4.2. Note that the paleodemographic analysis of the Health and Nutrition in the Western Hemisphere data is based on the latter figure, as is the discussion that follows.

Fertility

The narrow range of fertility estimates for individual sites is striking, but one should not place too much confidence in the absence of variation. No variation at all is found among seven grouped sites contributed by Walker, but none should be expected because 68.6% of the specimens are assigned a single age, 35 years. Accounting for one-third of the database population ages five years and above, these sites are excluded from further discussion in this chapter, although their results are reported in Table 4.2.

Of the remaining 58 sites, 38 (66%) report fewer than 100 individuals ages 5 years or older (see Table 4.2). Demographic estimates from these small collections are particularly conjectural. Fourteen of the 17 sites with the lowest fertility (82%) are represented by meager collections. If the data and analysis are to be trusted, this suggests that low fertility is associated with tiny sites (or collections). The only truly large collection ($n > 125$) with low fertility (GRR = 2.0–2.1) is the ancient Mesoamerican population at Tlatilco (~3100 BP).

The correlation between low fertility and size should not be surprising. In the demographic lottery of the ancient world, small communities had more to gain, and to lose, than larger ones. The discovery or development of a new ecological niche could lead to a baby boomlet, the incorporation of outsiders, or the retention of the native born. Microcommunities were as easily extinguished by the sudden exhaustion of food supplies, the loss of a water supply, mass violence, an outbreak of botulism, or simply a hiving-off to a more promising site. Smaller populations were both blessed and cursed by greater variability in underlying demographic dynamics. If small populations were to survive, better-than-average mortality was required. Yet, as we shall see below, life expectancies of 30 years or more were uncommon for all sites, both large (19%) and small (23%).

Moderately high fertility was the norm in the collection as a whole (average GRR for the three best-fitting models for 58 sites = 2.9 female children), but given the great variety of sites, an overall average is meaningful only for establishing a yardstick.

Ancient American Fertility

During ancient times, lower fertility was the rule (Figure 4.4). Lowest fertility characterized sites from more than 1,500 years ago (GRR = 2.1–2.3, pooled data). The great transformation in fertility came 1,500 years ago, when fertility seems to have increased almost by half (GRR = 2.9). Grouping sites from more recent times into classic (1,500 BP–500 BP) and modern (500 BP–present) reveals a great plateau over

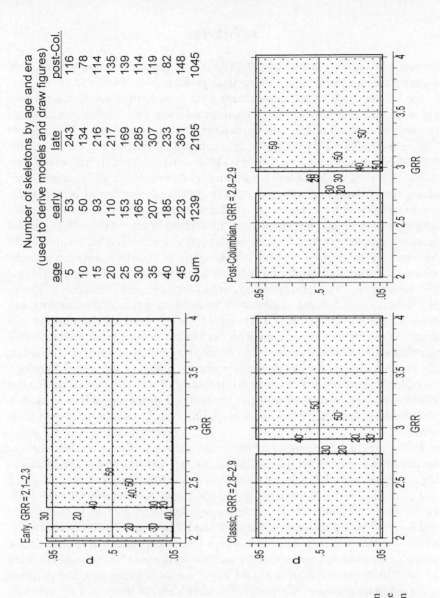

Number of skeletons by age and era
(used to derive models and draw figures)

age	early	late	post-Col.
5	53	243	116
10	50	134	78
15	93	216	114
20	110	217	135
25	153	169	139
30	165	285	114
35	207	307	119
40	185	233	82
45	223	361	148
Sum	1239	2165	1045

Figure 4.4. Fertility increased between ancient and classic eras; little change between classic and post-Columbian eras.

111

the past 1,500 years (GRR = 2.8–2.9). The critical variable seems to be time itself. Resource base and settlement type are less significant.

For ancient America, strikingly absent is the hypothesized association between higher fertility and horticulturally complex societies. Low fertility (GRR = 2.2) characterized both foragers and horticulturalists in ancient times ($n=356$ and 749, respectively). In classic times, the hypothesized relationship exists, but the differences are slight (2.8 vs. 3.0, $n=143$ and 1,467). Fertility variations were minimal or nonexistent between communities that exploited some domesticated plants versus those that cultivated corn or potatoes, regardless of period. If the spread of agriculture caused a demographic impact, it may have come nearer the beginnings of the development of horticulture, rather than with the emergence of complex systems. The critical difference in demographic regimes in the Americas, in contrast to the Old World, seems to have been between societies with no domesticated plants and those with some (GRR = 2.2, 3.0; $n=356$ and 134, respectively). The fertility of populations with complex cultivation technologies is similar to those with rudimentary horticultural practices. This finding supports the thesis that agricultural "revolution" in the Americas did not lead to a dramatic rise in fertility or a swell in population growth rates. Here the shift to complex horticultural systems was retarded by ecological obstacles, including day length, posed by the North–South pattern of diffusion. Additional osteological collections are needed to confirm this finding. Then, too, if evidence for Old World sites were reanalyzed with fertility-centered proportional hazard models, what would global comparisons of demographic transformations in ancient times reveal?

In the Americas, absence of domesticated animals is also associated with low fertility from earliest times (GRR = 2.1 vs. 2.3, $n=193$ and 1,046), as well as during the climax period of Native American demographic development (GRR = 2.7 and 2.9; $n=175$, 1,648). In the historical era, Native American fertility was highest for those sites where both European and American animals were exploited (GRR = 3.0 vs. 2.7 for others; $n=1,095$ and 579). Since fertility probably declined slightly for Native American groups wholly dependent upon New World animals, the most important fertility increase in the past 500 years is explained by the shift to the exploitation of Old World animal domesticates. The statistical effect is 3 times stronger than time (pre/modern), and 10 times stronger than horticultural type (none, some, or complex – maize or potatoes, beans, and squash). Highest fertility among Native Americans for any period (GRR = 3.2) is associated with the exploitation of European animals, particularly on the Great Plains where some agriculture was practiced, but none based on corn or potatoes. Other contextual variables are weak in comparison to the effect associated with domesticated animals.

Pooling the data by settlement type (Figure 4.5) reveals surprising fertility differences as well, but it is unclear whether settlement density has any effect independent of resource base. Higher fertility is associated with village settlements (GRR = 2.7), while both forager and urban groups are characterized by lower fertility (2.3–2.6).

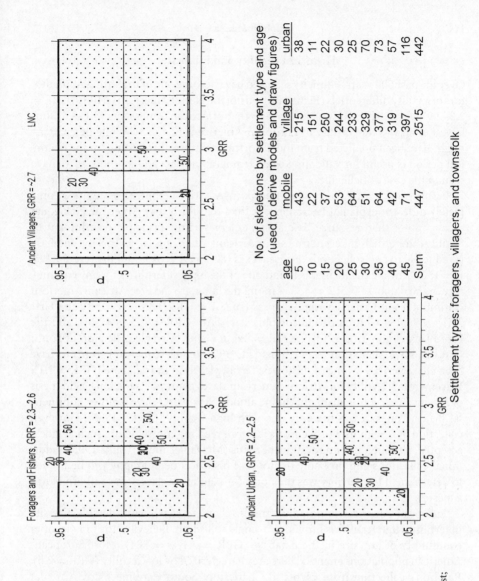

No. of skeletons by settlement type and age
(used to derive models and draw figures)

age	mobile	village	urban
5	43	215	38
10	22	151	11
15	37	250	22
20	53	244	30
25	64	233	25
30	51	329	70
35	64	377	73
40	42	319	57
45	71	397	116
Sum	447	2515	442

Settlement types: foragers, villagers, and townsfolk.

Figure 4.5. Village fertility is highest; urban lowest.

Historical Fertility and Ethnicity

Over the past 500 years, ethnicity seems to have become one of the strongest predictors of fertility differentials (Figure 4.6). Historical Native American fertility (GRR = 2.8–2.9), although high, was lower than that of African-Americans (3.1–3.3), but lowest of all was the fertility of European-Americans (2.4–2.5). While this pattern might have been predicted from the historical literature, this finding for the historical period is useful for validating paleodemographic data and method, as we have seen in the case of Belleville.

Fertility levels for African- and European-American ethnicities require a completely different explanatory framework than that for Native Americans. Unequal access, rather than resource base alone, emerges as the principal determinant of fertility differentials in recent times. For African-Americans ($n = 765$), the database is reducible to two collections: Dallas, Texas (80.1%, $n = 613$) and the rest (19.1%, $n = 152$). Among the former is found one of the highest fertilities for any community in the database (GRR = 3.3). Among the latter are the Free African-American communities at Cedar Grove, Arkansas (site 3LA: GRR = 3.1, $n = 59$), the First African Baptist Church of Philadelphia (site FAB: GRR = 2.5, $n = 46$), and the Free Black Union Troops (3C9, GRR = 2.6, $n = 19$). A single collection of South Carolina slave plantation populations (site 3C7, Remeley: $n = 31$) seems to have been characterized by one of the lowest fertility levels in the database (GRR = 2.1). Extremely low fertility for African-American slaves contradicts the long-held thesis of American exceptionalism, that alone among New World slave regimes, continental British-America was the only one with high fertility (Steckel 1985). However, collection 3C7 with its 31 specimens is a frail reed for contradicting such a widely accepted, although not unquestioned, thesis (McDaniel and Grushka 1995). Additional collections and probably the tools of historical demography will be needed to determine if low fertility was the norm for plantation slavery in southern North America.

European-American populations are also characterized by considerable diversity in fertility. High fertility is limited to a single collection, Belleville, the only frontier community of any size in the database (GRR = 3.1, $n = 284$). Most European-American populations analyzed here are characterized by low fertility (GRR = 2.0): Rathbun's collection from crypts in Charleston, South Carolina ("cry," Circular Congregational Church, $n = 29$), Sirianni's study of a Rochester, New York, poorhouse ($n = 30$), and Ubelaker's Quiteñan elites from both the early colonial and national periods ($n = 91$ and 53, respectively, for the Church of San Francisco). A third collection from the same site, from the late colonial period, suggests somewhat higher fertility, but the size of the collection is small ($n = 31$). Soldier outposts in North America seem to have come from moderately higher fertility populations (GRR = 2.7), according to this analysis of Sledzik's collections from Ft. Laurens, Ohio (late eighteenth century, $n = 44$), Snake Hill (early nineteenth century), and Glorietta Pass (Confederate Army, $n = 39$). Fertility levels derived from European-American skeletal populations are difficult to relate to the findings from historical demography on the same subject. Historical studies are many, and they are often

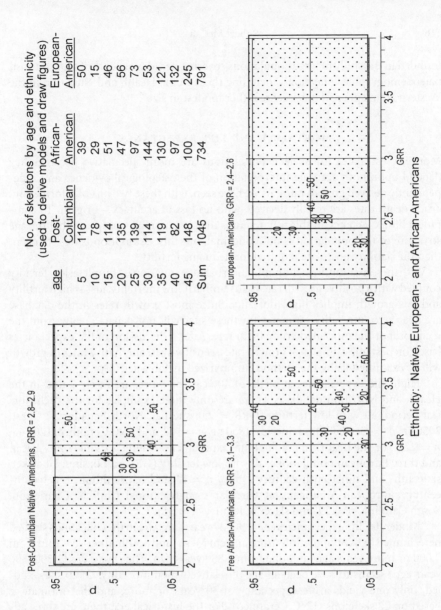

No. of skeletons by age and ethnicity
(used to derive models and draw figures)

age	Post-Columbian	African-American	European-American
5	116	39	50
10	78	29	15
15	114	51	46
20	135	47	56
25	139	97	73
30	114	144	53
35	119	130	121
40	82	97	132
45	148	100	245
Sum	1045	734	791

Figure 4.6. Fertility of African-Americans was highest; Euros-, lowest.

115

founded in the study of large populations covering decades or centuries. In contrast, paleodemographic collections, including those in the Health and Nutrition in the Western Hemisphere database, are rather modest in size.

MORTALITY AND LIFE EXPECTANCY

Mortality estimates for skeletal populations are more speculative because they depend upon both accurate interpretation of the osteological evidence and independently derived growth rates. As we have seen, with these two bits of information, crude death rates are readily derived, with no loss of accuracy – or gain. To compute a life expectancy in this way requires the simplifying assumption that the age structure of the population is not abnormal, but this assumption is less stringent than the stability postulate required for deducing fertility.

With these assumptions the population balance equation is complete: low fertility coupled with a positive growth rate yields similarly low mortality, just as high fertility and low growth implies high mortality. Since most growth rates in the database are near zero, mortality estimates for these sites will not depart greatly from the reciprocal of the estimated crude birth rate. After a discussion of life expectancies based on best guesstimates of growth rates, sensitivity to alternative rates of growth will be examined using the method summarized in Table 4.1.

"High" life expectancies at birth, of 40 years or more, are rarely found in the Health and Nutrition database. There are only three examples for the prehistorical period, all with low fertility (GRR = 2.0: site Lat, North Ecuadorian Coast, 2050 BP, $n = 45$; CUI, Mesoamerica, 1850 BP, $n = 108$; and LNC Ceramico, 1200 BP, $n = 22$). For the historical era, high life expectancies emerge for only one African and three European populations, all with low fertility (GRR = 2.0, sites: Ubelaker, sixteenth- and nineteenth-century Quito, $n = 91$ and 53; Rathbun, nineteenth-century European-Americans at Circular Congregational Church, Charleston, South Carolina, $n = 29$, and slaves at Remley, $n = 31$).

"Moderate" life expectancies ($e_0 = 30$–37 years) are rare in the collections studied here, limited to five populations from ancient Meso- and South America – four from 3,000 or more years ago, and one from 1,850 years ago. The classic era (1,500–500 years ago) seems to have been an age of relatively high mortality. Of 20 sites studied, only one yields a life expectancy of 30 years or more, and that estimate is based on 22 skeletons (LNC Ceramico). For the historical era, there are three additional examples with moderate life expectancies: a Native American population (3AM, Oneota, Arikara, 418 BP, $n = 31$), and two European-American populations (Belleville, Ontario, and the Glorietta Pass collection, $n = 39$). Low life expectancies are the norm for paleodemographic populations, and that is the rule in the Health and Nutrition database, even with proportional hazard methods. The average life expectancy at birth for sites where growth rates have been supplied by the investigators (4,736 cases) is 25.4 years. Ancient Americans were the longest-lived, according to the methods used here, averaging 34 years. This figure is based on 1,020 skeletons from sites occupied 1,500 years ago or more. The great discontinuity in mortality occurred not 500 years ago, with demographic catastrophe following the collision of the European and American biospheres, but more than a millennium ago with a startling fertility transformation discussed above. For the period 1500–500 BP, average life expectancy was 23 years, about one-third less than in ancient times ($n = 838$). In the historical era, the osteological data suggest a slight decline to 22 years for Native American populations ($n = 1,602$) to the same level as for African-Americans ($n = 765$). In comparison, the average for European-Americans approached 30 years.

These averages conceal substantial differences from earliest to modern times. In ancient times, the emergence of cities seems to have occasioned a fall in life expectancy ($e_0 = 21$ years), but there was no penalty for villages or towns ($e_0 = 33$ years or more). In classic times, life expectancy was substantially reduced for all settlement types ($e_0 = 23$–25, $n = 650$), but the worst conditions continued to be associated with urban centers ($e_0 = 20$, $n = 178$). If, however, one postulates an overall quickening of growth rates during classic times and accepts the fertility estimates presented here, then mortality conditions perhaps did not worsen as much as suggested by these life expectancy figures.

With the clash of the biospheres from 1492, "normal" mortality did not worsen significantly for Native Americans, according to the skeletal evidence ($e_0 = 23, 22$; $n = 838, 1,602$, respectively), unless one postulates worse "growth" rates than those provided by the site investigators. Catastrophic mortality, such as that caused by exogenous epidemics (e.g., smallpox), leaves little imprint on bones nor on the age distribution of skeletal remains, and consequently cannot be assessed by these data.

For African-Americans, higher densities were associated with higher mortality ($e_0 = 21$ years for Dallas, Texas, vs. 29 for others), but this was not the case for European-Americans, if the skeletal evidence and growth rates are accepted at face value. Life expectancy for European-Americans was remarkably uniform, regardless of settlement type. If life expectancy was better in Belleville (36 years) than for other urban and village settlements, the differences were slight (33 and 32 years, respectively; $n = 175$ and 68).

If fertility establishes the foundation for deriving life expectancies, growth rates fix the surface contours. Table 4.3 helps the reader to visualize these constraints and assess the sensitivity of life expectancy estimates to alternative growth rates. For the first site in the table, KIT (Scuilli's study of a late archaic Native American population), high fertility means that life expectancy at birth probably ranged between 13 and 31 years, if the rate of population change per annum (r) was within plus or minus 2%. If r was zero, then e_0 was 19 years. Seventeen other sites display grim life expectancies of 20 years or less, when r is zero. Under the best conditions ($r = 2\%$), 35 years was the upper bound; under the worst, the lower bound was 13 years ($r = -2\%$). Of twenty-one sites with high fertility (GRR $= 3.0$ or greater), the best guesstimate of the growth rate points to a life expectancy greater than 25 years in only two cases, Belleville and the Arikara on the Great Plains (247 BP, WW7, $n = 125$, GRR $= 3.0$, $r = 15$, $e_0 = 30$).

At the other extreme, low fertility populations with gross reproduction ratios of 2 (crude birth rates of 30), good estimates of growth rates are even more essential. Otherwise, with growth rates ranging between plus or minus 2%, life expectancy

Table 4.3: Sensitivity of Life Expectancy at Birth Estimates to Alternative Growth Rates

Year BP/AD	Code	Site: Investigator place	Cases: Age 5+	Guesstimated crude rates				Best guess*	Life expectancy in years at various birth and growth rates				
									Alternative growth rates				
				GRR	Birth	Death	Growth		−2%	−1%	0%	1%	2%
ANCIENT (BP)													
Foragers													
7425	osg	Ubelaker Sta. Elena	68	2.1	32	27	5	37	19	23	31	45	83
3000	LNP	Neves Pre-ceramico	125	2.1	32	32	0	31	19	23	31	45	83
2564	KIT	Sciulli Late Archaic	101	3.2	52	.	.	.	13	16	19	23	31
Villagers													
6015	MR1	Arriaza Pre-Ceramic	118	2.6	42	.	.	.	16	19	23	31	45
4663	rea	Ubelaker Realto	45	2.1	32	27	5	37	19	23	31	45	83
3100	TL2	Marquez Tlatilco	306	2.1	32	27	5	37	19	23	31	45	83
2278	cot	Ubelaker Highland	161	2.5	40	35	5	29	16	20	25	33	50
2050	lat	Ubelaker N. Coast	45	2.0	30	25	5	40	20	25	33	50	100
1835	lib	Ubelaker S. Coast	129	2.3	36	31	5	32	17	21	27	38	62
Townsfolk													
1850	CUI	Marquez Cuicuilco	108	2.0	30	25	5	40	20	25	33	50	100
1625	teo	Storey Tlatinja	33	2.6	42	47	−5	21	16	19	23	31	45
CLASSIC (BP)													
Foragers													
1350	101	Larsen 101–110	75	2.7	43	38	5	26	15	18	23	30	43
1350	111	Larsen 111–121	78	3.0	48	43	5	23	14	17	20	26	35
Villagers													
1200	LNC	Neves Ceramico	22	2.0	30	25	5	40	20	25	33	50	100

118

1200	QUI	Neves Tiwanaku	182	2.7	43	43	0	23	15	18	23	30	43
1175	AZ1	Arriaza Maitas Chribaya	96	2.6	42	·	·	·	16	19	23	31	45
1125	co9	Storey Copan Rural	144	2.7	43	48	−5	21	15	18	23	30	43
1050	dol	Martin Dolores	36	2.7	43	38	5	26	15	18	23	30	43
900	PEA	Sciulli Pearson	73	3.3	53	·	·	·	13	15	18	23	30
750	SUN	Sciulli Sunwatch	70	3.8	62	·	·	·	12	13	16	19	23
700	CHB	Buikstra Chiribaya	249	3.2	52	·	·	·	13	16	19	23	31
700	ESB	Buikstra Estuquina	319	3.0	48	·	·	·	14	17	20	26	35
700	SGB	Buikstra San Geronimo	69	2.8	45	·	·	·	15	18	22	28	40
700	Y1B	Buikstra Yaral	50	3.1	50	·	·	·	14	16	20	25	33
650	MON	Sciulli Monongahela	90	3.1	50	·	·	·	14	16	20	25	33
600	201	Larsen 201–223	280	2.9	47	42	5	24	15	18	21	27	37

Townsfolk

1350	J73	Marquez Jaina	53	3.4	55	55	0	18	13	15	18	22	28
1125	cop	Storey Copan Urban	37	2.0	30	35	−5	29	20	25	33	50	100
990	XCA	Marquez Xcaret	33	2.0	30	35	−5	29	20	25	33	50	100
790	CO1	Marquez Cholula	178	2.8	45	50	−5	20	15	18	22	28	40

HISTORICAL (AD)

Native Americans

448	la8	Martin San Cristobal	193	3.0	48	53	−5	19	14	17	20	26	35
418	3AM	Owsley Oneota, Arikara	31	2.1	32	27	5	37	19	23	31	45	83
401	snt	Ubelaker Historic	38	2.3	36	41	−5	24	17	21	27	38	62
398	haw	Martin Hawikku	146	3.0	48	53	−5	19	14	17	20	26	35
350	BUF	Sciulli Buffalo	72	3.2	52	·	·	·	13	16	19	23	31
325	301	Larsen 301–302	294	3.0	48	53	−5	19	14	17	20	26	35
325	303	Larsen 303	95	2.2	34	39	−5	26	18	22	29	41	71
247	WW7	Owsley Plains-Arikara	125	3.0	48	33	15	30	14	17	20	26	35
179	DW2	Owsley Plains-Arikara+C19	45	4.6	75	75	0	13	10	11	13	15	18
167	BU2	Owsley Plains-Pawnee	98	3.0	48	38	10	27	14	17	20	26	35

continued

Table 4.3 (continued)

Year BP/AD	Site: Investigator place	Code	Cases: Age 5+	Guesstimated crude rates				Best guess*	Life expectancy in years at various birth and growth rates				
				GRR	Birth	Death	Growth		Alternative growth rates				
									−2%	−1%	0%	1%	2%
155	Owsley Plains-Omaha	dk2	55	3.9	63	48	15	21	12	13	15	18	23
155	Owsley Plains-Ponca	KX1	34	3.5	57	42	15	24	13	14	17	21	27
75	Owsley Nomad-Blackfeet	BFT	61	2.0	30	35	−5	29	20	25	33	50	100
75	Owsley Nomad-Crow	CRW	66	2.0	30	35	−5	29	20	25	33	50	100
71	Owsley Nomad-Cheyenne	CHY	41	2.0	30	35	−5	29	20	25	33	50	100
European-Americans													
290	Ubelaker Eur. 1595–1690	sfc	91	2.0	30	25	5	40	20	25	33	50	100
179	Ubelaker Eur. 1690–1800	sfa	31	2.5	40	45	−5	22	16	20	25	33	50
150	Sledzik Ft Laur., Sn.	fti	44	2.7	43	.	.	.	15	18	23	30	43
128	Rathbun Crypt	cry	29	2.0	30	25	5	40	20	25	33	50	100
108	Sirianni Highland Park	HPK	220	2.0	30	.	.	.	20	25	33	50	100
102	Saunders Belleville	stt	284	3.0	48	28	20	36	14	17	20	26	35
97	Ubelaker Eur. 1800+	SF1	53	2.0	30	20	10	50	20	25	33	50	100
84	Sledzik Glor. Pass	GPS	39	2.7	43	33	10	30	15	18	23	30	43
African-Americans													
Enslaved													
95	Rathbun Remeley	3C7	31	2.0	30	25	5	40	20	25	33	50	100
Free													
105	Rathbun 1st. Afr. Bapt.	FAB	59	2.5	40	35	5	29	16	20	25	33	50
97	Rathbun Folly	3C9	16	2.7	43	.	.	.	15	18	23	30	43
62	Condon Dallas City	41D	613	3.4	55	40	15	25	13	15	18	22	28
42	Rose Cedar Grove	3La	46	3.1	50	40	10	25	14	16	20	25	33

* "Best" life expectancy is derived from the guesstimate of the crude rates in the immediately preceding columns.

balloons to a not very helpful range of between 20 and 100 years. This is the case for 13 sites in the database. An additional 8 sites with birth rates in the mid- or high 30s yield life expectancies ranging from 16 to 80 years. Only with moderately high fertility, that is, with crude birth rates in the 40s or higher, does the range of life expectancies contract to any significant degree (to a range of 14 and 50 years).

Table 4.3 demonstrates the critical importance of ascertaining a valid growth rate if an estimate of life expectancy from skeletal data is to be bounded by a reasonable range. Fortunately, archaeologists collect a great deal of material evidence with valuable clues to settlement history. This handle opens the window on life expectancies that has proven so elusive to researchers who rely on the mean age at death.

CONCLUSIONS

Skeletal demography is as much art as science. If it is to be done well, the findings of physical anthropology must be integrated with those of skeletal biology (Paine 1997a); otherwise, only the fertility half of the demographic equation can be known. Then, too, fertility findings are less contentious because the methodological chain of reasoning is both shorter and stronger than for mortality.

One of the major contributions of this project to our knowledge of the demography of the past is the uncovering of great variations in fertility. In the Ancient Americas (that is, more than 1,500 years ago), fertility seems to have been surprisingly low (GRR $= 2.3$), and the brake on explosive population growth was fertility rather than mortality ($e_0 = 34$ years). Consequently, the ancient demographic regime was a relatively low-pressure system.

A high-pressure system, which we have long presumed to characterize much of antiquity, dates from the middle period in the Americas (1500 BP–500 BP). A demographic system of high fertility and high mortality, which characterized only simple horticulturists in ancient times, seems to have become more general during the middle period, intrinsic to complex agrarian systems as well as to foragers and fishers (GRR $= 3.0$ and 2.8, respectively). Fertility surged from ancient times by more than 50% for both groups, if we may generalize from the collections in the Health and Nutrition in the Western Hemisphere database. Agriculture was not the engine of demographic transformation in prehistoric America because nonhorticulturists also experienced a substantial rise in fertility. Instead, agriculture may have been the caboose. Agricultural innovations may have occurred in response to rising demographic densities and shifts in scale.

A second great demographic transformation began 500 years ago with the intrusion of Old World populations and technologies. While these changes were sweeping, indeed many peoples were thrust to the verge of extinction, the fundamental demography of the survivors did not change greatly. The old demographic regime persisted into the nineteenth century, if the osteological evidence is trustworthy. Likewise, African-American demographic systems seem to have been under high pressure: very high fertility and high mortality, with the highest pressures characteristic of free populations. European-American demographic systems, as measured here, were decidedly low pressure, with relatively moderate mortality and moderately higher fertility. For these more recent times, historical demography, because of the large volume of extant written records, may have more to teach about diverse ethnic systems than paleodemography due to the paucity of skeletal material (Shoemaker 1999).

REFERENCES

Bocquet-Appel, J. P., and J. N. Bacro. 1997. Brief communication: Estimates of some demographic parameters in a neolithic rock-cut chamber (approximately 2000 B.C. using iterative techniques for aging and demographic estimators). *American Journal of Physical Anthropology* 102:569–575.

Bocquet-Appel, J. P., and C. Masset. 1982. Farewell to paleodemography. *Journal of Human Evolution* 11:321–333.

Buikstra, Jane E. 1997. Paleodemography: Context and promise. In Richard R. Paine (ed.), *Integrating Archaeological Demography: Multidisciplinary Approaches to Prehistoric Population*. Carbondale, IL: Center for Archaeological Investigations, 367–380.

Buikstra, J. E., and L. W. Konigsberg. 1985. Paleodemography: Critiques and controversies. *American Anthropologist* 87:316–333.

Coale, A., and P. Demeny. 1983. *Regional Model Life Tables and Stable Populations.* New York: Academic Press.

Gage, T. B. 1988. Mathematical hazard models of mortality: An alternative to model life tables. *American Journal of Physical Anthropology* 76:429–441.

Gage, T. B., and B. Dyke. 1986. Parameterizing abridged mortality tables. *Human Biology* 58:275–291.

Hammel, E. A. 1996. Demographic constraints on population growth of early humans: With emphasis on the probable role of females in overcoming such constraints. *Human Nature: An Interdisciplinary Biosocial Perspective* 7(3), 217–255.

Horowitz, S., G. Armelagos, and K. Wachter. 1988. On generating birth rates from skeletal populations. *American Journal of Physical Anthropology* 76:189–196.

Howell, N. 1976. Toward a uniformitarian theory of human paleodemography. In R. H. Ward and K. M. Weiss (eds.), *The Demographic Evolution of Human Populations.* New York: Academic Press, 25–40.

——— 1982. Village composition implied by a paleodemographic life table: The Libben site. *American Journal of Physical Anthropology* 59:263–269.

Jackes, M. K. 1992. Paleodemography: Problems and techniques. In S. R. Saunders and M. A. Katzenberg (eds.), *Skeletal Biology of Past Peoples: Research Methods.* New York: Wiley-Liss, 189–224.

——— 2000. Building the bases for paleodemographic analysis: Adult age determination. In M. A. Katzenberg and S. R. Saunders (eds.), *Biological Anthropology of the Human Skeleton.* New York: Wiley-Liss, pp. 407–456.

Johansson, S. Ryan, and S. Horowitz. 1986. Estimating mortality in skeletal populations: Influence of the growth rate on the interpretation of levels and trends during the transition to agriculture. *American Journal of Physical Anthropology* 71:233–250.

Konigsberg, L. W., and S. R. Frankenberg. 1992. Estimation of age structure in anthropological demography. *American Journal of Physical Anthropology* 89:235–256.

Konigsberg, L. W., S. R. Frankenberg, and R. B. Walker. 1997. Regress what on what? Paleodemographic age estimation as a calibration problem. In Richard R. Paine (ed.), *Integrating*

Archaeological Demography: Multidisciplinary Approaches to Prehistoric Population. Carbondale, IL: Center for Archaeological Investigations, 64–88.

Lovejoy, C. O., R. S. Meindl, R. P. Mensforth, and T. J. Barton. 1985. Multifactorial determination of skeletal age at death: A method and blind tests of its accuracy. *American Journal of Physical Anthropology* 68(1):1–14.

McCaa, R. 1989. Populate: A microcomputer projection package for aggregative data applied to Norway, 1736–1970. *Annales de Démographie Historique,* 287–298.

McCaa, R., and J. W. Vaupel. 1992. Comment la projection inverse se comporte-t-elle sur des données simulées? In Alain Blum, Noël Bonneuil, and Didier Blanchet (eds.), *Modèles de la Démographie Historique.* Paris: Institut National des Etudes Démographiques, Congrès et Colloques N° 11, 129–46.

McDaniel, Antonio, and Carlos Grushka. 1995. Did Africans live longer in the antebellum United States? The sensitivity of mortality estimates of enslaved Africans. *Historical Methods* 28(2):97–105.

Meindl, R. S., and Katherine F. Russell. 1998. Recent advances in method and theory in paleodemography. *Annual Review of Anthropology* 27:375–399.

Mensforth, R. P. 1990. Paleodemography of the Carlston-Annis (Bt-5) Late Archaic skeletal population. *American Journal of Physical Anthropology* 28:81–99.

Milner, G. R., D. A. Humpf, and H. C. Harpending. 1989. Pattern matching of age-at-death distributions in paleodemographic analysis. *American Journal of Physical Anthropology* 80:49–58.

Paine, R. R. 1989. Model life table fitting by maximum likelihood estimation: A procedure to reconstruct paleodemographic characteristics from skeletal age distributions. *American Journal of Physical Anthropology* 79:51–61.

1997a. The need for a multidisciplinary approach to prehistoric demography. In Richard R. Paine (ed.), *Integrating Archaeological Demography: Multidisciplinary Approaches to Prehistoric Population.* Carbondale, IL: Center for Archaeological Investigations, 1–18.

1997b. Uniformitarian models in osteological paleodemography. In Richard R. Paine (ed.), *Integrating Archaeological Demography: Multidisciplinary Approaches to Prehistoric Population.* Carbondale, IL: Center for Archaeological Investigations, 191–204.

Paine, R. R., and H. C. Harpending. 1996. The reliability of paleodemographic fertility estimators. *American Journal of Physical Anthropology* 101:151–160.

1998. Effect of sample bias on paleodemographic fertility estimates. *American Journal of Physical Anthropology* 105: 231–240.

Preston, S. H., A. McDaniel, and C. Grushka. 1993. New model life tables for high-mortality populations. *Historical Methods* 26(4):149–160.

Sattenspiel, L., and H. Harpending. 1983. Stable populations and skeletal age. *American Antiquity* 48:489–498.

Saunders, S. R., A. Herring, L. A. Sawchuk, and G. Boyce. 1995. The nineteenth-century cemetery at St. Thomas' Anglican church, Belleville: Skeletal remains, parish records and censuses. In S. R. Saunders and A. Herring (eds.), *Grave Reflections: Portraying the Past through Cemetery Studies.* Toronto: Canadian Scholars' Press Inc., 93–117.

Shoemaker, Nancy. 1999. *American Indian Population Recovery in the Twentieth Century.* Albuquerque: University of New Mexico Press.

STATA reference manual release 4. 1995. College Station, Tex: STATA Press.

Steckel, R. H. 1985. *The Economics of U.S. Slave and Southern White Fertility.* New York: Garland Press.

Van Gerven, D. P., S. Guise Sheridan, and W. Y. Adams. 1995. The health and nutrition of a medieval Nubian population: The impact of political and economic change. *American Anthropologist* 97(3):468–480.

Weiss, K. M. 1973. *Demographic Models for Anthropology. Memoirs of the Society for American Archaeology*, No. 27. *American Antiquity*, 38, supplement.

Wood, J. W. 1998. A theory of preindustrial population dynamics: Demography, economy, and well-being in Malthusian systems. *Current Anthropology* 39:99–121.

Wood, J. W., G. R. Milner, H. C. Harpending, and K. M. Weiss. 1992. The osteological paradox: Problems of inferring prehistoric health from skeletal samples. *Current Anthropology*, 33:343–370.

PART III

EURO-AMERICANS AND AFRICAN-AMERICANS IN NORTH AMERICA

Introduction

All remaining sections of the book assume that readers are familiar with the methodology outlined in Part II. Much of what follows will be unintelligible without an understanding of basic skeletal indicators of nutrition and disease. In particular, we suppose that all who venture forward comprehend our measures of childhood stress, which are average stature (a measure of a society's history of net nutrition in childhood), linear enamel hypoplasias (somewhat like tree rings, but in teeth), and anemia (porotic hyperostosis and cribra orbitalia, which are identified by pitting of the skull or eye orbits, respectively). We also take for granted a familiarity with our measures of health deterioration that accompany aging, including dental decay and degenerative joint disease. Infections that penetrate the bone and trauma, such as broken bones or weapon wounds, can occur at any age but are most frequent among adults.

To facilitate comparisons, the seven component measures of health have been scored on a scale of 0 (lowest or worst) to 100 (highest or best). These scores are then averaged or weighted equally to form our Mark I version of the health index.[1] Bear in mind that the index and its components have been adjusted for variations in the age distributions of deaths across sites. The scores reflect only the age-specific rates at which pathologies occurred. Though a desirable component of any health index, longevity is not included because the data are too fragile at most sites for formal incorporation into the index. Therefore the index likely understates the variation in health that existed in the Western Hemisphere. For this reason it is also possible that the Mark I version of the index is somewhat inaccurate in its ranking of health across sites. Qualifications and limitations of the procedure, as well as possible extensions and refinements, are discussed in Chapters 2 and 3 of Part II.

As a general rule, much more is known about the recent than the more distant past simply because information is more abundant. Thus, economic, social, and health

---

[1] At a few sites, some components are missing, in which case the available components are weighted equally in tabulating the health index.

Table III.1: Health Index and Component Scores of Blacks and Whites in North America during the Eighteenth and Nineteenth Centuries

Investigator	Age BP	Group	Index	Stature	Hyp.	Anemia	Dental	Inf.	DJD	Trauma
Blacks										
Rathbun	0105	Baptist Church, Philadelphia	73.8	49.3	66.4	96.9	64.9	81.5	69.1	88.6
Condon	0062	Texas frontier	69.5	42.8	53.9	94.5	85.9	46.6	74.0	89.0
Rathbun	0097	Folly Island Union troops	68.5	41.6	39.0	100.0	74.9	46.9	82.5	94.3
Rose	0042	Cedar Grove, Arkansas	65.5	67.8	9.8	87.2	77.6	55.0	85.6	75.6
Rathbun	0095	Plantation slaves, South Carolina	58.4	3.2	42.7	57.1	81.3	49.5	77.0	98.3
		Average, blacks	67.1	40.9	42.4	87.1	76.9	55.9	77.6	89.2
		Std. dev., blacks	5.7	23.6	21.1	17.4	7.9	14.7	6.6	8.6
Whites										
Walker	0075	Northern California	72.8	36.1	60.4	97.2	81.3	89.0	68.5	77.1
Sirianni	0108	Rochester, N.Y., poorhouse	72.3	33.0	80.1	96.1	71.7	54.0	79.3	92.1
Rathbun	0100	Eastern United States	71.3	28.2	43.3	96.9	73.6	68.6	88.7	100.0
Sledzik	0150	Military, East	70.4	31.7	98.6	64.8	74.0	84.1	85.1	24.8
Saunders	0102	Belleville, Ontario, Canada	69.3	36.0	71.8	93.9	71.2	81.5	41.6	89.2
Sledzik	0080	Military, West	66.2	40.6	70.8	96.4	74.3	92.1	78.1	10.8
		Average, whites	70.4	34.3	70.8	95.9	74.4	78.2	73.6	65.7
		Std. dev., whites	2.4	4.3	18.6	1.3	3.6	14.4	17.1	38.1
		Average, 65 sites	72.6	20.7	71.1	90.5	81.8	75.1	78.9	85.7
		Std. dev., 65 sites	8.0	16.9	24.6	11.5	10.4	17.0	12.3	16.1
		Minimum, 65 sites	53.5	0.4	9.8	53.2	53.3	44.1	41.6	10.8
		Maximum, 65 sites	91.8	67.8	99.7	100.0	100.0	98.7	100.0	100.0

Source: Consolidated database.

conditions of the nineteenth century are better known than those of the seventeenth century. Readers familiar with the history of the past two centuries, but new to physical anthropology, can link their knowledge of the past to our skeletal indicators of health. By connecting the familiar with the less familiar, these readers will more easily absorb the meaning of our skeletal measures. Similarly, their knowledge of skeletal biology will help physical anthropologists unfamiliar with recent history to link their knowledge of skeletal biology with historical developments. It is therefore useful to begin the discussion of health at individual sites with Euro-Americans and African-Americans who lived in the past two centuries.

For the readers of the chapters in Part III it is helpful to recognize the unusual aspects of health at each site. Table III.1 shows that blacks (index = 67.1) and whites (index = 69.9) as groups were slightly less healthy (as measured by skeletal lesions) than the average of all 65 sites in the project (index = 72.6). Blacks tended to score well (lower incidence of) on trauma, but compared to the average, tended to have more infections, worse dental health, and more hypoplasias. Whites had greater stature and less anemia than average, but had more trauma and worse dental health.

It is notable, however, that the averages disguise considerable variation within groups. The plantation slaves, for example, scored poorly on indicators of health in childhood (stature, hypoplasias, and anemia), but the free blacks from Philadelphia did much better than average in this category. The slaves scored poorly on infections but did well on trauma, while free blacks from the Southwest were relatively tall but susceptible to hypoplasias and infections.

Remarkably, the poorhouse residents of Rochester, New York, scored higher on the health index than the middle class of Belleville, Ontario, whose overall score was brought down by the worst score among 65 sites on degenerative joint disease. The poorhouse residents benefited from good scores on childhood indicators, which suggests that they experienced considerable downward mobility, that is, they had relatively healthy childhoods but suffered reversals as adults, scoring low in dental health and infections. Unsurprisingly, the military samples had relatively good scores on childhood indicators, which is consistent with minimum health standards for entry, but performed among the worst of all groups on trauma. As noncombatants, the Folly Island troops had relatively little trauma.

## CHAPTER FIVE

The Health of the Middle Class

The St. Thomas' Anglican Church Cemetery Project

Shelley R. Saunders, Ann Herring, Larry Sawchuk,
Gerry Boyce, Rob Hoppa, and Susan Klepp

ABSTRACT

The economic record establishes the mid–nineteenth century as a time of prosperity according to growth in incomes, wealth per capita, and technology. Less is known about the record on health, and that which is available suggests that improvements in the quality of life did not extend to mortality rates and morbidity levels. The population investigated here consists of almost 600 skeletons out of more than 1,500 individuals buried at St. Thomas' Anglican Church cemetery in Belleville, Ontario, between 1821 and 1874. Our investigations show that mortality rates, especially for infants, did not improve over the period of greatest cemetery use, from 1850 to 1874. Skeletal investigations support the interpretation of the importance of acute versus chronic infections and the significance of environmental conditions affecting infant morbidity and mortality. The skeletal variables identified as significant contributors to the quality of life index for St. Thomas' may fit with the conclusion that healthwise, life in the mid-nineteenth century was not measurably better for the middle to upper class at St. Thomas' and may coincidentally reflect a broader North American phenomenon related to urbanization. Nevertheless, these observations are also uniquely reflective of the church and town alone.

INTRODUCTION

Historians and other social scientists have been interested in the fate of various classes or socioeconomic groups during the transition from a settled agricultural to an urban-industrial way of life, a change that occurred in North America during the middle of the nineteenth century. The economic record clearly establishes the mid-nineteenth century as a time of prosperity according to growth in incomes, wealth per capita, and technology. In the United States, for example, real gross national product per capita grew at about 1.6% per year – an unprecedented doubling within a typical person's working life – during the middle decades of the nineteenth century (Atack and Passell, 1994, Chap. 1).

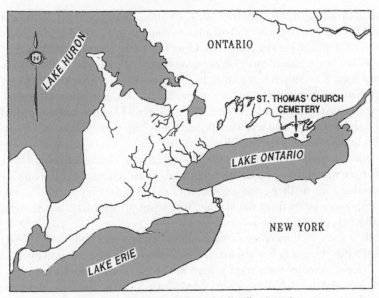

Figure 5.1. Map of location of Belleville, Ontario.

Less is known about the record on health, and that which is available suggests that improvements in the quality of life did not extend to mortality rates and morbidity levels. Studies of mortality rates, as estimated from genealogies, and studies of changes in stature, as a reflection of the effects of poor nutrition and disease on growth, suggest that health levels declined for all income groups in the United States through midcentury (Steckel, 1995; Pope, 1992). Improvements in growth and reductions in mortality did not begin until the closing decades of the century.

This paper examines a different source of evidence relevant to the standard of living debate – skeletal indicators of chronic biological stress. The population investigated here consists of almost 600 skeletons out of over 1,500 individuals buried at St. Thomas' Anglican Church cemetery in Belleville, Ontario, between 1821 and 1874 (Figure 5.1). The Anglican Church was the state church of Upper Canada at the time, and the members of the parish represented many of the most politically and socially influential members of the community. The question pertinent to the debate is whether the skeletal sample from the cemetery reflects this presumed group of middle- to upper-class Anglicans and thus a materially more prosperous and possibly healthier subset of Belleville society. Settlement and economic development began later in Canada than in the eastern United States although the two regions traded and interacted intensively. It is not clear whether the proposed general declines in health in mid-nineteenth-century United States would also have been felt in Upper Canada. We consider these questions by making comparisons of the St. Thomas' sample's skeletal indicators to those of other nineteenth-century groups to determine if they are informative about the ways that health and material prosperity coexisted in Belleville during the transition to an urban-industrial economy.

The excavation of the cemetery at St. Thomas' developed out of the church's decision to construct a parish hall on adjacent land that was used as a burial ground between 1821 and 1874. The church building had been reconstructed twice over the previous 175 years, and all but 15 gravestones in the cemetery were disturbed due to two past fires. The church hired an archaeological contract firm in 1989 to excavate a portion of the abandoned cemetery to make way for construction. Ultimately, 579 grave shafts were located and excavated and a total of 577 individuals were identified. Consequently, the St. Thomas' skeletal sample is one of the largest historic period samples in North America (McKillop et al., 1989).

Detailed investigations of the skeletal sample were carried out over a one-year period after which the remains were reburied. However, numerous tissue samples were retained for further analyses, and over 400,000 data observations and measurements were taken from the sample, including primary data in the form of X rays, photographs, and casts.

While a map of the cemetery interments has not survived, a complete set of parish records recording burials, marriages, and baptisms for the entire period during which the cemetery was used is kept in the Anglican Church Archives. These records indicate that 1,564 individuals were buried, and so the skeletal sample represents almost 40% of all interments for the 53-year period (Saunders et al., 1995b). A number of other historical documents survive for parts of the period of cemetery use, including censuses, municipal assessment rolls, newspapers, directories, and some personal letters and accounts. In addition, some of the skeletons from the excavation were personally identified from preserved coffin plates with associated inscriptions indicating name and date of death. These inscriptions were checked against the parish records, producing an "identified" sample of 72 individuals. It became clear that this was an excellent opportunity for comparing biological reconstructions of the St. Thomas' burial population from the skeletal sample to historical reconstructions of the parish and community from various documents. A research group was organized and funding obtained from the Canadian Social Sciences and Humanities Research Council beginning in 1991. The initial goal was to complete transcriptions of parish records and censuses, as well as to complete some of the skeletal analyses. It was during this period of research that we were invited to participate in the Health and Nutrition in the Western Hemisphere Project.

TRADITIONAL SOURCES OF EVIDENCE AND METHODS OF ANALYSIS

Historians

In their investigations of temporal changes in nineteenth-century Upper Canada[1] and North America in general, historians have tended to focus on the apparent transformation from rural to urban society and the growth of industrial capitalism with

---

[1] In 1791 the British parliament enacted the Constitutional Act to establish two provinces, Upper Canada and Lower Canada. In 1840, the two provinces came under a central government and were named Canada West and Canada East. Canada West ultimately became the province of Ontario.

the appearance of large cities. This emphasis on "urbanization" or "modernization" usually disregards more complex relationships between population growth, developing economies, and changing social structures, but this approach has been changing in American and Canadian historical research. More recently, historians have argued that past emphases on central-place theory and metropolitan dominance mask the regional and local variations that were occurring in pioneer settlements and developing communities of the last century (Widdis, 1991).

General historical information about Upper Canada is vast and includes documentation that began as early as the appearance of the first settlers and local and regional governments. A broad perspective of these sources of information can be found in the edited *Historical Atlas of Canada* for the nineteenth century (Gentilcore, 1993). More detailed demographic reconstructions of the mortality and fertility experience of early populations in the United States have been increasing in recent years. Interest in the transition from rural to urban living continues, as well as attempts to understand the health implications of that trend. While some very detailed analyses of eighteenth- and nineteenth-century population change have been carried out in Quebec, progress in our knowledge of the demographic changes in communities in Ontario has been correspondingly slow for various reasons, including difficulties with documentary records and lack of sufficient research (Sawchuk et al., n.d.). Nevertheless, there are investigations of the relationship between economic trends and land tenure in local nineteenth-century communities (Gagan, 1981) and also detailed assessments of the demographic, social, and economic impact of the emigration of specific groups (Akenson, 1984; Elliot, 1988).

Historical demographic studies of the relationships between mortality and health in the United States are abundant (Meeker, 1972; Condron and Crimmins, 1979; Crimmins and Condran, 1983; Cheney, 1984; Swedlund, 1990; Preston and Haines, 1991; Haines, 1994). In Canada, often because of the difficulties with the quality of records, much of the work focuses on the mid-nineteenth century and beyond (MacMurchy, 1910; Robert, 1988; Emery and McQuillan, 1988; Gagan, 1989; Thornton and Olson, 1993) and can be compared to the more extensive historical demographic studies carried out in Europe. In addition, a considerable body of literature on fertility exists for nineteenth-century Europe, a lesser amount for the United States, and an even smaller amount for Canadian populations (Beaujot and McQuillan, 1986; Bouchard and Roy, 1991; Vanderlinden, 1995).

General historical studies of diet and nutrition, health, illness, and epidemics in the nineteenth century in North America abound. While there is a fairly extensive literature on these topics for Upper Canada in general and several of the larger communities (Barkin and Gentles, 1990; Bliss, 1991; Duffin, 1997), there are no such studies for Belleville.

Bioarchaeologists

Until recently, relatively little bioarchaeological investigation of historical populations in North America has taken place. But over the past two decades, urban growth and renewal has fostered archaeological excavations and analyses of some historic cemeteries and mortuary sites in the United States and Canada.

In Ontario, several bioarchaeological studies of human skeletal remains from historic cemeteries have been conducted by archaeological and environmental assessment firms as a result of regional and municipal master plans (Cook et al., 1985; Cybulski, 1988; Pfeiffer et al., 1989; Spence, 1989; Saunders and Lazenby, 1991; Pfeiffer and Williamson, 1991). However, most of these excavations have been small, the cemeteries are unmarked and unregistered under provincial statutes, and in some cases biological research was very limited. The closing, excavation, and moving of registered historic cemeteries in Ontario requires provincial permission. Cultural attitudes toward burial excavation and general ignorance of bioarchaeology as a scientific field contribute to these limitations.

Studies of the physical remains of Upper Canada pioneer populations in the nineteenth century can also be compared to several of those in nearby American communities (see Higgins et al., this volume; Elia and Weslowsky, 1991; Grauer, 1995). Since the majority of the original settlers and migrants to Upper Canada were British Loyalists from the United States or British subjects, it also makes sense to compare bioarchaeological studies of nineteenth-century Upper Canada pioneers to those of related populations in Britain. Presently, there are two major skeletal samples in England coming from church crypt excavations dating into the nineteenth century, and for both there are personally identified individuals.[2] Otherwise, nineteenth-century preserved skeletal samples are rare, no doubt because of the relatively short time period which has passed since their interment.

Bioarchaeological studies of historical samples apply the same methods of analysis used on prehistoric samples. The advantage of historical samples is the ability to directly compare results to documented information about demography, health, population relationships, and personal information. A critical factor is the degree of preservation of the skeletal remains, since even when sample sizes are large, damaged, or fragmentary, skeletons yield relatively little useful information (Walker et al., 1988; Jackes, 1992; Walker, 1995; Ubelaker, 1995; Nawrocki, 1995). One of the advantages of the St. Thomas' sample is its good state of preservation. The cemetery location at the top of a well-drained sandy glacial shoreline meant that the condition of the bones was excellent. Only 3% of skeletons were too fragmentary for detailed sex and age determinations (Saunders et al., 1995a).

STATE OF KNOWLEDGE

Historical

As noted above, a dominant theme in the literature on nineteenth-century North American populations is that of the transition from rural to urban living and the

---

[2] The St. Bride's Church, Fleet Street, City of London skeletal collection contains the remains of 237 personally identified individuals who died between 1730 and 1867 (Scheuer and Bowman, 1995). The Christ Church, Spitalfields, East London sample consists of almost 400 personally identified individuals named from coffin plates who died between 1729 and 1852 (Molleson et al., 1993; Molleson, 1995). A third large collection has been mentioned briefly in the literature but only to record evidence of dental disease (Corbett and Moore, 1976).

health implications of such a change. Observations from studies in Europe and the United States have provided some general trends. First of all, there were marked differentials in rural/urban mortality, with childhood mortality significantly lower in rural areas and little evidence for real improvements in life expectancy until the 1880s. Although adult survivorship may have been improving from 1850 onward, infant mortality was not declining and probably increased in many regions prior to 1880.

Cities in the United States and Britain differed in their levels of mortality and the timing of the decline in mortality in accordance with changes in public health, sanitation, and the environment in conjunction with regional, economic, and cultural differences (Lee, 1991). Like a number of cities in the United States, Canadian urban areas seemed unable to turn their attention to sanitation until quite late. In Belleville, lack of a proper water supply was identified as a significant problem in the mid-1870s and again in the mid-1880s (Bell, 1876; Tracy, 1885), even though the town was located on the fast-flowing Moira River and the Bay of Quinte, a bay of Lake Ontario. Nevertheless, from an early period, the populace relied on local stream and spring sources for their water because of easier transport than water from the river or bay. The safety of this practice was not assured; a prominent Belleville resident, the author Susanna Moodie, noted in 1853 that the main underground water source flowed directly beneath St. Thomas' cemetery (Moodie, 1853).

The regions of Canada, both urban and rural, experienced a variety of epidemics throughout the century, including smallpox, typhus, and cholera, a disease which returned several times from the 1830s to the 1860s (Godfrey, 1968; Bilson, 1975, 1977). In the Belleville area, accounts record that the town avoided the effects of the major 1832 cholera epidemic because barricades were drawn around the community (Boyce, 1967), although William Hutton noted the occurrence of one case of cholera (Boyce, 1972). Tuberculosis was clearly present as was venereal syphilis (Saunders et al., 1991; Jimenez, 1991). Malaria appeared in Upper Canada with the arrival of Loyalist settlers from America and was a major problem until its gradual decline after 1850 (Fallis, 1984). Yet, even beginning in 1829, people in the Belleville area were said to be free from "ague" or "fever" even while it (and many mosquitoes) plagued settlers in the woods (Moodie, 1852; Boyce, 1972). The low level of malaria in Belleville was probably related to extensive land clearing, few swampy areas, advanced building construction, and the presence of domestic animal vectors.[3] Accidental and traumatic deaths and injuries were also of importance in early Canadian settlements but perhaps particularly so in Belleville both prior to and after 1850 (Jimenez, 1991, 1995; Saunders et al., 1995b).

While the diet of early-nineteenth-century European settlers to Upper Canada was often monotonous and heavy with fat and starches, food was always abundant

---

[3] While Susanna Moodie noted many cases of "fever" during her bush settlement, the title of her second book set in Belleville is *Life in the Clearings*. By the 1850s, Belleville was depicted as having a number of excellent stone or brick buildings (Smith, 1851), in contrast to the more poorly constructed log houses of bush settlement (Fallis, 1984). The Moira River was fast flowing with flooding occurring early in the spring, while the Bay of Quinte was not swampy but deep enough for steamships. Quinine became cheaper and more readily available as a prophylactic by midcentury (Fallis, 1984).

and undernutrition for even the poorest was usually not a problem (Saunders et al., 1997). Meat was an important dietary component, providing more than sufficient protein, and Canadian settlers also took advantage of fresh and preserved fruits and vegetables. Several grain crops were important, particularly wheat made into bread and alcohol, and Indian corn, which was often used as a porridge (Boyce, 1972). The variety of the diet was greater in towns and larger urban centers, and by the 1830s many different products were available in Belleville as a result of its importance as an export–import distribution center (Boyce, 1972). At a fairly early date, refined flour products, particularly breads and cakes, became very important in Belleville, as did the use of sugar. The dietary characteristics of nineteenth-century Canadians, not surprisingly, were intermediate to their major political and economic sources, resembling those of their American neighbors to the south as well as the preferences and influences of the mother country, England (Saunders et al., 1997).

Bioarchaeological

Historical skeletal samples have offered the opportunity for researchers to investigate the quality and representativeness of these data sources in greater detail (Saunders et al., 1995a; Grauer and McNamara, 1995; Hoppa, 1996). This work demonstrates that caution is necessary since skeletal samples are usually small, *biased*, and limited by techniques of biological investigation (Cook et al., 1985; Walker, 1995; Scheuer and Bowman, 1995; Molleson, 1995). Often, all that can be expected is a brief glimpse of the lives and deaths of some of the populace. The St. Thomas' cemetery sample, by its size, has already contributed substantially to this literature. Previous St. Thomas' bioarchaeological results and those of the present study are discussed later in this chapter.

Historical samples from the United States constitute mainly military examples (see Sledzik and Sandberg, this volume), slave and free black cemeteries (see Rathbun and Steckel, this volume), and poorhouse/almshouse cemeteries, most in the U.S. North (see Higgins et al., this volume), although there are also a number of small family cemeteries which have been investigated (see Bell, 1994, and Grauer, 1995, for some examples). Since studies of large nineteenth-century church or municipal cemetery samples are lacking, the St. Thomas' sample might be compared to those from the poorhouse cemeteries. For the Highland Park Cemetery, which is associated with the Monroe County Poorhouse of Rochester from the 1820s through the 1860s, researchers have observed apparently high infant and young-adult female mortality, which corresponds to observations from town and cemetery records. The high prevalence of enamel hypoplasias in the deciduous teeth of the subadults from Highland Park suggests poor prenatal conditions for mothers and stressful childhood living conditions. A study of subadult mortality in a small skeletal sample from the Dunning cemetery associated with a nineteenth-century poor farm and almshouse in Chicago found a similar subadult age distribution to that for Highland Park, but significant differences from the demographic data reported for Chicago and Cook County (Grauer and MacNamara, 1995). These authors conclude that this sample is not an adequate reflection of subadult mortality patterns at the Dunning poorhouse.

Studies of the St. Bride's and Spitalfields' crypt samples from England, as well as simulation studies, have shown clearly how skeletons that belong to a particular sample may not be representative of a smaller or larger group to which they bear a relation (Scheuer and Bowman, 1995; Molleson, 1995; Hoppa and Saunders, 1998). A number of detailed biological studies have been and continue to be conducted on the two English samples. This work has suggested that there are temporal differences in the biological processes of aging, growth, and skeletally manifested disease in these samples as compared to modern populations.

The few investigations of nineteenth-century Canadian samples show some similarities to American and British studies. Infant mortality appears to be substantial. One study of a midcentury Methodist cemetery found juvenile long bone lengths to be shorter than modern standards, and this was interpreted to be due to chronic or acute growth retardation (Pfeiffer et al., 1989). Evidence of healed and unhealed trauma is common (Saunders and Lazenby, 1991), while skeletal signs of infection are often associated with earlier trauma, age-related diseases, or congenital problems (Cybulski, 1988; Pfeiffer et al., 1989; Saunders and Lazenby, 1991).

An interesting approach to analyses of historical skeletal samples involves recent attempts to detect patterns of infant feeding. In the 1980s, researchers discovered that stable isotopes of nitrogen could be used to evaluate nursing and weaning (Fogel et al., 1989). Following studies which showed that animals at successively higher levels in the food chain (trophic levels) exhibit enrichment of ^{15}N relative to ^{14}N, it was thought that infants feeding on their mothers' milk might exhibit a similar enrichment. Fogel and colleagues analyzed fingernail clippings as a source of protein from nursing infants and documented an increase in the ratio of ^{15}N to ^{14}N (referred to as "delta" ^{15}N) over the period of nursing and a decline in values beginning at the process of weaning. These same authors then showed a similar pattern of increasing, then decreasing, nitrogen isotope values in infants and older children in two skeletal samples (Fogel et al., 1989; Tuross and Fogel, 1994). Weaned infants and children should show values corresponding to adults in the sample. A definite trophic-level shift was demonstrated for infants from the Prospect Hill nineteenth-century Methodist Cemetery in Ontario (Katzenberg and Pfeiffer, 1995), as well as for the St. Thomas' sample (Herring et al., 1994; Katzenberg et al., 1996; Herring et al., 1998). A more recent study (Wright and Schwarcz, 1998) has looked at carbon and oxygen stable isotope ratios from the carbon dioxide component of the apatite in tooth enamel in earlier- and later-developing teeth to identify the introduction of solid foods and the decline in breast-feeding within the same individuals. This area of research is important because of the effects of feeding practices on infant health and survival and on population fertility (Katzenberg et al., 1996).

DESCRIPTION OF THE SITE

Location

Belleville is located on the north shore of the Bay of Quinte, a protected bay which separates the mainland from the Prince Edward Peninsula, a major body of land which juts into Lake Ontario (Figure 5.2). St. Thomas' Anglican Church was one of

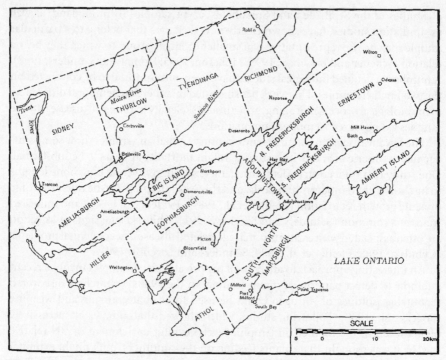

Figure 5.2. Map of townships in the Belleville area.

the first churches established in the community.[4] Founding of the parish occurred on December 26, 1818, and construction of a building began in 1819. The first church service in the building was held in June 1821. St. Thomas' Church cemetery was the first public burial ground established in the town although an earlier private burial ground had been used since the 1790s (Boyce, 1967).

Ecological Variables

Belleville is part of the geographical area of southern Ontario known as the Great Lakes Lowlands (Putnam et al., 1952). These lowlands are underlaid by an ancient limestone bedrock. Toward the end of the last major glaciation, the melting glacier formed a much larger lake. Consequently, old lake margins composed of dense layers of sand and clay deposits can be found less than a kilometer or so from the present Lake Ontario shoreline while the remainder of the Lowlands is covered in glacial till deposits. St. Thomas' Church and cemetery stand on a crest of part of this old shoreline, one of the highest points of land in the Belleville district.

The Moira River flows through the middle of Belleville and forms a large drainage basin to the north of Lake Ontario, extending for more than 1,000 square miles. The headwaters of the Moira rise in the area known as the Canadian Shield. The Shield

---

[4] Since the Church of England was the state church for the colony, a parcel of land was assigned to the C. of E. at survey. This became St. Thomas' Church.

is a region of ancient Precambrian granitic rock with little soil cover and dense coniferous forest, which begins only 18 miles north of Belleville. The last 18 miles from north to south form the limestone-based Lowlands, which fall a little more than 80 feet in elevation toward Lake Ontario. Locally, physiography on the east side of the river is identified as beveled till plain, while on the west side, the land is clay plain which extends onto the Prince Edward Peninsula to the south of Belleville (Chapman and Putnam, 1984).

Climatically, the area is known as the North Shore Lake Ontario climatic zone (Chapman and Brown, 1966). This is a typical eastern North America temperate climate moderated by proximity to the lake. Currently, the mean temperature in January is 21°F (−10°C) and 70°F (21°C) in July. Precipitation averages around 32 inches (81 mm) per year with a slightly greater amount of that (19 inches/48 mm) received as snow in the winter months.

Climatic reconstructions of nineteenth-century weather in eastern North America rely on instrument records and tree ring data (Baron, 1992; Cook et al., 1992). The early nineteenth century ushered in some relief from the "Little Ice Age," which began back in the thirteenth century. A warming trend at the beginning of the 1800s brought temperatures close to current averages. The reconstructions also identify a period of severe drought from 1814 to 1822 and subsequently an extremely wet decade from 1827 to 1837. This high level of precipitation also brought the return of colder weather, however, and the period from 1840 to 1860 is considered to have been the coldest in eastern North America for 1,000 years. A second warm-up began after 1860 and continued through to the present time, while precipitation also returned to normal after 1860. It would be useful to know if these regional trends coincide with local climate in the Belleville area for the time. There is some information on local climatic conditions derived from letters written by an early settler, William Hutton, to his relatives back in Ireland (Boyce, 1972). Hutton arrived in Belleville in 1834 and proclaimed his satisfaction with clear, dry, frosty winter weather in Belleville because of its contrast with drearier, wetter weather in Ireland. He noted the wetness of the seasons in the late 1830s and 1840s and also observed that winter conditions did get much colder throughout the 1840s, except for the winter of 1842.

As a result of glacial deposits, the north shoreline areas around Lake Ontario contain sufficiently arable land for agriculture. Soils in the Belleville district are gray-brown podzols. The native forest is categorized as the Huron-Ontario forest region consisting of broad-leafed hardwoods. In well-drained areas, sugar maples and beech are the dominant trees, while elms, ashes, blue beech, silver maple, and yellow birch are found on imperfectly drained clay plains (Rowe, 1959). This narrow band of sufficiently arable land around the lake margin meant that nineteenth-century settlement in Belleville began for agricultural reasons, but always with the influence of the exploitable forest and mineral resources to the north.

Size and Density of Settlement

Belleville's population was not much more than 100 at the time of its founding in 1816 but grew to about 700 by the end of the 1820s (Boyce, 1967; Mika and

Thousands

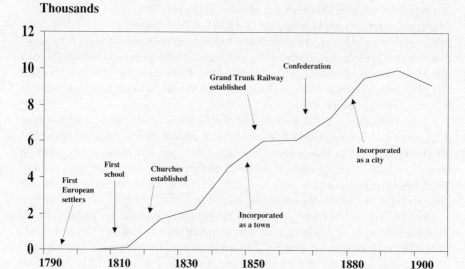

Figure 5.3. Belleville, Ontario: Population size and some landmark events.

Mika, 1986). In 1836, Belleville became an independent municipality or "police village," and the population stood at approximately 1,800 individuals (Boyce, 1967). The population expanded rapidly to 4,569 people by 1851 as it became a hub for marketing farm and lumber products. This was typical of many other Canadian communities of the time that served as collection and distribution centers for the produce of the surrounding countryside (Widdis, 1991). Population size recorded by the censuses in 1861 and 1871 was 6,081 and 7,302, respectively. By 1874, when St. Thomas' cemetery was closed, Belleville had grown from a small village to a bustling urban and industrial community. Figure 5.3 provides a general summary in diagram form of Belleville's history and population growth.

Age of Settlement

The site at Belleville was occupied for many years prior to 1800. Mississauga Indians used it as a temporary campsite and burying ground at least as far back as the seventeenth century (Boyce, 1967). After 1784, the first Loyalists established themselves along the front of Thurlow and Sidney Townships (Figure 5.2), while for some time the land where the center of Belleville is now found was reserved for the Mississaugas. However, various white settlers established small trading posts near the mouth of the river toward the end of the eighteenth century. Disenfranchised supporters of the King, the Loyalists, were called to Upper and Lower Canada after the American Revolution to serve in British regiments there. Families were maintained in refugee camps mainly near Montreal and later given land grants and annual allowances. Many of these earliest settlements were established on the Prince Edward Peninsula, south of the area where Belleville would become established.[5]

In 1792, the first Lieutenant-Governor of Upper Canada, John Graves Simcoe, established 200-acre allotments of free land to the so-called late Loyalists (both civilian and military settlers) on the condition of a loyalty oath and agreement to clear and build. This policy attracted settlers but also angered earlier colonists and fostered various rivalries. Nevertheless, the land policy introduced extensive surveys so that the town of Belleville itself was first surveyed and named in 1816, at which time it occupied less than 200 acres. Further waves of settlement occurred after the War of 1812 and into midcentury. These settlers were mainly British subjects (Saunders and Sawchuk, 1995). A large component of Irish immigrants, mostly Roman Catholic, settled in Belleville in the early to mid-nineteenth century.

As both agricultural resources from farms along the north Lake Ontario shore and forest products from the Shield area were produced, Belleville became a convenient distribution center for the import and export of goods into and out of its hinterland. While wheat was the main agricultural crop in most of Upper Canada, Quinte region farmers never specialized in it, and its importance never exceeded that of lumbering in the Belleville district. Wheat production suffered further when the wheat midge reached the area in 1849 (Gentilcore, 1993). Rye was an important crop through midcentury and, in fact, one of the largest North American distilleries was established just north of Belleville by the Corby family. During the American Civil War, when a tax was placed on whiskey, barley grown to make beer became a major crop of the region. In the 1850s, dairying also became an important economic activity, and to this day, the Belleville district is noted for its butter and cheese production.

Besides his writings about climate, William Hutton was a noted farmer in the district throughout midcentury. He wrote an agricultural and economic report for the district in 1852 which provides a great deal of information (Boyce, 1972). Farmers generally remained diversified, raising cattle, sheep, oxen, horses, and hogs. Besides wheat, rye, barley, and fodder crops, other important produce included peas, oats, Indian corn, buckwheat, root and green vegetables, and maple sugar. It seems that potatoes were very difficult to grow in the district and never achieved any importance.

Economic and Social Activities

As can be seen from the above historical account, Belleville was not a planned community or military center, in contrast to larger colonial Upper Canadian settlements, such as Kingston and Toronto. While the local farming and lumber industries were the mainstays of Belleville's economy, growth was further stimulated by the establishment of the Grand Trunk Railway in 1856 and by the Ontario mining boom of the 1860s (Boyce, 1992). The economic prosperity of the mid-nineteenth century that characterized the growth of Victorian England was amply reflected by events in Canada (Best, 1979). Population growth was fueled by moderately high

[5] By 1785 there were 6,000 Loyalists living in all of southern Ontario (Gentilcore, 1993).

fertility (Vanderlinden, 1995) and by substantial migration. Long-distance immigration played a major role in the development of the community. In particular, severe economic distress in the British Isles during the 1840s led to increased emigration to North America (Cowan, 1928; Guillet, 1937; MacDonagh, 1961; Ellis, 1977; MacKay, 1990).

In 1846, Belleville had four flour mills, four grist mills, two carding and cloth dressing mills, and three tanneries, as well as several carriage works (Boyce, 1967). By 1860, Belleville's industries included three agricultural implements factories, two axe and edge tool factories, two distillieries, seven carriage makers, four flour mills, five iron founders, five lumber companies, and three saw mills (Widdis, 1991). The largest employers were the lumber companies. The post-1850 prosperity which occurred throughout North America and Europe was also experienced by Belleville, and fortunes for the town did not really start to decline until the recession period of 1874, after St. Thomas' cemetery had been closed.

Related Sources

As was noted above, a complete set of parish records survives for St. Thomas' Anglican Church over the period that the cemetery was used. Parish records began to be maintained with some degree of regularity among Anglican, Methodist, Presbyterian, and Roman Catholic congregations in Belleville in the 1820s, but the completeness of parish records from other denominations besides the Anglicans is limited or the records are just beginning to be studied.

The full set of parish registers for St. Thomas' from 1821 to 1900 was transcribed from microfilm copies held at the Anglican Church Archives. These registers were scrutinized and checked twice for precision of transcription as well as document accuracy, following the method of Drake (1974). A second Anglican congregation, Christ Church, was formed in 1863, resulting in a significant drop in baptisms at St. Thomas'. Consequently, parish records for Christ Church congregation were collected for the period 1863 to 1900. The personal information contained in the parish records is quite comprehensive with the exception of causes of death, which are recorded for only 12% of all burial records. In addition, information has been collected from city directories dating from 1860 to 1885, Government of Canada Sessional Papers dating from 1871 to 1904, newspaper articles and obituaries from Belleville for the period 1857 to 1900, and newspaper articles from Kingston for the period 1810 to 1848. After the failure of three local newspapers in the 1820s and 1830s, *The Belleville Intelligencer* was founded in 1834 and continues to this day, although complete, archived copies of the newspaper only date as early as 1857. Copies of decennial censuses for Belleville (and the two bordering townships of Sidney and Thurlow) were obtained for the years 1851 (but the 1851 census is incomplete), 1861, 1871, and 1881. These censuses have also been transcribed and some preliminary analyses have been completed (Saunders and Sawchuk, 1995; Saunders et al., 1995a; Vanderlinden, 1995).

A detailed history of the first Methodist Church in Belleville (later to become the United Church) has been written (Lamb, 1990), as well as shorter histories of

St. Andrew's Presbyterian Church (Boyce, 1978) and St. Thomas' (Bellestedt, 1969). Copies of vestry minutes dating to the beginning of the parish also survive.

Personal historical accounts include the compiled letters of William Hutton (Boyce, 1972), as well as the writings and letters of Susanna Moodie, a noted English emigrant to Upper Canada who lived in Belleville from 1840 to the 1870s (Moodie, 1852, 1853; Ballstadt et al., 1985, 1993). There are also accounts and surviving papers of a number of other successful and distinguished figures from Belleville, including members of parliament, lawyers, doctors, businessmen, and a former prime minister of Canada (see, for example, Canniff, 1869; Fryer, 1983; Godfrey and Godfrey, 1991; Boyce, 1992). The Archives of Ontario also holds copies of estate records for some of the early Belleville doctors, but these have not been examined as yet by our research group (Connor, 1993).

RESULTS

Demographic Findings: Previous and Current

The ideal study is a comparison of calculations of demographic characteristics from the St. Thomas' skeletal sample to those determined from the historical documents. In skeletal samples, reliability of reconstruction is tied to quantity and quality of bone preservation, as well as to the precision and accuracy of methods of sex and age at death determination. It has already been demonstrated that the St. Thomas' sample is so well preserved as to provide one of the best historical examples of skeletal reconstruction (Saunders et al., 1995a). Methods of sex and age determination are moderated in more complex ways by preservation quality. In the St. Thomas' sample, all subadult skeletons could be aged from teeth or long bones, and fully 86% could be assessed by means of dental development, currently the most appropriate method for chronological age estimation (Saunders et al., 1995a; Saunders, 2000). For the adults, ages have been estimated from the average of two morphological methods (pubic symphysis metamorphosis and auricular surface metamorphosis), while ideally, a broad series of methods should be applied (Saunders et al., 1992; Bedford et al., 1993; Houck et al., 1996). Certain aging techniques are inappropriate to this sample (i.e., dental wear), while analyses have not yet been completed for some other methods (i.e., histological) (Saunders et al., 1995a).

Morphological changes at the symphyseal face of the pubic bone (anterior cartilaginous joint where the two hip bones meet) have received a great amount of attention in North America. The method has been seen as the most reliable for adult age estimation, although there are clearly limitations with applying it to older adults (Meindl and Russell, 1998). Each pubic symphysis was scored according to the Suchey-Brooks standards (Suchey and Katz, 1986; Brooks and Suchey, 1990), and photographs and dental stone casts were also prepared from each skeleton. The joint surface alters from a deeply ridged and horizontally furrowed system to the gradual buildup of bone over the dorsal and then ventral parts, which later break down. The auricular surface of the hip bone (the iliac side of the sacroiliac joint) also exhibits systematic age-related changes, which, while

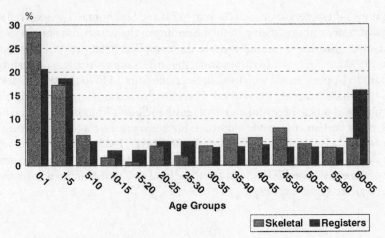

Figure 5.4. Comparisons by age group of skeletal and parish record samples in the St. Thomas' Anglican Church cemetery sample.

demonstrating senescent changes into the sixth decade, is more complex and often more difficult to score. The joint surface changes from a billowed, developing joint surface to one more coarsely granulated in appearance. In late metamorphosis there is a change from a smooth, dense face to one of increasingly degenerative irregularity (Meindl and Russell, 1998). Proponents of this method point out that intrasample seriation is necessary for approximating true age distributions more closely.

Initial comparisons of the skeletal and parish record samples for broad demographic categories, such as adult sex ratios and adult to subadult ratios, were encouraging (Saunders et al., 1991). But when a comparison is made of five-year-age categories of subadult and adult age estimates, it is clear that the skeletal sample has an excess of infants compared to the parish records and a deficiency of elderly adults (Figure 5.4). In addition, using the two combined morphological aging methods, the skeletal sample has fewer young adults but more middle-aged adults than the parish records. Consquently, the skeletal sample age distribution by present criteria does not adequately reflect the age distribution of all individuals buried in the cemetery.[6] If only the pubic symphysis aging method is used for adult age estimates, the observable sample decreases substantially and the proportions of young adults are overestimated in the skeletal sample, while middle-aged and old adults are severely underestimated.

Early on in the St. Thomas' project we decided to focus on the infant category since infant mortality is accepted by demographers as a proxy measure for a community's social and sanitary conditions. Furthermore, the magnitude of infant mortality, defined as the number of deaths under one year per 1,000 live births, is independent of the age structure of the population, allowing for demographic comparisons in populations experiencing migration. The greater proportion of infants in the

[6] In fact, exact ages at death are reported for 92% of all burial entries (Saunders et al., 1995a).

skeletal sample might be explained by a bias in excavation and recovery. This is surprising since infants are typically lacking from archaeological sites because of poor preservation or imperfect excavation techniques (Saunders, 1992). However, in the St. Thomas' case, it appears that the excavation selectively recovered more infants from the latter part of the 53-year time period. This is not surprising since 67% of all burials (and 71% of all infant burials) took place after the midpoint of the cemetery interval, or after 1848.

Despite the differences in the proportions of total infants in the two skeletal and parish record samples, the proportion of neonates (≤ 28 days) and postneonates (>28 days, <1 year) is the same in the two sources (Herring et al., 1991). Postneonatal mortality predominates in both data sets, indicating the greater impact of environmental factors, such as poor sanitation and poor nutrition on infant mortality. Our analysis of the dates of death from the burial records also showed that infant deaths clustered in the summer months when the risks of the weanling diarrhea complex were highest (Herring et al., 1991; Saunders et al., 1995a). A further, more detailed examination of the distribution of infant ages at death in the skeletal sample, by month, is representative of all infants listed in the burial register (Herring et al., 1994; Saunders et al., 1995b). In this case, a demographic method was applied to the two data sets for inferring breast-feeding and weaning practices (Katzenberg et al., 1996). Both the skeletal and burial record samples indicated that mothers of St. Thomas' parish were breast-feeding their babies and that the weaning process began around five to seven months of age for many infants.

Infant mortality rates (IMR) cannot be calculated from skeletal samples because the total numbers of births are not known. Certainly, little is known about the health of infants and children in Upper Canada beyond what can be gleaned from letters and diaries (Siegel, 1984; Thornton et al., 1987; Vanderlinden, 1995; Duffin, 1997). Infant mortality rates in nineteenth-century Europe and North America are high, ranging from 94/1,000 to 250/1,000 (Hibbs, 1916; Swedlund, 1990), although levels fluctuated considerably in industrial nations in the latter half of the nineteenth century depending upon varying ecological conditions.

In the case of St. Thomas', the number of live births can be derived from baptismal records for the same period for which infant deaths are recorded. But while baptisms are treated as proxies for births, large lapses of time between births and baptisms are common in parish records. In the St. Thomas' sample, 95% of baptisms have separate birth date information and of these, 70% were baptized in their first year of life. Preliminary calculations of IMRs showed no differences in the rates for males and females (as was also suggested for raw counts of burials), but IMRs appeared to increase dramatically from the first to the second half of the cemetery interval (Saunders et al., 1995b). If valid, these increases could be due to continually deteriorating local conditions in Belleville throughout the century.

A recent, more detailed investigation of infant mortality in the latter half of the time period determined that IMRs based on the raw data from the parish registers are underestimates because counting all recorded baptisms as births inflates the calculated number of births. There is also underreporting of the actual number of infant deaths in the parish records (Sawchuk et al., n.d.). When adjusted IMRs were

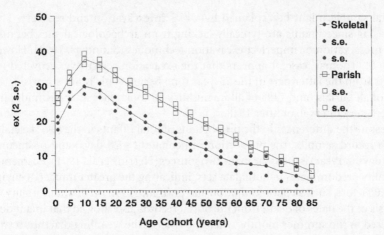

Figure 5.5. Initial life expectancy estimates from St. Thomas' Anglican Church parish records and skeletal sample.

calculated, they were found to be comparable to those reported for other American and Canadian communities of the time (average value from 1856 to 1875 is 143.5 infant deaths per 1,000 births), though perhaps in the lower part of the range.

Studies of overall mortality began with calculations of life expectancy in the skeletal and parish record samples. The overall mortality profile of the community was based on period life expectancy estimates following the methodology of Chiang (1984). The advantage of the Chiang method is that it allows for the computation of the standard error of the q_x and e_x columns of the life table, which are critical when dealing with the small sample sizes encountered with skeletal studies. The skeletal and parish record life expectancies at birth (e_0) are significantly different from one another, with the skeletal results depicting a grimmer life course (21 years for the skeletal sample and 26.5 years for the records (Saunders et al., 1995a) (Figure 5.5)). Both sets of data show higher survivorship in the early age groups and lower survivorship in the older categories. Underestimating adult age is clearly one source of error in the skeletal sample (as shown by Figure 5.4), but this cannot be the case for the records. Another source of error in skeletal samples is the exclusion of indeterminately aged adults, and this can also have a significant effect on the calculation of e_0 (Jackes, 1992). Fifty-four adults from the skeletal sample were of indeterminate age and had not been included in the original e_0 estimate. These individuals were proportionately distributed into the sample based on the estimated age distribution of the older (50+) age intervals of the initially analyzed sample. When this was done, e_0 increased to 24.2 years (Sawchuk et al., n.d.).

Another factor that affects the calculation of life expectancy is population growth. Without the knowledge of growth rates, be it through births and/or migration, any estimate of mortality is highly suspect and should be treated with a high degree of caution. As Sattenspeil and Harpending (1983) and Johansson and Horowitz (1986) have shown, skeletal ages reveal fertility better than mortality. The strategy employed here is to utilize the parish registers as well as the nominative census to get at a "reasonable" measure of mortality, using this as our benchmark to evaluate how the skeletal sample compares.

In the St. Thomas' case it is possible to estimate a rate of increase from completed census returns available for the latter part of the cemetery interval. The annual rate of change was calculated on the basis of the number of people present at the different census points following the method of Barclay (Barclay, 1958) ($r = 0.0261$). When this estimated rate of change was applied to the skeletal sample, life expectancy increased to 35 years (Sawchuk et al., n.d.). One only has to refer back to the previous discussion on population size increase in Belleville over the century to see why the increase is so substantial.

Meanwhile, detailed evaluations of life expectancy were carried out on the parish records for the latter half of the cemetery interval. Estimates of the overall mortality profile of the community were based on period life expectancy estimates following the Chiang method referred to above (1984). A significant contribution to overall mortality can derive from infant mortality. As described above, we adopted two strategies for reassessment of infant mortality. The first involves recomputing infant mortality rates using only those baptisms that took place within one year of birth, since late baptisms typically reflect the reporting of only surviving children and will decrease the estimate of infant mortality. The strategy employed to address underreporting of infant deaths is based on the widely accepted biometric method developed by Bourgeois-Pichat (1946, 1950, 1952).

Assuming that the issue of underestimation of the infant mortality rate was resolved, the point values of e_0 for males and females from the parish records for the period 1856–1875 ranged from 33.5 years to 44.3 years (there were increases over the two decades in this period). These values are quite comparable to those reported for a variety of American and Canadian cities and regions for a similar time period.

In addition to the birth rate, a population can also grow through migration. We have a number of indications of the importance of migration to Belleville from several sources. Certainly, historians have discussed the importance of population turnover in Canadian communities throughout the nineteenth century (Gagan, 1981; Osborne and Swainson, 1988; Gentilcore, 1993). Our examination of census returns for Belleville shows that substantial numbers of individuals do not persist from one census to the next (Vanderlinden, 1995; Beckett et al., 1998). In addition, our preliminary attempts to reconstitute St. Thomas' families by linking vital events from the parish records and examining census data were hampered by significant movements of people into and out of the community.

The Anglican population pyramids for 1861 to 1881 conform to the growing population model with its broad base in the younger age groups, which tapers off with increasing age (Saunders et al., 1995a; Sawchuk et al., n.d.). A statistical evaluation of the age structure revealed that the male composition remained stable over the three census points (Likelihood Ratio Chi Square = 33.91, $p = .284$), while the female composition underwent significant change over the two periods (Likelihood Ratio Chi Square = 76.64, $p = .00001$). Closer inspection of the growth rates for females and males aged 20 to 50 revealed some basic similarities. However, there are pronounced increases in the growth rate among women aged 15 to 19 as well as 30 to 34. An examination of the nominative census returns shows that these increases can be attributed to influx of women seeking work in Belleville as household servants, dressmakers, and milliners.

Further life expectancy calculations were run for the skeletal remains based on a differential growth rate for the population under 15 years compared to those 15 years and older in order to take into account increased growth fueled by immigration. A life table for the skeletal sample was calculated with a correction factor to accommodate natural increase noted earlier following the methodology of Henneberg and Steyn (1994). When this was done, life expectancy rose to 38 years and showed a closer fit to the survivorship distribution obtained from the parish records (Sawchuk et al., n.d.). Depending on the chosen rate of growth at given age intervals, the skeletal estimates of life expectancy, at least in the latter part of the cemetery interval, could range anywhere from 38 to 46 years. In sum, it is clear from these investigations that bone preservation, biological techniques of the analysis of skeletal remains, and demographic forces all influence efforts to evaluate the demographic structure of St. Thomas' parish from skeletal remains and, indeed, of any population.

With the parish records we have a good idea of the population at risk, and we have a good idea of the number of births as well as immigration and derive a "best estimate" of vital rates. We are comparing a skeletal sample of all of the deaths over a limited 53-year period to reasonable estimates of population dynamics from the parish records.

DISCUSSION OF HEALTH INDEX

The St. Thomas' sample has a health score of 18.28, which represents 69.3 % of the possible maximum score. In the overall rankings of sites for percent maximum score, the St. Thomas' sample is 46 out of the total of 65 sites. This is 3.5 points below the median percent maximum score and 3.3 points below the mean, placing St. Thomas' below the average for all sites, although within one standard deviation of the mean. More surprisingly, the St. Thomas' sample has the second lowest percent maximum score of all of the samples of European origin.

The one site that would make the most appropriate comparison to St. Thomas' because of geographic proximity and the northwest European origins of the individuals is the Highland Park cemetery. The health index for Highland Park is 3 percentage points higher than that of St. Thomas'. Recognizing the general effect of socioeconomic levels on health, this is quite surprising, since the Highland Park skeletons represent inmates of the Monroe County poorhouse established in 1826 to give aid to paupers (Higgins and Sirianni, 1995). A major proportion of these included Irish, German, and other European immigrants who came to the United States with nothing and soon sought aid or shelter in the only available social welfare institutions. On the other hand, Higgins and Sirianni (1995) note that disease-specific mortality listed in a set of records dating from 1847 to 1850 for the Monroe County poorhouse does not differ considerably from that recorded for the greater Rochester area, except for a higher rate of deaths due to consumption. However, age-at-death profiles suggest that more poorhouse women were dying before age 40, while a greater proportion of Rochester women survived to older ages. This would lead us to infer that the age-adjusted health index from skeletal remains between nineteenth-century Belleville and Rochester might not differ dramatically if residents of the two communities were experiencing similar patterns of health and disease. Certainly, it is presently impossible to evaluate the significance of the magnitude of the differences between health indexes as calculated for this project. As an aggregate index it provides only relative comparisons.

But based on general historical comparisons, it seems likely that people in Belleville, as members of a smaller community than Rochester over the time period, would have fared better healthwise simply because of less severe effects of urbanization on health. We have evidence that socioeconomic levels among St. Thomas' parishioners were generally higher than those of other inhabitants of the town of Belleville and, probably, mid–nineteenth-century Rochester in general (Burke, 1994). Also, our demographic analyses have shown that the adjusted infant mortality rate increased over the latter half of the cemetery interval from 97.3/1,000 to 157/1,000 (Sawchuk et al., n.d.). Infant mortality rates, while high, are in the lower half of the full range reported for nineteenth-century communities. Life expectancy at birth from the 1850s through 1870s was also higher than 30 years.

Consequently, a more detailed consideration of the attributes and their scores in the index seems warranted. If Table 3.3 in Chapter 3 ("Health Index as a Percent of Maximum, Attribute Scores, and Person-Years Observed by Site") is examined, it can be seen that the St. Thomas' attribute scores for stature, anemia, bone infection, and trauma fall very close to or above their medians. Obviously, it is the scores for degenerative joint disease and less so for dental pathology and hypoplasia which affect the relatively low score of St. Thomas' among all sites.

Dental Pathology

A separate study of dental pathology in the St. Thomas' sample has been carried out (Saunders et al., 1997). In this case, caries rates and antemortem tooth loss rates were calculated for individuals and compared to a variety of historical samples. In addition, aggregate percentages of caries and antemortem tooth loss were examined for samples where individual rates were not calculated. The comparisons show that the St. Thomas' sample is closest to a British series (the Ashton-under-Lyne cemetery sample) in terms of occurrence of caries, particularly to a pre-1850 subgroup from this cemetery (Figure 5.6). Caries values reported for other historic British series are lower, but these skeletal samples date to earlier time periods, for example, the late eighteenth and early nineteenth century in the case of the Spitalfields sample. It is likely that these earlier groups represent individuals whose diets contained relatively low amounts of processed foods, such as refined sugars.

Except for one sample from New Orleans, caries values are much lower in the American historical samples. The eighteenth-century St. Peter's sample from New Orleans dates to an era and region with a highly cariogenic diet of cane sugar, cornmeal, fine flour, and molasses (Owsley et al., 1987). Yet, caries percentages in this group are still not as high as for the St. Thomas' or Ashton-under-Lyne samples.

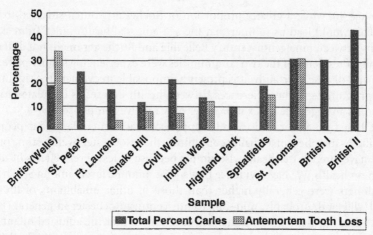

Figure 5.6. Intersample comparisons of total percent caries and antemortem tooth loss for a number of eighteenth- and nineteenth-century skeletal samples (see Saunders, De Vito, and Katzenberg, 1997).

This might be explained by a lower life expectancy in the New Orleans samples, who were urban slaves. Since caries rates increase with age, a mortality sample of individuals who died fairly young would show lower levels of caries.

The specific diets of the individuals from the Highland Park sample are not known, but the impact of a developing nineteenth-century cariogenic diet is thought to be present (Sutter, 1995). But diseased and missing tooth indices show that antemortem tooth loss, when added to caries rates, still does not exceed that for either the overall or the age-adjusted St. Thomas' sample. This suggests that there were real differences in the cariogenicity of the diets between the St. Thomas' and Highland Park people, with the St. Thomas' sample experiencing greater rates of disease. In fact, the attribute scores calculated for the quality of life index for these two samples are only .5 percentage points apart, reflecting the fact that the Highland Park score for dental pathology is also below the median for all samples or has relatively high rates of dental disease. However, the comparison also demonstrates how the index does, in fact, dampen the magnitude of differences between paired samples since a separate investigation has found it to be notable.

But what does this mean in terms of quality of life? It might be suggested that higher caries rates are reflective of middle- to higher-class individuals who had access to processed foods, such as the most highly refined flours and pastries from town and city bakeries. While during the Industrial Revolution in England the poor workers lived on treacle and bread, in North America the poor or rural farmers might be less likely to eat processed foods and get as much sugar because of their cost.

With dental disease, the risks to severely compromised health or even survival occur when chronic and severe infections track from the mouth through the facial network of veins to reach brain tissues, the heart, or other parts of the body (Calcagno and Gibson, 1995). Yet, particularly with recent populations, we would expect that tooth extraction would be the most common method used to arrest developing dental infections. While the recognition of the mechanisms of the spread of infection came quite late in the nineteenth century, dentists came quite early to provide responsive treatment to pain. Mr. G. V. N. Relyea, who was born in Albany, New York, in the early 1800s, attended lectures at the Albany Medical College and later studied dentistry for a year with a practicing dentist. Relyea settled in Belleville in 1843, where he practiced until 1874, commanding patient clients from a wide area. In published newspaper advertisements he offered to extract, restore, regularize, and replace teeth, to prepare dental plates and to treat periodontal disease (Saunders et al., 1997), but we do not know exactly who his patients were or what proportion of the population could afford to pay.

Hypoplasia

The St. Thomas' sample falls below the median, but just above the mean, for the distribution of attribute scores for hypoplasia. Of the eight European samples it ranks fifth for hypoplasia. While the statistics for the distribution of hypoplasia attribute scores place St. Thomas' in the upper 58%, it should be noted that the distribution is highly variable (S.D. = 24.59, 50% more than the next highest attribute S.D.) and highly skewed. The lowest value is 9.8 while the highest is 99.7, and more than half of the scores fall above 70. This means that a difference between sites of 10 percentage points for hypoplasia is not as significant as a smaller difference between sites for other attributes. Consequently, it can be said that St. Thomas' actually scores well for hypoplasia in comparison to the other sites. In addition, there are 16 sites which lack a hypoplasia attribute score, the highest number of missing values for any of the attributes. This lack of data must surely have some impact on the comparisons that can be drawn for this trait.

In a separate analysis we have examined published hypoplasia frequencies in a variety of historical samples dating from medieval times through the nineteenth century (Saunders and Keenleyside, 1999). The St. Thomas' sample fares well, with one of the lowest frequencies of hypoplasia of all sites at around 35%. Goodman and Rose (1990) have noted that expectations of hypoplasia prevalence for developed countries, where living conditions are good, are less than 10%. Previous work has shown that long bone growth sizes in children from the St. Thomas' sample are comparable to healthy twentieth-century children, suggesting that acute conditions, rather than chronic ones, were most often associated with the deaths of the children in the skeletal sample (Saunders et al., 1993). From these observations we would suggest that the low to moderate levels of hypoplasia in the St. Thomas' skeletal sample are consistent with a developing pioneer community, where the quantities of food were generally sufficient and chronic disease levels were relatively low but acute infectious diseases common.

Studies of the etiology of enamel hypoplasia have shown that a variety of both acute and chronic factors are implicated in the production of these defects (Goodman et al., 1989; May et al., 1993; Zhou and Corruccini, 1994). If acute infant and childhood infections were relatively common in Belleville (as discussed above), then certainly hypoplastic defects would be expected. It should be noted that a somewhat different picture might have resulted if deciduous tooth hypoplasias had been recorded for this sample.

Degenerative Joint Disease (DJD)

St. Thomas' scored the lowest of all sites in the entire sample for this attribute, receiving a score of 41.6. Since all attributes are contributing equally to the overall index, the DJD score should make quite a difference to the St. Thomas' percentage of maximum score. In fact, this score is so low compared to the rest of the distribution for DJD that it is a statistical outlier. Further scrutiny of the site scores for DJD shows that several sites scored 100%, indicating that there were no cases of degenerative joint disease in these samples. This seems surprising since it is the most pervasive of conditions to be found on bones. These observations lead us to suggest that the nature of the skeletal samples may affect the resultant attribute scores. Even though the quality of life index is age-adjusted, observations are aggregate, sampling only those skeletal cases from the original samples which could be age-estimated, and for which observations were made because the bony parts had survived burial and excavation. Since the St. Thomas' sample is so well preserved, it actually includes fairly complete observations on most bones and also includes a relatively good proportion of older adults whose ages *could* be estimated (although 54 were not so aged). This suggests that biased sampling might partly explain the very low attribute score (highest age-adjusted proportion) for degenerative joint disease for the St. Thomas' sample. That is, more older adults are preserved in the St. Thomas' sample than in many of the other archaeological samples so that degenerative joint disease is well represented (Figure 5.7).

The clinical literature identifies DJD as affected by a variety of predisposing factors. Climate and hormonal factors have been implicated (Hough and Sokoloff, 1989; Rogers and Waldron, 1995), but the mechanic stress of physical activity has been identified as the primary contributing factor to the development of DJD (Larsen, 1997). DJD is rarely found before the age of 30 years in urban, industrialized

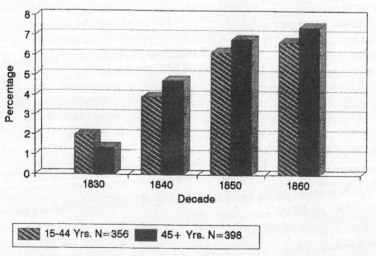

Figure 5.7. Deaths by decade for age groups over 15 years of age taken from parish records from St. Thomas' Anglican Church.

societies, but industrial laborers show patterns of articular degeneration that are directly related to their particular physical activities in the workplace. On the other hand, young adults and juveniles of some prehistoric societies show a high prevalence of DJD (Larsen, 1997). Was hard, physical labor common among the parishioners of St. Thomas' Church?

In the early years of pioneering in Upper Canada, life on small farms in cleared bush land was hard and required backbreaking effort from the entire family unit, men, women, and children. But by 1850, Belleville was a prosperous town of 5,000, and it had grown into a much larger rail and manufacturing center by the 1870s. Even in 1834, the settler William Hutton could write the following to his wife in Ireland, prior to her departure for Canada:

Do not encumber yourself with much. Everything can be had here reasonably. . . . I had not the most remote idea that this country had approached so far to civilization. The children as well as the ladies are most beautifully dressed in silks with their veils and parasols.

On the other hand, the various cottage industries and manufacturing activities of the town still demanded physical labor. Separate studies of the St. Thomas' skeletons showed that healed trauma of the upper limbs was common in the males (Jimenez, 1995), and males commonly showed moderate to severe bony changes at muscle attachment sites (Saunders and Sawchuk, 1995). Yet, we would emphasize that the burial sample is probably heterogeneous. A limited linking of 25% of the burial register names to the censuses indicates a diversity of male occupations at St. Thomas', from blacksmiths to barristers.

The domestic labor required of females was still demanding by the end of the nineteenth century. Even by the end of the 1870s, women on farms and in towns were still responsible for a great deal of the spinning, the sewing of most clothes, quilting of bedding, and fabricating of carpets and other floor coverings. The lack of refrigeration meant daily preparations of all meal requirements, including killing and plucking of fowl, cleaning and preparation of raw foods, baking of bread and pastries, and the churning of butter. Laundry required a major effort, and housecleaning included the preparation of lamps and mattress stuffing. On the other hand, domestic female servants constituted a significant component of Belleville's mid-nineteenth-century community (Saunders and Sawchuk, 1995). Without full family reconstitutions derived from marriages, baptisms, burials, and censuses (as well as municipal assessment rolls), it is not possible to know which individuals benefited from having servants to do much of the work.

While people in this pioneering community probably worked their bodies harder than the average twentieth-century urbanite, it is unlikely that physical labor would have been more strenuous for them than for some of the hunting and gathering peoples examined elsewhere in this volume. The relationship between DJD and physical activity is neither simple nor straightforward (Waldron, 1994). We would argue that sample composition (the presence of larger proportions of older adults) in the St. Thomas' sample is a major contributing factor to the attribute score for DJD.

Implications

It has been shown that a combination of several age-estimation techniques for skeletons usually produces age estimates that are closer to chronological age than are single techniques (Meindl and Russell, 1998; Jackes, 2000). Alternative statistical techniques are now being explored to deal with and compensate for the problems of adult underestimation and the influence of reference standards (Paine, 1997; Milner et al., 2000; Jackes, 2000). Nevertheless, it appears from our demographic explorations of the St. Thomas' skeletal sample that biased exclusion of indeterminately aged adults is a significant problem. Most of these unaged adults are older. The skeletons of the elderly (as is usually the case with infant skeletons) are often totally lost due to poor preservation. This suggests that what is also needed are better age-estimation techniques for fragmentary remains. Techniques developed for teeth and microscopic sections of bone show promise. Jackes (2000) has also suggested that in group comparisons, biologically aged, rather than chronologically aged, distributions should be compared. But even if developed laboratory techniques and enhanced statistical approaches solve the problems of distributional evaluations for these methods, if the biological aging process has altered over the millennia or even the centuries, then we will still face problems.

Simple issues of sampling are more crucial than refined techniques of biological aging. It has been shown that skeletal samples of less than 100 cannot accurately estimate mean age-at-death of a sample, regardless of whether it reflects the death rate, the birth rate, or migration (Hoppa, 1996; Hoppa and Saunders, 1998). To overcome these problems, the quality of life index is calculated as an aggregate or site-specific method which records all information for skeletons *for which age-at-death is available*. As was noted above, if a skeletal sample is lacking a large proportion of adults (or other age groups) simply because of problems with assigning them to even a general age category, then resultant attribute scores are affected.

CONCLUSIONS

Our investigations of St. Thomas' parish and cemetery have shown that mortality rates, especially for infants, did not improve over the period of greatest cemetery use, from 1850 to 1874. While this was a time of continental and regional prosperity, the failure to deal with social and sanitary conditions affecting the opportunities for acute infections concomitant with the developing urbanization of Belleville meant a continued rise in morbidity rates just before and after the cemetery closed. But this picture is derived from historical and demographic analyses independent of the skeletal analysis, since demographic calculations require knowledge of the living population and not just the dead.

Some of the skeletal investigations support the interpretation of the importance of acute versus chronic infections (the study of subadult long bone growth) and others the significance of environmental conditions affecting infant morbidity and mortality (investigations of weaning).

The skeletal variables identified as significant contributions to the quality of life index for St. Thomas' may fit with the conclusion that healthwise, life in the mid-nineteenth century was not measurably better for the middle to upper class at St. Thomas'. Enamel hypoplasias appear to be more common than in modern, healthy industrial populations, and high dental caries, because of its direct relation to foods eaten, may actually be an accurate portrayal of the dietary habits of a wealthier class. Interpretations of the relationship of degenerative joint disease to prosperity are even more tenuous and complex. Of course, none of these observations takes into account the heterogeneity (intragroup variability) of the frailties expressed in the skeletons from St. Thomas' (see Milner et al., 2000). The lack of improvement in health at St. Thomas', or even the town of Belleville, may coincidentally reflect a broader North American phenomenon that may be related to urbanization, but it is also uniquely reflective of the church and town alone. Current research efforts on the St. Thomas' data are directed toward investigating individual and intragroup expressions of stress.

REFERENCES

Akenson, D. (1984) *The Irish in Ontario*. Kingston: McGill-Queen's University Press.

Atack, J., and Passell, P. (1994) *A New Economic View of American History*. New York: W. W. Norton, 1994.

Ballstadt, C., Hopkins, E., and Peterman, M., eds. (1985) *Susanna Moodie: Letters of a Lifetime*. Toronto: University of Toronto Press.

(1993) *Letters of Love and Duty: The Correspondence of Susanna and John Moodie*. Toronto: University of Toronto Press.

Barclay, G. W. (1958) *Techniques of Population Analysis*. New York: Wiley.

Barkin, R., and Gentles, I. (1990) Death in Victorian Toronto, 1850–1899. *Urban History Review/Revue d'histoire urbaine* 19, 14–29.

Baron, W. R. (1992) Historical climate records from the northeastern United States, 1640–1900. In *Climate Since A.D. 1500*, ed. R. S. Bradley and P. D. Jones, pp. 74–91. London: Routledge.

Beaujot, R. P., and McQuillan, K. (1986) The social effects of demographic change: Canada, 1851–1981. *Journal of Canadian Studies* 21, 57–69.

Beckett, K., Crinnion, C., Farmer, T., Neill, C., and Pratte, D. (1998) The Irish population of 19th century Belleville: "Stepping stone" migrants? Paper presented at the Annual Meeting, Canadian Association for Physical Anthropology, Calgary, Alberta.

Bedford, M.E., Russell, K.E., Lovejoy, C.O., Meindl, R.S., Simpson S.W., and Stuart-Macadam, P.L. (1993) A test of the multifactorial aging method using skeletons with known ages-at-death from the Grant Collection. *American Journal of Physical Anthropology* 91, 287–297.

Bell, E. L. (1994) *Vestiges of Mortality & Remembrance: A Bibliography on the Historical Archaeology of Cemeteries*. Metuchen, N.J.: The Scarecrow Press, Inc.

Bell, J. T. (1876) *Epidemic Disease and their Prevention in Relation to the Water Supply of the Town of Belleville*. Archives of Ontario, Pamphlet no. 29.

Bellstedt, I. (1969) *St. Thomas' Anglican Church, 1818–1968: The Parish Story*. Belleville: Ontario.

Best, G. (1979) *Mid-Victorian Britain 1851–75*. London: Fontana Press.

Bilson, G. (1975) Cholera in Upper Canada, 1832. *Ontario History* 67(1), 15–30.

(1977) The first epidemic of Asiatic cholera in Lower Canada, 1832. *Medical History* 21(4), 411–433.

Bliss, M. (1991) *Plague: A Story of Smallpox in Montreal*. Toronto: HarperCollins Publishers.

Bouchard, G., and Roy, R. (1991) Fécondité et alphabetisation au Saguenay et au Québec (XIXe–XXe siècles). *Annales de démographie historique* 1991, 173–201.

Bourgeois-Pichat, J. (1952) Essai sur la mortalité "biologique" de l'homme. *Population* 7, 381–394.

Boyce, B. D. (1992) *The Rebels of Hastings*. Toronto: University of Toronto Press.

Boyce, G. (1967) *Historic Hastings*. Belleville: Hastings County Council.

(1972) *Hutton of Hastings*. Belleville: Hastings County Council.

(1978) *The St. Andrew's Chronicles: An Account of Presbyteriansim before 1879 in the Belleville-Hastings County-Quinte Area*. Belleville: St. Andrew's Presbyterian Church.

(1992) *Eldorado: Ontario's First Gold Rush*. Toronto: Natural Heritage/Natural History Inc.

Brooks, S.T., and Suchey, J.M. (1990). Skeletal age determination based on the os pubis: A comparison of the Acsadi-Nemeskeri and Suchey-Brooks methods. *Human Evolution* 5, 227–238.

Burke, S. D. A. (1994) The Anglicans of Belleville, 1861–1881: Defining the population at risk. M.Sc. Research Paper, University of Toronto.

Calcagno, J. M., and Gibson, K. R. (1995) Selective compromise: Evolutionary trends and mechanisms. In *Advances in Dental Anthropology*, ed. Kelley, M. A., and Larsen, C. S., pp. 59–76. New York: Wiley-Liss.

Canniff, W. (1972) *The Settlement of Upper Canada*. Toronto, 1869; reprint, Belleville, Ont.: Mika Silk Screening.

Chapman, L., and Brown, D. M. (1996) *The Canada Land Inventory. Report No. 3: The Climates of Canada for Agriculture*. Toronto: Department of Forestry and Rural Development.

Chapman, L., and Putnam, D. (1984) *The Physiography of Southern Ontario*. Toronto: Geological Survey of Ontario, Ministry of Natural Resources.

Cheney, R. A. (1984) Seasonal aspects of infant and childhood mortality: Philadelphia, 1865–1920. *Journal of Interdisciplinary History* 14, 561–585.

Chiang, C. L. (1984) *The Life Table and Its Applications*. Malabar, Fl.: Robert E. Krieger Publishing Company.

Condran, G.A., and Crimmins, E. (1979) A description and evaluation of mortality data in Federal Census: 1850–1900. *Historical Methods* 12, 1–23.

Connor, J. J. (1993) Estate records and the history of medicine in Ontario. *Canadian Bulletin of Medical History* 10, 97–114.

Cook, E. R., Stahlem, D. W., and Cleaveland, M. K. (1992) Dendroclimatic evidence from eastern North America. In *Climate since A.D. 1500*, ed. Bradley, R. S., and Jones, P. D., pp. 331–348. London: Routledge.

Cook, M. L., Gibbs, L., and Spence, M. W. (1985) Age and sex identification in the Stirrup Court Cemetery. *Kewa* (The Newsletter of the London Chapter of the Ontario Archaeological Society) 1985, 3–19.

Corbett, M. E., and Moore, W. J. (1976) Distribution of dental caries in ancient British populations. IV: The 19th century. *Caries Research* 10, 401–414.

Cowan, H. I. (1928) *British Emigration to North America 1783–1837*. Toronto: University of Toronto Press.

Crimmins, E., and Condran, G. A. (1983) Mortality variation in U.S. cities in 1900. A two-level explanation by cause of death underlying factors. *Social Science of History* 7, 31–60.

Cybulski, J. S. (1988) Skeletons in the wall of Old Quebec. *Northeast Historical Archeology* 17, 61–84.

Drake, M. (1974) *Historical Demography: Problems and Prospects*. Milton Keynes, Eng.: The Open University Press.

Duffin, J. (1997) Census versus medical daybooks: A comparison of two sources on mortality in nineteenth-century Ontario. *Continuity and Change* 12, 199–219.

Elia, R. J., and Wesolowsky, A. B. (1991) *Archaeological Excavations at the Uxbridge Almshouse Burial Ground in Uxbridge, Massachusetts.* BAR International Series 564.

Elliot, B. (1988) *Irish Migrants in the Canadas: A New Approach.* Montreal: McGill-Queen's University Press.

Ellis, E. (1977) *Emigrants from Ireland, 1847–1852: State-Aided Emigration Schemes from Crown Estates in Ireland.* Baltimore: Genealogical Pub. Co.

Emery, G., and McQuillan, K. (1988) A case study approach to Ontario mortality history. *Canadian Studies in Population* 15, 135–175.

Fallis, A. M. (1984) Malaria in the 18th and 19th centuries in Ontario. *Canadian Bulletin of Medical History* 1(1), 25–38.

Fogel, M., Tuross, N., and Owsley, D. W. (1989) Nitrogen isotope tracers of human lactation in modern and archaeological populations. Carnegie Institution, Annual Report of the Director; Geophysical Laboratory.

Fryer, M. B. (1983) *John Walden Meyers: Loyalist Spy.* Toronto: Dundurn Press.

Gagan, D. (1981) *Hopeful Travellers: Families, Land and Social Change in Mid-Victorian Peel County, Canada West.* Toronto: University of Toronto Press.

Gagan, R. R. (1989) Mortality patterns and public health in Hamilton, Canada, 1900–14. *Urban History Review* 17, 161–175.

Gentilcore, R. L., ed. (1993) *Historical Atlas of Canada,* vol. 2. Toronto: University of Toronto Press.

Godfrey, C. M. (1968) *The Cholera Epidemics in Upper Canada, 1832–1866.* Toronto: Secombe House.

Godfrey, S., and Godfrey, J. (1991) *Burn This Gossip: The True Story of George Benjamin of Belleville, Canada's First Jewish Member of Parliament, 1857–1863.* Toronto: The Duke & George Press.

Goodman, A. H., Martin, D. L., Perry, A., Martinez, C., Chavez, A., and Dobney, K. (1989) The effect of nutritional supplementation on permanent tooth development and morphology. *American Journal of Physical Anthropology* 78, 229. [Abstract]

Goodman, A. H., and Rose, J. C. (1990) Assessment of systemic physiological perturbations from dental enamel hypoplasias and associated histological structures. *Yearbook of Physical Anthropology* 33, 59–110.

Grauer, A. L. ed. (1995) *Bodies of Evidence: Reconstructing History through Skeletal Analysis.* New York: Wiley-Liss.

Grauer, A. L., and McNamara, E. M. (1995) A piece of Chicago's past: Exploring subadult mortality in the Dunning poorhouse cemetery. In *Bodies of Evidence: Reconstructing History through Skeletal Analysis,* ed. Grauer, A. L., pp. 91–103. New York: Wiley-Liss.

Guillet, E. C. (1937) *The Great Migration: Atlantic Crossing by Sailing Ship 1770–1860.* Toronto: T. Nelson.

Haines, M. R. (1994) *Estimated Life Tables for the United States, 1850–1900.* Cambridge: National Bureau of Economic Research.

Henneberg, M., and Steyn, M. (1994) Preliminary report on the paleodemography of the K2 and Mapungubwe populations (South Africa). *Human Biology* 66, 105–120.

Herring, D. A., Saunders, S.R., and Boyce, G. (1991) Bones and burial registers: Infant mortality in a 19th-century cemetery from Upper Canada. *Northeast Historical Archaeology* 20, 54–70.

Herring, D. A., Saunders, S. R., and Katzenberg, M. A. (1994) Investigating the weaning process in a cemetery sample from 19th-century Upper Canada. *American Journal of Physical Anthropology Supplement* 18, 106. [Abstract]

(1998) Investigating the weaning process in past populations. *American Journal of Physical Anthropology* 105, 425–439.

Hibbs, H. H. (1916) *Infant Mortality: Its Relation to Social and Industrial Conditions.* New York: Russel Sage Foundation.

Higgins, R. L., and Sirianni, J. E. (1995) An assessment of health and mortality of nineteenth century Rochester, New York using historic records and the Highland Park skeletal collection. In *Bodies of Evidence: Reconstructing History through Skeletal Analysis,* ed. Grauer, A. L., pp. 121–138. New York: Wiley-Liss.

Hoppa, R. D. (1996) Representativeness and bias in cemetery samples: Implications for paleodemographic reconstructions of past populations. Ph.D. dissertation, Department of Anthropology, McMaster University, Canada.

Hoppa, R. D., and Saunders, S. R. (1998) The MAD legacy: How meaningful is mean age-at-death in skeletal samples. *International Journal of Anthropology* 13(3), 1–14.

Houck, M. M., Ubelaker, D. H., Owsley, D., Craig, E., Grant, W. E., Fram, R., Woltansky, T., and Sandness, K. (1996) The role of forensic anthropology in the recovery and analysis of Branch Davidian compound victims: Assessing the accuracy of age estimations. *Journal of Forensic Sciences* 41, 796–801.

Hough, A. J., and Sokoloff, L. (1989) Pathology of osteoarthritis. In *Arthritis and Allied Conditions,* 11th ed., ed. McCarthy, D. J., pp. 1571–1594. Philadelphia: Lea & Febiger.

Jackes, M. (1992) Paleodemography: Problems and techniques. In *The Skeletal Biology of Past Peoples: Advances in Research Methods,* ed. Saunders, S. R., and Katzenberg, M. A., pp. 189–224. New York: Wiley-Liss.

——— (2000) Building the bases for paleodemographic analysis: Adult age and sex determination. In *The Skeletal Biology of Past Peoples: Advances in Research Methods,* 2d ed., ed. Katzenberg, M. A., and Saunders, S. R., pp. 417–466. New York: Wiley-Liss, Inc.

Jimenez, S. B. (1991) Analysis of patterns of injury and disease in an hisotric skeletal sample from Belleville, Ontario. Master's thesis, Department of Anthropology, McMaster University, Canada.

Johansson, S., and Horowitz, S. (1986) Estimating mortality in skeletal populations: The influence of the growth rate on the interpretation of levels and trends during the transition to agriculture. *American Journal of Physical Anthropology* 71, 233–250.

Katzenberg, M. A., Herring, D. A., and Saunders, S. R. (1996) Weaning and infant mortality: Evaluating the skeletal evidence. *Yearbook of Physical Anthropology* 39, 177–199.

Katzenberg, M. A., and Pfeiffer, S. (1995) Nitrogen isotope evidence for weaning age in a nineteenth century Canadian skeletal sample. In *Bodies of Evidence: Reconstructing History through Skeletal Analysis,* ed. Grauer, A. L., pp. 221–235. New York: Wiley-Liss.

Lamb, J. W. (1990) *Bridging the Years: A History of Bridge Street United/Methodist Church, Belleville, 1815–1990.* Winfield, B.C.: Wood Lake Books.

Larsen, C. S. (1997) *Bioarchaeology: Interpreting Behavior from the Human Skeleton.* Cambridge: Cambridge University Press.

Lee, R. D. (1991) Method and models for analyzing historical series births, deaths, and marriages. In *Population Patterns in the Past,* ed. Lee, R. D., pp. 337–370. New York: Academic Press.

MacDonagh, O. (1961) *A Pattern of Government Growth: Passenger Acts and Their Enforcement 1800–1860.* London: MacGibbon & Kee.

MacKay, D. (1990) *Flight from Famine: The Coming of the Irish to Canada.* Toronto: McClelland and Stewart.

MacMurchy, H. (1910) *Infant Mortality: Special Report.* Toronto: L. K. Cameron.

May R. L., Goodman, A. H., and Meindl, R. S. (1993) Response of bone and enamel formation to nutritional supplementation and morbidity among malnourished Guatemalan children. *American Journal of Physical Anthropology* 92, 37–51.

McKillop, H., Marshall, S., Boyce, G. E., and Saunders, S. R. (1989) Excavations at St. Thomas' Church, Belleville, Ontario: A 19th-century cemetery. Paper presented to the Ontario Archaeology Society Symposium, London, Ontario.

Meeker, E. (1972) The improving health of the United States, 1800–1915. *Explorations in Economic History* 9, 353–373.

Meindl, R. S., and Russell, K. F. (1998) Recent advances in method and theory in paleodemography. *Annual Reviews of Anthropology* 27, 375–399.

Mika, N., and Mika, H. (1986) *Belleville, the Seat of Hastings County.* Belleville: Mika Publishing Co.

Milner, G. R., Wood, J. W., and Boldsen, J. L. (2000) Paleodemography. In *The Skeletal Biology of Past Peoples: Advances in Research Methods,* 2d ed., ed. Katzenberg, M. A., and Saunders, S. R., pp. 467–498. New York: Wiley-Liss, Inc.

Molleson, T. I. (1995) Rates of aging in the eighteenth century. In *Grave Reflections: Portraying the Past through Cemetery Studies,* ed. Saunders, S. R., and Herring, D. A., pp. 199–222. Toronto: Canadian Scholar's Press.

Molleson, T. I., and Cox, M. (1993) *The Spitalfields Project,* vol. 2: *The Anthropology, The Middling Sort.* CBA Research Reports 86. York: Council for British Archaeology.

Moodie, S. (1970, 1852) *Roughing It in the Bush: Of Forest Life in Canada.* Toronto: McClelland and Stewart.

—— (1989, 1853) *Life in the Clearings versus the Bush.* Toronto: McClelland and Stewart, 1853, New Canadian Library Edition, 1989.

Nawrocki, S. P. (1995) Taphonomic processes in historic cemeteries. In *Bodies of Evidence: Reconstructing History through Skeletal Analysis,* ed. Grauer, A. L., pp. 49–66. New York: Wiley-Liss.

Osborne, B. S., and Swainson, D. (1988) *Kingston: Building on the Past.* Westport, Ont.: Butternut Press.

Owsley, D. W., Orser, Jr., C. E., Mann, R. W., Moore-Jansen, P. H., and Montgomery, R. L. (1987) Demography and pathology of an urban slave population from New Orleans. *American Journal of Physical Anthropology* 74, 185–197.

Paine, R. R. (1997) *Integrating Archaeological Demography: Multidisciplinary Approaches to Prehistoric Population.* Center for Archaeological Investigations, Occasional Paper No. 24, Southern Illinois University at Carbondale.

Pfeiffer, S., Dudar, J. C., and Austin, S. (1989) Prospect Hill: Skeletal remains from a 19th-century Methodist cemetery, Newmarket, Ontario. *Northeast Historical Archeology* 18, 29–48.

Pfeiffer, S., and Williamson, R. W. (1991) *Snake Hill: An Investigation of a Military Cemetery from the War of 1812.* Toronto: Dundurn Press.

Pope, C. L. (1992) Adult mortality in America before 1900: A view from family histories. In *Strategic Factories in Nineteenth Century American Economic History,* ed. Goldin, C., and Rockoff, H., pp. 267–296. Chicago: University of Chicago Press.

Preston, S. H., and Haines, M. R. (1991) *The Fatal Years: Child Mortality in Late Nineteenth-Century America.* Princeton, N. J.: Princeton University Press.

Putnam, D. F. (1952) *Canadian Regions: A Geography of Canada.* Toronto: Dent.

Robert, J.-C. (1988) The city of wealth and death: Urban mortality in Montreal, 1821–1871. In *Essays in the History of Canadian Medicine,* ed. Mitchinson, W., and McGinnis, J. D., p. 18–38. Toronto: McClelland and Stewart.

Rogers, J., and Waldron, T. (1995) *A Field Guide to Joint Disease in Archaeology.* Chichester and New York: J. Wiley & Sons.

Rowe, J. S. (1959) *Forest Regions of Canada.* Forestry Branch Bulletin. 123, Canada.

Sattenspiel, L., and Harpending, H. (1983) Stable populations and skeletal age. *American Antiquity* 48, 489–498.

Saunders, S. R. (1992) Subadult skeletons and growth related studies. In *The Skeletal Biology of Past Peoples: Advances in Research Methods,* ed. Saunders, S. R., and Katzenberg, M. A., pp. 1–20. New York: Wiley-Liss.

Saunders S. R. (2000) Subadult skeletons and growth related studies. In *The Skeletal Biology of Past Peoples: Advances in Research Methods,* 2d ed., ed. Katzenberg, M. A., and Saunders, S. R., pp. 135–162. New York: Wiley-Liss.

Saunders, S. R., DeVito, C., Herring, D. A., Southern, R., and Hoppa, R. D. (1993) Accuracy tests of tooth formation age estimations from human skeletal remains. *American Journal of Physical Anthropology* 92(2), 173–188.

Saunders, S. R., DeVito, C., and Katzenberg, M. A. (1997) Dental caries in nineteenth century Upper Canada. *American Journal of Physical Anthropology* 104(1), 71–87.

Saunders, S. R., FitzGerald, C. M., Rogers, T., Dudar, C., and McKillop, H. R. (1992) A test of several methods of skeletal age estimation using a documented archaeological sample. *Canadian Society of Forensic Sciences Journal* 25, 97–118.

Saunders, S. R., Herring, D. A., and Boyce, G. (1991) Testing theory and method in palaeodemography: The St. Thomas' Anglican Church cemetery. Paper presented at the Canadian Archaeological Association Meetings, St. John's, Nfld.

(1995b) Can skeletal samples accurately represent the living populations they come from? The St. Thomas' cemetery site, Belleville, Ontario. In *Bodies of Evidence: Reconstructing History through Skeletal Analysis,* ed. Grauer, A. L., pp. 69–89. New York: Wiley-Liss.

Saunders, S. R., Herring, D. A., Sawchuk, L. A., and Boyce, G. (1995a) The 19th-century cemetery at St. Thomas' Anglican Church, Belleville: Skeletal remains, parish records, and censuses. In *Grave Reflections: Portraying the Past through Cemetery Studies,* ed. Saunders, S. R., and Herring, D. A., pp. 93–118. Toronto: Canadian Scholar's Press.

Saunders, S. R., and Keenleyside, A. (2000) Enamel Hypoplasia in a Historic Sample. *American Journal of Human Biology* 11, 513–524.

Saunders, S. R., and Lazenby, R. A. (1991) *The Links That Bind: The Harvie Family 19th-Century Burying Ground.* Occasional Papers in Northeastern Archaeology. Dundas, Ont.: Copetown Press.

Saunders, S. R., and Sawchuk, L. A. (1995) Women's bodies, women's lives: Biological indicators of labour and occupational stress, gender comparisons in a nineteenth century pioneer community. Paper presented at the American Association for Physical Anthropology Meetings, Oakland, Calif.

Sawchuk, L. A., Burke, S. D. A., and Choong, H. (n.d.) Migrant shock and shifting patterns of mortality in early 19th century Ontario: The Belleville Anglicans, a community in transition (1856–1875). Unpublished manuscript.

Scheuer, J. L., and Bowman, J. E. (1995) Correlation of documentary and skeletal evidence in the St. Bride's Crypt population. In *Grave Reflections: Portraying the Past through Cemetery Studies,* ed. Saunders, S. R., and Herring, D. A., pp. 49–70. Toronto: Canadian Scholar's Press.

Siegel, L. S. (1984) Child health and development in English Canada, 1790–1850. In *Health, Disease and Medicine: Essays in Canadian History,* ed. Roland, C. G., pp. 360–380. Hamilton: The Hannah Institute of Medicine.

Sirianni, J. E., and Higgins, R. L. (1995) A comparison of death records from the Monroe County almshouse with skeletal remains from the associated Highland Park cemetery. In *Grave Reflections: Portraying the Past through Cemetery Studies,* ed. Saunders, S. R., and Herring, D. A., pp. 71–92. Toronto: Canadian Scholar's Press.

Smith, W. H. (1851) *Canada: Past, Present and Future, Being a Historical, Geographical, Geological and Statistical Account of Canada West.* Toronto: Thomas Maclear.

Spence, M. W. (1989) The osteology of the Wise cemetery. Manuscript on file, Museum of Indian Archaeology, London, Ontario.

Steckel, R. H. (1994) Census manuscript schedules matched with property tax lists: A source of information on long-term trends in wealth inequality. *Historical Methods* 27, 71–85. (1995) Stature and the Standard of Living. *Journal of Economic Literature* 33, 1903–1940.

Suchey, J., and Katz, D. (1986) Skeletal age standards derived from an extensive multiracial sample of modern Americans. *American Journal of Physical Anthropology* 69, 269. [Abstract].

Sutter, R. C. (1995) Dental pathologies among inmates of the Monroe County poorhouse. In *Bodies of Evidence: Reconstructing History through Skeletal Analysis,* ed. Grauer, A. L., pp. 185–196. New York: Wiley-Liss.

Swedlund, A. C. (1992) Infant mortality in Massachusetts and the United States in the Nineteenth Century. In *Diseases in Populations in Transition,* ed. Swedlund, A. C., and Armelagos, G. J., pp. 161–182. New York: Bergin & Garvey.

Thornton, P. S., and Olson, S. (2001) A deadly discrimination among Montreal infants, 1860–1900. *Continuity and Change* 16:95–135.

Thornton, P., Olson, S., and Thach, Q. T. (1987) Infant mortality in Montreal in 1860: The role of culture, class and habitat. Shared Spaces, No. 9, Département de Géographie, Université de McGill.

Tracy, R. (1885) *Third Annual Report of the Provincial Board of Health of Ontario being for the Year 1884.* Toronto: Grip Printing.

Tuross, N., and Fogel, M. L. (1994) Stable isotope analysis and subsistence patterns at the Sully site. In *Skeletal Biology in the Great Plains: Migration, Warfare, Health and Subsistence,* ed. Owsley, D. W., and Jantz, R. L., pp. 283–289. Washington D.C.: Smithsonian Institution Press.

Ubelaker, D. H. (1995) Historic cemetery analysis: Practical considerations. In *Bodies of Evidence: Reconstructing History through Skeletal Analysis,* ed. Grauer, A. L., pp. 37–48. New York: Wiley-Liss.

Vanderlinden, L. D. (1995) Reckless or prudent propogation: A biocultural analysis of marriage & fertility patterns in 19th-century Upper Canada, Belleville, Ontario. Ph.D. dissertation, Department of Anthropology, University of Toronto, Canada.

Waldron, T. (1994) *Counting the Dead: The Epidemiology of Skeletal Populations.* New York: John Wiley & Sons.

Walker, P. L. (1995) Problems of preservation and sexism in sexing: Some lessons from historical collections for paleodemographers. In *Grave Reflections: Portraying the Past through Cemetery Studies,* ed. Saunders, S. R., and Herring, D. A., pp. 31–48. Toronto: Canadian Scholar's Press.

Walker, P. L., Johnson, J. and Lambert, P. (1988) Age and sex biases in the preservation of human skeletal remains. *American Journal of Physical Anthropology* 76(2), 183–188.

Widdis, R. W. (1991) Belleville and environs: Continuity, change and the integration of town and country during the 19th century. *Urban History Review/Revue d'histoire urbaine* 19, 181–208.

Wright, L. E., and Schwarcz, H. P. (1998) Stable carbon and oxygen isotopes in human tooth enamel: Identifying breastfeeding and weaning in prehistory. *American Journal of Physical Anthropology* 106, 1–18.

Zhou, L., and Corruccini, R. S. (1994) Dental enamel hypoplasia and historical famine in China (1959–1961). *American Journal of Physical Anthropology Supplement* 18, 214.

CHAPTER SIX

The Poor in the Mid-Nineteenth-Century Northeastern United States

Evidence from the Monroe County Almshouse, Rochester, New York

Rosanne L. Higgins, Michael R. Haines,
Lorena Walsh, and Joyce E. Sirianni

ABSTRACT

Data were collected from 254 skeletons at the Monroe County Almshouse in Rochester, New York, dating from 1826–1863. Additional evidence was used to calculate mortality rates for paupers (Brighton Town Clerk's Records) and the general population of the City of Rochester (Mount Hope records and census data). Because death rates were so high at the almshouse, the signs of biological stress observed in the skeletons, with the possible exception of infants, were probably not the result of institutionalization but, rather, the result of nutritional inadequacies or diseases experienced outside the almshouse. Documentary evidence indicates that mortality in the City of Rochester around the middle of the nineteenth century was highly variable and characterized by considerable infectious and parasitic diseases. Infant and early childhood mortality was severe. At the Monroe County Almshouse almost one-half of the subadults (as evidenced in both the skeletal collection and the BTC Record) died within the first year of life.

The health index for the sample is 72.3% of the possible maximum score, which is higher than that for the St. Thomas' Anglican Church sample. Documentary evidence, when available, should be included in the overall assessment of health among skeletal samples. It is evident from the Brighton Town Clerk's record that acute infectious disease played a major role in the mortality experience of almshouse residents, a situation that was not incorporated into the Mark I version of the index. In some respects, inmates of the almshouse do not appear much different from the population in general, for example, with respect to the stature of adult males. In other respects, they were different, for example, the chance of being an immigrant or illiterate. Also, almshouses most likely did not provide the relief people were seeking. Even if the almshouse did provide adequate food and shelter, it was often overcrowded, with no separate quarters for those suffering from highly contagious infectious diseases.

I. INTRODUCTION

Over the past decade, the Rochester Museum and Science Center and the University at Buffalo have undertaken the excavation and analysis of 300 human skeletons from a cemetery at Highland Park in Rochester, New York. The burial ground was likely to have been used by the Monroe County Almshouse between 1826 and 1863. The cemetery was unearthed accidentally in 1984 when the Monroe County Parks Department began construction of a public facility at Highland Park, an area now part of the city of Rochester. Initially the remains were thought to be part of a private family cemetery belonging to Erastus Stanley, an adjacent landowner. The 300 skeletons excavated represent approximately one-third of the total burials in the cemetery. The sheer number of burials soon led to the conclusion that this was instead the burial site used by the adjoining Monroe County Almshouse from its establishment in 1826 (and, from the 1850s, by an adjoining penitentiary and insane asylum) up to 1863. The almshouse, penitentiary, and insane asylum were actually located in the adjacent town of Brighton. There is no absolute historical or archaeological proof that the Highland Park burials were the potter's field for these institutions. However, there is no reasonable alternative explanation for the presence of so many burials at a site for which there is no record of any established city, county, or church cemetery. The absence of datable artifacts associated with the skeletons precludes any closer dating of the remains. Nevertheless, since some later burials were superimposed on earlier ones, the collection must represent a reasonably long span of time (Steegmann, 1991).

Unlike many of the historical groups studied in this project, primary documentary records are relatively abundant for public paupers in the mid-nineteenth-century Northeast, as are secondary historical analyses of the living standards of the urban poor. The Highland Park collection is the largest of nineteenth-century pauper skeletal collections. While more skeletal samples are needed to better represent the paupers of the Northeast, this collection offers an excellent opportunity for direct comparisons between discrete, comparable physical and documentary evidence. In addition, the skeletal evidence serves to modify some of the assumptions that historians have drawn about some aspects of quality of life on the basis of documentary records alone. The analysis of skeletal lesions provides the opportunity to document the health of individuals within a group. Some lesions indicate prolonged illness (those associated with tuberculosis or syphilis), while others chronicle episodes of physiological stress that had occurred during childhood (enamel hypoplasia, cribra orbitalia), thus giving us a source of longitudinal data for individual inmates. This, in turn, may suggest that some inmates experienced periods of physiological stress throughout their entire lives, while others may have remained relatively healthy.

Historical Background

ROCHESTER

Nonnative settlements had first been established in the upper Genesee River Valley in the late 1780s, and the town of Rochester was laid out in 1811. Six years later, when the village was incorporated, residents numbered only about 700. The population grew rapidly, however, particularly upon completion of the Erie Canal in 1825. The Village of Rochester first appeared separately enumerated in 1830, when it had a population of 9,207. It became a city shortly thereafter (in 1834) and had grown to 20,191 by 1840 and 43,877 by 1855 (*Census of the State of New York for 1865*).

Initially, the local economy centered around flour milling, trade with the hinterland tapped by the Genesee River and with Canada across Lake Ontario, and the East-West canal trade. During the boom years of the 1820s, building and canal construction, milling, and local and interregional trade including the provisioning of westward migrants usually afforded ample employment. Even in these good years, however, the poor faced seasonal unemployment in winter when the canal was frozen over. By the mid 1830s, the economic stimuli provided by early rapid population growth and development of the local infrastructure had begun to subside, and the pace of growth slowed. The population growth rate slowed from 7.8% per annum in the 1830s to 5.9% per year in the 1840s to 2.8% per year in the 1850s (*Census of the State of New York for 1865*).

In 1845, approximately one-third (31%) of the city's residents were foreign born, many of them, as well as many of the native born, recent migrants to the city. British, and especially Irish, accounted for 23% of Rochester's total population, and Germans were also numerous (at 5.2% of the population). Subsequently immigration diminished; by 1865 the absolute number of foreign born in Rochester had declined (relative to 1855). The Germans were now the largest ethnic group (6,388 residents), nearly matched by the Irish (5,823), followed by 4,703 from Great Britain and Canada, slightly more than 1,000 from other European countries, and 429 African-Americans (*Census of the State of New York for 1865*).

The very circumstances that favored Rochester's growth in the first half of the nineteenth century at the same time increased chances of premature death for many of its residents. Foreign-born immigrants carried cholera and typhus into the city, as did groups of migrants heading for the West who passed through the city by road or on the Erie Canal. High levels of transience within the general population also favored the circulation of disease. Of the adults listed in a city directory of 1827, for example, 70% moved on or died before the next listing in 1834, as did 60% between listings of 1838 and 1844, and 55% between 1844 and 1849. Out-migration again accelerated in the 1850s, with only 34% of a sample of residents listed in the 1849–1850 Rochester City directory reappearing in the directory of 1853–1854 (McKelvey, 1945).

POOR RELIEF

After the Revolutionary War, officials and social reformers in the larger northeastern cities moved to establish tighter control over the poor. Rapidly growing urban populations and influxes of new immigrants exacerbated concerns among the ruling classes about rising welfare costs and about an apparent increase in the numbers of paupers, beggars, and vagrants. Worries about social disorder, crime, and drug abuse – in this case, increased alcohol consumption within the lower classes – intensified the perceived need for controlling behavior and for reforming the habits of the poor (Katz, 1983).

Wage laborers in the Genesee Valley, many of them dependent on the seasonal canal and lake trades, as well as on seasonal employment on farms, seem to have been increasingly vulnerable to short-term periods of destitution. In 1823, just 3.44 residents per 1,000 population required public assistance, a figure similar to that prevailing in the rest of the state outside of the New York City area. Almost three-quarters of those receiving relief were supported throughout the year, suggesting that most were either elderly or disabled adults or children who could not support themselves. By the early 1840s, however, the figure increased to 19.3 per 1,000, and subsequently rose to 28.28 in 1845–1849, and then to about 45.0 between 1850 and 1859. Although well below the more than 100 welfare recipients per 1,000 residents prevailing in New York City between 1840 and 1859, it was considerably higher than in other longer-settled regions in the state (Hannon, 1984).

Beginning in the 1790s, outdoor relief (primarily cash, food, and fuel supplied to indigents in their own homes or lodgings), the most extensive colonial remedy, was curtailed in the major cities, and new almshouses were constructed where destitute people could be segregated in a workshop environment. Further cost cutting and efficiencies were anticipated by including a public hospital, an insane asylum, and a penitentiary in the new centralized almshouse complexes. By the 1820s and 1830s, smaller towns and rural counties followed suit, abolishing home relief and the annual auction of able-bodied paupers to the lowest bidder willing to care for them in favor of institutional aid (Cray, 1988). In Rochester, a workhouse (soon upgraded to a penitentiary) was built adjacent to the almshouse in 1854, and an insane asylum in 1857. Previously the mentally ill had been housed in the almshouse (McKelvey, 1947, 1956, 1972).

The goals of the almshouse movement appear contradictory. While the main priority was to relieve poverty, equally important was the goal of using the threat of entering the almshouse as a deterrent to public dependency. Humane treatment of the "worthy" poor could not be combined with the threat of the unpleasant consequences of applying for relief, and the aged and infirm ended up being held hostage to "the war on able bodied paupers" (Katz, 1996). By the 1850s, almshouse inmates often endured worse treatment than did criminals. From a survey of the early nineteenth-century New York poor relief system, Michael Katz concluded, "[A] preoccupation with order, routine, and cost replaced the founders' concern with the transformation of character and social reform. Everywhere, reform gave way to custody as the basis of institutional life" (Katz, 1996).

Some destitute men and women from surrounding rural areas sought relief in both of these county-administered almshouses, but they were apparently primarily the refuge of last resort for the urban poor of the lake port cities of Buffalo and Rochester. In order better to understand the demographics of the almshouse, the Brighton Almshouse was located in the manuscripts of the federal censuses of 1850 and 1860. The information was coded into machine-readable form. The census was, unfortunately, taken in June of those years (officially June 1), which was likely a low point for inmate population for the year. Nonetheless, these data do provide some insight into the nature of the population of paupers.

The population of the almshouse numbered 323 in 1850 (excluding the almshouse superintendent and his wife and four children). Of these, 168 were males and 155 females. The age structure included a significant number of children – 36% of the inmates were aged 0–14 years. A perusal of the names, ages, and nativities of the inmates points to a number of families (in contrast to unrelated individuals), many of them single-parent, female-headed families. The population was disproportionately foreign born: 66% of the overall population of inmates was foreign born and 76% of the population aged 15 years and older. The City of Rochester in 1855 was only about 44% foreign born. The overwhelming number of the foreign born were Irish (71%), with about 9%–10% each for Canadians, Germans, and English. Occupations were listed only as "Inmate," and literacy was not recorded. Thirty-one of the inmates (1%) were listed as disabled, half being recorded as "Insane." All the inmates were white.

In contrast, in June, 1860, the almshouse was recorded as having had fewer inmates, 277 in number, along with 7 administrative staff (the superintendent, his wife and child, a matron, a female teacher, and a farmer and his wife). The inmates consisted of slightly more males (117 or 62%). No occupations were listed. All inmates were once again white. The age structure seemed regular with 31% children aged 0–14 years. The foreign born were again mostly Irish (65% of the foreign inmates), along with 17% from Germany, 8% from England, and 6% from Canada. The proportion of inmates in families seemed less, and the number of children without apparent adult relatives seemed greater. About 77% of the inmates aged 20 years and over were illiterate (72% among males and 84% among females). Only 20 (.7%) were recorded as disabled.

The overall impression is of a varied group of individuals by age and sex occupying the almshouse. They were more likely to have been foreign born, especially Irish, particularly in 1850, a date close to the Great Famine. Adults were considerably more likely to have been illiterate in 1860 (77%) than among the general population, which was only about 8% illiterate among whites aged 20 years and older in 1860. This was even lower in New York State, about 5% (these estimates were based on the preliminary IPUMS sample of the 1860 Federal Census). Female-headed, single-parent families and children without apparent adult relatives were quite common. It is unknown whether any of these children were, in fact, orphans. Ostensibly unrelated individuals were somewhat more common in 1860 than in 1850. This was a population on the margins, with many recent immigrants and illiterate individuals.

HEALTH AND MORTALITY

High mortality in the middle of the nineteenth century was apparently characteristic of the nation as a whole. Expectation of life at birth for the total population (both sexes combined) was 38.3 years in 1850, and the infant mortality rate was 229

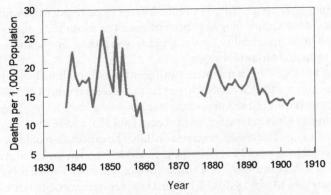

Figure 6.1. Crude death rate for Rochester, N.Y., 1837–1904.

infant deaths per 1,000 live births (Haines, 1998). Despite high rates of economic growth, between 1840 and 1860, adult mortality was significantly higher than at the beginning of the century, even for native-born whites (Pope, 1992). Rapid population growth due especially to heavy European immigration outstripped the abilities of city administrators to handle complex problems, such as financing public water works, sewage systems, fire prevention, refuse removal, poor relief, and facilities to care for other members of the population in need. Most poor people endured appalling living conditions that included unventilated, damp, cramped, and dirty dwellings surrounded by human and animal wastes. Clothing and fuel were often inadequate, particularly in winter. More often than not, water supplies were polluted, as was milk, which typically sat on delivery wagons all day exposed to the heat of the sun. At the height of the epidemics, city governments made half-hearted efforts to clean up some of the filth, but as soon as the contagion subsided, so did most public health initiatives (Rosenberg, 1962).

Conditions in Rochester were especially bad in the areas of the city where recent immigrants lived in crowded tenements. The immigrant poor suffered disproportionately from cholera epidemics that struck the city in 1832, 1849, and 1852 (McKelvey, 1945; Rosenberg-Naparsteck, 1983). Some idea of the mortality regime in Rochester in the nineteenth century may be seen in Figure 6.1, which traces the crude death rate for the city from 1837 to 1860 and again from 1877 to 1904. The data on annual deaths for the period 1837–1860 come from interment records kept by the city sexton with the records of the Mount Hope Cemetery, whether or not the burials were in that cemetery (Higgins and Sirianni, 1995). The series for the years 1877 to 1904 are based on the official vital statistics for the City of Rochester as reported by Hoffman (Hoffman, 1906). For the 1830s to the 1850s (the period of interment of most of the skeletal remains), the base mortality rate was not particularly high – a crude death rate of 18 deaths per 1,000 population per year for 1837 to 1859. There was, however, great variability, especially in the late 1840s and early 1850s when cholera visited and revisited the city in 1849, 1852, and 1854 [the coefficient of variation (the standard deviation divided by the mean) for the crude death rate was .217 for 1837–1859 and .118 for 1877–1904]. While some deaths in

Rochester may have been omitted from the Mount Hope register and while the last several years of the sample may have been increasingly incomplete, the age and sex patterns and annual variability appear quite reasonable, as do the cause-of-death results (Higgins and Sirianni, 1995).

The Mount Hope Cemetery interment records were combined with published age distributions for the City of Rochester from the federal census of 1840 and the New York State census of 1855 to produce a set of abridged life tables. They apply to the deaths from 1838/42 (centered on the census of 1840) and 1853/57 (centered on the census of 1855). The results seem reasonable. The expectation of life at birth for both sexes combined was 41 in 1840 and 45 in 1855, although the latter may be a bit too high. The infant mortality rate (infant deaths per 1,000 live births) estimated by this means was 132 in 1840 and 145 in 1855. Female mortality was expectedly lower than male mortality at both dates. (The life tables, Tables 6.A.1–6.A.6, are reproduced in Appendix A.)

Overall, then, mortality in the City of Rochester around the middle of the nineteenth century was highly variable and characterized by considerable infectious and parasitic disease (tuberculosis, cholera, typhoid and typhus fever, gastritis, croup, bronchitis). It might actually have worsened between the 1830s and the 1850s with the influx of immigrants, urban growth without adequate sanitary infrastructure, and increased mobility of both people and commodities (Pope, 1992).

However bad living conditions may have been in the city at large, the historic records for the Monroe County Almshouse suggest that conditions may have been worse there. Infant and early childhood mortality was severe, with almost one-half of the subadults (as evidenced in both the skeletal collection and the Brighton Town Clerk's Record) dying within the first year of life. Other documentary evidence indicates that infants and young children, in both the almshouse and general Rochester population, regularly succumbed to consumption, gastrointestinal disorders, respiratory ailments, and childhood diseases. Convulsions, worms, teething, and accidents were the cause of some additional deaths, as was cholera in the Rochester population and typhus at the almshouse. Among adults, consumption was the leading cause of death among women in the 20–29 age category and among males between 30 and 39 and 50 and 59. Typhus and cholera, diseases that result in deaths so quick as to leave no trace in the skeletal record, emerge in the documents as the second- and third-leading causes of death in early Rochester (Higgins and Sirianni, 1995).

Higgins and Sirianni's (1995) analysis of the dental health of women and children at the almshouse suggests that life may have been particularly stressful for these two groups. Approximately one-third of the children in the skeletal collection exhibited enamel hypoplasia. Among those children showing hypoplastic lesions, over 59% had deciduous dentitions. This suggests that not only did children at the almshouse experience nutritional stress but so did expectant mothers.

These death records by age and sex for the Monroe County Almshouse for 1847/50 were related to the tabulations of the almshouse population from the 1850 federal census. The indicated death rate was stunning: 19% of the average population of the almshouse died in any given year. This represents a crude death rate of 193. And this was even more extreme for the very young and the very old. For those over age 60, 51% died in any given year; and for those under age five, it was 38%. This may represent an upper bound, since the census was taken in June, likely when the almshouse population was smaller. Clearly, however, this institution was a pesthouse. Some inmates likely entered because they were ill and simply died there rather than elsewhere; but the almshouse was also a focus for infection. Many otherwise healthy new inmates contracted infectious diseases in those close quarters and consequently died.

A similar result obtains using published data for the Monson, Tewksbury, and Bridgewater state almshouses in Massachusetts for the censuses of 1855 and 1860 and vital statistics for surrounding years (Abstract of the Census of the Commonwealth of Massachusetts, 1855, 1856, 1859, 1860, 1861). There about 30% of inmates died in the average year 1855/56 and 26% during 1859/61. The conclusion must be reached that almshouses in the United States were distinctly dangerous and unhealthy places in the middle of the nineteenth century.

II. SKELETAL ANALYSIS

The Sample

Two hundred and ninety-six skeletons were excavated by the Rochester Museum and Science Center. Of these, 67 are subadults and 229 are adults. Among the adults, 72 are female, and 103 are male (Table 6.1). Sex could not be estimated for 28 adult individuals. For analysis the categories of female and probable female ($N = 11$) and male and probable male ($N = 15$) were combined.

The average age at death for subadults is 3 years old. For the total group of adults, the average age at death is 40 years old, for males, 44 years, and for females, 35 years.

The distribution of age estimates for subadults is based on dental and skeletal development (Demirjian, 1986; Krogman and Iscan, 1986). Age estimates for adults is based on a multiregional approach, which focused on changes in cranial sutures, the pubic symphysis, the auricular surface of the ilium, and dental wear (Brothwell, 1981; Meindl and Lovejoy, 1985; Meindl et al., 1985; Lovejoy et al., 1985).

Table 6.1: Sample

	Females	Prob. females	Males	Prob. males	Subadults	Unknown	Total
Adult	72	11	103	15		28	229
Subadult					67		67
TOTAL	72	11	103	15	67	28	296

Infectious Disease

ADULTS

The frequency and severity of periosteal reaction on the tibiae and the broader category of periosteal reaction on other bones of the skeleton measured the presence of infectious disease for this project. Table 6.2 shows the frequency of periosteal reaction on adult tibiae. There were 194 adults who had at least one bone for analysis. Twenty-three males exhibited a slight periosteal reaction, compared to 16 females. The remaining four observations occurred in individuals of unknown sex. Although listed in Table 6.2 separately, moderate and severe categories were combined to maximize sample size for statistical analysis; 20 males were observed in this category, compared to 10 females. Chi-square tests revealed no significant differences at the 0.05 level between the sexes.

The frequency of periosteal reaction in bones other than the tibiae are found in Table 6.3. Of the 229 adult skeletons examined in this study, 112 did not show signs of skeletal infection. A mild skeletal response was recorded for 91 adults (39%), while 26 (11%) individuals showed evidence of systemic infection. When broken down by sex, 49 males, 37 females, and 5 unknown individuals showed evidence of periosteal reaction. The bones of 16 males, 9 females, and 1 unknown individual indicated that these individuals suffered from systemic infection. Chi-square tests again revealed no significant differences between the sexes in these two categories.

Table 6.2: Periosteal Reaction of the Tibia

	Males	Females	Unknown	Total
No reaction	64	49	6	119
Slight reaction	23	16	4	43
Moderate reaction	6	2	1	9
Severe reaction	14	8	1	23
TOTAL	90	92	12	194

Table 6.3: Periosteal Reaction in Other Bones of the Skeleton

	Males	Females	Unknown	Total
No reaction	53	37	22	112
Periosteal reaction	49	37	5	91
Systemic infection	16	9	1	26
TOTAL	118	83	28	229

Table 6.4: Frequency of Periosteal Reaction in
the Tibia among Subadults

	N	%
No skeletal response	22	81
Slight skeletal response	5	19
Moderate skeletal response	0	0
Severe skeletal response	0	0
TOTAL OBSERVED	27	100

Table 6.5: Periosteal Reaction in Other Bones of
the Skeleton among Subadults

	N	%
No skeletal response	54	81
Skeletal response	13	19
Systemic infection	0	0
TOTAL OBSERVED	67	100

SUBADULTS

Twenty-two of the 27 subadults observed did not show evidence of periosteal reaction of the tibia (Table 6.4). Mild periosteal reaction was observed in 5 subadults, but no evidence of a moderate or severe reaction in any of the subadult tibiae observed. There was no indication of periosteal reaction in the other bones of 54 subadults (Table 6.5). Thirteen showed some periosteal reaction, and no individuals had a severe skeletal response indicative of systemic infection.

Nutritional Deficiency

ADULTS

Iron deficiency anemia, as suggested by the presence and severity of cribra orbitalia and porotic hyperostosis, was observed and recorded as part of this study. A summary of these two conditions for adults can be found in Table 6.6. One hundred and eighty-three adult skeletons had at least one orbit present for the scoring of cribra orbitalia. Of these, 165 showed no evidence of the condition. A slight / moderate reaction was observed in 18 skeletons, 12 of which were determined to be female. None of the skeletons observed showed a reaction that could be considered severe. Similarly, the frequency of porotic hyperostosis is also very low among adults. Only 3 of the 193 individuals with intact crania showed evidence of a slight/moderate lesion; 2 were female and 1 was male.

Table 6.6: Frequency of Iron Deficiency Anemia

	Cribra orbitalia				Porotic hyperostosis			
	Males	Females	Unknown	Total	Males	Females	Unknown	Total
No lesion	86	52	27	165	104	71	15	190
Slight moderate	5	12	1	18	1	2	0	3
Severe lesion	0	0	0	0	0	0	0	0
TOTAL	91	64	28	183	105	73	15	193

Table 6.7: Frequency of Iron Deficiency Anemia in Subadults

	Cribra orbitalia		Porotic hyperostosis	
	N	%	N	%
No skeletal lesion	24	83	35	92
Slight moderate lesion	5	17	2	5
Severe lesion	0	0	1	3
TOTAL OBSERVED	29	100	38	100

SUBADULTS

The frequency of iron deficiency anemia in subadults is shown in Table 6.7. Of the 36 individuals who had at least one orbit for observation, 5 showed evidence of a slight/moderate skeletal response. None of these individuals showed any signs of a severe skeletal response. Three out of the 38 subadults analyzed showed evidence of porotic hyperostosis. Of these, 2 showed a slight to moderate skeletal response and 1 showed a severe response.

Dental Health

ADULTS

The dental health for males and females is reported in Table 6.8. Approximately 37% of the female skeletons exhibited dental caries, compared to 27% observed among males. In both males and females, mandibular molars had the greatest number of carious lesions. The percentage of dental calculus was higher among males in all teeth except the mandibular incisors. The percentage of adult teeth that showed evidence of enamel hypoplasia was low for both sexes, except for the mandibular canines.

Degenerative Joint Disease (DJD)

A total of 184 individuals were observed for DJD of the shoulder or elbow. Of these, 95 skeletons showed no evidence of the pathology. Seventy-eight individuals had

Table 6.8: Frequency and Percentage of Caries, Dental Calculus, and Enamel Hypoplasias in Adults

		Males				Females		
Teeth	N	Caries %	Calculus %	Hypoplasia %	N	Caries %	Calculus %	Hypoplasia %
Maxillary								
Incisors	179	18.4	15.6	5	165	29.7	11.5	3
Canines	114	19.2	16.7	4.4	94	17.2	11.7	2.1
Premolars	194	23.2	28.4	1.5	153	40.5	21.6	2
Molars	267	46.4	44.2	1.9	214	61.7	34.1	1.9
SUBTOTAL	754	29.7	29	2.9	626	41.4	21.7	2.2
Mandibular								
Incisors	289	11.4	42.9	7.3	219	12.3	45.2	6.4
Canines	164	15.8	42.1	12.2	117	20.5	37.6	13.7
Premolars	291	19.2	36.1	1.7	222	30.3	33.3	3.6
Molars	291	51.5	38.5	1.7	223	66.8	24.7	1.8
SUBTOTAL	1035	25.6	39.6	4.9	781	34.2	34.8	5.4
TOTAL	1789	27.3	35.2	4.1	1407	37.4	29	4

Table 6.9a: The Frequency of Degenerative Joint Disease of the Shoulder/Elbow

	Males	Females	Unknown	Total
No DJD	44	41	10	95
Slight DJD	54	23	1	78
Severe DJD	4	1	0	5
Immobile joint	0	2	0	2
Systemic DJD	3	1	0	4
TOTAL	105	68	11	184

initial osteophyte formation, 5 showed evidence of eburnation, and the joints of 2 individuals were determined to be immobile. Evidence of systemic DJD was present in 4 skeletons (Table 6.9a). The higher frequency of DJD at this region in males ($N = 60$ for males, $N = 27$ for females) was significant at the 0.05 level.

The age and sex distribution can be seen in Table 6.9b. The highest percentages of DJD in this region occurred in individuals 35–64 years of age among males and 25–54 years of age for females. A chi-square test revealed no significant differences in the frequency of DJD between males and females between the ages of 25 and 34. However, the higher frequency observed in males for all the older age groups was significant at the .05 level.

Two hundred seven individuals were complete enough to record DJD of the hip/knee. The frequency of this pathology can be seen in Table 6.10a. Ninety-two

Table 6.9b: DJD of the Shoulder/Elbow by Age and Sex

Age	Under 2	25–34	35–44	45–54	55–64	65+
Males						
N	0	3	17	17	15	8
%	0	5	28.3	28.3	25	13
Females						
N	1	5	8	6	3	4
%	3.7	18.5	29.6	22.2	11.1	14.8

Table 6.10a: The Frequency of Degenerative Joint Disease of the Hip/Knee

	Males	Females	Unknown	Total
No DJD	41	46	8	95
Slight DJD	58	28	6	92
Severe DJD	11	4	1	16
Immobile joint	0	1	0	1
Systemic DJD	3	0	0	3
TOTAL	113	79	15	207

Table 6.10b: DJD of the Hip/Knee by Age and Sex

Age	Under 2	25–34	35–44	45–54	55–64	65+
Males						
N	0	2	22	19	17	11
%	0	2.8	31	26.8	23.9	15.5
Females						
N	0	5	9	10	5	4
%	0	15.1	27.2	30.3	15.1	12.1

individuals showed evidence of initial osteophyte formation, 16 showed eburnation, and 1 individual indicated immobility of the joint. Again, a chi-square test revealed that the higher frequency of DJD at this region in males ($N = 71$ for males, $N = 33$ for females) was significant at the 0.05 level. When broken down by age and sex (Table 6.10b), again there is a pattern of DJD occurring in this region earlier in females. Of the DJD of the hip/knee recorded for females, 15% occurred between the ages of 25 and 34, in comparison to 2.8% in males. Of the female skeletons scored for DJD in this region, 57% were between 25 and 54 years of age. Among males, the largest percentage of DJD in this region occurred between the ages of 35 and 64 (82%). A chi-square test revealed no significant differences in the frequency of DJD between males and females between the ages of 25 and 34. However, the higher frequency observed in males for all the older age groups was significant at the 0.05 level.

Table 6.11: Stature Estimates for the Highland Park Skeletons

Sample	N	Mean stature (cm)	S.D.
Females	57	160.1	6.2
Females and probable females	64	160.5	6.2
Males	86	171.9	6
Males and probable males	94	171.7	6.1
TOTAL	156	167.1	8.3

Adult Heights

The mean statures for the Highland Park skeletal collection are presented in Table 6.11. An average height of 160.1cm was recorded for females. This figure changes very little when the "probable females" are added to the female sample (160.5cm). The same similarity in stature is apparent for the male samples. The specimens for which the category of "male" is certain show a mean stature of 171.9cm. When the "probable" males are added to the sample, height shows little change (171.8cm).

III. DISCUSSION

In interpreting the results of this research, focusing particularly on health, it is important to understand the nature of the almshouse system during this period. Documentary evidence from both the Erie (Buffalo, New York) and Niagara (Lockport, New York) County almshouses suggests that the duration of stay at these institutions for adults was usually not longer than two weeks (Katz, 1983; Higgins, 1996, 1998). In fact, most people stayed only a few days. It seems reasonable to assume that the duration and pattern of occupation at the Monroe County Almshouse would not be much different. Therefore, the evidence of poor health that was observed in the skeletons of almshouse inmates, with the possible exception of infants, was probably not the result of institutionalization, but rather the result of nutritional or disease stress experienced outside the almshouse.

The records from Erie and Niagara Counties also indicate that the majority of people who sought relief during this period did so because they were destitute and/or sick. These conditions would have undoubtedly left them susceptible to whatever contagions they would have been exposed to during their brief stay at the almshouses.

Subadults

Children who came to the Monroe County Almshouse with destitute parents certainly would have been at risk, particularly if they were already suffering from acute nutritional stress. In light of this, the presence of cribra orbitalia and porotic hyperostosis among subadults is not surprising. Higgins and Sirianni's analysis of the deciduous dentitions in subadults also suggests that many children at the almshouse were suffering from nutritional deficiencies at birth (actually before birth because the deciduous dentition forms in utero) (Higgins and Sirianni, 1995). Nevertheless, researchers suggest that adequate food was available at the Monroe County Almshouse during this period (Rosenberg-Naparsteck, 1983). Similarly, documentary evidence from the Erie County Almshouse suggests that adequate food was also available there. However, newspaper reports of the period report that appalling diets were provided to all almshouse residents in Buffalo, often consisting of nothing more than spoiled, undercooked bread and coffee (Katz, 1983). Archival data are unclear regarding the availability of good-quality food at almshouses. However, skeletal data indicate the presence of nutritional stress in women and children at the Monroe County poorhouse. One explanation is that they arrived at the almshouse in a nutritionally deprived state, a condition that did not improve during their stay, perhaps even leading to their death.

The frequencies of skeletal infection are low among the almshouse children represented in this collection. This is not unusual given that the major causes of death among children were acute infectious diseases like measles, cholera, and typhus fever (Higgins and Sirianni, 1995). The types of prolonged infections that leave evidence in the skeleton were not common among children at the almshouse. Once again, acute nutritional stress could have increased susceptibility to infectious diseases, and led to a quick death.

Adults

The high frequencies of skeletal infection among adults is not surprising considering what is known from the Brighton Town Clerk's Record. Consumption (pulmonary tuberculosis) was the leading cause of death for both males and females at the almshouse (27.7% of all deaths). Also, the frequency of tuberculosis observed in the skeletal sample is approximately what would be expected given the documentary evidence. Although syphilis was seldom recorded as a cause of death in the Brighton Town Clerk's Record for the almshouse, it was observed in the skeletal sample. Given the presence of skeletal infection, a strong indication of prolonged illness, some people may not have been seeking relief at the almshouse until they were too ill to care for themselves. Diseases such as tuberculosis were likely contracted outside of the institution, as it was the leading cause of death in the city of Rochester, as well as in the almshouse (Sirianni and Higgins, 1995).

The frequency of iron deficiency anemia was low in this sample, observed in only 9% of the adult population. The higher frequency among females could be due to anemic stress during pregnancy (Lanphear, 1988). Eight out of 10 of the women were aged between 15 and 39 years. The high rate of childbed fever at the Monroe County Almshouse indicates that many women were having children there (Sirianni and Higgins, 1995). This condition, usually resulting in death, is associated with unsanitary conditions during childbirth. The historic records from both the Erie and Niagara County Almshouses also indicate that many women came to almshouses to give birth.

The low frequency of enamel hypoplasia in both sexes is indicative of a physiologically stress-free childhood for most of the adults who died at the almshouse. The high frequency of caries in both sexes may be indicative of their depressed socioeconomic status. It is probable that these people could not afford dental care. Also, they were probably forced to rely on high carbohydrate food sources. A diet consisting largely of processed grains (bread, etc.) has the potential to produce a high incidence of dental caries. The higher frequency of caries in females may be attributed to reproductive stress.

The demographic pattern of older males at the almshouse is evident from the presence of degenerative joint disease in the long bone joints observed in this collection. The higher frequency among males in the region of the hip/knee and shoulder/elbow is not unusual given the older males in residence at the almshouse. Also, according to the Brighton Town Clerk's Record, many of these men had been employed as laborers (70% of adult males), so it is likely that a great deal of stress was placed on these joints during the course of their working lives.

It is interesting to note that the mean stature among males in this collection was similar to recruits from the Union army of roughly the same period. The sample of Union army recruits was originally collected by Robert Fogel and has now been linked to their medical, pension, and census records. The original sample is available from the Interuniversity Consortium for Political and Social Research in Ann Arbor, MI (ICPSR 9425). The linked sample is now available as a set of public-use files from the Center for Population Economics, Graduate School of Business, University of Chicago. Adult males from the Highland Park collection are 1.1cm taller, on average, than the total sample of recruits from New York State (170.6cm). When the soldiers are broken down into occupational categories, the Highland Park males are taller than the New York recruits who previously worked as laborers (169.6cm), but are shorter, on average, than those who had worked as farmers (172.0cm). The results are not much changed if recruits from New York and Kings (Brooklyn) Counties are excluded. The mean difference of 1.1cm between the Highland Park males and the total sample of recruits is not significant at the 0.05 level, nor is the difference between almshouse males and soldiers who had been employed as farmers (the tallest soldiers). The mean difference of 1.9cm between the Highland Park males and those soldiers who had worked as laborers is statistically significant at the 0.05 level.

These results support the earlier work of Steegmann (1991), who compared the heights of both males and females in this collection to other contemporary nonpoor samples, and found no significant differences. The majority of linear growth occurs prior to adulthood (usually by the late teens). The life experiences of the paupers prior to entering the almshouse are unknown. Many of them may have experienced adequate health and nutrition during their years of growth. The lack of stunting in this sample suggests that the resources needed to attain maximum stature were available to many of these people when they needed them.

When comparing stature between the Highland Park skeletal collection and the Uxbridge Almshouse (Elia, 1991) collection, there is little difference in the overall mean height among these groups (1.1cm). Males from the Highland Park collection are taller than males from the Uxbridge Almshouse by 2.0cm, while females from

Highland Park are shorter than those at Uxbridge by 2.9cm. None of these results are statistically significant at the 0.05 level. It should be noted that the Uxbridge sample is very small and may not accurately represent a true population mean. Nonetheless, Weslowsky (1991) maintains that estimates of stature for both males and females from the Uxbridge Almshouse do compare favorably with other nineteenth-century skeletal samples.

Health Index

The results of the health index developed by Steckel, Sciulli, and Rose (this volume) place the Highland Park collection just about average in terms of the possible maximum score attainable. The quality of life score for this sample is 19.08, which represents 72.3% of the possible maximum score. This quality of life score is higher than that for the St. Thomas' Anglican Church sample which scored 18.28 or 69.9% of the maximum possible score. At first this may seem surprising. Nevertheless, the nature of the almshouse system discussed above, particularly during this period, may place this result in a better perspective. Also, we know that many of the individuals at the Monroe County Almshouse, both adult and subadult, were dying of acute infectious diseases, such as typhus fever, cholera, and measles, which typically do not leave evidence in the skeletal record. It is also important to note that this pattern of infectious disease, with the exception of typhus fever, was typical of the City of Rochester during this period. It is the general conclusion of Sirianni and Higgins (1995) that the overall health status of inmates at the Monroe County Almshouse did not differ that much from the rest of the city, which was generally poor. Perhaps if the documentary record could be factored into the health index, we would see the scores for this collection decline somewhat.

IV. CONCLUSIONS

The combination of archaeological remains and historic documentation provide insight into poverty during the nineteenth century. The skeletal evidence for both adults and subadults indicates that economic distress took a toll on the health of people during this period. The most seriously affected group were children, many of whom began their lives in a state of nutritional stress, only to have them cut short by acute infectious diseases. The documentary evidence from the Monroe County Almshouse, which reports high rates of infectious diseases for all age groups, adds to a bleak picture. It is important to remember, however, that such conditions were not unique to almshouses. It is more likely that infectious diseases were brought to these institutions from people seeking relief from the harshness of poverty. The presence of infectious diseases, like tuberculosis, in the skeletons attests to this because they indicate prolonged illness.

In some respects, inmates of the almshouse do not appear much different from the population in general, for example, with respect to the stature of adult males. In other respects, however, they were rather different, for example, in the chance of being an immigrant or illiterate. Equally important is the idea that almshouses appear to have been ineffective in buffering the problems associated with poverty. They most likely did not provide the relief people were seeking. Even if the almshouse did provide adequate food and shelter, it was often overcrowded, with no separate quarters for those suffering from highly contagious infectious diseases.

With regard to the health index, it would seem that documentary evidence, when available, should be included in the overall assessment of health among skeletal samples. It is evident from the Brighton Town Clerk's Record that acute infectious disease played a major role in the mortality experience of almshouse residents, a situation that could not be realized by the index as it stands. Nevertheless, in terms of measuring lifetime biological stress, the index has merit. The average score for the sample, in general, is not unusual for a group of people who may have spent most of their lives in relatively good health until unfortunate circumstances (such as illness or destitution) resulted in their admission into the almshouse.

The skeletal data are also a valuable addition to the study of poverty during the nineteenth century because they provide information on the health status of individuals. The lesions identified in adult skeletons suggest that either they had been ill for a long period or that they experienced episodes of physiological stress during childhood. Similarly, some of the lesions identified in subadult skeletons suggest that stress occurred in utero (either due to poor nutrition or disease experienced by the mother). Therefore, the presence of skeletal lesions implies that some individuals were sick and/or nutritionally stressed before they entered the almshouse, perhaps because they had lived a lifetime in poverty, or at least experienced conditions of poverty several times during their lives.

APPENDIX A. LIFE TABLES: ROCHESTER, N.Y., 1838–1857

Table 6.A.1: Rochester, N.Y., 1838–1842: Males (Mount Hope Cemetery data)

Age	Population	Deaths	M(X)	Q(X)	L(X)	LL(X)	T(X)	E(X)
0	379.0	52.9	.139578	.127272	100000.00	90963.68	4023411.00	40.23
1	1318.0	50.6	.038392	.139206	87272.79	316447.10	3932447.00	46.06
5	1134.0	13.9	.012257	.058335	75123.91	364663.70	3616000.00	48.13
10	941.0	4.0	.004251	.020963	70741.59	350000.50	3251336.00	45.96
15	1044.0	5.7	.005460	.026419	69258.60	341718.70	2901336.00	41.89
20	2515.0	19.1	.007594	.072914	67428.89	649706.50	2559617.00	37.96
30	1506.0	17.5	.011620	.111291	62512.41	590338.80	1909911.00	30.55
40	757.0	11.3	.014927	.143931	55555.35	515572.90	1319572.00	23.75
50	322.0	9.8	.030435	.281119	47559.22	408743.20	803998.80	16.91
60	118.0	9.1	.077119	.546590	34189.41	248456.20	395255.50	11.56
70	54.0	3.9	.072222	.540938	15501.82	113090.60	146799.40	9.47
80	9.0	1.9	.211111	1.000000	7116.30	33708.79	33708.79	4.74
TOTALS	10097.0	199.7						

CDR = 19.778.
Births = −1.0.

Table 6.A.2: Rochester, N.Y., 1838–1842: Females (Mount Hope Cemetery data)

Age	Population	Deaths	M(X)	Q(X)	L(X)	LL(X)	T(X)	E(X)
0	362.0	44.7	.123481	.113398	100000.00	92175.55	4180788.00	41.81
1	1174.0	42.0	.035775	.130598	88660.23	323655.90	4088612.00	46.12
5	1141.0	12.1	.010605	.051130	77081.39	375554.00	3764956.00	48.84
10	985.0	4.4	.004467	.022120	73140.22	361656.50	3389402.00	46.34
15	1223.0	8.3	.006787	.032646	71522.37	351774.50	3027746.00	42.33
20	2339.0	25.5	.010902	.103289	69187.45	656142.80	2675971.00	38.68
30	1221.0	15.9	.013022	.123244	62041.12	582180.10	2019828.00	32.56
40	654.0	10.1	.015443	.146756	54394.91	504035.30	1437648.00	26.43
50	322.0	9.0	.027950	.248850	46412.15	406373.30	933612.90	20.12
60	153.0	5.5	.035948	.308177	34862.50	294905.90	527239.60	15.12
70	62.0	3.3	.053226	.474099	24118.67	184013.60	232333.80	9.63
80	8.0	2.1	.262500	1.000000	12684.05	48320.18	48320.18	3.81
TOTALS	9644.0	182.9						

CDR = 18.965.
Births = −1.0.

Table 6.A.3: Rochester, N.Y., 1838–1842: Both Sexes (Mount Hope Cemetery data)

Age	Population	Deaths	M(X)	Q(X)	L(X)	LL(X)	T(X)	E(X)
0	741.0	97.6	.131714	.120507	100000.00	91564.54	4104358.00	41.04
1	2492.0	92.6	.037159	.135165	87949.34	319914.60	4012793.00	45.63
5	2275.0	26.0	.011429	.054738	76061.66	369899.70	3692879.00	48.55
10	1926.0	8.4	.004361	.021569	71898.21	355614.20	3322979.00	46.22
15	2267.0	14.0	.006176	.029776	70347.47	346500.70	2967365.00	42.18
20	4854.0	44.6	.009188	.087679	68252.80	652606.40	2620864.00	38.40
30	2727.0	33.4	.012248	.116666	62268.48	586361.80	1968258.00	31.61
40	1411.0	21.4	.015167	.145191	55003.89	510108.60	1381896.00	25.12
50	644.0	18.8	.029193	.263761	47017.84	408171.00	871787.30	18.54
60	271.0	14.6	.053875	.424255	34616.36	272732.80	463616.30	13.39
70	116.0	7.2	.062069	.505125	19930.20	148965.80	190883.50	9.58
80	17.0	4.0	.235294	1.000000	9862.97	41917.61	41917.61	4.25
TOTALS	19741.0	382.6						

CDR = 19.381.
Births = −1.0.

Table 6.A.4: Rochester, N.Y., 1853–1857: Males (Mount Hope Cemetery data)

Age	Population	Deaths	M(X)	Q(X)	L(X)	LL(X)	T(X)	E(X)
0	730.0	117.3	.160685	.145345	100000.00	89680.52	4391700.00	43.92
1	2536.6	71.2	.028069	.104402	85465.53	317886.60	4302019.00	50.34
5	2501.6	16.4	.006556	.032125	76542.75	376566.30	3984133.00	52.05
10	2412.4	8.8	.003648	.018040	74083.79	367077.70	3607566.00	48.70
15	2067.0	9.8	.004741	.023495	72747.29	359463.40	3240489.00	44.54
20	2166.1	20.1	.009279	.045321	71038.07	347141.50	2881025.00	40.56
25	2138.1	20.5	.009588	.046814	67818.55	331155.60	2533884.00	37.36
30	1890.7	18.3	.009679	.047344	64643.70	315567.30	2202728.00	34.07
35	1489.1	18.7	.012558	.061130	61583.23	298504.70	1887161.00	30.64
40	1152.6	17.6	.015270	.073528	57818.64	278464.90	1588656.00	27.48
45	886.3	11.5	.012975	.062854	53567.34	259419.30	1310191.00	24.46
50	1085.5	22.1	.020359	.185493	50200.39	455444.90	1050772.00	20.93
60	445.6	14.1	.031643	.293245	40888.59	348934.00	595326.70	14.56
70	157.2	14.3	.090967	.636241	28898.20	197050.80	246392.70	8.53
80	23.0	4.9	.213043	1.000000	10511.97	49341.89	49341.89	4.69
TOTALS	21681.8	385.6						

CDR = 17.785.
Births = −1.0.

Table 6.A.5: Rochester, N.Y., 1853–1857: Females (Mount Hope Cemetery data)

Age	Population	Deaths	M(X)	Q(X)	L(X)	LL(X)	T(X)	E(X)
0	768.3	99.7	.129767	.118828	100000.00	91800.86	4699559.00	47.00
1	2494.3	61.0	.024456	.091814	88117.19	330818.80	4607758.00	52.29
5	2531.3	14.2	.005610	.027587	80026.77	394614.50	4276939.00	53.44
10	2408.1	8.8	.003654	.018108	77819.04	385572.30	3882324.00	49.89
15	2434.2	15.0	.006162	.030324	76409.89	376256.90	3496752.00	45.76
20	2606.5	15.1	.005793	.028580	74092.88	365170.40	3120495.00	42.12
25	2249.8	23.1	.010268	.050150	71975.30	350852.60	2755325.00	38.28
30	1704.9	14.5	.008505	.041796	68365.75	334685.30	2404472.00	35.17
35	1386.4	18.7	.013488	.065377	65508.35	316835.00	2069787.00	31.60
40	1105.9	13.6	.012298	.059807	61225.64	296973.80	1752952.00	28.63
45	755.3	12.5	.016550	.079433	57563.90	276388.40	1455978.00	25.29
50	1055.8	15.5	.014681	.137222	52991.45	493556.40	1179589.00	22.26
60	514.9	17.1	.033210	.300123	45719.84	388590.40	686032.90	15.01
70	143.2	11.7	.081704	.599671	31998.24	224040.30	297442.60	9.30
80	36.1	6.3	.174515	1.000000	12809.82	73402.28	73402.28	5.73
TOTALS	22195.0	346.8						

CDR = 15.625.
Births = −1.0.

Table 6.A.6: Rochester, N.Y., 1853–1857: Both Sexes (Mount Hope Cemetery data)

Age	Population	Deaths	M(X)	Q(X)	L(X)	LL(X)	T(X)	E(X)
0	1498.4	217.0	.144821	.131772	100000.00	90775.97	4546057.00	45.46
1	5030.9	132.2	.026278	.098190	86822.81	324426.80	4455281.00	51.31
5	5032.9	30.6	.006080	.029847	78297.66	385645.90	4130854.00	52.76
10	4820.6	17.6	.003651	.018083	75960.71	376369.60	3745208.00	49.30
15	4501.1	24.8	.005510	.027177	74587.12	367868.00	3368838.00	45.17
20	4772.5	35.2	.007376	.036217	72560.07	356230.60	3000970.00	41.36
25	4387.9	43.6	.009936	.048515	69932.18	341179.10	2644739.00	37.82
30	3595.6	32.8	.009122	.044715	66539.45	325258.90	2303560.00	34.62
35	2875.5	37.4	.013006	.063176	63564.13	307781.40	1978301.00	31.12
40	2258.5	31.2	.013814	.066827	59548.42	287793.60	1670520.00	28.05
45	1641.4	24.0	.014620	.070517	55569.00	268048.60	1382727.00	24.88
50	2141.4	37.6	.017559	.162027	51650.42	474660.30	1114678.00	21.58
60	960.5	31.2	.032483	.296978	43281.64	368547.90	640017.60	14.79
70	300.5	26.0	.086522	.618390	30427.93	210197.80	271469.80	8.92
80	59.1	11.2	.189509	1.000000	11611.62	61272.01	61272.01	5.28
TOTALS	43877.0	732.4						

CDR = 16.692.
Births = −1.0.

REFERENCES

Brighton Town Clerk's Record of Births, Deaths, and Marriages for the Years 1847–1850. Local History Division, Rochester Public Library.

Brothwell, D. R. 1981. *Digging Up Bones.* London: Oxford University Press.

Clement, Priscilla F. 1985. *Welfare and the Poor in the Nineteenth Century City, Philadelphia, 1900–1854.* Cranbury NJ: Associated Press, Inc.

Costa, Dora L. 1993. "Height, Wealth, and Disease among the Native-born in the Rural, Antebellum North." *Social Science History* 17: 355–383.

Cray, Robert E., Jr. 1988. *Paupers and Poor Relief in New York City and Its Rural Environs, 1700–1830.* Philadelphia: Temple University Press.

Demirjian, A. 1986. "Dentition." In F. Falkner and J. M. Tanner, eds. *Human Growth.* Vol. 2: *Post Natal Growth,* 2d ed. New York: Plenum Press, pp. 269–298.

Elia, Ricardo J. 1991. "The Uxbridge Almshouse Burial Project," in Ricardo J. Elia and Al B. Wesolowsky, eds. *Archaeological Excavations at the Uxbridge Almshouse Burial Ground in Uxbridge, Massachusetts.* BAR International Series 564, pp. 1–11.

French, J. H. 1860. *Gazetteer of the State of New York.* Syracuse, NY: R. Pearsall Smith.

Haines, Michael R. 1998a. "Estimated Life Tables for the United States, 1850–1910." *Historical Methods* 31: 149–169,

1998b. "Health, Height, Nutrition, and Mortality: Evidence on the 'Antebellum Puzzle' from Union Army Recruits for New York State and the United States." In John Komlos and Joerg Baten, eds., *The Biological Standard of Living in Comparative Perspective.* Stuttgart: Franz Steiner Verlag, pp. 155–180.

Hannon, Joan Underhill. 1984. "Poverty in the Antebellum Northeast: The View from New York State's Poor Relief Rolls." *Journal of Economic History* 44: 1007–1032.

1985. "Poor Relief Policy in Antebellum New York State: The Rise and Decline of the Poorhouse." *Explorations in Economic History.* 22: 233–256.

HEA Newsletter. Richard H. Steckel, ed. (1996). Columbus, Ohio.

Higgins, Rosanne L. 1996. "Estimates of Mortality in the Erie and Niagara County Poorhouses: 1870–1886." *American Journal of Physical Anthropology.* Supplement 22, p. 124.

1998. "The Biology of Poverty: Epidemiological Transition in Western New York. Ph.D. diss., State University of New York at Buffalo.

Higgins, Rosanne L., and Joyce E. Sirianni. 1995. "An Assessment of Health and Mortality in Nineteenth Century Rochester, New York, Using Historic Records and the Highland Park Skeletal Collection." In A. L. Grauer, ed., *Bodies of Evidence: Reconstructing History through Skeletal Analysis.* New York: Wiley Liss and Sons, Inc., pp. 121–136.

Hoffman, Frederick L. 1906. "The General Death-Rate of Large American Cities." *Publications of the American Statistical Association.* New Series, No. 73 (March): 1–75.

Katz, Michael B. 1983. *Poverty and Policy in American History.* New York: Academic Press.

1996. *In the Shadow of the Poorhouse.* Rev. ed. New York: Basic Books, Inc.

Krogman, W. M., and M. Y. Iscan. 1986. *The Human Skeleton in Forensic Medicine.* Springfield, IL: Charles Thomas.

Lanphear, K. M. 1988. "Health and Mortality in a Nineteenth Century Skeletal Sample." Ph.D. diss., SUNY Albany.

Lovejoy, C. O., R. S. Meindl, T. R. Pryzbeck, and R. O. Mensforth. 1985. "Chronological Metamorphosis of the Auricular Surface of the Ilium: A New Method for the Determination of Age at Death." *American Journal of Physical Anthropology* 68: 15–28.

Massachusetts. Secretary of the Commonwealth. 1856–1862. *Report to the Legislature of Massachusetts Relating to the Registry and Returns of Births, Marriages, and Deaths, in the Commonwealth for the Year Ending December 31, 1855, 1856, 1859, 1860, 1861.* Boston.

1857. *Abstract of the Census of the Commonwealth of Massachusetts, taken with reference to facts existing on the First Day of June, 1855.* Boston: W. White.

1863. *Abstract of the Census of Massachusetts, 1860: From the Eighth U.S. Census, with Remarks on the Same.* Prepared under the direction of Oliver Warner, Secretary of the Commonwealth by George Wingate Chase. Boston: Wright and Potter.

McKelvey, Blake. 1945. *Rochester: The Water-Power City, 1812–1854.* Cambridge, MA: Harvard University Press.

1947. "Historic Origins of Rochester's Social Welfare Agencies." *Rochester History* 9, nos. 2 and 3: 6–11.

1956. "The History of Public Health in Rochester, New York." *Rochester History* 18, no. 3: 3–28.

1972. "A History of Penal and Correctional Institutions in the Rochester Area." *Rochester History* 34: 3–24.

Meindl, R. S., and C. O. Lovejoy. 1985. "Ectocranial Suture Closure: A Revised Method for the Determination of Skeletal Age at Death and Blind Tests of its Accuracy." *American Journal of Physical Anthropology* 68: 57–66.

Meindl, R. S., C. O. Lovejoy, R. O. Mensforth, and R. A. Walker. 1985. "A Revised Method of Age Determination Using the Os Pubis, with a Review and Tests of Accuracy of Other Current Methods of Pubic Symphyseal Aging." *American Journal of Physical Anthropology* 68: 29–45.

Mount Hope Cemetery Records. 1837–1850. Vol. 1, Mount Hope Cemetery, Rochester, NY.

New York State. 1867. *Census of the State of New York for 1865.* Albany, NY: Charles van Benthuysen & Son.

Pope, Clayne L. 1992. "Adult Mortality in America before 1900: A View from Family Histories." In Claudia Goldin and Hugh Rockoff, eds. *Strategic Factors in Nineteenth Century American Economic History: A Volume to Honor Robert W. Fogel.* Chicago: University of Chicago Press., pp. 267–296.

Rosenberg, Charles E. 1962. *The Cholera Years: The United States in 1832, 1849, and 1866.* Chicago: University of Chicago Press.

Rosenberg-Naparsteck, Ruth. 1983. "Life and Death in Nineteenth Century Rochester." *Rochester History* 45, nos. 1 and 2: 2–24.

Sirianni, Joyce E., and Rosanne L. Higgins. 1995. "A Comparison of Death Records from the Monroe County Almshouse with Skeletal Remains from the Associated Highland Park Cemetery." In Shelley R. Saunders and Ann Herring, eds. *Grave Reflections, Portraying the Past through Cemetery Records.* Toronto: Canadian Scholars Press, pp. 71–92.

Steegmann, A. Theodore. 1991. "Stature in an Early Mid-nineteenth Century Poorhouse Population: Highland Park, Rochester, New York." *American Journal of Physical Anthropology* 85: 261–268.

Wesolowsky, Al B. 1991. "The Osteology of the Uxbridge Paupers." In Ricardo J. Elia and Al B. Wesolowsky, eds., *Archaeological Excavations at the Uxbridge Almshouse Burial Ground in Uxbridge, Massachusetts.* BAR International Series 564.

CHAPTER SEVEN

The Effects of Nineteenth-Century
Military Service on Health

Paul S. Sledzik and Lars G. Sandberg

War is delightful to those who have had no experience of it. –
Desiderius Erasmus

ABSTRACT

During the nineteenth century, soldiers lucky or clever enough to avoid a bullet endured physical hardships that took a serious toll on their skeletons. The remains of 83 soldiers, spanning the Revolutionary War to the Battle of Little Bighorn, display the effects of these hardships. Conditions such as porotic hyperostosis, vertebral lesions, and dental caries and abscesses appeared at an early age among these soldiers. Low frequencies of chronic infection and moderate-to-severe skeletal deformities indicate that men with these conditions were not allowed to serve. The health index used in this study places the soldiers among the least healthy groups, supporting the conclusion that nineteenth-century military service turned relatively healthy young men into physical wrecks, unless they perished in combat first.

I. INTRODUCTION

As human endeavors go, war is particularly unsavory. Health and disease have impacted on the outcome of important battles and military campaigns at least until this century. Sick soldiers do not fight well.

Modern interpretations of the life of nineteenth-century soldiers are colored by firsthand accounts and broadly written historical works, usually focused on tactics and battles. Soldiers' diaries and generals' recollections rarely present the effects of military service on the bodies of young men. Certainly, military life was hard during the nineteenth century, but just how did it affect the musculoskeletal system of the soldiers? The skeletons of nineteenth-century soldiers provide unique evidence regarding the physical effects of military life.

Most of the substantial amount of work recently done on the level and rate of change of health and welfare in Europe and North America since the middle of

185

the eighteenth century relies primarily on data obtained from body measurements, particularly the stature, of individuals. The principal keepers of these data were prisons, schools, slave traders and, most importantly, military authorities. The chief motive for these, not surprisingly, was the identification of living individuals.

Unfortunately, these data sources do not represent random samples of the entire population. In the case of the military, it is clear that the soldiers were taller, and indeed were healthier, than the general population (Costa, 1993; Sandberg and Steckel, 1980). Various statistical devices, therefore, have been developed to draw inferences concerning the state of health and nutrition of the entire population from evidence on the state of this healthier than average subset of the population (Komlos and Kim, 1990, and Wachter and Trussell, 1982).

Given this background, it is, at least initially, startling to learn that the sample of skeletons of American soldiers available for analysis, within the confines of this project, yields distinctly mediocre results in terms of the health index developed in other parts of this book. On the basis of their skeletal records, these supposedly healthier than average Euro-Americans have a health index that places them below many Native American groups and well below the overall median. This remains true even if the soldier's low age at death is disregarded. It is made no less startling by the fact that these soldiers clearly were of above-average stature relative to the already very tall Euro-American population. Is it really possible that the Euro-American population in North America during the period between roughly the 1770s and the 1870s was tall but unhealthy?

Almost certainly this was not the case. Rather, the skeletal remains analyzed in this chapter are striking evidence of the truly ghastly conditions under which North American soldiers served during the wars of the eighteenth and nineteenth centuries. Granted, the fact that life in the military was hard is no surprise. Literary and other evidence has long made it clear that the soldier's life involved bad food, hard work, and an appalling lack of sanitation. That many, often most, wartime fatalities were the result of disease, rather than combat, is also not news. When recruits entered the military, they quickly encountered deterioration in diet, increased exposure to disease, and constant physical and psychological stress. John Shaw Billings, the military officer responsible for many improvements in the U.S. Army military health system in the nineteenth century, described the situation as follows in an 1875 report on U.S. Army hygiene:

It is sufficient for the purposes of this report to say that the standard of health and physical perfection of the enlisted men on entering the service is above the average. . . . [S]etting aside injuries, to which the soldier is specially liable, the mortality from disease among these picked men is distinctly greater than among men of the same age in civil life, under the same conditions of climate. – It is, I think, sufficiently evident . . . that the hygienic conditions under which our troops are placed cannot be considered satisfactory. (Billings, 1875, p. viii)

Certainly Billings's observations were not well suited for inclusion in the army's recruitment literature. Nonetheless, the situation he describes is much less drastic than the conditions at least hinted at by the state of the skeletons of 83 individuals from four battle sites dating from the Revolutionary War period to the Battle of the Little Bighorn analyzed in this chapter. In a fairly modest amount of time, the army apparently had managed to take healthier-than-average young men and convert them into distinctly unhealthy soldiers. The fact that these particular individuals then suffered a miserable death serves to make their particular lives especially tragic, but there is no reason to believe that their more fortunate surviving comrades (whose skeletons obviously are not available from the sites in question) were any healthier. The unfortunate 83 did not die because of the health problems revealed by their skeletons (excluding their final trauma). While a larger sample of skeletons certainly would be helpful in more firmly establishing our conclusions, there is little doubt that at least the remains examined here were of men who could truly say "army life is a bitch, and then you die."

II. TRADITIONAL SOURCES OF EVIDENCE AND METHODS OF ANALYSIS

Information about life in the nineteenth-century United States military comes primarily from historical records. Recruit enlistment information often reveals name, age, stature, occupation, geographic origin of birth, and race or ethnic group. Military medical manuals, recruit selection criteria, food ration orders, and reports on disease prevalence among troops offer insight into the military procedures that impacted the health of the soldier. Personal biological information gleaned from recruit lists provides raw data for analysis, but age and stature data are limited measures of health. As supportive documentation, military reports and regulations are windows into the practices that shaped the health of the soldier.

A review of the sources indicates that there was a trend in the type of data available over the course of the nineteenth century. Early in the century, data exists in the form of stature, age, birth origin, and occupation at the time of enlistment. Some recruit selection information is available. As the nineteenth century progressed, the physical condition of soldiers was documented more thoroughly. The publication of the *Medical and Surgical History of the War of the Rebellion* (1879) and research by Gould (1869) were exhaustive analyses and interpretations of health and stature, respectively. The *Medical and Surgical History* is both a list of individual patient information and an interpretive epidemiological study. This focus on individual health information and comprehensive epidemiological analysis continued into the beginning of this century. Modern researchers have used these nineteenth-century sources to examine the quality of life of soldiers during and after military service (Costa, 1993; Fogel et al., 1986).

In recent years, access to the skeletons of soldiers has provided another source of data about the health of soldiers and the effects of military service on the skeleton. The information residing in the human skeleton is limited. In some situations, it can provide a "reality check" for the historical data. In other areas, the historical data are used to help interpret what the skeletal biologist sees in the skeleton.

A. Military Bioarchaeology

The analysis of skeletal remains from historic military sites is a recent addition to the bioarchaeological literature. As with any unique skeletal series, military skeletal samples offer information in terms of age, sex, and physical stressors. The few dozen reports and publications that have presented data from military skeletal samples have focused largely on the health of the soldiers. The number of skeletons examined in these reports and publications is small. As a group, they show the physical toll of life as an American soldier in the eighteenth and nineteenth centuries. Many of these reports also reveal that the final insult to their brief, hard life was a fatal bullet. One bioarchaeologist has noted: "A skeletal series from a battlefield offers the opportunity to study the effects of field conditions and physical stress (acute or chronic excessive biomechanical strain or injury) in a specially selected subset of the general population in which age, sex, and other physical characteristics are relatively consistent as a result of induction standards" (Owsley, 1997, p. 8).

Angel (1976) reviewed skeletal change from colonial times to the modern era. He compared 82 individuals dating from 1675 to 1879 with individuals from the modern anatomical collections and with forensic cases. Several crania from nineteenth-century military settings were also analyzed. Angel's study provides data on stature, skeletal anthropometry, and pathological conditions for the general population during the relevant time period. He notes that both skeletal and historic data do not support an expected significant increase in stature from the colonial period to the modern period (ca. 1950–1975).

In 1986, Steegman examined the remains of mid-eighteenth-century British soldiers buried at Fort William Henry (ca. 1757) on Lake George, New York. A total of 14 individuals were examined for stature; no other information was collected. Steegman compared these skeletal statures to anthropometric statures taken on recruits (Steegman, 1986). He notes that the skeletal sample was a select group, significantly taller than the provincial troops. In an earlier study, Steegman (1985) examined eighteenth-century British military stature, noting variation in stature with cold, migration, place of residence, and occupation. He and Haseley presented similar results in an analysis of American colonial data (1988). Baker and Liston (1995) and Liston and Baker (1995; 1996) reanalyzed the skeletons from Fort William Henry and also studied additional remains. Their reports focus primarily on traumatic injuries and skeletal infections. Although a total of 30 individuals, aged 14 to 45, were analyzed by the authors for the 1995 studies, only 5 individuals were reported in the 1996 article. The traumatic injuries documented on these individuals included cuts, gunshot wounds, and decapitation.

Remains from the Battle of the Little Bighorn have been analyzed by several authors (Scott and Willey, 1997; Snow and Fitzpatrick, 1989; Willey, 1997; Willey and Scott, 1996; Willey et al., 1997). Snow and Fitzpatrick analyzed skeletal remains representing 34 incomplete individuals recovered from various places on the battlefield. Estimates of age at death ranged from 15 to 19 years for the youngest, and 35 to 45 for the older soldiers. Mean stature of the nine measurable individuals was 169.67cm. These remains exhibit various types of perimortem traumatic injuries, including gunshot wounds, blunt force trauma, and incised wounds. Antemortem pathology consisted of two healed fractures of two metatarsals and one lumbar vertebra. No evidence of nutritional deficiency, infectious disease, or dental caries was noted. Information from the remaining reports by Willey and Scott are used in the present study.

In 1991, Sledzik and Moore-Jansen examined dental health among eighteenth- and nineteenth-century military skeletal samples. Their results revealed that changes in diet throughout the eighteenth and nineteenth centuries were responsible for the increase in caries frequency observed in Civil War soldiers. In addition, recruit selection guidelines eliminated men with missing anterior teeth; the results of these guidelines are seen in reduced rates of antemortem loss.

Ratliff (1993) reported on a mass grave of Mexicans killed in the battle of Resaca de la Palma near Brownsville, Texas, in 1846. This abstract indicates that 28 individuals, including 4 females, were analyzed. The soldiers from the sample revealed healed fractures, degenerative lesions, and ligamentous avulsions, largely of the lower limbs.

The analysis of military remains is complemented by the availability of historical documents. These give the bioarchaeologist powerful evidence for the interpretation of skeletal data. This is particularly true of studies of military skeletal samples. In the United States since at least the eighteenth century, nearly every aspect of military life has been documented: diet, disease, weather, clothing, place of origin of recruits, anthropometric data on soldiers, and other quantitative and qualitative information. These data, collected largely to increase military readiness, exist both in raw and in tabular form. These documentary data comprise health and anthropometric standards for military recruitment, statistical analyses of anthropometric measurements, tabulations of morbidity and mortality, and requirements for rations, clothing, housing, and military exercises. For over 100 years, researchers have exhaustively analyzed the anthropometric data gathered on recruits. Older studies tended to be tabular listings of data, while modern researchers have used these tabular data to draw inferences concerning health, economic status, and response to environmental and physical factors.

It is well known that not just anyone could become a soldier. Recruitment standards called for the selection of soldiers well suited to the specific physical demands of military service (Friedl, 1992). The impact of the standards was to assure relatively good health and a reasonable distribution of heights and weights. The screening effect of selection standards provides the skeletal biologist with a tool for interpreting the differences in frequency of various skeletal measures of health. The existence of recruit selection guidelines presumes an adequate state of health at the time of entry into the military and can thus act as a standardized point of departure for interpretations of the physical effects of military service.

B. Historical Evidence for Nineteenth-Century Military Health

During the eighteenth and nineteenth centuries, as well as in all earlier centuries, military service was not the route to better health. Even aside from the possibility of crippling injury or a miserable death on the battlefield, this was especially the case during wartime. Although this study deals with North America, it should at least be noted that this health-destroying effect was a worldwide phenomenon. It is only in recent times that some armies have been able to claim with any degree of truthfulness that they take youths and "build men." In the past, they took young men and built physical wrecks.

Recruits experienced a combination of dietary, health, and physical stressors that acted to lower their quality of life and their state of health, regardless of their origin. Rural residents, used to eating fresh vegetables and unprocessed grains, suffered an especially sharp decline in their dietary standard. Recruits from urban areas probably experienced a somewhat lesser deterioration in diet. As soldiers were assigned to quickly erected camps with a high population density and minimal sanitary facilities, disease exposure increased substantially. Even the more permanent forts reported high rates of infectious disease (Billings, 1875). While exposure to diseases and physical stress increased for both rural and urban recruits, it seems highly likely that the former, in particular, came into contact with new pathogens. Of course, once the recruits had been trained and sent into the field, things only got worse. The physical and psychological stress was especially severe during actual campaigns and in combat situations.

With recruit selection standards acting as a screening device, men who entered the military must have been in relatively good health at the time of enlistment. The rigor with which these standards were applied is open to debate, but it seems reasonable to assume that as a group, new recruits were healthier than the general population. Information on the standards can be found in manuals used for recruit selection (Hamilton, 1861; Hammond, 1863; Henderson, 1840). Several biological characteristics were used as standards: age, stature, weight, diseases, physical deformities, and oral health.

Mid-nineteenth-century U.S. standards required recruits to be between 18 and 35 years of age, with parental or guardian consent required for those under age 21. By 18 years of age, recruits would have experienced childhood diseases, and the consequences of their nutritional standard should have been apparent. Most would have reached their final adult stature. In 1790, the minimum height for recruits was set at 5 feet, 6 inches. During the Mexican-American War, a minimum standard of 5 feet, 3 inches was applied. By 1854, this standard had risen to 5 feet, 4 1/2 inches. Weight standards as a function of height were also established. Thus, for example, a 6-foot recruit was not to exceed 220 pounds in weight. By 1874, the standards for the artillery and infantry were at least 5 feet, 4 inches tall, with a weight of between 120 and 180 pounds. Cavalrymen had to be between 5 feet, 5 inches and 5 feet, 10 inches tall, and they could not weigh more than 155 pounds (Billings, 1875).

Since the nineteenth century was a time when bodily deformities were thought to have a great impact on overall health and physical capacity, much attention was devoted to such deformities. Recruits could be excluded from service if their heads were too large or too small, if their arms or legs were too short or too long, or if their limbs or their chest were misshapen. Too many missing or unsound teeth was also grounds for rejection. Sound teeth were needed not just to chew the virtually unchewable food (e.g., salted meat and "hard tack") but also to bite the paper off the ends of cartridges (Hamilton, 1861; Lewis, 1865.)

Certain fractures, dislocations, or amputations were the basis for rejection from service. Examiners could disqualify recruits whose fractures could result in future lameness. Fractures not expected to cause lameness, such as fractures of the radius, the ulna, the fingers, the shaft of the humerus, and some fractures of the femoral shaft, were not cause for disqualification. Certain spinal deformities affecting the curvature of the spine were also unacceptable. Diseases such as syphilis, epilepsy, paralysis, itch and other incurable skin diseases, defects in hearing and sight, goiter, deformities of the mouth or nose, chronic asthma, and a variety of other conditions affecting overall health or potential performance as a soldier were grounds for rejection.

III. DESCRIPTION OF SITES

Four samples, dating from 1778 to 1876, were used in the present study. A total of 83 male Euro-American individuals were coded for analysis. General information on each site is presented in Table 7.1. Given the small sample size, these four sites will be considered as one for the purposes of comparison with other samples.

A. Fort Laurens

Fort Laurens was a Revolutionary War era stockade located in the town of Bolivar, Ohio, about 60 miles south of Cleveland on the Tuscarawas River (Sciulli and Gramly, 1989). Construction on the fort began in late 1778 and involved regiments from Pennsylvania, Virginia, and North Carolina. By early December 1778, only the Pennsylvania and Virginia regiments remained at the fort. Between 20 and 27 deaths occurred during the nine months the fort was occupied, including a period of siege by the British and their Native American allies. A majority of these fatalities occurring between January and March of 1779 were soldiers from the Virginia and Pennsylvania regiments. Sciulli and Gramly report that these deaths were either the result of accidents or of ambushes by Native Americans. Seven individual graves and a single mass grave were exhumed and analyzed. For the present study, 19 individuals were coded for analysis by Paul Sciulli.

The troops stationed at Fort Laurens marched from the Pittsburgh area through the frontier, and they began to build Fort Laurens in mid-November of 1778. Rations were very scarce during the march and at the fort. The diet at the fort consisted mainly of cornmeal and other grains, infrequently supplemented by fresh meat obtained from the native tribes. Just before arriving at the site of the fort, the troops' flour rations were reduced. Future rationing reductions followed, with soldiers being allowed just four ounces of spoiled flour and eight ounces of rancid beef

Table 7.1: Military Skeletal Sample Information

Site name	Location	Date	Regiment locations	Sample size	Mean age at death	Mean stature (cm)
Fort Laurens	Ohio	1778	PA, VA, NC	19	23.9 years	171.7
Snake Hill	Ontario	1812–14	NY, PA	25	24.9 years	174.3
Glorieta Pass	New Mexico	1862	TX	30	23.5 years	172.9
Little Bighorn	Montana	1876	Unknown	9	27.4 years	175.5

daily (Pieper and Gidney, 1976). The situation was even worse during the winter, conditions being described as near starvation.

Physical stresses included the march to the garrison and the building of the fort. During the siege, there was little strenuous physical activity, a result of the small size of the fort and the overall poor nutrition of the troops. Sciulli and Gramly report that, based on the osteological evidence, the individuals in the present study were exposed to at least moderate levels of mechanical stress. They also suggest that high levels of mechanical stress may have been experienced. This conclusion is based on the frontier experience of the soldiers before enlistment, and on the fact that men could serve up to one and a half years, during which time they constructed two forts. Weakness and sickness were prevalent inside the fort. Given the diet and poor sanitation, diarrheal and camp diseases were no doubt common.

B. Snake Hill

The Snake Hill site is located in Fort Erie, Ontario, across Lake Erie from Buffalo, New York. Fort Erie was captured by American troops on July 3, 1814, and was later besieged by the British from August 5, 1814, to September 21, 1814. The fort cemetery contained the remains of 28 individuals, all members of the American force. Presumably, the remains in the cemetery were interred during the siege. Volunteer regiments from New York and Pennsylvania were stationed at Fort Erie. British, German, Polish, and Spanish prisoners were also held at the fort. The cemetery was excavated in 1987 by a joint Canadian-U.S. team of archaeologists and physical anthropologists.

An edited volume by Pfeiffer and Williamson (1991) presents historic, archaeological, and skeletal information concerning this site. Reports on medical and military history, as well as the archaeology of the site, yield additional information. These reports provide an in-depth examination of life and death among the soldiers at Snake Hill. For the present study, Paul Sledzik recoded the original data sheets to fit the project requirements. A total of 25 skeletons were complete enough to be included in the present study.

In the months before the American forces captured Fort Erie, they underwent a rigorous training and drilling program ordered by Brigadier General Winfield Scott. By early June of 1814, their typical day included at least eight hours of drill. Their packs weighed close to 20kg, in addition to the weight of their rifles. During the siege, the digging of trenches and repairing earthwork and building damage took place between bombardments.

Soldiers were required to bathe three times a week and their food was inspected by an officer assigned to that task. Concerning the state of the enlisted soldiers, Whitehorne (1991) has written: "There can be no doubt that under Scott's direction, Brown's force was as close to the ideal in training, discipline, and equipment as any organization fielded by the U.S. during the War." The volunteer units faced the same drilling requirements, although their equipment and supplies were of lower quality than that of the U.S. soldiers.

Regimental surgeons reported cases of illness or disease even prior to the attack on Fort Erie. During the siege, men were pushed to their physical and emotional limits, performing heavy labor for extended periods under perilous conditions (Whitehorne, 1988). Dysentery, diarrhea, and typhus were common afflictions. The effects of extreme physical activity and exposure to the elements resulted in bouts of intermittent, acute rheumatism. The basic ration during the siege consisted of salt pork and hard bread. Rum, whiskey, brandy, molasses, salt, and vinegar were added to the rations when available. On occasion, butter, onions, and potatoes could be purchased, although at great cost, from local settlers. The risk of scurvy was great, at least one captain being ordered to procure potatoes regardless of price.

C. Glorieta Pass

On February 28, 1862, Union and Confederate forces clashed at the battle of Glorieta Pass, about 20 miles east of Santa Fe, New Mexico. One of five battles fought in the New Mexico campaign, this battle involved 1,000 Confederates from Texas and 850 Union troops. Records indicate that the Confederates suffered 40 killed and 60 injured; the Union forces had 38 fatalities and 64 casualties. In 1987, 31 Confederate burials were located and excavated. Owsley (1994) and London and Oakes (1989) have reported on the site. For the present study, Owsley's original data sheets were recoded by Paul Sledzik.

The soldiers who died at Glorieta Pass were Confederate enlistees. In his report on the osteology of these soldiers, Owsley (1994) includes the description of physical hardships taken from the diaries of two survivors of the New Mexico campaign. The campaign began late in 1861 and ended in the spring of 1862. The winter weather resulted in difficult conditions, particularly with regard to shelter.

Water was scarce, and the diet consisted of bread, coffee (when water was available), a small ration of dried beef, and, on occasion, mutton or beans. Diseases encountered during the campaign included smallpox, pneumonia, and measles.

Physical activity was intense because most of the pack animals had been killed early in the campaign. Aided only by small teams of animals, the men themselves were obliged to push and pull wheeled vehicles and artillery pieces over very rough terrain. Given the adverse climatic conditions, even walking proved difficult. Owsley presents both documentary and osteological evidence supporting his claim that the physical stresses endured in the six months prior to their deaths affected the skeletons of the Glorieta soldiers. Schmorl's nodes in the vertebrae, vertebral fusion and compression, joint and vertebral osteophytosis, and other indicators of skeletal stress are cited as osteological evidence.

D. Little Bighorn

The Battle of Little Bighorn, perhaps the most legendary nineteenth-century encounter with Native Americans, took place on June 25, 1876, in southern Montana. The battle resulted in the deaths of over 210 U.S. soldiers and of hundreds of Sioux and Cheyenne warriors. In 1991, eight graves were exhumed from the Custer National Cemetery by a team of archaeologists. These burials had originally been discovered on the battlefield in the first half of this century and then interred at the cemetery. The project osteologist, P. Willey of Chico State University, completed the original analysis on the burials. Some of the data have been previously published (Scott and Willey, 1997; Willey, Glenner, and Scott, 1996; Willey and Scott, 1996). Data on nine individuals were coded for the present study.

Willey et al. (1996) reported on the dental health of the Little Bighorn skeletons used in the present study. They extracted dietary information from Billings (1875). Daily rations consisted of 18 ounces of beef or pork, 2 ounces of beans, peas or rice, 2 ounces of sugar, 1 ounce of coffee, and some vinegar as a condiment. Billings notes that the caloric requirements of the typical soldier were not met by this diet. As in most military situations, soldiers supplemented their rations with other foods. Antiscorbutics were missing from the rations. Willey observed that while the men did not starve or suffer true malnourishment, they were certainly not well fed.

The physical stresses on these men included horseback riding (documented by Willey, 1994) and other military-related activities. The areas of osteological evidence are degenerative changes in the joints and vertebrae. Willey argues that, based on the low frequency of enamel hypoplasias and Harris lines, the childhood and adolescent health of these men was moderately good.

IV. RESULTS

A. Stature and Age at Death

Table 7.2 provides information on mean age at death and mean stature. Table 7.2 reveals additional age information. A total of 83 individuals were available for age assessment and analysis. Ages ranged from 13 years to 40 years for the combined sample. Table 7.2 presents age frequency data using the age categories in the present study. The mean age for the entire sample was 24.4 years ($n = 83$). The mean age for the samples varied by only 3.9 years, from 23.5 to 27.4 years. The Fort Laurens sample included two individuals 13 and 14 years of age. Eleven of the 30 Glorieta

Table 7.2: Age Category Frequency Data

Age category	Fort Laurens	Snake Hill	Glorieta Pass	Little Bighorn	Total
10–14.99	2	0	0	0	2
15–19.99	4	6	11	1	14
20–24.99	3	10	7	2	21
25–29.99	7	3	6	3	17
30–34.99	1	2	4	1	6
35–39.99	2	3	1	2	7
40–44.99	0	1	1	0	2
45–49.99	0	0	0	0	0
50+	0	0	0	0	0
TOTAL	19	25	30	9	83
MEAN	23.9	24.9	23.5	27.4	24.4

soldiers (36.7%) were between 15 and 19.99. As a whole, more than half (52/83 or 62.7%) of the sample ranged between 15 and 29.99 years. There were no individuals older than 45 years.

Mean stature is 173.4 centimeters, or slightly taller than 5 feet, 8 inches. The tallest soldiers were from the Little Bighorn site, while the shortest were from Fort Laurens. When the samples are compared, it is striking to note that the sample means vary by only 3.6cm. The statistics for each site indicate little variation from the mean in both these categories of data.

B. Skeletal Pathology

The data for pathological skeletal conditions in the military samples are provided in Table 7.3. Data are grouped by type of pathology (anemia, trauma, osteoarthritis, infectious disease, and dental disease). Given the small sample size of the combined sample, we did not analyze the severity of pathological lesions, but rather scored

Table 7.3: Pathological Conditions in the Military Skeletal Samples

Pathological condition	Fort Laurens		Snake Hill		Glorieta Pass		Little Bighorn		Total	
	N	%	N	%	N	%	N	%	N	%
Anemia										
Cribra orbitalia	7	0.0	20	0.0	28	7.2	8	0.0	63	3.2
Porotic hyper.	18	0.0	15	46.6	28	7.2	8	0.0	70	5.7
Trauma										
Vault	18	22.2	24	4.2	30	0.0	8	25.0	65	10.8
Arm	6	16.7	25	0.0	30	3.3	9	11.1	70	4.3
Leg	16	0.0	25	12.0	30	0.0	9	0.0	80	3.8
Weap. wound	19	94.7	25	48.0	30	93.3	9	33.3	83	73.5
Osteoarthritis										
TMJ	9	0.0	23	0.0	30	3.3	8	37.5	70	5.7
Shoulder	9	0.0	25	16.0	30	10.0	9	22.2	83	10.8
Wrist	1	0.0	25	8.0	30	3.3	9	11.1	65	6.2
Hip/Knee	16	0.0	24	20.8	30	6.7	9	44.4	79	13.9
Cervical vert.	11	0.0	22	4.5	30	0.0	8	0.0	71	1.4
Thoracic vert.	10	0.0	24	12.5	30	10.0	8	37.5	72	12.5
Lumbar vert.	8	25.0	24	20.8	30	13.3	8	25.0	70	18.6
Infectious disease										
Tibial infection	7	0.0	25	24.0	30	0.0	9	22.2	71	11.3
Skeletal infect.	19	10.5	25	8.0	30	10.0	9	0.0	83	8.4
Dental pathology										
LEH incisor	13	0.0	19	5.3	30	40.0	4	0.0	66	19.7
LEH canine	16	0.0	19	5.3	30	50.0	4	50.0	69	26.1
Caries	416	16.6	541	11.6	795	17.9	113	22.1	1865	16.0
Abscess	434	4.8	554	5.4	806	3.2	177	0.6	1971	4.0
Antemort. loss	434	4.1	554	8.8	806	2.2	177	7.3	1971	5.0

them as either present or absent. Dental disease will be examined separately below. The small sample sizes comprising each group make comparisons of the data between groups problematic. The data on the four samples combined, however, can be used for comparison with other groups.

The frequencies of the two anemic conditions included in this study (cribra orbitalia and porotic hyperostosis) are quite different. The frequency of cribra orbitalia in the combined military sample was relatively low (3.2%; 2/63). Both cases were from the Glorieta series. The frequency of porotic hyperostosis in the combined sample was 13% (9/69), with the Snake Hill soldiers accounting for 7 of the 9 cases. Tibial and skeletal infection frequencies were similar when the combined sample is examined. Tibial infections were observed in 8 of 71 skeletons (11.3%). As in the porotic hyperostosis data, Snake Hill soldiers comprised a majority of these cases (6 of the 8 cases). The frequency of skeletal infection in the combined sample was 8.4% (7/83). Such skeletal infections were noted in the Fort Laurens, Snake Hill, and Glorieta series.

Frequencies of degenerative joint disease indicates that the most common arthrodial joint affected was the hip/knee complex, followed by the shoulder and the wrist. In the vertebrae, the lumbar vertebrae show the highest frequency of disease (13/70 or 18.6%), followed by the thoracic and cervical vertebrae. Temporomandibular joint disease was evident in 5.7% (4/70) of the entire sample.

Data concerning the frequency of healed traumatic injuries and unhealed weapon wounds reveal that cranial trauma was the most common type of healed trauma, affecting 7 of 65 individuals, or 10.8% of the combined sample. Of note is the frequency of leg trauma in the Snake Hill soldiers (3/25; 12.0%) and the high frequency of healed cranial vault trauma encountered in the Fort Laurens sample (4/18; 22.2%). The frequency of unhealed weapon wounds is remarkably high, as is to be expected in these samples. Two samples show a lower frequency of weapon-related deaths. Almost half of the Snake Hill soldiers (12/25; 48.0%), as well as one-third of the Little Bighorn soldiers, presented weapon wounds. In the Snake Hill series, archaeological and documentary evidence reveals that several soldiers died in the hospital.

C. Dental Pathology

Linear enamel hypoplastic defect data are also provided in Table 7.3. The Glorieta soldiers reveal the highest frequency, while the Fort Laurens soldiers exhibited no enamel defects. The frequencies for the combined sample were 19.7% for incisors and 26.1% for canines.

Dental disease data are presented in Table 7.3. For the combined sample, carious lesions were observed in 16% of 1865 teeth. Individual site rates vary from 11.6% (Snake Hill) to 22.1% (Little Bighorn). Dental abscesses affected 4% of 1971 tooth sockets. The highest individual site rate was among the Snake Hill soldiers (5.4%). Only 1 socket of the 177 observed in the Little Bighorn soldiers exhibited an abscess. Antemortem loss frequency was observed in 5% of the 1971 sockets. The lowest antemortem tooth loss rate was observed in the Glorieta soldiers (2.2%).

V. DISCUSSION AND COMPARISON

In order to better understand the impact of military life on the skeleton, we need to establish some basis for comparison with the stresses of military life. The documentary and archaeological evidence from these samples indicates that these soldiers probably were not career servicemen. They enlisted at a young age and died, usually from a bullet, soon thereafter. Were the enlistees young men of good health or poor health? How did their military service impact their skeletons? Can the effects of recruit selection be detected in the frequencies of certain pathological conditions?

To answer these questions, we selected several different samples for comparison. Table 7.4 compares the military sample to two samples of males from the study in this volume. St. Thomas and Highland Park, similar in terms of ancestry (European) and time period (nineteenth century), also represent the upper and lower ends of socioeconomic status. St. Thomas is the site of an upper- to middle-class nineteenth-century cemetery from Ontario. Highland Park is a nineteenth-century poorhouse cemetery from New York. In Table 7.5, we compare the military sample to the three large ancestry groups represented in the present study: Euro-American, Native American, and African-American. The military samples were removed from these large groups, and comparisons were made only with adult males. Table 7.6 presents information on the samples broken down by two age categories, allowing for comparison between younger and older groups of military and Euro-American males. This may give some indication of the age-related changes to the skeleton. Lastly, Table 7.7 provides comparative data for stature from military and nonmilitary samples. Following a brief discussion of some broad issues of interpreting the skeletal evidence, each disease category will be examined with a focus on the questions posed above.

Examination of the differences within each pathology category reveals some indication of the hardships of military life, as well as an indication of childhood health. Two pathological conditions can be considered reflective of poor childhood health. Both cribra orbitalia and linear enamel hypoplasia are believed to be associated with stress events (e.g., malnutrition or a severe bout of diarrheal disease) in childhood. As such, if these conditions are prevalent in a skeletal population, poor childhood health can be inferred. Reduced adult stature can also be indicative of poor nutrition as a child, but recruit selection criteria may have eliminated such men.

There are also certain pathological conditions related to the health of the individual as an adult. For the military sample, interest centers on those pathological conditions that produce skeletal lesions in a relatively short period of time. It is not known how long any of these men spent in the military, and so the best indicators of health are those conditions that produce skeletal lesions in a short time. Of the conditions examined for the present study, four meet this criteria: osteoarthritis, porotic hyperostosis, dental caries, and dental abscesses. Trauma and infectious disease are less of a concern here, since an individual may have had these conditions previous to military service.

Table 7.4: Comparison of Pathological Conditions

	Military		St. Thomas'		Highland Park	
Pathological condition	N	%	N	%	N	%
Anemia						
Cribra orbitalia	63	3.2	91	5.5	113	3.5
Porotic hyperostosis	70	5.7	106	0.9	118	0
Trauma						
Vault	65	10.8	99	2.0	108	1.9
Nose	65	0.0	106	4.7	82	1.2
Face	63	0.0	97	2.0	81	0
Arm	70	4.3	116	9.5	108	8.3
Hand	—	—	4	50.0	107	1.9
Leg	80	3.8	129	12.4	109	6.4
Weapon wound	83	73.5	139	0.7	108	0.9
Osteoarthritis						
TMJ	70	5.7	129	10.9	72	9.7
Shoulder	83	10.8	133	88.7	105	58.1
Wrist	65	6.2	132	86.4	101	25.7
Hand	—	—	—	—	102	20.6
Hip/Knee	79	13.9	132	90.2	120	60.0
Cervical vertebrae	71	1.4	—	—	95	26.3
Thoracic vertebrae	72	12.5	—	—	92	41.3
Lumbar vertebrae	70	18.6	—	—	95	44.2
Infectious disease						
Tibial infection	71	11.3	135	9.6	107	40.2
Skeletal infection	83	8.4	143	25.9	118	54.2
Dental pathology						
LEH incisor	66	19.7	78	26.9	82	22.0
LEH canine	69	26.1	107	36.4	82	22.0
Caries	1865	16.0	2739	4.0	1826	4.5
Abscess	1971	4.0	3814	2.0	2624	5.3
Antemortem loss	1971	5.0	3814	19.5	2624	17.5

The guidelines intended to select healthy recruits for service eliminated men with gross physical abnormalities and debilitating physical conditions. As noted above, ongoing infections, lameness, or any other condition preventing normal activity was grounds for exclusion. Although the military sought healthy recruits – the healthier the man, the better the soldier – keeping the men fit to fight was not a high priority. Certainly recruit selection guidelines were not applied equally to all men at all times during the nineteenth century. Still, the guidelines can be used as a baseline from which to understand the frequency of pathological conditions seen in the military skeletal sample.

Table 7.5: Comparison of Pathological Conditions

Pathological condition	Military N	Military %	Euro-Americans N	Euro-Americans %	Native Americans N	Native Americans %	African Americans N	African Americans %
Anemia								
Cribra orbitalia	63	3.2	266	7.1	1266	17.2	148	11.5
Porotic hyperostosis	70	5.7	280	1.8	1287	16.2	261	6.1
Trauma								
Vault	65	10.8	252	5.2	1249	8.6	303	5.6
Nose	65	0.0	220	4.1	912	2.0	112	1.8
Face	63	0.0	209	1.0	983	3.9	122	0.8
Arm	70	4.3	274	9.1	1110	0.5	287	4.9
Hand	—	—	145	4.1	659	2.4	153	9.2
Leg	80	3.8	285	9.5	1243	2.8	312	5.7
Weapon wound	83	73.5	412	15.5	2194	2.8	37	0
Osteoarthritis								
Temporomandibular joint	70	5.7	232	58.2	813	16.7	175	36.6
Shoulder	83	10.8	177	57.6	1157	34.7	219	50.2
Wrist	65	6.2	266	56.4	930	17.6	1590	26.4
Hand	—	—	117	27.4	757	15.6	182	34.1
Hip/Knee	79	13.9	288	74.7	1167	36.4	224	49.1
Cervical vertebrae	71	1.4	130	30.8	912	39.8	158	38.6
Thoracic vertebrae	72	12.5	124	41.9	851	48.5	130	33.1
Lumbar vertebrae	70	18.6	122	45.9	909	58.4	142	42.3
Infectious disease								
Tibial infection	71	11.3	1462	79.9	1330	31.5	293	52.9
Skeletal infection	83	8.4	341	34.3	2243	19.6	350	45.1

As the data are examined and interpreted, it must be remembered that some of the differences observed may be the result of both scoring problems and of small sample size. Each sample was analyzed by a different physical anthropologist or team of anthropologists. The original data sheets for three of the sites were translated into the project data coding scheme. These three sites were analyzed before the project was initiated. The resulting possibility of interobserver error should be noted. Additionally, the sample of 83 individuals spans nearly 100 years. Thus, a very small number of individuals have to represent the hundreds of thousands of men who served over the course of a century.

A. Anemic Conditions

Taken together, the frequencies of the anemic conditions of cribra orbitalia and porotic hyperostosis in the military sample indicate differences in adult nutrition.

Table 7.6: Age Comparison of Pathological Conditions

	15–25-year-olds				26–45-year-olds			
	Military		Euro-Americans		Military		Euro-Americans	
Pathological condition	N	%	N	%	N	%	N	%
Anemia								
Cribra orbitalia	37	2.7	56	7.1	21	4.8	99	15.1
Porotic hyperostosis	43	16.2	61	11.5	24	8.3	94	25.5
Osteoarthritis								
Temporomandibular joint	39	0.0	56	14.3	22	9.0	86	59.3
Shoulder	39	5.1	56	8.9	25	12.0	90	61.1
Wrist	37	5.4	52	7.7	23	8.7	90	52.2
Hip/Knee	42	2.4	61	6.6	26	15.4	94	64.9
Cervical vertebrae	40	2.5	44	2.3	24	0	41	14.6
Thoracic vertebrae	41	2.4	45	2.2	24	25.0	39	28.2
Lumbar vertebrae	39	5.1	44	4.5	23	39.1	36	38.9
Infectious disease								
Tibial infection	43	7.0	65	7.1	26	3.8	99	15.1
Skeletal Infection	44	16.2	68	22.1	27	3.7	94	25.5
Linear enamel hypoplasia								
Incisor	35	22.9	54	25.9	21	14.3	62	22.6
Canine	38	31.6	47	38.3	22	13.6	89	32.6

Cribra orbitalia frequencies for the military samples are comparatively low. In Table 7.4, the three samples are not statistically significantly different (chi-square = .68, df = 2). When compared to the larger project samples (Table 7.5), however, the differences are significantly different (chi-square = 26.43, df = 4). The age breakdown in Table 7.6 indicates that both groups of soldiers show a lower frequency of cribra orbitalia. Conversely, the prevalence of porotic hyperostosis in the military sample is significantly greater (chi-square = 25.60, df = 2) than the two nineteenth-century samples. Additionally, when the military rate is compared to the three large samples, military frequency is equivalent to that of African-Americans and is much greater than that of Euro-Americans. In the age-separated analysis, both age groups show a lower frequency of cribra orbitalia. However, when examining porotic hyperostosis, it can be seen that the younger military age group has a higher frequency than the young Euro-Americans and the older military group.

The low frequency of cribra orbitalia may indicate that these men suffered from less nutritional deficiency as older children or teenagers, given their younger age at death. This is also supported by the fact that men with poor childhood nutrition likely would not have reached their maximum adult stature and may well have suffered from other diseases. The resulting short stature or physical problems associated with disease may have excluded them from service. In other words, the low

Table 7.7: Eighteenth- and Nineteenth-Century Male Stature Comparisons

Site name	Description	Dates	N	Mean stature (cm)	SD	Reference
Fort Laurens	U.S. Military	1779	13	171.7	6.8	Current study
Snake Hill	U.S. Military	1814	23	174.3	6.2	Current study
Glorieta Pass	U.S. Military	1862	24	172.9	5.6	Current study
Little Bighorn	U.S. Military	1876	8	175.5	4.7	Current study
	U.S. Military-site average	1779–1876	68	173.4	6.0	Current study
Osteometric Statures						
Highland Park	Rochester, NY, poorhouse	1820–1850	93	170.1	6.4	This volume
St. Thomas'	Ontario middle/upper class	1820–1860	127	171.9	5.3	This volume
Various	Colonial–Civil War skeletons	1675–1879	21	173.4	N/A	Angel, 1976
Ft. William Henry	British troops	1775	14	177.3	3.9	Steegman, 1986
Prospect Hill	Southern Ontario immigrants	1824–1879	17	173.4	4.4	Pfeiffer et al., 1992
Quebec City	POWs	1746–1747	30	173.3	6.09	Cybulski, 1988
Uxbridge poorhouse	Central Mass. poorhouse	1831–1872	9	169.7	N/A	Weslowsky, 1989
Documentary statures						
Civil War enlisted	White troops	1862–1865	150,000	171.4	N/A	Gould, 1869
Civil War enlisted	New England natives	1862–1865	33,783	173.5	N/A	Gould, 1869 (Table 11)
Civil War enlisted	NY/NJ/PA natives	1862–1865	61,351	173.0	N/A	Gould, 1869 (Table 11)
Civil War enlisted	British Province natives	1862–1865	6,667	171.6	N/A	Gould, 1869 (Table 11)
Bradford's Company	21st Mass. Regiment	1812–1814	180	173.9	6.89	Williamson, 1988

frequency of cribra orbitalia may be the result of selection for men who were healthy and tall as recruits. These men, no doubt, also had been healthy as older children.

The porotic hyperostosis evidence indicates that once in the service, these men did undergo nutritional stress. If porotic hyperostosis is taken to be a condition of fairly rapid onset, particularly the lesions seen in the early stages of the condition, then this explanation is plausible. Tables 7.4 and 7.5 indicate that the porotic hyperostosis frequency is significantly greater than in the contemporaneous St. Thomas' and Highland Park samples. If these samples are viewed as upper- and lower-class Euro–North American populations, respectively, then the high frequency of porotic hyperostosis in the military sample must be the result of some stress after the beginning of military service. Additionally, this disease frequency approximates more closely that seen in the nutritionally stressed African-American sample, thus arguing for some similarity in causation. The difference in porotic hyperostosis frequency between the older and the younger soldiers presented in Table 7.6 may be due to the weeding out of young soldiers by disease. Over the course of the Civil War, the decrease in morbidity and mortality was partly attributable to young soldiers with "less experienced" immune systems being killed off by disease early in the war. This left a larger number of men with more "experienced" immune systems. Nutrition level is directly tied to immune response. Thus, the high rate of porotic hyperostosis in the young age group may be interpreted as the skeletal response of a nutritionally "less experienced" group of soldiers.

B. Trauma

The trauma data reveal several points. The frequency of healed cranial trauma (10.8%) is the highest among any of the comparative samples. Although previous head trauma is probably not indicative of those desirous of military service, it may be the result of the rural background of many recruits. Subtle cranial injuries may not have been noticed by the recruit examiner, particularly not ones that left little soft-tissue damage. On the other hand, obvious deformities from a fracture of the face, of the arm, or of the leg were grounds for disqualification. The data reveal that the military sample has lower frequencies of nasal, facial, arm, and leg fractures than the European counterpart samples. For all of the fractures observed in the military sample, it is impossible to determine if they were the result of military service. It is impossible to accurately determine when a fracture occurred. It is known, however, that men were discharged from service if they became incapacitated by a fracture, and so fractures occurring during military service should not be represented. If the cranial fractures were received during military service, they were not severe enough to lead to discharge. This is not surprising, given that severe fractures to the skull result in death, whereas minor vault fractures present only pain that can be alleviated by drugs. A fractured leg or arm leaves a soldier unable to fight, but a minor skull fracture is only an inconvenience.

What makes the frequency of weapon wounds intriguing is that the number is so small. The presence of shroud pins makes it clear that in at least one of the samples (Snake Hill), several skeletons were buried in shrouds. Shroud burials were indicative of a hospital, not a battle, death. In fact, at least one of these skeletons showed evidence of an active bone infection. The types of injuries that resulted in these deaths were not from bullets alone. Shrapnel and artillery may have killed several. It is also important to note that in the nineteenth century, more soldiers died from disease than from bullets.

C. Osteoarthritis

Osteoarthritis is a condition related to activity and to age. The more there is of either, the more the osteoarthritis evident on the skeleton. In the military sample, the young age of these men and their hard physical activity seem to be at odds in terms of osteoarthritis evidence. Marching, carrying packs, digging, and drilling were the typical physical activities of the soldier, but did they affect the skeleton?

The frequency of all types of osteoarthritis is lower in comparison to the five groups in Tables 7.4 and 7.5. This is largely a function of the young age of these soldiers at the time of their deaths – they had not used their joints long enough to allow lesions to develop. Controlling for age, as in Table 7.6, the rates of nonvertebral osteoarthritis are lower in both military age groups when compared to the Euro-American male samples. The vertebral data differ less. This latter evidence might be interpreted to indicate that the physical activity in the military did not surpass that of civilian life. Recruit selection, however, would have eliminated most of the severe cases of osteoarthritis – those soldiers who had severe joint pain or were unable to move a joint.

The pathology coding requirements for the present study did not include two other indicators of physical activity: Schmorl's nodes of the vertebrae and enthesophytes (cortical lesions) of the proximal humerus. These lesions are indicative of, respectively, stress to the vertebrae and biomechanical stress to the upper arm and shoulder (Mann and Murphy, 1990; Owsley, Mann, and Murphy, 1991). Schmorl's nodes were noted in the vertebrae of many of the soldiers from all four sites. In addition, enthesophytes were reported for the Snake Hill and Glorieta sites. We argue that this evidence indicates that the soldiers in the sample were under physical stress, but that this stress is not represented in the project pathology coding scheme. Given the young age of the soldiers, subtle osseous changes related to physical stress, not osteoarthritic lesions, would be expected.

D. Infectious Disease

The frequency of bone infections of the tibia and other elements of the skeleton in the combined military samples are lower than for Native Americans, Euro-Americans, African-Americans, and the Highland Park sample. Severe infectious disease is incompatible with the physical demands of military life, and so it is likely that men who had experienced such diseases were excluded from service. The infections seen in the military samples are of a generalized nature, usually idiopathic periosteal reactions. Of the seven cases of skeletal infection noted in the military samples, five are described as periosteal reactions. In the Snake Hill and Glorieta samples, there are more healed than active infectious lesions (Owsley, Mann, and Murphy, 1991; Owsley, 1994). On their own, tibial infections may not have been visible enough to exclude men from service. Of the eight cases noted in the sample, only two show a severity greater than slight periosteal reaction.

When the sample is broken down by age, it can be seen that the younger soldiers had a higher rate of skeletal infection than did their older military counterparts. This might be attributed to the "weeding out" process mentioned above. The immune systems of these young soldiers were being "tested" by infectious diseases.

E. Dental Pathology

Linear enamel hypoplastic lesions are indicative of poor childhood health. As we see from the comparison with the nineteenth-century samples, the frequency of these lesions is not significantly different, either for the incisor (chi-square = 1.12, df = 2) or for the canine (chi-square = 5.14, df = 2). The low prevalence of these lesions in the military sample argues for relatively good childhood health. Linear enamel hypoplasia was not a factor in recruit exclusion, but men who had shorter stature or were "sickly" because of nutrition problems as children would have been excluded.

When carious lesions, abscesses, and antemortem loss are examined, two points may be noted. First, the caries rate is significantly different (chi-square = 263.18, df = 2). This is probably the result of a diet higher in sugar among these two samples. Sugar was not a common dietary item in military rations (Smith, 1875). Saunders, De Vito, and Katzenberg (1997) examined dental disease in the St. Thomas sample and indicate that the increase is the result of a greater intake of sugar. The other difference is the variation in the rate of antemortem tooth loss. This is probably the result of the military selection bias against men with anterior teeth missing (Sledzik and Moore-Jansen, 1991).

F. Stature

Adult stature reflects biological and social factors, such as genetics, health, and nutrition (Steckel, 1995). Stature is positively correlated with income or wealth and nutrition. Chronic poor nutrition and chronic and acute diseases during childhood result in decreased adult stature.

Stature among the military has been examined using documentary and skeletal evidence. Steegman (1985), in his studies of the skeletal and documentary stature data of eighteenth-century British and Irish troops, concludes that among the British military, measurements were taken in order to eliminate men of short stature from military service. The U.S. military did not collect stature data on officers (Gould, 1869). As far as can be ascertained from available documentary and archaeological evidence, the soldiers in this study were not officers.

Comparative data on contemporaneous military and nonmilitary samples are provided in Table 7.7. These data represent statures calculated from skeletal samples, as well as those derived from documentary sources. The military statures indicated by the present study were equivalent to statures from other military and nonmilitary samples. In fact, taken as a whole or individually, the military samples from the current study were higher than documented European military statures, and equivalent to those of U.S.-born military samples, both skeletal and documentary. This is strong evidence indicating that the soldiers in the current study had achieved their maximum adult statures before entering military service.

VI. IMPLICATIONS AND CONCLUSIONS

For thousands of years, the outcomes of battles and wars frequently have been determined by the presence of disease. The plague saved Rome from Attila the Hun. More recently, in the nineteenth century, Napoleon, like his eighteenth-century predecessor Charles XII, was defeated by the malnutrition and disease engendered by the Russian winter. Even in a more salubrious Russian climate during the Crimean War (1853–1856), more than 50,000 soldiers died from disease, compared with approximately 2,000 killed by bullets. During the American Civil War, more than 400,000 men expired from disease, while less than half that number were killed by ordnance. Only in recent times has modern medicine been able to reverse this ratio.

The effects of marching, drilling, and other types of physical activity on nineteenth-century, and earlier, soldiers can be gleaned from personal accounts. These effects, however, are not usually documented in the medical accounts of the wars. The present study of human remains thus provides both strong and unique evidence of the extraordinary stresses of, at least, military life. The comparatively high rates of dental caries and porotic hyperostosis, as well as the presence of stress-related lesions not included in the overall project's scoring scheme (i.e., Schmorl's nodes), reveals that these men were under intense physical and nutritional stress.

It must be admitted that, in general terms, this conclusion is not entirely new or startling. What is perhaps startling, however, is exactly how very unhealthy life, even ignoring the high possibility of death, was in the military. These men had entered the service with above-average health and in short order had had that health seriously undermined. For most of the soldiers included in this study, the bullet that killed them was just the last, if the most serious, in a long series of physical insults. Although it would certainly have been preferable if this study had been based on a larger sample of military skeletons, nonetheless, we believe that some conclusions can be drawn. It seems clear that these soldiers were healthy as recruits. In addition to being quite tall, these skeletons reveal low frequencies of markers indicative of severe childhood stress events. Quite clearly they had not greatly suffered from nutritional deficiencies or chronic disease loads. It is also clear from the low frequency of certain disease conditions, such as skeletal infections and healed trauma, that the published recruit selection standards did, in fact, play an important role.

Finally, the question must be asked: If life in the nineteenth-century American military was so difficult, why did these young men enlist? Clearly, some answers can be suggested. The chance to earn a steady paycheck might have attracted some, especially immigrants. Others may have been fervent believers in the "cause," while yet others may have been enticed by the prospect of adventure and by the apparent romance of war. Unquestionably, recruiters played on such juvenile sentiments. Ultimately, however, some nineteenth-century men and boys took up the cause and suffered physically through the experience.

REFERENCES

Baker, Brenda J., and Maria A. Liston. "Infection in Eighteenth-Century Military Remains at Fort William Henry." *American Journal of Physical Anthropology*, Supplement #20 (1995): 61.

Billings, John Shaw. *A Report on the Hygiene of the U.S. Army with Descriptions of the Military Posts.* Surgeon General's Office, Circular No. 8. Washington, D.C: GPO, 1875.

Costa, Dora L. "Height, Weight, Wartime Stress, and Older Age Mortality: Evidence from the Union Army Records." *Explorations in Economic History,* 30 (1993): 424–449.

Friedl, Karl E. "Body Composition and Military Performance: Origins of the Army Standards." In *Body Composition and Physical Performance: Applications for the Military Services,* ed. Bernadette M. Marriott and Judith Grumstrup-Scott, 31–55. Washington, D.C.: National Academy Press, 1992.

Gould, B. A. *Investigations in the Military and Anthropological Statistics of American Soldiers.* Published for the U.S. Sanitary Commission. New York: Hurd and Houghton, 1869.

Hamilton, Frank H. *A Practical Treatise on Military Surgery.* New York: Bailliere Brothers, 1861.

Hammond, William A. *A Treatise on Hygiene.* Philadelphia: J. B. Lippincott, 1863.

Henderson, T. *Hints for the Medical Examination of Recruits for the Army.* Philadelphia: Haswell, Barrington, and Haswell, 1840.

Karlen, Arno. *Man and Microbes.* New York: G. P. Putnam's and Sons, 1995.

Komlos, John, and Joo Han Kim, "Estimating Trends in Historical Heights." *Historical Methods,* 23 (1990): 116–120.

Lewis, J. R. "Exemption from Military Service on Account of Loss of Teeth." *American Dental Association Transactions,* July 1865: 164–169.

Liston, Maria A., and Brenda J. Baker. "Trauma in Eighteenth-Century Military Remains at Fort William Henry." *American Journal of Physical Anthropology*, Supplement #20 (1995): 135–136.

"Reconstructing the Massacres at Fort William Henry, New York. "*International Journal of Osteoarchaeology,* 6 (1996): 28–44.

Mann, Robert W., and Sean P. Murphy. *Regional Atlas of Bone Disease: A Guide to Pathologic and Normal Variation in the Human Skeleton.* Springfield, Ill.: Charles C. Thomas, 1990.

McNeill, William. *Plagues and Peoples.* Garden City, N.Y.: Anchor, 1976.

Medical and Surgical History of the War of the Rebellion, Part 2, Volume 1. Washington, D.C.: Government Printing Office, 1879.

Owsley, Douglas W. *Bioarchaeology on the Battlefield: The Abortive Confederate Campaign in New Mexico.* Archaeology Notes #142. Santa Fe: Museum of New Mexico, Office of Archaeological Studies, 1994.

"New Perspectives on the Past." In *In Remembrance: Archaeology and Death,* ed. David A. Poirier and Nicholas F. Bellantoni, 1–16. Westport, Conn.: Bergin and Garvey, 1997.

Owsley, Douglas W., Robert A. Mann, and Sean P. Murphy. "Injuries, Surgical Care, and Disease." In *Snake Hill: An Investigation of a Military Cemetery from the War of 1812,* ed. Susan Pfeiffer and Ronald F. Williamson, 198–226. Toronto: Dundurn Press, 1991.

Pfeiffer, Susan, and Ronald F. Williamson, eds. *Snake Hill: An Investigation of a Military Cemetery from the War of 1812.* Toronto: Dundurn Press, 1991.

Ratliff, E. A. "Resaca de la Palma (41CF3): A Mass Grave from the Mexican-American War." *American Journal of Physical Anthropology,* Supplement #16 (1993): 162.

Sandberg, Lars G., and Richard H. Steckel. "Soldier, Soldier, What Made You Grow So Tall? A Study of Height, Health, and Nutrition in Sweden, 1720–1881." *Economic History,* 23, no. 2 (1980): 91–105.

Saunders, Shelley R., Carol De Vito, and M. Anne Katzenberg. "Dental Caries in Nineteenth Century Upper Canada." *American Journal of Physical Anthropology,* 104 (1997): 71–87.

Sciulli, Paul W, and Richard M. Gramly. "Analysis of the Fort Laurens Skeletal Sample." *American Journal of Physical Anthropology,* 80, no. 1 (1989): 11–24.

Scott, Douglas D., and P. Willey. "Little Bighorn: Human Remains from the Custer National Cemetery." In *In Remembrance: Archaeology and Death,* ed. David A. Poirier and Nicholas F. Bellantoni, 155–171. Westport, Conn.: Bergin and Garvey, 1997.

Sledzik, Paul S., and Peer H. Moore-Jansen. "Dental Disease in 19th Century Military Skeletal Samples." In *Advances in Dental Anthropology,* ed. Marc A. Kelley and Clark Spencer Larsen, 215–224. New York: Wiley-Liss, 1991.

Smith, Joseph R. "Food in the Army." In *A Report on the Hygiene of the U.S. Army with Descriptions of the Military Posts,* ed. John Shaw Billings, xix–xxv. Surgeon General's Office, Circular No. 8. Washington, D.C.: GPO, 1875.

Snow, Clyde Collins, and John Fitzpatrick. "Human Osteological Remains from the Battle of the Little Bighorn." In *Archaeological Perspectives on the Battle of the Little Bighorn,* ed. Douglas D. Scott, Richard A. Fox, Jr., Melissa A. Connor, and D. A. Harmon, 243–282. Norman: University of Oklahoma Press, 1989.

Steckel, Richard H. "Stature and the Standard of Living." *Journal of Economic Literature,* 33 (1995): 1903–1940.

Steegman, Jr., A. Theodore. "18th Century British Military Stature: Growth Cessation, Selective Recruiting, Secular Trends, Nutrition at Birth, Cold, and Occupation." *Human Biology,* 57 (1985): 77–95.

Steegman, Jr., A. Theodore, and P. A. Halseley. "Stature Variation in the British American Colonies: French and Indian War Records." *American Journal of Physical Anthropology,* 75 (1988): 413–421.

Wachter, Kenneth W., and James Trussell. "Estimating Historical Heights." *Journal of the American Historical Assocation,* 77 (1982): 279–293.

Whitehorne, Joseph W. A. "The Battle of Fort Erie: Reconstruction of a War of 1812 Battle." *Prologue,* 1990: 129–148.

Willey, P., and Douglas D. Scott. " 'The Bullets Buzzed Like Bees': Gunshot Wounds in Skeletons from the Battle of the Little Bighorn." *International Journal of Osteoarcheology,* 6 (1996): 15–27.

CHAPTER EIGHT

The Health of Slaves and Free Blacks in the East

Ted A. Rathbun and Richard H. Steckel

ABSTRACT

Because the vital registration system evolved slowly in the United States, and was not complete in the South until the second quarter of the twentieth century, historical evidence on the health of blacks is meager. This chapter incorporates skeletal indicators of health and compares results with traditional sources. Free blacks were remarkably healthy in early-nineteenth-century Philadelphia, despite obstacles to their social and economic mobility. The number of slave skeletons studied here is small, but they contain many lesions indicating biological stress and considerable physical exertion. If this was true more generally, then intense physical labor, rather than organizational efficiency, could have been an important source of the greater output per worker on slave as opposed to free farms.

Controversy over the health and mortality of slaves and free blacks can be traced to the abolitionist era when critics of slavery included charges of poor living conditions and poor nutrition as part of their attack (Weld, 1839). Although these claims were secondary issues in the attack against the institution in the United States, they nevertheless defined an agenda for later research by historians, economists, and other social scientists. Virtually all comprehensive twentieth-century works on slavery address the issues of health and nutrition against a backdrop of whites or of free blacks.[1]

Despite remarkable efforts by historians and economists to understand slavery and to interpret and analyze some of the features of the experience of African slaves of the nineteenth century through numerous sources, several points or issues of controversy remain over health. As part of the overall research objective of this project, our goal is to bring bioarchaeological evidence into the debate and to compare results with other historical skeletal samples. In addition to the common data elements of the project, we present evidence supplementary to the conclusions regarding health, nutrition, and work effort of pre-twentieth-century U.S. groups east

---

[1] See, for example, Stampp (1956); Fogel and Engerman (1974); David et al. (1976).

of the Mississippi River. The analysis focuses on the most surprising and interesting findings – the health of free blacks in early-nineteenth-century Philadelphia and on the health and work effort of southern slaves.

I. EARLIER APPROACHES AND RESULTS

Quantitative knowledge of health and nutrition among slaves has traditionally been informed by plantation records of births and deaths, model life tables estimated from federal census records, and information on stature gathered from shipping manifests. These sources have been supplemented by reports of southern medical observers, statements by plantation owners on health characteristics and medical practices, and information on the diet and work routine.

We do not review the evolution of thought on slave health, but instead attempt a concise statement of the current stage of knowledge and the issues or outstanding questions on which bioarchaeology evidence may be of value.[2] Height data suggest that slave children had extraordinarily poor health, with an average stature that fell below the first percentile of modern National Center for Health Statistics (NCHS) standards. In addition, mortality rates of slave children were approximately double those of the free population and less than one-half of the live births survived to age 5 (Steckel, 1986). Among adults, mortality rates were approximately equal in the slave and free populations, and as teenagers, slaves experienced a remarkable catch-up growth to nearly the 20th percentile of modern NCHS standards. Working slaves were remarkably productive, and on large plantations, slaves produced approximately 35 percent more per hour than did free farmers. In one interpretation of these productivity results, specialization and division of labor – the factory in the field – have been suggested as an explanation (Fogel and Engerman, 1974). They argue that coordination of effort, not harder or longer work, made slaves so productive. Thus, the analysis of the skeletal samples here can confirm or deny the unusual age pattern of slave health. Moreover, if it was coordination of labor rather than effort that produced so much output, slaves should have left skeletons whose signs of degeneration and stress were little different from the free population.

Though not invisible to historians, much less research has been done on free blacks compared with slaves and Anglo-American workers.[3] This state of affairs is partly the result of scholarly interest that was defined by the legacy of the debate over slavery and abolition. Free blacks were also numerically much smaller, comprising much less than 10 percent of the black population in most southern states. Moreover, the information base available for study is much smaller for free blacks and lacks plantation records, manifests, and other sources specific to slaves. Nevertheless, some evidence is available from bills of mortality and from registration records, or identification papers that provide stature information (Margo and Steckel, 1982; Klepp, 1988; Komlos, 1992). Unfortunately, the dynamic nature of the free black population – its changes in size and composition associated with various

---

[2] For discussions of the evolution of thought, see Steckel (1986a, 1986b).
[3] See, for example, Berlin (1974).

emancipations – has made it difficult for study using model life tables for demography. Instead, free blacks are often combined with slaves for study by these means. The volume of information on blacks grew considerably during the late nineteenth century, beginning with records of the Freedmen's Bureau and continuing with the applicability of model life tables and the diffusion of vital registration.

In the absence of other information, scholars have tended to assume that free blacks fared worse than whites and little better than slaves, a general conclusion indicated by Ira Berlin's title, *Slaves Without Masters.* Constraints on mobility, limits on education, restricted access to the political system, and upper bounds on social mobility support this view. Two nineteenth-century skeletal samples from the Philadelphia First African Baptist Church considered here provide information relevant to this point (Angel et al., 1987; Kelley and Angel, 1989; Crist et al., 1995).

The bills of mortality suggest that slave health suffered in colder climates, probably from nutritional deficiencies and respiratory illnesses (Warren, 1997). Turmoil during and following the Civil War could have elevated the mortality of blacks, particularly adults, who migrated to cities or otherwise traveled more widely and sought new employment or attempted to reconnect with family members (Donald, 1952). Comparing results from samples in rural Arkansas (Cedar Grove) and western urban groups (Dallas Freedman's Cemetery) is relevant to this point. Improvements in health may have been realized after the 1880s when labor markets and institutions stabilized and public health measures were becoming somewhat effective (Meeker, 1976).

Thus, skeletal materials may shed light on questions of health by region and condition of the population. Some relevant questions that might be addressed include: Did health of African-American groups vary by region and, in particular, did they fare less well in cold areas compared with warm climates? Did the rural/urban contrast dramatically affect health conditions? How did the health of free blacks compare with that of whites and slaves? What can be said about the temporal pattern of health? Did the biological quality of life deteriorate and eventually recover following the Civil War? How was stress on health of African-Americans expressed in terms of length of life versus quality of life while living?

II. HISTORIC CEMETERIES

Although physical anthropologists, especially skeletal biologists, paleopathologists, and bioarchaeologists, have worked extensively on the prehistoric period, only recently has attention been given to the wealth of data available from historic groups, especially in the United States. Until recently, either historic cemeteries were relocated without analysis of the human remains (Phelphs, Green, and Hartsell, 1979), frequently as a salvage mitigation project, or descriptive accounts of the biological profile and burial information were included in less accessible formats, such as an appendix in contract or archaeological reports (Rathbun, 1991). The latter are particularly difficult to locate as part of the "gray, semipublished literature" that is not readily located through typical library or archival search resources.

Academic journal and monographic publications of historic cemetery projects are increasing, however. Recent conference symposia and subsequent published volumes have dealt explicitly with historic mortuary information from a physical anthropological perspective (Grauer, 1995; Saunders and Herring, 1995). Although J. Lawrence Angel tried to synthesize temporal trends using historical skeletal material, much of the physical anthropological and archaeological literature focused on individual topical questions, such as stature, demography, or infection, at specific geographic sites (Angel, 1976).

In the 1970s, a number of historians and economists, frequently members of the Social Science History Association, began to use biological data, especially human stature, to address topics in slavery, mortality, inequality, and the standard of living during industrialization (Steckel, 1998). Only in recent years has this group acquired an interest in skeletal analysis to address topics of interest in their field (Steckel, Sciulli, and Rose, 1998). In a reciprocal manner during the 1980s, physical anthropologists began to appreciate more fully the significance of historical data for understanding more of the biological nature of their samples. In 1985, Ted Rathbun and Jerome Rose (Rose and Rathbun, 1987) organized a symposium on Afro-American biohistory (one of the earliest uses of this term) for the meetings of the American Association of Physical Anthropology, with publication of the symposium papers in 1987 in the *American Journal of Physical Anthropology*, vol. 74, no. 2. Although individual papers covered a range of topics, the synergistic nature of the biological and historical data was stressed. Rose also made a cogent argument for the utility of skeletal data to address historical and archaeological questions (Rose, 1989). Areas of common concern would include medical questions (Rose, 1989), dietary sufficiency (Gibbs et al., 1980; Kiple and King, 1981; Kiple, 1984), growth, health and stature, and demographic considerations (Steckel, 1979a, 1979b; Fogel, 1986).

Anthropological Findings for Historical Groups

A short review of some of the anthropological findings related to health and nutrition in other studies is relevant for understanding results under study here. Archaeological investigation of a plantation cemetery in Barbados (Handler and Lange, 1978) revealed a discrepancy between plantation records and cemetery findings for demography, especially the historical underreporting of births and of infant and early childhood deaths. This potential bias for demographic reconstruction and comparison of diverse groups may be critical. Subsequent studies of the Barbados cemetery revealed much developmental disruption and dental pathology (Corruccini et al., 1982; Corruccini, Jacobi, and Handler, 1985; Corruccini et al., 1987), evidence for congenital syphilis (Jacobi, 1992), and lead poisoning (Handler, Aufderheide, and Corruccini, 1986). Due to a number of unresolved questions, the postcranial skeletal material was recently reexcavated and is currently being analyzed for health-related attributes in a doctoral dissertation (Herndon and Corruccini, 1996).

Comparative studies of African- and European-American samples by Angel revealed a decline in dental health and an increase in frequency of fractures related to selection and cultural change (Angel, 1976). Other sites with relevant skeletal data include colonial ironworker slaves at College Landing, Maryland (Kelley and Angel, 1983), colonial whites in Virginia (Kelley and Angel, 1981), and nineteenth-century free blacks at College Landing, Virginia (Hudgins, 1977). These groups and others, including Clift's Plantation in Virginia (Aufderheide et al., 1981, 1985) and the eighteenth-century elite planter's family at Belleview Plantation, South Carolina (Rathbun and Scurry, 1991), experienced considerable variation in the lead burden similar to that found at Newton Plantation in Barbados. Studies of African-American urban groups in New Orleans, paupers in Atlanta, and free blacks in Philadelphia reflect a high mortality rate, low life expectancy, extensive physical labor, elevated infection burdens, and inadequate nutrition. In a comparative study of eighteenth- and nineteenth-century northeast urban, rural, free, and enslaved African-Americans and poor European-Americans, T. E. Leslie suggested that economic and social status, rather than biological "race" or ancestry, was most significant with similar patterns of biological and health stress among the poor (Leslie, 1996).

III. THE SAMPLES

Surprisingly, few systematic excavations and analyses of eighteenth- and nineteenth-century mortuary samples have been undertaken. As is typically the case, the majority of the samples included in this study were the result of salvage situations after accidental discovery during construction operations. The initial interest from the owners, authorities, and public was usually the relocation of the skeletal remains, and only secondarily the systematic study and analysis of them for either humanistic or scientific pursuits. Table 8.1 lists the samples. Those analyzed by Rathbun and associates are discussed below, and the other samples are described elsewhere in this volume.

The largest and most complete sample included in this study, the First African Baptist Church in Philadelphia, derives from the 1990 mitigation excavations by John Milner Associates, Inc., and subsequent analysis and preliminary publication of findings by Crist et al. (1995). This is the second cemetery sample excavated in Philadelphia, Pennsylvania, that has been associated with the First African Baptist Church. This cemetery included graves of 89 African-Americans, buried between 1810 and 1822 (38 female and 18 male adults and 33 infants and children), recovered from the cemetery located at Tenth and Vine Streets. An earlier 1983–1984 cemetery excavation at Eighth St. and Vine, dated between 1823 and 1841 (Parrington and Robers, 1984), produced 140 burials of which 75 adults were suitable for osteological analysis (Angel et al., 1987). Unfortunately, the original data for these individuals were not available for inclusion in this study. Nonetheless, the nineteenth-century cemeteries associated with the First African Baptist Church of Philadelphia represent the largest sample of urban free blacks in the eastern United States for which results have been published. Earlier research on this data source discussed issues of African-American biohistory (Rose and Rathbun, 1987), but the data analyzed here for the second cemetery are included in a preliminary analytical report

Table 8.1: Health Index and Component Scores of Blacks and Whites in the Eighteenth and Nineteenth Centuries

Investigator	Age BP	Group	Index	Stature	Hyp.	Anemia	Dental	Inf.	DJD	Trauma
		Blacks								
Rathbun	0105	Baptist Church, Philadelphia	73.8	49.3	66.4	96.9	64.9	81.5	69.1	88.6
Condon	0062	Texas frontier	69.5	42.8	53.9	94.5	85.9	46.6	74.0	89.0
Rathbun	0097	Folly Island Union troops	68.5	41.6	39.0	100.0	74.9	46.9	82.5	94.3
Rose	0042	Cedar Grove, Arkansas	65.5	67.8	9.8	87.2	77.6	55.0	85.6	75.6
Rathbun	0095	Plantation slaves, South Carolina	58.4	3.2	42.7	57.1	81.3	49.5	77.0	98.3
		Average, blacks	67.1	40.9	42.4	87.1	76.9	55.9	77.6	89.2
		Whites								
Sirianni	0108	Rochester, NY, poorhouse	72.3	33.0	80.1	96.1	71.7	54.0	79.3	92.1
Rathbun	0100	Eastern U.S.	71.3	28.2	43.3	96.9	73.6	68.6	88.7	100.0
Sledzik	0150	Military, East	70.4	31.7	98.6	94.8	74.0	84.1	85.1	24.8
Saunders	0102	Belleville, Ontario, Canada	69.3	36.0	71.8	93.9	71.2	81.5	41.6	89.2
Sledzik	0080	Military, West	66.2	40.6	70.8	96.4	74.3	92.1	78.1	10.8
		Average, whites	69.9	33.9	72.9	95.6	73.0	76.1	74.6	63.4

Age BP denotes number of years before 1950.
Source: Consolidated database.

213

(Crist et al., 1995) and graciously made available for our use. The skeletal remains of all these individuals have been reinterred in Philadelphia.

The slave sample consists of two groups. One group worked at Belleview Plantation of South Carolina, which was owned by Edward Croft between 1738 and 1756. The sample consists of 9 white adults (3 males, 4 females, 2 sex unknown), 5 white subadults, and at least 2 black adult slaves, which were excavated in 1979 by Rathbun and his undergraduate students as a salvage project and subsequently analyzed (Rathbun and Scurry, 1991). The burials were recovered along the Wando River in Charleston County, South Carolina, during the construction of a marine terminal and docking facility by the Port's Authority. A vault marker for Croft and several smaller crypt fragments were initially located, but the skeletal remains were excavated only later when construction equipment accidentally disturbed one of the burials. In the comparison with other available African- and European-American samples, it appeared that the health similarities were more pronounced than were differences of groups of clearly unequal social status. However, analysis of the lead burden revealed by bone chemical analysis showed a higher burden for the white sample. With the cooperation of the Port's Authority and the descendants of Edward Croft, the skeletal remains are curated at the South Carolina Institute of Anthropology and Archaeology of the University of South Carolina.

The African-American slaves at the Paul Remley Plantation near Charleston, South Carolina, were excavated by Rathbun as part of a construction project in 1984, and subsequently analyzed (Rathbun, 1987). The primary date of the plantation cemetery as indicated by archival research and analysis of coffin hardware, including one nameplate with an 1863 date, appears to range from 1840 to 1870. At the plantation site, a total of 36 individuals (8 subadults and 28 adults – 13 male and 15 female) were recovered from individual primary inhumations. The former slaves exhibited signs of childhood stress and anemia, and among adults the women had shorter life spans. Poor diets and parasite loads provoked anemia, as indicated by the frequency of cribra orbitalia and porotic hyperostosis, and infection with subsequent recovery appears in over 60 percent of the sample. About 15 percent of the adults expressed expanded diploe, which suggests sickle-cell anemia, a disease elevated in modern times in the Charleston area relative to the national average. Skeletal changes associated with demanding physical labor were ubiquitous, as shown by arthritic changes at the major joints and by the early onset of vertebral degeneration. Benign cortical defects of the humerus, as well as a number of extremely large rhomboid sulci of the clavicle, suggested both heavy physical labor and strength. Initial chemical analyses indicated a relatively high exposure to lead and a diet high in plant foods (Rathbun, 1987). More extensive analysis of the bone chemical data (Crist, 1991) revealed dietary variations along gender and age parameters. Older individuals as a whole, and females in general, appeared to have eaten less meat, while nuts and seafood were common in the diet.

The last nineteenth-century African-American sample includes 19 adult male soldiers from a Union troop cemetery on Folly Island near Charleston, South Carolina. The graves were located during construction activities and subsequently excavated in 1987 by the South Carolina Institute of Archaeology and Anthropology (Legg and Smith, 1989). Only 2 of the 19 graves contained skeletons sufficiently complete to allow an assessment of ancestry from the cranial morphology. It is quite probable that the graves had been disturbed by removal companies hired to relocate bodies after the war, and thereafter some of the skeletal material was reburied at the National Cemetery in Beaufort. The soldiers were probably federal troops of the 55th Massachusetts, the 1st North Carolina Colored Infantry, and the 2nd U.S. Colored Infantry who died during their stay in 1863. Basic osteological analysis of the skeletal remains revealed a relatively healthy, young (average age 25) and vigorous group of African-American males (Rathbun, 1989). Other physical attributes included moderate height and significant markers of great muscularity and strength. The upper arms had deep enthesopathies at the insertion of the teres major and pectoralis muscles, and hands had hypertrophic tendon sheathes that were strikingly large. At the conclusion of the archaeological and osteological analysis, the skeletal remains were interred in the National Cemetery in Beaufort, South Carolina.

For comparative purposes, Rathbun also analyzed a collection of European-Americans (Rathbun, Eastern U.S. in Table 8.1), which includes urban elite nineteenth-century European-Americans recovered from an underground crypt in the cemetery of the Circular Congregational Church of Charleston, South Carolina. Rathbun opened this crypt and removed selected skeletal remains for study in the midst of renovation activities during the summer of 1984. Interred from the late eighteenth to the mid-nineteenth centuries, the remains reputedly include the family and descendants of William Hutson, a pastor of the church who died in 1761 (Edwards, 1947). Complete individuals could not be reconstructed, but cranial samples representing 5 male, 7 female and 5 subadult individuals and some postcranial remains probably associated with them were retrieved, analyzed, and subsequently returned to their original position in the crypt. Because of poor condition and incompleteness, not all individuals are equally represented in the data for this project. Recognizing possible sample bias, demographic features of this group should be viewed with caution. We note that an adult female exhibited one of the earliest examples in South Carolina of gold foil fillings (Jennings, Herschaft, and Rathbun, 1988). The data for other individual skeletal samples in this group were provided by Paul Sciulli (1994) and represent 6 nineteenth-century European-Americans buried in three Ohio sites (Sandusky, Dark, and Holmes Counties) and in Beaver, Pennsylvania.

IV. COMPARATIVE ANALYSIS

Although it is unsurprising that whites fared better than blacks in the health index rankings, the margin of advantage was low (69.9 versus 67.1) and the diversity across groups is remarkable. Surprisingly, the healthiest population was free blacks who lived in early-nineteenth-century Philadelphia. They were not only the best off among the blacks, but their health index exceeded that of any of the European-Americans, including the upper-middle-class group from Belleville, Ontario.

Table 8.2: Mean Values of Characteristics at Eighteenth- and Nineteenth-Century Samples

Site	Age	Height, cm	Humerus cir., mm	No. teeth lost	No. cavities	No. abscesses
Remley Plantation						
Male	33	168	67	7	2	0.5
Female	40	158	62	12	4	0.1
Belleview Plantation						
Male	33	164	62	5	6	0
Female	33	162	58	6	3	0.3
Charleston elites						
Male	34	175	n.a.	0	0	0.3
Female	33	166	n.a.	2	1	1
FABC, Phila.						
Male	44	171	71	7	7	1
Female	36	158	63	5	9	1
Black soldiers						
Male	25	169	72	1	2	1
Blacks, Arkansas						
Male	43	177	74	6	5	0.6
Female	38	163	66	8	4	0.4
Blacks, Texas						
Male	37	171	74	3	4	0.1
Female	33	159	64	3	4	0.1
Rochester poorhouse						
Male	44	170	68	5	5	1
Female	37	160	60	5	6	0.9
Middle class, Canada						
Male	42	171	n.a.	8	6	0.6
Female	42	160	n.a.	8	7	0.6
Military						
Ft. Laurens, Ohio	24	171	71	1	4	1
Glorietta Pass, N.M.	23	185	66	4	5	0.8
Snake Hill, Ont.	25	174	71	2	3	1

It is less surprising that slaves ranked at the bottom (58.4) of all groups in Table 8.1, but the extent of their shortfall is worth noting. They fell 7.1 points below the next higher group (free blacks in Cedar Grove, Arkansas), and 15.4 points behind the free blacks in Philadelphia. In fact, the health index of slaves places them in the company of pre-Columbian populations facing extinction or demographic disaster (see Chapter 3).

The components of the health index display interesting patterns. The Philadelphia blacks were not uniformly well-off, but they did rank first by large margins in hypoplasias and infections and also performed well in stature and anemia. Among blacks, however, they were last in dental health and degenerative joint disease. The slaves did poorly in early childhood indicators of health – hypoplasias, stature, and

Table 8.3: Frequency (%) of Skeletal Lesions at Various Sites

Site	Hyp. incisor	Hyp. canine	Cribra orb.	Tibial inf.	Trauma
Remley Plantation					
Male	23	80	27	67	33
Female	7	50	36	57	0
Belleview Plantation					
Male	25	50	0	0	0
Female	40	40	0	0	0
Charleston elites					
Male	n.a.	36	0	10	0
Female	0	20	20	20	0
FABC, Phila.					
Male	6	31	0	31	44
Female	16	30	3	27	21
Black soldiers					
Male	33	50	n.a.	40	7
Blacks, Arkansas					
Male	67	80	20	67	87
Female	48	62	5	43	19
Blacks, Texas					
Male	24	58	4	44	23
Female	17	45	3	39	6
Rochester poorhouse					
Male	18	18	4	36	19
Female	14	16	15	31	2
Middle class, Canada					
Male	15	28	10	9	28
Female	12	17	12	11	14
Military					
Ft. Laurens, Ohio	0	0	0	0	87
Glorietta Pass, N.M.	40	50	7	0	97
Snake Hill, Ont.	4	4	0	24	64

anemia – ranking last by large margins in the last two categories. The Folly Island Union troops faired well in childhood, recording no anemia, but carried a heavy burden of skeletal infections.

Tables 8.2 through 8.4 provide additional details on health and physical activity. The midshaft dimensions of the femora, an indicator of robusticity, did not appear to vary significantly across samples, except that (as expected) males were larger than females. Humerus (upper arm) circumference varied little across females groups, with the plantation elite having the smallest values. Among the males, plantation slaves were larger than the elite, but the urban African-Americans and soldiers had the most robust upper arms. The African-American soldiers also had the highest arm values among all the soldier samples. This robust pattern is consistent with the prevalence of benign cortical defects and rhomboid sulcus enthesopathies discussed

Table 8.4: Frequency of Degenerative Joint Disease at Various Sites (%)

Site	Shoulder	Hip-Knee	Wrist	Hand	Cervical	Thoracic	Lumbar
Remley Plantation							
Male	67	73	13	33	20	20	27
Female	79	93	14	21	43	28	21
Belleview Plantation							
Male	50	25	0	0	25	0	25
Female	20	20	0	0	0	0	20
Charleston elites							
Male	n.a.	20	n.a.	n.a.	n.a.	n.a.	n.a.
Female	n.a.	20	n.a.	n.a.	n.a.	n.a.	n.a.
FABC. Phila.							
Male	44	56	31	0	50	38	38
Female	38	34	16	0	13	34	13
Black soldiers							
Male	13	27	0	0	7	13	13
Blacks, Arkansas							
Male	7	26	13	13	43	40	46
Female	29	20	10	24	24	24	29
Blacks, Texas							
Male	31	29	12	19	16	9	14
Female	16	17	7	9	10	6	11
Rochester poorhouse							
Male	51	60	22	18	12	19	23
Female	33	40	12	10	12	19	23
Middle class, Canada							
Male	83	83	80	0	1	n.a.	n.a.
Female	79	82	74	0	3	1	1
Military							
Ft. Laurens, Ohio	0	0	0	0	n.a.	n.a.	n.a.
Glorietta Pass, N.M.	10	7	3	0	n.a.	n.a.	n.a.
Snake Hill, Ont.	16	20	8	0	n.a.	n.a.	n.a.

n.a.: Not available.

earlier. It should be noted, however, that the other African-American samples from Arkansas and Texas also had large humerus circumference values.

The cumulative effects of age, diet, disease, and hygiene typically influence the antemortem loss of teeth. In several series, antemortem tooth loss was frequent. Although the average number of antemortem missing teeth for all adults was approximately 5, plantation females had the highest average (12 missing teeth). Historical sources frequently contain references to both toothache and expenses of extraction. In contrast, the elite Charlestonians had the lowest rate of missing teeth. We add that this series also contained an early example of dental restoration.

Tables 8.3 and 8.4 present additional results on the frequency of lesions by class, region, and sex. The main points to note here are the obvious male–female differences across all samples. Unfortunately, no statistical evaluation by sex or age was possible due to the nature of the samples. It is interesting to note that Remley Plantation, which grew rice, had the highest incidence of cribra orbitalia, quite possibly for genetic, dietary, and parasitic reasons. Moreover, the incidence was higher for males than females in Rose's post-reconstruction black sample, while the reverse pattern prevailed at the Rochester poorhouse. Males generally did worse than females on the score of hypoplasias. With regard to degenerative joint disease (Table 8.4), relatively few problems appeared for hands, with the exception of Remley Plantation, among the Arkansas blacks, and at the Rochester poorhouse. Shoulder problems were confined primarily among males, except at Remley. The Remley females may have been carrying considerable weights on their heads. Black males in Arkansas and in Philadelphia were apparently engaged in heavy lifting with the lower back.

V. EXPLANATIONS

Some outcomes given in Table 8.1 may be so startling that they border on the unbelievable. Among these, the most surprising is the relatively good health of Philadelphia blacks. How could free blacks living in or near a large urban area have been better off than middle- and upper-class whites living in a small town, in view of the fact that free blacks faced social and economic discrimination and elevated mortality risks in northern cities (Klepp, 1994, 1988; Warren, 1997; Nash, 1988; Nash and Soderlund, 1991)?

While some readers may dismiss this result as an artifact of some weakness in the data or methods, first it is worthwhile to ponder why the result may be so surprising. Many modern studies show that the rich and the well educated live longer and have better health than the poor and the less well educated. In the absence of other information, many scholars tend to presume that such connections also existed in the past. Several recent studies show, however, that no such correlation existed, or was considerably diminished within populations that lived prior to the twentieth century. In the absence of a reliable theory of disease causation, the rich and the well educated did not know how to spend their wealth to improve health. Using a national sample of households matched in the 1850 and 1860 censuses, Richard Steckel found that the survival of young children and of wives was largely uncorrelated with literacy, wealth, or occupation of the household head (Steckel, 1988). Eric Davin replicated these results in a large study for Pittsburgh (Davin, 1993). Samuel Preston and Michael Haines found that the correlation between socioeconomic status and survival was weak as late as the turn of the twentieth century (Preston and Haines, 1991). Thus, socioeconomic status was probably a poor indicator of health in the nineteenth century.

It is also important to note that the burials in the sample of Philadelphia free blacks occurred early in the nineteenth century, all prior to 1841. The timing is significant because social and economic conditions were relatively good early in the century (Hershberg, 1981). Thus, general perceptions of the free black experience may be heavily shaped by the deteriorating conditions near midcentury created by immigration, industrialization, and growing discrimination. Consistent with the importance of this time trend to black health, the bioarchaeologists conducting the examinations noted that the skeletons interred early in the century (years 1810–1822 at Tenth St. and Vine site) were significantly healthier than those examined from the second site (Eighth St. and Vine, buried from 1823–1841) (Crist et al., 1997).

A census conducted by the Pennsylvania Abolition Society in 1838 shows that church membership was vital to free blacks (Crist et al., 1997). As members of the First African Baptist Church, the sample under study had some advantages over blacks more generally. Though organized around spiritual fulfillment, the church was also important in creating a social and economic safety net for its members. Through its networks, members in need could find basic necessities of life. Indeed, church membership was a valuable index of general social condition.

The benefits of church membership and living in the early nineteenth century contributed to the relatively good health of Philadelphia free blacks. It is also notable that many of the church members were involved in the food provisioning and catering business (Nash, 1988). Thus, they and their families probably had regular access to a variety of foods, which is central to good health. Importantly, the First African Baptist Church members all scored well on indicators of childhood stress (stature, hypoplasias, and anemia) and on infections, which is consistent with a good diet that could have been provided through their occupations.

In contrast to the free blacks of Philadelphia, the South Carolina slaves displayed the worst levels of childhood stress in the modern populations and among the worst in the entire set of 65 sites. The slaves scored in the midrange on other attributes of health. This asymmetry in health would have been surprising, if not stunning, 25 years ago. The pattern, however, is consistent with a large volume of data on stature assembled beginning in the late 1970s from the slave manifests (Steckel, 1986b). In these data, the children were among the smallest ever measured, while adults caught up by approximately 10 centimeters in stature as teenagers. Plantation lists of births and deaths, records of cotton picked during and after pregnancy, and seasonal patterns of diet, work, and disease suggest that significant problems in child health originated with seasonal deprivation in utero. Newborns then faced attenuated breast-feeding and endured a low protein diet as young children. The dietary situation did not improve, and significant catch-up growth did not occur until regular rations of meat were provided to young slaves when they began working around age 10.

Robust bones and large muscle attachments document the arduous work of slaves, and the results do raise the possibility that physical effort was a source of higher measured productivity of slaves compared with whites in agriculture. While not denying that organization may have contributed to high output, we note that nineteenth-century planting and weeding required a given number of hoe strokes per acre – an amount that could not be changed by organization. Analogies to the factory depicted in *Time on the Cross* describe the planting operation, which occupied only a few weeks of labor per year. From an annual perspective, most labor effort was expended on other tasks less amenable to factory methods, such as plowing, thinning cotton, weeding, harvesting, or clearing land. Consistent with the robust skeletal remains, the "factory in the field" may have achieved some of its superior output simply through speedup. This result could have been obtained by more labor effort per hour, and need not have required a longer workday.[4] The tight-knit structure of the gang system meant that laggards could be forced to keep up with the most productive or those who were feeling the most fit on a particular day. If exertion was the source of higher productivity, it is understandable why free workers resisted the system.

The Folly Island troops had reasonably healthy childhoods, as indicated by moderate to very high scores on childhood stress (stature, hypoplasias, and anemia), which is consistent with minimum health standards for entrance into the army. These troops also had remarkably high trauma scores (i.e., a low incidence of trauma), much above those for other military samples given in Table 8.1. The Folly Island troops were noncombatants who provided support for military operations (Rathbun and Smith, 1997). They died from infectious diseases, such as dysentery, that were spread by unsanitary camp life (Legg and Smith, 1989).

VI. CONCLUDING REMARKS

The most interesting findings of this chapter are the relatively good health of early-nineteenth-century free blacks who lived in Philadelphia and the remarkably poor health and evidence of hard work by plantation slaves who lived in South Carolina. In terms of chronic health conditions visible on skeletons, time period was important. Those who lived early in the century were much better off than those who faced discrimination, immigration, and industrialization that began in the 1830s. Networks provided by the church and occupations associated with food production or distribution also protected their health. Early-nineteenth-century residents were also less likely to have been escaped slaves, who displayed the skeletal scars of the institution. Deteriorating social and economic conditions that began in the 1830s may be responsible for images of distress faced by free blacks.

Considerable effort has been expended by economic historians on the question of the slave diet. Now that the dust has settled somewhat, it appears that working slaves may have consumed roughly 4,200 calories per day, which appears to have been significantly above that consumed by the free population (Fogel and Engerman, 1974; David et al., 1976; Fogel, 1989). This fact, combined with information on the physical degeneration of slaves, particularly from work through the shoulders, and with knowledge that slaves produced approximately one-third more output than free farmers, suggests that much of the higher slave output may have originated with work effort, rather than with organizational efficiency.

The samples under study in this chapter are small, and it is an open question whether the results apply to the larger black population. We hope that excavations underway or planned for the future may help to address this need. With larger samples, it will be possible to investigate patterns in health by region or crop produced, by time period, and by age and sex. Potentially, skeletal data have much to offer in clarifying the controversies of history.

[4] For a discussion of the debate over the length of the workday, see Olsen (1992) and references therein.

REFERENCES

Angel, J. Lawrence. "Colonial to Modern Skeletal Change in the U.S.A." *American Journal of Physical Anthropology* 45 (1976): 723–736.

Angel, J. Lawrence, Jennifer Olsen Kelley, Michael Parrington, and Stephanie Pinter. "Life Stresses of the Free Black Community as Represented by the First African Baptist Church, Philadelphia, 1823–1841." *American Journal of Physical Anthropology* 74, no. 2 (1987): 213–230.

Aufderheide, Arthur C., Fraser D. Neiman, Lorentz E. Wittmers Jr., and George Rapp. "Lead in Bone II. Skeletal Lead Content as an Indicator of Lifetime Lead Ingestion and the Social Correlates in an Archaeological Population." *American Journal of Physical Anthropology* 55, no. 3 (1981): 285–291.

"Lead in Bone III. Prediction of Social Correlates from Skeletal Lead Content in Four Colonial American Populations (Catoctin Furnace, College Landing, Governor's Land and Irene Mound)." *American Journal of Physical Anthropology* 66 (1985): 353–361.

Berlin, Ira. *Slaves Without Masters.* New York: Pantheon Books, 1974.

Corruccini, Robert S., Jerome S. Handler, Robert J. Mutaw, and Frederick W. Lange. "Osteology of a Slave Burial Population from Barbados, West Indies." *American Journal of Physical Anthropology* 59, no. 4 (1982): 443–459.

"Implications of Tooth Root Hypercementosis in a Barbados Slave Skeletal Collection." *American Journal of Physical Anthropology* 74 (1987): 179–184.

Corruccini, Robert S., Keith P. Jacobi, and Jerome S. Handler. "Distribution of Enamel Hypoplasias in an Early Caribbean Slave Population." *American Journal of Physical Anthropology* 66, no. 2 (1985): 158.

Crist, Thomas A. J. "The Bone Chemical Analysis and Bioarchaeology of an Historic South Carolina African-American Cemetery." *Historical Archaeology*, Vol. 18. Columbia: South Carolina Institute of Archaeology and Anthropology, 1991. Also in 1990 M.A. thesis, University of South Carolina-Columbia.

Crist, Thomas A. J., et al. "A Distinct Church of the Lord Jesus." *The History, Archeology, and Physical Anthropology of the Tenth Street First African Baptist Church Cemetery, Philadelphia, Pennsylvania, Site Number 36PH72.* Vine Expressway (I-676), L.R. 67045, ER #82-101-0133. Philadelphia: John Milner Associates, Inc., 1995.

"The First African Baptist Church Cemeteries: African-American Mortality and Trauma in Antebellum Philadelphia." In *Remembrance: Archaeology and Death*, ed. David A. Poirier and Nicholas F. Bellantoni. Westport, Conn.: Bergin & Garvey, 1997. Pp. 17–49.

David, Paul A., Herbert G. Gutman, Richard Sutch, Peter Temin, and Gavin Wright. *Reckoning with Slavery.* New York: Oxford University Press, 1976.

Davin, Eric Leif. "The Era of the Common Child: Egalitarian Death in Antebellum America." *Mid-America* 75 (1993): 135–163.

Donald, Henderson H. *The Negro Freedman.* New York: Henry Schuman, 1952.

Edwards, George N. *A History of the Independent or Congregational Church of Charleston South Carolina, Commonly Known as Circular Church.* Boston: The Pilgrim Press, 1947.

Fogel, Robert William. "Nutrition and the Decline in Mortality since 1700: Some Preliminary Findings." In Stanley L. Engerman and Robert E. Gallman (eds.), *Long-Term Factors in American Economic Growth.* Chicago: University of Chicago Press, 1986. Pp. 439–527.

Without Consent or Contract. New York: W. W. Norton, 1989.

Fogel, Robert William, and Stanley L. Engerman. *Time on the Cross: The Economics of American Negro Slavery.* Boston: Little, Brown and Co., 1974.

Gibbs, Tyson K., Kathleen Cargill, Leslie Sue Lieberman, and Elizabeth Reitz. "Nutrition in a Slave Population: An Anthropological Examination." *Medical Anthropology* 4, no. 2 (1980): 175–262.

Grauer, Anne E. *Bodies of Evidence, Reconstruction History Through Skeletal Analysis.* New York: Wiley-Liss, 1995.

Handler, Jerome S., Arthur Aufderheide, and Robert S. Corruccini. "Lead Contact and Poisoning in Barbados Slaves: Historical, Chemical and Bioanthropology Evidence." *Social Science History* 10 (1986): 399–425.

Handler, Jerome S., and Frederick W. Lange. *Plantation Slavery in Barbados.* Cambridge, Mass.: Harvard University Press, 1978.

Herndon, Kristi S., and Robert S. Corruccini. *Post Cranial Skeletal Analysis of Newton Plantation Slaves.* NSF Doctoral Dissertation Improvement Proposal, 1996.

Hershberg, Theodore. "Free Blacks in Antebellum Philadelphia: A Study of Ex-Slaves, Freedom, and Socioeconomic Decline." In *Philadelphia: Work, Space, Family, and Group Experience in the 19th Century*, ed. Theodore Hershberg. New York: Oxford University Press, 1981. Pp. 368–391.

Hudgins, C. L. *Historical Archaeology and Salvage Archaeology Excavations of College Landing. An Interim Report.* Yorktown: Virginia Research Center for Archaeology, 1977.

Jacobi, Keith P., Della Collins Cook, Robert S. Corruccini, and Jerome S. Handler. "Congenital Syphilis in the Past: Slaves at Newton Plantation, Barbados, West Indies." *American Journal of Physical Anthropology* 89, no. 2 (1992): 145–158.

Jennings, Deborah, Edward Herschaft, and Ted Rathbun. "A Comparison of Dental Diseases Between Black and White Populations in Antebellum S.C." *American Academy of Forensic Sciences Abstracts* (1988): 84.

Kelley, Jennifer O., and J. Lawrence Angel. "The Armor and Drummond-Harris Sites, Governor's Land, Virginia." Unpublished report to Alain Outlaw at Virginia Historical Landmarks Commission's Research Center for Archaeology, 1981.

"Workers for Catoctin Furnace." *Maryland Archaeology* 19 (1983): 2–17.

"Life Stresses of Slavery." *American Journal of Physical Anthropology* 74, no. 2 (1987): 199–213.

"The First African Baptist Church Cemetery: Bioarchaeology, Demography, and Acculturation of Early Nineteenth Century Philadelphia Blacks." *Osteological Analysis,* Vol 3. Department of Anthropology, National Museum of Natural History and Man. Washington, D.C.: Smithsonian Institution, 1989.

Kiple, Kenneth F. *The Caribbean Slave.* Cambridge: Cambridge University Press, 1984.

Kiple, Kenneth F., and Virginia H. King. *Another Dimension to the Black Diaspora.* Cambridge: Cambridge University Press, 1981.

Klepp, Susan. "Black Mortality in Early Philadelphia, 1722–1859." Paper given at the Social Science History Association meetings, Chicago, 1988.

"Seasoning and Society: Racial Differences in Mortality in Eighteenth-Century Philadelphia," *William and Mary Quarterly* 51 (1994): 473–506.

Komlos, John. "Toward an Anthropometric History of African-Americans: The Case of the Free Blacks in Antebellum Maryland." In *Strategic Factors in Nineteenth Century American Economic History,* ed. Claudia Golden and Hugh Rockoff. Chicago: University of Chicago Press, 1992. Pp. 297–329.

Legg, James B., and Steven D. Smith. "The Best Ever Occupied . . ." *Archaeological Investigations of a Civil War Encampment on Folly Island, South Carolina.* Research Manuscript Series 209. Columbia: South Carolina Institute of Archaeology and Anthropology, 1989.

Leslie, Teresa. "Problematics in Approach: An Analysis of Historic Health Patterns." M.A. thesis, Department of Anthropology, University of South Carolina, Columbia, S.C., 1996.

Margo, Robert A., and Richard H. Steckel. "The Heights of American Slaves: New Evidence on Slave Nutrition and Health." *Social Science History* 6 (1982): 516–538.

Meeker, Edward. "Mortality Trends of Southern Blacks, 1850–1910: Some Preliminary Findings." *Explorations in Economic History* 13 (1976): 13–42.

Nash, Gary B. *Forging Freedom: The Formation of Philadelphia's Black Community, 1720–1840.* Cambridge, Mass.: Harvard University Press, 1988.

Nash, Gary B., and Jean R. Soderlund. *Freedom by Degrees: Emancipation in Pennsylvania and Its Aftermath.* New York: Oxford University Press, 1991.

Olsen, John F. "Clock Time Versus Real Time: A Comparison of the Lengths of the Northern and Southern Agricultural Work Years." In *Without Consent or Contract: Markets and Production, Technical Papers,* Vol. 1, ed. Robert William Fogel and Stanely L. Engerman. New York: W. W. Norton, 1992. Pp. 216–240.

Parrington, Michael, and Daniel G. Roberts. "The First African Baptist Cemetery." *Archaeology* 37, no. 6 (1984): 26–32.

Phelphs, David S., J. B. Green, and K. C. Hartsell. *An Archaeological-Historical Study of the Bryan Cemetery and Site 31CV25, Simmons-Nott Airport, New Bern, North Carolina.* Publication No. 10. Raleigh: North Carolina Archaeological Council, 1979.

Preston, Samuel H., and Michael R. Haines. *Fatal Years: Child Mortality in Late Nineteenth-Century America.* Princeton, N.J.: Princeton University Press, 1991.

Rathbun, Ted A. "Health and Disease at a South Carolina Plantation: 1840–1870." *American Journal of Physical Anthropology* 74, no. 2 (1987): 239–254.

——— "Human Remains from 38CH920." In "The Best Ever Occupied . . .," by James B. Legg and Steven D. Smith, A1–A4. *Archaeological Investigations of a Civil War Encampment on Folly Island, South Carolina.* Research Manuscript Series 209. Columbia: South Carolina Institute of Archaeology and Anthropology, 1989.

Rathbun, Ted A., and James D. Scurry. "Status and Health in Colonial South Carolina: Belleview Plantation, 1738–1756." In *What Mean These Bones? Studies in Southeastern Bioarchaeology,* ed. J. L. Powell, P. S. Bridges, and A. M. W. Mires, 148–164. Tuscaloosa: University of Alabama Press, 1991.

Rathbun, Ted A., and Steven Smith. "Folly Island: An African-American Union Brigade Cemetery in South Carolina." In *In Remembrance: Archaeology and Death,* ed. David A. Poirier and Nicholas F. Bellantoni. Westport, Conn.: Bergin & Garvey, 1997.

Rose, Jerome C. "Biological Consequences of Segregation and Economic Deprivation: A Post-Slavery Population from Southwest Arkansas." *Journal of Economic History* 44, no. 2 (1989) : 351–360.

Rose, Jerome C., and Ted A. Rathbun. "Preface: Afro-American Biohistory Symposium." *American Journal of Physical Anthropology* 74, no. 2 (1987): 177–179.

Saunders, Shelley R., and Anne Herring. *Grave Reflections: Portraying the Past Through Cemetery Studies.* Toronto: Canadian Scholars Press, 1995.

Savitt, Todd L. *Medicine and Slavery.* Urbana: University of Illinois Press, 1978.

Sheridan, Richard B. *Doctors and Slaves.* Cambridge: Cambridge University Press, 1985.

Stampp, Kenneth M. *The Peculiar Institution: Slavery in the Ante-Bellum South.* New York: Random House, 1956.

Steckel, Richard H. "Slave Mortality: Analysis of Evidence from Plantation Records." *Social Science History* 3 (1979a): 86–114.

——— "Slave Height Profiles from Coastwise Manifests." *Explorations in Economic History* 16 (1979b): 363–380.

"Birth Weights and Infant Mortality among American Slaves." *Explorations in Economic History* 23 (1986): 173–198.

"A Dreadful Childhood: The Excess Mortality of American Slaves." *Social Science History* 10 (1986a): 427–465.

"A Peculiar Population: The Nutrition, Health, and Mortality of American Slaves from Childhood to Maturity." *Journal of Economic History* 46 (1986b): 421–441.

"The Health and Mortality of Women and Children, 1850–1860." *Journal of Economic History* 48 (1988): 333–345.

"Stature and the Standard of Living." *Journal of Economic Literature* 33 (1995): 1903–1940.

"Strategic Ideas in the Rise of the New Anthropometric History and Their Implications for Interdisciplinary Research." *Journal of Economic History* 58 (1998): 803–821.

Steckel, Richard H., Paul Sciulli, and Jerome C. Rose. "Skeletal Remains, Health, and History: A Project on Long-Term Trends in the Western Hemisphere." In *The Biological Standard of Living in Comparative Perspective*, ed. John Komlos and Joerg Baten. Stuttgart: Franz Steiner Verlag, 1998. Pp. 139–154.

Warren, Christian. "Northern Chills, Southern Fevers: Race-Specific Mortality in American Cities, 1730–1900." *Journal of Southern History* 63 (1997): 23–57.

Weld, Theodore D. *Amercian Slavery As It Is: Testimony of a Thousand Witnesses*. New York: American Anti-Slavery Society, 1839.

CHAPTER NINE

The Quality of African-American Life in the Old Southwest near the Turn of the Twentieth Century

James M. Davidson, Jerome C. Rose, Myron P. Gutmann,
Michael R. Haines, Keith Condon, and Cindy Condon

ABSTRACT

This chapter examines the quality of life of African-Americans in the historic West between the Mississippi River and the Rocky Mountains in the late nineteenth and early twentieth centuries. The primary data come from two sites: Cedar Grove Cemetery in rural southwest Arkansas, and Freedman's Cemetery, an urban graveyard located in downtown Dallas, Texas. We compare these skeletal series to archival and other demographic data sets and to a smaller composite skeletal series derived from sites in Illinois and the Great Plains. Issues examined include demography, childhood health and nutrition, growth and development, diet, infection, degenerative joint disease, and trauma. Since Freedman's Cemetery has a relatively precise chronology, the changing health of the African-American community in Dallas is emphasized. Key measures of health declined in urban Dallas during much of the late nineteenth century before improving at the turn of the century, a pattern that likely resulted from improvements in public health infrastructure.

INTRODUCTION

Certainly for many inhabitants of Europe, emigration to the United States seemed a dream given form – the American western frontier was a vast land of opportunity containing a wealth of exploitable resources.[1] The essential story was the same – from the founding of the American colonies, to the Virginians moving into the

This research was partially supported by Grant Number 5 R01-HD32325 from the National Institute of Child Health and Human Development. Excavations conducted at Cedar Grove Cemetery in 1982 were performed under contract to the U.S. Army Corps of Engineers, New Orleans district. The Freedman's Cemetery Project excavations were sponsored by the Texas Department of Transportation (TxDOT). We are also grateful to Sara Pullum for helping with the research about the historical living conditions of African-Americans in Texas and Arkansas.

[1] This utopian situation applied only to the Old World immigrants and not to the Native Americans who originally resided in this region and who, if they would not move off their land, were often killed. This chapter will not include Native Americans whose biohistory is well covered elsewhere (Owsley and Jantz 1994; Owsley and Rose 1997).

Appalachians, and finally on to the land rushes of the western prairies – the frontier was where fortunes were to be made and, on a simpler level, where farmland could be obtained with little or no capital. This uncritical view of the American West is the same that many still retain today. However, although the American West is traditionally romanticized through the lens of history as a vast land of limitless opportunity, clearly life in "the West" was often less than idyllic. At its worst, the frontier environment was unbelievably harsh – the weather unpredictable and deadly, infectious disease rampant, and medical care virtually nonexistent. Moreover, through the introduction of slavery as an American institution and, further, the creation of a codified means of oppression based along socially constructed racial lines, opportunities for some groups, especially African-Americans, in reality fell far short of "limitless."

This chapter will examine the frontier health experience in the American West, from the Mississippi River to the Continental Divide. Here we will attempt to weave the analysis of skeletal remains into the unfinished tapestry of knowledge begun by more traditional historical resources. Although some of the skeletal data utilized here dates to the early nineteenth century, our principal focus will be the late nineteenth and early twentieth centuries, utilizing data derived from archaeological investigations of two historic African-American cemeteries: Cedar Grove and Freedman's Cemetery.

Cedar Grove (site number 3LA97) is a rural burial ground in southwest Arkansas that served the congregation of the Cedar Grove Baptist Church between 1881 and 1927. In 1982 approximately 28% of the cemetery was excavated and moved as part of construction for a revetment on the Red River, yielding a total of 80 skeletons; 72% of the cemetery remains undisturbed. Only that portion of the cemetery endangered by construction was excavated, analyzed, and relocated. A recent reanalysis of the associated mortuary hardware suggests a date range of the exhumed graves from circa 1900 to 1915 (Davidson, unpublished manuscript). All skeletons were analyzed in an on-site field laboratory, and the detailed methodology is available in Rose (1985).

The other cemetery utilized in this study is Freedman's Cemetery (site number 41DL316), in Dallas, Texas, located just north of the city's downtown district. Freedman's Cemetery is an historic African-American cemetery originally founded in 1869 within the fledgling settlement of Freedman's Town, a community formed of ex-slaves. Freedman's Cemetery saw continuous use as the primary burial ground for virtually all of the black communities of Dallas from 1869 until its forced closure in 1907. Due to expansion needs of the North Central Expressway (U.S. Hwy 75), intensive archaeological investigations sponsored by the Texas Department of Transportation were conducted between 1991 and 1994. These resulted in the excavation of approximately 25% of the cemetery and yielded a total of 1,150 burials (containing 1,157 individuals), while the remaining portions of the cemetery remain undisturbed and protected.[2]

---

[2] A detailed methodology for age, sex, and stature, as well as a summary of the date of interment rationale, is available in Condon, et al. (1998), while a more in-depth appraisal regarding the chronology of the

One aspect of Freedman's Cemetery must be stressed – the site was the only public burial ground available for blacks in Dallas, from its inception in 1869, until early 1902, when Woodland Cemetery was opened. Thus, for 34 of its 39 years of operation, Freedman's Cemetery was the only burying place for virtually all of black Dallas. Therefore, the skeletal population derived from the archaeological investigations is an inclusive one, simultaneously containing the graves of paupers and stillborns (buried in plain boxes at county and later city expense), as well as the more elaborate resting places of Dallas's ruling black elite (Davidson 1999). Another advantage of the Dallas sample is that although all of the graves at Freedman's Cemetery were unmarked and undated, it was still possible to assign narrow date ranges to virtually all of the recovered burials using records of land utilization, associated temporally diagnostic artifacts, seriation of mortuary hardware, and a correlation of archaeological data with the archival record. This analysis resulted in the designation of three major time periods. The Early Period spans 16 years, from the cemetery's founding in 1869 until 1884 ($n = 64$ individuals; 5.5%), the Middle Period lasts for 15 years (1885–1899) ($n = 171$ individuals; 14.8%), while the Late Period covers only an 8-year interval between 1900 and 1907 ($n = 884$; 76.4%). Burials interred during Freedman's Late Period are contemporaneous with those recovered from Cedar Grove.[3]

Since Freedman's and Cedar Grove lie on nearly the same latitude, are largely contemporaneous, and have similar physical environments, comparison of the two sites offers insight into the quality of life and economic effects on the health of African-Americans living in the late nineteenth and early twentieth centuries. While the economy of rural Cedar Grove was essentially static, dominated primarily by sharecropping (Rose 1985), the economy of Dallas was a dynamic one – the city transformed itself from a rural agricultural community of some 800 inhabitants at the eve of the Civil War, to a major trade center and the second largest city in the state (with a population approaching 100,000) by circa 1907 (Kimball 1927:25; Holmes and Saxon 1992:85). Whereas some of the individuals (and especially the older adults) interred during the Early Period at Freedman's had lives associated with agricultural pursuits (paralleling the later Cedar Grove economy), individuals whose deaths occurred during the Middle and Late Periods would have participated primarily in an urban cash economy, working as laborers and domestics. In both the urban and rural economies of this time period, physical labor played a major role in employment for African-Americans. For example, in the 1875, 1889/90, and 1909 Dallas City Directories, approximately 90% of the occupation entries for African-Americans involved some degree of physical labor.[4] Assessment of the health of these

---

cemetery and individual burials is available in Davidson (1999). The reader is also referred to Chapter 3 in this volume for a discussion of the other data set collection protocols.

[3] Although Freedman's three major temporal periods account for 1,119 (or 96.7%) of excavated burials, there is an additional time period designation, termed simply "Pre-1900," into which were placed 37 (3.2%) burials that while dating before 1900, could not be further subdivided into either the Early or Middle Periods. Finally, there is a single burial (1,127), which could not be dated by any means, and so could conceivably have occurred anytime during the 39-year span of the cemetery (Davidson 1999).

[4] These data are described more fully below.

two skeletal populations will be based upon the following parameters: demography, growth and development, diet, infection, degenerative joint disease, and trauma.

Although this chapter's principal concern is African-American health in Texas and Arkansas during the late nineteenth and early twentieth centuries, to contextualize the relative health of these communities we first begin with brief reference to the skeletal biology of western frontier immigrants derived from the published, as well as the unpublished ("gray"), literature of cultural resource management archaeology. These skeletal studies are temporally situated between 1830 and 1900 and serve to set the stage for an intensive study of Cedar Grove and Freedman's Cemetery.

PIONEERS OF THE WESTERN FRONTIER

The western frontier was not a fixed, static boundary; rather, the border between the settled East and the western frontier was a dynamic one that shifted ever westward over time. Excavations at the Cross Family homestead Cemetery, located near Springfield, Illinois, yielded 29 graves dated between 1820 and 1846 and represents the mortality experience of a single tenant farm family on the western edge of the settled East (Larsen et al. 1995). Some of the general conclusions derived from the Cross skeletal analysis are: 1) high mortality and low life expectancy; 2) degenerative disease rates indicating a demanding and physically active life; 3) a 28.6% cribra orbitalia rate indicating iron deficiency anemia derived from either an iron-poor diet or extensive infection/parasitism; 4) frequent dental caries and abscesses indicating poor oral health; and 5) 67% of the people with one or more enamel hypoplasias indicating high levels of childhood disease and/or nutritional stress (Larsen et al. 1995).

The Dunning Poorhouse Cemetery, located just outside of historic Chicago and in use between 1851 and 1869, yielded 106 human skeletons whose ages at death could be determined. Analysis suggests relatively high levels of childhood stress, disease, and mortality for those entering the poorhouse with their families (Grauer and McNamara 1995). In 1867, 49.1% of all of the recorded deaths in Chicago were of children younger than 5 years of age, and this high childhood mortality rate was a consequence of historically reported epidemics of cholera and smallpox that were common along the western frontier (Grauer and McNamara 1995).

The total number of skeletal analyses presently available for the western frontier are few, but they illustrate the range of living conditions during the nineteenth century. These samples include small family cemeteries, ranging from those living in settled areas to very remote and isolated locations (e.g., East Texas), which have been aggregated here for comparison.[5] There were numerous deaths during the westward migration, and there are examples of graves along the various wagon routes.[6] The

[5] These data representing families residing in the frontier have been reorganized from data provided in Winchell et al. (1995:164) and which originally derive from cultural resource management contract reports by Ferguson (1983); Fox (1984); Taylor et al. (1986); Lebo (1988); and Burnett (1988).

[6] These data derive primarily from the excellent summary of skeletal injuries of pioneers in the Great Plains by Gill (1994), with supplementation of data from Finnegan (1976, 1980, 1984); Gill and Smith (1989); Gill et al. (1984); Buff (1990); and a bioarchaeology overview project edited by Owsley and Rose (1997), which reviews all the extant literature and data from the Plains region.

conflict between indigenous inhabitants and the Euro-American invaders is represented by wagon train massacres and battlefield deaths. These skeletons (primarily, but not exclusively, male) derive from the excavation of boot hill cemeteries. Non-Europeans are also found throughout the West and were important in its changing economic character. African-Americans were brought in as slaves and, after emancipation, played important roles as they sought their fortunes in the frontier. Chinese laborers were important in the construction of the railroads.

Available published skeletal analyses have been synthesized, and Table 9.1 summarizes their paleopathology data. The families represent settled farm families (summarized in Winchell et al. 1995), and Utah Mormons (from Tigner-Wise 1989). The Frontier group represents the cowboys, "gunfighters," and wagon train deaths (synthesized from Finnegan 1976; Finnegan 1980; Gill et al. 1984; Bluff 1990; Gill 1994; Owsley and Rose 1997). Taken from the same sources, but kept separate from the frontier group, are frontier blacks. Chinese immigrants are also represented in Table 9.1 (taken from Tigner-Wise 1989). Finally, these groups are contrasted with the Cross skeletal sample from Illinois (Larsen et al. 1995).

The major differences in age-specific number of skeletons is the higher number of middle-aged adults in the frontier, African-American, and Chinese groups. These groups represent the transients of the frontier, including the miner, wagoneer, laborer, and cowboy. In Gill's (1994) study of 18 isolated burials from Wyoming and Texas, 84.3% showed some trauma, 38.9% died of trauma, and 33.3% of these died of gunshot wounds. The one female in the group had been crushed by a wagon (Buff 1990), and the Texas cowboys appeared to show injuries consistent with trampling (Gill 1994). Finnegan (1976) examined a group of wagoneers (including two blacks) who had been killed by Indians; the Chinese were railroad laborers killed in a civic

Table 9.1: Percentage of Skeletons with Skeletal Pathological Lesions

Group	PHSb	PHAd	Infec	Arth	Trau	Weap	Caries
Family	—	12.5	5.0	15.4	12.5	9.3	34.2
Mormon	—	0.0	0.0	67.0	11.1	0.0	88.9
Frontier	—	0.0	—	66.7	27.3	45.4	54.6
Blacks	—	0.0	—	33.3	0.0	50.0	100.00
Chinese	—	—	—	—	—	100.0	—
Cross	Yes	Yes	18.8	72.7	0.0	0.0	Many

PHSb = Porotic Hyperostosis in subadults.
PHAAd = Porotic Hyperostosis in adults.
Infec = Infectious lesions.
Arth = Degenerative joint disease.
Trau = Trauma indicated by broken bones.
Weap = Weapon wounds including gunshot, arrows, and knives.
Caries = Dental decay.
Source: Families, Winchell et al. (1995); Mormon, Tigner-Wise (1989); frontier and blacks, Buff (1990), Finnegan (1976, 1980), Gill et al. (1984, 1994), Gill and Smith (1989), Rose and Owsley (1997); Chinese, Tigner-Wise (1989); Cross, Larsen et al. (1995).

uprising (Tigner-Wise 1989). These mature adults did not die of disease but of the violence and danger associated with life on the frontier. Consequently, they differ from the settled farmers. However, the family farmers were not immune to violence: one of the adult women from a farmstead in East Texas was killed by what appears to be both barrels of a 10-gauge shotgun (Winchell et al. 1995). In another study, two adult male farmers were ambushed, killed, and buried beside the trail (Fox 1984).

The skeletal lesions document the hardships of frontier life. Porotic hyperostosis indicates the presence of anemia, probably due to a combination of an iron-poor diet associated with corn (maize) and high parasitism due to unsanitary conditions. The low rate of infectious lesions, in comparison to the Cross cemetery, is attributed to death by acute infections (documented for western Mormons; Tigner-Wise 1989) and rapid death from bacterial infections due to the high-stress loads. Resistance was likely so low that individuals simply died of bacterial infections before visible impact to the skeleton could occur. The high degenerative joint disease rates (arthritis) are associated with the heavy workloads of frontier life. The rate is lower (15.4%) for the family group because of the inclusion of many late-nineteenth-century skeletal series where the workloads may have been reduced. The categories that stand out as the most important are the trauma and weapon wound rates. Lastly, dental health was poor, which led to loss of teeth. Even after an intensive search for all pertinent osteological analyses, our knowledge of nineteenth-century western pioneers derives from the analysis of only 131 skeletons. It is true that there are more individuals discussed in the literature and unpublished reports, but the extent of the analyses is so cursory that they could not be used even in a limited fashion.

We will now turn to the interpretation of two large and well-studied African-American skeletal series that will serve as our primary sources of skeletal data for discussing the quality of life in the terminal phase of the western frontier.

LATE-NINETEENTH AND EARLY-TWENTIETH-CENTURY AFRICAN-AMERICANS

Assessment of the health of the skeletal populations at Freedman's Cemetery and Cedar Grove is based upon the following parameters: demography, growth and development, diet, infection, degenerative joint disease and trauma. Comparisons are made between individuals interred during Freedman's three major temporal periods (i.e., Early, Middle, Late) and also to the more temporally homogeneous Cedar Grove population. While a more fine-grained analysis would have been achieved by calculating estimated birth years for each individual (from the estimated age-at-death and established interment date range), the broad comparisons made here between Freedman's three sequential temporal periods represent a positive first step toward establishing diachronic trends in demography and health.

Demography

The demographic composition of the skeletal remains at the two sites is shown in Table 9.2. Both sites are characterized by a large proportion of subadults and relatively low mean ages at death. It is interesting to note that as observed in the Freedman's Cemetery population, the trend for the mean age-at-death is one of continual increase, from the amazingly low 13.6 years in the Early Period and the slightly higher 17.7 years during the Middle Period, to a relative high of 23.1 years in the turn-of-the-century dead of Freedman's Late Period. The mean age-at-death for Freedman's Late Period population, at 23.1 years, is higher than the 19.6 years exhibited at Cedar Grove. While the mean age-at-death exhibited for Freedman's Early Period might seem unusually low, Dallas County's slave population itself was relatively youthful. Of the 1,074 slaves recorded in the 1860 Federal Census, 17% were between 1 and 5, 46% were between 1 and 14 years, and 40% between the ages of 15 and 40 years (Smith 1985). The mean ages-at-death calculated for Freedman's and Cedar Grove are the lowest of all eighteenth- and nineteenth-century skeletal samples reported by Rathbun and Steckel (this volume), except the military personnel at Glorieta Pass, New Mexico. Both of these findings suggest populations with relatively high fertility (Sattenspiel and Harpending 1983), resulting in large numbers of subadult deaths (younger than 15 years). This interpretation is supported by the estimates of birthrate (Deaths over 30 years/Deaths over 5 years, or D30+/D5+) devised by Buikstra and co-workers (1986) for skeletal series and shown in Table 9.2. According to Buikstra, since there is an inverse relationship between the measure D30+/D5+ and the birthrate, a decrease in the proportion of D30+/D5+ translates into a proportional increase in the number of births. Given this, the trend exhibited temporally at Freedman's Cemetery (e.g., Early = 0.533; Late = 0.7) seems to represent a decline in the birthrate within the African-American community of Dallas. This trend corresponds to that known historically, with the documented decrease in overall fertility occurring nationally among African-American women between 1880 and 1920 (Rose 1985:150).

Overall, however, both Freedman's and Cedar Grove yield estimates of high birthrates that, for Freedman's, can be supported by census data. Between 1870 and 1900, the African-American population of Dallas grew from 1,200 to 9,000 (Condon et al. 1998). While immigration undoubtedly played a role in this explosive growth, the skeletal data clearly suggests a correspondingly high birthrate as a contributing factor. The African-American population of nineteenth-century Dallas was a somewhat stable one, with migration out of the city being relatively low.[7] The high birthrate of the black population is further supported by data in Tables 9.3 and 9.4. Table 9.3 presents information on the fertility and mortality of the white and black populations of the United States for the period 1860 to 1930. Table 9.4 presents child-woman ratios (children aged 0–4 per 1,000 women aged 15–44) as a measure of fertility and some selected life table data for Arkansas, Texas, and some large

---

[7] Engerrand (1978) examined the stability of residence for blacks and mulattos living in Dallas between 1880 and 1910, revealing that the persistence rate for these combined groups (32%), by continuing to reside in Dallas over the course of 30 years, exceeded that of whites by about 10%.

Table 9.2: Demographic Composition of Freedman's and Cedar Grove Collections

| | Freedman's Cemetery | | | | | | | | | | Cedar Grove (1900–1915) | |
| | Early (1869–1884) | | Middle (1885–1899) | | Pre-1990 (1869–1899) | | Late (1900–1907) | | All Freedman's | | | |
Group	N^a	%	N^a	%	N^a	%	N^a	%	N^a	%	N^a	%
Males	11	17.2	38	22.2	6	16.2	233	26.4	288	24.9	15	18.8
Females	10	15.6	32	18.7	4	10.8	232	26.2	278	24.0	21	26.2
Indet. adults	2	3.1	10	5.8	1	2.7	91	10.3	104	9.0	0	0.0
Subadults	41	64.1	91	53.2	26	70.3	328	37.1	486	42.0	44	55.0
Total	64	100.0	171	99.9	37	100.0	884	100.0	1156*	99.9	80	100.0
Infants (age < 1 year)	22	34.4	58	33.9	19	51.4	209	23.6	309	26.7	22	27.5
Mean age at death	13.6		17.7		—		23.1		21		19.3	
D30+/D5+^{b}	0.533		0.756		—		0.7				0.652	

*Note: 1 burial recovered from Freedman's could not be assigned to any of the above temporal periods; hence 1,156 burials (in the four temporal periods) +1 = 1157.

^{a}Sample size.

^{b}Deaths aged 30+ divided by deaths aged 5+.

Source: See text.

Table 9.3: Fertility and Mortality in the United States, 1860–1930

Approximate date	Birthrate[a]		Child-woman ratio[b]		Total fertility rate[c]		Expectation of life[d]		Infant mortality rate[e]	
	White	Black[f]	White	Black	White	Black[f]	White	Black[f]	White	Black[f]
1860	41.4	55.0[g]	905	1072	5.21	7.58[g]	43.6		181.3	
1870	38.3	55.4[h]	814	997	4.55	7.69[i]	45.2		175.5	
1880	35.2	51.9[i]	780	1090	4.24	7.26[i]	40.5		214.8	
1890	31.5	48.1	685	930	3.87	6.56	46.8		150.7	
1900	30.1	44.4	666	845	3.56	5.61	51.8[j]	41.8[j]	110.8[j]	170.3[j]
1910	29.2	38.5	631	736	3.42	4.61	54.6[k]	46.8[k]	96.5[k]	142.6[k]
1920	26.9	35.0	604	608	3.17	3.64	57.4	47.0	82.1	131.7
1930	20.6	27.5	506	554	2.45	2.98	60.9	48.5	60.1	99.9

[a] Births per 1,000 population per annum.
[b] Children aged 0–4 per 1,000 women aged 15–44, taken from U.S. Bureau of Census (1975), Series B67–68.
[c] Total number of births per women if she experienced the current period age-specific fertility rates throughout her life.
[d] Expectation of life at birth for both sexes combined.
[e] Infant deaths per 1,000 live births per annum.
[f] Black and other population for CBR (1920–1970), TFR (1940–1990), e_0 (1950–1960), IMR (1920–1970).
[g] Average for 1860–1869.
[h] Average for 1870–1879.
[i] Average for 1880–1884.
[j] Approximately 1895.
[k] Approximately 1904.

Sources: U.S. Bureau of the Census (1975, 1985, 1997); Coale and Zelnik (1963); Coale and Rives (1973); Haines (1998); Preston and Haines (1991), Table 2.5.

234

Table 9.4: Fertility and Mortality by Race, Arkansas and Texas, 1860–1930

Date	Location	Child-woman ratio[a]		Expectation of life[b]		Infant mortality rate[c]		q(5)[d]	
		White	Black	White	Black	White	Black	White	Black
Arkansas									
1860	State	898.4	798.9						
1870	State	719.4	785.5						
1880	State	887.5	975.1						
1890	State	856.3	850.6						
	Little Rock	457.5	455.3						
1900	State	723.8	690.0	42.7	35.4[e]	159.5	210.3[e]	0.24611	0.32444[e]
	Little Rock	391.2	302.5						
1910	State	809.1	653.5	49.4	38.8[f]	131.8	194.6[f]	0.18294	0.28621[f]
	Little Rock	359.8	265.1						
1920	State	638.7	481.1						
	Fort Smith	393.0	263.6						
	Little Rock	316.3	234.3						
Texas									
1860	State	956.9	861.8						
1870	State	708.9	844.4						
1880	State	895.9	982.0						
1890	State	837.7	883.7						
	Dallas	503.6	435.6						
	Galveston	528.0	368.4						
	Houston	512.5	449.2						
	San Antonio	565.4	526.5						
1900	State	732.6	725.0	49.0	38.6[e]	114.8	176.9[e]	0.18715	0.28831[e]
	Dallas	391.7	269.3						
	Fort Worth	435.3	298.6						
	Galveston	456.2	279.9						
	Houston	421.6	269.2						
	San Antonio	437.3	361.1	35.3[g]		191.8[g]		0.28708[g]	
1910	State	722.4	658.9	54.0	45.6[f]	97.0	148.5[f]	0.14270	0.21849[f]
	Austin	341.0	329.4						
	Dallas	345.6	230.8						
	El Paso	445.1	258.7	29.1[g]		247.6[g]		0.36722[g]	
	Fort Worth	397.1	286.0						
	Galveston	389.2	231.8	48.7	38.2	117.3	167.7	0.16178	0.21494
	Houston	357.6	249.1						
	San Antonio	413.8	280.9	40.1	37.5	173.5	215.0	0.24300	0.26479
	Waco	397.9	284.8						
1920	State	525.0	459.1						
	Austin	287.4	206.4						
	Beaumont	409.6	290.9	57.5	44.2	72.0	166.8	0.09832	0.21340
	Dallas	302.3	207.1	53.8	41.2	96.7	159.6	0.13295	0.20183
	El Paso	401.5	211.2	33.6[g]		227.4[g]		0.31625[g]	

(continued)

Table 9.4 *(continued)*

Date	Location	Child-woman ratio[a]		Expectation of life[b]		Infant mortality rate[c]		q(5)[d]	
		White	Black	White	Black	White	Black	White	Black
	Fort Worth	323.6	216.4						
	Galveston	372.7	204.9	54.1	42.3	93.2	108.7	0.11328	0.15556
	Houston	325.2	206.8	53.7	43.3	85.2	130.6	0.11474	0.16852
	San Antonio	372.1	231.0	47.0	45.0	144.0	124.8	0.20018	0.16302
	Waco	351.5	262.8						
	Wichita Falls	398.8	172.4						

[a] Children aged 0–4 per 1,000 women aged 15–44.
[b] Expectations of life at birth for both sexes combined.
[c] Infant deaths per 1,000 live births per annum.
[d] Probability of surviving between birth and age 5.
[e] For approximately 1895.
[f] For approximately 1904.
[g] For the total population.

Sources: (*a*) Child-woman ratios. 1860: U.S. Bureau of the Census (1984), Table 1. 1870: U.S. Bureau of the Census (1872), Tables XXVI & XXIX. 1880: U.S. Bureau of the Census (1883), Table XXI. 1890: U.S. Bureau of the Census (1897), Tables 2 & 8. 1900: U.S. Bureau of the Census (1902), Tables 2 & 9. 1910: U.S. Bureau of the Census (1913), Tables 7 & 13. 1920: U.S. Bureau of the Census (1923), Tables 13, 15, 16.
(*b*) Expectation of life at birth, infant mortality rate, and q(5). For states, 1900 and 1910, calculated by indirect methods of estimation described in Haines and Preston (1997). The results for expectation of life at birth are extrapolations from childhood mortality in the West Model life table system. For individual cities, life tables were calculated by standard methods from census data on population by age, sex, and race for 1900 to 1920 and from deaths by age, sex, and race from U.S. Bureau of the Census, *Mortality Statistics of the United States,* various volumes. For the methods of constructing life tables, see Shryock, Siegel, and Associates (1971), chap. 15.

cities in those states for the period 1860 to 1920. Since most blacks during this period were in the rural South, the fertility measures were probably not untypical of the Cedar Grove population. As can be seen, black fertility was relatively high over this period, substantially higher than for the white population. This was not as true for Arkansas and Texas, however, where the fertility of the white population was considerably higher than that for the whole United States (Tolnay 1996). Both tables also support the notion of declining black fertility from the era of the Civil War to the 1920s. Finally, it should be noted that the child-woman ratio data do not support a view of especially high fertility in the black population of Dallas, Texas, although these ratios might not be accurate in terms of differentials if the correction for the relative underenumeration of children aged 0–4 was not enough in that urban environment (Coale and Zelnik 1963; Coale and Rives 1973).[8] The high proportion of subadults in the burials is due to rather high mortality among black children in Dallas and in Arkansas, which is supported by the data in infant mortality rates and q(5) values in Table 9.4 [q(5) is the probability of dying between birth and age 5].

Census sample data from 1880 and 1910 shed further light on the demography of urban and rural populations in Texas and Arkansas. Table 9.5 presents age structure

---

[8] All the data were corrected upwards by 5% for whites and 13% for blacks for the relative underenumeration of children.

data (by gender, racial, and ethnic group) for urban and rural Texas and Arkansas for the two years. The table also shows the age distribution of urban and rural inhabitants of Dallas County, Texas, in 1910 (Dallas County is too small in 1880 to make a similar analysis). The age structure data contradict the skeletal data to some extent, because the African-American population did not usually have an excessively large population of individuals under age 20. Published census data for the City of Dallas from the 1890 U.S. Census, however, do show relatively high proportions of the black population below age 20 (39% for males and 43% for females) (U.S. Bureau of the Census, 1897, Table 10). In general, the age data tend to confirm a high birthrate implied by the skeletal data earlier in the period. But as the birthrate fell, the proportion of subadults also fell. By 1910, for example, the proportion of subadults in the black population was about 31% (30.7% for males and 31.8% for females; U.S. Bureau of the Census, 1913, Table 53).

We can learn still more by examining the results in Table 9.6, which present the Preston-Haines Child Mortality Index for selected states for 1910. The child mortality index is a ratio of actual deaths to expected deaths in a population, given certain assumptions. The data in Table 9.6 confirm results that have been reported elsewhere (Preston and Haines 1991; Preston, Ewbank, and Hereward 1994; Gutmann and Fliess 1996; Haines and Preston 1997; Gutmann et al. 1998). In the populations of the Southwest (and especially the South), as well as in urban areas, the African-American population had high rates of child mortality. These high levels of child mortality combined with relatively high fertility to produce the large number of subadult skeletons in the analysis of Freedman's and Cedar Grove. The high childhood mortality in the black population of Arkansas and Texas, as well as some cities in Texas (including Dallas for 1920), for the period roughly 1890 to 1920 is also seen in Table 9.4. Comparisons to the white populations in those states, as well as to the white population of the nation as a whole (Table 9.3) for the infant mortality rate (as well as expectation of life at birth), show that blacks in Arkansas and Texas were much worse off than whites in this area of human well-being and were worse off than blacks in the nation as a whole.

According to Gutmann and Fliess (1996), rural African-Americans in Texas had better life chances than did African-Americans in the national samples described by Preston and Haines (1991), as well as by Glover (1976), who report expectations of life at birth for African-American children of under 35 years. Moreover, the life chances of African-American children in rural Texas appear to have been improving slightly in the early twentieth century.

Drawing distinctions between the mortality of Texas families in the early twentieth century, Gutmann and Fliess showed that other factors beyond race and ethnicity were significant. Health was dependent on household wealth, as measured by tax assessments. The children of well-to-do families were more likely than those of poor families to survive to adulthood. The impact of wealth had much to do with living conditions. In another article, Fliess (1992) showed that the Wendish population of Serbin, Texas, improved their levels of infant mortality between the 1850s and the 1880s, largely by reducing air- as well as waterborne contagious diseases. By the 1890s, the larger German-origin population analyzed by Gutmann and Fliess had probably

Table 9.5: Percent in Age Groups, 1880 and 1910 (Census Data)

| Age group | Arkansas | | | | Texas | | | | Dallas County | | | |
| | Rural | | Urban | | Rural | | Urban | | Rural | | Urban | |
	White, non-Hispanic	African-American	White, non-Hispanic	African-American	White, non-Hispanic	African-American	White, non-Hispanic	African-American	White, non-Hispanic	African-American	White, non-Hispanic	African-American
1880												
Male												
0–19	53.9	56.1	44.0	35.9	52.4	60.4	41.6	49.1				
20–39	31.6	28.6	32.7	43.6	32.6	23.8	37.4	34.0				
40–59	11.5	13.1	17.8	20.5	11.7	10.8	18.0	14.5				
60+	3.0	2.2	5.6	0.0	3.3	5.0	3.0	2.5				
N	289,000	103,200	10,700	3,900	595,300	191,100	62,800	15,900				
Female												
0–19	55.3	60.1	45.5	38.0	55.8	58.8	45.7	45.5				
20–39	29.4	27.2	36.4	40.0	30.3	27.3	36.5	37.0				
40–59	12.2	10.2	16.9	14.0	11.3	10.0	14.5	13.2				
60+	3.1	2.5	1.3	8.0	2.6	4.0	3.3	4.2				
N	264,700	102,500	7,700	5,000	498,100	184,000	54,500	18,900				

1910

Male

0–19	52.3	50.3	33.3	35.7	51.4	53.2	38.7	38.7	15.2	15.8	33.9	30.3
20–39	28.4	30.8	39.9	40.2	28.9	29.0	38.5	42.3	37.0	68.4	46.2	45.5
40–59	14.1	13.9	21.0	20.5	14.5	12.5	17.5	15.4	15.1	10.5	15.2	18.2
60+	5.2	5.0	5.7	3.6	5.2	5.3	5.3	3.6	2.7	5.3	4.7	6.1
N	485,92-	187,893	83,884	28,207	1,187,883	257,027	346,037	92,659	18,387	4,787	43,072	8,314

Female

0–19	54.7	53.7	41.1	40.3	53.0	55.1	40.5	35.6	50.8	60.0	42.0	27.3
20–39	23.5	30.6	38.4	36.6	29.7	29.7	37.8	43.9	27.7	26.7	40.4	50.0
40–59	11.9	11.7	14.2	16.4	12.8	10.7	16.6	16.4	15.4	6.7	14.3	20.4
60+	4.9	4.0	6.3	6.7	4.4	4.5	5.2	4.1	6.2	6.7	3.1	2.3
N	443,828	182,612	83,378	33,744	1,053,670	260,665	307,233	101,706	16,374	3,776	40,549	11,086

Sources: Calculated from data in Ruggles and Sobek (1997). The procedure for determining Hispanic ethnicity is described in Gratton and Gutmann (2000). The Ns reflect the approximate number of cases multiplied by the sampling weights.

Table 9.6: Child Mortality by Race/Ethnic Group, State and Urban/Rural Status, 1892–1910

| | Race/Ethnic Group | | | | | | | | | | | | | | |
| | Hispanic | | | White, non-Hispanic | | | African-American | | | Other races | | | All race/ethnic groups | | |
	Rural	Urban	Total	Rural	Urban	Total	Rural	Urban	Total	Rural	Urban	Total	Rural	Urban	Total
Five states	1.12	1.10	1.11	0.91	0.88	0.91	1.42	1.85	1.48	0.94		0.94	1.04	1.11	1.05
Arkansas				1.04	1.14	1.05	1.63	1.76	1.65				1.18	1.30	1.20
Louisiana				0.95	0.99	0.96	1.65	2.23	1.76				1.25	1.35	1.27
Mississippi				0.88	0.71	0.86	1.31	1.11	1.30				1.10	0.82	1.07
Oklahoma				1.02	1.11	1.03	1.40	2.60	1.72	0.95		0.95	1.03	1.28	1.07
Texas	1.15	1.22	1.17	0.81	0.71	0.79	1.16	1.58	1.27				0.88	0.93	0.89

Notes: Empty cells are based on fewer than 40 children ever born.

Child mortality is measured by a Child Mortality Index, which is the ratio of actual to expected child deaths in each group or category. Actual child deaths are calculated as the difference between children ever born and children surviving to women in the group or category. Expected child deaths are calculated by multiplying the children ever born for women in the marriage duration categories 0–4 years, 5–9 years, . . . , 20–24 years by the proportion of children dead expected under indirect mortality estimation using the Coale and Demeny West Model life table level 13.5 (males and females combined). The women were chosen as currently married, once-married women of marriage durations less than 25 years with at least one birth. A child is defined as the children of those women. The period of the estimation dates from 1910 back to 1892, but the mean date to which the estimates apply is about 1903–1904.

Sources: Basic census data from Ruggles and Sobek (1997), samples ip19001, ip19101, and ip19103 (Hispanic oversample). The procedure for determining Hispanic ethnicity is described in Gratton and Gutmann (2000). The Child Mortality Indexes for 1900 and 1910 were calculated by indirect methods of estimation described in Preston and Haines (1991), pp. 88–90.

done the same. The higher-mortality Mexican-American and African-American families, by 1910, had not had the opportunity to experience those improvements in living conditions. Studies of rural living conditions elsewhere in the South (Bradley and Williamson 1918) suggest that the poorest whites and African-Americans may have been ignorant of ways to improve their health, too poor to do much about it, and living in tenancy arrangements that made improvements difficult.

The demographic data provide some insight into the quality of life for African-Americans near the turn of the century. The age distribution of skeletons for both Cedar Grove and Freedman's suggests high fertility comparable to frontier families of European descent, but far less than for the Mormons. The average age of skeletons from both cemeteries places them below all but one of the eighteenth- and nineteenth-century samples included in this project. In contrast, the census data indicate that the life expectancy at birth for rural African-Americans in Texas (44.9 years) was lower than for European-Americans in Texas (58 years), but better than for African-Americans from other areas of the United States, which could be as low as 35 years. The increase in life expectancy from 1900 to 1910 indicates that life conditions were improving, likely due to public health officials' attempts at reducing air- and waterborne diseases. Overall, then, the demographic data tend to confirm the representativeness of the age distribution of the skeletal remains in both Cedar Grove and the Freedman's Cemetery.

Childhood Health and Nutrition

Evaluating the quality of childhood health and nutrition from a skeletal sample must of necessity use indirect measures, some of which are total cumulative outputs, such as adult height; others are partially cumulative, such as achieved height at a given age; while others are age specific, such as an enamel hypoplasia that indicates a disease episode that occurred at a specific age. In addition, none of these indicators have direct linear relationships to either health or nutrition, but are instead the final product of a synergistic interaction of nutrition and health. For example, final adult height is the end result of a given intake of protein, but if protein was used to fight frequent infections or to make up for deficient calories when workloads were high, then height is reduced. We must interpret all of our skeletal markers for health and nutrition as an array of interacting data points that together permit an assessment of both nutrition and health.

Growth and Development

Differences in skeletal growth and development between Cedar Grove and Freedman's are assessed using three measures: femoral growth velocity, adult stature, and developmental enamel defects.

Femoral Growth Velocity. Table 9.7 compares the femoral velocity (growth per age interval) and the femur length equations for data from both Freedman's and Cedar

Table 9.7: Femur Velocity and Femur Length Equations
in Centimeters

	Age			
Site	2 years	5 years	8 years	11 years
Freedman's	23.7	23.0	20.6	19.7
Cedar Grove	26.9	22.2	21.0	20.4
Freedman's	$FL = 110.64 + 17.95$ (age) $+ 16.68$ (Ln age); $N = 92, r^2 = 0.978$			
Cedar Grove	$FL = 103.68 + 18.98$ (age) $+ 15.87$ (Ln age); $N = 32, r^2 = 0.988$			

Source: See text.

Grove. While the values for Cedar Grove are slightly higher for the youngest age intervals, the values thereafter are alike and show a similar pattern of growth. This suggests that the net effects of nutrition and health influencing skeletal growth at the two sites was nearly identical. This is surprising, given the evidence for poor nutritional status of Cedar Grove presented later. When these data are compared to other samples in the project, childhood growth at both sites seems remarkably good. Both cemeteries display greater growth at all ages than the preagricultural Native Americans from Ohio, which were better off than all other Native American groups in the project. Furthermore, growth at both sites is similar (given the small sample sizes which necessitate curve smoothing) to the nineteenth-century European-Canadians from the Belleville Cemetery. This suggests that the outcomes of western African-American nutrition and health were not dissimilar to the nineteenth-century settled East.

Adult Height. Despite similar juvenile skeletal growth velocities observed at the two sites, Table 9.8 shows that for both males and females, adults at Cedar Grove were taller on average than their counterparts at Freedman's, but that the level of size sexual dimorphism (m/f × 100) did not differ significantly (approximately 1.08). The differences in achieved stature at the two sites arose during pubertal growth, which cannot be measured because of the few individuals who died at these ages.

The stature of individuals at Cedar Grove is truly remarkable. As seen in Table 9.8, both the males and females are almost as tall as modern African-Americans. Cedar Grove males are 13cm taller than the project mean for Native Americans and 5cm taller than the project mean for European-Americans, while the females are 4cm taller than the Native Americans and the same as the Europeans. Comparisons with the nineteenth-century project samples show that the Cedar Grove males and females are taller than Remley and Belleview Plantation slaves, free African-Americans from Philadelphia, the Monroe County Poorhouse, and middle-class Canadians (see Rathbun and Steckel, this volume). The males are taller than or as tall as the military samples. The Cedar Grove females are taller than the slaves, and

Table 9.8: Adult Stature in Centimeters

Site	Males N^a	Mean	SE^b	Females N^a	Mean	SE^b
Freedman's	98	171.1	4.7	84	159.3	4.6
Cedar Grove	14	177.8	6.9	19	162.8	5.6
U.S. modern African-American	75	179.0	6.5	67	165.2	5.9

^{a} Sample size.
^{b} Standard error.
Source: See text.

shorter than the Charleston elites, Monroe County Poorhouse, and middle-class Canadians. The explanation for the abnormal height of males at Cedar Grove remains unclear.

Freedman's males are only 7 cm taller than the project mean for Native Americans and the same as the project mean for European-Americans. Comparison to the nineteenth-century samples show them to be taller than the slaves and the inhabitants of the Monroe County Poorhouse, shorter than the Charleston elites, and the same as Philadelphia African-Americans, middle-class Canadians, and the military samples. Freedman's females are slightly taller than one slave group and shorter than the other, taller than Philadelphia African-Americans, while shorter than the Monroe Country Poorhouse and middle-class Canadians. In summary, the heights of both males and females at Freedman's are normal for their time period, do not differ significantly from any other historic African-American skeletal sample, except Cedar Grove, and are indistinguishable from Higman's (1979) estimates for U.S. African slaves between 1828 and 1860.

Because growth rates are similar for Cedar Grove and Freedman's, while Cedar Grove heights remain so much greater, the major difference in nutrition and health seems to have occurred during the teenage years, or the adults at Cedar Grove were children during a time of plenty that was not represented by the subadult skeletons at Cedar Grove. This later alternative appears to be the most compelling at this time.

Enamel Defects. Linear enamel hypoplasias (or LEH) are deficiencies in the thickness of the enamel and appear as horizontal grooves across the surface of the tooth. These result from specific disease episodes, such as diarrhea, or infectious diseases, such as measles. Thus, enamel defects document the frequency of these diseases during childhood. The sensitivity of the tooth to the disease episode is determined by the overall nutrition of the child, especially with respect to protein. The lower the quality of the nutrition, the more frequently do the disease episodes show up as hypoplasias. Table 9.9 shows the proportion of individuals possessing 1 or more linear enamel hypoplasias on the most sensitive tooth types (i.e., incisors and canines) of the deciduous and permanent dentitions. Defects in the deciduous teeth would suggest stress sufficient to disrupt enamel formation (i.e., deposition) during

Table 9.9: Proportion of Individuals with One or More Linear Enamel Hypoplasias (LEH)

| | Freedman's Cemetery | | | | | | | | | | | | | | | Cedar Grove | | |
| | Early | | | Middle | | | Pre-1900 | | | Late | | | All periods | | | | | |
	N^a	1 or more LEH	%	N^a	1 or more LEH	%	N^a	1 or more LEH	%	N^a	1 or more LEH	%	N^a	1 or more LEH	%	N^a	1 or more LEH	%
Max. decid. incisor	19	0	0	41	4	9.8	8	0	0	130	3	2.3	198	7	3.5	9	2	22.2
Max. decid. canine	17	0	0	34	2	5.9	6	0	0	97	3	3.1	154	5	3.2	8	3	37.5
Max. perm. incisor	25	3	12.0	71	20	28.2	9	4	44.4	471	123	26.1	576	150	26.0	40	32	80.0
Max. perm. canine	29	14	48.3	71	43	60.6	9	7	77.8	486	296	60.9	595	360	60.5	42	35	83.3

[a] Sample size.
Source: See text.

the period just before and after birth, whereas defects in the permanent incisors and canines indicate stresses during the first 4 years of life.

The diachronic trend in the rate of deciduous hypoplasia experienced in Dallas is an intriguing one (Table 9.9). Of subadults dying during Freedman's Early Period, the deciduous hypoplasia rates are zero, with no teeth affected. These rates, however, jump during Freedman's Middle Period to 9.8% (maxillary deciduous incisor) and 5.9% (mandibular deciduous canine), before declining during the Freedman's Late Period to a more modest 2.3% and 3.1%, respectively. Since major elements of the deciduous dentition are formed prior to birth (especially the deciduous incisor), in large part what is being reflected here is the health and well-being of the mother, prior to the birth of the child. Further, even after birth, infants are provided partial protection from infectious disease through breast-feeding. Thus, the marked increase in deciduous rates between the Early and Middle Periods suggests, in part, an increase in the overall stress levels of women of childbearing age during the 1880s and 1890s, while the decline in deciduous hypoplasia rates in the turn of the century Late Period suggests a decline in overall stress (i.e., lowering of workloads, improvements in sanitation and nutrition, etc.). It is interesting to note that this overall trend (i.e., of greatest stress during Freedman's Middle Period) is also seen in the rates of degenerative joint disease experienced by women (detailed below).

The pattern in the hypoplasia rates observed in the Freedman's permanent dentition only somewhat parallels that found in the deciduous. The permanent hypoplasia rates are lowest during the Early Period, and then rise sharply in the Middle Period. Although *deciduous* hypoplasias declined in the Late Period, the hypoplasia rates in the permanent dentition remain essentially unchanged from the Middle Period to Freedman's Late Period. Since permanent dentition is formed after birth (to approximately 4 years), the increase of hypoplasias from the Early to Middle Periods suggests a significant increase in the overall stress levels (e.g., poor sanitation, nutrition, etc.) experienced by infants and young children (especially between 2 and 4 years), and that these environmental factors remained essentially unchanged from the 1890s into the early 1900s.

Examination of Table 9.9 shows that for both the deciduous and permanent dentitions, individuals at Cedar Grove have a much higher frequency of enamel defects than experienced during any of the three major temporal periods at Freedman's. In fact, between Cedar Grove and Freedman's Late Period, there is a nearly tenfold difference in the deciduous hypoplasia rate. Additionally, of the sample of teeth from Cedar Grove exhibiting LEH, *all* of the deciduous canines displayed 2 or more hypoplasias ($n = 3$), demonstrating repeated stress episodes, while only one of the Freedman's examples had 2 or more LEH (occurring during the Late Period). Overall, these profound disparities may suggest differences in the causes of infant mortality, given the similar rates of infant mortality seen in the demography.

The same trend seen in deciduous LEH rates is present in the permanent dentition. Compared to Dallas, the rates of LEH at Cedar Grove are extremely high, and as before, the rate of teeth with 2 or more hypoplasias is much greater at Cedar Grove. For example, of the 296 permanent canines in Freedman's Late Period exhibiting LEH, only 42% had 2 or more hypoplasias ($n = 125$), demonstrating repeated stress episodes. For Cedar Grove, the rate for 2 or more LEH affecting the same tooth is 94%. These significantly higher rates of enamel defects in the permanent dentition at Cedar Grove may reflect a poorer diet and corresponding increased susceptibility to disease after 2 years of age. The diet of the sharecroppers at Cedar Grove may have been derived from subsistence agriculture and thus subject to seasonal fluctuation, whereas the cash economy in Dallas may have permitted a more stable, consistent, and nutritionally superior diet. This supposition is supported by the evidence for dietary anemia presented later.

Comparison with other groups in the project sample requires using data obtained only from adults over 20 years of age and counting those with 1 or more hypoplasias on the permanent central incisors and canines. This procedure produces incisor hypoplasia rates of 18.5% for the combined Freedman's sample and 78.3% for Cedar Grove, which compare with 28.2% for all Native Americans and 22.8% for all European-Americans in the project sample. Freedman's is slightly lower than, but essentially similar to, both groups, while Cedar Grove is much higher than both. When the permanent canines are compared, the combined Freedman's sample has 46.5% and Cedar Grove 66.7%, which are both higher than the total Native American sample with 40.9% and the European-Americans with 27.5%.

These data suggest that childhood nutrition and disease was far worse for the people of rural Cedar Grove than for those of urban Dallas. Additional evidence for this urban/rural disparity can be found in the presence of microscopic enamel defects (Wilson bands are also associated with disease events). Wilson bands are twice as common at rural Cedar Grove as among the urban African-Americans from the nineteenth-century First African Baptist Church of Philadelphia, again demonstrating the disadvantages of the rural diet and environment (Marks 1993). In order to allay the notion that this was just an African-American experience, we can note that the hypoplasia rates at Cedar Grove, as alarmingly high as they were, are still lower than those from a rural, nineteenth-century European-American family cemetery in East Texas (located not very far from Cedar Grove), where poor nutrition and repeated epidemics produced *highly stressful* childhoods (Winchell et al. 1995). Comparisons of hypoplasia rates to the combined project samples demonstrates that both Cedar Grove and Freedman's experienced higher childhood stress than the Native American and European-American samples as a whole.

Diet

Possible differences between the diets at Cedar Grove and Freedman's are assessed on the basis of dental caries and skeletal pathologies associated with anemia. Analysis of the diet of historical African-American populations, based on skeletal remains, reflects on our broader knowledge of diet in this community. While there has been less systematic analysis of the diet of African-Americans than would be desirable, most researchers have described the rural sharecropping population in the terms used by Levenstein (1993), consisting of "salt meat, corn bread, and syrup of sorghum, with a bit of milk here and there – many rarely ate vegetables, even in the summer." What is striking in all these reports is the absence of vegetables in the diet, a result either of lack of time or financial reasons to tend a home garden (Jones 1985; Levenstein 1993). The consequence of this aspect of the poor diet was shortages of protein and vitamins, leading to pellagra, scurvy, and other deficiency diseases.

Dental Caries. Table 9.10 compares the proportion of individuals with 1 or more caries (dental decay) in the permanent teeth at the 2 sites. At Freedman's, there are slight differences in the caries rates from the Early to Late Periods. Viewing all adults together as a single sample, the trend is for a relatively lower rate of caries experienced during the Early Period (77.3%), with this rate climbing to a relative higher rate during the Middle Period (87.5%), and then declining in the Late (79.3%) to nearly those levels experienced in the Early. This trend is especially pronounced in adult women. In men alone, this trend is reversed, with the highest rates observed during the Early Period (91%), and a drop in the Middle (81.1%) and Late Period (80.4%) caries rates.

One possible explanation for the relatively lower caries rate experienced overall in the Early Period might be found in the circumstances of that time, when most African-Americans in the vicinity of Dallas lived outside the city limits in a number of Freedman's Towns, established for mutual protection. Such isolation, necessary to avoid the worst effects of racism, would have limited access to jobs and the means to purchase cariogenic foods, such as molasses. Greater access to town jobs and a wider variety of highly sugared foods (especially for women working as domestics in the homes of wealthy whites) during the Middle Period in the late 1880s and 1890s would have caused a higher caries rate. Viewing the caries rate overall, the frequencies are high and do not differ much when comparing Cedar Grove to either the Freedman's Late Period (its contemporary) or the combined Freedman's sample. These data suggest no significant differences in the caries-causing properties of the diet at the two sites. It is highly likely that corn, starches, and sugars (e.g., molasses) were a major component of the diet of both populations, contributing to the high caries rates observed.

It is interesting to note that access to dental care as evidenced by dental work did not differ significantly between the rural Cedar Grove and urban Freedman's Cemetery. Of the 24 individuals exhibiting dental work at Freedman's Cemetery, 23 date to the Late Period (2.6% of total). Only a single burial with dental work dates to the Middle Period. This increase in dental work corresponds to the arrival of African-American dentists serving the Dallas community in 1894 (Dallas City Directory 1894–1895; McKnight 1990; Barr 1995:95). At Cedar Grove, fewer than 4% of the adults exhibited dental work. For both populations, the majority of dental care was vanity work, in contrast to restorative (e.g., false teeth). Because both sites predate the onset of modern prophylactic dentistry, availability of dental care was probably only a minor factor in altering dental health.

Cribra Orbitalia and Porotic Hyperostosis. The association of cribra orbitalia and porotic hyperostosis with anemia has been extensively documented (see Larsen 1997:29–40). Cribra orbitalia is pitting on the bone surface and expansion of the marrow-containing portion of the bone within the eye orbits. Porotic hyperostosis

Table 9.10: Proportion of Adults with One or More Dental Caries

| | Freedman's Cemetery | | | | | | | | | | | | | | | | | | Cedar Grove (1900–1915) | | |
| | Early (1869–1884) | | | Middle (1885–1899) | | | Pre-1900 (1869–1899) | | | Late (1900–1907) | | | All periods | | | | | |
	N^a	1 or more caries	%	N^a	1 or more caries	%	N^a	1 or more caries	%	N^a	1 or more caries	%	N^a	1 or more caries	%	N^a	1 or more caries	%
Males	11	10	91.0	37	30	81.1	5	5	100.0	225	181	80.4	278	226	81.3	15	12	80.0
Females	10	6	60.0	30	29	96.7	4	3	75.0	224	185	82.6	268	223	83.2	21	18	85.7
Sex unknown	1	1	100.0	5	4	80.4	1	1	100.0	58	36	62.1	65	42	64.6	—	—	—
TOTAL ADULTS	22	17	77.3	72	63	87.5	10	9	90.0	507	402	79.3	611	491	8.04	36	30	83.3

[a] Sample size.

Source: See text.

248

is pitting of the surface and thickening of the cranial bones caused by a similar expansion of the marrow-containing portion of the bone. Table 9.11 shows the proportion of individuals with cribra orbitalia and porotic hyperostosis at Freedman's and Cedar Grove by temporal period, age, and sex groups.

Overall, there is a very clear trend at Freedman's of increasing frequency of both porotic hyperostosis and cribra orbitalia. During Freedman's Early Period, there are no affected individuals with either porotic hyperostosis or cribra orbitalia. In regard to cribra orbitalia alone, the Middle Period marks its first appearance in the Freedman's population, though only within the subadults (15.4%). In the Late Period, the rates of cribra orbitalia increase substantially in all individuals, more than doubling in the subadults and increasing from no cases (in either the Early or Middle Periods) to 12.1% in the combined adults.

The basic trend exhibited by porotic hyperostosis in Dallas is the same as that seen with cribra orbitalia. There are no cases in Freedman's Early Period, with its first appearance in the Middle, though notably occurring only in subadults (4.3%) and adult women (3.4%). In the turn-of-the-century Late Period, all age and gender groups are affected to some degree; subadults see a slight decline from the Middle Period, while adult females, with 11.4% affected, exhibit twice the rate seen in men (5.1%).

Except for females, the frequencies for cribra orbitalia are twice as high at Cedar Grove as in Freedman's. The evidence for increased levels of anemia at Cedar Grove is much stronger with regard to porotic hyperostosis. Here, all sex and age subgroups at Cedar Grove show a significantly higher proportion, with nearly triple the frequency seen at Freedman's. These data strongly suggest iron-deficiency anemia at rural Cedar Grove. A diet dependent upon corn, which inhibits iron absorption from all foods passing through the gut, combined with a deficiency of red meat (pork and chicken were the typical meat sources) would produce iron-deficiency anemia. High frequencies of infections (evidenced by the increased frequencies of dental defects at Cedar Grove), combined with an iron-poor diet, would synergistically increase the anemia rates. Furthermore, parasites, such as the pork tapeworm (*Taenia solium*), roundworm (*Trichinella spiralis*), and hookworm (*Necator americanus*), common in the rural South, are another cause of anemia, and their impact is far worse in conjunction with an iron-poor diet (Krupp and Chatton 1976). Skeletal evidence for other dietary deficiencies such as vitamins C and D is also present at Cedar Grove (Rose 1985). The data for anemia corroborates the hypoplasia data in suggesting a diet more nutritionally deficient at Cedar Grove than at Freedman's.

The trend in iron deficiencies occurring within Freedman's African-American Dallas population is clear, although the reasons for the deficiencies are more difficult to discern. Dallas County was an important agricultural center from the time of settlement in the 1840s, and it is known that area farmers produced substantial quantities of wheat (Cochran 1928:59; Holmes and Saxon 1992:127). In fact, in 1873 it was reported that, "as a wheat growing county, Dallas is second to none in the state, and to prepare this crop for market, at least a dozen flouring mills have already been erected" (Anonymous 1873). With flour a significant commodity in the formative years of Dallas, corn may not have been a major part of the diet during

Table 9.11: Proportion of Individuals with Porotic Hyperostosis or Cribra Orbitalia

Freedman's Cemetery: porotic hyperostosis

	Early period			Middle period			Pre-1900 period			Late period			All periods			Cedar Grove		
	N^a	Number affected	%	N^a	Number affected	%	N^a	Number affected	%	N^a	Number affected	%	N^a	Number affected	%	N^a	Number affected	%
Subadults	16	0	0.0	23	1	4.3	4	0	0.0	79	2	2.5	122	3	2.5	43	6	14.0
Males	11	0	0.0	31	0	0.0	3	0	0.0	176	9	5.1	221	9	4.1	14	5	35.7
Females	10	0	0.0	29	1	3.4	4	0	0.0	176	20	11.4	219	21	9.6	21	5	23.8
Sex unknown	0	0	0.0	3	0	0.0	0	0	0.0	28	4	14.3	31	4	12.9	—	—	—
TOTAL ADULTS	21	0	0.0	63	1	1.6	7	0	0.0	380	33	8.7	471	34	7.2	35	10	28.6
TOTAL SAMPLES	58	0	0.0	86	2	2.3	11	0	0.0	459	35	7.6	614	37	6.0	78	16	20.5

Freedman's Cemetery: cribra orbitalia

	Early period			Middle period			Pre-1900 period			Late period			All periods			Cedar Grove		
	N	Number affected	%	N	Number affected	%	N	Number affected	%	N	Number affected	%	N	Number affected	%	N	Number affected	%
Subadults	4	0	0.0	13	2	15.0	1	1	100.0	38	13	34.2	56	16	28.6	42	18	42.9
Males	7	0	0.0	13	0	0.0	1	0	0.0	90	10	11.1	111	10	9.0	14	3	21.4
Females	6	0	0.0	12	0	0.0	1	0	0.0	75	9	12.0	94	9	9.6	21	1	4.8
Sex unknown	0	0	0.0	0	0	0.0	0	0	0.0	8	2	25.0	8	2	25.0	—	—	—
TOTAL ADULTS	13	0	0.0	25	0	0.0	2	1	50.0	173	21	12.1	213	21	9.9	35	4	11.4
TOTAL SAMPLES	17	0	0.0	38	2	5.3	3	1	33.0	211	37	16.1	269	37	13.8	77	22	28.6

^{a} Sample size.
Source: See text.

Freedman's Early Period. However, the increased occurrence of iron deficiencies in the Middle Period, affecting subadults and adult women, could suggest diet as a possible (though perhaps minor) contributing factor, because the diets of women and their dependent children may have been more alike than those of adult males.

Beyond a purely dietary etiology, internal parasites may have been a *significant* contributing factor toward the increase in iron-deficiency anemias in Dallas. In the early 1920s in Charleston, South Carolina, a study of preschool African-American children documented a 28% rate of malnutrition and a 6% anemia rate. Further, the primary cause for both conditions was traced to internal parasites; 45% of the children had evidence of hookworm, pinworms, and so forth (Beardsley 1987:18). During the late nineteenth and early twentieth centuries, Dallas experienced huge population increases, concurrent with a well-documented lag in establishing an adequate public health infrastructure. The African-American populations located in the cramped and segregated communities of North Dallas Freedman's Town, String Town, and Deep Ellum, among others, would have suffered the worst under such conditions, where free-roaming livestock, unpaved streets, standing water, and backyard privies were commonplace, creating ideal conditions for parasitism to occur (Anonymous 1941). While parasitism was likely the most important factor in the anemia rates in Dallas, another possible contributing factor cannot be ignored: the genetic predisposition for sickle-cell anemia present within populations of African ancestry (Gibbs et al. 1980). Finally, it should be noted that none of the examples of either cribra orbitalia or porotic hyperostosis observed at Freedman's or Cedar Grove were extreme, debilitating cases; rather, all were scored as mild to moderate.

Comparisons of both Cedar Grove and Freedman's to other groups in the study enable us to interpret these data within a broader context. The Cedar Grove anemia rates are about the same as those for the African-American slaves reported from South Carolina, when the small sample sizes are taken into consideration. This reflects a similarity in climate, diet, and a rural environment. Both Freedman's and Cedar Grove anemia rates are much lower than those for the corn-dependent and prehistoric Native Americans from the American Southwest, who also experienced high rates of parasite infestation. In this context, African-Americans did not experience the most debilitating level of stress. Nevertheless, both rates are much higher than the Monroe County Poorhouse sample and middle-class Canadians, where anemia was low. These differences reflect variations in climate (warm temperate versus cold temperate) which reduces exposure to parasites, settlement pattern (rural versus urban and long-settled versus frontier), diet (wheat based in the North, with beef more plentiful), and access to economic resources that could provide a more balanced diet.

Infection

Periosteal Reactions. The proportion of individuals with periosteal lesions (i.e., periostitis) on the tibia at both sites by age and sex groups is shown in Table 9.12. Periosteal lesions are areas where either new bone was added to the surface, or bone was being resorbed (removed) when the skeleton responded to bacterial infection.

Table 9.12: Proportion of Individuals with Tibial Periostal Reactions

| | Freedman's Cemetery | | | | | | | | | | | | | | | Cedar Grove | | |
| | Early | | | Middle | | | Pre-1900 | | | Late | | | All periods | | | | | |
	N^a	Number affected	%	N^a	Number affected	%	N^a	Number affected	%	N^a	Number affected	%	N^a	Number affected	%	N^a	Number affected	%
Subadults	8	3	37.5	23	16	70.0	5	2	40.0	88	59	67.0	124	80	64.5	42	24	57.1
Males	11	8	72.7	34	21	61.8	6	3	50.0	190	94	49.5	241	126	52.3	15	10	66.7
Females	10	4	40.0	28	13	46.4	4	0	0.0	172	91	52.9	214	108	50.5	20	9	45.0
Sex unknown	0	0	0.0	3	1	33.3	0	0	0.0	27	17	63.0	30	18	60.0	—	—	—
TOTAL ADULTS	21	12	57.1	65	35	53.8	10	3	30.0	389	202	51.9	485	252	52.0	35	19	54.3
TOTAL SAMPLES	29	15	51.7	88	51	58.0	15	5	33.3	477	261	54.7	609	332	54.5	77	43	55.8

^{a} Sample size.
Source: See text.

252

At Freedman's Cemetery, subdividing individuals by gender and age groups, as well as by temporal period, reveals two basic (and opposing) patterns. In adult males, tibial periosteal reactions are highest in the Early Period (72.7%), and then decline somewhat in the Middle (61.8%) and Late (49.5%) Periods, though never declining to less than half of all men. This trend is reversed in adult women, where tibial periosteal reactions are at their lowest levels during Freedman's Early Period (40%), then increase in the Middle (46.4%) and Late (52.9%). The rate of tibial periosteal lesions in the subadult population basically follows the pattern seen in adult women, except that the increase in the rate from the Early (37.5%) to Middle (70%) Periods is far greater, and there is an insignificant decline in the rate experienced during Freedman's Late Period (67%).

When not only the presence but also the severity of periosteal lesions is considered (scored as either mild, moderate, or severe), these general trends are seen with greater clarity. For Freedman's subadults, the Early Period had both the fewest and least severe cases (all cases scored as mild). In the Middle Period, the rates of tibial periosteal lesions are at their highest, and the greatest rate of severe cases are also present (of the tibiae with lesions, 25% are severe cases, 31% moderate). While there is virtually no decline in the simple presence or absence of subadult tibial periosteal lesions between Middle and Late, there is a significant decline in the rate of severe cases (of the Late Period tibiae with lesions, only 7% are severe). For Cedar Grove's subadult population, not only is the rate of tibial periosteal lesions higher than any of the Freedman's periods, but the rate of severe cases is also extremely high (46% of the cases are severe).

The high frequency of skeletal infection at both sites suggests the presence of widespread chronic infectious diseases. More specifically, possible factors contributing to the significant increase in tibial periosteal reactions observed with the Freedman's subadults from the Early to Late Periods may include an overall increase in environmental pathogens present in the soils. Such pathogen increases likely were the inevitable result of an increasingly urban environment that forced more and more people into the near finite spaces of Dallas's African-American enclaves. These often squalid conditions were commonly combined with the worst unsanitary aspects of much more rural landscapes, especially intimate and daily contact with domestic animals, including pigs, horses, and cows. However, the clear decline in the rate of *severe cases* of tibial infection between the Middle and Late Periods (across all age and gender groups) suggests that these or other etiologies were mitigated.

Specific Infectious Diseases. In a detailed analysis at Cedar Grove of periostitis with new bone (active infections at the time of death, rather than healing infection with old bone), by the specific bone affected, Rose and Hartnady (1991) identified four major disease clusters: congenital syphilis among neonates, weanling diarrhea syndrome, an age-cumulative increase of tibial lesions among adults, and, lastly, a frequent rib infection which is consistent with a high rate of tuberculosis. An equally complete analysis of Freedman's has yet to be done. However, as with Cedar Grove, at Freedman's the pattern of periosteal lesions in the subadults matches the expected distribution for a diagnosis of congenital syphilis (Condon et al. 1994).

Moreover, the dental evidence for congenital syphilis at Freedman's is much more abundant. Only one individual at Cedar Grove exhibited a classically diagnostic dental defect of the incisors characteristic of congenital syphilis (Rose and Hartnady 1991) (although a later study of the dental casts identified three more cases), while this later analysis found none at the nineteenth-century urban First African Baptist Church skeletal series (Jacobi et al. 1992). In contrast, at Freedman's, 110 cases show one or more probable or possible indicators of congenital syphilis. This likely greater frequency of congenital syphilis at Freedman's may be a result of greater population density and urban social structure that increased the risk of transmitting this infection among adults. Among African-Americans, this treponemal infection (and its debilitating and eventual lethal effects) was of great concern to health officials in the nineteenth and early twentieth centuries (Frazier 1957:572–575; Beardsley 1987:11–13, 16). Indeed, before effective methods to treat or cure the disease developed in the early twentieth century, syphilis was likely endemic within *any* nineteenth-century population center. In fact, one study estimated that in the early twentieth century, approximately 10% of the urban population of Western Europe was infected (Ortner and Putschar 1985:182). As for other historic cemetery studies, syphilis was also found at the European-American Monroe County Poorhouse (Higgins et al. this volume). At both Freedman's and Cedar Grove, congenital syphilis is a logical possibility for the high rates of infant mortality and decreased fertility.

Periosteal lesions on the medial surface of the ribs (within the rib cage) are characteristic of pulmonary tuberculosis and were found on 6% of the Cedar Grove skeletons (Rose and Hartnady 1991). Because these lesions occur on only a small percentage of tuberculosis cases, the actual tuberculosis rate at Cedar Grove would have been higher. Similar rib lesions have also been observed at Freedman's, but their frequency has yet to be calculated. However, Dallas City death records from 1900 to 1907 reveal tuberculosis as the cause of 25% of adult deaths, consistent with national findings that reported deaths from tuberculosis as the most numerous among African-Americans in U.S. southern cities in 1910 (U.S. Department of Commerce 1918). Both skeletons and records indicate that tuberculosis was also a major problem at the Monroe County Poorhouse (Higgins et al. this volume).

Degenerative Joint Disease and Trauma

Degenerative Joint Disease (DJD). The trend in the rate and type of DJD in the Freedman's Cemetery population reveals a number of patterns (Tables 9.13, 9.14, 9.15; Figures 9.1, 9.2). Generally speaking, in women the rates of DJD are relatively low in the Early Period, reach their highest levels during the Middle, and decline during the Late Period (Table 9.13; Figure 9.1). This is true for every category except for shoulder/elbow. Rates of DJD in these joints increase from a low level of 12.5% in the Early Period, to 15% in the Middle, and more than double during the Late Period (33.9%).

For men at Freedman's Cemetery, the overall pattern is the reverse of that in women (Table 9.13; Figure 9.2). Rates of DJD are relatively high in the Early Period, decrease during the Middle Period, and then increase again in the Late Period, in

Table 9.13: Proportion of Adults with DJD at Various Joints

		Freedman's Cemetery										
	Early			Middle			Late			Cedar Grove		
	N^a	Number affected	%	N^a	Number affected	%	N^a	Number affected	%	N^a	Number affected	%
Shoulder/elbow DJD												
Males	8	5	62.5	22	9	40.9	123	73	59.3	14	1	7.1
Females	8	1	12.5	20	3	15.0	115	39	33.9	20	6	30.0
Indet. adults	0	0	0.0	1	0	0.0	13	8	61.5	—	—	—
TOTAL ADULTS	16	6	37.5	43	12	27.9	251	120	47.8	34	7	20.6
Hip/knee DJD												
Males	8	4	50.0	23	8	34.8	121	70	57.9	15	4	26.7
Females	10	3	30.0	18	9	50.0	108	32	29.6	19	4	21.1
Indet. adults	0	0	0.0	1	0	0.0	8	4	50.0	—	—	—
TOTAL ADULTS	18	7	38.9	42	17	40.5	237	106	44.7	34	8	23.5
Cervical vertebrae DJD												
Males	6	2	33.3	12	5	41.7	74	39	52.7	15	5	33.3
Females	4	0	0.0	9	4	44.4	82	24	29.3	20	5	25.0
Indet. adults	0	0	0.0	1	0	0.0	8	4	50.0	—	—	—
TOTAL ADULTS	10	2	20.0	22	9	40.9	164	67	40.9	35	10	28.6
Thoracic vertebrae DJD												
Males	4	2	50.0	8	3	37.5	53	21	39.6	15	6	40.0
Females	1	0	0.0	6	3	50.0	57	14	24.6	20	5	25.0
Indet. adults	0	0	0.0	0	0	0.0	3	2	66.7	—	—	—
TOTAL ADULTS	5	2	40.0	14	6	42.9	113	37	32.7	35	11	31.4
Lumbar vertebrae DJD												
Males	4	3	75.0	11	4	36.4	59	32	54.2	15	7	46.7
Females	—	—	—	10	5	50.0	61	24	39.3	20	6	30.0
Indet. adults	—	—	—	—	—	—	5	3	60.0	—	—	—
TOTAL ADULTS	4	3	75.0	21	9	42.9	125	59	47.2	35	13	37.1

^{a} Sample size.
Source: See text.

most cases to levels approaching that seen during the Early. As with Freedman's women, there is one category of male DJD that does not follow this temporal trend. Cervical vertebrae DJD increases in every period, from the low level of 33.3% during the Early Period (which matches the rate at Cedar Grove), to 41.7% for the Middle Period, and finally to 52.7% in the Late Period.

Census sample data for the region (Table 9.14) show that African-American men and women were disproportionately employed in unskilled manual occupations in both 1880 and 1910. These employment rates are consistent with the high rates of DJD in the skeletal data. To better interpret the temporal trends of DJD observed at Freedman's Cemetery, we further examined occupations within the African-American community of Dallas. Three Dallas City Directories (1875, 1889–1890, and 1909) served as a source of information, yielding direct comparisons to the three major temporal periods defined for Freedman's Cemetery. To minimize

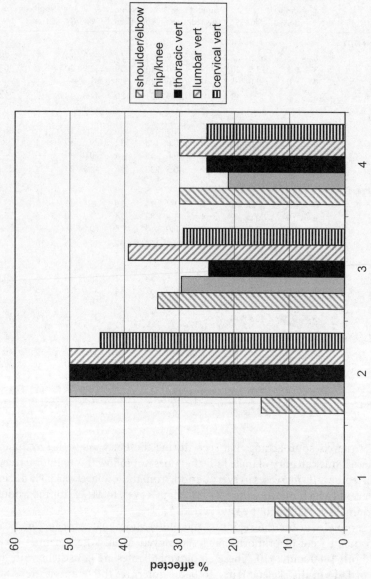

Figure 9.1. Degenerative joint disease in women at Freedman's and Cedar Grove. Key: 1. Freedman's Early Period (1869–1884); 2. Freedman's Middle Period (1885–1899); 3. Freedman's Late Period (1900–1907); 4. Cedar Grove (1900–1915). *Source:* See text.

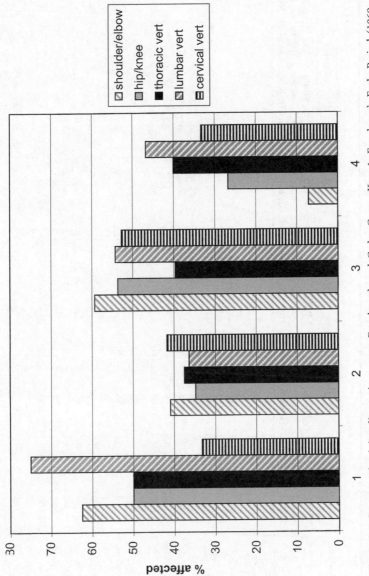

Figure 9.2. Degenerative joint disease in men at Freedman's and Cedar Grove. Key: 1. Freedman's Early Period (1869–1884); 2. Freedman's Middle Period (1885–1899); 3. Freedman's Late Period (1900–1907); 4. Cedar Grove (1900–1915).
Source: See text.

Table 9.14: Occupational Distribution (in Percent) by Major Race/Ethnic Groups and Sex, 1880 and 1910 (Age 15 and Over)

| | Arkansas | | | | Texas | | | | Dallas County | | | |
| | Rural | | Urban | | Rural | | Urban | | Rural | | Urban | |
Occupation	White non-Hispanic	African-American	White non-Hispanic	African-American	White non-Hispanic	African-American	White non-Hispanic	African-American	White non-Hispanic	African-American	White non-Hispanic	African-American
1880												
Male												
High white collar	4.9	0.7	26.5	11.5	5.0	1.2	21.1	3.2				
Farmers	55.1	38.3	8.8	11.5	51.7	44.9	5.2	1.1				
Lower white collar	1.9	0.0	11.8	0.0	1.8	0.2	15.7	1.1				
Skilled manual	4.8	2.0	29.4	23.1	6.4	3.7	27.7	20.2				
Unskilled manual	25.5	42.0	14.7	53.9	26.8	43.3	19.0	70.2				
Other occupations	7.9	6.9	8.8	0.0	8.4	6.8	11.3	4.3				
N^a	161,700	54,800	6,800	2,600	337,600	94,500	42,600	9,400				
Female												
High white collar	0.4	0.0	0.0	0.0	0.4	0.2	1.4	1.7				
Farmers	1.7	2.5	0.0	0.0	1.4	2.7	0.0	0.0				
Lower white collar	0.0	0.0	0.0	0.0	0.0	0.0	0.3	0.0				
Skilled manual	0.3	0.2	10.2	5.6	0.3	0.6	5.4	0.0				
Unskilled manual	2.8	33.7	2.0	38.9	2.9	30.0	7.7	53.3				
Other occupations	94.8	63.7	87.9	55.6	95.0	66.4	85.1	45.0				
N^a	141,600	52,000	4,900	3,600	267,500	94,900	34,900	12,000				

1910

Male

High white collar	5.9	0.9	24.5	3.6	6.3	0.9	19.3	2.9	8.7	5.6	16.0	0.0
Farmers	45.4	48.6	0.8	1.2	44.1	45.3	1.8	0.8	39.1	22.2	0.0	0.0
Lower white collar	2.5	0.0	22.5	2.4	4.2	0.0	19.8	0.8	4.3	0.0	25.6	0.0
Skilled manual	8.6	4.3	30.4	19.1	7.3	2.7	29.0	13.3	13.1	16.7	36.0	15.4
Unskilled manual	30.7	41.4	11.9	69.0	28.9	45.9	17.0	75.2	32.6	55.6	14.4	76.9
Other occupations	6.9	4.8	9.9	4.8	9.1	5.3	13.1	7.1	2.2	0.0	8.0	7.7
N^a	287,165	116,11	63,733	21,156	700,840	150,461	242,472	65,816	11,587	4,535	31,486	6,500

Female

High white collar	1.9	0.5	3.5	0.0	1.8	0.2	3.4	1.0	0.0	0.0	2.8	0.0
Farmers	2.5	5.5	0.0	0.0	1.6	3.6	0.0	0.0	0.0	0.0	0.0	0.0
Lower white collar	0.5	0.2	5.2	5.3	0.9	0.0	5.1	0.0	7.1	0.0	11.1	0.0
Skilled manual	1.0	0.5	3.0	6.3	1.1	0.1	5.1	4.6	2.4	0.0	13.0	5.1
Unskilled manual	11.8	5.5	7.8	49.5	9.8	56.8	1.7	59.6	0.0	42.9	5.6	71.8
Other occupations	82.3	37.9	30.5	39.0	84.8	39.4	81.6	34.8	90.5	57.1	67.6	23.1
N^a	251,646	106,293	58,187	23,925	614,197	148,397	213,636	78,473	10,581	1,763	27,203	9,826

[a] Sample size.

Source: Calculated from data in Ruggles and Sobek (1997).

259

Table 9.15: Selected Black Occupation Categories in Dallas, Texas

Major occupations	1875 City Directory		1890 City Directory		1909 City Directory	
	#	%	#	%	#	%
Men	$n = 91$	100.0	$n = 2049$	100.0	$n = 5892$	100.0
Porter	8	8.8	235	12.1	831	15.4
Teamster	2	2.2	45	2.3	237	4.4
Other drivers (expressmen, etc.)	0	0.0	73	3.8	252	4.7
Combined total heavy lifting jobs	10	11.0	353	18.2	1320	24.5
General laborers	54	59.3	831	42.8	2194	40.7
Women	$n = 17$	100.0	$n = 532$	100.0	$n = 2724$	100.0
Cook	3	17.6	19	3.6	829	30.4
Domestic	1	5.9	456	58.7	710	26.1
Laundress	12	70.6	21	3.9	1016	37.3
Combined total jobs	16	94.1	496	93.2	2555	93.7

For males, the categories involve heavy work, and for women, the most common occupations.
Source: Dallas City Directories, various years.

sampling bias, every African-American enumerated was entered into a database: 1875 ($n = 138$), 1890 ($n = 3,189$), 1909 ($n = 9,394$). Table 9.15 lists the major occupations for both men and women for the three Dallas City Directories examined.

For women, three occupations account for over 90% of listings within each directory: cook, domestic, and laundress. All three were typical of African-American Texas women for the period (Winegarten 1995:47–50).[9] With the caveat that the 1875 directory listings for women are highly inflated and hence not representative, Table 9.15 displays a trend in which the occupation of laundress grows to become, by

---

[9] Despite the fact that it is one of the few available sources regarding occupations in 1870s Dallas, there is a critical flaw inherent within the 1875 City Directory (or for that matter, any other document of the period): its probable lack of representation. From the time of emancipation into the early 1870s, most of the area's African-American population did not reside within the boundaries of Dallas proper, but instead within a number of Freedman's Towns ringing the city (e.g., Frogtown, Deep Ellum, etc). This settlement pattern was likely one formed for mutual protection, in part to circumvent the harsh vagrancy laws established by the Dallas City Council immediately following emancipation, that explicitly targeted freedmen (and women) by name (Dallas *Weekly Herald,* November 25, 1865). The total number of African-Americans listed in the 1875 city directory was 138, and only 17 of these are known to be women. By comparison, in 1873 Freedman's Town alone, the African-American settlement located just one and one-half miles north of Dallas and in which Freedman's Cemetery was located, held in excess of 500 individuals (Dallas *Daily Herald,* April 27, 1873). Hence, the number of commercial laundresses working within the Dallas city limits, although a majority of women listed in the directory, is actually only a small minority of the total number of African-American women within the Dallas area, and it is from this larger, more inclusive population that Freedman's Cemetery derived its demographic makeup. This problem of nonrepresentation is likely to be much less a factor for the 1890 or 1909 directories, as the North Dallas Freedman's Town had, by 1887, found itself squarely within the municipal boundaries of Dallas proper (Davidson 1999:34–35).

1909, one employing nearly 40% of all working African-American women in Dallas. This conclusion essentially corresponds with other studies. Using a 10% sample of the 1900 U.S. Census, Scott (1979) found that 42.6% of Dallas women had occupations listed as laundress. The increasing number of commercial laundresses within Dallas's African-American community would seem to correlate well with the continually increasing degenerative joint disease affecting the shoulder and elbow within the Freedman's population.

For Freedman's males, the only category of DJD that shows a continual increase from the Early to Late Periods is in the cervical vertebrae. This could correspond with the increase in the numbers of men specifically involved in the driving, loading, and unloading of wagons, such as teamsters, as well as similar jobs, most notably porters. Teamsters and porters account for 11% of all listed occupations during the Early Period. This rate nearly doubled by 1890 (18.2%), and by 1909 became the occupation of one-quarter of all African-American men in Dallas (24.5%).

The overall temporal trend in Freedman's DJD rates, as viewed by gender (Figures 9.1 and 9.2), is more difficult to interpret, but is so consistent that it cannot be ignored. DJD levels in women are mostly at their lowest levels during the Early Period, increase sharply in the Middle Period, and decline to more moderate levels in the Late Period. It is interesting to note that in men there is a complementary pattern: a relative high during the Early Period, a drop in all categories (save for cervical DJD) during the Middle Period, and then an increase during Freedman's Late Period.

The increase in rates of DJD in women, as seen from the Early to the Middle Period, would suggest an increase in workloads experienced by African-American women during the late 1870s and 1880s. Conversely, there would seem a lessening in the workloads of African-American men for this same time period, due to the more moderate amounts of DJD recorded. As further outlined below, it is possible that the ultimate causes in the broad patterns of DJD exhibited at Freedman's Cemetery can be attributed to a few key social trends experienced during Reconstruction (relative lack of employment for men, employment of women as domestics, large numbers of women as single heads of households), as well as the immediate post–Reconstruction era (lessening of workloads through organized labor).

During the time of Reconstruction and into the late 1870s, a great deal of animosity was focused upon freedmen by the white majority, likely to the point of excluding many from obtaining or keeping jobs within Dallas (Smallwood 1981). This supposition seems borne out by the 1870 federal census manuscript for Dallas. Under the heading of occupation, Smith (1985) found that most African-American men had blank entries. Smith gives three scenarios to explain the lack of stated occupations for African-American males: unemployment, unskilled labor, or carelessness on the part of the enumerator. Given the relative lessening in the rates of DJD seen in African-American males in Freedman's Middle Period, it is possible that workloads decreased, due to the lack of opportunity for steady employment afforded African-American men in Dallas, from Reconstruction into the late 1870s.

The second critical trend occurring during this same time period is that African-American women, as a whole, were an exception to the lack of employment within the African-American community. African-American women were employed quite commonly as domestics, cooks, and nursemaids in the homes of wealthy whites, as well as domestic and commercial laundresses (Smith 1985). A third point that could be offered as partial explanation for the heightened DJD rates in women during the Middle Period is that due to the social instability experienced during Reconstruction and for years beyond (with the separation of families and all-too-common death of husbands), over 30% of African-American women recorded in the 1880 federal census were enumerated as heads of households. Thus, as much as a third of all African-American women in Dallas were single parents, faced with the heavy burden of both raising a family and providing, in the process, clothing, food, and shelter (Engerrand 1978).

Finally, one possible mitigating factor in the lessening of DJD rates for African-American men during the Middle Period is that of moderation of workloads. The 1880s in Dallas mark the beginnings of organized labor in the city. There were early efforts to unionize African-Americans in the 1880s, which bore some fruit (such as the establishment of a legislated eight-hour workday), before failing during the depression of the 1890s (Hill 1996). Temporally, the fall in the rates of DJD experienced by men during the Middle Period goes hand in hand with the years when organized labor held some sway in the politics of the city. The mid-to-late 1890s, then, marking the decline in the benefits of organized labor, greater competition for fewer jobs, the rise of Jim Crow legislation, and a real drop in wages as a result of an economic depression, also marks the increase in workloads and the accompanying higher rates of DJD, as witnessed in the dead of Freedman's Late Period.

To better define the parameters of the rates of degenerative joint disease in the Freedman's Cemetery population, two additional factors were examined: the severity of DJD and the mean age-at-death of affected individuals (Tables 9.16 and 9.17). The temporal pattern of DJD, as discussed thus far, has focused solely upon the presence or absence of DJD in individuals within each time period, and has not taken into account either the age of the individuals at the time of death or the severity of DJD. This is a critical point, because DJD is a progressive condition, and its presence and severity is determined by both the age of an individual and his or her workload. Thus, the trend defined for women at Freedman's (an overall increase of DJD in the Middle Period) could also be accounted for if workloads remained constant and mean age-at-death simply increased. Tables 9.16 and 9.17 display the number of affected individuals, degree of severity of DJD, and the mean age-at-death for each category of joint.

Broadly speaking, the trend exhibited in this more detailed assessment parallels the simple presence or absence of the disease. For example, the trend in Freedman's men of a continual (though mild) increase in the rate of DJD of cervical vertebrae is displayed both in the age-at-death of affected individuals, as well as by its severity (Table 9.16). From the Middle to Late Period, the mean age-at-death decreases from 49.5 to 46.6 years, and two severe cases are reported for the Late Period, where none were present in the previous periods. Another example can be seen in Freedman's women, where in some categories there is a marked increase in the severity of DJD during the Middle Period, from mild to moderate cases (Table 9.17); this is the same period for which the workloads seem to have increased historically for women in Dallas.

Table 9.16: Freedman's Cemetery: Diachronic Trend in Severity of DJD and Mean Age (Adult Males)

DJD	Total observable	Number affected	Mild			Moderate			Severe		
			#	%	Mean age	#	%	Mean age	#	%	Mean age
Shoulder/elbow											
Early	8	5	2	40.0	49.4	3	60.0	41.7	0	0.0	—
Middle	22	9	6	66.7	45.8	3	33.3	39.4	0	0.0	—
Late	123	73	66	90.4	43.6	7	9.6	45.4	0	0.0	—
Hip/knee											
Early	8	4	3	75.0	43.1	1	25.0	42.5	0	0.0	—
Middle	23	8	6	75.0	44.0	2	25.0	49.2	0	0.0	—
Late	121	70	58	82.9	42.8	12	17.1	42.6	0	0.0	—
Cervical vertebrae											
Early	6	2	0	0.0	0.0	2	100.0	49.4	0	0.0	—
Middle	12	5	3	60.0	38.4	2	40.0	49.5	0	0.0	—
Late	74	39	23	59.0	43.0	14	35.9	46.0	2	5.1	51.2
Thoracic vertebrae											
Early	4	2	1	50.0	39.8	1	50.0	44.1	0	0.0	—
Middle	8	3	3	100.0	41.5	0	0.0	—	0	0.0	—
Late	53	21	14	66.7	42.3	7	33.3	46.6	0	0.0	—
Lumber vertebrae											
Early	4	3	1	33.3	39.8	2	66.7	49.4	0	0.0	—
Middle	11	4	3	75.0	40.6	1	25.0	42.4	0	0.0	—
Late	59	32	14	43.8	44.6	18	56.2	45.0	0	0.0	—

Source: See text.

Table 9.17: Freedman's Cemetery: Diachronic Trend in Severity of DJD and Mean Age (Adult Females)

DJD	Total observable	Number affected	Mild			Moderate			Severe		
			#	%	Mean age	#	%	Mean age	#	%	Mean age
Shoulder/elbow											
Early	8	1	1	100.0	36.8	0	0.0	—	0	0.0	—
Middle	20	3	3	100.0	39.5	0	0.0	—	0	0.0	—
Late	115	39	37	94.9	37.8	2	5.1	35.9	0	0.0	—
Hip/knee											
Early	10	3	2	66.7	33.5	1	33.3	38.9	0	0.0	—
Middle	18	9	6	66.7	38.3	3	33.3	43.1	0	0.0	—
Late	108	32	26	81.3	38.5	6	18.8	44.3	0	0.0	—
Cervical vertebrae											
Early	4	0	0	0.0	—	0	0.0	—	0	0.0	—
Middle	9	4	2	50.0	33.2	2	50.0	42.5	0	0.0	—
Late	82	24	18	75.0	38.8	6	25.0	41.4	0	0.0	—
Thoracic vertebrae											
Early	1	0	0	0.0	—	0	0.0	—	0	0.0	—
Middle	6	3	3	100.0	39.3	0	0.0	—	0	0.0	—
Late	57	14	13	92.9	35.1	1	7.1	42.9	0	0.0	—
Lumber vertebrae											
Early	0	0	0	0.0	—	0	0.0	—	0	0.0	—
Middle	10	5	3	60.0	41.0	2	40.0	45.8	0	0.0	—
Late	61	24	20	83.3	37.2	4	16.7	43.9	0	0.0	—

Source: See text.

With such comparisons between archival documentation and bioarchaeological data, problems attributing ultimate cause and effect to one phenomenon or another are inherent. One difficulty that cannot be avoided is the variability of employment over a person's life. An article appearing in a turn-of-the-century Dallas newspaper details the scarcity of labor within the city, blaming a portion of the problem on a flight of the urban labor force to adjacent cotton fields, where jobs, at one dollar per 100 pounds of cotton picked, paid more than the $1.50 to $2.00 per-day rate routinely paid to common laborers (Dallas *Times-Herald,* November 11, 1906). Thus, within at least a portion of Dallas's African-American community, the urban work regime was sporadically supplemented with agricultural work. However, overall trends, both within a single individual's lifetime and within a population as a whole, have a smoothing effect. The general trend shown in the skeletal remains of Freedman's Cemetery probably reflects true conditions.

While the occupations of the majority of individuals at both Freedman's and Cedar Grove involved physical labor, it might be argued that the physical stresses borne out by agricultural labor would be greater than urban manual labor, and that this would be reflected in a greater incidence of arthritis in the rural population. The data in Table 9.13 would seem to suggest that this scenario was not the case. On the whole, rates of DJD at Freedman's Cemetery are higher than those observed at Cedar Grove.

Farm work is hard, but it is also seasonal with periods of light activity interrupting periods of heavy activity involving lifting and carrying. In addition, the farmer can moderate the pace of work to fit his abilities by working more slowly, but for longer hours. None of these factors are characteristic of urban labor. The pace of urban work may have been set by the employer or the group of laborers as a whole, rather than by the individual worker. As more skeletal series are analyzed, we predict that this rural/urban contrast will be confirmed. Comparison to the Monroe County Poorhouse, where records show that the majority of the inhabitants were laborers, shows that the males have higher arthritis rates than the females, and the rates of arthritis are high, with 49% of the adults displaying arthritis of the hip and knee. This pattern is very similar to Freedman's, but much less than Cedar Grove (Higgins et al. this volume). It also might be assumed that the African-Americans were working harder than those of European ancestry, but examining the entire project database shows that African-American arthritis rates exceed the European-Americans only for those older than 40 years and then not by much.

Trauma. The frequencies of healed bone fractures by sex and site are shown in Table 9.18. Here a clear urban/rural difference can be seen with a higher proportion of arm fractures in the Cedar Grove females and a higher proportion of leg fractures in the Cedar Grove males. An increased frequency of trauma, especially to the arm, would be expected in the higher-risk rural environment. Accidents were a major problem everywhere on the frontier, because contact with animals and heavy equipment was common (West 1989).

There are differences in the rates of trauma in the Freedman's population, as measured by gender and time period. The decrease in the rates of leg trauma in

Table 9.18: Proportion of Adults with Trauma

| | Freedman's Cemetery | | | | | | | | | Cedar Grove | | |
| | Early | | | Middle | | | Late | | | | | |
	N^a	Number affected	%	N^a	Number affected	%	N^a	Number affected	%	N^a	Number affected	%
Arm trauma												
Males	11	0	0.0	32	0	0.0	171	7	4.1	15	1	6.7
Females	10	0	0.0	26	0	0.0	155	2	1.3	20	3	15.0
Indet. adult	—	—	—	2	0	0.0	17	1	5.9	—	—	—
TOTAL ADULTS	21	0	0.0	60	0	0.0	343	10	2.9	35	4	11.4
Hand trauma												
Males	7	0	0.0	18	1	5.6	89	9	10.1	15	3	20.0
Females	6	0	0.0	16	0	0.0	75	0	0.0	20	0	0.0
Indet. adult	—	—	—	1	0	0.0	5	0	0.0	—	—	—
TOTAL ADULTS	13	0	0.0	35	1	2.9	169	9	5.3	35	3	8.6
Leg trauma												
Males	11	1	9.1	33	1	3.0	191	13	6.8	15	5	33.3
Females	10	0	0.0	28	0	0.0	172	5	2.9	20	0	0.0
Indet. adult	—	—	—	3	0	0.0	26	2	7.7	—	—	—
TOTAL ADULTS	21	1	4.8	64	1	1.6	389	20	5.1	35	5	14.3
Cranial vault												
Males	11	0	0.0	30	1	3.3	190	12	6.3	15	3	20.0
Females	10	0	0.0	29	2	6.9	187	5	2.7	21	0	0.0
Indet. adult	—	—	—	3	0	0.0	22	0	0.0	—	—	—
TOTAL ADULTS	21	0	0.0	62	3	4.8	399	17	4.3	36	3	8.3
Weapon Wounds												
Males	11	0	0.0	38	1	2.6	233	15	6.4	15	1	6.7
Females	10	0	0.0	32	0	0.0	232	2	0.9	20	1	5.0
Indet. adult	2	0	0.0	10	0	0.0	91	1	1.1	—	—	—
TOTAL ADULTS	23	0	0.0	80	1	1.3	566	18	3.2	35	2	5.7

[a] Sample size.
Source: See text.

males from the Early (9.1%) to the Middle Period (3%) may reflect the change from an emphasis on agricultural fieldwork to a more urban workplace. Generally speaking, the most common trend exhibited at Freedman's is an increase in trauma rates from the Early to the Late Period, although this simply may be an artifact of sample size. The critical difference between accidents in rural and urban settings is the greater likelihood that rural people were working alone and there was no one available to help with difficult tasks, prompting them to take chances. Nor was there someone to aid them when they got into trouble. These circumstances could change a minor difficulty into a major accident. Trauma to the heads and hands did not drastically differ between sites or sexes, except for a higher frequency of hand injuries among males at Cedar Grove.

While it might be postulated that African-Americans worked at more dangerous or more arduous tasks than their counterparts from other ethnic groups, the analysis does not validate this assumption. African-American female trauma frequencies are not that different from those of Native Americans and European-Americans. The African-American females have a slightly higher frequency of leg trauma only in the age groups below 35 years, but not for older ages. Trauma to the face and head is more frequent than among the European-Americans, but lower than among the Native Americans. Male arm trauma is slightly higher than for the Native Americans and lower than for the European-Americans. Here also the frequency of hand trauma stands out. The frequency of healed hand fractures is higher than for both Native Americans and European-Americans, especially in the youngest age groups where the rates are four times higher among the 10–25-year-old males. This could be associated with going to work at hazardous trades at much younger ages, and, of course, the lack of machinery among the Native Americans is obvious. In contrast, leg trauma is higher than for Native Americans, but lower than for European-Americans.

For Freedman's and Cedar Grove, the category of weapon wounds consists of individual skeletons recovered with bullets (in virtually all cases believed to be the cause of death). At Freedman's, no gunshot victims were identified for the Early Period and only 1 is dated to the Middle (1.25%); the remaining 18 gunshot victims were all interred during the Late Period (3.2%). Surprisingly, a slightly higher rate of gunshot victims was observed at the rural Cedar Grove, where 2 individuals were recovered with bullets (5.7% of total).

Health Index

The health index developed by Steckel et al. (this volume) provides a mechanism for comparing skeletal data between various samples and permitting an estimate of the quality of life by combining numerous variables, especially debilitating pathological lesions, into a single number. The health indexes are 65.5 for Cedar Grove and 69.5 for Freedman's, which are not appreciably different. Both of these samples rank close to the bottom of the 65 samples in the project. Cedar Grove ranks 56 and Freedman's 44. Most of the samples ranking in the vicinity of these 2 African-American groups are highly stressed Native Americans. Both do rank above the African-American slave samples, however. These comparisons clearly show that the quality of life for African-American slaves was relatively poor.

SUMMARY AND CONCLUSIONS

On the American western frontier, the skeletal remains of Old World immigrants that have been studied are relatively few, and yet they tell a consistent story of life and death in this land of opportunity during the nineteenth and early twentieth centuries. These few extant data document economic development from pioneer conditions to urbanization and its consequences for diet, health, and work during this short time period spanning nearly a century. Life for these people appears to be the same whether we look in western Illinois, East Texas, or even Chicago. Childhood was characterized by high mortality, accidents, anemia, and stress. The adults exhibit the skeletal markers of high workloads, accidents, and poor dental health. The historic records make it clear that life in these remote locations was subject to epidemics of acute infections, such as smallpox and cholera. By the end of the nineteenth century, these epidemics diminished in importance and more chronic diseases such as tuberculosis and syphilis replaced them as a primary health problem.

In Dallas, Texas, Freedman's Cemetery remained open as an active burial ground between 1869 and 1907, a span of some 39 years. Within that interval, Dallas grew from a sleepy agricultural village to a true city nearing 100,000 population. In concert with this increase in urbanism, the social and economic changes experienced by African-Americans were vast. Both variables (urbanism and socioeconomic change) are apparent from the skeletal data.

Figures 9.3 through 9.5 summarize the rates of three basic stress indicators or health proxies (porotic hyperostosis, cribra orbitalia, tibial periosteal), in the three temporal periods defined for Freedman's Cemetery, as well as at Cedar Grove. Overall, subadult stress levels reveal an increase from the Early to Late Periods in the Freedman's population (Figure 9.3). Further, the Late Period stress levels exhibited in Dallas are, on the whole, very similar to those seen in the Cedar Grove subadult population, if not in the exact percentages, then in the ratios between stress markers.

This trend is also found in adult women (Figure 9.4). The three stress markers chosen for inclusion are at their lowest levels in Freedman's Early Period, and they show a continuous rise within the population into the twentieth-century Late Period. These same stress markers are present, in much the same ratios, at rural Cedar Grove. This trend of increasing stress within Freedman's women and subadults is not entirely present in adult men (Figure 9.5). Rather, it is Freedman's Early Period that displays the highest levels of tibial periosteal reactions, with this rate falling to just under 50% in the Late Period. However, the Late Period does show the presence of both porotic hyperostosis and cribra orbitalia (though in relatively low levels) where none had been present previously. The levels of these same stress markers in the rural Cedar Grove population are much higher.

While the simple presence of these stress markers would seem to suggest that the quality of life in Dallas's African-American community worsened with increasing urbanism, there is also unambiguously clear evidence of an increasingly less stressed population in Freedman's Late Period. From the Middle to Late Periods, mean age-at-death increases (from 17.7 to 23.6 years), while the death rate of infants less than 1 year of age decreases (from 33.9% to 23.6%). These archaeologically defined trends are corroborated by the archival record through the U.S. census data (and discussed previously).

Further evidence for a less stressed population can be found in the dental hypoplasia rates; LEH in the deciduous dentition declines from the Middle to Late Periods, suggesting increased health in women of childbearing age, while neither the presence nor the severity of the permanent dentition rates changes from the Middle to Late Periods, suggesting that stress levels experienced by young children (between the ages of birth and 4 years) did not worsen from the 1880s through to the twentieth century.

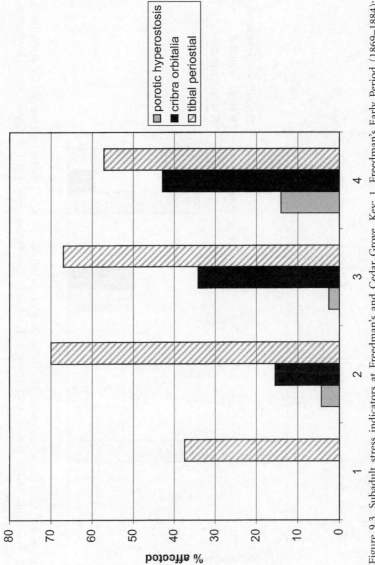

Figure 9.3. Subadult stress indicators at Freedman's and Cedar Grove. Key: 1. Freedman's Early Period (1869–1884); 2. Freedman's Middle Period (1885–1899); 3. Freedman's Late Period (1900–1907); 4. Cedar Grove (1900–1915). *Source:* See text.

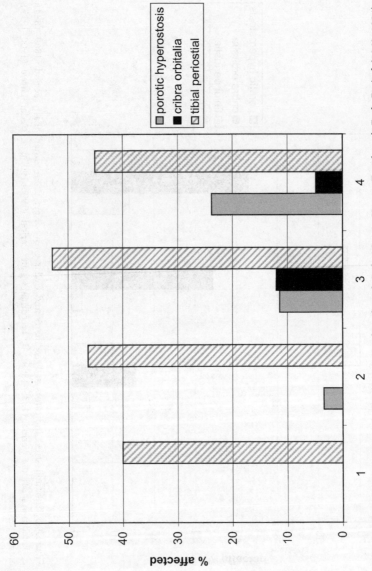

Figure 9.4. Adult female stress indicators at Freedman's and Cedar Grove. Key: 1. Freedman's Early Period (1869–1884); 2. Freedman's Middle Period (1885–1899); 3. Freedman's Late Period (1900–1907); 4. Cedar Grove (1900–1915). *Source:* See text.

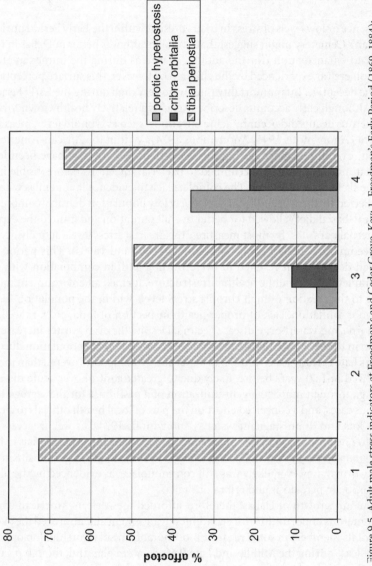

Figure 9.5. Adult male stress indicators at Freedman's and Cedar Grove. Key: 1. Freedman's Early Period (1869–1884); 2. Freedman's Middle Period (1885–1899); 3. Freedman's Late Period (1900–1907); 4. Cedar Grove (1900–1915).
Source: See text.

Turning to evidence from the postcranial skeleton, the rates of tibial periosteal lesions are high in the Middle Period subadults, and there is only a minor decline between the Middle and Late Periods. However, the rate of *severe* cases decreases dramatically between the Middle (25%) and Late Periods (7%). Finally, although there is a greater rate of anemias in Late Period subadults, all of the cases are mild expressions.

The absence or low levels of stress markers present within the Early Period burials at Freedman's Cemetery might suggest that overall health was better in Dallas in the time prior to emancipation (for the adults), as well as during the immediate Reconstruction era (as experienced by the children). However, this surface perception may well be deceptive. Infant mortality rates were very high during the Early Period (34.4%). Although early accounts describe Dallas as a relatively healthy town for its time, numerous deaths did occur by acute infections, such as typhoid fever, measles, and cholera (Anonymous 1941; Anonymous 1974). Within the African-American population, overall resistance during the Reconstruction era may have been low enough that most individuals succumbed to bacterial infections before visible impacts to the skeleton could occur. The complete lack of evidence for anemias within the Early Period further suggests that a relatively low population density (combined with a wheat-based diet) allowed for better overall sanitation and limited the exposure to internal parasites. By most measures, the greatest stress levels actually occur during Freedman's Middle Period (i.e., the late 1880s and 1890s). This period of rapid urban development resulted in overcrowding and, in combination with an almost complete lack of public health infrastructure, formed an environment most conducive to the creation of high chronic stress levels within the population (e.g., through poor sanitation, lack of proper health inspection of food, etc.), as well as acute airborne and waterborne disease vectors. Despite the even greater increase in population in the early twentieth century, the African-American population during Freedman's Late Period (1900–1907) had better survivorship rates overall than those who had lived just 20 years before, likely due to greater control over acute disease vectors (e.g., through more stringent utilization of a pesthouse for the segregation of infectious cases, and a concerted effort on the part of local health officials to clean up vacant lots and drain stagnant water) (Anonymous 1974), as well as access to overall better health care (with the establishment of black health professionals in the 1890s). *Chronic* stress among the African-American community (e.g., parasitism by intestinal worms), however, likely was still commonplace, as evidenced by the high rates of porotic hyperostosis and cribra orbitalia.

The dynamic growth of Dallas, therefore, afforded the African-American community numerous opportunities for economic advancement and improved the overall health of its members in some regards, most notably in survivorship. Job opportunities, at least during the Middle and Late Periods, were plentiful, though overall workloads experienced by African-American men seemed to have increased as well. All in all, there was a real price to be paid for "progress."

Comparisons between Freedman's and Cedar Grove do reveal both striking similarities and important differences that permit us to understand the contrasts between the rural and urban environments as they developed in the West. Demographically, the sites are similar, with high birthrates and many children's skeletons. At both sites congenital syphilis appears to play a role in infant mortality. In terms of diet, the urban population appears to have enjoyed some benefits of a consistent food supply, visible in fewer enamel defects and less anemia. Paradoxically, however, the rural population shows higher skeletal growth velocities with a greater attained stature. Whereas we might hypothesize a greater frequency of infectious disease in the denser urban population, both populations show high frequencies of chronic infectious pathology. There are nonetheless differences in specific diseases, with higher occurrences of syphilis and possibly tuberculosis in the denser urban population. In both communities, occupations involving physical labor dominated the economy. Degenerative joint disease was higher among urban males and showed no difference between rural and urban females, suggesting similar roles for the females in both situations. Conversely, and as expected, the frequency of healed fractures was greater in the rural population, consistent with a higher risk of injury associated with farm activities. These comparisons clearly show that while differences existed between urban and rural environments, overall the two populations are remarkably similar in their health status. To what extent they differ from contemporaneous European-American populations remains to be determined, but comparison with the earlier European-American skeletal data suggests that these differences might not have been as great as one may think.

For African-Americans, despite the incredible impediments first of enslavement and later open racism, the American "West" could still be a land of opportunity, much as it had been for European-Americans. Almost immediately after emancipation in 1865, blacks began to move from their former places of enslavement to seek lost family members, to find work, or simply to test the limits of their newfound freedom. Many migrated toward urban centers, such as Dallas. In the Reconstruction era, Dallas was a dirty frontier town with odd delusions of grandeur, where buffalo hunting was still a major source of income for many and where scores of pigs were allowed to roam the muddy streets at will (Holmes and Saxon 1992:58–65). The little town of Dallas was full of racism and open hostility toward freedmen that could, and oftentimes did, act itself out in violence and cruel death, again and again. And yet Dallas, like so many other towns and cities throughout the country, was also full of the possibility of advancement, and of escape from the new form of slavery that was tenancy. It offered free education, jobs that paid a living wage, the chance to buy a home of one's own, and the hope that all of the rhetoric of the late war, of equality and freedom for all people, might somehow still come into being.

Cedar Grove represents the other side of the coin – those who by choice (or perhaps its lack) never left the plantation and fell instead into the agricultural snare of tenancy. The comparisons made here between these two groups of people, one rural, the other urban, reveal that neither situation was ideal – both involved compromise, hard choices that had direct impact on the lives of these men, women, and children, and that all too often made indelible marks on their very bones.

REFERENCES

Anonymous. (1873, reprinted 1980). *Dallas in 1873: An Invitation to Immigrants.* Dallas: Stone-Inge Books.

Anonymous. (1941). *Safeguarding the Public Health in Dallas (1873–1941).* Compiled by Workers of the Dallas Unit, Writers' Program of the Works Projects Administration. Unpublished typewritten manuscript, Dallas Public Library.

Anonymous. (1974). *History of Dallas Health Department: 1870–1899.* Unpublished typewritten manuscript, Dallas Public Library.

Barr, A. (1995). *Black Texans: A History of African Americans in Texas, 1528–1995,* 2d ed. Norman: University of Oklahoma Press.

Beardsley, E. H. (1987). *A History of Neglect: Health Care for Blacks and Mill Workers in the Twentieth-Century South.* Knoxville: The University of Tennessee Press.

Bradley, F. S., and Williamson, M. A. (1918). *Rural Children in Selected Counties of North Carolina, U.S. Department of Labor Children's Bureau Rural Child Welfare Series,* 2. Washington, D.C.: G.P.O.

Buikstra, J. E., Konigsberg, L. W., and Bullington, J. (1986). Fertility and the Development of Agriculture in the Prehistoric Midwest. *American Antiquity* 51:528–546.

Buff, C. (1990). The Excavation of an Oregon Trail Burial. *Wyoming Archaeologist* 33(3): 51–62.

Burnett, B. A. (1988). Bioanthropological Patterns. In *An Archaeological and Bioarchaeological Perspective: The Tucker (41DT104) and Sinclair (41DT105) Cemeteries of Delta County, Texas,* ed. S. A. Lebo, pp. 95–114. Denton, Tex.: Institute of Applied Sciences, University of North Texas.

Coale, Ansley J., and Rives, Norfleet W. (1973). A Statistical Reconstruction of the Black Population of the United States, 1880–1970: Estimates of True Numbers of Age and Sex, Birth Rates, and Total Fertility. *Population Index* 39(1): 3–36.

Coale, Ansley J., and Zelnik, Melvin. (1963). *New Estimates of Fertility and Population in the United States.* Princeton, N. J.: Princeton University Press.

Cochran, J. H. (1928). *Dallas County: A Record of its Pioneers and Progress.* Austin: Service Publishing Co.

Condon, C. G., Becker, J. L., Edgar, H. J. H, Davidson, J. M., Hoffman, J. R, Kalima, P., Kysar, D., Moorhead, S., Owens, V. M., and Condon, K. (1998). *Freedman's Cemetery: Site 41DL316, Dallas, Texas, Assessments of Sex, Age at Death, Stature and Date of Interment for Excavated Burials.* Report No. 9. Archaeology Studies Program, Environmental Affairs Division. Austin, Tex.: Texas Department of Transportation.

Condon, K, Becker, J. L., Hoffman, J. R., and Condon, C. (1994). Dental and Skeletal Indicators of a Congenital Treponematosis. *American Journal of Physical Anthropology, Supplement* 17:73.

Dallas City Directories (on microfilm Dallas Public Library), 1875 through 1909.

Dallas Times Herald (microfilm, on file, Dallas Public Library).

Davidson, J. M. (1999). *Freedman's Cemetery (1869–1907): A Chronological Reconstruction of an Excavated African-American Burial Ground, Dallas, Texas.* M.A. thesis, University of Arkansas, Fayetteville.

Engerrand, S. W. (1978). Black and Mulatto Mobility and Stability in Dallas, Texas, 1880–1910. *Phylon* 39(3):203–209.

Ferguson, B. (1983). *Final Report on the McGee Creek Cemetery Relocations, Atoka County, Oklahoma.* Report on file. Ferris, Okla.: Bureau of Reclamation, Department of the Interior.

Finnegan, M. (1976). Walnut Creek Massacre: Identification and Analysis. *American Journal of Physical Anthropology* 45:737–742.

——— (1980). Osteological Examination and Possible Historical Record from Site 14BT478, Near Fort Zarah, Barton County, Kansas. *Journal of the Kansas Anthropological Association* 1(2):42–63.

——— (1984). Forensic Analysis of Osseus Material Excavated at the James Site, Clay County, Missouri. In *Human Identification*, eds. Ted A. Rathbun and Jane E. Buikstra, pp. 380–390. Springfield Ill.: Charles C. Thomas.

Fliess, K. H. (1992). Mortality Transition among the Wends of Serbin, Texas, 1854–1884: Investigation of Changes in the Pattern of Death Using Parochial Records. *Social Biology* 38:266–276.

Fox, A. A. (1984). *A Study of Five Historic Cemeteries at Choke Canyon Reservoir, Live Oak and McMullen Counties, Texas.* San Antonio, Tex.: Center for Archaeological Research, University of Texas at San Antonio.

Frazier, E. F. (1957). *The Negro in the United States,* rev. ed. New York: The Macmillan Company.

Gibbs, T., Cargill, K., Lieberman, L. S., and Reitz, E. (1980). Nutrition in a Slave Population: An Anthropological Examination. *Medical Anthropology* (4):175–262.

Gill, G. W. (1994). Skeletal Injuries of Pioneers. In *Skeletal Biology in the Great Plains: Migration, Warfare, Health, and Subsistence,* ed. Douglas W. Owsley and Richard L. Jantz, pp. 159–172. Washington D.C.: Smithsonian Institution Press.

Gill, G. W., Fisher, J. W., Jr., and Zeimens, G. M. (1984). A Pioneer Burial near the Historic Bordeaux Trading Post. *Plains Anthropologist* 29(105):229–238.

Gill, G. W., and Smith, C. S. (1989). The Divide Burial from near Wamsutter, Sweetwater County, Wyoming. *Wyoming Archaeologist* 32(3):61–80.

Glover, J. W. (1976). *United States Life Tables, 1890, 1901, 1910, and 1901–1910.* New York: Arno Press (reprint of United States Department of Commerce Publication, 1921).

Gratton, Brian, and Gutmann, Myron P. (2000). Hispanics in the United States, 1850–1990: Estimates of Population Size and National Origin. *Historical Methods.* 33:137–153.

Grauer, A. L., and McNamara, E. M. (1995). A Piece of Chicago's Past: Exploring Childhood Mortality in the Dunning Poorhouse Cemetery. In *Bodies of Evidence,* ed. Anne L. Grauer, pp. 91–103. New York: John Wiley and Sons Inc.

Gutmann, M. P., and Fliess, K. H. (1996). The Social Context of Child Mortality in the American Southwest. *Journal of Interdisciplinary History* 26:589–618.

Gutmann, M., Haines, M. R., Frisbie, W. P., and Blanchard, K. S. (2000). Intra-Ethnic Differences in Hispanic Child Mortality. *Demography* 37:467–475.

Haines, Michael R. (1998). Estimated Life Tables for the United States, 1850–1900. *Historical Methods* 31(4):149–169.

Haines, M. R., and Preston, S. H. (1997). The Use of the Census to Estimate Childhood Mortality: Comparisons from the 1900 and 1910 United States Census Public Use Samples. *Historical Methods* 30:77–96.

Higman, B. W. (1979). Growth in Afro-Caribbean Slave Populations. *American Journal of Physical Anthropology* 50:373–386.

Hill, P. E. (1996). *Dallas: The Making of a Modern City.* Austin: University of Texas Press

Holmes, M., and Saxon, G. D., ed. (1992). *The WPA Dallas Guide and History.* Denton, Tex.: Dallas Public Library and University of North Texas Press.

Jacobi, K. P., Cook, D. C., Corruccini, R. S., and Handler, J. S. (1992). Congenital Syphilis in the Past: Slaves at Newton Plantation, Barbados, West Indies. *American Journal of Physical Anthropology* 89:145–158.

Jones, J. (1985). *Labor of Love, Labor of Sorrow: Black Women, Work, and the Family from Slavery to the Present*. New York: Basic Books.

Kimball, J. F. (1927). *Our City – Dallas, A Community Civics*. Dallas: Kessler Plan Association of Dallas.

Krupp, M. A., and Chatton, M. J. (1976). *Current Medical Diagnosis and Treatment*. Los Altos, Calif.: Lange Medical Publications.

Larsen, C. S. (1997). *Bioarchaeology: Interpreting Behavior from the Human Skeleton*. New York and Cambridge: Cambridge University Press.

Larsen, C. S., Craig, J., Sering, L. E., Schoeninger, M. J., Russell, K. F., Hutchinson, D. L., and Williamson, M.A. (1995). Cross Homestead: Life and Death on the Midwestern Frontier. In *Bodies of Evidence*, ed. Anne L. Grauer, pp. 139–159. New York: John Wiley & Sons Inc.

Lebo, S. A. (1988). *An Archaeological and Bioarchaeological Perspective: The Tucker (41DT104) and Sinclair (41DT105) Cemeteries of Delta County, Texas*. Denton, Tex.: Institute of Applied Sciences, University of North Texas.

Levenstein, H. A. (1993). *Paradox of Plenty: A Social History of Eating in Modern America*. New York and Oxford: Oxford University Press.

Marks, M. K. (1993). *Dental Enamel Microdefects as Indicators of Childhood Morbidity Among Historic African Americans*. Ph.D. diss., University of Tennessee, Knoxville.

McKnight, M., ed. (1990). *African American Families and Settlements of Dallas: On the Inside Looking Out*. Dallas: Black Dallas Remembered, Incorporated.

Ortner, D. J., and Putschar, W. G. J. (1985). *Identification of Pathological Conditions in Human Skeletal Remains*. Washington, D.C.: Smithsonian Institution Press.

Owsley, D. W., and Jantz, R. L., ed. (1994). *Skeletal Biology in the Great Plains: Migration, Warfare, Health, and Subsistence*. Washington, D.C.: Smithsonian Institution Press.

Owsley, D. W., and Rose, J. C., ed. (1997). *Bioarcheology of the North Central United States*. A Volume in the Central and Northern Plains Archeological Overview, Research Series No. 49. Fayetteville, Ark.: Arkansas Archeological Survey.

Preston, S. H., Ewbank, D., and Hereward, M. (1994). Child Mortality Differences by Ethnicity and Race in the United States: 1900–1910. In *After Ellis Island: Newcomers and Natives in the 1910 Census*, ed. S. C. Watkins, pp. 35–82. New York: Russell Sage Foundation.

Preston, S. H., and Haines, M. R. (1991). *Fatal Years: Child Mortality in Late Nineteenth-Century America*. Princeton, N.J.: Princeton University Press.

Rose, J. C. (1985). *Gone to a Better Land. A Biohistory of a Rural Black Cemetery in the Post-Reconstruction South*. Research Series No. 25. Fayetteville: Arkansas Archeological Survey.

Rose, J. C., and Hartnady, P. (1991). Interpretation of Infectious Skeletal Lesions from a Historic Afro-American Cemetery. In *Human Paleopathology: Current Synthesis and Future Options*, eds. D. J. Ortner and A. C. Aufderheide, pp. 119–127. Washington, D.C.: Smithsonian Institution Press.

Ruggles, Steven, and Sobek, Matthew. (1997). *Integrated Public Use Microdata Series, Version 2.0*. Minneapolis, Minn.: Minnesota Historical Census Projects.

Sattenspiel, L., and Harpending, H. (1983). Stable Population and Skeletal Age. *American Antiquity* 48:489–498.

Scott, J. D. (1979). *Married Women at Work: Dallas, Texas 1880–1900*. M.A. thesis, The University of Texas at San Antonio.

Shryock, Henry S., and Siegel, Jacob S., and Associates. (1971). *The Methods and Materials of Demography*. Washington, D.C.: G.P.O.

Smallwood, J. M. (1981). *Time of Hope, Time of Despair: Black Texans during Reconstruction.* Port Washington, N.Y.: Kennikat Press.

Smith, T. H. (1985). Blacks in Dallas: From Slavery to Freedom. *(Dallas County) Heritage News* 10(1):18–22.

Summerville, J. (1983). *Educating Black Doctors: A History of Meharry Medical College.* University: University of Alabama Press.

Taylor, A. J., Fox, A. A., and Cox, I. W. (1986). *Archaeological Investigations at Morgan Chapel Cemetery (41BP200), A Historic Cemetery in Bastrop County, Texas.* Archaeological Survey Report No. 146. San Antonio: Center for Archaeological Research, University of Texas at San Antonio.

Thompson, W. S., and Whelpton. P. K. (1933) *Population Trends in the United States.* New York: McGraw-Hill.

Tigner-Wise, L. F. (1989). *Skeletal Analysis of a Mormon Pioneer Population from Salt Lake Valley, Utah.* M.A. thesis, Anthropology, University of Wyoming, Laramie.

Tolnay, Stawart E. (1996). Structural Change and Fertility Change in the South, 1910 and 1940. *Social Science Quarterly.* 77:559–576.

U.S. Bureau of the Census (1864). *United States Census of Population: 1860,* Vol. 1: *Population.* Washington, D.C.: G.P.O.

    (1872). *United States Census of Population: 1870,* Vol. 2: *The Vital Statistics of the United States.* Washington, D.C.: G.P.O.

    (1833). *United States Census of Population: 1880,* Vol. 1: *Population.* Washington, D.C.: G.P.O.

    (1897). *United States Census of Population: 1890,* Vol. 1, Part II: *Population.* Washington, D.C.: G.P.O.

    (1902). *United States Census of Population: 1900,* Vol. 1, Part II: *Population.* Washington, D.C.: G.P.O.

    (1913). *United States Census of Population: 1910,* Vols. 2 & 3: *Population by States.* Washington, D.C.: G.P.O.

    (1923). *United States Census of Population: 1920,* Vol. 2: *Population: General Report and Analytical Tables.* Washington, D.C.: G.P.O.

    (1975). *Historical Statistics of the United States.* Washington D.C.: GPO.

    (1985, 1997). *Statistical Abstract of the United States.* Washington, D.C.: GPO.

U.S. Department of Commerce. Bureau of the Census (1918). *Negro Population in the United States, 1790–1915.* Washington D.C.: U.S. Department of Commerce.

West, E. (1989). *Growing Up with Country: Childhood on the Far Western Frontier.* Albuquerque: University of New Mexico Press.

Winchell, F., Rose, J. C., and Moir, R. W. (1995). Health and Hard Times: A Case Study from the Middle to Late Nineteenth Century in Eastern Texas. In *Bodies of Evidence,* ed. Anne L. Grauer, pp. 161–172. New York: John Wiley & Sons Inc.

Winegarten, R. (1995). *Black Texas Women: 150 Years of Trial and Triumph.* Austin: University of Texas Press.

PART IV

NATIVE AMERICANS IN CENTRAL AMERICA

Introduction

All sites of the project in Central America were inhabited, and disappeared from our statistical view, before Columbus arrived in the Americas. It is known, however, that several of these sites were part of a larger hierarchical society that was in considerable distress. The chapters in this section consider environmental factors that may have been responsible for the high incidence of skeletal lesions. As a group they scored 64.0 on the health index, compared with the average of 72.6 across all sites (see Table IV.1). Moreover, no single site in the region exceeded the average, and the group with the best health, Tlatilco, fell more than 4 points below the mean. As a group, the Central Americans scored poorly on the childhood indicators, especially hypoplasias, and were laden with infections. No group even approached the average (75.1) in the latter category, and most fell very near the bottom. The only category in which the Central Americans did well was trauma, where they scored more than 6 points above average, and only one group (Cuicuilco) fell below average.

As a group, these Central Americans were less diverse in their health than the historic populations. With the exception of hypoplasias, the standard deviations for components of the health index were lower (often much lower) than the standard deviations for all sites. Only two sites, Xcaret and urban Copán, scored above average on stature. Some diversity prevailed in hypoplasias, however, where Tlatilco and Cuicuilo scored above average, whereas most groups scored well below average.

Table IV.1: Health Index and Component Scores of Central American Populations

Investigator	Age BP	Description	Index	Stature	Hyp.	Anemia	Dental	Inf.	DJD	Trauma
Marquez	3100	Tlatilco, Mexico	68.4	13.2	75.1	86.6	76.5	54.2	80.1	93.0
Marquez	0990	Xcaret, Mexico	67.7	28.4	67.3	70.3	81.8	50.5	79.1	96.8
Marquez	1850	Cuicuilo, Mexico	66.1	7.9	80.5	90.5	84.1	45.2	69.3	85.1
Marquez	0790	Cholula, Mexico	66.0	7.6	70.7	76.1	80.2	55.5	79.9	92.1
Marquez	1350	Jaina, Mexico	64.5	3.1	54.4	75.7	89.6	58.2	74.2	96.1
Storey	1625	Tlatinga, Mayan	61.7	12.5	20.3	89.2	88.5	59.7	72.5	89.1
Storey	1125	Copán, rural, Mayan	59.0	6.0	18.7	82.1	85.1	46.9	81.9	92.2
Storey	1125	Copán, Mayan	58.4	28.4	35.6	74.3	67.9	44.1	64.0	94.2
		Average Central America	64.0	13.4	52.8	80.6	81.7	51.8	75.1	92.3
		Std. dev., Central America	3.8	9.8	24.8	7.6	7.0	6.0	6.3	3.8
		Average, 65 sites	72.6	20.7	71.1	90.5	81.8	75.1	78.9	85.7
		Std. dev, 65 sites	8.0	16.9	24.6	11.5	10.4	17.0	12.3	16.1
		Minimum, 65 sites	53.5	0.4	9.8	53.2	55.3	44.1	41.6	10.8
		Maximum, 65 sites	91.8	67.8	99.7	100.0	100.0	98.7	100.0	100.0

Source: Consolidated database.

CHAPTER TEN

Social Disruption and the Maya Civilization of Mesoamerica

A Study of Health and Economy of the Last Thousand Years

Rebecca Storey, Lourdes Marquez Morfin, and Vernon Smith

ABSTRACT

The civilization of the Maya of Mesoamerica has experienced two major disruptions within the last thousand years. The effects of these disruptions were studied on skeletal samples and the patterns of morbidity and mortality reflected these times of trouble, although the time of the Classic collapse was the most stressful. The Maya have endured to the present day and are still facing many health problems in adjusting to the modern world. Comparison of some measures on living individuals that are equivalent to those on skeletal samples indicates that the Maya still suffer from quality-of-life problems. A perspective on Maya history using health indicators reveals that in spite of quite significant burdens of morbidity and probable high mortality at many points in their history, the Maya were able to build, intensify, and maintain a distinctive civilization.

The Maya are a well-known and distinct group of Native Americans that are presently concentrated in parts of Mexico, Guatemala, and Belize. Although they are one of the largest such indigenous groups surviving since the European discovery and settlement of the New World, they are probably best known because of one of the most famous collapses of a civilization revealed by archaeology. The present-day extent of the Maya is less than it was during the Late Classic Period (circa AD 700–1000), when there was a dense population in the lowlands of Mexico, Guatemala, Belize, El Salvador, and Honduras. This was definitely one of the most spectacular manifestations, in terms of architecture and art and complexity of society, of the pre-Columbian civilizations of Mesoamerica, and it has left some of the most famous ruins, places like Uxmal, Tikal, Palenque, and Copán. At the end of the Classic, most of the southern lowland area was abandoned by the Maya, not to be resettled again by people until recent times, but Maya civilization

We would like to thank the Instituto Nacional de Antropología e Historía, Mexico, for allowing access to the collections. The Copán study is done with the permission of the Instituto Hondureño de Antropología e Historía and with the financial support of the Instituto Hondureño, a Fulbright award, and the University of Houston. Many people are always involved in the study of skeletal collections; without their help this study could not have been done.

reformed itself in the Yucatan Peninsula and the highlands of Chiapas, Mexico, and Guatemala, where it continues to our day. The proper way to think about the Maya civilization is not that it disappeared suddenly, leaving mysterious and romantic ruins in the jungle at the end of the Classic Period, but that it has around 3,000 years of history. Maya civilization has survived two periods of severe disruption and is facing perhaps its greatest challenge now at the end of the twentieth century. The focus of this work is on the major disruptions of Maya civilization, comparing them for the effects that such events have on the humans going through them.

The pre-Columbian Maya have long been noted among Western scholars for their monumental architecture, sculpture and painting, sophisticated glyph writing and calendrical systems, and astronomical knowledge. These characteristics came to prominence during the Classic Period (AD 300–1000), when the Maya were divided into a number of competing polities of varying size. The recent decoding of the glyph writing has allowed insight into the politics of dynasties and warfare, such that the Maya can be said to have a history during this time, perhaps uniquely among the civilizations of the New World before the arrival of Europeans in the fifteenth century.[1]

Although the Maya have suffered a number of localized disruptions throughout their history, the first major disruption occurs at the end of the Classic Period. At this time, the most densely populated area of the Maya civilization, the southern lowlands of Mexico, Guatemala, Honduras, El Salvador, and Belize, was virtually abandoned by its people. The large centers that had been prominent during this period – Calakmul, Tikal, Copán, Palenque, and many others – were left to the rain forest and never reoccupied. This is the famous Classic Maya Collapse, which obviously involved the loss and movement of large numbers of people. This is the first disruption that will be investigated here.

After this collapse, the Postclassic Period lasts until the Spanish Conquest in the early sixteenth century. While the Maya thrived in large sites in the Guatemalan highlands and the northern Yucatan Peninsula, the civilization had changed. Gone were the prominent, charismatic, dynastic rulers of the Classic Period, to be replaced by more stratified polities where a larger number of political offices, and not dynasties, were important. The Maya were also more prominent in the larger Mesoamerican interaction sphere and in long-distance trade. Thus, the Maya civilization present when the Spaniards arrived was more complex economically and politically than during the Classic Period. It also was one that was not easily conquered and had several rebellions.[2] After Spanish domination, the Maya, like most Native Americans, were affected by the introduction of Old World diseases and the dislocations caused by the introduction of a new cultural and political system. This is the second disruption that will be investigated.

---

[1] For an interesting account of reading Maya glyphs, see Coe 1992. Books about Classic Maya civilization and its history include Schele and Friedl 1990 and Culbert 1991.

[2] For discussions of the Postclassic, see Sabloff and Andrews V 1985, and Chase and Rice 1986. There is a large literature on the ethnohistory of the Maya at Spanish contact, for example, Farriss 1984 and Jones 1988.

Unlike many other Native Americans, the Maya did not disappear as a people nor as a vibrant cultural tradition. The present-day Maya are noted for their beautiful folk art and their cultural cohesion in the face of 400 years of European domination. While the noble class that had been present since the Late Preclassic disappeared eventually after Spanish domination, the Maya remain today a recognizable and dynamic Native American group, especially in Guatemala and Mexico. Because of their marginal position and poverty in the nation-states of which they are a part, the present-day Maya are often used as an example of a biologically stressed and poorly nourished population by present-day health researchers.[3] While this is a situation which has been with the Maya for the last four centuries since conquest, it is one that the Maya themselves no longer wish to tolerate and that internationally is also something of a scandal, as the recent "uprising" in Chiapas and the battles between the Guatemalan government and Maya groups have so clearly demonstrated. Thus, modernization and greater participation in the modern world are changing the Maya civilization yet again, and this is the third and ongoing disruption.

These social disruptions involved cultural and population dislocations, new forms of government, rearrangement of settlements, economic changes, and adjustments to foreign cultures and peoples that also put strains on the health and well-being of the individuals undergoing such changes. Since the earlier two disruptions resulted in significant population losses, it is likely that they were also times of biological stress. However, our information about the past disruptions has to be based on different evidence than that available for the contemporary situation. While it is not possible to understand a contemporary situation more completely than a past one, modern peoples can be interviewed, observed, and medically evaluated. This allows nutrition, incidence and severity of illness or morbidity, developmental problems, causes of death, and life expectancies to be weighed in determining the biological stress suffered by modern Maya. For the past, traditional sources of evidence from archaeology and history have been used to understand past disruptions and postulate biological stress. These have clearly indicated the social disruptions and have provided some good evidence of the impacts upon the health, longevity, and population size of past Maya. According to these traditional sources, the Maya have survived two population crashes that involved high mortality, with accompanying problems of disease and malnutrition clearly indicated in historical sources and postulated in archaeological studies. Although precipitated by specific historical causes, these earlier disruptions had to have dramatic effects upon the health of individuals and were costly in terms of human lives.

The human skeletons recovered archaeologically have until recently been only sporadically, and often insufficiently, employed as evidence about the Maya past, although there has been a recent dramatic increase in the research involving Maya skeletons.[4] As has already been well detailed in this volume, skeletons have advantages and disadvantages as records of the past lifestyles, morbidity, and health of

[3] There has been extensive research on the Maya during the twentieth century available from both ethnographic and public health standpoints, and there is also an extensive literature to match. See Fash 1994 and Bogin and Loucky 1997 for examples.

[4] See Whittington and Reed (1997) for a discussion of the history of skeletal studies of the ancient Maya.

individuals, but they remain the best single source of information on what it was like to live in that past society. The Maya did have a dense population from the Classic Period onward, which would mean that skeletons should be available, but the humid tropical environment does make it difficult to recover good skeletal samples, as bone preservation is not of the best in such an environment. Nevertheless, skeletal samples are available and should be analyzed for the information they can provide about the chronic stresses that the Maya suffered. The advantage here is that it is possible – because of similar methodologies used to create the skeletal database that will be used here, plus published information on other skeletal samples – to look at the incidence of paleopathological indicators during times of past social disruption among the Maya in order to make comparisons. The skeletons can then be added to archaeological, historical, and medical evidence that is already available to improve knowledge of what happened in the past. For the Maya, we are fortunate that there is information on living and recent individuals that is comparable to information available from the skeletons, such as stature studies and incidence of enamel hypoplasias and anemia, to improve overall interpretations of the findings from archaeological contexts.

THE CLASSIC MAYA COLLAPSE

This is the most famous social disruption of Maya civilization, the one the general public thinks of whenever the Maya are mentioned. While this collapse has long been the focus of archaeological attention and explanation, recent scholarship has focused on the suitability of an ecological model of the collapse – overexploitation of the environment, coupled with overpopulation, leading to an unraveling of the economic and social organization and a demographic collapse – with evidence of a more varied and slower process of population decline and regional variability as possible precipitating factors.[5] While a large area was seemingly virtually abandoned as a result of the collapse, there was variability in the times of abandonment and the presence of bitter warfare, for example. Thus, to many Mayanists, there does not seem to be one model that will explain collapse at all polities. The ecological model certainly has had many adherents and would also be one that would postulate stress and health problems among skeletons from the Terminal Classic Period at various sites.

There seems to be evidence that much of the ecological model will explain the collapse at one well-investigated site, Copán, Honduras, in terms of the effects of deforestation, loss of agricultural potential, and abandonment of house groups.[6] There has recently been a reawakened interest among archaeologists in long-term climatic changes and how they might affect the humans in a particular area, as these might better explain periods of florescence and decline in societies. A recent study of a lake in the southern Yucatan Peninsula has found evidence of a drier climate

[5] Fash (1994) updates various areas of Maya scholarship and the collapse discussions; other information is found in White 1997.

[6] See Fash (1991) for an earlier formulation of a model and Paine and Freter 1996 for the most recent model.

between about AD 800 and 1000, the driest period of the last several thousand years,[7] which might explain why societies in the southern lowlands would have been under some agricultural and economic stress, which could have led to political and social problems. Such studies indicate that the debates about the causes of the Classic Maya collapse, and the suitability of an underlying ecological cause, will continue to be hotly contested for the near future.

In spite of the obvious relevance that osteological indicators of health and environment might have for understanding the period of the collapse, generally called the Terminal Classic (circa AD 800–1000), there are few populations presently available that focus on that period. The samples included here in the database are those available to the bioarchaeologists and are not by any means a representative sample of Maya skeletal populations. Three are from the Classic Period (AD 300 to 1000), both Copán samples and Jaina, and the fourth, Xcaret, is from the Late Classic into the Postclassic (see Figure 10.1 for location of the sites). The Lowland Maya Classic Period "collapse" is of particular interest as a distinctive historical event in the comparative study of civilizations. It is possible here to do a preliminary test of whether Terminal Classic populations from a center that definitely "collapsed," Copán, were more stressed than those from a site where the skeletal sample dates during its prosperity, Jaina, and from one that survived into the Postclassic Period, Xcaret.[8]

Description of the Classic Period Samples

Two of the samples are from Copán, Honduras, one of the major centers of the Lowland Classic Maya civilization. It is located on the southeastern periphery of the Maya world in a 24km^2 mountain valley nearly 600m above sea level. It is not coastal, as are Jaina and Xcaret, but is definitely tropical in climate with a pronounced wet and dry seasonality. Copán reached a peak population of about 27,000 during the ninth century and then started to decline, with less than a third present by AD 1000. The valley was finally abandoned around AD 1200. While the decline took perhaps two centuries to unfold, it nevertheless remains a dramatic example of a sociopolitical collapse and demographic loss. While some people undoubtedly migrated to more thriving Maya areas, the large population concentrated in the Copán Valley during the Classic Period did not all migrate; much of the population loss was due to mortality in the area. Archaeological excavations at Copán have concentrated on the Late/Terminal Classic Period (circa AD 800–1000), and the skeletal sample is dominated by individuals dated to this period. Thus, the skeletons can provide information about life during the time when the society peaks and declines.

Classic Maya societies were characterized by differences in status that are most simply contrasted as nobles and commoners, although there were rank distinctions

---

[7] Hodell, Curtis, and Brenner 1995.
[8] Information on the site of Copán can be found in Fash 1991 and on the 9N-8 sample from Webster 1989. Information on the Copán rural sample can be found in Webster and Gonlin 1988. For Jaina, see Piña Chan 1968, and for Xcaret, see Andrews and Andrews 1975.

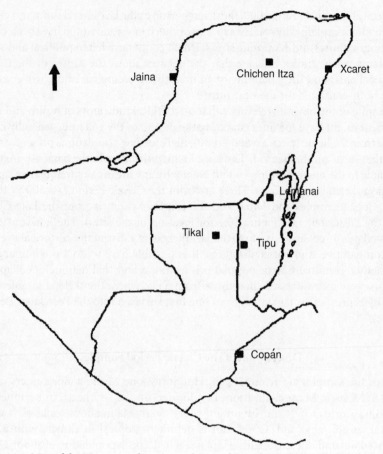

Figure 10.1. Map of the Maya area of Mexico and Central America with sites discussed in text.

within each group. The Copán samples capture what are believed to be the greatest status differences present in the society. The Copán Urban sample is from the 9N-8 compound, the "House of the Bacabs," the largest outside the royal Acropolis, containing 11 adjoining patios with over 50 masonry structures, housing around 200 individuals at one time. The compound is believed to have been occupied by families belonging to a prominent noble lineage. However, from mortuary characteristics, there was quite a range of statuses within the compound, from elaborate tombs with offerings to simple earthen pits with no offerings. Probably not all individuals from 9N-8 had a recognized elite rank. In spite of these differences, all individuals lived in elaborate stone masonry houses and probably shared in the obvious wealth of the lord of the compound, enjoying the best lifestyle that Late Classic Copán society could offer. Preliminary analysis by internal status divisions within 9N-8 revealed that there are not really any significant differences in paleopathological indicators among inhabitants of the compound. Thus, the sample will be treated as an example of privileged individuals within their society.

The Copán Rural sample is much smaller. These are individuals recovered from modest dwellings of perishable materials dispersed in rural areas away from the urban core of the site. These are reconstructed as probable agricultural laborers and part-time craftspeople, the poor commoners of the society. These should be the most different in status to the residents of 9N-8. Diet for all the Copán peoples was based on the Mesoamerican staples of maize, beans, and squash, with a few domesticated animals available for food, such as dog and turkey. The Copán diet was heavily dependent on maize, with relatively little protein, as there would be no wild game available to supplement any dogs or turkeys in a land long devoted so completely to agriculture. The elite may have had more access to a wider variety of other foods and slightly more protein during the course of a year. The other difference between the two samples is that the 9N-8 lived in a quite dense residential ward, with other elite compounds nearby but also with more modest families. The rural population comes from dispersed house groups, which would have had less problem with garbage buildup and fewer daily contacts with many people than did the elite sample.

Jaina is a small artificially constructed island 1km long off the coast of Campeche, Mexico, on the west coast of the Yucatan Peninsula. While there are definitely monumental structures and also some residences on the island, it has always been notable for the density and richness of its burials, including the famous ceramic Jaina figurines. Thus, the skeletal sample probably consists mostly of elite individuals. The dates from Jaina indicate that it is from the Late Classic but earlier than Copán, being at its height around AD 600 and ending before AD 1000. The nature of the construction and settlement on the island is not clear, and so it is unknown how many people lived there and for how long. From the density of burials, it has always been interpreted as a necropolis, an elite burial site, that drew on surrounding populations for several centuries. It was probably a very specialized site, primarily ritual in purpose, with a small residential population tending to the necropolis. The practice of burying people on Jaina seems to have stopped sometime in the Late Classic, but this does not appear to be linked with a collapse of population but probably instead with a change in important centers and new political arrangements. This was an area where there was continuity from the Classic to Postclassic, as the Maya continue on in the region today. After the Classic Period, it was probably used only sporadically as a fishing station. The diet on and around Jaina was maize and marine resources, and so would be considered a rich and balanced one. This sample should represent a thriving population, with those with the best lifestyle represented.

Xcaret is a site found on the eastern coast of the Yucatan Peninsula. It was apparently a fairly predominant port during the Late Postclassic and is one of a number of such sites found up and down that coast. These were undoubtedly tied in with long-distance canoe trading, an important economic activity of the Postclassic Maya, and this port was probably the main embarkation point for the island of Cozumel, an important pilgrimage destination. While settlement is dispersed rather than nucleated, the site would have been a large settlement in the area, although no population estimates are given presently. The skeletal sample is small and from Group B, a distinctive residential group in the core area of the site. While information is only preliminary at best, the skeletons are from the Late Classic to the Postclassic. Thus, Xcaret serves here as a sample from a Maya site with continuity over time from Classic to Postclassic. The skeletons range from those with elaborate offerings to none and will represent lifestyle in a site not threatened with collapse in the Classic but that, in fact, goes on to thrive in the Postclassic. As with Jaina, the diet should have been a good one, combining maize, other domesticated plants, and marine resources.

Results of Comparisons on Classic Period Samples

Further investigation of the pattern of stress in these populations should allow for more interpretation of what was happening during the Classic Period. The interpretation of paleopathological indicators is complicated, because there is no simple relationship between the morbidity they indicate and the mortality of the individual. A skeletal sample is a mortality sample of those dying at various ages that is not necessarily, and in fact is not likely, to be typical of the living population at those various ages. Skeletons should, in fact, be sicker than was generally true of the living population. For example, individuals dying as children should be different from those who lived to adulthood, probably more sickly, more stressed, and/or more frail. They cannot be taken as necessarily representative of what childhood was like for all individuals; although inasmuch as high childhood mortality was a very general premodern condition, the dead children are informative of the risks of that time. Thus, we need to contrast the patterns of those dying as children, as young adults, and as old adults to see if there are any patterns to age that might be the result of the mortality sample effect. In addition, the differences between males and females might also provide insight into the stressfulness of life that was probably typical of each gender role.

We can see by looking at broad demographic categories of these skeletal samples (Table 10.1), that Copán Rural and Xcaret have proportionately too few juveniles, a common problem with skeletal samples, and such small samples will make it difficult to make any interpretations about juveniles in these populations. Both Jaina and Copán Urban have large enough samples of both juveniles and adults to make comparisons. All sites have statistically equal numbers of males and females, except for Xcaret, where the greater number of males is evident. Both Copán samples obviously have more older than younger adults, while Jaina and Xcaret have about equal numbers of young and old adults. There are also no significant differences within each site as to the distribution of younger or older males and females in all but Xcaret. Here, not only is there a sexual imbalance, but females are also younger and males older. However, the Xcaret sample may reflect the characteristics of a living population primarily involved in sea trade, where male labor would be crucial and thus more males would be living in the settlement.

From the archaeological situations interpreted for the different sites, the Copán samples probably come from declining populations, while Jaina and Xcaret are probably at least growing slowly. This is likely because of the collapse of the society at Copán, while the Yucatan skeletons are from prospering populations. In the case of

Table 10.1: Breakdown by Age and Sex of the Maya Samples

	Copán Urban		Copán Rural		Jaina		Xcaret	
Age	N	%	N	%	N	%	N	%
0–14	112	47	10	22	59	58	4	12
Females								
15–40	25	10	2	4	15	15	7	21
41+	50	21	16	36	10	10	2	6
Males								
15–40	21	9	4	9	10	10	7	21
41+	31	13	13	29	8	8	13	39
TOTALS	239		45		102		33	

Note: Jaina had three adult individuals that could not be sexed but could be aged, and Xcaret had two. Jaina had one individual that could be sexed but not aged. These individuals will be left out of all analyses. $\chi^2 = .661$, p > .05 for Copán Urban; $\chi^2 = .085$, p > .05 for Jaina; Fisher's exact test, p = .40 for Copán Rural and p = .04 for Xcaret for tests of distribution of sexes by age.

a growing population, the skeletal sample should be young, to reflect the increasing numbers of young added to the population each year. The Jaina mortality sample would be that expected of a growing population, while a declining population would be older, to reflect the decreasing numbers of young added to the population and their corresponding lesser proportion of the deaths within such a society. The Copán Rural sample especially has the profile expected of a mortality sample from such a demographic situation. Comparisons across sites have no significant differences (according to chi-square) in the number of young and old males, but significant differences in the number of young and old females, as they tend to be young in Jaina and Xcaret and old in Copán Rural.[9] Thus, again Copán Rural probably reflects a population clearly in demographic trouble.

Porotic hyperostosis is a lesion on the cranial vault resulting from anemia during childhood for which 69% of the sample could be scored. Copán Rural has by far the most prevalence, with about 65% of the individuals having the lesions, while Copán Urban and Jaina only have around 25% of the population affected. Table 10.2 has the prevalences for age and sex in the samples. There are few severe examples and 7/10 are juveniles, indicating that this condition was probably more likely to lead to early death. Comparing across the sites by age, the incidence of porotic hyperostosis was not significantly different among the juveniles (in spite of the underrepresentations) or young adults, but was significant among old adults (Kruskal-Wallis,

[9] Issues about the interpretation of demographic profiles of skeletal samples are raised in Wood et al. 1992. All statistical tests discussed here were performed using SPSS, and because cell sizes in the contingency tables are small, all chi-square and Kruskal-Wallis tests were performed using the Exact Tests procedure, which uses a Monte Carlo procedure to estimate the exact probability within 99% confidence intervals. This allows determination of significance when conventional calculation would not, because the cell sizes violate statistical test assumptions. See Mehta and Patel 1996.

Table 10.2: Incidence of Porotic Hyperostosis by Age and Sex

Lesion severity	Juveniles		Young males*		Young females		Old males*		Old females*	
	N	%	N	%	N	%	N	%	N	%
Copán Urban										
None	60	76	12	75	13	68	14	70	29	83
Slight	17	22	4	25	6	32	6	30	6	17
Severe	2	2	0		0		0		0	
Copán Rural										
None	5	63	0		1	50	1	9	6	40
Slight	3	37	2	100	1	50	9	82	8	53
Severe	0		0		0		1	9	1	7
Jaina										
None	28	72	5	83	7	64	2	67	3	100
Slight	7	18	1	17	4	36	1	33	0	
Severe	4	10	0		0		0		0	
Xcaret										
None	1	33	1	25	5	100	5	63	0	
Slight	1	33	2	50	0		2	37	2	100
Severe	1	33	1	25	0		0		0	

*Indicates differences among the sites at the p < .05 level.

p < .004). Copán Rural was too affected, whereas old adults in Jaina and Copán Urban were little affected, in essence. Adding sex to the investigation of the pattern among adults, young females did not differ significantly across the sites, but young males, old males, and females were all significant (Kruskal-Wallis, p < .05). Again, Copán Rural has high incidence, and Jaina and Copán Urban relatively little for these groups. Thus, it appears as if some populations generally are free of this indicator, and it is not an important cause of morbidity among them. On the other hand, it is fairly common in Xcaret and Copán Rural in both young males and old adults, a marker of chronic stress, but certainly not incompatible with survival to old age.

Enamel hypoplasia is an indicator of chronic stress during childhood as well, and in this sample, hypoplasias on the canines could be scored on 54% of the sample. Just comparing incidence, there was more in both Copán samples and relatively less in Jaina and Xcaret. The Copán Urban sample was also distinguished by the highest percentage of individuals with two or more hypoplasias. The pattern by age and sex is given in Table 10.3. Comparing the prevalence and severity by age across the sites, juveniles were not significantly different, but the samples were very small except for Copán Urban. The incidence and severity is significantly different across the sites among young females, young males, old females, and old males (Kruskal-Wallis, p < .05). In these, the proportions of adults of both sexes with two or more hypoplasias is high in Copán Urban, while Xcaret had low proportions with lesions in all young adults and old males, and Jaina had also fairly low proportions in all but old males. In this indicator, there is more evidence of chronic stress and more

Table 10.3: Incidence and Severity of Enamel Hypoplasias on the Permanent Canine

No. of hypoplasias	Juveniles		Young males*		Young females*		Old males*		Old females*	
	N	%	N	%	N	%	N	%	N	%
Copán Urban										
None	6	14	1	6	4	17	2	7	0	
One	25	60	8	47	11	48	13	46	20	49
Two+	11	26	8	47	8	35	13	46	21	51
Copán Rural										
None	1	33	1	25	1	50	2	20	3	23
One	2	67	2	50	1	50	6	60	7	54
Two+	0		1	25	0		2	20	3	23
Jaina										
None	1	33	4	57	4	40	0		3	75
One	2	67	3	43	4	40	1	33	0	
Two+	0		0		1	20	2	67	1	25
Xcaret										
None	0		2	100	4	80	4	67	0	
One	0		0		1	20	2	33	1	50
Two +	0		0		0		0		1	50

*Significant differences among the sites at p < .05 level.

severity in Copán. Nevertheless, as with porotic hyperostosis, it is not incompatible with survival to older ages.

Infectious reactions are an indicator that can occur at any age. The distribution of prevalence and severity by age and sex is given in Table 10.4 for tibial infection and Table 10.5 for skeletal infection. This indicator is actually more evenly distributed across the sites, as in neither indicator was there any significant difference among the sites in incidence and severity for any age or sex (Kruskal-Wallis, p > .05). In these indicators, Jaina was quite similar to Copán Urban, for example. This reveals that the kinds of chronic, nonspecific infections that cause these lesions are a general risk of the environment in these Maya sites. There appears to be a burden of morbidity and probably some incapacity for work and normal activities as a result of these infections, especially for those with moderate and severe tibial infections and skeletal systemic involvement. However, those dying as children do not seem to be more susceptible to these lesions than those dying as old adults generally.

Trauma rates in these samples were generally quite low. There were only 24 examples of trauma, all healed, in the sample. However, 15 of the 24 cases with trauma are in females, including 8 of 13 with skull trauma, and so females are more at risk of having healed injuries. It is quite possible that male trauma would be underestimated in this population, because many males would not return from warfare to heal (i.e., the Classic Maya tended to sacrifice noble war captives). There were no examples of trauma to juveniles. While they may be accidental, the skull injuries to females could be examples of domestic violence. Life does not appear

Table 10.4: Incidence and Severity of Tibial Infection by Age and Sex

Lesion severity	Juveniles		Young males		Young females		Old males		Old females	
	N	%	N	%	N	%	N	%	N	%
Copán Urban										
None	29	54	12	60	14	74	11	39	15	40
Slight	14	26	5	25	4	21	12	43	17	45
Moderate	11	20	2	10	0		4	14	5	13
Severe	0		1	5	1	5	1	4	1	2
Copán Rural										
None	3	43	0		0		4	36	4	31
Slight	2	29	1	100	1	50	4	36	6	46
Moderate	2	29	0		1	50	3	27	3	23
Jaina										
None	21	49	4	50	6	50	2	40	5	63
Slight	17	40	3	38	4	33	3	60	2	25
Moderate	5	11	1	12	2	17	0		0	
Severe	0		0		0		0		1	12
Xcaret										
None	1	33	3	75	1	25	2	22	0	
Slight	2	66	0		2	50	5	56	2	100
Moderate	0		1	25	1	25	2	22		

Table 10.5: Incidence and Severity of Skeletal Infection by Age and Sex

Lesion severity	Juveniles		Young males		Young females		Old males		Old females	
	N	%	N	%	N	%	N	%	N	%
Copán Urban										
None	51	45	8	38	11	44	13	42	22	44
Slight	50	45	8	38	10	40	12	39	21	42
Systemic	11	10	5	24	4	16	6	19	7	14
Copán Rural										
None	5	50	3	75	0		5	39	8	50
Slight	4	40	1	25	0		5	39	6	38
Systemic	1	10	0		2	100	3	23	2	12
Jaina										
None	32	54	6	60	9	60	5	63	4	40
Slight	16	27	1	10	4	27	2	25	4	40
Systemic	11	19	3	30	2	13	1	12	2	20
Xcaret										
None	2	50	5	71	4	57	9	69	0	
Slight	2	50	1	14	2	29	3	23	2	100
Systemic	0		1	14	1	14	1	18	0	

Table 10.6: Robusticity Indexes for Maya Males and Females

	Femur index						Humeral index					
	Females			Males			Females			Males		
	Mean	SD	N	Mean	SD	N	Mean	SD	N	Mean	SD	N
Copán Urban	7.0	7.7	39	7.6	1.0	30	1.2	2.2	16	1.1	2.3	11
Copán Rural	7.7	1.0	11	9.6	1.5	6		None			None	
Jaina	7.3	1.2	11	7.4	.9	7	1.1	2.2	13	1.1	.25	5
Xcaret	7.8		2	7.1		2	1.6		3	1.3		2

to be unusually risky for those buried within these sites, although undoubtedly the amount of trauma is underestimated for these samples.

The physical activity of Maya males tends to fit with the robusticity indexes, which show a much greater range than among the Basin of Mexico populations who have similar diets and lifeways, especially in the Copán populations (see Table 10.6). Copán Rural males have the highest index in the femur, which probably reflects their activity in the very steep slopes of the rural areas of the region. Copán Urban males are more robust than the females, again probably reflecting their specialized activities as elite males in Classic Maya society, involving warfare and the ball game. All elite males were fairly active. In Jaina, the females were more robust in the femur, but the males less than the Copán Urban. The Jaina samples have low standard deviations, indicating that activity patterns were quite similar for the individuals in this population. Jaina shows less sexual dimorphism than Xcaret, where females have the higher index, both in arm and leg. The females are probably doing more strenuous activities here, including corn grinding and perhaps agricultural work. The males may have been involved in trading and fishing, using canoes, and thus had less femur use but more arm use. The Xcaret samples had the highest robusticity in the humerus. The Copán Urban females are the least robust and are probably the ones doing less physical activity than any other group. They also have a very high standard deviation, indicating that there is probably great variety in the amount of activity performed by these women. The highest ranked elite females may have done little strenuous domestic work, like corn grinding, while others may have been much more responsible for domestic tasks, although they probably did little work in agricultural fields, unlike the rural females.

For dental pathology, Table 10.7 has the indexes for the sexes. In general, the Copán samples have more pathology, while Jaina has little. Jaina probably reflects both a more varied diet and a younger overall population. Copán Rural, and especially the females, are the highest in caries and abscess indexes, reflecting poor hygiene and starchy diet. Males have higher indexes in Jaina and Xcaret, while males and females are about the same in Copán Urban. Copán has a high percentage of maize in the diet, which is reflected here, while the lower indexes for the coastal sites probably indicate their more varied diet and better protein sources from marine resources. The higher rate of male pathology in these coastal populations may indicate that they consumed more maize, perhaps as part of rituals and in the form of beer,

Table 10.7: Dental Pathologies in the Maya Skeletal Samples

	Copán Urban	Copán Rural	Jaina	Xcaret
Caries index	.13	.26	.05	.10
Males	.18	.26	.06	.12
Females	.17	.32	.03	.07
Abscess index	.02	.11	.02	.03
Males	.02	.09	.04	.03
Females	.02	.14	.02	.01
Decayed–missing index	.34	.41	.07	.25
Males	.34	.44	.09	.30
Females	.43	.38	.05	.16
Age-adjusted decayed–missing index	.75	.77	.23	.59
Males	.73	.83	.27	.64
Females	.95	.71	.16	.47

than did females. If the amount of teeth already lost before death is added to the caries index and adjusted for age, the burden of dental pathologies among these populations is better compared. As can be seen from the age-adjusted decayed–missing index, the Copán populations are very high, especially Copán Urban females and Copán Rural males. Jaina is low, but there is a difference between males and females. Xcaret is also moderately high, with males more impacted. Copán is an older adult population, but nevertheless seems to have been plagued with dental pathologies.

Discussion of Classic Period Patterns

Comparing these Classic Period skeletal samples, Copán is usually much more affected with skeletal indicators of stress and morbidity than are the coastal populations of Jaina and Xcaret. In general, the Maya sites are also more affected with some of these indicators than are the Basin of Mexico populations who are from similar societies and time periods, indicating that the humid tropical environment of the Maya was less healthy than the arid uplands. Of interest is that the Copán juveniles do not seem to have higher incidences of these indicators than do the other populations. The morbidity risks for juveniles appear similar for the various parts of the Classic Maya world, and these individuals are probably more frail than those that survive to adulthood, explaining why they died young. In comparison with other populations in the Hemisphere, these juveniles are burdened with chronic stressors that undoubtedly affect the mortality rates in these populations. Perhaps if there were larger samples for the various indicators, it would be possible to distinguish a higher incidence in the Copán juveniles. The differences are in the greater incidence, and usually greater severity, of the indicators on the Copán adults, especially the older ones. That means that the greater burden of these indicators of chronic stress is falling on the productive adults of the society. Individuals in Copán must survive the chronic stresses causing enamel hypoplasias and often porotic hyperostosis to reach over 40 years of age. These individuals also have dental pathology and at least slight infectious reactions. Individuals in Jaina and Xcaret generally have to survive fewer stresses as children, and while infection is as serious, dental pathology is less.

The Copán society collapsed and the population mostly disappeared, while those at Jaina probably continued on, and those at Xcaret certainly did. From looking at skeletal indicators here, the situation prior to the Classic Maya collapse in Copán was not one of a society with significantly sicker children, but with adults more burdened by chronic stress, and probably suffering more episodes of temporary disability and less productivity than adults in other societies. While Copán may turn out to be a particularly good example of collapse due to ecological factors, the information here may indicate how stresses were felt by different Maya groups living in different ecological situations. The chronic stress burden of adults at the levels present at Copán probably indicate how political and social stresses were interfering in the daily lives of the Copán Maya and ultimately influenced the viability of the Copán society. Further research is sorely needed using similar methodology, as well as information from archaeology at various sites, to test the variability in stresses by ecological and sociopolitical factors in Mayan societies and to ascertain whether high adult stress burdens reveal potential long-term adaptation problems for these societies.

THE SPANISH CONQUEST

History and ethnohistory, as well as some archaeological excavations, have shown the tremendous changes that accompanied the Spanish Conquest of Mesoamerica in the sixteenth century. There were definitely dramatic cultural changes, especially the introduction of Christianity and new forms of government and settlement, and the demographic disruptions of introduced diseases, such as smallpox, influenza, and so on, which caused so many populations of Native Americans over the whole Hemisphere to decrease dramatically. The Maya nevertheless were able to survive the period with some cultural continuity and reasonable population numbers, although exact figures and the extent of the depopulation are in question.[10] For much of the colonial period, the actual Spanish presence and degree of control were relatively little in the Yucatan Peninsula and Maya lowlands. There is resettlement of some populations and the construction of churches, but otherwise the evidence of Spanish material culture is fairly sparse. This area remained a frontier, where Spanish control was tenuous and the Maya were able to revolt and remain independent for several decades. Nevertheless, that does not means that these populations were isolated, cut off from the effects of conquest violence or disease. The Guatemalan highlands present a slightly different scenario, as there was more direct Spanish influence and

[10] See Farriss 1984; Jones 1988; and Lovell 1992.

definitely several deadly pandemics, but there also the Maya population survived. The contact period was one of stress for the Maya culturally and should also have been one biologically.

Description of Colonial Period Samples

There are several skeletal populations from the contact period from the Maya lowlands that can be used to look for the skeletal evidence of stress. The Colonial Period Xcaret population has just recently been excavated and the skeletons added to our database. Unfortunately, it is the only such population presently available to us, and so it must be compared with other populations known to us only from published sources. As the methodology and coding of paleopathological indicators will not be exactly the same, comparisons will be somewhat more tentative. From published sources, however, there is evidence from Tipu and Lamanai, Belize.

The Xcaret Colonial population comes from the same site as our Classic/Postclassic one. A thriving port in Postclassic times, this site is believed to be Pole, which was a Spanish/Colonial Maya port and church.[11] The church was a masonry structure but apparently with a thatched roof. The Spanish presence was not extensive at the site, and the church appears to have been visited by only itinerant friars. The skeletal sample consists of 131 individuals.

Tipu[12] was part of the southeastern frontier of colonial Yucatan and was a *visita* mission, as was probably Xcaret, with no permanent Spanish priest. The site was an important Postclassic site as well. Although there was a clear Spanish influence and presence, Tipu was mostly politically independent, and indigenous Maya practices certainly continued along with Christian rituals. In 1638, the Tipu Maya revolted and threw out the Spanish, remaining largely independent for about 50 years. The Spanish reasserted control and reestablished Christianity in the settlement, as part of a campaign to try to control this frontier area. The site was forcibly abandoned in 1707. A large skeletal population was recovered from the church itself and surrounding courtyard. While most are Christian burials, there are also some Maya burials, probably from the time after the revolt. Preservation is variable, but there are about 631 individuals, not all of which, unfortunately, can be used to look at health.

Lamanai[13] is one of those sites in the Maya lowlands that clearly survived the Classic Maya collapse and continued to thrive, though smaller, into the Postclassic and Early Colonial Periods. Thus, it is impressive for its long, continuous occupation, probably because of its strategic location on the New River. During the Colonial Period, it had a church but, like Tipu, relatively little direct Spanish presence; Maya lifeways generally predominate. In 1641, Lamanai apparently joined the general revolt against the Spanish, the same one as at Tipu, destroying the churches, and the inhabitants fled to Tipu. The Lamanai skeletal sample has both a Postclassic (115)

---

[11] See Andrews and Andrews 1975.

[12] More information on Tipu can be found in Jones 1988 and Cohen et al. 1997.

[13] Lamanai is discussed in Pendergast 1986 and White, Wright, and Pendergast 1994.

and Colonial component (179). The Postclassic is generally an elite one from the ceremonial core, and the Colonial from under the earlier church.

Results of Colonial Period Comparisons

The three Colonial samples to be compared thus are from very similar contact situations, where there was much continuity with the pre-Hispanic past, Spanish influence and contact were basically light and sporadic, but populations were likely exposed to the new diseases. These three sites had been part of trade networks in the Postclassic and continued to be so in Colonial times. While remote to the powerful Spanish settlements, these are not isolated populations by any means, but they remain very Mayan in many lifeways. At Lamanai, the evidence of stable isotopes and the caries rate indicate dietary stability from Postclassic to Colonial times, with a strongly maize-based diet that was not much affected by the introduction of new European crops and animals.[14] This is probably true of Tipu and Xcaret as well, indicating that differences with the Classic skeletal samples will not be confounded by a distinctly different subsistence regime.

Table 10.8 compares the three colonial populations on some of the possible pale-opathological indicators.[15] Unfortunately, the method by which Tipu and Lamanai were scored is not exactly the same as was done for the database for this project. The Xcaret Colonial population has 58 females, 37 males, and 36 juveniles. This sex ratio is significantly different. There are too many females, but in this it resembles Lamanai, which also has more females, although Tipu has more males. Xcaret has higher incidences of periosteal reactions and systemic infection than did Tipu. The hypoplasia rate at Xcaret is less than at Tipu, but unfortunately, the calculation for Lamanai is not comparable by individuals affected. Porotic hyperostosis is not very common at Lamanai but similar in Tipu and Xcaret. Caries rates are less at Xcaret than at Lamanai, but the former probably had more marine resources, and these are not particularly common at Lamanai, which has a large maize component in the diet. Thus, there are differences in the paleopathological indicators among the three sites, which probably do reflect slightly different conditions. Compared to the Classic Period samples discussed above, Xcaret is slightly worse in infectious incidence and porotic hyperostosis than Copán Urban, but better in canine hypoplasias. It still is generally better than Copán Rural. It has caries rates comparable to Xcaret Classic and Jaina. The infectious rates at Tipu and porotic hyperostosis at Lamanai are lower than for the Classic Period samples. The high infectious rate at Xcaret may be explained because as a port, it became a crossroads of various diseases, although the new diseases introduced by Spaniards cause acute morbidity that generally does not last long enough to be registered on the skeleton. However, such illnesses might make individuals more susceptible to the chronic infections revealed by the skeletons.

---

[14] White, Wright, and Pendergast 1994, "Biological Disruption."
[15] The data for Tipu are from Cohen et al. 1997. The data from Lamanai are from White, Wright, and Pendergast 1994, and White 1997.

Table 10.8: Paleopathological Indicators Found in Skeletal Samples from Colonial Maya Sites

	Xcaret Colonial	Tipu	Lamanai
Periosteal reactions	Males 84% Females 69% Juveniles 67%	Males 22.6% Females 13.8% Juveniles 2.2%	
Systemic infections	Males 49% Females 43% Juveniles 19%	Males 9.9% Females 7.5% Juveniles 1.6%	
Hypoplasias on canines and incisors	C – Males 40% Females 40% Juveniles 50% I – Males 15% Females 11% Juveniles 100%	C – 90.4% individuals I – 69% individuals	.31 (mean of means of observable teeth per individual)
Porotic hyperostosis	Males 62%, 4% severe Females 48%, 3% severe Juveniles 32%, 0 severe	Total 55.3%, 20% severe Juveniles 43%, 22% severe	
Caries index	Males .01 Females .15		Males 17% Females 11% Juveniles 13% .21 (mean of means of observable teeth per individual)

Discussion of Colonial Period Samples

The frequencies of most of these paleopathological indicators are indeed less than in most of the Classic Period samples discussed above. The researchers think that Tipu looks basically like a fairly healthy population. The only indication of problems is that it has a demographic profile that is younger than the Classic samples, with only 2 individuals, out of 492, over 50 years at death. After disallowing biases due to differential burial practices and the age estimation methods, the researchers thought that this youthful population indicates indeed the effects of successive waves of new diseases that allowed few individuals to live to old age. At Colonial Xcaret, 31% of the population was over 40 at death, and only 5 individuals were over 50, and so it also appears to be a younger population at death than the Classic Copán samples. The younger demographic profile may be due to the same reasons as at Tipu, although Xcaret individuals had a higher burden of chronic disease as well. At Lamanai, the paleopathological indicators of porotic hyperostosis and Wilson bands (a microscopic enamel defect caused by acute morbidity) increase from the Postclassic sample to the Colonial. Since the diet did not change, the researchers think that the difference is also due to the change in epidemiological patterns, where more acute morbidity would be present.

The information that is presently available from this important period of disruption indicates that there seems to be some increase in stress over the few Postclassic skeletal samples available. However, the nature of the stress seems to have changed from that which was more ubiquitous during the Late Classic. The Late Classic had common chronic stress indicators: enamel hypoplasias, infection, and porotic hyperostosis, especially in Copán. These Colonial populations show less evidence of chronic stress and possibly more evidence of acute stress, which would be consistent with morbidity and mortality due to waves of newly introduced highly infectious diseases brought by the Spaniards. These types of diseases tend to leave no skeletal indicators, as death or recovery is usually too quick for bone involvement. Individuals might die quickly of the first epidemic, or might survive one disease only to succumb to the next new epidemic a few years later. The strongest evidence in a skeletal sample of the effects of the new diseases would be a population dying at young ages, as few would survive the waves of new epidemics to reach old age. In both the Classic Collapse and Spanish Conquest, the effect on the Maya was of depopulation, rather rapidly over a couple of centuries. However, as the source of disruption in the two cases is quite different, one conquest and acculturation and the other probable social instability driven by historical and ecological factors, it is not surprising that the skeletal information available gives a different pattern of skeletal health. The information presently available is only suggestive; it is hoped that future research will allow a more detailed comparison of these disruptions of the Maya civilization.

MODERN MAYA HEALTH INDICATORS

The legacy of the Spanish Conquest has been impoverishment and marginality with some assimilation for Maya peoples in the colonies and independent nations of which they have been a part for over 400 years. The effects of this impoverishment and marginality have been detailed in the recent anthropometric, nutritional, and health studies of human biologists. Many of their findings parallel the problems seen in the pre-Columbian skeletons. Studies have linked malnutrition to the prevalence of hypoplasias on deciduous and permanent teeth among Guatemalan Maya children.[16] For example, in children with second-degree malnutrition, 43% had deciduous hypoplasias, while 73% of those with third-degree malnutrition had hypoplasias. For the study on permanent teeth, 38% of males and 58% of females had hypoplasias, and in this case, there was a general relationship of less nutritional supplementation, more illness, and higher incidence of hypoplasia. These prevalence figures definitely fall within the bounds seen in the skeletal samples.

A recent forensic study on crania of Maya has allowed comparison of rates of prevalence of porotic hyperostosis and anemia on modern versus past populations.[17] The rate of prevalence in the adult crania is 11%, and in surveys of Maya children around 30% are anemic. In comparison, at least 60% of adult crania from Copán have healed porotic hyperostosis, indicating that more individuals with anemia survived to adulthood in the past. The researchers hypothesize that the greater variety of infectious diseases and earlier weaning in modern groups may lead to higher childhood mortality than in prehistory. The Maya have through time actually had a deteriorating morbidity and mortality situation.

Studies of Maya children have found that they are small, short, and light compared to other children in Guatemala and Mexico.[18] They also appear to have low life expectancy for a modern population; at least it was so for the Tojolabal Maya of Chiapas, Mexico. An interesting point from this last study is that the people themselves indicated that disease and shortage of land were important preoccupations. One cannot help feeling that many Maya of the past may have said the same thing, especially before the Classic Period Collapse. The general shortness of adult stature and low fat-fold measures of children indicate the effects of poor nutrition, poor hygiene, and lack of medical care that still plague many Maya here at the beginning of the twenty-first century. In a nine-year study of Maya children in Guatemala, the deleterious effects of the synergistic interactions of common infection and malnutrition while ill were strongly indicated. The result was higher mortality of children with stunted growth for most of the survivors, which continued into the next generation in the stunted women who delivered small babies who were much more susceptible to infection and infant mortality. Again, this situation was probably found among the Maya of the Late Classic Period and in the early Colonial times.

The effects of the past and the coming changes are highlighted by evidence from Maya living in the United States, where the children are significantly taller and heavier, and they carry more muscle and fat mass than children in Guatemala.

---

[16] Data on hypoplasias of the deciduous dentition are from Sweeney, Saffir, and de Leon 1971, and those in the permanent dentition are from May, Goodman, and Meindl 1993.

[17] Wright and Chew 1998.

[18] Studies of growth of Maya children in Guatemala are from Bogin, Wall, and MacVean 1992, and on the growth of U.S. Maya children from Bogin 1995 and Bogin and Loucky 1997. The longitudinal study is from Mata 1995. Information on life expectancy and growth of Mexican Mayan children is from Furbee et al. 1988.

According to Barry A. Bogin: "The average increase of 5.5 cm in height for the Maya in the United States, in less than one generation, is perhaps the largest such increase recorded. The forces holding back growth were severe indeed."[19] The political and socioeconomic conditions of the Maya are changing again. Although still severely plagued by chronic and acute stressors, high mortality, and shorter life expectancy than many modern populations, the Maya, it is hoped, will face a more healthy and prosperous future.

CONCLUSIONS

The study of a thousand years of Maya civilization has shown that these populations have been plagued with high incidences of chronic stressors, especially during periods of social disruption. In some measures, such as stature, we can trace a trend of continued decrease in average stature of adults through time. Table 10.9 contains the information available on stature estimates based on skeletons.[20] The trend is a shortening through time, especially in males, although Postclassic, Colonial, and Modern statures are quite similar. As short adult stature would be the result of stunting due to malnutrition and illness during childhood, the Maya seem to have been deteriorating since early in their history of civilization. Other measures seem to be worse during the Classic Period Collapse, be better in at least some Postclassic populations, deteriorate again during the contact depopulation period, and still be bad when measured in the twentieth century. In comparison with other populations in this project, the Classic samples were all among the worst in terms of the overall health index. There is probably no reason to think that the contact period and modern populations would fare better.

The need for further research about the Maya is obvious. Actually, the numbers of osteological studies beginning to be published is increasing dramatically over just what was available 10 years ago. The number of Classic Period samples needs to be increased and compared, hopefully with the possibility of comparable measures of the incidence of paleopathological indicators, so as to investigate how different ecological, sociopolitical, and continuity factors affected Maya civilization and contributed to the collapse of the southern lowland area. Also, if possible, it would be good to have more colonial samples, possibly from areas with more direct Spanish contact, to better gauge what was happening with contact and the introduction of new diseases. Lastly, the overall declining trend in Maya stature through time may actually be mirrored in other indicators; it would provide time depth to the study of a civilization to look at how these stress markers increase and vary according to the vitality, size, and complexity of Maya societies. For this, Preclassic samples would need to be assembled and compared.

Nevertheless, the Maya have persisted as a people. While mortality was probably high during the Classic Collapse, was undoubtedly high during the contact period,

---

[19] Bogin 1995:65.

[20] Data for stature estimates are from the database used here, on Yucatan Maya and Modern Maya from Márquez and del Angel 1997, and the data on Tipu is from Cohen et al. 1994.

Table 10.9: Estimated Statures (in cm) for Maya Populations through Time

	Males		Females	
	Mean	N	Mean	N
Preclassic				
Altar de Sacrificios	166.6	4	148.3	2
Tikal	161.7	6	144.4	4
Yucatan Maya	164.4	7	151.2	2
Classic				
Jaina	160.6	12	151.0	12
Altar de Sacrificios	159.0	3		
Tikal	155.2	21	148.5	11
Xcaret	164.5	2	154.0	3
Copán Urban	162.8	36	155.5	46
Copán Rural	160.1	9	154.9	13
Yucatan Maya	162.1	22	151.8	14
Postclassic				
Yucatan Maya	161.5	25	148.4	5
Colonial Maya				
Tipu	160.3	149	148.3	106
Xcaret	157.3	15	145.5	31
Modern Maya				
Yucatan	160.0	4	150.9	3

and is high in relation to modern standards among contemporary Maya, the stressors discussed here are really of more importance as indicators of quality of life. Maya quality of life was not good in relation to that of modern industrial Western nations, and is not good in terms of other Native American populations in pre-Columbian times. For example, many of the incidences of chronic stress indicators discussed here are higher than was present in the Basin of Mexico, which had many cultural and social similarities. These people have been burdened with chronic stress that makes itself felt as periods of illness and disability, when they cannot take care of themselves and their families as well as would be liked. What the history of the Maya reveal is that in spite of chronic stress problems afflicting children and, more importantly, productive adults, their societies have been able to maintain a complex civilization in their tropical environment for a long time. While situations, probably largely caused by ecological and disease problems, overwhelmed their ability to persist in individual sites at times in the past thousand years, the Maya seem to regroup and go on. As they enter a new millennium of Maya civilization, it should be interesting to see how they are able to change some of the health stresses that have plagued them for so many years.

REFERENCES

Andrews, E. Wyllys IV, and Anthony P. Andrews. 1975. *A Preliminary Study of the Ruins of Xcaret, Quintana Roo, Mexico.* Middle American Research Institute Publication 40. New Orleans: Tulane University.

Bogin, Barry A. *Patterns of Human Growth.* 1988. Cambridge: Cambridge University Press.

——— 1995. Growth and Development: Recent Evolutionary and Biocultural Research. In *Biological Anthropology: The State of the Science,* ed. Noel T. Boaz and Linda D. Wolfe, pp. 49–70. Oregon: International Institute for Human Evolutionary Research.

Bogin, Barry A., and James Loucky. 1997. Plasticity, Political Economy, and Physical Growth Status of Guatemala Maya Children Living in the United States. *American Journal of Physical Anthropology* 102:17–32.

Bogin, Barry, M. Wall, and R. B. MacVean. 1992. Longitudinal Analysis of Adolescent Growth of Ladino and Mayan School Children in Guatemala: Effects of Environment and Sex. *American Journal of Physical Anthropology* 89:447–457.

Chase, Arlen F., and Prudence M. Rice. 1985. *The Lowland Maya Postclassic.* Austin: University of Texas Press.

Coe, Michael D. 1992. *Breaking the Code.* New York: Thames and Hudson.

Cohen, Mark, K. A. O'Connor, M. E. Danforth, K. P. Jacobi, and C. W. Armstrong. 1994. Health and Death at Tipu. In *In the Wake of Conquest,* ed. C. S. Larsen and G. R. Milner, pp. 121–133. New York: Wiley-Liss.

——— 1997. Archaeology and Osteology of the Tipu Site. In *Bones of the Maya,* ed. Stephen Whittington and David Reed, pp. 78–88. Washington, D.C.: Smithsonian Institution Press.

Culbert, T. Patrick. 1991. *Classic Maya Political History: Hieroglyphic and Archaeological Evidence.* Albuquerque: University of New Mexico Press.

Farriss, Nancy M. 1984. *Maya Society Under Colonial Rule.* Princeton, N.J.: Princeton University Press.

Fash, William L. 1991. *Scribes, Warriors, and Kings: The City of Copán and the Ancient Maya.* London: Thames and Hudson.

——— 1994. Changing Perspectives on Maya Civilization. *Annual Review of Anthropology* 23: 181–208.

Furbee, Louana, et al. 1988. Tojolabal Maya Population Response to Stress. *Geoscience and Man* 26:17–27

Hodell, David A., Jason H. Curtis, and Mark Brenner. 1995. Possible Role of Climate in the Collapse of Classic Maya Civilization. *Nature* 375:391–394.

Jones, Grant D. 1988. *Maya Resistance to Spanish Rule.* Albuquerque: University of New Mexico Press.

Lovell, W. George. 1992. Disease and Depopulation in Early Colonial Guatemala. In *"Secret Judgments of God": Old World Disease in Colonial Spanish America,* ed. N. D. Cook and W. G. Lovell, pp. 49–83. Norman: University of Oklahoma Press.

Marquez Morfin, Lourdes, and Andres del Angel. 1997. Height Among Prehispanic Maya of the Yucatán Peninsula: Reconsideration. In *Bones of the Maya,* ed. Stephen Whittington and David Reed, pp. 62–77. Washington, D.C.: Smithsonian Institution Press.

Mata, Leonardo. 1995. The Santa María Cauqué Study: Health and Survival of Mayan Indians Under Deprivation, Guatemala. In *Community-Based Longitudinal Nutrition and Health Studies,* ed. Nevin S. Scrimshaw, pp. 29–78. Boston: International Foundation for Developing Countries.

May, Richard, Alan Goodman, and Richard S. Meindl. 1993. Response of Bone and Enamel Formation to Nutritional Supplementation and Morbidity Among Malnourished Guatemalan Children. *American Journal of Physical Anthropology* 92:37–51.

Mehta, C. R., and N. R. Patel. 1996. *SPSS Exact Tests 7.0 for Windows*. Chicago: SPSS, Inc.

Paine, Richard R, and AnnCorinne Freter. 1996. Environmental Degradation and the Classic Maya Collapse at Copán, Honduras (A.D. 600–1250): Evidence from Studies of Household Survival. *Ancient Mesoamerica* 7:37–47.

Pendergast, D. M. 1986. Stability Through Change: Lamanai, Belize, from the 9th to the 17th Century. In *Late Lowland Maya Civilization*, ed. J. A. Sabloff and E. W. Andrews, pp. 223–249. Albuquerque: University of New Mexico Press.

Piña Chan, Roman. 1968. *Jaina: La Casa en el Agua*. Mexico City: Instituto Nacional de Antropología e Historía.

Sabloff, Jeremy A., and E. Wyllys Andrews V. 1986. *Late Lowland Maya Civilization: Classic to Postclassic*. Albuquerque: University of New Mexico Press.

Schele, Linda, and David Friedel. 1990. *A Forest of Kings: The Untold Story of the Ancient Maya*. New York: William Morrow.

Sweeney, E. A., A. J. Saffir, and R. de Leon. 1971. Linear Hypoplasia of Deciduous Incisor Teeth in Malnourished Children. *American Journal of Clinical Nutrition* 24:29–31.

Webster, David L., ed. 1989. *House of the Bacabs*. Studies in Pre-Columbian Art and Archaeology 29. Washington, D.C.: Dumbarton Oaks.

Webster, David L., and Nancy Gonlin. 1988. Household Remains of the Humblest Maya. *Journal of Field Archaeology* 15:169–190.

Wood, James W., G. R. Milner, H. C. Harpending, and K. M. Weiss. 1992. The Osteological Paradox: Problems of Inferring Prehistoric Health from Skeletal Samples. *Current Anthropology* 33:343–370.

White, Christine D. 1997. Ancient Diet at Lamanai and Pacbitun: Implications for the Ecological Model of Collapse. In *Bones of the Maya*, ed. Stephen Whittington and David Reed, pp. 171–180. Washington, D.C.: Smithsonian Institution Press.

White, Christine D., Lori Wright, and D. M. Pendergast. 1994. Biological Disruption in the Early Colonial Period at Lamanai. In *In the Wake of Conquest*, ed. C. S. Larsen and G. R. Milner, pp. 135–145. New York: Wiley-Liss.

Whittington, Stephen, and David Reed, eds. 1997. *Bones of the Maya: Studies of Ancient Skeletons*. Washington, D.C.: Smithsonian Institution Press.

Wright, Lori E., and Francisco Chew. 1998. Porotic Hyperostosis and Paleoepidemiology: A Forensic Perspective on Anemia among the Ancient Maya. *American Anthropologist* 100:924–939.

CHAPTER ELEVEN

Health and Nutrition in Pre-Hispanic Mesoamerica

Lourdes Marquez Morfin, Robert McCaa,
Rebecca Storey, and Andres Del Angel

ABSTRACT

Central Mexico witnessed the development and florescence of pre-Columbian Mesoamerican complex societies for over two thousand years, including several urban civilizations and centers of influential empires. Using four skeletal samples that span the Mesoamerican sequence from an early ranked village to a Postclassic urban society, we trace the health effects of living in such an arid highland environment. The small skeletal samples available here cannot provide more than hints as to quality of life, but comparisons with other hemispheric samples indicate that health problems are always present. There is moderate morbidity in the earliest, most simple society; however, as populations became more dense, urban, socially stratified, and militaristic, there is a general trend to greater burdens of morbidity through time as reflected in the various health indicators. Future research is needed to test the broad pattern of change portrayed here in this first attempt to look at the quality of life for all of pre-Columbian Central Mexico.

INTRODUCTION

Mesoamerica has been an important area for archaeological research for some time. Despite the amount of information that we have from these ancient societies, whether from small or grand monumental sites, our knowledge about their inhabitants is less developed: how they lived, what they ate, what kind of health problems they had, or what kind of activities they developed. We think that a helpful means of answering these questions is through the analysis of the way of life of these individuals. Our approach is to study the skeletons, searching for the multicausality of physiological adjustment with the material conditions of existence and lifestyle, which in turn shape culture, habits, and habitat. We selected

We gratefully acknowledge the help provided by Professors Ma. Teresa Jaen and Jose C. Jimenez (Direccíon de Antropología Física, INAH), and Vera Flores, Blanca Gonzalez, Laura Huicochea, Humberto Ortiz, Carlos Karam, and Ma. Lucia Plaza (Escuela Nacional de Antropología e Historía, INAH). The Tlajinga 33 study was supported by the National Science Foundation (BNS 80-05825 and 82-04862).

the Basin of Mexico for our analysis and applied the standard methodology developed for the overall Health and Nutrition in the Western Hemisphere Project.

The Basin of Mexico is a core area of one of a handful of regions of the world where complex cultures seem to have arisen from internal social and historical processes alone and not as a result of imposition or stimulus from other regions. It is also a place that witnessed the dramatic confrontation of biospheres: the New and the Old World, a place where civilizations literally collided and both sides emerged to tell the tale and eventually to found a new nation. As a result, the Basin holds an important place in anthropological and historical investigation.[1] The Basin has served and continues to serve as a place where the processes of cultural development and their impact on humans can be studied.

Questions concerning the health of populations, and thus of individuals, are today subjects of great public and political interest. Usually the past is thought of in one of two ways: either as a place where humans had fewer problems, and a simpler, more healthy life; or where humans were bedeviled by health problems, high mortality rates, and reduced life expectancy. However, the study of health and disease is necessarily tied to how human populations adapt to different physical environments, as well as to different modes of subsistence. The study of the way of life, health, and nutrition of past populations is important in the quest to understand the trends and relationships between society and health, as evidence of particular kinds of adaptations.

We know that one of the great epidemiological changes is related to the development of measures for public health during the nineteenth century. Started, if not from the spread of Jennerian vaccination for controlling smallpox, then as a result of the great pandemics of cholera that devastated many populations around the world, the establishment of institutions devoted to health care mushroomed in the twentieth century. We know that infectious diseases have been constant companions of humans and the cause of most infant and juvenile mortality. It is often assumed that the development of societies into civilizations brought with it an improvement in the quality of life. This leads to the question of exactly how social and economic development, which brings with it an increase in social inequality, improves the health of the most vulnerable people who occupy the bottom of the social hierarchy. The controversy is over whether the rise of civilization and urban centers actually causes health to deteriorate for the majority of the people, a position that has been supported among anthropologists by Cohen and that is widespread in the historical study of preindustrial cities.[2] The Basin of Mexico is a natural laboratory for investigating the effects of increasing social inequality and of the rise of cities on health.

Health problems seen today in the Basin of Mexico are due to high population density, air pollution, water contamination, and economic and social problems

---

[1] There is a wealth of books in English and Spanish available about the Spanish Conquest and about the importance of Mesoamerica in the history of civilizations. For the latter subject, consult Sanders, Parsons, and Santley (1979), and a recent history is Thomas (1993).

[2] See Cohen (1989), and among many possible sources for preindustrial cities, see de Vries (1984).

Table 11.1: Chronology of Pre-Hispanic Mesoamerica

Approximate years	Major Mesoamerican Period
1600–900 BC	Early Preclassic or Formative
900–300 BC	Middle Preclassic or Formative
300 BC–AD 300	Late Preclassic or Formative
AD 300–600	Early Classic
AD 600–900	Late Classic
AD 900–1200	Early Postclassic
AD 1200–1521	Late Postclassic

Source: See Blanton et al. 1993: 56.

associated with a megalopolis whose growth has outpaced the ability of government, private organizations, and citizens to meet their own needs. Here, it is possible to ask if the health of the ancient inhabitants of this same region, the center of the modern day Republic of Mexico, had better or worse living conditions and health, and which of their problems were similar. The Basin is a place where the past can lend context to the present.

The Basin of Mexico was also where the great civilizations of Teotihuacan and the Nahua (Aztecs) developed. The cultural evolution of this region accelerated with the appearance of settled hamlets. Here, human settlement was encouraged by the rich flora and fauna of this high intermontane valley (2,000 meters above sea level). Thanks to a temperate climate and the presence of large lakes, some of the highest population densities in the ancient Americas were attained. Here, too, agriculture slowly evolved. Along with it came larger and more complex societies. This process began in the Preclassic, almost 4,000 years ago (see periodization in Table 11.1). By the Classic Period, around 300 AD, the first urban complex society had appeared, that of Teotihuacan, which because of its size and splendor influenced much of Mesoamerica. After the fall of Teotihuacan, the Basin saw the appearance of other similarly complex societies, culminating in the Aztec, who ruled an empire from the island city, Tenochtitlan. This Postclassic florescence was interrupted by the Spanish Conquest in 1521, and for the next three centuries, the Basin of Mexico was the site of one of the most important of Spain's American colonies. The lifestyle of the indigenous ethnic groups that lived in the Basin was forever changed through the encounter with Europeans, Africans, and their descendants.

In this chapter, the results obtained from the analysis of skeletal indicators of health, nutrition, and lifeways of the different populations in and around the Basin show how cultural development and historical situations affected people. From our study of the first hamlets, then of societies where clear differences in social ranks appear, to centers of powerful states, and finally cities that are peripheral to but part of other regional powers, we discern the relationship among social complexity, health, and population density. The results from these case studies show that, at least in the Basin, there are no clear trends in health over the millennia, although the data do point to a striking deterioration in life expectancy. Nevertheless, we can identify certain patterns, such as the presence of infectious diseases in all groups and their greater ubiquity in larger cities. Problems of nutrition depended on resource base, as well as on technology and inequality. Although it is not possible here, with the generally small skeletal samples available, to fully investigate the implications of increasing urbanization and social complexity, it is possible to contrast living in the more urban and complex societies with living in less dense ones. There are differences among societies that are expressed as differential health risks for individuals.

At the start of this project, we had planned to analyze historical skeletal data from the Basin of Mexico, but soon realized that suitable samples were not yet available. A future project will look at the skeletal remains of the Mestizo populations that are common today in Mexico. Thus, unfortunately, it is not possible to address here the question of whether there are differences in skeletal patterns of stress that accompanied Spanish colonization and the change from an autonomous center of power to a colony. One of the important questions, likewise unexplored here, is how the introduction of new diseases – intertwined with colonial exploitation – caused the near catastrophic decline in native population. Or, in turn, how skeletal remains reflect the changed conditions of life. Although this question can and has been addressed in other parts of the Hemisphere, the Basin of Mexico was the central location for Spanish dominion over Meso- and North America. With its colonial importance and dense pre-Hispanic population, the Basin provides an important case study. It already figures importantly in the debates over the size of the hemispheric population at European contact, in the controversies of Cook and Borah and Dobyns versus Rosenblat, Sanders, and Henige.[3] Future studies on the Basin of Mexico will continue to shed light on the whole process of conquest and adaptation to new diseases and new ways of life.

SKELETAL SAMPLES

The samples selected for analysis consist of skeletal material curated at the laboratory for Human Osteology at the National Museum of Anthropology in Mexico City and at the Teotihuacan Center for Archaeological Research. Some samples were excavated decades ago. We selected representatives from various chronological periods and subsistence systems. In addition, the size of the sample, state of preservation of the skeletons, and the available archaeological data had to be adequate for the project (see Tables 11.1 and 11.2).

Tlatilco

This sample derives from a large burial collection of nearly 500 individuals excavated in San Luis Tlatilco, located in the west of the Basin of Mexico, during four field seasons: Tlatilco I, II, III, IV. We chose 343 individuals for analysis from the four

---

[3] Again, there are many texts on this controversial topic. For recent treatments, see Cook (1998) and Henige (1998), and for a summary that includes Mexican views, McCaa (2000).

Table 11.2: Skeletal Samples by Sex and Age

	Tlatilco		Cuicuilco		Tlajinga		Cholula	
	N	%	N	%	N	%	N	%
Male	116	33.8	49	41.1	18	36	54	22.8
Female	149	43.4	52	43.6	12	24	69	29.2
Juvenile < 15 years	57	16.6	12	10.0	20	40	82	34.7
Unidentified adult	21	6.1	6	5.0			31	13.1
TOTALS	343		119		50		236	

series. According to archaeological data, they represent the Formative Period or the Early Horizon (1400–900 BC) of the Basin of Mexico, as determined by radiocarbon date of 1150 BC ± 150 years.[4]

Cuicuilco

Cuicuilco is located in the south of the Basin of Mexico, near Lake Xochimilco, bordering the Sierra del Ajusco. The sample derives from archaeological excavations made some years ago in this early center. More than a hundred burials, accompanied by offerings, were excavated. From this sample, 119 burials were selected for study. They represent the Ticoman phase of the Formative (600–150 BC).

Teotihuacan (Tlajinga 33)

The Teotihuacan sample derives from an archaeological excavation carried out in a small residential compound named Tlajinga 33 on the southern edge of this big urban center. Even though the skeletal collection was composed of more than 200 individuals, for this research we selected only 50, in accordance with the methodology of this book to use only the best preserved skeletons. The site occupation was exclusively during the Middle Horizon or Classic Period, spanning about 350–400 years from AD 250 to 600.[5]

Cholula

This sample derives from archaeological excavations carried out in the site of Cholula in the 1960s, where 308 primary or anatomical-position burials and 120 secondary or bundle burials were recovered. From these, 94% of the primary burials correspond to the Postclassic period: 70% to the Cholulteca III phase (AD 1325–1500), 16% to the Cholulteca II phase (AD 900–1325), and 5% to Cholulteca IV (AD 1500–1521).

---

[4] General information about the Tlatilco burials can be found in Romano (1972). Dates for Tlatilco II and IV can be found in Tolstoy, "Coapexco and Tlatilco," p. 105, and the given date is from García Moll, Juarez Cossio, and Pijoan Aguade (1992:13). The skeletal remains were studied by Lourdes Marquez and Magalí Civera.

[5] Storey (1992).

The skeletal material used in this study is represented by 236 individuals, mostly from the Cholulteca III phase.[6]

The Basin of Mexico sits atop a highland block, the central highland of Mexico. In pre-Hispanic times, it was an internal drainage basin. The floor of the basin is at 7,000 feet above sea level, which gives it a cool climate. Frost is a severe problem for agriculture in the fall, winter, and spring. High mountains surround the valley, which, until the beginning of the twentieth century, was a closed hydrographic unit with a series of shallow, interconnected lakes. The valley constituted a unique ecology in Mesoamerica, one suitable for hunting, foraging, intensive farming, and waterborne transport. Resources included such lacustrine products as fish, insect larvae, reeds, and waterfowl. Figure 11.1 gives the location of the sites and their relation to the valley's lakes.

Tlatilco

The first Mesoamerican permanent settlements were the villages of the Formative Period (1600 BC–AD 300). The Basin's population density in the early phase of this period was quite low. Nineteen villages have been identified as belonging to this phase, all of them populated by a few hundred people, and generally situated in the middle and southern area of the basin. Sedentary groups lived in these villages, whose subsistence system was based on agriculture and the exploitation of lacustrine and terrestrial resources, adequate for the relatively small populations. El Arbolillo, Zacatenco, Tlapacoya, and Tlatilco are the main villages of this period. Tlatilco, located on the lower slopes of the Los Remedios Hill in the Rio Hondo Basin, was an important site in the region during the Early and Middle Formative Periods. In early times its soft soils and proximity to Lake Texcoco must have been attractive to agriculturalists. Paul Tolstoy[7] has shown that Tlatilco burials occur in groupings, suggesting that they may represent house subfloor burial clusters. Tlatilqueños often disturbed one grave to make another at greater depth. In fact, 13% of the graves were disturbed in this way. All the burials were made in a relatively short span of time, if dating by ceramic styles is a reliable guide. The alternative is that ceramic styles and techniques remained relatively stable throughout the Tlatilco occupation of the area.

Subsistence resources were quite varied, according to paleofauna and paleoflora analysis. Maize, squash, bean, and pepper cultigens were found, as well as plant items foraged from the rich environment. Some species of fishes were abundant in the lake, and animals were also numerous in the area, including small rodents,

---

[6] Lopez, Lagunas, and Serrano (1976).
[7] Tolstoy, "Coapexco and Tlatilco," p. 117. More information on Tlatilco can be found in Blanton et al. (1993) and Porter (1953).

Figure 11.1. Map of the Basin of Mexico and nearby valleys, with locations of sites discussed in the text.

deer, peccary, and rabbit. We do not know exactly how much of the Tlatilco economy was based on agriculture. A near but later site, Loma Torremote is said to have had an economy where subsistence was primarily derived from agriculture. Yet, the people of Torremote also relied on lacustrine and terrestrial plants and animals obtained through foraging. The faunal remains by weight were 50% mammal, 30% bird, 14% reptile, and 4% fish. Food sources at Tlatilco were probably similar.[8]

Tlatilco's population consisted of a few hundred inhabitants. While the burials were definitely associated with residences and probably storage pits, the number and floor plans of the houses are unknown. This kind of information is necessary for correct interpretation of the sanitary conditions of the settlement and its possible relation to health. Social organization at Tlatilco was characteristic of a simple chiefdom. These were "ranked" societies, where position was inherited through genealogical ties to important ancestors. Differences in wealth and status are

[8] The information on Tlatilco is from Alvarez in Garcia Moll et al. (1992), and from Loma Torremote in Serra Puche (1998).

measurable. Tolstoy[9] discovered an interesting series of developments at Tlatilco. He describes an increase in wealth in male graves from early to later settlement. For the early period, matrilineal kinship is clearly evident, as can be seen by the quantity and quality of items buried with females, by the position and location of the graves, and by the orientation of bodies. The in-marrying spouse was most often male, at least in the early period, and group membership was transmitted through females.

Cuicuilco

In the phase from 800–600 BC, villages emerged on the lakeshore plain and sloping piedmonts, mostly in the southern half of the Basin. The increasing complexity of village life stimulated the occupation of hillsides and basins where cultivable lands were found. The population of the Basin of Mexico in this period was about 20,000, based on the size and density of 75 settlements.[10] Cuicuilco, located in the southeast of the Basin, had its origins in the early phases of the Middle Formative (600–300 BC). This period was characterized by "rapid" population growth, the emergence of ceremonial architecture, and the first signs of an emerging hierarchy among different types of settlements. Cuicuilco acquired importance in the Ticoman phase (600–150 BC.). There is no available data on its population size or importance, due to the difficulties of excavating solid lava which lies over the site. Based on similar studies for other settlements, its population has been estimated at about 1,000 to 2,000 inhabitants in its initial phase, but it was later to acquire considerable regional importance. By the end of this phase, Cuicuilco had between 5,000 and 10,000 inhabitants and exerted control over at least five lesser centers, showing a great level of sociopolitical centralization. In the period from 300 BC to AD 1, Cuicuilco became, together with Teotihuacan, one of the most rapidly growing population centers. Estimated at 40,000 inhabitants, it occupied an area of 400 hectares. A city of this size would only have been matched by Teotihuacan, which was already growing at that time. In fact, both cities seem to be similar in size, nature, and regional impact. However, Cuicuilco declined in relation to Teotihuacan when the Xitle volcano erupted and covered a large part of the region with a thick blanket of lava. Its population decreased, as well as its regional political power. By the year AD 300, Cuicuilco was totally buried under a new cover of lava.

Cuicuilco subsistence was based on food production by intensive agriculture, using simple irrigation through canals and terracing, greatly complemented by hunting, gathering, and fishing. Artisan production and internal and external trade were also important. At the same time, economic surplus was extracted from neighboring villages. Cuicuilco was a center of an emergent complex chiefdom with the formation of permanent elites. All these factors must have had an impact on health conditions; if output per head did not rise, elites gained greater control over resources and their distribution grew increasingly unequal. We do not know much

---

[9] Tolstoy, "Coapexco and Tlatilco," p. 117.

[10] Blanton et al. 1993:116–117. Further information about Cuicuilco can be found in Sanders, Parsons, and Santley (1979) and Schavelson (1993).

about Cuicuilco settlement, households, or daily life. Information about burials is also scanty, although we do know that they were located in bell-shaped pits in different anatomical positions, all accompanied by offerings. We have inferred that some social differences must have been present in the population, but at the moment, we are not able to relate them to the skeletal remains of specific individuals.

Teotihuacan (Tlajinga 33)

In the period from 300 BC to AD 1, a series of socioeconomic transformations took place in the Basin. Population may have nearly doubled each generation or so, settlements in the alluvial plains increased, and toward the end of this period, at least half of the population was concentrated in a center, namely Teotihuacan in the northeastern part of the Basin. Here, a great urban center emerged. Its economy was based on specialized artisan production, trade, and agrictulture. Irrigation was used to intensify food production. Teotihuacan was a state with a hierarchical society internally differentiated into a number of social, political, and economic strata. Inhabitants of the urban center were distributed in residential units called apartment compounds, which were large structures with a complex pattern of rooms, patios, and central courtyards. These could have housed up to 100 people organized into 15 to 20 families. The apartment compounds would have been the locus of kinship, social, political, and religious organization within the city.

Tlajinga 33 is located on the southern edge of the ancient city in what has been identified as a ceramic craft-working neighborhood (barrio) in the later phases of the city's history, although they had been only general lapidary workers in earlier phases.[11] Its inhabitants were full-time craft specialists who would have been dependent upon some form of market exchange to acquire most of their food. Diet was based on maize, beans, squash, small mammals, and eggs. The Tlajinga 33 series selected for this analysis are representative of the lower social strata of society. The status of this site may be inferred from, first, its peripheral location to the administrative center; second, its architecture composed of insubstantial building materials of adobe brick instead of stone; and third, its rather haphazard layout. Since hierarchical societies like Teotihuacan have most of their population at the lowest social stratum, Tlajinga 33 may be more representative of the whole city than of a higher-status compound.

Cholula

It has been hypothesized that toward the end of the Classic Period, a series of crises occurred which may explain the collapse of Teotihuacan. Other centers extended their control through long-distance trade. Some groups moved out of the city in search of better conditions and greater stability. The ruling class faced difficulties in retaining power. Finally, soil exhaustion paved the way for the emergence of

---

[11] A recent description of Teotihuacan can be found in Cowgill (1996). Description of Tlajinga 33 can be found in Storey (1992) and Widmer and Storey (1993).

militarism. In the Postclassic Period after the fall of Teotihuacan, society succumbed to rule by a military or warrior class. The conquest of others became a common occurrence. Tribute was imposed, chiefdoms and lordships were integrated, leaders and divine heroes were created, and trade became monopolized. Society was deeply divided into groups that could be considered social classes. In the Postclassic, with the drainage of low-lying areas, much of the Basin was developed for farming, creating in the shallows of the lakes consolidated agricultural plots called *chinampas*. It was a complex labor-intensive system, but exceedingly productive.

Cholula emerged in this period as a prominent settlement with a great ceremonial center in the area of the current states of Puebla and Tlaxcala, in the basin of the same name just to the east of the Basin of Mexico. Cholula Basin had been populated since the Middle Formative Period (900–300 BC). During the Upper Formative Period (300 BC–AD 300) there were developments in architecture, which reached their apogee during the Classic Period (300–900 AD). Due especially to population displacements, during the post-Teotihuacan period, this site became an important supraregional axis and one of the most powerful states of the central plateau. Its two peak moments of development happened during the late Classic (AD 600 – 900) and the late Postclassic (AD 1200–1521) Periods.[12] The ancient city, which had been abandoned since the beginning of the Postclassic, resurfaced as a new center for ceremonial activities in what we know today as Cholula, which at the time of the Spanish Conquest was still densely populated. At that moment, Cholula constituted a thickly settled, nucleated urban community. In 1519, its society was generally divided into two large groups: the *tlatoani* [elites] and the *macehuales* [commoners], which were in turn divided into social strata according to both residence and occupation. Professional warriors, merchants, and full-time artisans lived in the city. Most of the macehuales were peasants living in the rural areas. There were also *mayeques* [temporary slaves] and prisoners of war *cum* permanent slaves. Each town had its own marketplace to facilitate the exchange of goods. Tribute was fundamental, although rates varied from village to village, indeed from household to household, paid from goods produced. Rural settlements were divided into *calpullis* based on kinship, although there is some controversy around this issue. According to some authors, calpullis were endogamous, patrilinear, and stratified residential units. Cholula, although not in the Basin of Mexico, is typical of the kinds of urban centers present during this later period. During the late Postclassic Period, Cholula was inhabited largely by common folk, if the type of construction and archaeological materials recovered from burials and sites are reliable guides.[13]

BIOARCHAEOLOGICAL INDICATORS FOR CENTRAL MEXICAN POPULATIONS

Paleodemography

For demographic patterns, the data available based on skeletons are the age distributions of deaths, which are related in complex ways to the living populations that

---

[12] Cholula is discussed in Sugiura (1993).   [13] See Lopez, Lagunas, and Serrano (1976).

produced them, as discussed in Chapter 4 in this volume. The current consensus seems to be that these age distributions of deaths are best interpreted as more accurate reflections of overall population fertility; these distributions cannot be used to study mortality without other archaeological information on population growth or decline. High-fertility populations would be expected to have large proportions of infants and children and few older adults. Lower-fertility populations have lower proportions of juveniles and higher proportions of old adults. The proportion of individuals dying at various ages can reflect preservation or excavation biases, rather than demographic effects, and these must always be considered. This is especially true for individuals less than 5 years old at death. For the individual sites, general interpretations can be offered. Here we have contrasted the proportions from each site in the database sample, which includes only the best-preserved skeletons, with the total series which have been analyzed in other publications (see Table 11.3a). In each case, except for Cuicuilco, the total sample has different proportions, including a higher proportion of subadults, reflecting the addition of less-complete skeletons of adults and children. The demographic information is better from the total sample.

The earliest sample, Tlatilco, is from what would be expected to be a growing population and might be expected to have a large proportion of children, but the sample seems to have moderate fertility. The relatively small proportion under 20 here may be affected by funerary practices that did not bury many individuals under the age of 5 where the excavations were done. Thus, although the fertility patterns look only moderate, it could have been high, and the skeletons do not accurately reflect this. The pattern of the adults is one of equal numbers of young and older adults, rather than few older adults. Thus, it is possible that what is reflected here might be a particular mortality pattern that affects younger adults more than might be expected, but it also might be that Tlatilco is a growing population but with good life expectancy for adults, so that many adults survive into the older years.

Next in time is Cuicuilco, from a settlement that is larger and more urban. Here again, the fertility looks moderate to low, but excavation bias (the skeletons are recovered from a lava flow which was probably very hard on the preservation of the small bones of children) probably underestimates the fertility of this population. However, the other proportions seem to indicate an older adult population, one more likely from a declining or very slowly growing population. From the archaeology of the Basin of Mexico, we know that Cuicuilco was an important settlement in the Late Formative, earlier than Teotihuacan, but was soon eclipsed by the latter. We cannot be sure if the population might have been growing or declining. While the exact chronology of the sample is not known, it appears to be from near the end, and the skeletal population probably reflects the decline of the settlement and perhaps the migration of younger individuals to Teotihuacan.

The Tlajinga sample is from the height of the urban settlement of Teotihuacan during the Classic Period and allows the study of at least one compound from this large, heterogeneous population. The other samples used here come from many different contexts and, thus, present less of an opportunity to look at individuals living and working in a delineated context with a known economic specialization and social status within the city. Because of both the excavation techniques and the

Table 11.3a: Interpretation and Comparison of Proportions of Deaths in
Various Age Groups

	Tlatilco	Cuicuilco	Tlajinga	Cholula
Database sample*				
< 20 years at death	22% (72)	21% (24)	42% (21)	37% (81)
20–35 years	36 (118)	32 (37)	6 (3)	37 (81)
> 35 years	42 (137)	47 (55)	52 (26)	26 (58)
Total Sample				
< 20 years at death	26% (97)	21% (24)	54% (111)	42% (191)
20–35 years	37 (137)	32 (37)	15 (31)	38 (173)
> 35 years	37 (137)	47 (55)	31 (64)	20 (91)

* Sample numbers are in parentheses. For the total sample of Tlatilco, Cuicuilco, Cholula, see Camargo
et al. 1999; for Tlajinga, see Storey 1992.

Teotihuacan practice of burying very young individuals in bowls, this sample is not
affected by underrepresentation of infants and young children. That is reflected in
the proportion under 20 years of age, which would seem to indicate a growing population with high fertility. The adult sample is definitely older with very few young
adults, an indication of a possibly declining population. The Tlajinga proportions
are so distinct because of the high numbers of subadults and high numbers of older
adults, such that it seems to give contradictory information. In fact, this is a sample
from the poorer statuses of a preindustrial urban center that was not growing during
the period. Thus, what is probably reflected here is a declining population with very
high subadult mortality, an urban society at the end of its florescence.

On the other hand, Cholula, from the Postclassic Period, is also an urban settlement, but it presents a very different pattern of proportions, which is that of a
high-fertility, growing population, even though Cholula is mostly also from artisans
and other workers of lower status. The difference is that Cholula is at this time a
dynamic, growing settlement, probably attracting much migration. Even though
the urban situation would have fostered high mortality, the fertility and migration
is such that the profile of the population is one of growth, not stagnation or decline.
The profile from Cholula is similar to that from the Aztec capital of Tenochtitlan,
where, using a stable life table methodology with a growth rate estimation of 0.4
in the adjustments to the age distributions, the life expectancy at birth is 25 years
for both, and crude fertility rate is 43 per 1,000 residents for both.[14] In fact, the
Postclassic cities of the area are obviously different from earlier Teotihuacan, and
the skeletal samples are from the dynamic, growing phases of these cities.

Based on the analysis of Chapter 4, further interpretations are possible. In theory,
if a collection of skeletal remains is representative of a living, quasi-stable population,
an age distribution of deaths is a robust measure of fertility. Surprisingly, any portion
of the age distribution is sufficient to estimate fertility. While the more data points
the better, it is important to understand that accurate estimates of fertility are readily

[14] The demographic modeling used here can be found in Camargo, Marquez, and Prado (1999).

Table 11.3b: Interpretation

Site	Crude rates (per 1,000 population)			Life expectancy at birth (years)
	Birth	Increase	Death	
Tlatilco	32	5	27	37
Cuicuilco	30	5	25	40
Tlajinga	42	−5	47	21
Cholula	45	−5	50	20

Source: "Paleodemography of the Americas," Chapter 4, this volume.

obtained without taking into account children, which tend to be poorly represented in skeletal collections. When fertility estimates are combined with archaeological information on population growth, such as expansion or decline of settlements, life expectancy is readily derived. Preservation or excavation biases may be severe and must always be kept in mind. This is especially true for specimens aged at less than 5 years at death, which are excluded from analysis by the most rigorous practitioners of this craft, and from this analysis and in Chapter 4.

The earliest sample, Tlatilco, points to moderate fertility with a crude birth rate in the low to middle-thirties and, for a paleopopulation, relatively high life expectancy at birth ($e_0 = 37$ years). Next in time is Cuicuilco, a settlement that is larger and more urban. Here again, the paleodemographic analysis suggests moderate to low fertility with a crude birthrate of 30. Excavation bias may be disguising a higher birthrate. Life expectancy is also surprisingly high at some 40 years at birth. Given the fact that the population was growing, but only slowly, this would indicate that growth was checked, not by mortality but by fertility. Unfortunately, the bones offer no evidence on how this might have been accomplished. The Tlajinga sample is from the height of the urban settlement of Teotihuacan during the Classic Period. This sample is not affected by underrepresentation of infants and young children. The age distribution for those over 5 points to high fertility, a crude birthrate of 42, and high mortality. Life expectancy at birth is estimated at only 21 years, one of the lowest life expectancies among the ancient populations in the Health and Nutrition in the Western Hemisphere database. On the other hand, Cholula presents a different pattern of proportions, which is that of high fertility. Its urban situation would have fostered high mortality, and this is confirmed by the estimate of life expectancy of 20 years.

The hypothesized crude birthrates for these samples are derived from the patterns in the age distributions of death from the skeletal database, with specimens under 5 years of age omitted (see Table 11.3b). Tlatilco and Cuicuilco are the lowest at 32 and 30 years, respectively, while Tlajinga at 42 and Cholula at 45 are the highest. Thus, the trend may be toward moderate fertility in the early history of the Basin, followed by higher fertility as the settlements and societies become more complex. Crude death rates are estimated as 27 for Tlatilco, 25 for Cuicuilco, 47 for Tlajinga, and 50 for Cholula, reflecting also a probable rise in mortality as the settlements become more urban. Thus, the early Tlatilco society of horticulturalists, with significant wild resources and low demographic densities, was one with moderate fertility and mortality and a slowly growing population. Life expectancy was good, although well below modern standards, even for the most severely AIDS-afflicted populations of Asia, Africa, or the Caribbean.

Stature

Stature is a valuable indicator of relative nutritional health, as poor childhood health and nutrition is reflected in stunted adult stature. In Mesoamerica, there is a long tradition of collecting these data. Previous research has produced two important generalizations: first, the existence of a northeast to southwest gradient in average stature, with more tropical and lowland populations having shorter statures; and second, a trend toward diminishing height over time.[15] The highest values of male height often occur during the Formative, but there is a clear decrease during the Classic Period, followed by a partial recovery or even further decline during the Postclassic, depending on the specific population studied. Del Angel has found proportionality changes, with a decrement in the relative size of legs in those populations through time in Central Mexican populations. In our database, both males and females show a trend toward shorter mean stature from the Formative to Postclassic, if it were not for the Tlajinga sample (see Table 11.4). However, Tlajinga is a small sample (eight males and two females) based on the best-preserved skeletons, which were usually the highest-status individuals and probably not typical of either the compound or that stratum in Teotihuacan. Thus, we think the Tlajinga data do not call into question the thesis of stature decline over time, but additional samples are needed to test the hypothesis. Comparison of series from the Maya area of Mesoamerica also show a decrease through time, for males (Table 11.4). This pattern is one of the indications of how the development of more urban and/or socially differentiated societies stunted the average individual in pre-Hispanic Mesoamerican societies.

Nutritional Evidence: Porotic Hyperostosis and Cribra Orbitalia

These lesions have been interpreted in other ancient populations of the New World as indicating the presence of iron-deficiency anemia caused by diets low in iron or possibly exposure to fish-borne parasites, where marine resources were available but water supplies show signs of contamination. Also, these lesions have been associated with higher densities and sedentarism, where an increase in viral, bacterial, and parasitic infection, possibly coupled with nutritional stress, would often to lead to anemia. Skeletal evidence of porotic hyperostosis was observed in the four series from the Basin of Mexico (Figure 11.2), with Cuicuilco having a much higher prevalence of slight to severe lesions than the other three sites. Only the difference between Tlajinga and Cuicuilco is statistically significant (P < .05). Cribra orbitalia has greater incidence than porotic hyperostosis in these populations, with Tlatilco having 25%

---

[15] Samples not from the database used here are from Marquez and Del Angel (1997) and Del Angel (1996). The Maya samples are discussed in Chapter 10 in this volume; for an English summary of this evidence, see McCaa (2000).

Table 11.4: Mean Stature (cm) by Site and Period

Period	Sample	Female	N	Male	N
Central Mexican populations					
Preclassic	Tehuacan*	158.5	6	167.2	7
Early/Middle Preclassic	Tlatilco	153.8	56	162.8	88
Late Preclassic	Cuicuilco	150.4	16	161.7	17
Classic	Tlajinga	153.0	2	166.0	8
Postclassic	Cholula	151.8	12	160.6	19
Maya Area populations*					
Preclassic	Tikal	144.4	4	161.7	6
Preclassic	Yucatan Maya	151.2	2	164.4	7
Classic	Tikal	148.5	11	155.2	21
Classic	Jaina	151.0	12	160.6	12
Classic	Copán Urban	155.5	46	162.8	36
Postclassic	Yucatan Maya	148.4	5	161.5	25

* For Tehuacan, see Anderson 1967; for the Maya area, see Storey, Marquez Morfin, and Smith, this volume.

of scorable individuals affected, Cuicuilco 33%, Tlajinga 13%, and Cholula 31%. Thus, three populations seem to have at least moderate amounts of anemia present, with Tlajinga the only one with low incidence. With regard to gender and age differences, 559 (75%) and 419 (56%) of the samples could be analyzed for the presence of anemia indicators (Table 11.5). In general, females and males have similar incidences within a site. Cuicuilco is distinctive, because here adults have higher incidences. This suggests that individuals are commonly able to survive into adulthood in spite of suffering from anemia. On the other hand, for cribra orbitalia, Tlatilco and Cholula have high incidences in subadults, perhaps indicating that this was an important cause of morbidity, and even an important cause of mortality, in children at these sites.

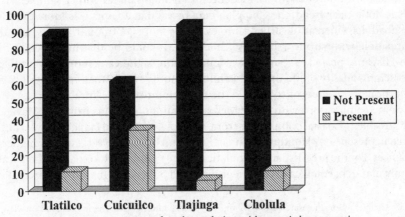

Figure 11.2. Percentage of total population with porotic hyperostosis.

Table 11.5: Incidence of Porotic Hyperostosis and Cribra Orbitalia by Sex and Age

Site	Females		Males		Subadults	
	No.	% affected	No.	% affected	No.	% affected
Porotic hyperostosis						
Tlatilco	128	10	88	14	51	10
Cuicuilco	29	38	33	36	10	20
Tlajinga	4	0	13	8	17	6
Cholula	57	9	43	5	62	19
Cribra orbitalia						
Tlatilco	96	19	66	23	42	43
Cuicuilco	24	38	29	31	8	25
Tlajinga	4	0	11	18	16	13
Cholula	43	21	31	19	43	54

Note: Individuals identified only as adults are not included, but there was only 1 of 5 individuals affected with cribra orbitalia and 1 of 24 with porotic hyperostosis, and so they do not affect the above patterns.

According to the paleopathological reports of other studies, we had expected to find an increase in these indicators, from Formative to Postclassic Mesoamerica, as populations became more dependent upon maize, or as infections and parasites increased with population density. Instead, Tlajinga presents low percentages of both porotic hyperostosis and cribra orbitalia for all age groups, in comparison with other series from the Basin of Mexico. All others, including the village site, have moderate incidences. The Tlajinga population seems to lack anemia problems in spite of its urban environment. This may be due to adequate iron in the diet, which buffered these individuals in spite of the other health problems they suffered, or else individuals tended to die of other causes before anemia was serious enough to be expressed in the cranium. For the Postclassic Period in the Basin of Mexico, Cholula displayed similar values as Cuicuilco in cribra orbitalia, although less porotic hyperostosis. Cholula subadults show more evidence of anemia than any other sample. While this is not a clear trend, the Cholulan data reveal that anemia was more prevalent in subadults, whereas in earlier samples, it was more common in adults, and thus compatible with survivorship past childhood. It could be that by the end of the pre-Hispanic period, anemia was a much more significant morbidity problem. Worsening quality of life impacted children more severely than in earlier times, a reflection of the effect of continued social development in Central Mexico.

Some comparisons with other Mesoamerican populations from the Maya area are possible.[16] Coastal populations from Yucatan, Xcaret, and Jaina, plus two sites located in present-day Honduras (Copán Rural and Urban) reveal generally higher incidences. For the pre-Hispanic population of the Quintana Roo coast of the Yucatan Peninsula, archaeological records register a high presence of marine resources. Playa

[16] See Chapter 10 on the Maya in this volume for further information. The information on Playa del Carmen is found in Marquez, Peraza, and Gamboa (1982).

del Carmen, a Maya Postclassic site located near Xcaret, has reported a 48% rate of healed porotic hyperostosis, including the subadults; for adults, the figures were 42% in males and 25% in females. Cribra orbitalia was present in 40% of the crania. The explanation for the high frequencies of cribra orbitalia and porotic hyperostosis could be related to diarrheal disease, as a result of water contamination and the exposure to fish-borne parasites, even though Playa del Carmen and Xcaret populations had rich diets based on marine resources. For the Maya sites, a more humid environment with greater numbers of parasites may account for the difference in rates. The more arid highland would have been less hospitable to the transmission of many parasites, and thus these Central Mexican populations suffered less from this problem.

Enamel Hypoplasia

The presence and frequency of dental enamel defects have been used as an index of the health status of archaeological populations and are among the most frequently studied indicators.[17] Tlatilco and Cuicuilco present similar frequencies of lines in permanent incisors, LPI (30% and 26%), and lines in permanent canines, LPC (43%); the values are slightly lower in Cholula (LPI 21% and LPC 33%). The prevalences in Tlajinga (LPI 81% and LPC 97%) are significantly higher (P < .05). Here the pattern is opposite that of iron-deficiency anemia, in that most samples have moderate incidences but Tlajinga is high.

Investigating differences by gender and age (Table 11.6), 51% of the sample could be scored for the permanent canine and 32% for the permanent incisor. The patterns are what would be expected, given the overall prevalences in the samples. Tlajinga is the only sample where having two or more hypoplasias is at all common, and this is true of all ages. Males and females within a site are again similar in prevalence. Subadults do not show greater frequencies in any of the populations over that of the adults, except Cuicuilco, but the sample is small. A hypoplastic prevalence greater than 40% might be considered as evidence of significant morbidity during tooth development from chronic nutritional and disease stress in a community. Only Cholula is below this level, although one-third of the sample is still affected. It is also possible that urban conditions at Cholula were such that more individuals died before such morbidity could be expressed on the teeth. Thus, this stress is significant, but certainly not excessive in comparison with many other prehistoric skeletal samples in the Western Hemisphere database, except Tlajinga. There is possibly a trend here, as the populations show increasing prevalence from Tlatilco to Tlajinga, although Cholula has less. In urban Tlajinga, the hypoplasias reflect a poor environment during childhood, but this does not further express itself as anemia nor does it prevent affected individuals from surviving to adulthood. In urban Cholula, the situation is more difficult to interpret, but it is possible that the higher prevalence of anemia, especially in subadults, made it harder to survive morbidity that causes hypoplasias. A deterioration of urban diets and environment through time would then be indicated.

---

[17] General information on hypoplasias can be found in this volume and in Martin et al. (1991).

Table 11.6: Comparison of Hypoplasias by Sex and Age

Site	Females			Males			Subadults			Unidentified adult		
	None	1 line	2+	None	1 line	2+	None	1 line	2+	None	1 line	2+
Permanent incisor												
Tlatilco	78%	18%	4%	67%	29%	4%	82%	18%	0	33%	67%	0
Cuicuilco	85%	15%	0	68%	32%	0	33%	33%	33%	100%		
Tlajinga	0	20%	80%	33%	33%	33%	20%	20%	60%			
Cholula	81%	16%	3%	82%	15%	4%	100%			56%	44%	
Permanent canine												
Tlatilco	62%	32%	6%	49%	42%	9%	69%	23%	8%	50%	50%	
Cuicuilco	60%	33%	7%	50%	38%	12%	50%	25%	25%	100%		
Tlajinga	0	40%	60%	0	47%	53%	25%	25%	50%	0		
Cholula	67%	31%	2%	70%	28%	2%	75%	13%	12%	58%	37%	5%

324

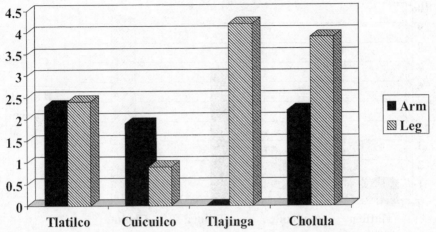

Figure 11.3. Percentages of individuals with arm and leg Trauma.

Traumas

Traumatic lesions are injuries primarily caused by physical force or by contact with blunt or sharp objects. Specific types of trauma provide a direct inference about specific behavior patterns. Certain activities predispose individuals to certain types of accidental trauma. Various forms of interpersonal violence (warfare, scalping, mutilation, lacerations) and surgical intervention (trepanation, amputation) may be identified. In Mesoamerican populations of the Basin of Mexico, traumas in general are low in the four series, and the evidence is from mostly healed bone fractures. Leg and arm traumas are similar in these populations (Figure 11.3); only Tlajinga and Cholula exhibit higher percents in the leg. From 160 Cholula cases observed, 3% ($n = 5$) show hand traumas. Cuicuilco had an even lower rate (2%) from 47 observed, and Tlatilco none. Skull, face, and nasal traumas have low frequencies, with the exception of face traumas in Cholula (Figure 11.4); Tlajinga exhibits the highest value of skull trauma, but the sample is small ($n = 4$). Cholula has higher percentages in arm, leg, skull, hand, and face traumas than the other populations. Traumatic lesion frequencies in this population, in comparison with the other periods, could be suggestive of changing behavior or activity.

Postclassic Mesoamerican societies have been characterized as militarist, involved in struggles and war. The Postclassic in the Basin of Mexico was a period of continuous change. There was great population mobility and participation in armed conflicts. The Cholula pattern may be a clear indication of intensification of various forms of interpersonal violence that were not present in the earlier societies, where militarism is late (Teotihuacan) or not very evident. We also found more traumas in urban populations, as in Tlajinga 33 (from Teotihuacan) and Cholula, than in the mixed-economy village of Tlatilco. There is a possibility that these could be related to violence, or to accidents from construction as a result of falling from a high structure, or merely by the vagaries of living. However, the Mesoamerican trauma frequencies are low in general, although females in Cholula have a higher rate of

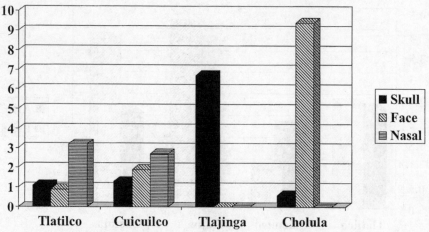

Figure 11.4. Percentages of individuals with skull, face, and nasal Trauma.

fracture, including the skull, 13%, than the 4% for males. Was skull and facial female trauma related to intentional domestic violence, the result of the general greater institutional violence of the Postclassic? Merbs's major finding in a survey of traumas among Aboriginal Australians was that as a general rule, female crania display more head trauma than males, but the same pattern is not found for other populations. He suggests that "women may not have been the victims of male attackers either, they could have been involved in arguments among themselves." We agree with Webb that the findings suggest that "there is no simple rule for interpreting what fracture patterns might represent in terms of a particular human activity or, if we want to be conservative, even basic behavior. One way of tackling the interpretative uncertainties of extrapolating behavior from bones is knowing something about the activities and lifestyle of the particular group in the first place."[18]

Degenerative Joint Disease

Degenerative joint disease has been reported in the majority of the archaeological populations, and the primary cause is related to biomechanical wear and tear and functional stress. Biomechanical stress is referred to as degenerative joint disease (DJD) and linked to activity. The pattern of degenerative joint disease can provide clues about the life of past individuals. For the arm, percents for shoulder and elbow frequencies of initial degenerative disease are highest for Tlajinga, and similar for Tlatilco, Cuicuilco, and Cholula (Figure 11.5). As osteoarthritis is age-related, comparisons must be age-controlled. Here, the proportion of young versus older adults is similar in the cases of Tlatilco, Cuicuilco, and Tlajinga. Only Cholula is a younger sample (see Table 11.3). Major DJD was found in Cholula (3%), including one case which exhibited immobilization. Wrist DJD percents in Cuicuilco and Tlajinga were twice those for Tlatilco and Cholula. Hand percents were again higher for Tlajinga and Cuicuilco and lower for Cholula and Tlatilco. This shows a trend toward greater

---

[18] Merbs (1989:204–205); Webb (1995:192) for the quotation.

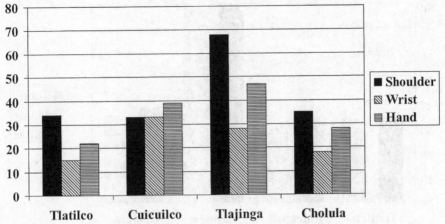

Figure 11.5. Percentages of individuals with DJD in the arm.

frequencies of stress in Tlajinga and Cuicuilco, suggesting more use of these joints. In the case of Tlajinga, these generally high indicators in relation to the similar ages at Tlatilco and Cuicuilco might be related to the artisanal activities, although occupation is not easily determined on the basis of just arthritic degeneration.[19] The involvement in Cholula is notable, as this is a younger sample, but still has similar prevalences to sites with older adults. For example, gender differences show greatest incidence in females in these joints in Cuicuilco and Cholula.

Hip and knee DJD is greater in Tlajinga and similar for Cholula, Cuicuilco, and Tlatilco (see Figure 11.6). The Tlajinga involvement is all light, while there is a low percentage of major involvement in the other samples. Cholula is the highest, and this may also reflect the effects of the greater institutional violence. Cervical, thoracic, and lumbar DJD present widely different ranges (see Figure 11.7). Cervical DJD has a higher prevalence in Cholula, while Tlajinga is higher in thoracic and lumbar. Again, the younger sample shows more involvement than might be expected, reflecting the biomechanical stress that the commoners of that late urban center might have experienced. In general, the dense urban populations of Tlajinga and Cholula have higher prevalences of DJD than do populations from earlier times. Gender differences in DJD across all four populations show greater prevalences in females, with the exception of thoracic and lumbar frequencies, which are higher for males.

Comparing populations, Tlatilco has the lowest values in general, and there is an increase through time in Cuicuilco, Tlajinga, and Cholula. The population of Tlatilco was not as dependent on maize consumption as that of Cuicuilco. In Tlajinga and Cholula, the basis of the diet was maize. The Mesoamerican series studied here show a rising rate of DJD with the shift from a hamlet-like subsistence economy to an urban one based on trade, such as Cholula's. The former, based as we said on foraging, fishing, and farming, was characterized by lower rates than the latter. Urban populations experienced greater stress, due not only to a more sustained struggle for subsistence, but also to mechanical demands in the construction of big buildings,

[19] See Waldron (1994).

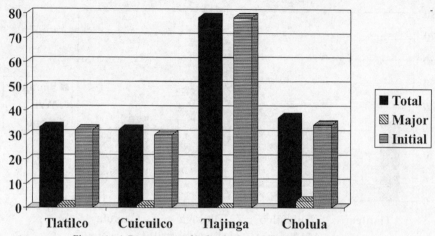

Figure 11.6. Percentages of individuals with DJD in hip and knee.

the manufacture of goods, and transportation. For females, in particular in societies heavily dependent upon maize as the principal source of calories, the preparation of food, such as making tortillas, was an arduous task that not only consumed great expenditures of time and energy but also produced severe degenerative disease at the wrist joints. The high male DJD at the cervical vertebrae for Cholula seems the result of greater mechanical stress, from carrying heavy loads with the "mecapal," a wide rope placed on the forehead to sustain a large, heavy bundle on the back. Archaeological information identifies Cholula as a stratified society. The skeletal series corresponds to common people, as is evidenced by the location of burials and the nature of the associated burial goods. These changes in the Postclassic may be related to the larger sphere in which Cholula was involved, such that transportion of goods was a more important activity in general than in earlier periods.

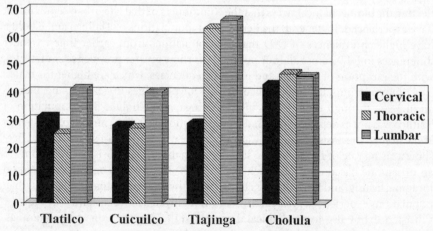

Figure 11.7. Percentages of individuals with DJD in the vertebrae.

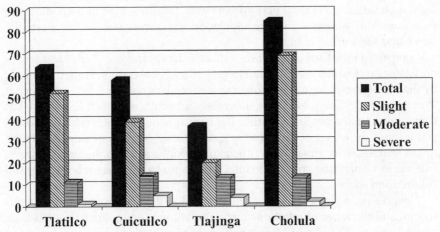

Figure 11.8. Percent of total population with tibial infection.

Infections

Periostitis in the tibia is reported here as frequencies and the degree of severity to characterize the prevalence of infections at the population level. In paleopathological research, tibia periostitis has been used as one of the best indicators of systemic infectious disease, but the presence of skeletal and systemic infection was also recorded for this project. Figure 11.8 presents the incidence of tibial periosteal reactions for pre-Hispanic populations of the Valley of Mexico, with the total representing the percent of scorable individuals with this indicator, and then broken into categories of severity. Cholula is the highest and Tlajinga is the lowest, although the proportions of individuals affected by moderate and severe cases are similar across all sites. Figure 11.9 presents the incidence of skeletal periostitis. Here Cuicuilco is the lowest, while the greatest proportion of systemic infection is at Tlajinga. Cholula has the

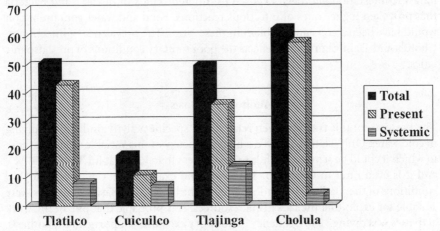

Figure 11.9. Percent of total population with skeletal periostitis.

highest prevalence of skeletal periostitis as well. Tlatilco is high in both infectious indicators, indicating that a village population was no more free of this morbidity factor than were urban ones.

Comparing incidence-of-infection indicators by age and sex (Table 11.7) reveals no significant sex differences by site. However, the Cholula sample is affected mostly by slight reactions, whereas the proportion of moderate/severe ones are greater at Tlajinga and Cuicuilco, especially for males. Subadults are much less affected at Cuicuilco than at other sites. Tlatilco has similar incidences across all categories, and it is not the lowest or highest in any. Adult males seem more impacted in the urban samples, which may reflect their more public activities in these societies, whereas in Tlatilco, the exposure to infections seems to be equal for both sexes and children and adults.

The presence of infections has been recorded in the majority of skeletal populations, and the range of infectious-disease response is quite varied. Pre-Hispanic populations of the Basin of Mexico were only moderately biologically stressed in terms of periosteal reactions, with incidences from 36% to 65% in tibial infection and 37% to 50% in skeletal infection in the Formative Period in Tlatilco and Cuicuilco and the Classic at Tlajinga. However, the situation became worse for the Postclassic population of Cholula, which presented the highest values in both tibial infection and skeletal infection, although most involvement was slight. Ecological conditions for Tlatilco and Cuicuilco were relatively similar. Infectious-disease rates in Tlatilco and Cuicuilco could be related to water contamination of the lake. Tlajinga appears not to have had as much infectious disease as Cholula, even though both are urban populations. However, Tlajinga had more serious involvement when disease was present. This could be related to lifestyle in that barrio of Teotihuacan and is another example of the high morbidity present in that sample. For Cholula, this population lived in the core of a big urban center with all the adverse sanitary circumstances of urban living. Population density was high, with more consumption and more garbage. Cholulans could have suffered from extreme parasitic infestation and been exposed to different kinds of diseases and bacteria that provoked higher rates of infectious reactions. Food and water contamination would have been a constant problem in these cities. The prevalence of infection in Cholula and Tlajinga probably reflects the poor sanitary conditions of pre-Hispanic cities.

Auditory Exostosis

The presence of this trait has been related to a specific activity: individuals diving in cold water. Only Tlatilco showed a high frequency of this variable (29%) in those in which it could be scored. Cholula's rate was less than half that for Tlatilco (12%), and it is even rarer in Cuicuilco. There were no examples at Tlajinga. Ecological conditions of the Tlatilco population, close to the lakes in the Basin of Mexico, were suitable for exploiting the lacustrine resources. It is probable that one of the work activities was diving. The frequency of auditory exostosis supports this hypothesis.

Table 11.7: Comparison of Infectious Reactions by Sex and Age

Site	Females			Males			Subadults		
	None	Slight	Mod/sev	None	Slight	Mod/sev	None	Slight	Mod/sev
Tibial infection									
Tlatilco	37%	51%	11%	32%	57%	11%	41%	41%	18%
Cuicuilco	25%	52%	23%	48%	33%	19%	67%	22%	11%
Tlajinga	60%	30%	10%	59%	12%	29%	68%	21%	11%
Cholula	11%	71%	18%	15%	60%	25%	22%	73%	5%
	None	Present	Systemic	None	Present	Systemic	None	Present	Systemic
Skeletal infection									
Tlatilco	52%	42%	6%	45%	47%	8%	40%	47%	12%
Cuicuilco	67%	12%	21%	74%	12%	14%	83%	0	17%
Tlajinga	58%	42%	0	50%	22%	28%	45%	45%	10%
Cholula	30%	62%	8%	30%	65%	5%	49%	49%	2%

Cavities and Abscesses

Dental caries are the result of disease produced by demineralization of the dental tissue by organic acids caused from the bacterial fermentation of dietary carbohydrates. Carious lesions were present among pre-Hispanic populations of the Basin of Mexico. Abscesses are another indicator of infection and sanitary conditions. Figure 11.10 compares the measures of dental pathology developed for the Western Hemisphere project. The caries index is the best comparative measure, and here Cuicuilco is highest, while the others are similar. The high Cuicuilco caries index could be related to porotic hyperostosis and cribra orbitalia frequencies that are highest for this population, and could indicate a starchy diet. Abscess rates in all populations are fairly similar. In recent population studies, tooth loss has been associated with carious lesions, and high loss could underestimate caries incidences. Here we are using a cavities-adjusted missing–decayed index (CAMDI), developed for this project, to allow better comparisons among different populations. Premortem tooth loss is associated with advancing age, as well as poor dental hygiene. At Tlajinga, we found the lowest CAMDI (0.56); at Tlatilco the highest (0.96). Cuicuilco and Cholula are indistinguishable at 0.79 and 0.77, respectively.

There are some interesting patterns by sex. Females have higher indexes compared to the males at Tlatilco (0.87 to 0.75) and Cuicuilco (0.91 to 0.68). The disparity is especially great at Cuicuilco. On the other hand, at Tlajinga and Cholula, no gendered differentiation is apparent in this regard (0.62 females to 0.63 males, and 0.65 females to 0.68 males, respectively). The earlier populations appear to have divergent diets by sex, with females probably more dependent on agricultural foods, while males had more access to meat. In Tlatilco, males probably did the bulk of wild resource harvesting and may have eaten more while doing so. This is a pattern often seen in mixed economies, such as this village. By the Classic Period with its fully developed urban environments, males and females shared similar diets. Access was probably determined more by economic status and earning potential to acquire

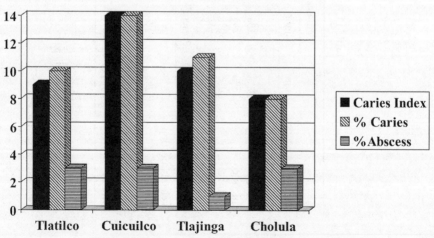

Figure 11.10. Comparison of dental pathology indexes.

food from markets than by any other single factor. Thus, Teotihuacan and Cholula are fairly similar. The overall index for Tlajinga is less than for the individual sexes, indicating not much dental pathology in subadults. The Cholula index is higher than for individual sexes, indicating that dental pathology among subadults increased in the Postclassic.

DISCUSSION

Health and nutrition of ancient populations have been among the most important issues of current bioarchaeology, but our knowledge about the health conditions of Mesoamerican pre-Hispanic populations remains shaky. The beginnings of the bioarchaeological integral approach are found at Altar de Sacrificios (first published in 1972).[20] Since then, only a few similar works have appeared. The Tlatilco, Cuicuilco, Tlajinga 33, and Cholula skeletal series, from the Basin of Mexico, were selected with the objective of characterizing population health conditions and to contrast the results of the diverse stress indicators within and among populations that had different ways of life, with a diversity of social, economic, and political conditions. All are located in a tropical, highland, arid environment. Tlatilco is one of the ancient villages from the Early and Middle Formative Period, where social and economical differentiation was present but not greatly elaborated, and where the way of life was subsistence horticulture supplemented by lacustrine resources and other wild resources regularly consumed in the diet. Cuicuilco represents a population living in one of the first ceremonial centers in the Middle Formative and continuing to the Late Formative. The Cuicuilco site probably represents a higher level of sociopolitical centralization, with more social differentiation than found in other contemporary regional centers in the Basin and at earlier Tlatilco. The Tlajinga 33 population, from Teotihuacan, represents a sample of the common people working in ceramics and lapidary in the biggest urban city of the Classic Period. Cholula was a major sociopolitical site in Central Mexico in two periods, the first during the AD 950–1150 phase and later during the late Postclassic. Cholula's inhabitants lived in a dense nuclear settlement and worked as artisans, merchants, and builders. Both the Tlajinga and Cholula samples are from highly complex social systems, with definite differences in social status that would affect access to resources, and both samples represent the less privileged members of their city. The general evaluation of the diverse stress indicators used in this research gives some insights about the adjustment of the Tlatilco, Cuicuilco, Tlajinga, and Cholula populations to their contexts.

In relation to other populations of the Basin of Mexico, Tlatilco presented low porotic hyperostosis frequencies, but cribra orbitalia rates were similar to all the others except Tlajinga. The highest frequencies for this indicator were for Cuicuilco. Enamel hypoplasia frequencies in Tlatilco were similar to those in Cuicuilco and Cholula, but by far the highest were in Tlajinga. On the other hand, the lowest percentage of porotic hyperostosis (6%) and cribra orbitalia (12%) was in Tlajinga.

---

[20] Saul (1972).

Tlatilco has greater stature in comparison with Cuicuilco and Cholula, among samples with reasonable sizes. Tlatilco infections were 65% for the tibia and 50% for skeletal reactions, little higher than in Cuicuilco and Tlajinga, but lower than in Cholula. Thus, in these indicators, there are some potentially confusing findings. The more egalitarian and smaller settlement of Tlatilco might have been expected to exhibit less of these skeletal indicators of stress than the later, more dense populations characterized by more status inequalities, whereas it usually is comparable to one or more of the urban populations. Conversely, the urban populations from Tlajinga and Cholula do have the highest frequencies of some indicators but are low on others. Comparison with the other indicators also reveals a complex picture.

In relation to general activities indicated through degenerative joint disease frequencies, the higher prevalences were generally among the later urban populations. Tlajinga is an older population, made up of lapidary and ceramic artisans, and so we are not surprised to find patterns of involvement of upper body and some vertebrae. This appears to be related to more stress due to the craft manufacture than to other activities developed by Tlatilco and Cholula populations, even though the activity pattern from all these populations is likely to be different. The surprise is that the younger adult sample has significant involvement in several joints higher than in the older adult samples from Cuicuilco and Tlatilco, indicating that more biomechanical stress was part of the way of life for these commoners. The Cholula population was more diversified than Tlajinga, and the skeletal collection corresponds to individuals with different occupations, although individuals involved in transportation of goods may be more represented than some other occupations.

Trauma is in general low, less than 6% of the samples. Only in Tlatilco were there a substantial fraction of individuals (almost 30%) with auditory exotosis, probably related to exploitation of lake resources. The low trauma values may seem surprising, because especially for the urban centers of the Classic and Postclassic, these were probably fairly militaristic societies. However, given the common Mesoamerican practice of capturing victims for human sacrifice in war, many war casualties would not have returned to their residences to be recovered in any skeletal series. Thus, most traumas are probably the result of accidents in daily life, although the nose fractures in Tlatilco and the face fractures and head trauma in Cholula are the best evidence present here for interpersonal violence.

Caries in the four populations reveal low values in a range from 8% to 14%, with the highest incidence of cavities found in Cuicuilco. The missing–decayed index is similar for Tlatilco, Cuicuilco, and Tlajinga from 0.24 to 0.29, while Cholula was the lowest at 0.19, probably because of its relative youth. The abscess index is low and quite similar for all four samples. The age adjusted missing–decayed index exhibits the highest for Tlatilco (0.96) and Cuicuilco, and Cholula had similar indexes (0.77, 0.79); the lowest was in Tlajinga (0.56). These indicate that at least part of the reason that caries rates are fairly low is that premortem tooth loss is quite common in these populations, perhaps because of carious teeth and/or heavy tooth attrition. Since all populations consumed maize, the high carbohydrate diet would have had a deleterious effect on dental health. Looking at the data by gender, females from Tlatilco and Cuicuilco have higher indexes than males, while Tlajinga and Cholula do not present gender differences (0.63, 0.62, 0.68, and 0.65 respectively). This indicates that for the earlier samples, the diets of males and females might have differed, probably because males might have done more collecting/hunting, and eaten more of the fruits of their foraging, while females were consuming proportionately more domesticated crops with the correspondingly higher carbohydrate diet. By the full Classic and later in these larger urban settlements, diets of males and females no longer reveal this distinction, probably because both sexes are getting their food from the market for the households. The Maya populations, which are also highly dependent on maize and other crops, have similar high missing–decayed indices (0.95 to 0.71). Coastal Yucatan populations have the lowest, probably due to substantial quantities of marine resources in the diet.

All of the populations presented in this chapter, in comparison with other populations studied in this volume, have, with few exceptions, mostly moderate to high frequencies of all indicators analyzed, and all present clear evidence that chronic stress was common in childhood and among adults. In general, we see a pattern of increase over time in cribra orbitalia and porotic hyperostosis from the village of Tlatilco to the great urban centers like Cholula. According to the infection results, with all frequencies between 60% and 80%, we observe poor sanitary conditions in these prehistoric groups. Stature, as a general indicator of health, exhibits a reduction from Formative Tlatilco to Postclassic Cholula, particularly in males, so that there is some overall deterioration in child health through time. The populations from the lower status of the great urban centers in this area, Tlajinga 33 and Cholula, often are those with the highest frequencies of various pathologies, although not for all. Tlajinga is low in porotic hyperostosis and cribra orbitalia, while Cholula has low frequencies of enamel hypoplasia, for example. The indicators thus do give evidence of the differences in the situations and environments of each of the various populations and do not just reflect increasing density and social inequality. Thus, the village of Tlatilco might have been expected to have the lowest indicators generally, because it is from the earliest and least complex society, but instead, it has generally moderate incidences of most pathologies. Tlatilco is always among the lower in prevalences, though, and is only high in the age-adjusted dental indexes, indicating the different and more varied diet of this earlier society. Thus, there is in general a trend of increasing burden of skeletal indicators of stress through time in the Basin of Mexico, culminating in the dense urban populations.

Mark Nathan Cohen has expressed a general hypothesis, discussed in the Introduction, that increasing social complexity, because of its inequalities of wealth and access to basic resources and increasing populations living in urban centers, leads to general declines in health and the quality of life for the average individual in past societies. The Central Mexican area, because of its long history as the center of Mesoamerican civilization, is a good place to test Cohen's hypothesis. Discussion of the individual indicators above revealed that while there is no uniform increase among the stress indicators with more complex, urban populations, the overall combination of indicators gives Tlajinga and Cholula more morbidity factors that impacted the quality of life. The comparative perspective afforded by the Western Hemisphere project does lead to a clearer overall picture. The health index, especially expressed as percent of maximum in the sample, clearly shows that the Central Mexican samples fall into the bottom third of the overall rankings. The highest is Tlatilco at 68% of maximum, Cuicuilco and Cholula similar at 66%, and Tlajinga lowest at 62%. Tlatilco is better here, even if not dramatically, over the three urban populations. The clearly lower-status urban population from Teotihuacan, the largest urban center in the sample, has the lowest quality of life, which is what might be expected. That Cuicuilco and Cholula are not much worse than Tlatilco is perhaps surprising. These might indicate that urban living in particular cases in Central Mexico was not so much more lacking in quality of life for its inhabitants as a large village with a mixed domesticated and wild subsistence, but more samples and knowledge from all sites is needed. On the other hand, it is possible that the dependence on agricultural products in an arid, highland environment, where crop reductions and failures from drought and frost may be common and where water was a scarce and too often contaminated resource, may make village life in the Basin of Mexico less healthy than in many other environments. Thus, the conditions at Tlatilco were not much better than at the other sites, because the Basin of Mexico is not an easy environment to live in with the pre-Hispanic technology. Nevertheless, although the quality of life was low compared to that of other parts of the Americas, it was not enough of a handicap to prevent the Basin of Mexico from becoming a locus of settlement and the center of dynamic civilizations. The overall trend present here is that as societies became more internally differentiated and more urban in settlement, there is a decline in the quality of life and life expectancy, much as Cohen's hypothesis would predict.

Among the pre-Columbian populations, the quality of life of individuals in the samples was certainly not as good as it might have been. That modern Mexico City has health problems resulting from intensive use of an arid environment and a dense urban population places it as the most recent example of a process that began with Teotihuacan and Cuicuilco around the beginning of the Common Era. Because of its long history of occupation and urban settlement, the Basin of Mexico is a crucial place to study what happens to people and society as they become parts of ever larger, denser, and hierarchically organized societies. Further research in health trends is needed. Especially important is the analysis and availability of more skeletal samples from the pre-Columbian societies, to test and refine the patterns depicted here. The historical demographic and epidemic records and skeletal research possible from the colonial period will help explain what happened at the time of contact of the Mesoamerican civilizations with Europeans. Integration of these data with public health information from Mexico City in the nineteenth and twentieth centuries will allow researchers to study and refine hypotheses and generalizations about the influence of urbanization and its effect on health under such different technological and historical circumstances. We have only made a small first step in this study and look forward to taking a second larger step in the future.

REFERENCES

Anderson, James E. 1967. The Human Skeletons. In *The Prehistory of the Tehuacan Valley*, vol. 1, ed. D. S. Byers, pp. 91–113. Austin: University of Texas Press.

Blanton, Richard E., Gary Feinman, and Laura Kowalski. 1993. *Ancient Mesoamerica*, 2d ed. Cambridge: Cambridge University Press.

Camargo, Lourdes, Lourdes Marquez, and Minerva Prado. 1999. Paleodemografía del México Prehispánico. In *Hacia la Demografía del Siglo* xx, vol. 3, pp. 227–248. Mexico City: SOMEDE.

Cohen, Mark Nathan. 1989. *Health and the Rise of Civilization*. New Haven, Conn.: Yale University Press.

Cook, Noble David. 1998. *Born to Die: Disease and New World Conquest, 1492–1650*. Cambridge: Cambridge University Press.

Cowgill, George L. 1996. State and Society at Teotihuacan, Mexico. *Annual Review of Anthropology* 26:129–161.

Del Angel, Andres. 1996. La Estatura de la Poblacíon Prehispánica de México. *Estudios de Antropología Física en México. Estudios sobre la Poblacion Antigua y Contemporanea*, ed. S. Lopez, C. Serrano, and L. Marquez, pp. 55–78. Mexico: Instituto de Investigaciones Antropológicas, UNAM.

De Vries, Jan. 1984. *European Urbanization 1500–1800*. Cambridge, Mass.: Harvard University Press.

Garcia Moll, Roberto, Daniel Juarez Cossio, Carmen Pijoan Aguade, et al. 1992. *Catálogo de Entierros de San Luis Tlatilco, México. Temporada IV*. México: Instituto Nacional de Antropología e Historía.

Henige, David. 1998. *Numbers from Nowhere: The American Indian Contact Population Debate*. Norman: University of Oklahoma Press.

Lopez, Sergio, Zaid Lagunas, and Carlos Serrano. 1976. *Enterramientos Humanos de la Zona Arqueológica de Cholula, Puebla*. Mexico: Coleccíon Cientifica no. 44, Instituto Nacional de Antropología e Historía.

Marquez, Lourdes, Ma. Elena Peraza, and Jose Gamboa. 1982. *Playa del Carmen: Una Poblacíon de la Costa Oriental en el Postclásico (Un Estudio Osteológico)*. Mexico: Coleccíon Científica no.119, Instituto Nacional de Antropología e Historía.

Marquez Morfin, Lourdes, and Andres del Angel. 1997. Height among Prehispanic Maya of the Yucatan Peninsula: A Reconsideration. In *Bones of the Ancestors*, ed. S. Whittington and D. Reed, pp. 51–61. Washington, D.C.: Smithsonian Institution Press.

Martin, L. Debra, Alan H. Goodman, George J. Armelagos, and Ann L. Magennis. 1991. *Black Mesa Anasazi Health: Reconstructing Life from Patterns of Death and Disease*. Occasional Paper No. 14. Carbondale: Center for Archaeological Investigations, Southern Illinois University at Carbondale.

McCaa, Robert. 2000. The Peopling of Mexico from Origins to Revolution. In *The Population History of North America*, ed. Michael Haines and Richard Steckel, pp. 241–304. Cambridge: Cambridge University Press.

Merbs, Charles F. Trauma. 1989. In *Reconstruction of Life from the Skeleton*, ed. M. Y. Iscan and K. A. R. Kennedy, pp. 161–190. New York: Alan R. Liss.

Porter, Muriel. 1953. *Tlatilco and the Pre-Classic Culture of the New World*. New York: Wenner Gren Foundation for Archaeological Research.

Powell, Mary Lucas. 1988. *Status and Health in Prehistory. A Case Study of the Moundville Chiefdom*. Washington, D.C.: Smithsonian Press.

Romano, Arturo. 1972. Sistema de Enterramientos en Tlatilco. *Religíon en Mésoamerica* (II Mesa Redonda de la Sociedad Méxicana de Antropología): 365–368.

Sanders, William T., Jeffrey R. Parsons, and Robert S. Santley. 1979. *The Basin of Mexico: Ecological Processes in the Evolution of a Civilization*. New York: Academic Press.

Saul, Frank P. 1972. *The Human Skeletal Remains of Altar de Sacrificios*. Papers of the Peabody Museum of Archaeology and Ethnology, vol. 63, no. 2. Cambridge, Mass.: Peabody Museum.

Schavelzon, Daniel. 1993. *La Píramide de Cuicuilco*. Mexico: Fondo de Cultura Económica.

Serra Puche, Mari Carmen. 1988. *Los Recursos Lacustres de la Cuenca de México Durante el Formativo*. Mexico: Universidad Nacional Autónoma de Mexico.

Storey, Rebecca. 1992. *Life and Death in the Ancient City of Teotihuacan: A Modern Paleodemographic Synthesis*. Tuscaloosa: University of Alabama Press.

Sugiura, Yoko. 1993. El Ocaso de las Ciudades y los Movimientos Poblacionales en el Altiplano Central. In *El Poblamiento de México, Tomo 1: El México Prehispánico*, pp. 190–213. Mexico: Consejo Nacional de Poblacíon.

Thomas, Hugh. 1993. *The Conquest of Mexico*. London: Hutchinson.

Tolstoy, Paul. 1989. Coapexco and Tlatilco, Sites with Olmec Materials in the Basin of México. In *Regional Perspective on the Olmecs*, ed. Robert J. Sharer and David Grove, pp. 85–121. Cambridge: Cambridge University Press.

Waldron, Tony. 1994. *Counting the Dead*. Chichester: John Wiley and Sons.

Walker, P. L. 1986. Porotic Hyperostosis in a Marine-Dependent California Indian Population. *American Journal of Physical Anthropology* 69:345–354.

Webb, Stephen. 1995. *Paleopathology of Aboriginal Australians: Health and Disease Across a Hunter-Gatherer Continent*. Cambridge: Cambridge University Press.

Widmer, Randolph, and Rebecca Storey. 1993. Social Organization and Household Structure of Teotihuacan Apartment Compound: S3W1:33 of Tlajinga Barrio. In *Prehispanic Domestic Units in Western Mesoamerica: Studies of Household, Compound, and Residence*, ed. R. Santley and K. Hirth, pp. 87–104. Boca Raton, Fl.: CRC Press.

PART V

NATIVE AMERICANS AND EURO-AMERICANS IN SOUTH AMERICA

Introduction

The oldest sites studied in the project were located in South America, and as a group the average age of the sites was about 2,200 years BP (before the present, which is taken as 1950). The skeletons of Santa Elena, Ecuador, are from sites inhabited about 7,500 years ago. The sites in the area are also characterized by ecological diversity, encompassing a wide range of habitats defined by topography, elevation, and proximity to water resources. This diversity is valuable for investigating possible causes or explanations for variations in health.

As a group, the South Americans studied in this project were reasonably healthy. Both Native Americans on this continent and the Euro-Americans in Ecuador scored above average on the health index despite slow growth in childhood (see Table V.1). Their uniformly low scores on stature were overcome by high results in other areas, particularly hypoplasias and infections. The low stature scores do not mesh with other indicators of early childhood health (hypoplasias and anemia), which suggests that growth failure may have occurred later in childhood, that is, adolescence. Indicators of chronic stress were virtually absent (scores equal or near 100) at several sites for hypoplasias, anemia, dental disease, and trauma. The group who lived in Brazil was among the healthiest populations in the 65 sites under study.

Not all South Americans were healthy, however, as indicated by results for several sites in Peru and Chile. These locations were unhealthy for a variety of reasons, including a high incidence of hypoplasias (Chiribaya), poor dental health (northern Chile), and frequent degenerative joint disease (Yaral and northern Chile).

Table V.1: Health Index and Component Scores of South American Populations

Investigator	Age BP	Description	Index	Stature	Hyp.	Anemia	Dental	Inf.	DJD	Trauma
		Native Americans								
Neves	1200	Coastal Brazil	91.8	*	88.4	100.0	82.9	*	93.4	94.4
Neves	3000	Shell mounds, southern Brazil	87.1	*	75.4	83.6	87.3	*	98.0	91.2
Buikstra	0700	Estuquina, Peru	85.0	*	60.3	92.7	100.0	78.1	86.1	92.6
Ubelaker	7425	Sta. Elena, Ecuador	83.4	8.7	99.7	100.0	91.1	98.7	94.8	90.8
Ubelaker	2160	Highland Ecuador	81.6	7.4	99.7	97.1	94.0	93.5	85.1	94.4
Ubelaker	4663	Realto, Ecuador	77.3	1.2	96.4	99.3	79.4	95.8	80.5	88.4
Ubelaker	1760	South coast, Ecuador	75.1	2.7	89.1	93.1	81.8	94.1	77.3	87.6
Ubelaker	2050	North coast, Ecuador	72.7	6.8	94.2	100.0	89.7	58.1	71.4	88.7
Ubelaker	0395	Quito convent, Ecuador	71.0	4.8	89.1	95.7	69.3	84.8	94.6	58.8
Arriaza	1175	Maitas Chirb., Chile	69.8	1.1	*	99.8	73.5	98.2	76.2	*
Buikstra	0700	Yaral, Peru	69.4	1.2	*	87.1	100.0	71.5	56.8	100.0
Arriaza	6015	Coastal Chile	68.6	0.4	*	88.4	86.4	86.1	81.5	*
Buikstra	0700	San Geron., Peru	67.8	4.0	48.4	79.6	89.3	72.7	61.3	100.0
Buikstra	0700	Chiribaya, Peru	67.5	3.2	48.4	87.5	86.4	80.1	67.7	98.8
Neves	1175	Northern Chile	59.1	1.9	71.2	90.0	55.3	64.1	51.4	80.2
		Average, Native Americans	75.1	3.6	82.9	92.9	84.4	82.8	78.4	89.7
		Std. dev., Native Americans	9.0	2.8	17.0	6.7	11.7	13.3	14.4	10.8
		Euro-Americans								
Ubelaker	0190	San Francisco church, Ecuador	76.9	16.9	99.4	99.6	62.1	98.3	89.8	72.2
Ubelaker	0090	San Francisco church, Ecuador	72.2	12.8	91.0	99.7	67.9	95.2	78.9	59.8
Ubelaker	0300	San Francisco church, Ecuador	70.9	3.7	98.6	94.6	71.8	72.8	79.8	75.0
		Average, Euro-Americans	73.3	11.1	96.3	98.0	67.3	88.8	82.8	69.0
		Std. dev, Euro-Americans	2.6	5.5	3.8	2.4	4.0	11.4	4.9	6.6
		Average, 65 sites	72.6	20.7	71.1	90.5	81.8	75.1	78.9	85.7
		Std. dev, 65 sites	7.98	16.86	24.59	11.53	10.39	16.97	12.26	16.12
		Minimum, 65 sites	53.5	0.4	9.8	53.2	55.3	44.1	41.6	10.8
		Maximum, 65 sites	91.8	67.8	99.7	100.0	100.0	98.7	100.0	100.0

* = not available.
Source: Consolidated database.

CHAPTER TWELVE

Patterns of Health and Nutrition in Prehistoric and Historic Ecuador

Douglas H. Ubelaker and Linda A. Newson

ABSTRACT

The prehistory and history of health and nutrition in Ecuador are examined from 22 samples of human remains drawn from sites that date from about 6000 BC to AD 1940 and come from diverse ecological environments. The study suggests a deterioration of health and nutrition with the beginnings of agriculture and increased sedentism. It also reveals less evidence of morbidity in prehistoric samples from the highlands compared to the coastal regions. However, within the coastal samples there were variations between the tropical humid north coast and the more arid south coast that related to differences in the natural environment and in the character of societies living there. Apart from the higher frequencies of periosteal lesions and evidence of trauma, generally the north coast samples revealed less evidence of morbidity than those from the south coast. The skeletal evidence reveals little change in health and nutrition following the Spanish Conquest. This may reflect in part the samples available, but also the fact that traumatic events, such as epidemics that are noted in the documentary sources, left no mark on the skeleton. The study suggests that health and nutrition in Ecuador were generally better than in other regions of Latin America, notably Mexico.

Scholars generally agree that when European explorers penetrated the New World it was already occupied by diverse peoples. Scholars also agree that their populations declined as a result of the introduction of new pathogens and the cultural changes brought by colonial rule. However, there is less agreement on the magnitude of the decline and on exactly what new pathogens were introduced, the extent of their impact, and their significance relative to others factors implicated in the decline. To some extent, the disagreement results from varying conceptions of the size of the New World populations prior to European contact and the state of their health. Some proponents of extensive population decline, such as Borah (1964), Crosby (1972), and Dobyns (1983), argue that population numbers were very large and, although they sometimes recognize that the environment was not completely disease-free, they often assume that death due to disease was minimal prior to European contact. From this perspective, the healthy environment allowed populations to increase to their full potential, but set them up for a tremendous mortality blow when the European pathogens arrived.

Others find the evidence for such large precontact numbers less compelling and suggest that the precontact New World populations suffered significant morbidity and mortality, similar to that sustained by their contemporaries in the Old World. All agree that the diseases introduced by Europeans created major problems for New World peoples, but this school would also argue that native populations were already in decline in some areas due to disease and other factors. Much of this evidence is archaeological in origin and is derived from the analysis of archaeologically recovered human remains. The study of human remains has not only documented the presence of significant morbidity and mortality in the Americas prior to European contact (see Larsen 1994), but also suggested a general temporal increase in these problems, again prior to the arrival of the European pathogens.

Most scholars suggest that this pattern of increasing morbidity is likely due to profound cultural changes and the gradual increase in population size and density, which in most areas of the New World have been associated with the development of agriculture (Cohen and Armelagos 1984; Cohen 1989). While agriculture offered its practitioners the advantage over hunting, gathering, and fishing of being able to control their food supply, in many cases, it often resulted in a less-diverse food supply and, in some areas, an overreliance on maize, a food with some nutritional disadvantages. The practice of agriculture also involved increased sedentism and population density, factors that favor the contamination of water and food sources and the general development and spread of infectious disease.

Works summarized by Cohen and Armelagos (1984), Verano and Ubelaker (1992), and others have suggested that whereas significant morbidity and mortality was present in the Americas prior to European contact, their expression varied regionally. Since the geographic setting and cultures of Native Americans varied enormously, it is not surprising that patterns of health also varied. To a large extent, this chapter, as well as the entire volume, explores the evidence for this variability in a systematic manner.

In Ecuador, enough historical, archaeological, and physical anthropological research has been done to enable preliminary examination of some of these problems. Do physical anthropological and historical studies document the disease impact of European contact? Does the evidence support a temporal increase in morbidity and mortality prior to European contact? If so, what geographic patterning is apparent, and can it be explained by geographical, cultural, or other factors? Skeletal collections from Ecuador span the course of human history in the region. The 22 samples analyzed here begin with those from the preceramic and preagricultural site of Las Vegas on the Santa Elena peninsula, dated about 6000 BC, and end with an historic series from the San Francisco church in Quito, which includes some remains as recent as AD 1940. The collections provide a unique opportunity to study temporal variations in health and nutrition that can be associated with major cultural changes, such as the beginnings of agriculture, increased sedentism, and the onset of social complexity. They can also throw light on the impact of the Spanish Conquest from 1534. The only major cultural changes for which the current skeletal evidence can

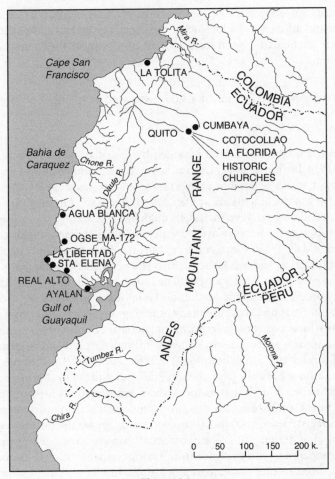

Figure 12.1.

provide few insights are those associated with Inca conquest, which began about 1460.

It is possible to examine not only temporal variations in health and nutrition but also geographical differences. Ecuador is a country of marked environmental diversity, and the sites (see Figure 12.1) are located at varying altitudes and in different climatic and ecological zones. In addition to the basic distinction between the coastal lowlands and the Andean highlands, where mountain peaks average 3,000 to 4,000 meters, there are marked climatic and ecological differences between the north and south coasts. The north coast has a tropical humid climate and supports a cloak of tropical rain forest, but within a few hundred miles to the south, the vegetation changes to desert-like scrub as the coast comes under the influence of the cool Humboldt current and conditions become drier. The nature of subsistence and settlement patterns in these regions differed, as did the opportunities for the spread of infections. Since few parts of the Americas are characterized by such marked environmental differences within such a small geographical area, the samples from Ecuador are particularly useful for exploring environmental influences on health and nutrition.

I. TRADITIONAL SOURCES OF EVIDENCE AND METHODS OF ANALYSIS

Historical

The Spanish Conquest of Ecuador headed by Sebastián de Benalcázar began in earnest in 1534, but the focus of historical research has extended back to the period of Inca conquest, which began about 1460 (Larrea 1971; Newson 1995; Salomon 1986). A wide variety of documents are available to the historian, but they vary considerably in kind and quality. Nevertheless, through our piecing together of fragmentary evidence, it is possible to reconstruct a general outline of demographic trends and the pattern of daily life in the region from the fifteenth century. In Ecuador the key archive for historical research is the Archivo Histórico Nacional in Quito, while for the colonial period, the Archivo General de Indias in Seville and the archives of the missionary orders, notably the Jesuits and Franciscans, in Rome, are also essential sources of information. There are many other regional, local, and private archives in Ecuador which also contain important materials. From the eighteenth century, local parish records are sufficiently complete for some areas to enable demographic analysis (Bromley 1977; Minchom 1984). All the colonial skeletal samples are from the Quito Basin, specifically from the San Francisco and Santo Domingo churches. The San Francisco church houses the Archivo Franciscano, which contains colonial documents, most of which date from the eighteenth century. It contains a few parish registers and *padrones* (censuses drawn up for the purposes of tribute assessment), but not on a sufficiently systematic basis to enable demographic analysis and comparison with evidence from skeletal remains from the same church. There have been studies of demographic trends, health, and living conditions in the highlands (Alchon 1991; Newson 1995; Tyrer 1976), but little has been written on the lowlands. In addition, the research has focused on native populations, and there have been only a few studies of other racial groups (for example, Minchom 1994). Historical research on social and economic conditions in Ecuador is still in its infancy.

Bioarchaeological

Bioarchaeology in Ecuador initially focused largely on assessments of population relationships based on skeletal measurements and observations and cultural effects on the skeleton. Gradually, these research problems expanded to include assessments of health and disease as large samples of human remains became available from multidisciplinary archaeological activity. These samples largely originate from coastal and highland areas. Skeletal remains from the interior tropical forest area have generally not been available due to poor skeletal preservation and comparatively less archaeological activity in that area. Information about skeletal biology of historical populations is confined to the Quito area in the highlands, where excavations associated with restoration efforts of the major churches made skeletal samples available.

II. THE BACKGROUND TO HEALTH AND NUTRITION
IN PREHISTORIC AND HISTORIC ECUADOR

Previous interpretative research suggests that until this century, health and nutrition in Ecuador declined with greater reliance on agriculture, sedentism, and increased population density (Ubelaker 1984, 1992a). Nutrition is thought to have worsened with greater specialization of production associated, among other things, with tribute demands and the development of market economies. Meanwhile, dental health is generally thought to have declined with increased food processing and the greater availability of cariogenic foods, such as sugar. Both nutrition and dental health are also likely to have been affected by health in general, including the presence of certain infections.

Archaeological evidence from prehistoric sites on the southern coast of Ecuador indicates a shift from an economy based on broad-spectrum hunting, fishing, and gathering to one based on agriculture, which on the south coast became increasingly specialized in the cultivation of maize (Byrd 1976; Pearsall 1988; Stothert 1985, 1988). On the north coast of Ecuador, cultivation was less permanent and based on a diversity of crops, including root crops and palms, and the diet was supplemented by the exploitation of a variety of wild food resources, particularly fish and shellfish (Alcina Franch and Peña 1979; DeBoer 1996). Diets in the highlands, although they emphasized different crops, were as diverse as those on the north coast. Highland communities were able to exploit different ecological niches at different altitudes, while supplementing their diets with animal protein obtained from hunting (Knapp 1991; Newson 1995; Salomon 1986). It might be expected, therefore, that in prehistoric times, nutrition was poorest on the south coast and that it declined over time.

Health was also significantly affected by the presence of infectious diseases. The prevalence of infections is influenced by environmental and cultural factors. Each parasite has certain environmental limits beyond which it cannot survive, of which perhaps the most obvious is climate. Those spread by insect vectors are particularly susceptible to changes of temperature, while many intestinal diseases, such as dysentery, typhoid, hookworm, and other helminthic infections, many of which are waterborne, thrive in humid tropical conditions. While the environment sets physical limits within which pathogens can survive, the incidence and spread of infections have commonly been correlated with population growth and sedentism (Cockburn 1971; Fenner 1970; McKeown 1988; McNeill 1976). More recently, attention has been drawn to the influence of other cultural factors, such as trade and religious practices that might facilitate their spread (for example, Newson 1998; Reynolds and Tanner, 1995; Wirsing 1985).

On the north coast, the hot, humid climate was conducive to the spread of disease. However, settlements were relatively small and dispersed, so that sanitary conditions might have been relatively good. In contrast, the semiarid conditions of the southern coast would have been less favorable for the spread of chronic infections, but the more permanent and nucleated settlement pattern may have engendered poorer sanitary conditions and encouraged their spread. Similar patterns of settlement probably existed in the highlands, but there the cooler climate of the Andean highlands would have inhibited the spread of those infections that thrive in hot, humid climates, though perhaps encouraged the spread of others. Whether or not infections were more prevalent in the highlands, high-altitude living is generally considered to have had an adverse effect on health (Monge and Monge 1966). Some of the samples included here are drawn from sites located at altitudes of over 2,800 meters.

The Spanish Conquest was a traumatic event in the history of native peoples. During the sixteenth century, the population of the highlands declined by over 80 percent (Newson 1995). The introduction of Old World diseases was clearly a major factor in the decline (see Table 12.1) (Alchon 1991; Newson 1992, 1995), but it is less clear whether the prevalence of chronic infections increased, perhaps encouraged by the Spanish policy of congregating Indians into larger settlements to facilitate their administration and conversion. Conquest itself led to battle casualties, and native peoples were subjected to tribute exaction and forced labor. These were not new to peoples of the Ecuadorian Andes, but the extent to which they increased under the Spanish is not clear. While it is generally held that the disruption to native subsistence systems, brought about by the alienation of Indian lands and increased demands for tribute and labor, may have reduced food supplies, it is also argued that the introduction of new crops may have enhanced dietary variety and that the introduction of chickens and cattle, among other things, may have increased the availability of animal protein (Cook and Borah 1974; Super 1988). The Quito Basin, which had natural advantages of an equable climate and fertile soils, has been identified as one region in the Spanish empire where food supplies may have improved in colonial times (Super 1988).

The skeletal samples from the highlands enable some comments to be made on these issues, but comparisons across the contact period are limited by the dates and ancestry of samples. First, the latest date for the prehistoric samples is AD 340, and so the impact of the Spanish Conquest cannot be isolated from other changes, such as those wrought by Inca expansion, that occurred during the intervening period. Second, while the earliest samples from the San Francisco and Santo Domingo churches in Quito are considered to be of Native American ancestry, the later samples are of predominantly non-Indian ancestry, including Europeans, persons of mixed race, and at least one individual of African ancestry.

Native American demographic trends in highland Ecuador are considered to be unusual in the context of colonial Spanish-American demography. The common pattern in highland regions of Spanish America was a dramatic decline that continued into the seventeenth century before the population began to recover

Table 12.1: Major Epidemics in Highland Ecuador

1524–1527	Smallpox epidemic, which kills Huayna Capac.
1531–1533	Measles and possibly plague introduced from Central America.
1546	Pneumonic plague, or possibly typhus. Present in Peru and southern Colombia, and hence probably in Ecuador.
1558	Smallpox, measles, and possibly influenza.
1585–1591	Smallpox, measles, and possibly mumps, spreading north from Cuzco; typhus moving south from Cartagena.
1604	Unidentified epidemic in Quito.
1606	Diphtheria outbreak in Quito.
1611	Outbreak of measles and typhus in Quito.
1612	Scarlet fever appears, and found with measles and typhus.
1614	Typhus and diphtheria present in Quito.
1618	Epidemics of measles and *mal del valle* (dysentery) in the province of Quito.
1634	Serious outbreak of typhus throughout the province.
1644–1645	German measles and diphtheria cause many deaths.
1648–1649	Major epidemic of smallpox and German measles kills 100,000 throughout the province.
1667	Typhus and pains in the side in the city of Quito.
1676–1677	Smallpox and other diseases in Quito.
1680	*Peste* in Quito.
1683	*Peste* in city.
1685–1689	Typhus and pains in the side kill Spaniards and Indians.
1691–1695	Major epidemics of measles, smallpox, typhus, and diphtheria claim the lives of between 25 to 50 percent of the native population.
1708	Outbreak of *catarros* (possibly influenza).
1709	Epidemic of smallpox in Quito and the surrounding area.
1746	Epidemic of smallpox throughout Ecuador claims many lives.
1759	Epidemic of smallpox and *peste de Japón* (possibly Asian flu).
1763	Epidemic that caused high mortality only among Indians and Mestizos.
1785–1786	Major outbreak of measles, which was the most important epidemic of the century.
1795–1796	Unspecified epidemic kills Indians and Mestizos in Quito.

Sources: Alchon, *Native Society* and "Disease"; Minchom, *People of Quito*; and Newson, *Life and Death.*

slowly during the eighteenth century (Newson 1985, 1993). By contrast, in Ecuador it is envisaged that there was an early recovery in the late sixteenth century that continued to the 1690s when a period of severe epidemics caused the population to plummet (Figure 12.2, Table 12.2). Beset by epidemics, economic decline, and earthquakes (Alchon 1991; Andrien 1995; Tyrer 1976), the native population of highland Ecuador failed to register the increases that were being experienced in other Andean regions in the eighteenth century. The early recovery of the Ecuadorian population was attributed by contemporary observers to the absence of harsh labor in mining and to better food supplies. More recent research has suggested that the

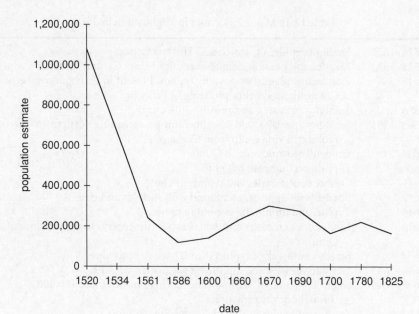

Figure 12.2. Native population decline in colonial Ecuador.

Table 12.2: Population Estimates for the North-Central Highlands
of Ecuador in the Colonial Period

Date	Estimate of the total population	Source
1520	1,080,00	Alchon, *Native Society and Disease*, 115
1534	667,600	Newson, *Life and Death*, 341
1561	240,670	Tyrer, "Demographic and Economic History," 79
1586	118,141	Tyrer, "Demographic and Economic History," 79
1600	140,233	Newson, *Life and Death*, 341
1660s	230,000	Tyrer, "Demographic and Economic History," 79
1670	300,000	Alchon, *Native Society and Disease*, 115
1690	273,000	Tyrer, "Demographic and Economic History," 79
1700	164,000	Tyrer, "Demographic and Economic History," 79
1779–1784	ca. 220,000	Alchon, *Native Society and Disease*, 115; Tyrer, "Demographic and Economic History," 79
1825	197,000	Alchon, *Native Society and Disease*, 115

early recovery was probably more apparent than real and that it reflected, at least in part, the more effective registration of the Indian population (Newson 1995; Powers 1995). However, the dramatic decline in the late seventeenth century has not been challenged.

Given the long time span covered by the skeletal remains, the question of the impact of environmental change needs to be considered. This has been afforded some attention in the context of the southern coast of Ecuador, which comprises an ecological transition zone that is particularly sensitive to climatic fluctuations. The climate of the Santa Elena Peninsula is affected by oceanic currents, notably the Humboldt current, whose position has experienced short-term fluctuations north and south, but on a longer timescale has shifted northward, resulting in the advance of desert-like conditions from the north of Peru to just north of the Santa Elena Peninsula. On the basis of archaeological evidence, Paulsen (1976) posits that during the two millennia before European contact, there were two pluvial periods of population expansion or repopulation between 500 BC to AD 600 and AD 1000 to AD 1400 that were separated by drier periods when settlements were abandoned. Paulsen argues that population growth in the pluvial periods created stress, conflict, and social change when conditions subsequently became drier. One sample from the Guangala site on the south coast dated at about 100 BC coincides with the proposed earlier pluvial period. There is some doubt as to whether settlements were abandoned in the subsequent dry period. For the second dry period immediately before the Spanish Conquest, historical sources indicate clearly that the peninsula was still densely settled, even though population levels may have been lower than in the preceding pluvial period (Newson 1995; Stahl 1984). All the samples analyzed here correspond to pluvial periods, with the dates of some extending into drier periods; none date exclusively from drier periods for which evidence of stress might be sought.

Paulsen notes that pluvial periods on the coast were often accompanied by periods of drought in the highlands and vice versa. Ice-core evidence from the Quelccaya glacier in southern Peru supports this assertion. It shows there were marked dry periods between AD 540–AD 610, AD 650–AD 730 , and AD 1040 to AD 1490, which were separated by wetter periods between AD 760 to AD 1040 and AD 1500 to AD 1720 (Thompson 1992; Thompson et al 1985). The skeletal samples from the prehistoric highlands predate these records, but there is paleoclimatic evidence from the Peruvian *cordillera* of a cold period between 1200 BC and 300 BC (Cardich 1985). Samples from the prehistoric highland sites of Cotocollao and Cumbayá broadly correspond with this cold period.

III. SITE AND SAMPLE CHARACTERISTICS

Twenty-two skeletal samples are considered in this study (Table 12.3). They have been grouped together chronologically to represent major cultural changes in the region. A basic distinction is made between prehistoric and historic sites. The latter are found only in the highlands, but sites on the coast have been grouped by geographical area, and within those regions, finer time periods have been distinguished to represent changes in subsistence patterns, population density, and

Table 12.3: Sample Group Characteristics

Sample group	Site	Period	Site code	Ancestry	Female	Male	Subadult	Unknown	Total
Santa Elena	Santa Elena	6300–4650 BC	osg	Native American	29	23	18	5	75
Real Alto	Real Alto	3400–1500 BC	rea	Native American	14	18	13	6	51
South Coast		900 BC–AD 1730		Native American	47	57	33	18	155
	La Libertad	900–200 BC	lib						
	Salango	300–200 BC	sal						
	Guangala	100–BC	gua						
	Ayalán	500 BC–AD 1730	AYA						
	Agua Blanca	AD 800–1500	AGB						
North Coast	La Tolita	600 BC–AD 400	lat	Native American	23	14	4	6	47
Prehistoric Highland		1000 BC–AD 450		Native American	58	49	16	41	164
	Cotocollao	1000–500 BC	cot						
	Cumbayá	400 BC–AD100	CUB						
	La Florida	AD 100–450	flo						
Historic Indian		AD 1500–1650		Native American	13	4	6	16	39
	San Francisco–Zaguan	AD 1500–1570	sab						
	Santo Domingo	AD 1500–1650	snt						
European 1		AD 1540–1858		Euro-American	25	19	14	46	104
	San Francisco	AD 1540–1650	sfc						
	San Francisco	AD 1580–1700	sfb						
	San Francisco	AD 1600–1725	SAA						
	San Francisco	AD 1540–1858	SA1						
European 2		AD 1670–1858		Euro-American	6	10	10	10	36
	San Francisco	AD 1670–1790	sfa						
	San Francisco	AD 1730–1858	SA2						
	San Francisco	AD 1750	sag						
European 3		AD 1770–1940		Euro-American	11	15	2	26	54
	San Francisco	AD 1770–1890	SF1						
	San Francisco	AD 1850–1940	sfo						

settlement characteristics. All but one of the historic samples are drawn from the San Francisco church (Ripley and Ubelaker 1992; Terán de Rodríguez 1988), and their burial dates have been estimated roughly from architectural features and radiocarbon methods, enabling them to be grouped into periods that broadly correspond with demographic trends that have been identified in the historical record. The earliest sample group is considered separately since it is the only one known to contain skeletal remains that are of definite Indian ancestry.

Skeletons from south-coast sites have been divided into three groups according to the character of native societies from which they were drawn. The earliest skeletons come from a preceramic Vegas Culture site on the Santa Elena Peninsula, which has been dated between 6300 BC to 4050 BC (Ubelaker 1980a, 1988d). These people exploited terrestrial mammals, marine fish, and shellfish from mangrove swamps. Although they may have also practiced some incipient cultivation, they were nomadic, possibly foraging as nuclear families, and population levels were low (Stothert 1985, 1988). Although the sample is large, the opportunities for observation and analysis are reduced by fragmentation and postmortem taphonomic change.

The second skeletal collection from the south coast is drawn solely from the site of Real Alto. This site (OSCH-12), which dates from the Early Formative Period between approximately 3400 BC and 1500 BC, represents the emergence of a sedentary and agriculturally based society that was characterized by increasing cultural complexity (Damp 1988; Lathrap et al. 1988; Marcos et al. 1976, 1988; Pearsall 1988).

The most recent group of skeletons from the prehistoric south coast (referred to here as South Coast) comprises samples from five sites – La Libertad (Ubelaker 1988a), Guangala (Ubelaker 1983, 1993), Ayalán (Ubelaker 1981), Agua Blanca (Ubelaker 1988c), and Salango – that are all located on or near the semiarid south coast. The data from Salango have not been published previously. These five samples are dated from 900 BC to as recent as AD 1730. However, they do not represent a continuous series, but are concentrated in two clusters, one between 1000 BC to 100 BC and the other between AD 800 to AD 1500. This group of samples is associated with societies firmly based on agriculture that were characterized by more permanent settlements, increased population density, and greater social complexity.

The North Coast sample comprises skeletons from the ceremonial site of La Tolita, located on the humid tropical north coast (Ubelaker 1988b; Valdéz 1987). The skeletons were derived from controlled excavations by the Banco Central and date between AD 90 and AD 190. Unfortunately, the sample is relatively small, limiting the generalizations that can be made.

The final group of skeletons from the prehistoric period derive from three sites in the forested highlands near Quito. They are the sites of Cotocollao (1000 BC to 500 BC) (Ubelaker 1980b, 1988e), Cumbayá (400 BC to AD 100) (Buys and Domínguez 1988a, 1988b; Ubelaker 1990a, 1990b), and La Florida (AD 340) (Doyon 1988; Ubelaker et al. 1995). The La Florida skeletons originate from deep shaft tombs that are thought to contain remains of the elite of the Quito Valley, as well as their subordinates. It is the one skeletal collection from Ecuador where the status of individuals can be differentiated.

Skeletal remains from the historic period derive primarily from excavations at the San Francisco convent in Quito, but include one from the Santo Domingo convent (Ubelaker 1994). The earliest sample (Zaguan) excavated from outside the entrance to the San Francisco convent is thought to represent local Indian populations and is considered separately. The other samples taken from the atrium, cloisters, and church appear to be of predominantly European origin, with at least a few of African or other descent. The eight European samples have been divided into three groups that correspond broadly with demographic trends identified from the historical record. European 1 is predominantly from 1540 to 1725, but one sample, SA1, extends to 1858. European 2 dates from 1670 to 1858, and European 3 from 1770 to 1940. Each sample was assigned to the broad chronological group based on the midpoint of the range of dates for the sample. The periods do not coincide exactly with demographic trends, partly because some samples extend beyond one demographic period, and partly due to the need to aggregate the small samples. While most of the samples appear to be representative of the population as a whole, one of the two samples in the most recent European group comprises mainly the remains of adult males who died and were deposited after AD 1770. An additional problem is the difficulty of determining the sex of many individuals, particularly in the earliest European group.

Skeletal remains can throw light on demographic trends, but the difficulties of demographic reconstruction and interpretation make it a hazardous exercise (Ubelaker 1994, 1995). Sources of error include the underrepresentation of certain age groups due to differential preservation or burial practices. Infants are often underrepresented, and in the case of the most recent European sample, middle-aged men, probably Franciscan monks, are overrepresented. In such cases, the presence of a disproportionate number of nonreproductive adults may render demographic reconstruction rather misleading. Another potential source of error is the estimation of age-at-death, which is difficult to assess for advanced adult years, particularly where preservation is poor. Finally, mortality statistics not only reflect death rates but are also influenced by fertility rates and possibly migration, about which little is often known (Johansson and Horowitz 1986; Sattenspiel and Harpending 1983).

The calculation of life expectancy for the Ecuadorian samples shows a slight decline on the south coast with the beginnings of agriculture (Table 12.4). Life expectancy at birth on the north coast is the highest of all the prehistoric samples, but it falls markedly to 17 years at age 20, suggesting that mortality focused on young adults, with the maximum longevity achieved of 48 years being the lowest of all samples.

The prehistoric highland group reveals the lowest life expectancy at birth, age 5, and age 15 of all the groups. The average age-at-death is also the lowest. This is surprising since the health index, which takes account of age distribution, suggests it was the healthiest of all the prehistoric groups that depended on agriculture. It is possible that the low average age-at-death is influenced by fertility in addition to mortality (Johansson and Horowitz 1986; McCaa this volume).

The historic series reveals a rather confused pattern. The low life expectancy at birth for the early colonial Indian and the European 2 groups is explicable in terms

Table 12.4: Life Expectancy and Average Age-at-Death

	Sample size	Life expectancy at birth	Life expectancy at 5 years	Life expectancy at 15 years	Life expectancy at 20 years	No. subadults	Ratio of subadults to adults	Maximum longevity	Average age-at-death
Santa Elena	75	31	31	22	19	18	.24	55.50	29.6
Real Alto	51	31	31	23	21	13	.25	55.00	30.3
South Coast	154	29	32	21	17	33	.21	57.50	27.8
North Coast	47	34	33	21	17	4	.09	47.50	32.4
Prehistoric Highland	164	28	27	15	13	15	.09	52.50	27.6
Historic Indian	39	29	28	18	14	6	.15	50.00	27.7
European 1	104	34	37	24	20	14	.13	57.50	32.1
European 2	36	29	28	21	17	10	.28	80.00	27.6
European 3	54	43	42	29	24	2	.04	70.00	40.8

of the epidemics and harsh labor, the latter revealed in fractures, among other things. However, the apparent improvement in the intervening European 1 sample is difficult to explain since similar conditions prevailed at that time. Furthermore, the health index suggests that health in this period was the poorest of all the historic periods examined. This suggests that the life expectancy values may have been affected by sampling error or by the manner in which the samples were aggregated. Although life expectancy at birth and the average age-at-death were similar for the early colonial Indian and the European 2 group, life expectancy at age 15 was slightly different, being 18 years in the case of the former and 21 years in the latter. Life expectancy values also might reflect patterns of population growth or decline that are otherwise not traceable.

IV. RESULTS

Living Stature

The skeletal remains indicate little variation in stature over time (Table 12.5). Male heights ranged between 157 and 170cm and female heights between 148 and 160cm. Stature was characteristically short and, indeed, comparable to modern Ecuadorian Indian populations (Gillin 1941). There appears to have been a slight increase in heights in the colonial period, but this could be due to sampling error or reflect the changing ancestry of individuals. Individuals comprising the three European samples are thought to be of predominantly non-Indian ancestry, and the significantly increased stature for the most recent group (European 3) is affected by the presence of a large number of adult males, probably Franciscan monks. Since the difference in stature between the prehistoric and colonial groups is slight, the non-Indian groups were also short. This is perhaps surprising since those associated with the church are likely to have had rather different diets than the population in general. Geographically there is a slight difference in stature between samples from the south and north coasts, with the latter being slightly taller. Perhaps the most

Table 12.5: Adult Height in Centimeters

	Male			Female		
	Mean	S. dev.	n	Mean	S. dev.	n
Santa Elena	160.0	4.2	5	148.2	8.2	11
Real Alto	156.8	7.1	11			0
South Coast	160.4	4.8	30	148.4	6.78	12
North Coast	162.3	4.5	8	154.6	7.9	10
Highland	160.6	5.6	18	151.1	7.2	16
Historic Indian	161.0		1	154.7	5.9	3
European 1	160.6	3.1	5	152.7	4.9	11
European 2	165.0	7.8	3	152.5	3.4	4
European 3	169.5	3.6	6	160.1	5.4	9

striking feature is the marked sexual dimorphism in all samples. Since this is lowest on the north coast where both males and females were the tallest of all prehistoric groups, there is a suggestion that this group may have had a better nutritional status.

Dental Health

Dental caries is the product of the demineralization of dental tissue caused by the action of bacteria. Although caries can be related to the structure of teeth and dental hygiene, the frequency of dental caries in early societies is related primarily to diet (Larsen et al. 1991) and, in particular, to an increasing reliance on agricultural foods, especially refined carbohydrates (Cohen and Armelagos 1984; Turner 1978; Ubelaker 1992c).

The samples from Ecuador suggest that although there was a general increase in carious teeth with the beginnings of agriculture, the frequency remained low until colonial times, when there was a marked increase that was probably associated with the availability of refined sugar (Table 12.6). The marked deterioration in dental health in postconquest times is apparent when scores for this attribute of below 71.8 for all the historic samples are compared with 94.0 for the prehistoric highland samples. However, geographical differences also appear to have been significant. The prevalence of caries in permanent teeth from the north coast and from prehistoric highland sites is considerably lower than from sites on the south coast. The rate of 1.2 percent for the north coast is even lower than that of 1.6 percent for the preagricultural Las Vegas site at Santa Elena, while the average of 2.6 percent for the prehistoric highland sites is low for communities with well-established agricultural economies. These differences may reflect dietary factors. Diets were more diversified on the north coast and in the highlands than on the south coast, where maize became increasingly dominant. Although maize was also grown on the northern coast, the more humid climate enabled the cultivation of root crops, such as manioc and plantains, as well as palms, while fishing and shellfish collection provided the bulk of protein (Alcina Franch and Peña 1979; DeBoer 1996). Highland groups were able to take advantage of the variety of ecological niches created by marked changes in altitude. The cultivation of cold-climate potatoes and the tuber ullucu (*Ullucus tuberosus* Caldas) could be combined with maize at intermediate altitudes, and at lower levels, sweet potatoes and arracacha (*Arracacha xanthorrhiza* Bancroft) were grown (Knapp 1991; Newson 1995). Since root crops are also starchy foods, differences in the prevalence of dental caries on the south coast compared to the north coast and the highlands might be related not so much to the buildup of plaque, which facilitates caries, but to attrition causing the destruction of the surface of the tooth, therefore decreasing the opportunity for caries. This type of wear might be caused by grit associated with grinding maize or with the consumption of shellfish. The highest prevalence of alveolar abscesses (of 13.2 percent) is also found in agricultural sites on the south coast, but this figure, like that of antemortem loss, may have been affected by the slightly older populations.

Table 12.6: Dental Health of Adults

Carious teeth	Adult* Percent	n	Male Percent	n	Female Percent	n
Santa Elena	1.6	737	2.3	303	1.3	378
Real Alto	10.5	362	10.7	149	8.7	161
South Coast	6.4	1673	5.6	756	7.6	724
North Coast	1.2	507	0.8	236	1.7	234
Prehistoric Highland	2.6	2283	1.5	799	3.5	857
Historic Indian	7.3	164	12.0	25	4.7	64
European 1	34.0	93	40.0	10	0.0	15
European 2	8.3	336	9.0	167	12.5	64
European 3	16.1	124	21.7	69	10.6	47

n = number of teeth.
Percent = carious teeth as a percent of total permanent teeth in adult individuals.

Premortem loss	Adult* Percent	n	Male Percent	n	Female Percent	n
Santa Elena	21.5	353	17.6	102	24.6	236
Real Alto	15.8	550	12.3	285	24.4	209
South Coast	39.7	766	39.5	428	42.0	276
North Coast	7.1	617	6.3	252	9.5	296
Prehistoric Highland	8.9	1095	10.5	400	10.2	518
Historic Indian	34.4	180	25.0	16	30.3	109
European 1	57.9	335	68.6	70	69.6	46
European 2	39.3	425	33.7	208	23.0	135
European 3	52.8	492	52.6	215	51.2	207

n = number of sockets.
Percent = percent of permanent teeth of adult individuals lost before death.

Abscesses	Adult* Percent	n	Male Percent	n	Female Percent	n
Santa Elena	3.7	353	4.9	102	3.4	236
Real Alto	9.1	550	8.8	285	12.0	209
South Coast	13.2	766	11.2	428	12.3	276
North Coast	4.9	617	0.8	252	8.1	296
Prehistoric Highland	1.3	1095	1.3	400	1.5	518
Historic Indian	2.8	180	0.0	16	3.7	109
European 1	1.2	335	4.3	70	0.0	46
European 2	7.5	425	8.7	208	0.0	135
European 3	1.6	492	0.5	215	2.9	207

n = number of sockets.
Percent = percent of sockets of adult individuals with evidence of abscesses.

* Includes males, females, and those of unspecified sex.

The pattern of antemortem loss generally follows that of the prevalence of caries, with lower rates on the north coast and in the prehistoric highlands, and a marked increase in colonial times and more recently. The main deviation from this pattern is found in dental remains from the preagricultural site at Santa Elena, where antemortem loss was 21.5 percent despite a low caries rate of 1.6 percent. This could reflect the presence of shell, bone, and grit associated with the exploitation of marine resources and game, but the figure is significantly higher than the 4.6 percent found among similar preagricultural groups in coastal Brazil (calculated from data provided by Neves and Wesolowski, this volume).

In prehistoric times, dental health seems to have been slightly poorer for women. Antemortem loss was higher among women in all environments, and once agriculture had become established, the prevalence of dental caries was also slightly higher. This accords with research elsewhere (see Larsen et al. 1991) that relates the higher prevalence of carious lesions among women to greater exposure to cariogenic foods through their greater involvement in cultivation and food preparation. Unfortunately, differences in the dental health of men and women that may have occurred with the Spanish Conquest are difficult to ascertain because of the difficulties of determining the sex of many individuals in the colonial samples.

Nutritional Status

Evidence for nutritional status can be found in the prevalence of porotic hyperostosis and cribra orbitalia, as it is known when occurring in the orbital roof of the cranium. These have been related to iron-deficiency anemia, which in the Americas has been associated with diets that are heavily dependent on maize. While these features have been associated with nutrition, the prevalence of anemia may also be induced by blood loss associated with some forms of parasitism.

In Ecuador, cribra orbitalia is found primarily among subadults (Table 12.7). The small size of the samples makes it difficult to establish temporal trends, but a comparison of the prehistoric samples indicates a higher frequency in the two agricultural groups on the south coast, where maize cultivation formed the basis of subsistence, and in the prehistoric highland sample. Porotic hyperostosis is also more common in the coastal agricultural samples, although this condition is also present in adults. It has been suggested that the prevalence of porotic hyperostosis on the coast of Ecuador may be related to the presence of intestinal diseases, especially hookworm (*Necator americanus* and *Ancylostoma duodenale*), which may cause anemia through blood loss and diarrhea (Ubelaker 1992b). Intestinal infections thrive in hot, moist climates, and they are associated with poor sanitation that can result from increased sedentism and population density. The higher prevalence of cribra orbitalia and porotic hyperostosis on the south coast could be related to the accumulation of human wastes associated with the more nucleated settlement pattern, which was encouraged, in part, by the restricted availability of water at wells, which itself may also have become contaminated. However, their absence from the north coast sample is surprising, particularly given that other evidence suggests higher levels of infection in this area despite the more dispersed settlement pattern.

Table 12.7: Cribra Orbitalia and Porotic Hyperostosis

Cribra orbitalia	Male Percent	n	Female Percent	n	Subadults Percent	n	Total* Percent	n
Santa Elena	0	1	0	6	0	3	0	10
Real Alto	0	10	0	3	20.0	10	8.0	24
South Coast	0	10	0	7	33.3	6	8.7	23
North Coast	0	5	0	2	0	2	0	10
Prehistoric Highland	0	9	25.0	8	0	1	8.3	21
Historic Indian	0	0	0	1	50.0	2	33.3	3
European 1	0	7	0	4	16.7	6	5.9	17
European 2	0	3	0	3	20.0	5	18.2	11
European 3	0	8	0	6	100.0	1	6.7	15

* Includes those of unspecified sex.
n = number of observable orbits.
Percent = percent of orbits with a lesion.

Porotic hyperostosis	Male Percent	n	Female Percent	n	Subadults Percent	n	Total* Percent	n
Santa Elena	0	7	0	16	0	3	0	26
Real Alto	0	14	0	6	0	8	0	30
South Coast	7.1	14	22.2	9	42.9	7	22.6	31
North Coast	0	7	0	9	0	2	0	19
Prehistoric Highland	14.3	7	0	4	0	0	8.3	12
Historic Indian	0	0	0	0	0	1	0	1
European 1	11.1	9	0	6	33.3	3	10.5	19
European 2	0	2	0	3	0	4	0	9
European 3	0	8	0	7	0	0	0	15

* Includes those of unspecified sex.
n = number of observable parietals.
Percent = percent of parietals with a lesion.

The prevalence of cribra orbitalia and porotic hyperostosis appears to increase in the colonial period, but the samples are small.

The prevalence of cribra orbitalia and porotic hyperostosis is comparable to Native American populations examined in the project as a whole (20.3 percent and 16.4 percent, respectively). However, no evidence of "gross lesions" of cribra orbitalia or porotic hyperostosis was recorded from any sample from Ecuador, although lesions from the Ayalán site approached that severity of expression. Also the prevalence is considerably lower than for maize-dependent groups in Mesoamerica (see Marquez Morfin et al., this volume) and coastal Chile (calculated from data provided by Arriaza in Table V.1 in the Introduction to Part V). Experimental evidence suggests that maize consumption with fish promotes iron absorption (Layrisse et al. 1986). There is considerable evidence that fish supplemented the diet on the coast of Ecuador, and this might account for the low prevalence of cribra orbitalia and porotic hyperostosis in the prehistoric coastal sites.

The prehistoric highland group includes a sample from the site of La Florida, where clear status differences are discernible. Stable isotope evidence indicates a slightly higher, though significant, consumption of maize by the higher-status group (Ubelaker et al. 1995). In Ecuador, maize was not only a daily food but also a ceremonial one that was consumed in the form of beer (Salomon 1986). Most likely this was prepared under the sponsorship of the elite, who possessed surplus maize to distribute. Its ceremonial use at La Florida is supported by archaeological evidence in the form of large jars used to brew beer. Although the sample contains only 19 observable orbits, the only 2 cases of cribra orbitalia are associated with high-status women.

Infections

Skeletal remains may provide insights only on certain features of the disease environment. Evidence for the presence of infectious disease is found in the form of periosteal lesions produced by the abnormal stimulation of the periosteum by infections and, less commonly, by trauma (Ortner and Putschar 1981). Acute infections that result in high mortality often leave little evidence of their occurrence since death occurs before the periosteal lesions have had time to develop. This probably accounts for the marked absence of periosteal lesions in subadult populations and in the early colonial sample. The skeletal evidence suggests that in the early colonial, the Indian population was relatively free from infections when it is known from archival sources that this was the period of highest disease mortality (Table 12.1). Conversely, the higher prevalence of periosteal lesions for non-Indian groups may reflect greater levels of survival that are also suggested by higher life expectancy and longevity. Given that the eighteenth century was one of epidemics and economic decline, the almost total absence of periosteal lesions from the European 2 sample is surprising, and most likely it reflects the relatively small size of the sample. In the later colonial period, even though chronic infections resulting from crowding and poor sanitation persisted despite some public health measures (Alchon 1991, 1992), by then populations would have acquired some immunity to acute infections and, compared to the early colonial period, nutrition may have improved. As the colonial period progressed, the frequency of severe periosteal lesions appears to have declined. However, the most recent European sample indicates an increase in both tibia and nontibia lesions that is likely to have been associated with the growth of Quito from the latter part of the nineteenth century (Saint-Geours 1989).

While the presence of tibia lesions shows a general increase through the prehistoric period, it reveals greater geographical variations (Table 12.8). The highest prevalence of tibia lesions is on the north coast where, as noted earlier, the moist tropical climate would have favored the spread of infections. The score of 58.1 for infections for this region is the lowest of any Ecuadorian sample, including the colonial period, and is considerably less than that for other prehistoric samples, which

Table 12.8: Skeletal Evidence of Infections

Tibia lesions	n	Percent			
		Slight	Moderate	Severe	Total
Santa Elena	28	3.4	0.0	0.0	3.4
Real Alto	34	0.0	5.9	0.0	5.9
South Coast	73	1.4	5.5	1.4	8.2
North Coast	23	21.7	4.3	8.7	34.8
Prehistoric Highland	81	1.2	4.9	3.7	9.9
Historic Indian	6	0.0	0.0	0.0	0.0
European 1	34	11.8	14.7	8.8	35.3
European 2	11	0.0	0.0	0.0	0.0
European 3	19	21.1	5.3	0.0	26.3

n = number of individuals with observable tibia(e).
Slight = percent with periosteal reaction involving less than one-quarter of the tibia(e) surface.
Moderate = percent with periosteal reaction involving less than one-half of the tibia(e) surface.
Severe = percent with periosteal reaction involving more than one-half of the tibia(e) surface.

Skeletal infections	n	Percent	
		Nontibia lesions	Systemic reaction
Santa Elena	75	0.0	0.0
Real Alto	51	0.0	2.0
South Coast	155	5.8	1.9
North Coast	47	8.5	2.1
Prehistoric Highland	164	3.0	0.0
Historic Indian	39	2.6	0.0
European 1	104	16.3	4.8
European 2	35	0.0	2.9
European 3	54	11.1	7.4

n = number of individuals.
Nontibia lesions = percent of individuals with periosteal reaction on bones other than the tibiae.
Systemic reaction = percent of individuals with perisoteal reaction on any bones, including the tibiae.

all register scores of over 93.5. Since this region was one of dispersed settlement and of relatively balanced diets, it suggests that in pre-Columbian times, at least climate may have played a more significant role than cultural factors in the spread of disease. Tibia infections are slightly more common in the highlands than the south coast, but in both cases, the higher prevalence of infection compared to earlier periods might be explicable in terms of poorer sanitary conditions resulting from increased population density.

There is little evidence for periosteal lesions on the skeleton, and so far no evidence for tuberculosis has been reported from Ecuador.

Enamel Hypoplasia

Enamel hypoplasia refers to defects in the development of tooth enamel, which are believed to be caused by stress during tooth development (Goodman and Rose 1991; Ubelaker 1992c). The growth of permanent tooth crowns normally occurs between birth and 15 years. In prehistoric populations, disruption to growth is generally considered to be the result of systemic metabolic stress that can be indicative of general living conditions, including nutrition.

In the Ecuadorian samples, hypoplastic defects found on permanent canines and incisors show an increase over time on the south coast (Table 12.9). The prevalence of hypoplasia in the most recent prehistoric group from the south coast is higher than that found among prehistoric samples from the north coast or the highlands. Since infections appear to have been less common on the south coast, but cribra orbitalia and porotic hyperostosis suggestive of iron-deficiency anemia were more prevalent there, the stress may have been, at least in part, nutritional. The

Table 12.9: Linear Hypoplasia

Canines	Male		Female		Subadults		Total	
	Percent	n	Percent	n	Percent	n	Percent	n
Santa Elena	0.0	14	0.0	16	14.3	7	2.6	39
Real Alto	9.1	11	9.1	11	16.7	6	8.8	34
South Coast	23.3	43	13.5	37	16.7	6	19.6	97
North Coast	22.2	9	0.0	15	50.0	2	11.1	27
Prehistoric Highland	0.0	33	0.0	40	8.3	12	1.8	111
Historic Indian	50.0	2	25.0	4	0.0	2	27.3	11
European 1	0.0	2	0.0	2	0.0	0	0.0	8
European 2	0.0	6	0.0	0	0.0	2	0.0	11
European 3	0.0	5	25.00	4	0.0	0	20.0	10

Incisors	Male		Female		Subadults		Total	
	Percent	n	Percent	n	Percent	n	Percent	n
Santa Elena	0.0	12	0.0	13	0.0	4	0.0	31
Real Alto	0.0	6	0.0	6	0.0	7	0.0	20
South Coast	12.5	16	8.0	25	0.0	5	9.4	53
North Coast	0.0	6	0.0	8	50.0	2	5.9	17
Prehistoric Highland	0.0	19	0.0	26	0.0	12	0.0	77
Historic Indian	0.0	1	0.0	3	50.0	2	12.5	8
European 1	0.0	0	0.0	1	0.0	0	0.0	2
European 2	0.0	1	0.0	0	0.0	1	0.0	2
European 3	0.0	1	0.0	1	0.0	0	0.0	2

n = number of observable teeth.
Percent = percent of observable teeth with hypoplasia.

significance of nutritional stress is further suggested by the relatively low frequency of hypoplasias in the North Coast group despite the high prevalence of tibia lesions. Here, nutritional status, as evidenced by taller stature and the low prevalence of anemia, was significantly better than on the south coast. With the exception of the South Coast group, subadults appear to have been most affected. Adult males had a slightly higher prevalence than females, with the exception of the most recent European sample, which is small, and Real Alto, where the values are the same. This runs counter to summary evidence for Native Americans, which shows a higher prevalence of 47.1 percent for women, in contrast to 36.1 for men.

The highest prevalence of hypoplasia is to be found among Indians in the early contact period. Although this is not unexpected since it was a period of epidemics and disruption to subsistence activities, the early colonial sample is small. Overall there are only 3 cases of multiple hypoplasia in all the 560 teeth examined, and the prevalence of single hypoplasias is generally lower than that for Native American populations as a whole, where hypoplasias were found on 23.1 percent of incisor teeth and on 38.2 percent of canines. This is also reflected in the high scores for hypoplasia of above 89.1 for all samples, when the median for the project as a whole is 77.8.

Trauma

Traumatic lesions are caused by external force, including the use of sharp or blunt objects as weapons. When these are considered by age and sex, they can throw light on the activities in which individuals participated and, in terms of the pain and discomfort they caused, give some indication of the quality of life. In particular, they can inform on patterns of violence, either domestic or intergroup, and the hazardous nature of daily subsistence activities. While the prehistoric evidence from Ecuador reveals some interesting patterns, for the historic period, the small size of the early European samples and the large proportion of individuals whose sex cannot be determined limits the generalizations that can be made.

During the prehistoric period, the prevalence of arm and leg fractures on observable bones generally increased on the south coast to 7.6 and 5.8 percent, respectively, in the sites where agriculture was well established (Table 12.10). Although generalizations are difficult due to the small size of samples, at the preagricultural site of Santa Elena, the fractures are located in the arm bones at sites suggestive of blows (Ubelaker 1980a), whereas at Ayalán, they were Colles fractures suggestive of falls (Ubelaker 1981). The prevalence of arm and leg trauma is higher on the north coast, where all the fractures are found on female skeletons. This extreme difference between the sexes, which extends to vault and weapon trauma, to be discussed below, suggests that women were disproportionately recipients of violence. Overall, the Ecuadorian samples reveal slightly higher levels of arm and leg trauma than those found among Native Americans as a whole, where fractures to observable arm and leg bones were 3.3 percent and 1.9 percent, respectively.

In the Ecuadorian samples, head fractures are largely confined to the vault, there being no observable facial fractures and only two nasal fractures in all the samples.

Table 12.10: Fractures on Observable Arm and Leg Bones

Arm bones	Male Percent	n	Female Percent	n	Subadults Percent	n	Total Percent	n
Santa Elena	16.7		0.0	11	0.0	5	4.5	
Real Alto	0.0	14	9.1		0.0		2.5	40
South Coast	9.4	32	11.11	18	0.0	14	7.6	66
North Coast	0.0	7	15.4	13	0.0	2	9.1	22
Highland	0.0	16	3.6	28	0.0	5	3.6	56
Historic Indian	0.0	0	33.3	3	0.0	0	33.3	3
European 1	33.3	3	0.0	1	0.0	1	50	8
European 2	25.0	4	0.0	3	0.0	2	10	10
European 3	20.0	5	20.0	5	0.0	1	35.7	14

Leg bones	Male Percent	n	Female Percent	n	Subadults Percent	n	Total Percent	n
Santa Elena	0	3	0.0	11	0.0	6	0.0	20
Real Alto	8.3	12	0.0	10		7	2.9	34
South Coast	9.1	33	5.9	17	0.0	17	5.8	69
North Coast	0.0	7	22.2	9	0.0	2	11.1	18
Highland	5.3	19	3.3	30	0.0	5	3.1	65
Historic Indian	0.0	0	0.0	3	0.0	0	0.0	3
European 1	0.0	1	0.0	1	0.0	0	0.0	2
European 2	0.0	5	0.0	3	100.0	1	9.1	11
European 3	16.7	6	0.0	7	0.0	1	23.5	17

n = number of individuals with observable bones.
Percent = percent of individuals with fractures.

The prevalence of vault trauma reveals no temporal or geographical pattern, or differences between the sexes. Contrary to what might be expected, there is no marked increase in the prevalence of vault and weapon trauma in the early colonial period. This could reflect the small size of the samples and/or the fact that the sample is drawn from persons associated with the church, who were perhaps less likely to have been involved in physical violence than the population in general. Two of the only four cases of weapon trauma encountered in all samples come from the prehistoric highland site of La Florida. They are found on lower-status males, and since they are found with an elite group, it has been speculated that these may have been war captives (Doyon 1988).

Degenerative Joint Disease

Degenerative joint disease is age progressive and mostly confined to adults. It is related to regular activity patterns and may have an important influence on the quality of life.

Table 12.11: Degenerative Joint Disease and Vertebral Osteophytosis

| | Shoulder/elbow | | | | Hip/knee | | | |
| | Male | | Female | | Male | | Female | |
	Percent	n	Percent	n	Percent	n	Percent	n
Santa Elena	0.0	1	0.0	2	0.0	3	0.0	3
Real Alto	66.7	12	50.0	6	66.7	6	33.3	6
South Coast	50	12	83.3	6	66.7	9	40.0	5
North Coast	0.0	1	0.0	0	0.0	1	100.0	1
Prehistoric Highland	25.0	4	37.5	8	80.0	5	16.7	6
Historic Indian	0.0	0	0.0	1	0.0	0	0.0	0
European 1	0.0	0	0.0	0	100.0	1	0.0	0
European 2	33.3	3	100.0	1	25.0	4	100.0	1
European 3	60.0	5	50.0	2	20.0	5	33.3	3

| | Wrist | | | | Thoracic | | | |
| | Male | | Female | | Male | | Female | |
	Percent	n	Percent	n	Percent	n	Percent	n
Santa Elena	0.0	1	50.0	2	50.0	4	0.0	1
Real Alto	55.6	9	0.0	3	60.0	5	100.0	1
South Coast	44.4	9	16.7	6	62.5	8	100.0	6
North Coast	0.0	1	0.0	0	33.3	3	0.0	2
Prehistoric Highland	0.0	2	14.3	7	20.0	5	25.0	4
Historic Indian	0.0	0	0.0	1	100.0	1	0.0	0
European 1	0.0	0	0.0	0	50.0	2	0.0	1
European 2	0.0	1	0.0	1	0.0	2	100.0	1
European 3	20.0	5	50.0	2	60.0	5	100.0	2

| | Cervical | | | | Lumbar | | | |
| | Male | | Female | | Male | | Female | |
	Percent	n	Percent	n	Percent	n	Percent	n
Santa Elena	33.3	3	50.0	2	0.0	2	0.0	1
Real Alto	100.0	5	50.0	2	100.0	5	100.0	2
South Coast	66.7	9	50.0	6	62.5	8	83.3	6
North Coast	33.3	3	25.0	4	0.0	3	0.0	4
Prehistoric Highland	50.0	4	25.0	8	0.0	2	50.0	4
Historic Indian	0.0	0	0.0	0	0.0	0	0.0	0
European 1	100.0	1	0.0	0	0.0	0	0.0	0
European 2	33.3	3	0.0	0	100.0	1	0.0	1
European 3	40.0	5	0.0	2	60.0	5	100.0	2

n = number of observable joints (shoulder, elbow, hip, knee, wrist) or vertebrae (cervical, thoracic, lumbar).

Percent = percent of joints with degenerative joint disease or vertebrae with osteophyte formation.

The prehistoric samples reveal an increase in thoracic and cervical degenerative changes with the beginnings of agriculture (Table 12.11). The activities in which the preagricultural groups at Santa Elena were involved were not particularly arduous. Hunting focused on small game, and the diet was highly dependent on the collection of shellfish, fishing, and the exploitation of wild plant resources. Agricultural labor may have been more strenuous. Women, who were probably the cultivators, were those who suffered most from thoracic degenerative changes, whereas cervical osteophytosis was more prevalent among men. This suggests that women may have been more involved in bending and lifting.

Degeneration of the shoulder and elbow joints, and osteophytosis on the lumbar vertebrae, appears to have been more prevalent on the south coast. The higher prevalence could be related to the process of grinding maize, and this argument is perhaps strengthened by the fact that these forms of joint deterioration are less prevalent on the north coast and in the highlands where a greater variety of crops was grown. Also, they are slightly more common among women. Comments on the colonial period are restricted by the small size of samples, but the deterioration of shoulder, elbow, and lumbar joints appears to have been comparable to that found in prehistoric south coast populations, but greater than among prehistoric highland groups. This suggests that for highland groups, colonial rule involved more arduous forms of labor, most likely as household servants, though there are no cases of extensive deterioration of these joints.

The deterioration of hip and knee joints reveals no temporal or geographical pattern, except that its absence from the preagricultural site of Santa Elena is not surprising. It might be expected that degeneration of the hip and knee might have been more common among highland dwellers because of their constant movement between different altitudes. Male skeletons from the prehistoric highlands do have the highest prevalence of hip and knee degeneration (80 percent), but the sample is small.

V. CONCLUSION

The skeletal remains from Ecuador confirm a number of findings made by archaeologists and historians. In general, they suggest a deterioration in health with the beginnings of agriculture and increased sedentism (Table 12.12). The preagricultural site of Santa Elena has the highest health index (83.4) of all of the Ecuadorian samples and one of the highest of all sample groups examined in this volume. While health may have deteriorated with the development of agriculture, the factors contributing to the decline varied between different cultures and environments. A comparison of the health indexes for prehistoric agricultural communities suggest that highland groups were healthier than those on the coast. Nutrition appears to have been better and infections less prevalent, and there is little evidence, except perhaps from life expectancy, that high-altitude living had a negative impact on health. This is especially noteworthy since some of the skeletons comprising the prehistoric highland group date from a proposed cold period, which might have adversely affected agricultural production.

On the coast, the factors responsible for the poorer health of agricultural groups differed. North Coast populations had taller stature, good dental health, and no

Table 12.12: The Health Index and Attribute Scores for Ecuador

	Health index	Stature	Enamel hypoplasia	Dental disease	Infections	Anemia	Degenerative joint disease	Trauma	Years
Santa Elena	83.4	8.7	99.7	91.1	98.7	100	94.8	90.8	4643
Real Alto	77.3	1.2	96.4	79.4	95.8	99.3	80.5	88.4	4786
South Coast	75.1	2.7	89.1	81.8	94.1	93.1	77.3	87.6	9730
North Coast	72.7	6.8	94.2	89.7	58.1	100	71.4	88.7	3306
Prehistoric highland	81.6	7.4	99.7	94.0	93.5	97.1	85.1	94.4	7991
Historic Indian	71.0	4.8	89.1	69.3	84.8	95.7	94.6	58.8	849
European 1	70.9	3.7	98.6	71.8	72.8	94.6	79.8	75.0	3482
European 2	76.9	16.9	99.4	62.1	98.3	99.6	89.8	72.2	1536
European 3	72.2	12.8	91.0	67.9	95.2	99.7	78.9	59.8	3563

For the calculation of the health index and attribute scores, see Steckel, Sciulli, and Rose, this volume.

revealed evidence of anemia, but they suffered to a greater degree from infectious diseases. The score for infections for the North Coast sample is only 58.1, which is the lowest score calculated for any attribute and any sample; it is primarily responsible for the placing of the health index of 72.7 below that of 75.1 for the South Coast. Agricultural populations on the South Coast had the highest prevalences of hypoplasia, cribra orbitalia, and porotic hyperostosis of all Ecuadorian groups, and had poorer dental health. Many of these features can be related to the greater dependence of these societies on maize cultivation. However, as might be expected from the semiarid environment in which they lived, these societies appear to have suffered less from infectious diseases, with all samples scoring over 94.1 for this attribute. This is perhaps surprising since settlements in this area were larger and more nucleated, and it suggests that climatic factors may play a more significant role in the spread of infections than population size and settlement patterns until much higher population thresholds are reached.

While health and nutrition appear to have declined during the prehistoric period, it is difficult to ascertain what impact this might have had on population growth. As yet there is insufficient evidence for nutritional stress or social conflict, which might be indicative of population pressure on resources, for the immediate pre–Spanish Conquest period. A larger sample of skeletal remains from this period would provide a clearer picture. At present the increase in health problems in the prehistoric period seems to relate more to shifts in the nature of subsistence activities and environmental conditions than to changes associated with population growth and density.

Unfortunately, the available skeletal samples generally do not permit an analysis of changing health and nutrition that might be linked to climatic change. The samples from the south coast all correspond to pluvial periods, so that it is not possible to ascertain whether health and nutrition declined when conditions became drier. Although the samples from the prehistoric highlands date from different climatic periods, there is no evidence that those from Cumbayá and Cotocallao, which date from the cold period 1200 BC to 300 BC, were characterized by greater nutritional stress or social conflict than those from La Florida. However, it is possible that the differences between the climatic periods may have been minimized by social changes that counteracted any benefits that might have accrued from improved environmental conditions.

Changes to health and nutrition as a result of the Spanish Conquest are difficult to detect in the skeletal record. This derives in part from the size, origin, and nature of the samples, and the fact that events such as epidemics and military conquest are largely unrecorded on skeletal remains. Bioarchaeological evidence can therefore throw little light on the impact of these episodes or on the level of population decline suggested by the historical record. However, as the study suggests, it can provide more evidence on nutritional status and chronic conditions. It would appear that in highland Ecuador, there was little change in nutritional status in the colonial period as evidenced by stature and iron-deficiency anemia. Although the colonial samples are drawn largely from the European population, which might be expected to have enjoyed a better diet than Native Americans, the one sample group of Native American ancestry does have a slightly higher at-tribute score for anemia than its contemporary European sample. This is perhaps surprising since it is generally considered that the Spanish Conquest resulted in subsistence activities being undermined by population losses, the alienation of Indian lands, and demands for labor which in some regions resulted in food shortages and even famines (Super 1988). The small size of the Native Ameri-can sample urges caution in concluding that the impact of the Spanish Conquest on nutritional levels was minimal. Even if this could be demonstrated, it seems likely that the impact of colonial rule was moderated by the natural fertility of the Quito Basin and the diversity of crops grown. For this reason and the relatively limited Spanish presence in the region, any conclusion that might be made should not be extrapolated to other parts of Spanish America. The experience of other regions and cultures is likely to have been different. Indeed, even for Ecuador, a differ-ent conclusion might emerge if colonial samples were available for the coastal region.

While nutritional levels may have changed little, in the colonial period dental health did deteriorate and levels of trauma appear to have increased, though the samples are small. Similarly, the prevalence of infections increased, with the attribute score for infections declining from 93.5 in the prehistoric highlands to 84.8 in the early colonial period. Although these scores are well above the average (75.1) for all samples analyzed in this volume, they are misleading, for they fail to take account of acute infections that are well documented in the historical sources. In addition, early death from epidemics or conflict would have resulted in fewer persons registering age-related conditions, such as degenerative joint disease. For reasons such as these, some attribute scores and the health index probably portray an overoptimistic view of health conditions among early colonial populations.

Evidence from skeletal remains suggests that in common with other Native Ameri-can societies, health in Ecuador deteriorated with the beginnings of agriculture and later with the Spanish Conquest. In prehistoric times, nutritional levels appear to have declined as people turned from hunting, fishing, and gathering to agriculture and increasingly focused on the cultivation of maize. The evidence also suggests that over time, as populations grew and became sedentary, infections became more prevalent. However, this study shows that environmental factors were also important and that in particular circumstances, perhaps below certain population thresholds, they might be more significant in determining the prevalence of infection than demographic factors. Taken a step further, it suggests that from an early date, en-vironmental factors exerted a negative influence on health in the tropical lowlands and that they may have contributed to the holding back of population growth in those regions.

Whether cultural or environmental factors were primarily responsible, it is clear that Native American populations did not live in a disease-free paradise, but suf-fered from a range of diseases that often resulted in premature death. Nevertheless, societies in prehistoric Ecuador do appear to have been healthier than in many other parts of the Americas. The health index for the prehistoric samples from Ecuador does not fall below 72.7, whereas the highest index for Central Mexican groups is 68.4 and for the Maya of Honduras 61.7.

Although there are suggestions that health declined with the Spanish Conquest, the Native American sample from the colonial period is too small on which to base any firm conclusions. A larger sample would throw light on nutrition and chronic conditions, which often receive at best only passing reference in the documentary record. At the same time, stable carbon isotope analysis of skeletal remains from both the late prehistoric and the early colonial periods would throw light on the nature and extent of changes to nutritional patterns consequent upon colonial rule. While further bioarchaeological research is likely to yield the best evidence for chronic conditions, at present it can provide only a limited insight on traumatic events, such as epidemics, and to a lesser extent, wars. It is perhaps in such conditions of rapid cultural change that the complementarity of bioarchaeological and historical research is most evident.

REFERENCES

Alchon, S. A. *Native Society and Disease in Colonial Ecuador*. Cambridge: Cambridge University Press, 1991.

"Disease, Population, and Public Health in Eighteenth-Century Quito." In *"Secret Judgments of God": Old World Disease in Colonial Spanish America*, ed. N. D. Cook and W. G. Lovell, 159–182. Norman: University of Oklahoma Press, 1992.

Alcina Franch, J., and R. de la Peña. "Patrones de asentamiento indígena en Esmeraldas durante los siglos XVI y XVII." *Proceedings of the 42nd International Congress of Americanists* (Paris) 9A (1979): 283–301.

Andrien, K. J. *The Kingdom of Quito, 1690–1830*. Cambridge: Cambridge University Press, 1995.

Borah, W. "America as Model. The Demographic Impact of European Expansion upon the Non-European World." *Actas y Memoria del XXXV Congreso Internacional de Americanistas*. Mexico, 1964.

Bromley, R. "Urban Growth and Decline on the Central Sierra of Ecuador." Ph.D. diss., University of Wales, 1977.

Byrd, K. "Changing Animal Utilization Patterns and Their Implications: Southwest Ecuador (6500 BC–AD 1400)." Ph.D. diss, University of Florida, 1976.

Buys, J., and V. Domínguez. "Un cementerio de hace 2000 años: Jardin del Este." In *Quito antes de Benalcázar*, ed. I. C. Cevallos, 31–50. Quito: Centro Cultural Artes, 1988a.

Hace dos mil años en Cumbayá. Proyecto arqueológico "Jardín del Este," Cumbayá, provincia de Pichincha, Ecuador. Quito: Instituto Nacional de Patrimonio Cultural, 1988b.

Cardich, A. "The Fluctuating Upper Limits of Cultivation in the Central Andes and Their Impact on Peruvian Prehistory." *Advances in World Archaeology* 4 (1985): 293–333.

Cockburn, A.T. "Infectious Diseases in Ancient Populations." *Current Anthropology* 12 (1971): 45–62.

Cohen, M. N. *Health and the Rise of Civilization*. New Haven, Conn.: Yale University Press, 1989.

Cohen, M. N., and G. Armelagos, eds. *Paleopathology at the Origins of Agriculture*. New York: Academic Press, 1984.

Cook, S. F., and W. Borah. *Essays in Population History*, vol. 2. Berkeley and Los Angeles: University of California Press, 1974.

Crosby, A. W. *Ecological Imperialism: The Biological Expansion of Europe: 990–1900.* New York: Cambridge University Press, 1986.

Damp, J. *La primera ocupación Valdivia de Real Alto: Patrones económicos, arquitectónicos e ideológicos.* Guayaquil: Escuela Politecnica del Litoral, 1988.

DeBoer, W. R. *Traces Behind the Esmeraldas Shore: Prehistory of the Santiago–Cayapas Region.* Tuscaloosa and London: University of Alabama Press, 1996.

Dobyns, H. F. *Their Number Become Thinned: Native American Population Dynamics in Eastern North America.* Knoxville: University of Tennessee Press, 1983.

Doyon, L. G. "Tumbas de la nobleza el La Florida." In *Quito ante de Benalcázar*, ed. I. C. Cevallos, 51–66. Quito: Centro Cultural Artes, 1988.

Fenner, F. L. "The Effects of Changing Social Organisation on the Infectious Diseases of Man." In *The Impact of Civilisation on the Biology of Man*, ed. S. Boyden, 48–76. Canberra: Australian National University Press, 1970.

Gillin, P. *Quichua-speaking Indians of the Province of Imbabura (Ecuador). Bulletin of the Bureau of American Ethnology*, no. 128, 1941.

Goodman, A. H., and J. C. Rose. "Dental Enamel Hypoplasias as Indicators of Nutritional Status." In *Advances in Dental Anthropology*, ed. M. Kelley and C. Larsen, 279–293. New York: Wiley-Liss, 1991.

Johansson, S. R., and S. Horowitz. "Estimating Mortality in Skeletal Populations: Influence of the Growth Rate on the Interpretation of Levels and Trends During the Transition to Agriculture." *American Journal of Physical Anthropology* 71 (1986): 233–250.

Knapp, G. W. *Andean Ecology: Adaptive Dynamics in Ecuador.* Boulder, Colo.: Westview Press, 1991.

Larrea, C. M. *Notas de prehistoria e historia Ecuatoriana.* Quito: Corporación de Estudios y Publicaciones, 1971.

Larsen, C. S. "In the Wake of Columbus: Native Population Biology in the Postcontact Americas." *Yearbook in Physical Anthropoplogy* 37 (1994): 109–154.

Larsen, C. S., R. Shavit, and M. C. Griffin. "Dental Caries Evidence for Dietary Change: An Archaeological Context." In *Advances in Dental Anthropology*, ed. M. A. Kelley and C. S. Larsen, 179–202. New York: Wiley-Liss, 1991.

Lathrap, D. W., J. G. Marcos, and J. A. Zeidler. "Real Alto: An Ancient Ceremonial Center." *Archaeology* 30 (1) (1977): 2–13.

Layrisse, M., C. Martínez-Torres, and M. Roche. "Interaction of Various Foods on Iron Absorption." *American Journal of Clinical Nutrition* 21 (1968): 1175–1183.

Marcos, J. G. *Real Alto: La historia de un centro ceremonial Valdivia.* Guayaquil: Escuela Politécnica del Litoral, 1988.

Marcos, J. G., D. W. Lathrap, and J. A. Zeidler. "Ancient Ecuador Revisited." *Field Museum Natural History Bulletin* 47 (1976): 3–8.

McKeown, T. *The Origins of Human Disease.* Oxford: Basil Blackwell, 1988.

McNeill, W. M. *Plagues and Peoples.* Oxford: Oxford University Press, 1976.

Minchom, M. *The People of Quito, 1690–1810: Change and Unrest in the Underclass.* Boulder, Colo.: Westview Press, 1994.

Monge, C. and Monge, C. *High Altitude Diseases: Mechanisms and Management.* Springfield, Ill.: Thomas, 1966.

Newson, L. A. "Indian Population Patterns in Colonial Spanish America." *Latin American Research Review* 20 (3) (1985): 41–74.

"Old World Epidemics in Early Colonial Ecuador." In *"Secret Judgments of God": Old World Disease in Colonial Spanish America*, ed. N. D. Cook and W. G. Lovell, 84–112. Norman: University of Oklahoma Press, 1992.

"The Demographic Collapse of Native Peoples of the Americas, 1492–1650." *Proceedings of the British Academy* 81 (1993): 247–288.

Life and Death in Early Colonial Ecuador. Norman: University of Oklahoma Press, 1995.

"A Historical Ecological Perspective on Epidemic Disease." In *Advances in Historical Ecology*, ed. W. Balée, 42–64. New York: Columbia University Press, 1998.

Ortner, D., J. and W. G. J. Putschar. *Identification of Pathological Conditions in Human Skeletal Remains*. Washington, D.C.: Smithsonian Institution Press, 1981.

Paulsen, A. C. "Environment and Empire: Climatic Factors in Prehistoric Andean Culture Change." *World Archaeology* 8 (2) (1976): 121–132.

Pearsall, D. M. *La producción de alimentos en Real Alto*. Quito: Biblioteca Ecuatoriana de Arqueología, 1988.

Powers, K. *Andean Journeys: Migration, Ethnogenesis and the State in Colonial Quito*. Albuquerque: University of New Mexico, 1995.

Reynolds, V., and R. Tanner. *The Social Ecology of Religion*. Oxford: Oxford University Press, 1995.

Ripley, C., and D. H. Ubelaker. "The Ossuary of San Francisco Church, Quito, Ecuador (abstract)." *American Journal of Physical Anthropology*, Supplement 14 (1992): 139.

Saint-Geours, Y. "L'évolution démographique de l'Equateur au XIXe siècle." In *L' Equateur*, vol. 1, ed. D. Dilemma and M. Portals, 197–207. Paris: Editions de l'ORSTOM, 1989.

Salomon, F. L. *Native Lords of Quito in the Age of the Incas: The Political Economy of Northern Andean Chiefdoms*. Cambridge: Cambridge University Press, 1986.

Sattenspiel, L., and H. Harpending. "Stable Populations and Skeletal Age." *American Antiquity* 48 (1983): 489–498.

Stahl, P. "On Climate and the Occupation of the Santa Elena Peninsula: Implications of Documents for Andean Prehistory." *Current Anthropology* 25 (3) (1984): 351–332.

Stothert, K. E. "The Preceramic Las Vegas Culture of Coastal Ecuador." *American Antiquity* 50 (3) (1985): 613–637.

"La cultura Las Vegas." In *La prehistoria temprana de la peninsula de Santa Elena, Ecuador: Cultura Las Vegas*, ed. K. E. Stothert, Miscelánea Antropológica Ecuatoriana, Serie Monográfica 10, 237–260. Quito: Banco Central-Abya-Yala, 1988.

Super, J. *Food, Conquest, and Colonization in Sixteenth-Century Spanish America*. Albuquerque: University of New Mexico Press, 1988.

Terán de Rodríguez, P. "Estudio de investigación arqueológica, convento de San Francisco de Quito, sitio: OPQSF-2." Unpublished report presented to Instituto de Cooperación Ibero Americana de España, Quito, 1988.

Thompson, L. G. "Ice Core Evidence from Peru and China." In *Climate Since AD 1500*, ed. R. S. Bradley and P. D. Jones, 517–548. London: Routledge, 1992.

Thompson, L. G., E. Moseley-Thompson, J. F. Bolzan, and B. R. Koci. "A 1500-year Record of Tropical Precipitation in Ice Cores from the Quelccaya Ice Cap, Peru." *Science* 229 (1985): 971–973.

Turner, C. G. "Dental Caries and Early Ecuadorian Agriculture." *American Antiquity* 43 (4) (1978): 694–697.

Tyrer, R. B. "The Demographic and Economic History of the Audiencia of Quito: Indian Population and the Textile Industry, 1600–1800." Ph.D. diss., University of California, Berkeley, 1976.

Ubelaker, D. H. "Human Skeletal Remains from Site OGSE-80, a Preceramic Site on the Sta. Elena Peninsula, Coastal Ecuador." *Journal of the Washington Academy of Sciences* 70 (1980a): 3–24.

"Prehistoric Human Remains from the Cotocollao Site, Pichincha Province, Ecuador." *Journal of the Washington Academy of Sciences* 70 (1980b): 59–74.

"The Ayalán Cemetery: A Late Integration Period Burial Site on the South Coast of Ecuador." *Smithsonian Contributions to Anthropology* 29 (1981).

"Human Skeletal Remains from OGSE-MA-172, an Early Guangala Cemetery Site on the Coast of Ecuador." *Journal of the Washington Academy of Sciences* 73 (1983): 16–26.

"Human Remains from OGSE-46, La Libertad, Guayas Province, Ecuador." *Journal of the Washington Academy of Sciences* 78 (1988a): 3–16.

"Prehistoric Human Biology at La Tolita, Ecuador, a Preliminary Report." *Journal of the Washington Academy of Sciences* 78 (1988b): 23–37.

"A Preliminary Report of Analysis of Human Remains from Agua Blanca, a Prehistoric Late Integration from Coastal Ecuador." *Journal of the Washington Academy of Sciences* 78 (1988c): 17–22.

"Restos esqueletos humanos del sitio OGSE-80." In *La prehistoria temprana de la peninsula de Santa Elena, Ecuador, Cultura Las Vegas*, ed. K. E. Stothert, Miscelánea antropológica ecuatoriana, serie monográfica 10, 105–132. Quito: Banco Central-Abya-Yala, 1988d.

"Restos humanos prehistóricos del sitio Cotocollao, provinicia de Pichincha, Ecuador." In *Una aldea formativa del Valle de Quito*, ed. M. Villalba, Miscelánea antropológica ecuatoriana, serie monográfica 2, appendix II, 557–571. Quito, Banco Central del Ecuador, 1988e.

"Human Skeletal Remains from 'Jardín del Este,' Cumbayá, Pichincha, Ecuador." In *La preservación y promoción del patrimonio cultural del Ecuador*, Cooperación tecnica Ecuadorian-Belga no. 4, 22–39. Quito: Institutio Nacional de Patrimonio Cultural, 1990a.

"Restos humanos provenientes de 'Jardín del Este,' Cumbayá, Pichincha, Ecuador." In *La preservación y promoción del patrimonio cultural del Ecuador*. Cooperación tecnica Ecuadorian-Belga no. 4, 40–52. Quito: Institutio Nacional de Patrimonio Cultural, 1990b.

"Porotic Hyperostosis in Prehistoric Ecuador." In *Diet, Demography and Disease: Changing Perspectives on America*, ed. P. Stuart-Macadam and S. Kent, 201–217. New York: Aldine de Gruyter, 1992a.

"Temporal Trends of Dental Disease in Ancient Ecuador." *Anthropologie* 30 (1992b): 99–102.

"Restos humanos esqueletícos de OGSE-MA-172, un sitio 'Guangala temprano' en la costa del Ecuador." In *Un sitio de Guangala temprano en el suroeste del Ecuador*, 99–112. Guayaquil: Banco Central del Ecuador, 1993.

"The Biological Impact of European Contact in Ecuador." In *In the Wake of Contact: Biological Responses to Conquest*, ed. C. S. Larsen and G. R. Milner, 147–160. New York: Wiley-Liss, 1994.

"Osteological and Archival Evidence for Disease in Historic Quito, Ecuador." In *Grave Reflections*, ed. S. R. Saunders and A. Herring, 222–239. Toronto: Canadian Scholars' Press Inc., 1995.

Ubelaker, D. H., M. A. Katzenberg, and L. G. Doyon. "Status and Diet in Precontact Highland Ecuador." *American Journal of Physical Anthropology* 97 (1995): 403–411.

Valdez, F. *Proyecto arqueológico La Tolita (1983–1986)*. Quito: Museo del Banco Central, 1987.

Verano, J. W., and D. H. Ubelaker, eds. *Disease and Demography in the Americas*. Washington, D.C.: Smithsonian Institution Press, 1992.

Wirsing, R. L. "The Health of Traditional Societies and the Effects of Acculturation." *Current Anthropology* 26 (3) (1985): 304–322.

CHAPTER THIRTEEN

Economy, Nutrition, and Disease in Prehistoric Coastal Brazil

A Case Study from the State of Santa Catarina

Walter Alves Neves and Verônica Wesolowski

ABSTRACT

The Northern Coast of the State of Santa Catarina, Southern Brazil, was first occupied around 5000 BP by populations of preceramic shellfishers, who were partially replaced by ceramist groups around AD 1000. Most Brazilian archaeologists assume that there is a strong correlation between pottery making and plant cultivation. Therefore, these later groups are said to have introduced agriculture to the region. In this chapter we explore temporal health trends among these prehistoric populations in order to test the hypothesis that ceramist groups introduced plant cultivation into the region. We also survey the general health status of these coastal Brazilian populations, comparing them with other archaeological samples represented in the joint project. To do so, we used the following osteological markers of quality of life: incidence of dental caries, degree of tooth wear, incidence of linear enamel hypoplasias, and incidence of porotic hyperostosis in the orbits. Two of the preceramic sites showed a high incidence of dental caries, demonstrating that in specific moments of the preceramic period, some of the groups relied on plant resources at least as much as they did on animal sources. None of the osteological markers traditionally associated with the adoption of agriculture showed higher frequencies in the ceramic level compared to the preceramic level. Thus, we conclude that although pottery making was introduced on the Northern Shore of the State of Santa Catarina by AD 1000, our data do not support that the adoption of agricultural practices was associated with this introduction. We found that the populations of both prehistoric occupations attained very high indexes of health and quality of life. When compared to the other populations represented in the

We want to express our deepest gratitude to Museu Arqueológico de Sambaqui de Joinville and Museu Nacional do Rio de Janeiro for permission to study the skeletal collections involved in this work. Thanks are also due to FAPESP for financial aid in different phases of this study and to Ohio State University for financial aid during its terminal phase. We also want to pay a tribute to Selma Marcus da Silva for her efficient assistance during the analysis of the collections housed at Museu de Joinville, to Maria do Carmo Zanini for her assistance during the statistical analysis of the data, to Herbert Klein for his comments on the first manuscript, to Eugene Harris for reviewing the English, and, last but not least, to Richard Steckel and Jerome Rose for their invitation to participate in the joint project and to write this chapter. This chapter is dedicated to Tânia A. Lima in recognition of her efforts in developing a theoretical-based archaeology in Brazil.

joint project, they ranked among the highest indexes of health and quality of life. We suggest that an explanation for this achievement is primarily related to the favorable environmental conditions along the coast enjoyed by these groups.

INTRODUCTION

Since 6000 BP the Southern Brazilian seashore was densely occupied by preceramic prehistoric groups specializing in shellfishing and fishing. These groups produced highly visible mound sites that have been known to naturalists since the first Europeans arrived in the country in the sixteenth century. Since the mid-twentieth century, several archaeologists have excavated these shell-mounds, which are among the most intensively studied archaeological sites in Brazil (André Prous, 1990). As pointed out by Maria D. Gaspar (1998), 91 sites have been extensively reported in the literature, and 231 radiocarbon dates have been generated for 121 sites.

The amount of processual knowledge we have about the groups who occupied these sites is meager (see Maria D. Gaspar, 1991; Tânia A. Lima, 1991; Tânia A. Lima et al., 1999, and Marco N. De Masi, 1999, for exceptions). This is especially difficult to understand if one considers the great number of excavations already undertaken in the southern coast of Brazil (Tânia A. Lima, 1999–2000). The main reason for this paradox is that most of the archaeological work carried out thus far at these sites has been of a descriptive nature. Brazilian archaeologists are still discussing basic questions about the formation, stratigraphy, and sociological functions of the mounds, and only recently have these sites become the object of processual and postprocessual analytical approaches (for a review, see Maria D. Gaspar, 1998, and Tânia A. Lima, 1999–2000). As a result, we still do not have a comprehensive understanding of the cultural variability of these sites, in space and time, and much less about their sociological meanings.

This situation limits significantly the kind of anthropological studies that can be carried out with the human skeletal remains recovered from the Brazilian shell-mounds, because problem-solving research projects are difficult to design and carry out in this context. One of the few specific areas that can be addressed by physical anthropologists, besides trying to describe very general temporal or spatial trends in the incidence of skeletal traits, is to test if the appearance of pottery in the upper layers of some of these sites also represents a marked change in the subsistence economy of these populations.

The question of plant domestication and intensification of food production among the prehistoric populations that occupied Brazilian territories is among the most important themes of investigation currently explored in Brazilian archaeology. A common assumption among local archaeologists is that the presence of pottery making is a direct indicator of cultivation practices (André Prous, 1990). Current anthropological knowledge about contemporary Brazilian indigenous groups seems to indicate that most human societies that practice agriculture in lowland South America, even on a small scale, also make pottery. However, there is no direct evidence to support the same correlation for precolonial times, and in our opinion, we may be dealing with a good example of how dangerous the use of simple direct ethnographic analogy in archaeology can be (see H. M. Wobst, 1978, for a review of this issue).

Among Brazilian Southern Coast groups, pottery making first appeared around 1000 BP. The assumption that ceramic production and agriculture are always associated led long ago to the hypothesis that cultivators of the southern Brazilian hinterland plateau migrated in late prehistoric times to the coast, replacing the former specialized gatherer-hunters (Anamaria Beck, 1972; Igor Chmyz, 1976; Pedro I. Schmitz, 1988). In the specific case of the Northern Coast of the State of Santa Catarina, one of us (Walter A. Neves 1982, 1988a) has demonstrated through paleogenetic studies that, indeed, the presence of pottery in the upper levels of some shell-mounds can be explained by migration from the hinterlands, while in others, the adoption of pottery making by the local shellfishers could also be a feasible explanation. In other words, Walter A. Neves (1988a) has built a model including partial population replacement and acculturation to account for the changes in material culture and site formation observed in late prehistoric times in Santa Catarina. Assuming that the newcomers were plant cultivators in their homeland, indeed a fact also still open to debate,[1] it remains to be proved that these people introduced food production along with pottery making in the economy of the coast of Santa Catarina.

Taking into account the relevance of this problem for Brazilian prehistory, and the inefficacy of archaeologists to examine it so far, we decided to approach this problem from the perspective of physical anthropology. In doing so, we assumed the efficacy of a number of osteological markers as indicators of biological stress and, more specifically, those derived from economic transitions from hunting-gathering to food production (M. N. Cohen and George J. Armelagos, 1984; Alan H. Goodman and Debra Martin, this volume).

The data used in this work, supplemented by a few other osteological markers analyzed for the same skeletal samples, were used as well to feed the general data bank of the joint project, where the health status of the coastal populations (preceramic and ceramic) of the State of Santa Catarina could be compared with other skeletal populations of the Western Hemisphere. The insertion of our data into such a comprehensive database is of interest because of the nature of the material in itself, and because of its transitional historical context. As we mentioned before, the seashore of Lowland South America has been intensively occupied by different groups since at least 6000 BP. They represent an important demographic segment of the human societies that occupied the subcontinent. The investigation of their lifestyles, their economic strategies, and their health status is of significance for understanding the diversity of prehistoric human adaptation in the Western Hemisphere, as a whole. The second reason why the inclusion of these populations in a comprehensive project is important is that very little has been published thus far, outside of Portuguese- and Spanish-speaking countries, concerning the skeletal biology of Lowland South American prehistoric skeletal populations. Last, if the pottery-making groups which arrived on the coast of the State of Santa Catarina by AD 1000 brought the practice

[1] De Masi (1999) has obtained isotopic evidence for the cultivation of maize by these pottery-making groups in the highlands beginning around 1200 BP.

of settled agriculture to the seashore and continued to practice it as a major subsistence activity, this could have had important consequences for the local health patterns, as has been shown in several other geographic areas (M. N. Cohen and George J. Armelagos, 1984). If only pottery making with no agriculture was brought by these newcomers, it may prove to be of importance to investigate the health impact of this technological novelty per se in a fishing-gathering context. In other words, would the introduction of pottery (with uses for food collecting, carrying, storing, and processing) be enough to impact the nutritional status of a prehistoric group, even if this innovation was not associated with major changes in its food repertoire?

In summary, the aim of this work is threefold: to compare the health status of the prehistoric populations of the Brazilian Southern Coast with other skeletal populations of the Western Hemisphere, to explore health trends along time in the region, and to test the hypothesis that besides pottery making, the newcomers to the Northern Coast region of Santa Catarina also introduced plant cultivation as a major subsistence strategy around 1000 BP.

SYNOPSIS OF THE STATE OF KNOWLEDGE ON THE REGIONAL PREHISTORY

The first archaeological investigations of the Northern Coast of the State of Santa Catarina, Southern Brazil, date back to the 1940s and were carried out primarily by Guilherme Tiburtius, a self-trained archaeologist. Most of these investigations were, in fact, carried out in the process of destruction of shell-mounds for commercial purposes (for example, in the use of shells for the pavement of roads and buildings, and in the industrialization of lime). For some key sites that were destroyed, these short reports will be forever the only archaeological information available. During the 1960s, however, systematic archaeological work proliferated, reaching its climax in the early 1970s, and declining again in the 1980s (Anamaria Beck, 1972, 1974; Alan L. Bryan, 1977, 1993; Mariland Goulart, 1980). Currently, little archaeological research is being carried out in the region.

The local prehistoric record is mainly composed of two distinct kinds of occupations, one dating back to around 5000 BP, characterized by the construction of huge shell-mounds, and another dating back to about 1000 BP, characterized by the abandonment of the practice of mound building, and by the formation of flat, mainly sedimentary campsites. The location of both occupations in the local landscape was very similar, and it is not uncommon to find settlements of the second occupation established on top of the shell-mounds.

There is a vast descriptive archaeological literature concerning these sites, not only for the specific region treated in this work but also for the whole Southern Brazilian Shore (see Tânia A. Lima, 1999–2000, and André Prous, 1990, for a synthesis). But, as mentioned before, processual archaeology still figures very meagerly in archaeological research in Brazil, and as a result, we are far from understanding the basic characteristics of the social and economic systems of the human populations that occupied the Northern Coast of Santa Catarina.

The earliest date for the occupation of shell-mound builders in this region is 4815 BP, and both cultural and biological information indicate that these populations came from northern regions of Brazil's coast. The sites are located primarily along the Babitonga Bay, near streams of fresh water that cross extensive areas of swamp forest, the predominant landscape. This location permitted populations to reach, within a short walking distance, the open ocean, the tropical rain forest in the nearby backhills, and the mangrove itself. One of the most intriguing practices of the people living in this period is the great investment of labor to build mounds of food debris, primarily comprised of mollusk shells (mainly *Ostraea* sp., *Anomalocardia brasiliana*, and *Modiolus* sp.). These moundlike sites are referred to as *sambaquis* in the local literature. The size of these mounds sometimes reached huge dimensions, but on average they were approximately 10 meters in height and 100 meters in length across the base (André Prous, 1990; Tânia A. Lima, 1999–2000).

Amid the shell debris, several other archaeological elements can be found, including habitation structures and hearths; a vast number of human burials; a diversity of instruments made of stone, bone, teeth, and shells; debris of lithic and bone industries; as well as food debris comprised primarily of animal remains and, more rarely, plant remains. The lithic industry is characterized by polishing and puncturing techniques, rather than flaking techniques. These latter techniques are very difficult to apply to the available raw materials, such as diabase and quartz. Among the lithic instruments, zoomorphs, named *zoólitos* in the local literature, are the most striking because of their fine elaboration. Regarded as ritual artifacts, zoólitos are pieces of rock sculpture, noted for their uniqueness in morphology and treatment. The bone and teeth industry was also very diversified, showing a tendency for more refined elaboration and complexity in more recent times. The most frequent artifacts are projectile points, adornments, spatulas, and atlatl propellers. Shells were used primarily in the elaboration of adornments (necklaces, bracelets, etc.) and scrapers.

Besides the abundance of artifacts, most archaeologists involved in the study of these sites are amazed by the huge amount of shellfish debris they contain. Although other animal remains are often found, including fish, these items are believed to be secondary components in the everyday diet of these people, who are also supposed to have ingested meager amounts of plant-food items. The predominance of shellfish over other animal resources in the diet of these peoples has for a long time been assumed. However, in most cases, such an assumption is based only on visual inspection of the stratigraphy. In other words, the importance of shellfish in the diet could be illusory, resulting from impressionistic assessment and differential preservation of shells and fish bones in tropical climates (Marco Aurélio N. De Masi, 1999). Few studies have tried to quantify the real amount of meat derived from shellfish, fish, and other animal sources by evaluating the net relation between the edible and the nonedible portions of the species involved (Maria D. Gaspar, 1998). Marco Aurélio N. De Masi (1999), for instance, has suggested recently that shellfishes were rarely consumed by this people as food. Taking into account his analysis based on isotopic proportions on human bones, he concluded that shellfishes were collected primarily to be used as fish bait.

The most striking difference between the later occupation and the one comprised of classic shell-mounds is the absence of shell accumulations to form vaultlike platforms. In the coastal campsites of the late horizon, the cultural debris are dispersed in a sedimentary matrix, and mollusk shells appear in small amounts, concentrated in pits or small lenses. When compared to the true shell-mounds, these sites are very shallow and do not surpass one meter of height. As mentioned before, it is not uncommon for these campsites to be placed on the top of a shell-mound. The only absolute date for this occupation is 880 ± 100 BP obtained by Allan Bryan (1977, 1993) for the site of Forte Marechal Luz, a campsite that sits above a true shell-mound top.

Artifacts from the flat campsites are very similar to those found in the true shell-mounds, but sometimes they suggest, as in the case of the bone industry, a higher degree of sophistication. However, as pointed out by André Prous (1990), this improvement in the bone industry can also be found in late classic shell-mounds, and consequently cannot be regarded as characteristic of the second occupation only. Some authors have suggested that the number of artifacts related to fishing seems to increase with the advent of the campsites. For example, fishhooks made of bone appear in the stratigraphy at this time.

The most dramatic difference between the two occupations regarding technology is the occurrence of pottery in the later one, and its complete absence among the true shell-mounds. The amount of potsherds varies from site to site, running from only a handful at some sites to thousands of fragments at others. The vessels appear to be of small size, being deeper than wide. The same pottery industry, known as the Itararé tradition, has been recognized in the nearby hinterlands (Igor Chmyz, 1976) and has been assigned older dates. Other archaeological features like burials and hearths are very similar in both occupations.

Some authors (Anamaria Beck, 1972, 1974; Allan Bryan, 1977, 1993) have also suggested that fishing and hunting became increasingly important in the late horizon, with a concomitant decrease in the importance of shellfishing. However, these assessments are also not based on quantitative methods and therefore need to be verified. Wild plant items, on the other hand, remained scanty and were mainly represented by small coconuts. Based on the presence of pottery, slash-and-burn cultivation is tradionally assumed to have been an important source of staple food.

DESCRIPTION OF SITES AND METHODS OF ANALYSIS

The human skeletal remains analyzed in this study are part of the collections housed at Museu Arqueológico de Sambaqui de Joinville and Museu Nacional do Rio de Janeiro. They total 164 individuals, whose state of preservation allowed the observation of at least one of the markers used in the project. The individuals studied were grouped in eight different groups, five of which were recovered from preceramic classic shell-mounds, and three from ceramic campsites. One of the preceramic groups is comprised of individuals recovered from several sites, as shown in Table 13.1, and has been referred to as a composite sample. All remaining groups correspond to a specific site. Basic information about the archaeological sites studied is supplied in Table 13. 1, while their location is shown in Figure 13.1.

Table 13.1: General Information about the Archaeological Samples

Samples	Site/source	Site type/dimensions (length, width, height)	Absolute dating	Main stratigraphic content	Number of individuals
Composite	*Cubatãozinho* Bigarella, Tiburtius & Sobanski (1954)	Preceramic shell-mound; dimensions unknown	Not available	*Anomalocardia brasiliana; Ostrea* sp.; *Mytilus* sp.; fish remains	1
Composite	*Conquista* Bigarella, Tiburtius & Sobanski (1954)	Preceramic shell-mound; dimensions: 75m × 70m × 6.5m	Not available	*Anomalocardia brasiliana; Ostrea* sp.	3
Composite	*Linguado* Prous & Piazza (1977); Bigarella, Tiburtius & Sobanski (1954)	Preceramic shell-mound; dimensions: 60m × 40m × 8m	2830 ± 145 BP	*Anomalocardia brasiliana; Ostrea* sp; fish remains	5
Composite	*Areias Pequenas* Bigarella, Tiburtius & Sobanski (1954)	Preceramic shell-mound; dimensions: 170m × 80m × 15m	Not available	*Anomalocardia brasiliana; Ostrea* sp.; animal remains; fish remains	5
Composite	*Costeira* Bigarella, Tiburtius & Sobanski (1954)	Preceramic shell-mound; dimensions: 50m × 23m × 4.5m	Not available	*Anomalocardia brasiliana;* whale bones	1
Composite	*Araquari* Bigarella, Tiburtius & Sobanski (1954)	Preceramic shell-mound; dimensions: 70m × 20m × 4m	Not available	*Anomalocardia brasiliana*	3
Composite	*Enseada I* (Lower level) Bigarella, Tiburtius & Sobanski (1954)	Preceramic shell-mound; dimensions unknown	Not available	*Anomalocardia brasiliana*	3

Composite	*Pernambuco* Bigarella, Tiburtius & Sobanski (1954)	Preceramic shell-mound; dimensions: 110m × 100m × 12m	Not available	*Anomalocardia brasiliana*	2
Composite	*Porto do Rei* Bigarella, Tiburtius & Sobanski (1954)	Preceramic shell-mound; dimensions: 100m × 60m × 15m	Not available	*Anomalocardia brasiliana*; *Ostrea* sp; whale bones and fish bones	1
TOTAL OF COMPOSITE SERIES					24
Rio Comprido	*Rio Comprido* Bibliographic sources not available; personal information from excavators	Preceramic shell-mound; dimensions not available	4815 BP	Mollusk shells	19
Morro do Ouro	*Morro do Ouro* Bigarella, Tiburtius & Sobanski (1954); Beck, Duarte & Reis (1969); Beck (1972); Beck, Araújo & Duarte (1970); Prous & Piazza (1977); Goulard (1980)	Preceramic shell-mound; dimensions not available	4050 BP ± 80	Mollusk shells, animal bones	61
Ilha de Espinheiros II	*Ilha de Espinheiros II* Bibliographic sources not available; personal information from excavators	Preceramic shell-mound; dimensions: 40m × 26m × 6m	2710 BP ± 80	*Anomalocardia brasiliana*; *Ostrea* sp; *Modiolus brasiliensis*	7

(continued)

383

Table 13.1 (*continued*)

Samples	Site/source	Site type/dimensions (length, width, height)	Absolute dating	Main stratigraphic content	Number of individuals
Forte Marechal Luz PR	*Forte Marechal Luz* (Lower level) Bryan (1977, 1993)	Preceramic shell-mound; dimensions not available	4290 BP ± 130 (first occupation)	*Ostrea arborea; Ostrea sp;* mussel shells; mammal; reptile, bird, and fish bones; crustacean remains	9
Enseada I	*Enseada I* (Upper level) Beck (1972, 1974)	Ceramic campsite; dimensions unknown	Not available	Fish bones, mollusk shells	20
Itacoara	*Itacoara* (Upper level) Tiburtius, Bigarella & Bigarella (1951); Chmyz (1976)	Ceramic campsite; dimensions: 20m × 15m × 1.2m		Not available	17
Forte Marechal Luz CR	*Forte Marechal Luz* (Upper level) Bryan (1977, 1993)	Ceramic campsite; dimensions not available	880 BP ± 100 (last occupation)	*Ostrea arborea; Ostrea sp;* mussel shells (*Mytilus perna and/or Modiolus brasiliensis*); mammal; reptile, bird, and fish bones; crustacean remains	7
TOTAL					164

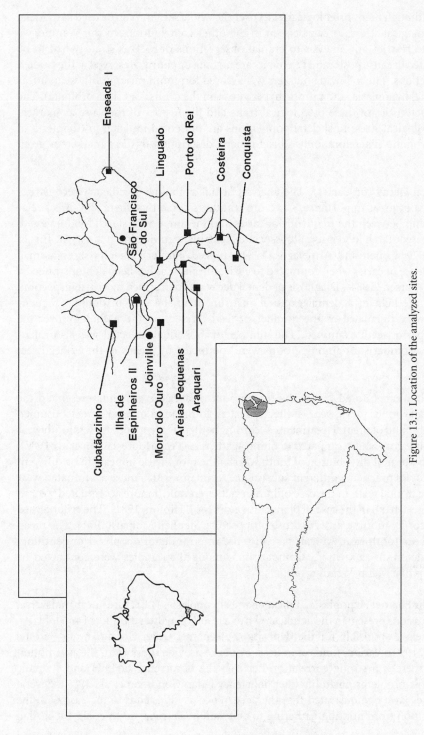

Figure 13.1. Location of the analyzed sites.

385

Although many osteological traits over the whole skeleton can be used as markers of biological stress, as can be seen in the other contributions to this volume, we had to restrict our analysis to cranial observations only. This strategy had to be adopted because postcranial elements are missing or poorly preserved in the studied collections. The following markers were scored for: tooth caries, tooth wear, linear enamel hypoplasia, and porotic hyperostosis in the orbits (or cribra orbitalia). The characteristics of these osteological traits and the history of their use as markers of biological stress in skeletal populations are presented in detail in Chapter 2 of this volume. Therefore, only a brief general description of these markers is given here.

Dental Decay (or Caries). The analysis of this pathology for dietary reconstruction is of great importance, since most authors agree that there is a direct relationship between the frequency of caries and the amount of starch food ingested. Increased starch food is usually associated with plant cultivation (Christy G. Turner II, 1979; Cohen and Armelagos, 1984). Indeed, hunter-gatherers show a small incidence of caries when compared to agriculturalists, as has been demonstrated by Clark Larsen (1984). Diagnosis of dental decay was performed by visual inspection, with the help of a dental explorer instrument in the case of doubt. Frequencies were calculated as the number of teeth presenting the pathology over the number of teeth examined. The number of individuals affected was also calculated. Comparisons among groups were conducted by means of the Fisher Exact Test.

Tooth Wear. Caused mainly by the amount of abrasive elements present in the everyday food, tooth wear is directly related to the kind of food items consumed and the kind of preoral treatment. Accordingly, there is a tendency for less tooth wear in cultivators when compared to hunter-gatherers (Peer Moore-Jansen et al., 1982). The pattern of distribution of tooth wear in the mouth also appears to be different in peoples practicing different subsistence regimens, with a more accentuated wear in the frontal teeth in the case of hunter-gatherers, and a more accentuated wear in the cheek teeth in the case of plant cultivators (R. J. Hinton, 1981). The criteria used for scoring tooth wear were those proposed by Stephen Molnar (1971). The mean degree of tooth wear was calculated for the anterior dentition, posterior dentition, and dentition as a whole. Comparisons among the samples were conducted by means of a Mann-Whitney test.

Linear Enamel Hypoplasia. Linear enamel hypoplasias (LEH) are linear transversal depressions present in the dental crown as a result of malfunctioning of ameloblasts, the cells responsible for the deposition of enamel (Alan Goodman and Jerome Rose, 1990). Various kinds of indirect evidence provide support for the assumption that there is a strong correlation between the occurrence of LEH and systemic organic problems, including diet deficiency (Alan Goodman et al., 1987). Several studies have demonstrated that the occurrence of LEH tends to increase with the transition from hunting-gathering to cultivation (Patricia Smith et al., 1984; Alan

Goodman et al., 1980, 1984). Only bilateral manifestations were considered systemic hypoplasias. Due to the degree of preservation, only presence/absence was scored, and the final frequency was calculated as the number of teeth affected divided by the number of dental pieces inspected. Number of individuals affected were also calculated. Comparisons among the samples were conducted by means of a Fisher Exact Test.

Porotic Hyperostosis. A human organism with iron-deficiency anemia responds through an intensification of red cell production, which provokes an expansion of the hematopoietic marrow and of the spongiosa of the bone. In the skull, the result is the appearance of porotic areas in the outer table of the vault and orbits, due to the exposition of the underlying trabeculae. In fact, several kinds of anemia can trigger this mechanism. However, hereditary anemia is associated with extreme responses, while more discrete manifestations are probably related to environmental stress, nutritional deficiency being an example. Several studies have demonstrated that the incidence of porotic hyperostosis increases with the adoption of cultigens as a main staple (Mahmoud Y. El-Najjar et al., 1976; Ann Palkovich, 1987; Patricia Stuart-Macadam, 1987). Diagnosis of porotic hyperostosis was carried out by means of visual inspection alone and was restricted to the orbits. An individual was included in the analysis if at least one of the orbits was present. Frequencies were calculated in terms of number of individuals affected. Comparisons among samples were also conducted by means of Fisher Exact Tests.

Our data as a whole (which includes the osteological markers analyzed in this chapter, plus other cranial traits required by the joint project) were also processed in such a way as to allow for comparisons with prehistoric and historic groups from other parts of the Western Hemisphere. In order to facilitate the comparison of traits, our observations followed strictly the recommendations and criteria defined by Alan Goodman and Debra Martin in Chapter 2. Results were expressed as an index called QALY (Maximum Quality Adjusted Life Years), and as percentages of the maximum possible obtainable value for this index. Separate QALY indexes were obtained for preceramic sites, on the one hand, and ceramic sites, on the other.

Results

Caries. Tables 13.2, 13.3, and 13.4 summarize the results obtained with respect to dental decay. Figure 13.2 illustrates a case of dental cavity from Morro do Ouro. Only two samples showed significantly greater incidence of caries (Rio Comprido and Morro do Ouro), both of them corresponding to preceramic shell-mounds. No significant increase in the incidence of cavities was observed for the ceramic period (Late Occupation).

Tooth Wear. Tables 13.5, 13.6, and 13.7 summarize the results obtained with respect to the amount of tooth wear. As can be perceived, there are significant differences in tooth wear in several pairwise comparisons, but it cannot be said that there

Table 13.2: Incidence of Teeth with Caries in Each Sample

	Total number of observed teeth	Absolute frequencies of carious teeth	Relative frequencies of carious teeth (%)
Preceramic samples			
Rio Comprido	258	15	5.81
Morro do Ouro	1142	85	7.44
Composite	318	7	1.74
Ilha de Espinheiros II	133	1	0.75
Forte Marechal Luz PR	109	0	0
Ceramic samples			
Enseada I	391	3	0.76
Itacoara	315	8	3.67
Forte Marechal Luz CR	73	0	0

Table 13.3: Incidence of Individuals Affected by Carious Lesions in Each Sample

	Total number of observed individuals	Absolute frequencies of affected individuals	Relative frequencies of affected individuals
Preceramic samples			
Rio Comprido	14	7	50.00
Morro do Ouro	54	27	50.00
Composite	16	3	18.75
Ilha de Espinheiros II	7	1	14.28
Forte Marechal Luz PR	8	0	0
Ceramic samples			
Enseada I	20	3	15.00
Itacoara	16	5	31.25
Forte Marechal Luz CR	6	0	0

is a systematic decrease when the ceramic sites are compared to the preceramic shell-mounds. The distribution of tooth wear in the anterior and posterior dentitions are approximately the same for both periods.

Linear Enamel Hypoplasia. Tables 13.8, 13.9, and 13.10 summarize the results obtained with respect to the incidence of linear enamel hypoplasia. Figure 13.3 illustrates a case of linear enamel hypoplasia from Morro do Ouro. No differences between the samples reached significant levels.

Porotic Hyperostosis. Tables 13.11 and 13.12 summarize the results obtained with respect to the incidence of porotic hyperostosis. Figure 13.4 illustrates a case of

Table 13.4: Comparison of Incidence of Carious Teeth
Between Samples (Fisher Exact Test)

Samples	P values
Rio Comprido × Morro do Ouro	0.4226
Rio Comprido × Composite	0.0125
Rio Comprido × Ilha de Espinheiros II	0.0148
Rio Comprido × Forte Marechal Luz PR	0.0072
Rio Comprido × Enseada I	0.0003
Rio Comprido × Itacoara	0.0550
Rio Comprido × Forte Marechal Luz CR	0.0488
Morro do Ouro × Composite	0.0001
Morro do Ouro × Ilha de Espinheiros II	0.0014
Morro do Ouro × Forte Marechal Luz PR	0.0005
Morro do Ouro × Enseada I	< 0.0001
Morro do Ouro × Itacoara	0.0010
Morro do Ouro × Forte Marechal Luz CR	0.0076
Composite × Ilha de Espinheiros II	0.6696
Composite × Forte Marechal Luz PR	0.3286
Composite × Enseada I	1.0000
Composite × Itacoara	0.5824
Composite × Forte Marechal Luz CR	0.5876
Ilha de Espinheiros II × Forte Marechal Luz PR	1.0000
Ilha de Espinheiros II × Enseada I	1.0000
Ilha de Espinheiros II × Itacoara	0.2916
Ilha de Espinheiros II × Forte Marechal Luz CR	1.0000
Forte Marechal Luz PR × Enseada I	1.0000
Forte Marechal Luz PR × Itacoara	0.1201
Forte Marechal Luz PR × Forte Marechal Luz CR*	—
Enseada I × Itacoara	0.0707
Enseada I × Forte Marechal Luz CR	1.0000
Itacoara × Forte Marechal Luz CR	0.3613

* Both samples do not present carious teeth.

porotic hyperostosis from Morro do Ouro. In all cases reaching significance, where one sample of each occupation is involved, the tendency was always in the direction of a lesser incidence in the ceramic period, and not the reverse.

Health Index. As can be seen in the summary chapter of this book, where the results of all sites included in the joint project are presented, the skeletons from classic preceramic shell mounds obtained a QALY index of 22.97, corresponding to 87.1% of the maximum possible score, while the skeletons recovered from the ceramic occupation obtained a QALY index of 24.22, corresponding to 91.8% of the maximum possible. In other words, the populations of both occupations presented very similar results regarding quality of life.

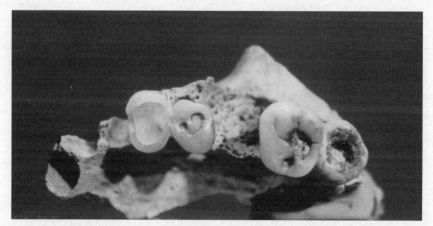

Figure 13.2. Upper jaw with small cavities in the second premolar and with extensive carious lesions in second and third molars (Sambaqui Morro do Ouro). (Photo: V. Wesolowski.)

Table 13.5: Descriptive Statistics for Anterior and Posterior Dentition Tooth Wear

	Rio Comprido	Morro do Ouro	Composite	Ilha de Espinheiros II	Enseada I	Itacoara
Anterior dentition						
Means	2.80	3.68	3.25	3.69	4.42	2.97
Sample size	79	290	101	39	147	145
Standard deviations	0.94	1.42	1.27	1.06	1.58	1.55
Median	3	3	3	4	4	3
Minimum	1	1	1	2	1	1
Maximum	5	7	8	5	7	7
Posterior dentition						
Means	3.23	4.97	4.19	4.94	5.34	3.92
Sample size	60	239	99	34	135	145
Standard deviations	0.67	1.51	1.35	1.25	1.44	1.87
Median	3	5	4	5.5	5	5
Minimum	2	3	2	2	2	1
Maximum	5	8	7	6	8	7

IMPLICATIONS AND CONCLUDING REMARKS

This chapter was designed to investigate three archaeological issues: (1) the temporal trends in health among preceramic shell-mound populations of the Brazilian Southern Coast; (2) to test the hypothesis that together with pottery making, people that arrived in the Northern Coast of Santa Catarina around 1000 BP also introduced plant cultivation as an important subsistence strategy; and (3) to compare the health status of both coastal populations (preceramic and ceramic) with those of the other populations included in the joint project. These tests were carried out assuming the efficacy of a number of osteological markers as indicators of biological

Table 13.6: Descriptive Statistics for Overall Tooth Wear in Each Sample

	Rio Comprido	Morro do Ouro	Composite	Ilha de Espinheiros II	Enseada I	Itacoara
Means	2.99	4.47	3.71	4.27	4.86	3.44
Sample size	139	529	200	73	282	290
Standard deviations	0.86	1.60	1.39	1.30	1.58	1.78
Median	3	4	4	4	5	3
Minimum	1	1	1	2	1	1
Maximum	5	8	8	6	8	7

Table 13.7: Comparison of Degree of Overall Tooth Wear Between Samples (Mann-Whitney Test)

Samples	P values
Rio Comprido × Morro do Ouro	0.0000
Rio Comprido × Composite	0.0000
Rio Comprido × Ilha de Espinheiros II	0.0000
Rio Comprido × Enseada I	0.0000
Rio Comprido × Itacoara	0.0000
Morro do Ouro × Composite	0.0000
Morro do Ouro × Ilha de Espinheiros II	0.7004
Morro do Ouro × Enseada I	0.0000
Morro do Ouro × Itacoara	0.0000
Composite × Ilha de Espinheiros II	0.0031
Composite × Enseada I	0.0000
Composite × Itacoara	0.0000
Ilha de Espinheiros II × Enseada I	0.0000
Ilha de Espinheiros II × Itacoara	0.8472
Enseada I × Itacoara	0.0000

stress. In the case of the second point, we were especially interested in the biological stresses associated with the transition from hunting-gathering to cultivation (Rebecca Huss-Ashmore et al., 1982).

No significant increase of dental cavities was observed for the ceramic period. In fact, some preceramic samples (Rio Comprido and Morro do Ouro) showed a significant higher incidence of this pathology when compared to any of the ceramic skeletal samples. This seems to indicate that the amount of carbohydrates ingested in the later period of the local prehistory was even smaller than that consumed during archaic times, at least when the classic shell-mounds are taken as a whole. The degree of tooth wear does not allow for the conclusion that preoral treatment of food items was intensified during the ceramic period. Accordingly, Enseada I, a ceramic sample, presented the most marked degree of tooth wear. Also, the distribution of tooth wear in the different tooth categories in the ceramic period remained the

Table 13.8: Incidence of Teeth Showing Linear Enamel Hypoplasia (LEH) in Each Sample

	Total number of observed teeth	Absolute frequencies of affected teeth	Relative frequencies of affected teeth (%)
Preceramic samples			
Rio Comprido	21	4	19.00
Morro do Ouro	142	28	20.00
Composite	29	3	10.00
Ilha de Espinheiros II	26	7	26.00
Forte Marechal Luz PR	—	—	—
Ceramic samples			
Enseada I	19	3	16.00
Itacoara	52	6	12.00
Forte Marechal Luz CR	14	1	7.00

Table 13.9: Incidence of Individuals Showing Linear Enamel Hypoplasia (LEH) in Each Sample

	Total number of observed individuals	Absolute frequencies of affected individuals	Relative frequencies of affected individuals (%)
Preceramic samples			
Rio Comprido	8	4	50.00
Morro do Ouro	40	17	42.50
Composite	10	3	30.00
Ilha de Espinheiros II	5	2	40.00
Forte Marechal Luz PR	—	—	—
Ceramic samples			
Enseada I	6	3	50.00
Itacoara	14	4	28.57
Forte Marechal Luz CR	3	1	33.33

same as that of the earlier period. The figures obtained indicate strongly that pre-oral and oral food processing were similar in groups of both occupations. Linear enamel hypoplasias showed no significant difference between preceramic and ceramic levels, also indicating that the degree of stress arising from unspecific causes was similar in both periods. The expression of porotic hyperostosis showed a clear, significant decrease with the advent of pottery making. This suggests that the preceramic archaic peoples suffered more significantly from iron-deficiency anemia.

Regarding the health index, the values obtained for the preceramic and ceramic populations treated in this study are both very high and very similar, and can be said to be among the first three high scores obtained in the joint project. They are

Table 13.10: Comparison of Incidence of Teeth Showing
Linear Enamel Hypoplasia (LEH) Between Samples
(Fisher Exact Test)

Samples	P values
Rio Comprido × Morro do Ouro	1.0000
Rio Comprido × Composite	0.4341
Rio Comprido × Ilha de Espinheiros II	0.7310
Rio Comprido × Enseada I	1.0000
Rio Comprido × Itacoara	0.4593
Rio Comprido × Forte Marechal Luz CR	0.6272
Morro do Ouro × Composite	0.2975
Morro do Ouro × Ilha de Espinheiros II	0.4336
Morro do Ouro × Enseada I	1.0000
Morro do Ouro × Itacoara	0.2082
Morro do Ouro × Forte Marechal Luz CR	0.4698
Composite × Ilha de Espinheiros II	0.1644
Composite × Enseada I	0.6690
Composite × Itacoara	1.0000
Composite × Forte Marechal Luz CR	1.0000
Ilha de Espinheiros II × Enseada I	0.4805
Ilha de Espinheiros II × Itacoara	0.1108
Ilha de Espinheiros II × Forte Marechal Luz CR	0.2216
Enseada I × Itacoara	0.6928
Enseada I × Forte Marechal Luz CR	0.6197
Itacoara × Forte Marechal Luz CR	1.0000

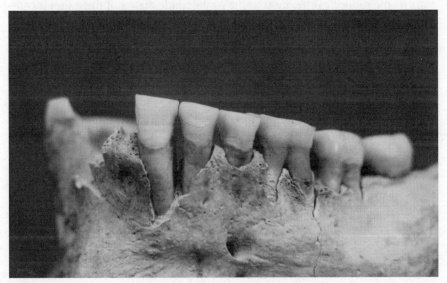

Figure 13.3. Lower jaw showing a series of linear enamel hypoplasia in canine, first and second premolars (Sambaqui Morro do Ouro). (Photo: V. Wesolowski.)

Table 13.11: Incidence of Individuals Affected by Porotic Hyperostosis in Each Sample

	Total number of observed individuals	Absolute frequencies of affected individuals	Relative frequency of affected individuals (%)
Preceramic samples			
Rio Comprido	12	8	66.66
Morro do Ouro	40	8	20.00
Composite	20	4	20.00
Ilha de Espinheiros II	4	3	75.00
Forte Marechal Luz PR	7	3	42.00
Ceramic samples			
Enseada I	16	0	0
Itacoara	17	4	23.54
Forte Marechal Luz CR	3	1	33.33

only paralleled by another coastal sample, from California (see Chapter 17 for more detail).

The first result from the present study that deserves discussion is the high prevalence of dental cavities detected among some of the preceramic samples, indicating a high consumption of carbohydrates. As previously emphasized, these sites have been repeatedly described in the Brazilian archaeological literature as the product of a highly specialized hunter-gatherer tradition, with meager intake of carbohydrates (André Prous, 1990; Maria D. Gaspar, 1998; Tânia A. Lima, 1999–2000).

As we mentioned before, most of the stratigraphic matrix of these sites is composed of shell refuse, and the conclusions reached by the excavators about the subsistence of these groups have been heavily influenced by this fact. Levy Figuti (1993), however, has demonstrated that when quantitative faunal analyses are performed on similar shell-mounds from the State of São Paulo, conclusions about the subsistence at these sites change dramatically, with the most important food source appearing to be fish, and not shellfish, as has been traditionally assumed. Tânia A. Lima (1991) has also emphasized that subsistence among the coastal preceramic populations could have been much more varied and locally adapted than previously thought, taking into account her experience with similar sites in the coast of Rio de Janeiro, further north.

Our results seem to add to the diversity of subsistence patterns that is emerging in the literature. At least in specific moments of their existence, the shell-mound builders of the Northern Coast of Santa Catarina relied significantly on vegetable food items for their survival. Unfortunately, we have very few dates for the region, and one of our preceramic samples is composed of skeletons recovered from several classical sites. As a result, the suggestion of any kind of temporal trend for the Santa Catarina population seems to us to be risky. On the other hand, our results suggest that the two most affected sites are the oldest preceramic shell-mounds. Would this

Table 13.12: Comparison of Incidence of Individuals
Showing Porotic Hyperostosis Between Samples
(Fisher Exact Test)

Samples	P values
Rio Comprido × Morro do Ouro	0.0041
Rio Comprido × Composite	0.0213
Rio Comprido × Ilha de Espinheiros II	1.0000
Rio Comprido × Forte Marechal Luz PR	0.3765
Rio Comprido × Enseada I	0.0002
Rio Comprido × Itacoara	0.0287
Rio Comprido × Forte Marechal Luz CR	0.5253
Morro do Ouro × Composite	1.0000
Morro do Ouro × Ilha de Espinheiros II	0.0425
Morro do Ouro × Forte Marechal Luz PR	0.3296
Morro do Ouro × Enseada I	0.0892
Morro do Ouro × Itacoara	0.7371
Morro do Ouro × Forte Marechal Luz CR	0.5151
Composite × Ilha de Espinheiros II	0.0593
Composite × Forte Marechal Luz PR	0.3278
Composite × Enseada I	0.1131
Composite × Itacoara	1.0000
Composite × Forte Marechal Luz CR	0.5392
Ilha de Espinheiros II × Forte Marechal Luz PR	0.5455
Ilha de Espinheiros II × Enseada I	0.0035
Ilha de Espinheiros II × Itacoara	0.0877
Ilha de Espinheiros II × Forte Marechal Luz CR	0.4857
Forte Marechal Luz PR × Enseada I	0.0198
Forte Marechal Luz PR × Itacoara	0.3742
Forte Marechal Luz PR × Forte Marechal Luz CR	1.0000
Enseada I × Itacoara	0.1046
Enseada I × Forte Marechal Luz CR	0.1579
Itacoara × Forte Marechal Luz CR	1.0000

mean that plant resources were more important for the groups that first settled the new region?

When we consider that cavity rates reach the relatively high levels of 5.8% in Rio Comprido and 7.4% in Morro do Ouro, two preceramic shell-mound groups, and taking into account what is known about the relationship between intake of carbohydrates and dental decay, we believe a less normative thinking about these sites should be adopted. That is, archaeologists should be much more open to the possibility of a wider range of subsistence patterns among the classical shell-mound builders of Southern Brazil.

The second point that deserves discussion is that none of the markers that usually increase in incidence with the adoption of plant cultivation showed such a tendency

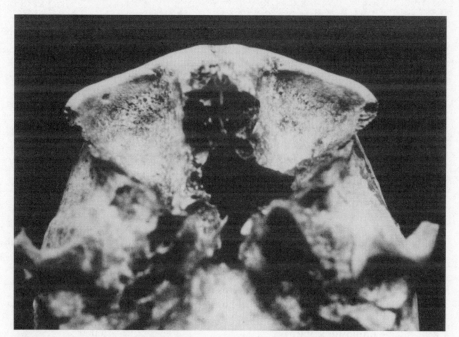

Figure 13.4. Cranium seen from below showing both orbits affected by porotic hyperostosis (Sambaqui Morro do Ouro). (Photo: W. Neves.)

when the early and the late occupation samples were compared. The incidence of dental cavities declined in the ceramic period, suggesting that the ingestion of carbohydrates diminished with the introduction of pottery in the area; tooth wear increased, indicating no intensification of pre-oral preparation of the food items ingested; linear enamel hypoplasias showed a very similar incidence among all samples; and porotic hyperostosis declined in the second period. We think these results taken together allow us to conclude that it is very unlikely that the introduction of pottery making in the Northern Coast of Santa Catarina around AD 1000 was also accompanied by the adoption of plant cultivation as a major subsistence strategy.[2] This conclusion is consistent with the general fact that the pottery vessels encountered in the ceramic sites are very small in size, and would be inadequate to process and store great amounts of plant items (Igor Chmyz, personal communication; Anamaria Beck, personal communication).

The last point that deserves consideration is the general health status of the populations analyzed in this chapter when compared among themselves, and vis-à-vis the other samples included in the joint project. As we remarked previously, the populations corresponding to both occupations from Santa Catarina, South Brazil, are among the healthiest populations in the project, and the values attained by them are very similar. This is clear when one considers the QALY index

---

[2] Marco N. De Masi (personal communication) has recently analyzed the isotopic content of some human skeletons from the ceramic level of Enseada I and reached the conclusion that at least no C_4 plant was systematically cultivated and ingested by the pottery-making group that occupied the site.

itself, or the percentage of the maximum reached (see Chapter 3 for the details). Taking into account their similarity in terms of health status and that no systematic plant cultivation seems to have been introduced in the area around AD 1000 by the pottery makers, two things are suggested: first, that the newcomers abandoned their original subsistence strategies (developed when they were in the hinterlands, far from the seashore) in favor of the one traditionally practiced by the coastal pre-ceramic populations since 6000 BP; and second, that the introduction of pottery-making technology alone does not seem to have been of major positive impact in the already excellent health status of the coastal populations of Santa Catarina.

How can we explain the fact that both populations are among the healthiest skeletal populations studied in the Western Hemisphere? Our belief is that the high quality of health attained by the individuals in these populations is primarily related to three different environmental factors. The first factor is primary and secondary productivity: tropical estuary zones are nutrient-rich environments and are among the most productive landscapes of the planet (Michael J. Kennish, 1990; Howard T. Odum, 1994). A complex food web exists in estuarine ecosystems structured by two major interlocking components of energy flow, that is, detrital and grazing pathways (Michael J. Kennish, 1990). As such, a high-quality and nutrient-rich diet was easily obtainable at a close distance using simple technological devices.

The second factor is predictability: the availability of the invertebrate and ver-tebrate faunas is very similar over the whole year, because seasonality has little influence on the overall productivity of mangrove swamps and associated microen-vironments. Even if some species, mainly of fish, have a seasonal behavior in terms of reproduction and, consequently, availability, the wide range of potential nutritional sources would compensate for this (Francis D. Por, 1994; George K. Reid, 1964).

The third factor is the presence of a natural system of waste removal, asso-ciated with the tide cycles (Michael J. Kennish, 1990). This minimizes the risks of contamination by human and animal parasites. Even if these populations were demographically denser than what we normally assume for hunter-gatherer groups, as seems to have been the case for the Northern Coast of Santa Catarina, their waste would not accumulate around their living areas for more than a few hours.

This explanation is reinforced by the fact that among the first 15 groups scored as the healthiest in the joint project, 9 refer to coastal populations of different parts of the American continent, with totally different cultural trajectories (see Chapter 3 for more information about the health score ranking). As a result, an environmental explanation seems to us to be more feasible than one of cultural or social nature.

We hope that the reader has realized that even under very unfavorable condi-tions in terms of archaeological context, such as is the case for the coast of Santa Catarina, studies of human skeletal remains based on osteological markers of quality and style of life can still be very informative. Future joint efforts between physical anthropologists and archaeologists will be of paramount importance in improving our understanding of human adaptation and social organization along the Brazilian Southern Coast, and especially on the Northern Coast of Santa Catarina. However, Brazilian archaeologists will have to move to a more theoretically based research strategy, and abandon their long tradition of digging first and thinking after.

In the last four decades, archaeological method and theory have advanced substantially. However, few if any of these advancements have been absorbed by the Brazilian senior archaeological community, as has been pointed out on several occasions by Walter A. Neves (1988b, 1999–2000), Cristiana Barreto (1998, 1999–2000), and Francisco Noelli (1999–2000). It is not just a matter of generating quantitatively better samples of human skeletal remains to be analyzed by well-trained skeletal biologists; it is also a matter of generating good samples of skeletons that can be used to test specific hypotheses raised by archaeological information. Without these changes, anthropological research in the area will remain very limited.

REFERENCES

Barreto, Cristiana. "Brazilian archaeology from a Brazilian Perspective." *Antiquity* 72 (1998): 573–581.
   "A construção de um passado pré-colonial: Uma breve história da arqueologia no Brasil." *Revista USP* 44 (1999–2000): 32–51.
Beck, Anamaria. "A variação do conteúdo cultural dos sambaquis. Litoral de Santa Catarina." Ph.D. diss., University of São Paulo, 1972.
   "O Sambaqui de Enseada I – SC LN 71 – um estudo sobre tecnologia pré-histórica." Full Professorship diss., University of Santa Catarina, 1974.
Beck, Anamaria, E. M. Araújo, and G. M. Duarte. "Síntese da arqueologia do litoral norte de Santa Catarina." *Anais do Museu de Antropologia da UFSC* 3 (1970): 23–48.
Beck, Anamaria, G. M. Duarte, and M. J. Reis. "Sambaqui do Morro do Ouro. Nota prévia." *Pesquisas Série Antropologia* 20 (1969): 31–40.
Bigarella, Jose J., Guilherme Tiburtitus, and A. Sobanski. "Contribuição ao estudo dos sambaquis do litoral norte de Santa Catarina I. Situação geográfica e descrição sumária." *Arquivos de Biologia e Tecnologia* 9 (1954): 99–140.
Bryan, Alan L. "Resumo da arqueologia do sambaqui do Forte Marechal Luz." *Arquivos do Museu de História Natural da UFMG* 2 (1977): 9–30.
   The Sambaqui at Forte Marechal Luz, State of Santa Catarina, Brazil. Brazilian Studies. Corvallis: Center for the Study of the First Americans, and Oregon State University, 1993.
Chmyz, Igor. "A ocupação do litoral dos estados do Paraná e Santa Catarina por povos ceramistas." *Estudos Brasileiros* 1 (1976): 7–43.
Cohen, M. N., and George J. Armelagos. "An introduction to the symposium." In *Paleopathology at the Origins of Agriculture*, ed. M. N. Cohen and G. J. Armelagos, 1–11. New York: Academic Press, 1984.
De Masi, Marco A. N. "Prehistoric hunter-gatherer mobility on the Southern Brazilian coast: Santa Catarina Island." Unpublished Ph.D. diss., Stanford University, 1999.
El-Najjar, Mahmoud Y., et al. "The etiology of porotic hyperostosis among the prehistoric and historic Anasazi Indians of southwestern United States." *American Journal of Physical Anthropology* 44 (1976): 477–487.
Figuti, Levy. "O homem pré histórico, o molusco e o sambaqui: considerações sobre a subsistência dos povos sambaquieiros." *Revista do MAE* 3 (1993): 67–80.
Gaspar, Maria D. "Aspectos da organização de um grupo de pescadores, coletores e caçadores: Região compreendida entre a Ilha Grande e o Delta do Paraíba do Sul, Estado do Rio de Janeiro." Unpublished Ph.D. diss., University of São Paulo, 1991.
   "Considerations of the sambaquis of the Brazilian coast." *Antiquity* 72 (1998): 592–615.

Goodman, Alan H., and Jerome Rose. "Assessment of systemic physiological perturbations from dental enamel hypoplasias and associated structures." *Yearbook of Physical Anthropology* 33 (1990): 59–110.

Goodman, Alan H., L. H. Allen, G. P. Hernandez, A. Amador, L.V. Arriola, A. Chavez, and G. H. Pelto. "Prevalence and age at development of enamel hypoplasias in Mexican children." *American Journal of Physical Anthropology* 72 (1987): 7–19.

Goodman, Alan H., George J. Armelagos, and Jerome C. Rose. "Enamel hypoplasias as indicators of stress in three prehistoric populations from Illinois." *Human Biology* 52, no. 3 (1980): 515–528.

Goodman, Alan H., J. Lallo, George J. Armelagos, and Jerome C. Rose. "Health changes at Dickson Mounds, Illinois (AD 950–1300)." In *Paleopathology at the Origins of Agriculture*, ed. M. N. Cohen and G. J. Armelagos, 271–306. New York: Academic Press, 1984.

Goulart, Mariland. "Tecnologia e padrões de subsistência de grupos pescadores-coletores pré-históricos, habitantes do sambaqui do Morro do Ouro – Joinville – Santa Catarina." Unpublished manuscript, Joinville, Santa Catarina, 1980.

Hinton, R. J. "Form and patterning of anterior tooth wear among aboriginal human groups." *American Jounal of Physical Anthropology* 54 (1981): 555–564.

Huss-Ashmore, Rebecca, Alan H. Goodman, and George J. Armelagos. "Nutritional inference from paleopathology." *Advances in Archaelogical Method and Theory* 5 (1982): 395–474.

Kennish, Michael J. *Ecology of Estuaries.* Boca Raton, Fla.: CRC Press, 1990.

Larsen, Clark. "Health and disease in prehistoric Georgia: The transition to agriculture." In *Paleopathology at the Origins of Agriculture,* ed. M. N. Cohen and G. J. Armelagos, 367–392. New York: Academic Press, 1984.

Lima, Tânia A. "Dos Mariscos aos peixes: Um estudo zooarqueológico de mudança de subsistência na pré-história do Rio de Janeiro." Ph.D. diss., University of São Paulo, 1991.

——— "Em busca dos frutos do mar: Os pescadores-coletores do litoral centro-sul do Brasil." *Revista USP* 44 (1999–2000): 270–327.

Lima, Tânia A., Walter A. Neves, and André Prous. "Projeto Babitonga: Uma proposta de releitura dos sambaquis do litoral meridional brasileiro." *Revista do CEPA* 23 (1999): 124–130.

Molnar, Stephen. "Human teeth wear, tooth function and cultural variability." *American Journal of Physical Anthropology* 34 (1971): 175–190.

Moore-Jansen, Peer, et al. "A model for dietary reconstruction of the prehistoric Caddo Indians." *51st Annual Meeting of the American Association of Physical Anthropology*, Eugene, Ore., 1982.

Neves, Walter A. "Variação métrica nos construtores de sambaquis do sul do Brasil: Primeira aproximação multivariada." *Revista de Pré-História* 4 (1982): 83–108.

——— "Paleogenética dos grupos pré-históricos do litoral sul do Brasil (Paraná e Santa Catarina)." *Pesquisas Série Antropologia* 43 (1988a).

——— "Arqueologia Brasileira: Algumas considerações." *Boletim do Museu Paraense Emilio Goeldi, Antropologia* 2 (1988b): 200–205.

——— "Antes de Cabral: A arqueologia e a sociodiversidade no passado." *Revista USP* 44 (1999–2000): 6–9.

Noelli, Francisco S. "A ocupação humana da região sul do Brasil: arqueologia, debates e perspectivas – 1872–2000." *Revista USP* 44 (1999–2000): 218–269.

Odum, Howard T. *Ecological and General Systems. An Introduction to Systems Ecology.* Denver: University Press of Colorado, 1994.

Palkovich, Ann. "Endemic disease patterns in paleopathology: Porotic hyperostosis." *American Journal of Physical Anthropology* 74 (1987): 527–537.

Por, Francis D. *Guia Ilustrado do Manguezal Brasileiro.* São Paulo: Instituto de Biociências da USP, 1994.

Prous, André. *Arqueologia Brasileira.*Brasíla: Editora da Universidade de Brasília, 1990.

Prous, André, and Walter F. Piazza. "Documents pour la préhistoire du Brésil Méridionel 2. L'état de Santa Catarina." *Cahiers d'Archéologie d'Amérique du Sud* 5 (1977).

Reid, George K. *Ecology of Inland Waters and Estuaries.* London: Chapman & Hall, 1964.

Schmitz, Pedro I. "As tradições ceramistas do planalto sul-brasileiro." *Documentos* 2 (1988): 75–130.

Smith, Patricia, Ofer Bar-Yosef, and A. Sillen. "Archaeological and skeletal evidence for dietary change during the Late Pleistocene/Early Holocene in the Levant." In *Paleopathology at the Origins of Agriculture,* ed. M. N. Cohen and G. J. Armelagos, 101–127. New York: Academic Press, 1984.

Stuart-Macadam, Patricia. "Porotic hyperostosis: New evidence to support the anemia theory." *American Journal of Physical Anthropology* 74 (1987): 521–526.

Tiburtius, Guilherme, João J. Bigarella, and Iris K Bigarella. "Nota prévia sobre a jazida paleoetnográfica de Itacoara, Joinville, Santa Catarina." *Ciência e Cultura* 3, no.4 (1951): 267–268.

Turner, Christy G., II. "Dental anthropological indications of agriculture among the Jomon people of Central Japan." *American Journal of Physical Anthropology* 51 (1979): 619–636.

Wobst, H. M. "The archeo-ethnology of hunter-gatherers or the tyranny of the ethnographic record in archaeology." *American Antiquity* 43 (1978): 303–309.

PART VI

NATIVE AMERICANS IN NORTH AMERICA

Introduction

Native Americans of North America are the largest group in this project, involving 52 percent of the individuals and 43 percent of the 65 sites under study. These sites were also diverse, chronologically ranging in age from about 3000 BC to the late nineteenth century, and they encompass a wide variety of habitats from temperate coastal areas to the high Plains. The region from the Great Lakes to the southern Atlantic coast was home to 10 of the 28 sites in this group, and most of the rest were concentrated in the Plains east of the Rockies. The single largest group in the entire study (about one-quarter of the entire database), however, was located in Southern California.

Table VI.1 shows that the North American natives were relatively healthy (as measured by skeletal lesions), particularly those who lived in the East. In that region, the health index was 78.1, which exceeds the average for all sites by 5.5 points. In sharp contrast to sites in Central and South America, the natives of eastern North America were remarkably tall, a phenomenon that may have been related to greater access to dietary protein from game. It is notable that scores on childhood indicators of health were high at most sites in the East. The region fell (slightly) below average only on dental health. Only one site in this region had below-average health – SunWatch, which was brought down by particularly low (for the region) scores on dental health and infections.

Many sites in the West were also healthy. All but 3 out of 18 sites scored above average, and the index exceeded 80 at 4 sites. Three sites with very poor health were located in New Mexico, where the individuals had high rates of biological stress in childhood and carried a heavy load of degenerative joint disease. These sites were above average in only one category – infections. Among the sites outside New Mexico, the component scores fell more than 15 points below average only for trauma (Cheyenne), infections (Crow and Blackfoot), and stature (village Ponca).

Table VI.1: Health Index and Component Scores of North American Populations

Investigator	Age BP	Description	Index	Stature	Hyp.	Anemia	Dental	Inf.	DJD	Trauma
		East								
Larsen	1350	Coastal South Carolina	89.2	59.8	*	98.6	99.9	92.9	91.1	93.2
Larsen	0325	Coastal South Carolina	83.8	31.7	92.4	92.6	93.7	92.2	100.0	*
Larsen	0600	Coastal South Carolina	80.9	24.3	*	98.4	94.5	83.3	88.2	96.8
Larsen	1350	Coastal South Carolina	80.3	9.3	*	100.0	99.7	96.6	90.4	86.0
Sciulli	2600	Treglia, Great Lakes region	77.9	48.2	92.2	94.5	75.2	83.1	67.8	84.2
Sciulli	0350	Buffalo, Great Lakes region	77.3	36.5	88.3	91.9	64.4	86.2	79.3	94.9
Sciulli	0900	Pearson, Great Lakes region	73.7	33.9	70.5	97.1	67.3	79.7	76.4	90.9
Larsen	0325	Coastal South Carolina	73.6	22.4	*	92.9	90.7	53.8	82.2	99.5
Sciulli	0650	Monongahela, Great Lakes region	72.9	24.5	93.5	92.0	62.8	81.0	73.1	83.2
Sciulli	0750	SunWatch, Great Lakes region	71.6	31.6	83.3	89.3	68.9	66.7	75.2	86.5
		Average, East	78.1	32.2	86.7	94.7	81.7	81.6	82.4	90.6
		Std. dev., East	5.6	14.1	8.8	3.6	15.3	12.9	9.9	5.9
		West								
Walker	1075	Coastal Southern California	82.4	42.8	85.0	96.1	97.4	83.8	78.6	93.4
Owsley	0075	Equestrian nomad, Blackfoot	81.5	*	*	95.2	86.6	52.5	87.8	85.5
Owsley	0200	Plains village, Pawnee	80.4	21.0	*	99.2	89.0	89.9	90.6	92.5
Walker	5250	Coastal Southern California	80.0	18.6	81.6	95.5	84.5	92.0	100.0	87.7

Walker	3834	Coastal Southern California	79.0	12.6	89.4	*	95.0	*	100.0	98.1
Owsley	0155	Plains village, Omaha	78.9	27.2	*	99.8	91.0	86.3	82.4	86.8
Owsley	0155	Plains village, Ponca	76.4	2.7	*	100.0	92.5	78.8	89.1	95.5
Walker	1625	Coastal Southern California	76.3	20.4	82.7	87.6	80.7	89.5	91.8	81.6
Owsley	0075	Equestrian nomad, Crow	75.9	49.9	*	93.0	90.6	49.3	82.3	90.2
Walker	0434	Coastal Southern California	75.7	12.2	87.2	90.5	83.9	84.6	85.2	85.8
Owsley	0170	Plains village, Arikara	75.1	16.8	*	99.3	83.1	87.1	72.6	92.0
Owsley	0475	Plains Arikara & Oneota	74.5	23.7	*	94.0	78.7	67.4	90.6	92.7
Owsley	0240	Plains village, Arikara	74.4	17.2	*	97.4	84.3	87.0	76.8	83.6
Owsley	0071	Equestrian nomad, Cheyenne	72.9	47.8	*	99.2	89.5	76.3	81.4	43.4
Walker	0075	Northern California	72.8	36.1	60.4	97.2	81.3	89.0	68.5	77.1
Martin	1050	Dolores, New Mexico	59.8	7.9	34.8	55.0	79.1	91.0	66.8	83.8
Martin	0448	San Cristobel, New Mexico	57.3	1.7	46.5	53.2	78.5	88.1	52.8	80.2
Martin	0398	Hawikku, New Mexico	53.5	4.0	26.9	55.8	73.6	80.0	50.0	84.3
		Average, West	73.7	21.3	66.1	83.8	85.5	80.7	80.4	85.2
		Std. dev, West	8.3	15.1	24.5	16.6	6.4	12.8	14.1	11.8
		Average, 65 sites	72.6	20.7	71.1	90.5	81.8	75.1	78.9	85.7
		Std dev, 65 sites	8.0	16.9	24.6	11.5	10.4	17.0	12.3	16.1
		Minimum, 65 sites	53.5	0.4	9.8	53.2	55.3	44.1	41.6	10.8
		Maximum, 65 sites	91.8	67.8	99.7	100.0	100.0	98.7	100.0	100.0

* = not available.

Source: Consolidated database.

405

CHAPTER FOURTEEN

A Biohistory of Health and Behavior in the Georgia Bight

The Agricultural Transition and the Impact of European Contact

C. S. Larsen, A. W. Crosby, M. C. Griffin, D. L. Hutchinson,
C. B. Ruff, K. F. Russell, M. J. Schoeninger, L. E. Sering,
S. W. Simpson, J. L. Takács, and M. F. Teaford

ABSTRACT

This chapter tracks temporal and regional trends in health in the midregion of the Georgia Bight, a large embayment extending from northern coastal Atlantic Florida to North Carolina. The study explores changes in health in precontact and contact-era native populations that in historic times were known as Guale. Comparison of prehistoric foragers (1100 BC–AD 1150) and prehistoric farmers (AD 1150–1550) and early mission (AD 1550–1680) and late mission (AD 1686–1702) intensive agriculturalists reveals a clear reduction in health and an increase in workload and physical activity in this subtropical coastal setting. In comparison with other regions of the Western Hemisphere, the health index of the Georgia Bight populations was relatively high, with the exception of the late mission group. The latter's position relative to other regions reflects a decline in health with long-term interaction with and exploitation by Spaniards. The trends identified in this study are generally consistent with other patterns identified elsewhere in North and South America, especially regarding health decline with the shift to an agricultural economy and increased population sedentism and aggregation.

INTRODUCTION

Human remains from the Georgia Bight offer a rich record for tracking and interpreting the biohistory of human populations in North America (Figure 14.1). This chapter recounts this record, especially with regard to how bioarchaeological study informs our understanding of two major events and their impact on health and

We thank the organizers of the History of Health and Nutrition in the Western Hemisphere Project – Richard Steckel and Jerome Rose – for their invitation to join their ambitious effort and for allowing us to offer our perspective on human health. Funding for analysis came from the National Science Foundation. The Department of Anthropology, University of North Carolina, Chapel Hill, provided graduate assistant support for data coding. We especially thank Joseph Herbert for his assistance in the compilation of the data set. The data were originally gathered under the auspices of the La Florida Bioarchaeology Project, directed by C. S. Larsen. We gratefully acknowledge the contributions to the project by the following individuals: Amy Bushnell, Inui Choi, John H. Hann, Kenneth W. Hardin, Dawn Harn, Bonnie G. McEwan, Jerald T. Milanich, Rebecca Shavit, David Hurst Thomas, and Nikolaas J. van der Merwe.

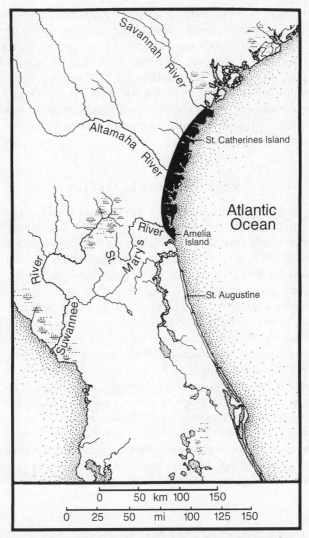

Figure 14.1. Map showing the location of the Georgia Bight.

behavior/activity in this setting: (1) the adoption and intensification of maize agri-culture, and (2) the arrival of Europeans and the establishment of Roman Catholic missions. These events mark major departures from previous lifeways both in this area and the Western Hemisphere generally (Reitz 1988; Larsen 1994). The shift from foraging to farming has been studied by archaeologists and others from a range of settings around the world. Traditionally, most scholars and others have regarded the shift to have been very beneficial for humankind, setting the stage for the rise of civilization and complex societies, urbanization, writing, art, and so forth. Evidence from human remains in the Georgia Bight and elsewhere in the Western Hemisphere allows us to address this long-held assumption. The arrival of Europeans in the New

World and its impact on the health of native populations is known mostly from written sources. These sources generally focus on the impact of the introduction of Old World diseases and demographic collapse. The bioarchaeological record suggests reduction in health. However, the range of information provided from study of skeletons provides new insight into adaptations that native peoples make to new and novel circumstances, such as increased workload. Extensive samples of human remains from contact-era sites in coastal Georgia and northern Florida help us to develop a broader picture of biological change in native populations in ways not possible from written documents alone.

THE ENVIRONMENTAL SETTING

The Georgia Bight is a large embayment extending from Cape Hatteras, North Carolina, to Cape Canaveral, Florida (Larsen 1994, 1995). A dominant feature is the chain of barrier islands sharing similar Pleistocene and Holocene depositional and ecological histories. Lying between the outermost barrier islands and the mainland are various marsh islands. The barrier islands and marsh islands are separated by sounds, salt marshes, and tidal creeks. The topography of the islands and adjacent mainland is characterized by very low relief with a diverse subtropical flora and fauna. Primary plant communities on the islands are maritime oak and pine forests. The inshore zone includes a tremendously rich and variable estuarine fauna, including numerous fishes, such as red drum (*Sciaenops ocellatus*), mullets (*Mugil* spp.), and flounders (*Paralichthys* spp.), and invertebrates, such as oyster (*Crassostrea virginica*), shrimp (*Penaeus* spp.), and hard clams (*Mercenaria* spp.). These resources played a crucial role in the foodways of native populations living in the tidewater zone following the establishment of post-Pleistocene sea levels. The remains of terrestrial species of plants (e.g., acorns from live oaks) and animals (e.g., deer) are frequently encountered in archaeological sites, indicating the important role of these resources. Marine foods, however, appear to have been a primary focus of diet throughout prehistory and into the historic period.

THE POPULATION GROUPS

Three broad temporal groups, demarcated by the adoption of maize in later prehistory and the arrival of Europeans and establishment of missions, provide the basis for comparative analysis and identification of significant shifts in health. These groups include the precontact preagricultural, precontact agricultural, and contact samples. Within the contact group, identification of earlier and later mission native populations has been made possible by an abundant historical record. This record documents movement and resettlement of native populations from coastal Georgia to northern Florida in the late seventeenth century. Therefore, for the purposes of this discussion, we divide the contact samples into early contact and late contact groups. In all, the analysis presented here involves comparisons of four subsamples. A summary of the mortuary samples, site, and temporal associations is provided in Table 14.1 The following overview provides a description of each of the four population groupings, including economic and social activities, sources of evidence, dietary ecology, and other relevant information.

Precontact Preagricultural Group (1100 BC–AD 1150)

This series is drawn from 21 sites on the Georgia coast dating from circa 1100 BC to the middle to late twelfth century AD. This spans the Woodland period of eastern North America, known locally as the Refuge (1100–400 BC), Deptford (400 BC–AD 500), Wilmington (AD 500–1000), and St. Catherines (AD 1000–1150) periods. Although covering a lengthy time span, most of the remains postdate AD 700.

Analysis of plant and animal remains from a wide variety of sites indicates that diet was based exclusively on resources acquired through hunting, gathering, and fishing (Larsen 1982; Reitz 1988). These foods include the aforementioned terrestrial and marine flora and fauna. Dietary reconstruction using stable isotopes (carbon and nitrogen) and element (barium and strontium) analysis from human bone (collagen) shows a heavy reliance on marine foods, thus confirming dietary reconstructions based on study of archaeological food remains (Schoeninger et al. 1990; Larsen et al. 1990, 1992, 2000, 2001; Ezzo et al. 1995; Hutchinson et al. 1998).[1]

Analysis of settlement patterns, location of habitation sites, and size and density of habitation sites indicates that population during this time was small, dispersed, and probably highly transitory (Thomas, unpublished; Larsen 1982). This pattern suggests that populations were low in density and followed a foraging strategy involving movement, at least on a seasonal basis, prior to the twelfth century AD.

Precontact Agricultural Group (AD 1150–1550)

The later prehistoric series is from 23 mortuary sites on the Georgia coast dating from circa AD 1150 to 1550 or so. The populations these remains represent are from the earlier and later Mississippian occupations of the region known locally as the Savannah (AD 1150–1300) and Irene (AD 1300–1550) periods, respectively. Analysis of plant and animal remains from late prehistoric sites indicates a continued reliance on the same suite of food items eaten by earlier populations predating AD 1150, including especially marine and terrestrial fauna and nondomesticated plants. Archaeobotanical evidence for consumption of domesticated plants is

---

[1] The stable isotopes of carbon (^{12}C and ^{13}C) and nitrogen (^{14}N and ^{15}N) provide a wealth of information about past diets. The ratios of ^{12}C to ^{13}C reveal the kinds of plants eaten. In eastern North America, most economically important plants have a C_3 photosynthesis pathway, whereas maize has a C_4 pathway. Owing to the differences in photosynthesis, the stable isotope ratios of carbon are different. These differences are passed up the food chain to the consumers, leaving a distinctive signature in the bones. Similarly, land-based and marine-based plants utilize nitrogen differently, resulting in a distinction between the stable isotope ratios of nitrogen. These differences are also passed up the food chain, so that humans eating marine foods have different stable nitrogen isotope ratios than humans eating terrestrial foods. The amount of barium and barium/strontium ratios are considerably lower in marine organisms and people consuming these organisms than in people who eat predominantly terrestrial foods. With the combined information provided by stable isotope ratios and barium/strontium ratios, our picture of food use is established.

Table 14.1: Mortuary Localities, Georgia Bight

Site code	Site	N (1413)
Precontact preagricultural (pre-AD 1150)		
101	South New Ground Mound	1
102	Cunningham Mound C	4
103	Cunningham Mound D	2
104	Cunningham Mound E	1
105	McLeod Mound	14
106	Seaside Mound I	17
107	Seaside Mound II	8
108	Evelyn Plantation	3
109	Airport	54
110	Deptford (nonmound)	47
111	Walthour	2
112	Cannons Point	18
113	Cedar Grove, Mound B	2
114	Cedar Grove, Mound A	1
115	Sea Island Mound	33
116	Johns Mound	65
117	Marys Mound	5
118	Charlie King Mound	15
119	Cedar Grove Mound C	8
120	South End Mound II	25
121	Indian King's Tomb	5
Precontact agricultural (AD 1150–1550)		
201	North End Mound	1
202	Low Mound, Shell Bluff	1
203	Townsend Mound	2
204	Deptford Mound	5
205	Norman Mound	25
206	Kent Mound	25
207	Lewis Creek, Mound II	7
208	Lewis Creek, Mound III	10
209	Lewis Creek, misc.	3
	Lewis Creek, Mound E	2
210	Red Knoll	5
211	Seven Mile Bend	18
212	Oatland Mound	2
213	Seaside Mound II	2
214	Irene Mound	267
215	Grove's Creek	2
216	South End Mound I	19
217	Skidaway Mitigation 3	3
218	Little Pine Island	17
219	Red Bird Creek Mound	3

Table 14.1 (*continued*)

Site code	Site	N (1413)
220	Couper Field	44
221	Taylor Mound	30
222	Indian Field	22
223	Taylor Mound/Martinez Test B	2
Early contact (AD 1550–1680)		
301	Santa Catalina de Guale	335
302	Pine Harbor	109
Late contact (AD 1686–1702)		
303	Santa Catalina de Santa Maria	122

meager (Larsen 1982). However, carbon and nitrogen stable isotope analysis reveals the significant role of maize (Schoeninger et al. 1990; Larsen et al. 1992, 2000, 2001; Hutchinson et al. 1998). In the last prehistoric period, the Irene period, isotopic evidence indicates a clear decline in maize consumption at the principal Mississippian center, the Irene Mound site, which may reflect either environmental stress (e.g., drought) or social disruption or some combination thereof (Larsen et al. 1992; Anderson 1994). The adoption of maize as an important contribution to native diets during this time has important implications for nutritional quality. Protein in maize (zein) is deficient in essential amino acids tryptophan and lysine, and it is lacking in niacin (Food and Agricultural Organization 1953). Endemic in various human populations relying on maize in the twentieth century is pellagra, which is caused by a deficiency of this vitamin (Food and Agricultural Organization 1953). Pellagra may well have been a significant health burden during the precontact agricultural period (and in the contact period). However, pellagra is not identifiable in skeletal remains, since the major symptoms of this deficiency disease are not related to the hard tissues directly. However, the stress caused by the disease could potentially be exhibited as increases in dental defects and other nonspecific indicators of physiological perturbation.

The late prehistoric population shows a major departure from the earlier pattern of small, dispersed settlements: after the twelfth century AD, there is a marked increase in the number and spatial extent of habitation sites (DePratter 1976, 1978, n.d.). This shift in settlement pattern reflects the demographic transition taking place in other agricultural settings, namely, an increase in population size and density and increasing sedentism (Larsen 1982, 1984; Crook 1984). Moreover, evidence from site structure and mortuary archaeology indicates that these population changes coincided with the appearance of complex chiefdoms, evolving out of earlier tribal societies, and the elaboration of social order and structure generally (Caldwell and McCann 1941; Anderson 1994).

Early Contact Group (AD 1550–1680)

Interaction between native populations and Europeans in the Georgia Bight came in two primary stages, the first involving exploration and inchoate attempts at colonization during the first half of the sixteenth century by major powers, principally France and Spain (Jones 1978). Because the explorations were short-term affairs and none of the colonies continued for a significant amount of time, long-term biological changes linked with the contact experience in native populations are difficult to assess. Human remains included in this study dating to the exploratory period are from the Pine Harbor site.

The second stage of contact between Europeans and Indians began in 1565 with the ousting of the French from the region by the Spanish and the founding of the first permanent European colony at St. Augustine by Pedro Menéndez de Avilés (Jones 1978). After the founding of this settlement, a series of Roman Catholic missions were established northward along the Atlantic coastline of the present-day states of Georgia and Florida. The northernmost and principal outpost was located on St. Catherines Island at Mission Santa Catalina among the Indians known as Guale. Unlike the earlier contacts between Europeans and Indians, this and other missions involved long-term, sustained contact and interaction between members of two dramatically different societies – European and Indian – each having their own highly distinctive and contrasting biological, social, and cultural histories.

Santa Catalina de Guale was a functioning mission outpost – complete with resident priests and a small military garrison – from the 1570s to 1680 (Jones 1978; Thomas 1987). Archaeological excavations in the floor of the church produced a large and comprehensive skeletal sample, numbering minimally some 432 individuals (Larsen 1993). Analysis of the architecture and building sequence of the church suggests that most human remains postdate a native uprising that took place in 1597, with subsequent rebuilding of the church a decade later, thus bracketing the skeletal series between 1607 and 1680. Abundant archaeobotanical evidence shows an unambiguous record of maize consumption, along with some other domesticated plants, including several European imports (e.g., grapes, wheat) (Ruhl 1990). Isotopic (carbon and nitrogen) and elemental (barium and strontium) analyses confirm the presence of marked reorientation of diet during the seventeenth century, indicating significant increase in maize consumption. Moreover, shift to the softer diet is indicated by microscopic changes on chewing surfaces of teeth (Teaford 1991; Teaford et al. 2001). That is, the high frequency of microscopic features (pits, scratches) reflecting coarse diet (or consumption of foods containing numerous abrasive materials) reduces. The reduction in number of microwear features may have resulted from consumption of maize cooked into stews and soft mushes in the contact-era Indians.

Analysis of historical records and settlement patterns from this period reveals that populations were even more concentrated than in the late prehistoric period. This concentration of population likely reflects the relocation of native peoples to the immediate vicinity of the mission complex on St. Catherines Island, as is also the case in other areas of Spanish Florida and Spanish America generally (Hann 1988).

The historical documentary record provides a vivid picture of work and activity by the native populations in Spanish Florida. In this region – as is the case with other provinces of New Spain – *repartimiento* labor draft was practiced (Hann 1988; Worth 1995, 2001). In this system, able-bodied Indians, mostly adult males, were required to be available for obligatory labor for a range of activities, such as building projects, road construction, carrying materials over long distances, and agricultural labor. This labor draft frequently involved relocation of adult males from their home villages for lengthy periods of time. The compensation for these activities was marginal at best, and the physical toll was high (Hann 1988; Larsen 1994; Larsen and Ruff 1994; Ruff and Larsen 2001).

Late Contact Group (AD 1686–1702)

The native and European inhabitants of St. Catherines fled the island in 1680 following an attack by British troops and British-allied Indians. Within a few years, Great Britain controlled the area, forcing native groups and the mission effort south to Amelia Island, Florida, after 1685 (Bushnell 1994; Worth 1995, 2001). Archaeological excavations of the relocated mission of Santa Catalina de Santa Maria on Amelia Island resulted in the recovery of the remains of 122 individuals (Larsen 1993). Historical, archaeobotanical, archaeozoological, isotopic, elemental, and tooth microwear analyses indicate a basic continuation of subsistence patterns established in the foregoing early contact period (Larsen 1993). Isotopic analysis suggests, however, an increased emphasis on maize during this time. Population relocation to the mission center appears to have continued. Although historical sources do not mention work patterns on Amelia Island specifically, repartimiento was certainly well in place (Worth 1995, 2001), no doubt indicating continued excessive labor, along with other stressors (e.g., epidemics, warfare, and food shortages).

Although the mission effort appears to have been successful, it was a relatively short-lived affair. Britain's interest in the region continued to move southward from the Carolinas, forcing the abandonment of the mission and its inhabitants in 1702. Indians and Europeans hence moved to St. Augustine (Worth 1995, 2001). This abandonment marks the terminal date of the late contact period skeletal series.

Summary of Georgia Bight Skeletal Series

This chapter compares biological data from native populations representing 47 skeletal samples ($n = 1413$ individuals) distributed over four temporal periods. Assessment of health and behavioral temporal trends is made by comparing the precontact preagriculturalists ($n = 330$) with precontact agriculturalists ($n = 517$), precontact agriculturalists with early contact ($n = 444$), and early contact with late contact ($n = 122$). The first comparison identifies key biological concomitants of the adoption of maize agriculture; the second, the impact of European contact and missionization on native populations; and the third, the continued influence of the mission system and interaction of Europeans and Indians. Data are unavailable for some groups (e.g., degenerative joint disease for early contact). Owing to small sample sizes for some comparisons, periods are combined (e.g., early contact and late contact for femoral growth velocity).

HISTORY OF HEALTH IN THE GEORGIA BIGHT

Our assessment of the history of health in the Georgia Bight is based on the following parameters: demography (mean age-at-death, fertility), skeletal and dental growth (growth velocity, adult height, enamel defects, tooth size), oral health (dental caries, antemortem tooth loss), iron status (cribra orbitalia, porotic hyperostosis), and infection (periosteal reactions).

Demography

The age distribution expressed as number (D_x) and percentage (d_x) of individuals dying by age class is presented in Table 14.2. Temporal comparisons reveal that the precontact agriculturalists have a slightly younger mortality peak and mean age-at-death than the previous group. Although this trend has been documented in other regions and generally interpreted to reflect increasing mortality and declining life expectancy, reevaluation of demographic profiles by several investigators suggest that mean age-at-death in skeletal samples reflects fertility and birthrate, not mortality, especially in populations that are closed to migration and have highly fluctuating growth (Sattenspiel and Harpending 1983). In particular, population growth relating to increased birthrate will express a larger number of younger individuals in the death assemblage, and hence, lower mean age-at-death for the population.

Birthrates in archaeological samples have been estimated by Buikstra and co-workers (1986) as an inverse of the proportion of number of individuals older than 30 years (D_{30+}) to number of individuals older than five years (D_{5+}). Applied to the Georgia Bight, the proportions for the respective precontact preagriculturalists and agriculturalists show a decrease from 0.3790 to 0.3500. This reduction suggests an increase in birthrate in late prehistory in this setting. This finding is consistent with the presumed population increases suggested by the settlement changes observed archaeologically during the final centuries of prehistory.

The early contact group shows a continuation of the trend identified in the prehistoric populations. That is, the early contact series has an average younger age-at-death than the precontact agriculturalists. In the late contact period, however, there is a marked reversal of the trend. That is, mortality is high in the first decade or so – more than in any of the three antecedent periods – and relatively low during the inclusive 5- to 35-year cohorts. It is again elevated after age 40; nearly 40% of the population is older than 40 years. Given the high number of older adults, the traditional perspective on the age structure of this population would indicate a major rebound in population health and well-being. After all, isn't a sign of a healthy population having lots of people live into old age? New interpretations of skeletal assemblage demographic profiles indicate that archaeological skeletons actually provide relatively little information on mortality. Rather, a more likely explanation is that the late contact Indians experienced a significant

Table 14.2: Age-at-Death Distribution, Georgia Bight

Age group	PP D_x (d_x)	PA D_x (d_x)	EC D_x (d_x)	LC D_x (d_x)
Total sample[a]				
1: 0–4.99	15 (8.9)	36 (11.4)	22 (6.9)	19 (16.7)
2: 5–9.99	23 (13.7)	24 (7.6)	44 (13.9)	8 (7.0)
3: 10–14.99	10 (5.6)	15 (4.8)	22 (6.9)	4 (3.5)
4: 15–19.99	19 (11.3)	67 (21.2)	36 (11.4)	7 (6.1)
5: 20–24.99	24 (14.3)	56 (17.7)	58 (18.4)	1 (0.8)
6: 25–29.99	19 (11.3)	20 (6.3)	51 (16.1)	6 (5.3)
7: 30–34.99	15 (8.9)	24 (7.6)	33 (10.4)	5 (4.4)
8: 35–39.99	10 (5.9)	28 (8.8)	40 (12.6)	17 (14.9)
9: 40–44.99	12 (7.1)	24 (7.6)	8 (2.5)	20 (17.5)
10: 45+	21 (12.5)	22 (6.9)	2 (0.6)	27 (23.7)
TOTAL N	168	316	316	114
MEAN AGE	23.2	22.5	21.3	29.8
D_{30+}/D_{5+}	.3790	3500	.2823	.7263
Adult males (>16.0 years)				
16.1–20	2 (5.4)	12 (14.1)	2 (7.7)	3 (7.7)
20.1–25	11 (29.7)	22 (25.9)	6 (23.1)	1 (2.6)
25.1–30	5 (13.5)	6 (7.1)	6 (23.1)	4 (10.3)
30.1–35	4 (10.8)	13 (15.3)	5 (19.2)	3 (7.7)
35.1–40	3 (8.1)	11 (12.9)	6 (23.1)	7 (18.0)
40.1–45	6 (16.2)	12 (14.1)	1 (1.2)	11 (28.2)
45.1+	6 (16.2)	9 (10.6)	0 (0.0)	10 (25.6)
TOTAL N	37	85	26	39
MEAN AGE	32.1	31.4	30.5	38.9
Adult females (>16.0 years)				
16.1–20	12 (21.8)	27 (24.6)	6 (15.0)	2 (4.9)
20.1–25	12 (21.8)	23 (20.9)	8 (20.0)	2 (4.9)
25.1–30	7 (12.7)	18 (16.4)	6 (15.0)	1 (2.4)
30.1–35	2 (3.6)	14 (12.7)	12 (30.0)	4 (9.8)
35.1–40	7 (12.7)	13 (11.8)	5 (12.5)	9 (22.0)
40.1–45	4 (7.3)	8 (7.3)	3 (7.5)	11 (26.8)
45.1+	11 (20.0)	7 (6.4)	1 (2.5)	12 (29.3)
TOTAL N	55	110	41	41
MEAN AGE	30.9	28.9	30.3	41.0

[a] Juveniles, sexed and unsexed adults.

decline in birthrate. This is also indicated by a reduction in the D_{30+}/D_{5+} proportion in a comparison of the early contact group (0.2823) and the late contact group (0.7263).

An interpretation of decline in birthrate in the late contact period is also more in line with deteriorating conditions documented in historic sources, including

Table 14.3: Abbreviated Epidemic History
of Seventeenth-Century Spanish Florida

Year	Event
1613–1617	Epidemic (plague?)
1649–1650	Epidemic (yellow fever?)
1653	Epidemic (smallpox)
1657	Epidemic
1659	Epidemic (measles)
1672	Epidemic (influenza?)
1675	Epidemic
1686	Epidemic (typhus?)

Sources: Dobyns 1983; Hann 1986, 1988.

reduction in number of settlements. For example, from 1675 to 1686, there was a reduction from seven settlements containing fewer than 500 natives to virtually complete depopulation of the area north of Cumberland Island (Jones 1978). Some of the reduction in population size can be accounted for by significant out-migration, but other factors were also important, especially the ravages wrought by epidemic disease (Table 14.3). One Florida governor remarked in 1657 that the previous years for Guale and Timucua had been difficult, that Indians "have been wiped out with the sickness of the plague and small-pox" (Hann 1986).

Skeletal and Dental Growth

Femoral Growth Velocity. Suggestive trends regarding growth and development of juveniles are provided by observation of the amount of growth per age interval (Table 14.4). These comparisons reveal that for all but the first age cohort (2-year), precontact foragers have more growth per year than the other three samples. Although these findings can be interpreted in a variety of ways, we believe that elevated growth values in the post-2-year cohorts reflect the presence of more robust health in foragers than in later populations.

Adult Height. Comparison of the four periods reveals a reduction in height over time to the early contact period, followed by an increase in the late contact period (Table 14.5). These reductions may be linked to the adoption of maize, a food deficient in high-quality protein and iron bioavailability (Larsen, Ruff, et al. 1992). The increase in height in the late contact period seems on the surface to contradict our

Table 14.4: Femur Velocity (in mm), Georgia Bight

	2 yrs.	5 yrs.	8 yrs.	11 yrs.
PP	23.7	19.7	18.7	18.2
PA	28.0	15.3	12.1	10.7
EC/LC	27.9	17.8	15.2	14.1

Table 14.5: Adult Heights (in cm), Georgia Bight

	PP mean (s.d.)	PA mean (s.d.)	EC mean (s.d.)	LC mean (s.d.)	Significant change[a]
Adult[b]	158.6 (8.5)	156.4 (8.5)	151.7 (13.0)	157.6 (7.8)	PA/EC, EC/LC
n	56	219	44	69	
Male	164.8 (5.8)	163.4 (6.4)	160.8 (9.6)	163.3 (6.6)	None
n	15	83	16	33	
Female	154.8 (7.7)	151.8 (6.5)	148.4 (11.6)	152.6 (4.8)	PP/PA
n	30	109	23	36	

Note: Height calculated following formulae provided by Sciulli et al. 1990.
[a] Statistically significant change (t-test: $p \leq 0.05$, two-tailed).
[b] Includes adult females, males, indeterminate sex.

interpretation of reduced quality of health in the late seventeenth and early eighteenth centuries. However, Ruff and Larsen (1990; Larsen and Ruff 1994) indicate elsewhere that if the quantity of foods – in this case, carbohydrates – consumed increased appreciably during this time, then an increase in height might be expected. Protein consumption would also result in height increases, but stable isotope analysis points to reduced availability of animal protein in the diets of native populations in this setting. We suggest, therefore, that the confines of mission life, coupled with dietary change, led to gains in body mass. This interpretation is consistent with observations of body composition in historic sedentary Indians, such as those living on reservations or in urban settings (Hrdlicka 1908; Miller 1970; Johnston and Schell 1979). At least two seventeenth-century observers remarked on Indian body composition in Spanish Florida: Fray Francisco Alonso described the Indians as "corpulent," and Bishop Calderón stated that the Indians "are fleshy, and rarely is there a small one" (Hann 1988).

Enamel Defects. As with most other data reported in this chapter, enamel defect data were collected well prior to the inception of this volume and the associated project. Enamel defect data were collected with the use of a light microscope (10x), thus preventing comparison with other regions discussed in this book. Nevertheless, a number of observations and interpretations are possible with regard to prevalence of enamel defects on permanent mandibular and maxillary central incisors, lateral incisors, and canines (Hutchinson and Larsen 1988, 1990, 1992, 2001; Simpson et al. 1990; Larsen and Hutchinson 1992). The precontact preagriculturalists have the highest prevalence per tooth type, followed by a slight decrease in the precontact agriculturalists, a slight increase in the early contact group, and a dramatic decrease in the late contact group (Table 14.6). The earliest and latest periods express the strongest contrasts in frequency of defects. For example, maxillary central incisors express 92% and 21% of teeth that are hypoplastic for the precontact preagriculturalists and late contact mission Indians, respectively. These differences are highly statistically significant (chi-square: $p \leq 0.01$). Overall, then, these findings point to the presence of stress events which result in enamel hypoplasia occurring on a more

Table 14.6: Hypoplasia Frequency, Georgia Bight

Tooth	PP % (n)[a]	PA % (n)	EC % (n)	LC % (n)	Significant change[b]
Maxilla					
I1	81 (53)	66 (65)	71 (77)	36 (50)	EC/LC
I2	92 (49)	64 (66)	74 (77)	21 (47)	PP/PA, EC/LC
C	88 (67)	70 (81)	78 (128)	38 (45)	PP/PA, EC/LC
Mandible					
I1	58 (40)	40 (65)	43 (84)	19 (47)	EC/LC
I2	72 (57)	55 (77)	52 (90)	19 (53)	EC/LC
C	91 (79)	77 (97)	87 (138)	51 (51)	PP/PA, EC/LC

[a] Percent of teeth affected with at least one hypoplasia; $n =$ total number of teeth and number of individuals examined (hypoplastic + nonhypoplastic teeth).
[b] Statistically significant change (chi-square: $p \leq 0.05$, two-tailed).
Source: From Larsen and Hutchinson 1992.

frequent basis in prehistoric Georgia coastal foragers, with the smallest number in the late contact group.

Three alternative explanations emerge for this finding: (1) late contact populations saw a reduction in physiological perturbation; or (2) the late contact group had more successfully adapted to stressors than their predecessors; or (3) the most stressed component of the population is not present in the death assemblage studied from Amelia Island, thus providing a biased subsample of the population from which it was drawn. It is unlikely that the first or second alternatives are viable explanations, since overwhelming evidence indicates a deterioration in quality of health and well-being during the contact period. The third alternative seems the most likely. That is, we suspect that some type of sample bias affecting hypoplasia prevalence is present. Study of age-at-death profiles indicates that the late contact series is remarkably old in comparison with the three preceding periods (see above). Perhaps, individuals most stressed during childhood have been selected against in determining the composition of the cemetery sample. On the other hand, it is important to point out that there is some evidence for maintenance of high stress levels in the late contact period. We have measured the widths of hypoplasias, which are widest during the late contact period (Larsen and Hutchinson 1992). These greater widths may indicate either greater severity or duration of stress, suggesting that frequency of defects may be but one part of the picture of stress as it affects growth of the dental hard tissues. However, the true significance, causes, and implications of hypoplasia breadth remain uncertain.

Juvenile Adult Permanent Tooth Size. Although largely under genetic control, tooth size is also influenced by environmental factors. Physiologically stressed individuals in living populations have smaller teeth than nonstressed individuals (Larsen 1995). Thus, it is possible to document the effects of stress for the period of time

Table 14.7: Juvenile and Adult Dental Dimensions
(Breadths, in mm), Georgia Bight

	Juvenile mean (s.d.)	Adult mean (s.d.)
Maxilla		
I1	7.66 (.56)	7.48 (.40)
n	16	33
I2	6.94 (.39)	6.91 (.36)
n	23	37
C	8.59 (.66)	8.64 (.47)
n	28	55
P3	10.12 (.59)	10.09 (.49)
n	34	70
P4	9.77 (25)	9.89 (.64)
n	25	72
M1	11.93 (.68)	12.14 (.51)
n	38	77
M2	12.09 (.67)	12.01 (.68)
n	21	85
Mandible		
I1	5.84 (.38)	5.89 (.33)
n	20	22
I2	6.23 (.40)	6.34 (.38)
n	27	47
C	7.51 (.57)	7.85 (.53)[a]
n	32	77
P3	8.09 (37)	8.30 (.44)[a]
n	37	95
P4	8.42 (.52)	8.63 (.47)[a]
n	33	95
M1	11.11 (.49)	11.24 (.52)
n	45	72
M2	10.76 (.57)	10.76 (.61)
n	31	87

[a] Statistically significant difference (t-test: $p \leq 0.05$, two-tailed).
Source: From Simpson et al. 1990.

during which teeth develop, namely, from four months in utero to 12 years. Age comparison of tooth size in the early contact sample from St. Catherines Island shows a clear pattern of smaller mean breadths, especially in mandibular teeth, in juveniles than adults (Table 14.7) (Simpson et al. 1990). This suggests the failure of teeth to reach their genetic potential in stressed settings (and see Guagliardo 1982). Additionally, it implies the presence of a link between tooth size and life-span, a finding consistent with other stress indicators (Larsen 1997). This is not to

Table 14.8: Deciduous Dental Dimensions
(Breadths, in mm), Georgia Bight

	PP mean (s.d.)	PA mean (s.d.)
Maxilla		
I1	3.9 (.07)	3.8 (6.7)
n	2	4
I2	4.2 (.49)	4.0 (.22)
n	5	7
C	5.4 (.49)	5.5 (.40)
n	7	16
M1	7.3 (.26)	7.1 (.53)
n	13	28
M2	9.3 (.24)	9.0 (.56)[a]
n	15	27
Mandible		
I1	4.8 (.30)	4.9 (.74)
n	7	9
I2	5.0 (.27)	4.9 (.57)
n	4	9
C	5.9 (.50)	6.0 (1.09)
n	10	15
M1	9.1 (.39)	8.8 (.78)
n	10	23
M2	10.6 (.46)	10.3 (.62)
n	8	25

[a] Statistically significant change (t-test: $p \leq 0.05$, two-tailed).
Source: From Larsen 1983a.

say that small tooth size led to early death. Rather, tooth size is symptomatic of environmental factors (e.g., nutrition) that resulted in reduced tooth size during critical years of growth and development – smaller teeth are symptomatic of reduced health.

Deciduous Tooth Size. There is a general pattern of reduction of crown lengths and breadths in precontact agriculturalists relative to preagriculturalists (Table 14.8). Although the mechanism leading to this reduction is unclear, placental sufficiency and maternal health status strongly influence deciduous tooth size, since the crowns of these teeth begin formation well before birth, and they are completely formed during the first months of life (Garn and Burdi 1971; Garn et al. 1979).

Oral Health

Dental Caries. Dental caries is a highly sensitive indicator of carbohydrate consumption, especially maize in native populations of North America and elsewhere,

Table 14.9: Dental Caries Frequency, Georgia Bight

	PP % (n)[a]	PA % (n)	EC % (n)	LC % (n)	Significant change[b]
Total[c]	1.2 (2479)	9.6 (5984)	7.6 (4466)	19.6 (1548)	PP/PA, PA/EC, EC/LC
Males	0.3 (638)	8.3 (1931)	14.9 (441)	21.4 (754)	PP/PA, PA/EC, EC/LC
Females	1.1 (1034)	12.8 (2405)	11.0 (598)	21.1 (606)	PP/PA, EC/LC

[a] Percent of teeth affected with at least one carious lesion; n = total number of teeth examined (carious + noncarious teeth).
[b] Statistically significant change (chi-square: $p \leq 0.05$, two-tailed).
[c] Total = juveniles, unsexed adults, adult females, adult males (see also Larsen 1983b).

because of the presence of sugar (sucrose) and other confounding factors (e.g., food consistency) (Milner 1984; Larsen et al. 1991). In concert with the increased reliance on maize in the Georgia Bight, there is a general increase in prevalence of dental caries, including especially a moderate increase within the precontact agriculturalists and a marked increase in the late contact mission Indians (Table 14.9). The latter change is the most conspicuous in the entire temporal span. We regard this change as representing a marked increase in consumption of maize. It is possible that these increases were occasioned by importation of sugar to Amelia Island during the late seventeenth century. However, the historical records do not mention the use of sugar in this region. Therefore, the role of sugar – aside from its association with maize – was likely minimal or nonexistent, at least with regard to explaining high caries prevalence in the late contact group.

The increase in dental caries prior to contact is more pronounced in females than males (Table 14.9). Although many other populations, archaeological and living, express similar sex differences, the pattern is not related to some inherent physiological differences between females and males (Larsen et al. 1991). We conclude that females ingested relatively more carbohydrates than males in the precontact population, which is perhaps related to the sexual division of labor observed in southeastern U.S. native societies: females were responsible for plant gathering, planting, care of crops, and food preparation; males were responsible for hunting and protection of the village. Thus, the greater exposure of cariogenic foods by women in this and similar settings best explains sex differences in carious lesion prevalence.

Be that as it may, the pattern of greater female caries prevalence does not hold true for either the early contact period, where males have more carious teeth than females, or the late contact period, where prevalences are virtually identical. This postcontact pattern of dental caries prevalence suggests that other factors influencing the disease may be operating. The similarity of caries prevalence in the late contact period may very well reflect similarity in diet between males and females as agriculture became more intensified. This finding is also consistent with the similar values of carbon and nitrogen isotope ratios between females and males in these populations (Larsen et al. 1992, 2001; Hutchinson et al. 1998).

Antemortem Loss. Owing to the poor archaeological preservation of the bone tissue supporting teeth in many of the skeletons included for study, we were not able to systematically collect antemortem tooth loss data. Our impression of antemortem tooth loss, however, is that it was high in prevalence, especially in the late contact group. Several older adults with well-preserved crania show complete or near-complete tooth loss, a phenomenon not observed in the preceding periods (Figure 14.2).

Iron Status

Cribra orbitalia and Porotic Hyperostosis. Cribra orbitalia and porotic hyperostosis, pathological indicators of iron-deficiency anemia, show a shift from relatively low prevalence for precontact individuals to increases in the early and late contact groups (Table 14.10). With regard to the latter, prevalences surpass 20% for the total sample in the late contact group, showing an increase over the early contact group. Severity of cribra orbitalia and porotic hyperostosis also increases over the temporal span. These increases denote a transformation in iron status in native populations, especially during the mission period.

The generally low prevalence of this pathology in both premaize and maize consumers prior to contact suggests that maize, at least as it is viewed in this setting, is not the primary factor in determining iron status. Other factors likely came to play, including poor living conditions and sanitation (Walker 1985, 1986). Experimental studies suggest that diets combining maize with fish significantly promote iron absorption (Layrisse et al. 1968). It is possible that the strong dependence on marine resources in precontact populations may have served to increase the bioavailability of iron in precontact maize agriculturalists, thus resulting in low prevalence of porotic hyperostosis.

In the mission settings of St. Catherines and Amelia Island, the concentration of population around limited and heavily used water sources and contamination thereof likely caused diarrheal infections and parasitism, which have also been linked with iron-deficiency anemia (Walker 1986). Unlike prehistoric groups, mission groups in the Georgia Bight constructed wells for sources of potable water (Thomas 1988). Archaeological documentation indicates that these wells were quite shallow, which would have lent themselves to the introduction of anemia-causing parasites. Moreover, at the mission on St. Catherines Island, a freshwater stream appears to have been dammed and utilized as a primary water source. The perimeter of this area contains a profusion of midden and food remains. The presence of trash during the occupation of the mission may have led to contamination and a potential breeding ground for parasites, and hence, increased iron-deficiency anemia. The diagnosis for iron-deficiency anemia is also confirmed by histological analysis of cranial lesions from several individuals (Schultz et al. 2001). We note that the relative high

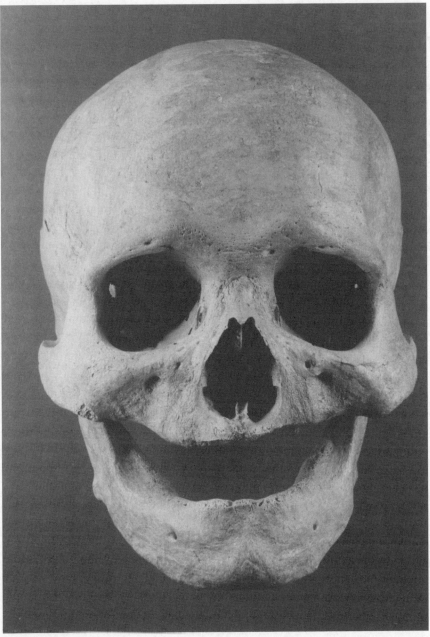

Figure 14.2. Individual from late-contact-period site, Santa Catalina de Guale de Santa Maria, Amelia Island, Florida, showing complete premortem loss of teeth.

Table 14.10: Cribra Orbitalia and Porotic Hyperostosis Prevalence
and Severity, Georgia Bight

	PP % (n)[a]	PA % (n)	EC % (n)	LC % (n)	Significant change[b]
Cribra orbitalia					
Total[c]	5.7 (104)	3.1 (287)	12.5 (32)	22.9 (70)	None
Juveniles[d]	38.5 (13)	6.1 (33)	60.0 (5)	73.3 (15)	PP/PA, PA/EC
Males	0.0 (29)	2.4 (84)	8.3 (12)	10.3 (29)	None
Females	0.0 (39)	2.4 (123)	0.0 (13)	4.2 (24)	None
Severity[e]	1.06 (104)	1.03 (287)	1.12 (32)	1.23 (70)	None
Porotic hyperostosis					
Total	0.0 (113)	3.3 (308)	9.4 (32)	21.1 (90)	None
Juveniles	0.0 (13)	0.0 (33)	0.0 (5)	50.0 (18)	EC/LC
Males	0.0 (35)	5.7 (88)	8.3 (12)	11.4 (35)	None
Females	0.0 (42)	0.7 (137)	15.4 (13)	11.4 (35)	PA/EC
Severity	1.00 (113)	1.03 (308)	1.09 (32)	1.21 (90)	None

[a] Percent of orbits/vaults affected; n = total number of orbits/vaults examined (pathological + non-pathological).
[b] Statistically significant change (chi-square: $p \leq 0.05$, two-tailed).
[c] Total = juveniles, unsexed adults, adult females, adult males.
[d] Juveniles < 10 years.
[e] Mean of severity scores: 1 = absent on at least one observable orbit or parietal; 2 = presence of lesion; 3 = gross lesions with excessive expansion and large areas of diploe exposed. All individuals combined.

prevalence of pathology in subadults less than 10 years of age (Table 14.10) is consistent with the general finding that porotic hyperostosis is a childhood condition (Stuart-Macadam 1988).

Infection

Periosteal Reactions. Periosteal lesions (periostitis) in this series range from vascular tracks and minimal inflammation to extensive bone involvement. Temporal comparisons show a general increase in prevalence and severity for the tibia (Table 14.11). The increase is especially marked for the late contact population. Relative to the early contact period, this represents a nearly threefold increase. The increase for adult females is not as great as observed in adult males (65.7% vs. 90.0% in late contact females and males, respectively).

The increase for the precontact agriculturalists is broadly similar to other New World groups undergoing the transition from foraging to farming (Larsen 1995). These changes are not linked with the dietary transition but, rather, with the increase in population sedentism and aggregation, seen both in the foraging-farming transition and in foragers undergoing decreases in mobility (Lambert and Walker 1991; Lambert 1993; Walker and Thornton this volume). For the Georgia Bight,

Table 14.11: Tibial Periosteal Reactions, Prevalence and Severity, Georgia Bight

	PP % (n)[a]	PA % (n)	EC % (n)	LC % (n)	Significant change[b]
Total[c]	9.5 (126)	19.8 (331)	15.4 (26)	59.3 (96)	PP/PA, EC/LC
Male[d]	9.3 (32)	23.6 (93)	23.1 (13)	70.0 (36)	PP/PA, EC/LC
Female[d]	4.3 (47)	24.1 (133)	14.3 (7)	65.7 (35)	PP/PA, EC/LC
Severity[e]	1.12 (126)	1.35 (331)	1.23 (26)	1.73 (96)	None

[a] Percent of tibiae/elements affected; n = total number of tibiae/elements examined (pathological + nonpathological).
[b] Statistically significant change (chi-square: $p \leq 0.05$, two-tailed).
[c] Total = juveniles, unsexed adults, adult females, adult males.
[d] Male = adult males; Female = adult females.
[e] Mean of tibial periosteal reactions severity scores: 1 = no lesions of the tibia(e) with at least one tibia available for observation; 2 = slight, discrete patch(s) of periosteal reaction involving less than one-quarter of the tibia(e) surface on one or both tibiae; 3 = moderate periosteal reaction involving less than one-half of the tibia(e) surface on one or both tibiae; 4 = severe periosteal reaction involving more than one-half of the tibia(e) surface (osteomyelitis). All individuals combined.

the dramatic increase in periosteal reactions in the late contact period is likely tied to reduction in mobility and aggregation of population in mission centers where living circumstances – especially sanitation – are less healthful. Additionally, the decline in nutrition with increased reliance on maize would likely have exacerbated deteriorating health. That is, there is a strong synergy between undernutrition or malnutrition and infection: individuals experiencing poor nutrition are less resistant to pathogens and are rendered more susceptible to infection; most infections worsen nutritional status (Scrimshaw 1975). The increase in infection in the contact period is different from other regions (e.g., South America). These differences are likely related to the fact that the populations in the Georgia Bight who came under Spanish control were living in mission settings where population was concentrated and living circumstances were of poorer quality than for those groups not living within the confines of the mission system.

Specific Infectious Diseases. Historical records indicate an abundance of infectious diseases in native New World populations in the Georgia Bight. Most of these diseases were introduced from the Old World, and are rarely registered osteologically. The pattern of skeletal involvement in populations from the precontact preagriculturalists from the Georgia coast indicates the presence of endemic treponematosis and tuberculosis (Powell 1990). Although probably not present prior to contact, venereal syphilis was likely a postcontact phenomenon, as indicated by the observation of René Laudonnière: "Most Indians were found to be diseased by the 'pox,' for they were exceedingly fond of the other sex, calling their female friends 'daughters of the sun'" (Gatschet 1880: 469).

Because periosteal reactions may also be caused by localized trauma, especially in relatively exposed areas such as the anterior surface of the tibia, some of the lesions observed in these skeletal samples may not be caused by infection. However, the overall deterioration in quality of living conditions suggests that infection – non-specific and specific – was the primary causative factor in explaining the profound increase in prevalence of periosteal reactions in this setting.

HISTORY OF BEHAVIOR AND ACTIVITY

Physical activity and behavior are an important component of the overall picture of health in human populations. For the Georgia Bight, activity and behavior are assessed from observation of pathology (degenerative joint disease, spondylolysis), long bone measurement (femoral subperiosteal diameter, humeral robusticity), and trauma (accidental injury, violence). These variables represent a cumulative history of the mechanical demands of daily living during the lifetime of an individual and the populations from which they are derived. The long-term consequences of physical activity loads on the structure of long bones provide additional perspective on behavior (see Ruff 2000; Ruff and Larsen 2001).

Pathology

Degenerative Joint Disease. Degenerative joint disease, or osteoarthritis, is an age-progressive disorder resulting in a deterioration of the articular joints of the skeleton. Although various factors are involved (e.g., heredity, blood supply, nutrition), the mechanical environment best explains most variation seen in human populations (Hough and Sokoloff 1989). The age-progressive nature of degenerative joint disease in precontact and contact-era native populations from the Georgia Bight is well illustrated by the increase in severity in vertebral joints – cervical, thoracic, and lumbar – from the younger to older age classes (Table 14.12).

Comparison of temporal periods in the Georgia Bight reveals two clear trends in prevalence of degenerative joint disease, including a decrease in precontact agriculturalists and a dramatic increase in the late contact population (Table 14.13). Consistent with these trends are respective decreases and increases in severity of degenerative joint disease in the precontact agricultural and late contact populations. These changes denote significant shifts in behavior after the adoption of maize agriculture and the subsequent period of missionization of native groups in the region. We regard the prehistoric decreases as representing a decline in workload, which is consistent with long bone structural analysis (Ruff and Larsen 2001). It is likely that the older nature of the adults in the late contact period contributed, in part, to the increase in prevalence of degenerative joint disease in them. However, comparison of the groups by subdividing into five-year age groups reveals that age is not the sole, or even most important, factor in explaining the changes in prevalence.

The increases in the contact population suggest a marked reversal in this pattern of behavior. Information provided from historical records supports this hypothesis. The labor demands of the repartimiento draft labor system in mission populations are well understood. Some adult males were required to make long-distance trips to various localities in the Spanish provinces of Florida (Hann 1988). These trips involved carrying heavy burdens over lengthy distances (Hann 1988), which would

Table 14.12: Degenerative Joint Disease Severity by Age Class, Georgia Bight (All Periods Combined)

	Total[a] mean (s.d.)	Females mean (s.d.)	Males mean (s.d.)
Cervical			
1: 0–4.99	1.00 (.0)	—	—
n	16		
2: 5–9.99	1.06 (.24)	—	—
n	17		
3: 10–14.99	1.00 (.0)	—	1.00 (.0)
n	8		1
4: 15–19.99	1.00 (.0)	1.00 (.0)	1.00 (.0)
n	40	18	11
5: 20–24.99	1.08 (.49)	1.00 (.0)	1.14 (.66)
n	37	15	21
6: 25–29.99	1.11 (.32)	1.00 (.0)	1.20 (.42)
n	19	9	10
7: 30–34.99	1.16 (.69)	1.00 (.0)	1.50 (1.23)
n	19	13	6
8: 35–39.99	1.22 (.61)	1.06 (.24)	1.40 (.83)
n	32	17	15
9: 40–44.9	1.56 (.72)	1.60 (.74)	1.53 (.72)
	32	15	17
10: 45 +	1.79 (.77)	1.67 (.73)	1.94 (.80)
n	39	21	18
Thoracic			
1: 0–4.99	1.00 (.0)	—	—
n	14		
2: 5–9.99	1.24 (.08)	—	—
n	17		
3: 10–14.99	1.00 (.0)	—	1.00 (.0)
n	8		1
4: 15–19.99	1.00 (.0)	1.0 (.0)	1.00 (.0)
n	35	17	9
5: 20–24.99	1.03 (.16)	1.06 (.25)	1.00 (.0)
n	38	16	19
6: 25–29.99	1.12 (.33)	1.00 (.0)	1.22 (.44)
n	17	8	9
7: 30–34.99	1.17 (.38)	1.17 (.38)	1.17 (.41)
n	18	12	6
8: 35–39.99	1.47 (.73)	1.25 (.58)	1.71 (.83)
n	30	16	14
9: 40–44.99	1.66 (.72)	1.60 (.74)	1.71 (.73)
n	29	15	14
10: 45 +	1.84 (.76)	1.75 (.64)	1.94 (.89)
n	37	20	17

(continued)

Table 14.12 *(continued)*

	Total[a] mean (s.d.)	Females mean (s.d.)	Males mean (s.d.)
Lumbar			
1: 0–4.99	1.00 (.0)	—	—
n	13		
2: 5–9.99	1.06 (.25)	—	—
n	15		
3: 10–14.99	1.00 (.0)	—	1.00 (.0)
n	7		1
4: 15–19.99	1.11 (.32)	1.11 (.32)	1.20 (.42)
n	37	18	10
5: 20–24.99	1.10 (.31)	1.06 (.25)	1.14 (.36)
n	39	16	21
6: 25–29.99	1.12 (.33)	1.00 (.0)	1.20 (.42)
n	17	7	10
7: 30–34.99	1.31 (.48)	1.31 (.48)	1.30 (.52)
n	19	13	6
8: 35–39.99	1.53 (.78)	1.29 (.58)	1.80 (.89)
n	30	17	13
9: 40–44.99	1.90 (.71)	1.73 (.59)	2.07 (.79)
n	30	15	15
10: 45 +	2.08 (.73)	1.95 (.67)	2.27 (.79)
n	36	21	15

[a] Total = juveniles, unsexed adults, adult females, adult males.
Severity scores: 1 = no lesions on at least two observable vertebrae; 2 = initial osteophyte formation along rim of the vertebral body(-ies); 3 = extensive osteophyte formation along rim of vertebrae; 4 = two or more vertebrae fused together.

have placed heavy demands on weight-bearing articular joints.[2] Thus, draft labor, a practice instituted by the Spanish crown, appears to have had major repercussions for labor and activity, resulting in an increase in labor demands. The osteological evidence clearly shows the change in activity in this setting of the Western Hemisphere.

Spondylolysis. Spondylolysis is a type of stress fracture involving a separation of the neural arches of vertebrae in the area between the superior and the inferior articular processes (called the pars articularis). Most commonly present in the fifth lumbar vertebra of the lower back, high frequencies of fractures have been reported in human populations engaged in physically demanding lifestyles (e.g., traditional Eskimos), or in components of populations with heavy workloads (e.g., athletes) (Stewart 1931; Semon and Spengler 1981). Although the condition is pathological,

---

[2] The greater labor demands on males in comparison with females is further indicated by the higher severity and prevalence of degenerative joint disease in males than in females; see Tables 14.12 and 14.13.

Table 14.13: Degenerative Joint Disease Prevalence and Severity, Georgia Bight

Articular joint	PP % (n)[a]	PA % (n)	LC % (n)	Significant change[b]
All adults				
Cervical	26.0 (50)	16.4 (189)	68.3 (60)	PA/LC
Thoracic	15.6 (32)	11.4 (175)	68.3 (60)	PA/LC
Lumbar	41.9 (43)	24.5 (163)	67.2 (58)	PP/PA, PA/LC
Shoulder	9.7 (113)	5.3 (207)	15.2 (66)	PA/LC
Hip	12.0 (108)	6.8 (206)	10.5 (67)	None
Wrist	5.9 (84)	1.1 (187)	13.2 (68)	PP/PA, PA/LC
Hand	5.0 (40)	3.0 (165)	5.9 (68)	None
Males				
Cervical	33.3 (18)	27.5 (80)	74.1 (27)	PA/LC
Thoracic	16.7 (12)	19.2 (73)	74.1 (27)	PA/LC
Lumbar	50.0 (14)	37.7 (69)	75.0 (28)	PA/LC
Shoulder	17.7 (34)	10.1 (79)	16.7 (30)	None
Hip	13.2 (38)	12.5 (80)	9.4 (32)	None
Wrist	15.4 (26)	2.7 (75)	16.1 (31)	PP/PA, PA/LC
Hand	8.3 (12)	5.8 (69)	3.3 (30)	None
Females				
Cervical	22.2 (27)	8.4 (95)	65.6 (32)	PA/LC
Thoracic	16.7 (18)	5.5 (91)	65.6 (32)	PA/LC
Lumbar	38.5 (26)	15.3 (85)	60.0 (30)	PP/PA, PA/LC
Shoulder	5.2 (58)	2.9 (105)	13.9 (36)	PA/LC
Hip	13.2 (53)	3.8 (105)	11.4 (35)	PP/PA
Wrist	2.3 (43)	0.0 (96)	10.8 (37)	PA/LC
Hand	4.0 (25)	1.2 (85)	7.9 (38)	None
Severity[c]				
Cervical	1.22 (58)	1.16 (223)	1.58 (55)	None
Thoracic	1.18 (38)	1.12 (215)	1.89 (62)	None
Lumbar	1.41 (49)	1.24 (119)	1.86 (59)	None

[a] Percent of articular joints affected; n = total number of joints examined (pathological + nonpathological).

[b] Statistically significant change (chi-square: $p \leq 0.05$, two-tailed); data for EC unavailable.

[c] Severity scores: 1 = no lesions on at least two observable vertebrae; 2 = initial osteophyte formation along rim of the vertebral body(-ies); 3 = extensive osteophyte formation along rim of vertebrae; 4 = two or more vertebrae fused together. All individuals combined.

it may contribute to an increase in flexibility of the lower back, thus enabling the individual to experience less discomfort during strenuous physical activity (Merbs 1983). The highest prevalence of spondylolysis is in the late precontact group from Amelia Island: the late precontact group has a prevalence of 9%, whereas earlier populations do not exceed 5% (Larsen and Ruff 1994).

Long Bone Size

Femoral Midshaft Subperiosteal Diameter. From the perspective of engineering principles, a long bone (e.g., femur) can be modeled as a hollow beam. In such a beam, the materials located farthest from an imaginary center running down the middle of the long bone are the strongest and stiffest. All else being equal – especially the total amount of bone in a cross section – a wider long bone will be able to resist the demands of heavy mechanical loading better than a narrower long bone.

Beam analysis involves the measurement of cross-sectional geometric properties from cross sections taken perpendicular to the long axis of the bone. These properties represent measures of the ability of the bone to resist forces placed on it in relation to the location of the cross section (e.g., femur midshaft) (Ruff 2000). Most of these properties require observation of the entire cross section of the bone. However, the external dimension, called total subperiosteal area, or TA, can be determined from external measurements of femoral midshafts. It is important to note that TA is a good general indicator of bone strength. We emphasize that TA or other properties are not qualitative assessments of bone tissue; rather, they are indicators of physical stress and lifestyle relating to the adaptation of bone to mechanical loading arising during physical activity. As with degenerative joint disease, it is not possible to identify specific activities from measurement of bone cross sections. Instead, cross-sectional geometric properties are an overall indicator of bone strength.

Comparison of femoral TA standardized for body mass (TA_{std}) for the four subsamples from the Georgia Bight reveals a pattern that closely parallels observations on degenerative joint disease. Prior to contact, there is a decline in TA_{std} for males and females (Table 14.14). Early and late contact males show appreciable increases, and females show an increase for the early group only, but the value is still high in the late contact group (Table 14.14). This pattern provides confirmation for the observations of degenerative joint disease, namely, that the adoption of an agricultural lifestyle prior to contact led to a decrease in physical demand, and the establishment of missions and accompanying labor demands entailed increased physical activity in native populations. This pattern of size increase and robusticity is also revealed in other measurements of the femora (e.g., midshaft anterior posterior diameter; Table 14.14).

Humeral Robusticity. Female and male humeral robusticity similarly shows declines prior to contact; both sexes show increases in the respective early and late contact periods (Table 14.14). The various measurements taken on the humeri from all periods show similar decreases, followed by increases in overall size of this skeletal element (Table 14.14). These changes reflect shifts in demands of use of the upper limb.

Trauma

Accidental Injury. The frequency of skeletal traumatic injuries due to accident are extremely low in the Georgia Bight populations (Table 14.15). Only seven

Table 14.14: Skeletal Size and Robusticity, Georgia Bight

	PP mean (s.d.)	PA mean (s.d.)	EC mean (s.d.)	LC mean (s.d.)	Significant change[a]
Male, Femur					
Length	452.9 (22.5)	446.5 (22.4)	436.9 (36.1)	446.7 (25.9)	None
n	15	84	16	33	
AP diameter	30.4 (2.9)	29.7 (2.9)	28.8 (1.5)	29.5 (2.5)	None
n	30	96	13	32	
ML diameter	27.0 (2.7)	25.8 (2.0)	26.1 (3.5)	27.1 (1.7)	PP/PA
n	30	96	13	32	
TA	6.45 (.82)	6.05 (.93)	5.90 (.80)	6.30 (.71)	PP/PA
n	30	96	13	32	
TA_{std}[b]	6.98 (1.0)	6.85 (.94)	6.87 (1.0)	7.17 (1.1)	None
n	15	83	13	32	
Male, Humerus					
Length	325.7 (15.4)	317.2 (16.1)	315.1 (15.8)	313.2 (16.4)	PP/PA
n	22	87	12	32	
Circumference	67.6 (7.4)	65.0 (5.5)	65.5 (3.4)	66.0 (5.1)	None
n	29	90	12	33	
Robusticity	20.8 (2.1)	20.6 (1.6)	20.8 (1.5)	21.1 (1.5)	None
n	22	87	12	32	
Female, Femur					
Length	428.7 (26.5)	418.1 (22.6)	406.7 (40.3)	420.2 (17.5)	PP/PA
n	30	111	23	37	
AP diameter	26.9 (2.3)	25.6 (2.3)	26.9 (2.3)	25.9 (1.9)	PP/PA, PA/EC
n	51	127	21	36	
ML diameter	24.8 (2.3)	23.4 (1.7)	23.5 (3.0)	25.4 (1.6)	PP/PA, EC/LC
n	51	127	21	35	
TA	5.26 (.68)	4.73 (.69)	4.97 (.86)	5.18 (.53)	PP/PA
n	51	127	21	35	
TA_{std}	6.71 (.98)	6.48 (.99)	6.85 (10.7)	7.01 (.81)	PA/EC
n	29	108	17	35	
Female, Humerus					
Length	299.1 (24.8)	298.6 (18.5)	296.3 (19.8)	296.8 (13.4)	None
n	39	112	17	37	
Circumference	60.1 (5.4)	57.4 (4.9)	58.2 (5.8)	58.8 (3.6)	PP/PA
n	48	119	17	36	
Robusticity	19.8 (1.8)	19.2 (1.6)	19.7 (1.7)	19.8 (1.3)	PP/PA
n	38	110	17	36	

[a] Statistically significant change (t-test: $p \leq 0.05$, two-tailed).
[b] TA_{std} = total subperiosteal diameter size-standardized by the formula: $(TA \div length^3) \times 10^8$; see Larsen and Ruff, 1994.

individuals, all from the precontact preagricultural period, have fractures. All fractures involve injuries to either the distal radius or ulna.

Violence (Weapon Wounds). Weapon wounds are also a very infrequent occurrence in this setting (Table 14.15). The few weapon wounds that are present include mostly

Table 14.15: Trauma and Weapon Wounds Frequencies, Georgia Bight

Location	PP % $(n)^a$	PA % (n)	LC % (n)	Significant change[b]
Trauma				
Arm	5.9 (118)	0.6 (331)	0.0 (91)	None
Hand	2.5 (40)	1.4 (139)	0.0 (85)	None
Face	0.0 (96)	0.4 (276)	0.0 (96)	None
Nasal	0.0 (94)	0.4 (276)	0.0 (95)	None
Skull	2.9 (104)	1.6 (307)	0.0 (94)	None
Leg	1.7 (118)	0.6 (331)	0.0 (92)	None
Weapon wounds				
All	1.9 (315)	1.3 (504)	0.8 (121)	None

[a] Percent of locations affected; n = total number in locations examined (pathological + nonpathological).

[b] Statistically significant change (chi-square: $p \leq 0.05$, two-tailed); data for EC unavailable.

cranial depressed fractures, all of which were well healed at the time of death. One individual – an adult female from the Sea Island Mound (ca. AD 1000–1150) from Sea Island, Georgia – shows extensive proliferative remodeling on much of the ectocranial vault (superior frontal, both parietals), which has been interpreted to represent postscalping modifications (Ortner and Putschar 1985). The presence of complete remodeling and no active infection indicates that the individual survived the trauma.

We expected to see an elevation in violence-related trauma in the contact period, especially in light of historical accounts of conflict (Bushnell 1994; Worth 1995, 2001). However, in this and all other mission samples from the Georgia Bight and other regions of Spanish Florida, only one individual displayed evidence of violent death, a high-status adult male from San Luis de Talimali (Larsen et al. 1996). This individual probably died from a gunshot wound to the abdomen. Additionally, several individuals display trauma from metal-edged weapons from the sixteenth-century nonmission Tatham Mound site on the Florida Gulf coast (Hutchinson and Norr 1994). These findings indicate that, at least with regard to the skeletal evidence, traumatic injury was relatively uncommon in native populations from the Georgia Bight, regardless of time period.

THE HEALTH INDEX: COMPARISONS BETWEEN THE GEORGIA BIGHT AND OTHER SETTINGS OF THE WESTERN HEMISPHERE

The four cultural/temporal samples discussed in this chapter fall within the upper half of 65 samples studied in the compilation of the health index by Steckel and co-workers (Steckel, Sciulli, and Rose this volume).[3] Three of the samples – precontact preagricultural, precontact agricultural, and early contact – are in the top 10 samples.

---

[3] The values for the health index in the Georgia Bight are: precontact preagricultural, 23.54; precontact agricultural, 21.34; early contact, 22.10; late contact, 19.41.

The fourth sample, late contact, is in the middle in position. On the whole, the general health differences between samples and their order of ranking in the health index are consistent with the results of this study. The precontact preagriculturalists rank at the top of the list of 65 (rank = 2), and the late contact is in the middle of the list (rank = 30). The order of the precontact agriculturalists and early contact population is reversed, however (ranks are 10 and 5, respectively).

As a group, the overall rankings would suggest that the Georgia Bight populations appear to be relatively healthy compared with other samples discussed in this volume. Indeed, prior to the late contact period, some pathological conditions appear to have lower prevalences than in other settings (e.g., dental caries, periosteal reactions). This relatively high level of health, for the precontact populations especially, may be related to living in a coastal setting where seafood and other resources are relatively rich. For example, the precontact populations have very low levels of porotic hyperostosis and cribra orbitalia, reflecting a virtual lack of iron-deficiency anemia or other factors that may affect iron status (e.g., parasitic infection is a known cause of iron-deficiency anemia). The Georgia Bight in particular is a highly economically productive region as it relates to seafood exploitation. Even today, the estuaries and ocean in the region are extremely productive in marine foods, including various shellfish and fish. The archaeological record also suggests a similar variety of foods available and high level of productivity. Compared to prehistoric populations from the American Southwest, where food sources are less predictable and lacking in the kinds of nutritional seafoods, the Georgia Bight had a range of foods available. Moreover, the prehistoric population density was likely relatively low, at least from what can be determined from settlement studies in the region (see above). Thus, we believe that the relatively better health in the Georgia Bight series – especially in regard to the prehistoric populations – reflects a combination of plentiful resources and low population density. The contact period, however, represents a clear decline in living circumstances, at least with regard to the last period, which is similar to regions experiencing prolonged interaction with Europeans.

SUMMARY, IMPLICATIONS, AND CONCLUSIONS

Comparisons of human skeletal remains from Native Americans from the Georgia Bight provide a compelling picture of alterations in health and lifestyle, with some variation by period (shown in parentheses below):

1. slight increase in fertility (precontact agricultural), followed by decrease in fertility (late contact);
2. reduction in femoral growth velocity (after precontact agricultural);
3. reduction in adult height (precontact agricultural and early contact), followed by increase in adult height (late contact);
4. reduction in enamel defects (especially in late contact);
5. reduction in deciduous tooth size (precontact agricultural);
6. increase in dental caries (precontact agricultural, late contact);
7. increase in antemortem tooth loss (late contact);

8. increase in iron deficiency anemia (early contact, late contact); and
9. increase in infection (precontact agricultural, late contact).

Shifts in workload and activity are indicated by pathology and external bone dimensions:

1. decrease in degenerative joint disease (precontact agricultural), followed by increase in degenerative joint disease (late contact);
2. decrease in subperiosteal diameter and long bone dimensions generally (precontact agricultural), followed by increase in subperiosteal diameter and long bone dimensions (early contact, late contact);
3. no change in hazards of lifestyle due either to accident or violence.

The trends relating specifically to health (e.g., dental caries) are broadly similar to other regions of the Eastern Woodlands and elsewhere in the Western Hemisphere, especially with regard to the effects of the adoption of agriculture prior to European contact, and the effects of contact (Larsen 1994, 1995). The earlier populations are healthier than the later populations. Contrary to popular and scholarly perceptions of the shift from foraging to farming, the change did not represent an improvement in the human condition. Agriculture certainly set the stage for the rise of complex societies and urbanization in the last five or so millennia of human history, but there was a health cost associated with the transition. When viewed within just the region of the Georgia Bight, skeletal and pathology findings suggest a decline in health. Broader comparison with other populations discussed in this volume indicates that the populations from the Georgia Bight were better off than most.

The trends observed here in workload and skeletal pathology and bone size appear to have a much more regional focus. For example, in contrast to our findings, Bridges reports increases in subperiosteal bone diameters (TA) and other external bone dimensions with the adoption of agriculture in other areas of the American Southeast (Bridges 1989). Comparisons of TA in the various populations discussed in this volume show a high degree of variability, which confirms the regional nature of skeletal robusticity. To a great extent, femoral robusticity is influenced by difficulty of terrain (e.g., mountains vs. coast), and less so by subsistence strategy per se (Ruff 2000). It is interesting to note that an increase in workload in the late contact Georgia Bight population appears to be accompanied by a decrease in mobility overall. Thus, the populations are working harder, but except for drafting of male laborers, essentially staying put throughout the year.

For historians, more often than not dependent on documentary evidence which can be discounted as at best impressionistic, the value of bioarchaeological research lends concreteness to such impressionistic accounts. Even so, "documentary" historians must determine if the skeletal data is representative of larger trends and longer periods. For instance, how do the results determined from the study of skeletal remains of native populations from the Georgia Bight fit with the impressions of literate witnesses contemporary with the bones?

The history conveyed to us by the human remains from the Georgia Bight represents two enormously important events, the coming of farming – maize in this setting – and the coming of Europeans. People all over the world have experienced the first event, and people all over the non-European world have experienced the second, representing what one of us has referred to as the "Neo-Europes" (Crosby 1986).

A generation ago, students were taught that both of the above experiences were positive. But human remains – from across the globe, and now in the Georgia Bight – tell us quite clearly that farmers, while greater in number than their hunter and gatherer ancestors, were less healthy. It turns out that being invaded by Europeans, though they be soldiers, traders, missionaries, or simply settlers, was pretty much a disaster for Native Americans. The newcomers might or might not be genocidal in intent, but they worked the aborigines hard, interfered with their food production, and – above all – brought them the communicable diseases of Eurasia and Africa. Europe's expansion was a glorious chapter in history for even its lower classes, but a tragedy for, to cite but one example, the peoples of the Georgia Bight. The stories of other Amerindians, Polynesians, and non-Eurasian peoples swept up in European imperialism were similar (Crosby 1986). History, it seems, was much more complicated and, perennially, tragic than what was taught to previous generations of students. Bioarchaeology makes that clear. On the other hand, study of bone structural changes indicates that native peoples adapted to changing circumstances, especially those involving workload and labor exploitation. Thus, we see a picture involving both decline in health and adaptation to changing behavioral conditions.

In summary, assessment of human remains from the Georgia Bight provides a picture of change in health and behavior in response to alterations in diet, disease, and lifestyle that coincides with major adaptive shifts. The broad temporal trends that emerge from the comparisons of skeletal indicators of health and behavior indicate that the human remains from this region provide a vital part of the history of the human condition in this region of the Western Hemisphere.

REFERENCES

Anderson, David G. 1994. *The Savannah River Chiefdoms: Political Change in the Late Prehistoric Southeast.* Tuscaloosa: University of Alabama Press.

Bridges, Patricia S. 1989. Changes in activities with the shift to agriculture in the southeastern United States. *Current Anthropology* 30:385–394.

Buikstra, Jane E., Lyle W. Konigsberg, and Jill Bullington. 1986. Fertility and the development of agriculture in the prehistoric Midwest. *American Antiquity* 51:528–546.

Bushnell, Amy Turner. 1994. *Situado and Sabana: Spain's Support System for the Presidio and Mission Provinces of Florida.* New York: Anthropological Papers of the American Museum of Natural History, No. 74.

Caldwell, Joseph, and Catherine McCann. 1941. *Irene Mound Site, Chatham County, Georgia.* Athens: University of Georgia Press.

Crook, Margan R., Jr. 1984. Evolving community organization on the Georgia coast. *Journal of Field Archaeology* 11:247–263.

Crosby, Alfred W. 1986. *Ecological Imperialism: The Biological Expansion of Europe, 900–1900.* Cambridge: Cambridge University Press.

DePratter, Chester B. n.d. An Archaeological Survey of Ossabaw Island, Chatham County, Georgia. Unpublished manuscript, on file, Department of Anthropology, University of Georgia, Athens.

1976. Settlement data from Skidaway Island: Possible implications. Paper presented, Southern Anthropological Society, Atlanta.

1978. Prehistoric settlement and subsistence systems, Skidaway Island, Georgia. *Early Georgia* 6:65–80.

Dobyns, Henry F. 1983. *Their Number Become Thinned: Native Population Dynamics in Eastern North America.* Knoxville: University of Tennessee Press.

Ezzo, Joseph A., Clark Spencer Larsen, and James H. Burton. 1995. Elemental signatures of human diets from the Georgia Bight. *American Journal of Physical Anthropology* 98: 471–481.

Food and Agricultural Organization. 1953. *Maize and Maize Diets: A Nutritional Survey.* Rome: FAO Nutritional Studies No. 9.

Garn, Stanley M., and Alphonse R. Burdi. 1971. Prenatal ordering and postnatal sequence in dental development. *Journal of Dental Research* 50:1407–1414.

Garn, S. M., R. H. Osborne, and K. D. McCabe. 1979. The effect of prenatal factors on crown dimensions. *American Journal of Physical Anthropology* 51:665–678.

Gatschet, Albert S. 1880. The Timucua language. *Proceedings of the American Philosophical Society* 18:465–502.

Guagliardo, Mark F. 1982. Tooth crown size differences between age groups: A possible indicator of stress in skeletal samples. *American Journal of Physical Anthropology* 58:383–389.

Hann, John H. 1986. Demographic patterns and changes in mid-seventeenth century Timucua and Apalachee. *Florida Historical Quarterly* 64:371–392.

1988. *Apalachee: The Land between the Rivers.* Gainesville: University Presses of Florida.

Hough, Aubrey J., and Leon Sokoloff. 1989. Pathology of osteoarthritis. In *Arthritis and Allied Conditions,* 11th ed., ed. D. J. McCarty, pp. 1571–1594. Philadelphia: Lea & Febiger.

Hrdlicka, Ales. 1908. *Physiological and Medical Observations among the Indians of the Southwestern United States and Northern Mexico.* Washington, D.C.: Bureau of American Ethnology, Bulletin No. 34.

Hutchinson, Dale L., and Clark Spencer Larsen. 1988. Determination of stress episode duration from linear enamel hypoplasias: A case study from St. Catherines Island, Georgia. *Human Biology* 60:93–110.

1990. Stress and lifeway change: The evidence from enamel hypoplasias. In *The Archaeology of Mission Santa Catalina de Guale: 2. Biocultural Interpretations of a Population in Transition,* ed. Clark Spencer Larsen, pp. 50–65. New York: Anthropological Papers of the American Museum of Natural History, No. 68.

2001. Enamel hypoplasia and stress in La Florida. In *Bioarchaeology of Spanish Florida: The Impact of Colonialism,* ed. Clark Spencer Larsen, pp. 181–206. Gainesville: University Press of Florida.

Hutchinson, Dale L., Clark Spencer Larsen, Margaret J. Schoeninger, and Lynette Norr. 1998. Regional variation in the pattern of maize adoption and use in Florida and Georgia. *American Antiquity* 63:397–416.

2000. Agricultural melodies and alternative harmonies in Florida and Georgia. In *Bioarchaeological Studies of Life in the Age of Agriculture: A View from the Southeast,* ed. Patricia M. Lambert, pp. 96–115. Tuscaloosa: University of Alabama Press.

Hutchinson, Dale L., and Lynette Norr. 1994. Late prehistoric and early historic diet in Gulf Coast Florida. In *In the Wake of Contact: Biological Responses to Conquest,* ed. Clark Spencer Larsen and George R. Milner, pp. 9–20. New York: Wiley-Liss.

Johnston, Frank E., and Lawrence M. Schell. 1979. Anthropometric variation of Native American children and adults. In *The First Americans: Origins, Affinities, and Adaptations*, ed. William S. Laughlin and Albert B. Harper, pp. 275–291. New York: Gustav Fischer.

Jones, Grant D. 1978. The ethnohistory of the Guale coast through 1684. In *The Anthropology of St. Catherines Island: Natural and Cultural History*, by David Hurst Thomas, Grant D. Jones, Roger S. Durham, and C. S. Larsen, pp. 178–210. New York: Anthropological Papers of the American Museum of Natural History, 55, part 2.

Lambert, Patricia L. 1993. Health in prehistoric populations of the Santa Barbara Channel Islands. *American Antiquity* 58:509–522.

Lambert, Patricia L., and Phillip L. Walker. 1991. Physical anthropological evidence for the evolution of social complexity in coastal Southern California. *Antiquity* 65: 963–973.

Larsen, Clark Spencer. 1982. *The Anthropology of St. Catherines Island: 3. Prehistoric Human Biological Adaptation*. New York: Anthropological Papers of the American Museum of Natural History 57, part 3.

———. 1983a. Deciduous tooth size and subsistence change in prehistoric Georgia coast populations. *Current Anthropology* 24:225–226.

———. 1983b. Behavioural implications of temporal change in cariogenesis. *Journal of Archaeological Science* 10:1–8.

———. 1984. Health and disease in prehistoric Georgia: The transition to agriculture. In *Paleopathology at the Origins of Agriculture*, ed. Mark Nathan Cohen and George J. Armelagos, pp. 367–392. Orlando, Fl.: Academic Press.

———. 1993. On the frontier of contact: Mission bioarchaeology in La Florida. In *The Spanish Missions of La Florida*, ed. Bonnie G. McEwan, pp. 322–356. Gainesville: University Press of Florida.

———. 1994. In the wake of Columbus: Native population biology in the postcontact Americas. *Yearbook of Physical Anthropology* 37:109–154.

———. 1995. Biological changes in human populations with agriculture. *Annual Review of Anthropology* 24:185–213.

———. 1997. *Bioarchaeology: Interpreting Behavior from the Human Skeleton*. Cambridge: Cambridge University Press.

Larsen, Clark Spencer, and Dale L. Hutchinson. 1992. Dental evidence for physiological disruption: Biocultural interpretations from the eastern Spanish borderlands, U.S.A. In *Recent Contributions to the Study of Enamel Developmental Defects*, ed. Alan H. Goodman and Luigi L. Capasso, pp. 151–169. *Journal of Paleopathology*, Monographic Publications, No. 2.

Larsen, Clark Spencer, Hong P. Huynh, and Bonnie G. McEwan. 1996. Death by gunshot: Biocultural implications of trauma at Mission San Luis. *International Journal of Osteoarchaeology* 6:42–50.

Larsen, Clark Spencer, and Christopher B. Ruff. 1994. The stresses of conquest in Spanish Florida: Structural adaptation and change before and after contact. In *In the Wake of Contact: Biological Responses to Conquest*, ed. Clark Spencer Larsen and George R. Milner, pp. 21–34. New York, New York: Wiley-Liss.

Larsen, Clark Spencer, Christopher B. Ruff, Margaret J. Schoeninger, and Dale L. Hutchinson. 1992. Population decline and extinction in La Florida. In *Disease and Demography in the Americas*, ed. John W. Verano and Douglas H. Ubelaker, pp. 25–39. Washington, D.C.: Smithsonian Institution Press.

Larsen, Clark Spencer, Margaret J. Schoeninger, Dale L. Hutchinson, and Lynette Norr. 2001. Food and stable isotopes in La Florida: Diet and nutrition before and after contact. In

Bioarchaeology of Spanish Florida: The Impact of Colonialism, ed. Clark Spencer Larsen, pp. 52–81. Gainesville: University Press of Florida.

Larsen, Clark Spencer, Margaret J. Schoeninger, Dale L. Hutchinson, Katherine F. Russell, and Christopher B. Ruff. 1990. Beyond demographic collapse: Biological adaptation and change in native populations of La Florida. In *Columbian Consequences*, Volume 2: *Archaeological and Historical Perspectives on the Spanish Borderlands East*, ed. David Hurst Thomas, pp. 409–428. Washington, D.C.: Smithsonian Institution Press.

Larsen, Clark Spencer, Margaret J. Schoeninger, Nikolaas J. van der Merwe, Katherine M. Moore, and Julia A. Lee-Thorp. 1992. Carbon and nitrogen stable isotopic signatures of human dietary change in the Georgia Bight. *American Journal of Physical Anthropology* 89:197–214.

Larsen, Clark Spencer, Rebecca Shavit, and Mark C. Griffin. 1991. Dental caries evidence for dietary change: An archaeological context. In *Advances in Dental Anthropology*, ed. Marc A. Kelley and Clark Spencer Larsen, pp. 179–202. New York: Wiley-Liss.

Layrisse, Miguel, Carlos Martínez-Torres, and Marcel Roche. 1968. Effect of interaction of various foods on iron absorption. *American Journal of Clinical Nutrition* 21:1175–1183.

Merbs, Charles F. 1983. *Patterns of Activity-Induced Pathology in a Canadian Inuit Population*. Toronto: Archaeological Survey of Canada, Mercury Series Paper No. 119.

Miller, Peter S. 1970. Secular changes among the Western Apache. *American Journal of Physical Anthropology* 33:197–206.

Milner, George R. 1984. Dental caries in the permanent dentition of a Mississippian period population from the American Midwest. *Collegium Antropologicum* 8:77–91.

Ortner, Donald J., and Walter G. J. Putschar. 1985. *Identification of Pathological Conditions in Human Skeletal Remains*. Washington, D.C.: Smithsonian Institution Press.

Powell, Mary Lucas. 1990. On the eve of conquest: Life and death at Irene Mound, Georgia. In *The Archaeology of Mission Santa Catalina de Guale: 2. Biocultural Interpretations of a Population in Transition*, ed. Clark Spencer Larsen, pp. 26–35. New York: Anthropological Papers of the American Museum of Natural History, No. 68.

Reitz, Elizabeth J. 1988. Evidence for coastal adaptation in Georgia and South Carolina. *Archaeology of Eastern North America* 15:137–158.

Ruff, Christopher B. 2000. Biomechanical analyses of archaeological human skeletons. In *Biological Anthropology of the Human Skeleton*, ed. M. Anne Katzenberg and Shelley R. Saunders, pp. 37–58. New York: Wiley-Liss.

Ruff, Christopher B., and Clark Spencer Larsen. 1990. Postcranial biomechanical adaptations to subsistence strategy changes on the Georgia coast. In *The Archaeology of Mission Santa Catalina de Guale: 2. Biocultural Interpretations of a Population in Transition*, ed. Clark Spencer Larsen, pp. 94–120. New York: Anthropological Papers of the American Museum of Natural History, No. 68.

     2001. Reconstructing behavior in Spanish Florida: The biomechanical evidence. In *Bioarchaeology of Spanish Florida: The Impact of Colonialism*, ed. Clark Spencer Larsen, pp. 113–145. Gainesville: University Press of Florida.

Ruhl, Donna L. 1990. Spanish mission paleoethnobotany and culture change: A survey of the archaeobotanical data and some speculations on aboriginal and Spanish agrarian interactions in La Florida. In *Columbian Consequences, Volume 2: Archaeological and Historical Perspectives on the Spanish Borderlands East*, ed. David Hurst Thomas, pp. 555–580. Washington, D.C.: Smithsonian Institution Press.

Sattenspiel, Lisa, and Henry Harpending. 1983. Stable population and skeletal age. *American Antiquity* 48:489–498.

Schoeninger, Margaret J., Nikolaas J. van der Merwe, Katherine M. Moore, Julia A. Lee-Thorp, and Clark Spencer Larsen. 1990. Decrease in diet quality between the prehistoric and contact periods. In *The Archaeology of Mission Santa Catalina de Guale: 2. Biocultural Interpretations of a Population in Transition*, ed. Clark Spencer Larsen, pp. 78–93. New York: Anthropological Papers of the American Museum of Natural History, No. 68.

Schultz, Michael, Clark Spencer Larsen, and Kerstin Kreutz. 2001. Disease in Spanish Florida: Microscopy of porotic hyperostosis and cribra orbitalia. In *Bioarchaeology of Spanish Florida: The Impact of Colonialism*, ed. Clark Spencer Larsen, pp. 207–225. Gainesville: University Press of Florida.

Sciulli, Paul W., K. N. Schneider, and M. C. Mahaney. 1990. Stature estimation in prehistoric Native Americans of Ohio. *American Journal of Physical Anthropology* 83:275–280.

Scrimshaw, Nevin S. 1975. Interactions of malnutrition and infection: Advances in understanding. In *Protein-Calorie Malnutrition*. ed. R. E. Olson, pp. 353–367. New York: Academic Press.

Semon, R. L., and D. Spengler. 1981. Significance of lumbar spondylolysis in college football players. *Spine* 6:172–174.

Simpson, Scott W., Dale L. Hutchinson, and Clark Spencer Larsen. 1990. Coping with stress: Tooth size, dental defects, and age-at-death. In *The Archaeology of Mission Santa Catalina de Guale: 2. Biocultural Interpretations of a Population in Transition*, ed. Clark Spencer Larsen, pp. 66–77. New York: Anthropological Papers of the American Museum of Natural History, No. 68.

Stewart, T. D. 1931. Incidence of separate neural arch in the lumbar vertebrae of Eskimos. *American Journal of Physical Anthropology* 16:51–62.

Stuart-Macadam, Patty. 1985. Porotic hyperostosis: Representative of a childhood condition. *American Journal of Physical Anthropology* 66:391–398.

Teaford, Mark F. 1991. Dental microwear: What can it tell us about diet and dental function? In *Advances in Dental Anthropology*, ed. Marc A. Kelley and Clark Spencer Larsen, pp. 341–356. New York: Wiley-Liss.

Teaford, Mark F., Clark Spencer Larsen, Robert F. Pastor, and Vivian E. Noble. 2001. Pits and scratches: Microscopic evidence of tooth use and masticatory behavior in La Florida. In *Bioarchaeology of Spanish Florida: The Impact of Colonialism*, ed. Clark Spencer Larsen, pp. 82–112. Gainesville: University Press of Florida.

Thomas, David Hurst. 1987. *The Archaeology of Mission Santa Catalina de Guale: 1. Search and Discovery*. New York: Anthropological Papers of the American Museum of Natural History 63, part 2.

———. 1988. Saints and soldiers at Santa Catalina: Hispanic designs for Colonial America. In *The Recovery of Meaning: Historical Archaeology in the Eastern United States*, ed. Mark P. Leone and Parker B. Potter, pp. 73–140. Washington, D.C.: Smithsonian Institution Press.

Walker, Phillip L. 1985. Anemia among prehistoric Indians of the American Southwest. In *Health and Disease in the Prehistoric Southwest*, ed. Charles F. Merbs and Robert J. Miller, pp. 139–164. Tempe: Arizona State University Anthropological Papers, No. 34.

———. 1986. Porotic hyperostosis in a marine-dependent California Indian population. *American Journal of Physical Anthropology* 69:345–354.

Worth, John E. 1995. *The Struggle for the Georgia Coast: An Eighteenth-Century Spanish Retrospective on Guale and Mocama*. New York: Anthropological Papers of the American Museum of Natural History No. 75.

———. 2001. The ethnohistorical context of bioarchaeology in Spanish Florida. In *Bioarchaeology of Spanish Florida: The Impact of Colonialism*, ed. Clark Spencer Larsen, pp. 22–51. Gainesville: University Press of Florida.

## CHAPTER FIFTEEN

Native Americans in Eastern North America

The Southern Great Lakes and Upper Ohio Valley

Paul W. Sciulli and James Oberly

ABSTRACT

A total of 469 individuals are sampled from three Late Archaic (ca. 3000 BP) and four Late Prehistoric (ca. 800–400 BP) Ohio Valley populations and are evaluated for health-related biological indicators.

These samples exhibit generally low frequencies of pathological conditions. Conditions associated with normal wear and tear (degenerative joint disease and, to some extent, trauma) are age associated and are of similar frequencies and severity in the samples. Linear enamel hypoplasia (LEH) is associated with growth depression in the samples, and although the samples exhibit a relatively large average stature, the somewhat smaller stature in Late Prehistoric samples is likely due to their higher frequency of LEH. The greatest difference in pathological conditions among the samples is in the increased incidence of acquired dental pathologies in the maize agricultural Late Prehistoric samples.

In the 2,500-year time span from which these populations were sampled, the overall differences in health indicators, aside from dental health, appear to be small and due to the generally similar biocultural conditions throughout the period.

INTRODUCTION

The culture-historical record of native populations of the middle and upper Ohio Valley is divided into five phases: Paleo-Indian (ca. 12,000–6000 BP), Archaic (ca. 6000–3000 BP), Woodland (ca. 3000–1100 BP), Late Prehistoric (ca. 1100–400 BP), and Proto-historic (400–200 BP). While a broad outline of the technological, subsistence, and organizational features of populations within these phases has been constructed, at present, biocultural studies are possible only for populations in and following the later part of the Archaic phase. The reason for the abrupt initiation of the biocultural record in the Late Archaic is that during this phase, populations began to dispose of their dead in relatively large, often conspicuous, cemeteries (Griffin, 1983). From the Late Archaic onward, cemeteries of various kinds are common and there is, thus, the potential for a fairly complete biocultural

record. However, due to the vagaries of preservation, the varying interests of investigators, and variations in mortuary ceremonialism (e.g., cremation), each phase
and all areas within the middle and upper Ohio Valley are not equally represented
bioculturally. Nevertheless, sufficient information has been accumulated to allow
initial inferences to be made concerning the general patterns of biocultural evolution of populations in the area subsequent to and including the Late Archaic
phase.

Culture-Historical Background

The region comprising the middle and upper Ohio Valley consists of areas of Pennsylvania, West Virginia, Ohio, and Kentucky, ranging from Pittsburgh in Pennsylvania to Cincinnati in Ohio (Figure 15.1). Most of the region adjacent to the valley and
its tributaries is part of the hilly, unglaciated Appalachian plateau. Soils in this area
have low to moderate fertility with low calcium content (except on valley floors).
To the west of the Appalachian plateau and extending through central and western
Ohio are glacial till plains resulting from the advance of the Pleistocene glaciers.
These till plains with fertile, high-calcium soils reach north and west to the Great
Lakes.

The entire region from the Appalachian plateau to the till plains supported a
mixed mesophytic forest. However, the forest was denser on the plateau; the till plains
contained more open forest as well as varying-sized islands of prairie vegetation. The
ecologically more diverse till plains, lake shores, and large alluvial valley bottoms
offered a great resource potential and appear to have been the foci of prehistoric
population concentrations.

Throughout the Archaic phase as modern ecological conditions were becoming
established, human populations appear to have been growing and were expanding
into regions little utilized previously (Brose, 1979). Although habitation sites are rare
for this phase in the middle and upper Ohio Valley, the evidence which does exist, as
well as evidence from surrounding regions, suggests that habitations were occupied
for multiple seasons, but not year-round, by sizable populations (compared to earlier
habitation sites) subsisting primarily by hunting, fishing, and gathering. Evidence
from regions surrounding the middle and upper Ohio Valley shows that native plants
of the Eastern Agricultural Complex (Smith, 1989) were under domestication by
this time and probably were included in the diet of Ohio Valley populations.

By about 3000 BP in the area between the Ohio River and the Great Lakes,
increased regionalization of populations is manifested in the recognition of a number of circumscribed mortuary complexes, such as "Glacial Kame," around western
Lake Erie and extending south and west into Michigan, Ohio, and Indiana, as well as
"Red Ocher," in south-central Ohio.

Populations of the Early Woodland phase (ca. 3000–2000 BP) in this area exhibit
strong biocultural similarities with preceding Late Archaic populations. In general,
the characteristic features of Early Woodland populations are simply elaborations
of features which first appeared in the Late Archaic. For example, ceramics, the
kinds of mortuary ceremonialism, the classes of raw materials, and artifacts used

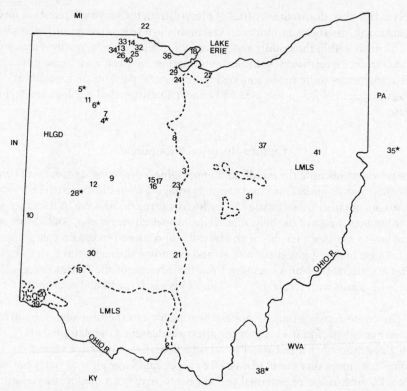

Figure 15.1. Map of Ohio showing the locations of samples from which data have been collected. (1) Dupont (2) Scioto County Homes (3) Davis (4) Duff (5) Boose (6) Kirian Treglia (7) Clifford Williams (8) Stratton Wallace (9) Muzzey Lake (10) McKee (11) Steck Shulte (12) Berry Hill (13) Willims Red Ocher (14) Hickory Island (15) Galbreath (16) Sidner (17) McMurray (18) Marblehead (19) Cowan Creek (20) Turner (21) Hopewell (22) Gord Island (23) Scioto Trails (24) Baker I (25) Waterworks (26) Reau (27) Taylor (28) SunWatch (29) Pearson (30) Anderson (31) Richards (32) Blacks Knoll (33) La Salle (34) Dodge (35) Monongahela (36) Peterson (37) Riker (38) Buffalo (39) Madisonville (40) Indian Hills (41) Maddie Stewart. Samples with a star are included in the data collection for the health index. HLGD is a soil region of high lime glacial drift. LMLS are soil regions of low and medium lime content.

in exchange systems are common to Late Archaic and Early Woodland peoples (Seeman, 1991). Aside from minor artifactual differences and the widespread use of ceramics, the primary change that marks the transition from Late Archaic to Early Woodland is the elaboration of mortuary ceremonialism. Early Woodland populations, especially Adena populations, placed great emphasis on burial mound building and associated activities.

Early Woodland habitation sites in the region indicate that economic units were relatively small, at most only a few houses in a hamlet. Subsistence data show that these populations continued the diffuse economic pattern of hunting-fishing-gathering while occupying sites for multiple seasons. In addition, it appears that

Eastern Agricultural Complex domesticates as well as cucurbits were widely utilized by Early Woodland populations.

The increasing elaboration of mortuary ceremonialism which continued through the Early Woodland reached a climax in the Middle Woodland, Hopewell phase (ca. 2000–1600 BP). Hopewell ceremonialism was the most complex and costly form of ritual behavior in the Woodland phase. Extensive time and labor were required to construct large earthen enclosures, measuring up to 5.2km^2, as well as huge burial mounds, up to 152m long by 55m wide by 11m high. In addition, large buildings were covered by the mounds which contained, aside from burials, great concentrations of exotic raw materials and artifacts.

The Hopewell settlement pattern appears generally similar to Early Woodland Adena's dispersed distribution of small hamlets. Subsistence data suggest a generally diffuse base (hunting-fishing-gathering) with the presence of Eastern Agricultural Complex domesticates and possibly maize. Although maize may be present in some Hopewell sites, there is no evidence that it comprised even a minor portion of the diet. In the upper Ohio Valley, Hopewell did not emerge and the basic cultural pattern of the Early Woodland persisted.

By about 1600 BP (Late Woodland phase) many populations within the middle and upper Ohio Valley exhibited characteristics of settlement pattern, material culture, and ritual activity that were fundamentally different from those that had been developed previously. Habitation sites were often much larger (up to 3.2ha), with some sites fortified with ditches and embankments and some organized around central plazas. Subsistence evidence, however, indicates a base essentially the same as in Middle Woodland times.

During the latter part of the Late Woodland (ca. 1300–1100 BP), populations begin to expand from primarily riverine localities to include upland sites. Ceramics were further developed at this time, and the presence of small triangular projectile points signals the introduction of the bow and arrow.

Beginning about 1100 BP, a new series of cultural features appear which relate to the adoption of intensive maize agriculture by populations of the region. Subsistence in the Late Prehistoric phase shifted from hunting-fishing-gathering and the cultivation of native domesticates to hunting-fishing-gathering and the focused cultivation of introduced, tropical domesticates: maize, beans, and curcurbits. Associated with this subsistence shift is the presence of relatively large, often fortified (palisaded) villages located in major river valleys. While large cemeteries are usually associated with these villages, mortuary ceremonialism of the kind seen in the Early and Middle Woodland periods is virtually absent. In the middle and upper Ohio Valley, the Late Prehistoric phase is represented by five cultural traditions: Fort Ancient in the south and southwestern areas, Sandusky in the northwest, Monongahela and Belmont in the east, and Whittlesey in the northeast. With some temporal variation, many features of these cultural traditions are evident in the area from their earliest appearance until Proto-historic times (400–200 BP). However, the period between about 600 and 300 BP is poorly known in this region and, thus, we are ignorant of the biocultural dynamics which produced the proto-historic groups.

Given this cultural historical background of native populations of the middle and upper Ohio Valley, we will now present the results of previous biocultural studies of these populations. Figure 15.1 shows the locations of the samples that will be described below.

PREVIOUS BIOCULTURAL INVESTIGATIONS

Biological Distance

An important first step in identifying potential sources of health differences among populations is the evaluation of the pattern of genetic similarities and differences among the populations. Because we are interested in the responses of populations to changing environments, we should consider, at least to some extent, the relative amount of genetic differentiation among populations since genetically different populations probably respond to environmental change in different ways. In the present context we will use the pattern of variation of cranial features as a representation of a population's genetic makeup.

Previous investigations of cranial metrics and nonmetric traits in Archaic (Sciulli and Schneider, 1985; Sciulli, 1990); Archaic, Middle, and Early Woodland (Sciulli and Mahaney, 1986); and Late Prehistoric to Proto-historic populations (Giesen, 1992) have shown that samples from the Late Archaic through the Middle Woodland phases are sampled from the same population. Since samples from these groups are sequential in time, these results indicate they form an ancestor-descendant chain of populations or an evolutionary lineage. Significant differences do exist, however, among some Late Prehistoric groups suggesting that contributions from genetically different lineages may have occurred in the Ohio Valley area at that time.

For the present study we have extended the comparisons of cranial metrics to include 19 samples ranging form the Late Archaic to the Proto-historic phases. We used the Box Test (Box 1949) to evaluate the homogeneity of the covariance matrices derived from 9 cranial measures and assumed, as in previous studies, that homogenous covariance matrices reflect similarities in cranial shape and thus genetic similarity.

Comparisons of Late Archaic ($n = 7$), Middle Woodland ($n = 2$), and Late Woodland ($n = 1$) samples reveal no heterogeneity among samples within the first two phases and no heterogeneity among samples when all three phases are considered together (Table 15.1). These results cannot refute the hypothesis that the Late Archaic through Late Woodland samples represent populations of a single lineage extending through approximately 1,800 years. Late Prehistoric samples ($n = 9$), on the other hand, are heterogeneous. However, within the northwest ($n = 3$) and southeast ($n = 3$) regions, the samples are homogeneous, and for both regions, the local samples and the Late Woodland sample are homogeneous. This indicates that populations of the northwestern and southeastern regions shared a Late Woodland ancestor (ca. 1300–1100 BP) but subsequently due to isolation, differential gene flow or possibly different types of selection, differentiated from each other. In the southwestern region, the three samples are heterogeneous. The source of the heterogeneity

Table 15.1: Result of the Box Test for Homogeneity of Variance–Covariance Matrices from 9 Cranial Measures per Sample

Comparison	Number of samples	D.F.	F.	P[7]
Archaic[1]	8	315, 17859	1.13	0.056
Hopewell[2]	2	45, 5460	0.86	0.738
Archaic–Hopewell	10	405, 24498	1.10	0.075
Archaic-Hopewell–Late Woodland[3]	11	450, 21359	1.16	0.012
Northwest[4]	3	90, 2762	1.31	0.026
Southwest[5]	3	90, 35593	1.91	0.000
Southeast[6]	3	90, 4775	1.17	0.130
Late Woodland–Anderson, SunWatch	3	90, 2694	1.34	0.0182
Late Woodland–Northwest	4	135, 3647	1.30	0.012
Late Woodland–Southeast	4	135, 4243	1.20	0.057

[1] Duff, Boose, Kirian Treglia, Clifford Williams, Davis, Muzzey Lake, William Red Ocher, Stratton Wallace.
[2] Hopewell Mound Group, Turner.
[3] Archaic and Hopewell samples plus Scioto Trails as Late Woodland representative.
[4] Pearson, Peterson, Indian Hills.
[5] Anderson, SunWatch, Madisonville.
[6] Buffalo, Monongahela, Maddie Stewart.
[7] A critical value of P = 0.01 is used due to the large number of degrees of freedom.

is the Madisonville sample since SunWatch and Anderson are homogeneous and homogeneous with the Late Woodland sample. Thus, there appears to have been a subdivision of the lineage into at least three local groups, northwest, southeast, and southwest, during or subsequent to the Late Woodland phase. The Madisonville population, a proto-historic group, may be intrusive to the area or may be an atypical population resulting from the amalgamation of numerous populations in the area (Drooker, 1997). For the purposes of the present chapter, these results indicate that the seven samples we have included in this study (see "Samples and Paleodemography") can be considered genetically similar, that is, sampled from the same evolutionary lineage.

Paleodemography

Previous paleodemographic studies of populations from the middle and upper Ohio Valley include the analyses of the Late Woodland Libben site sample (Lovejoy et al., 1977), the Late Archaic Duff site sample (Sciulli and Aument, 1987), and the Early Late Prehistoric Pearson Village sample (Sciulli et al., 1996). Although differing in time by up to 2,000 years, these three samples exhibit almost identical age-specific percentages of death. Lovejoy et al. (1977) and Sciulli and Aument (1987) interpreted their respective samples as being representative of the populations. Preservation was good, and archaeological methods were such as to recognize the extent of the cemeteries and to recover even the youngest infants. However, the demographic

feature of these samples did not conform to the patterns seen in historic populations (Coale and Demeny, 1966). Both the Libben and the Duff samples showed
low proportions of infants and older adults. To explain the differences between the
demographic profile of the Libben sample and historic populations, Lovejoy et al.
(1977) proposed the "immunological competence" theory. In this theory, historic
(and "anthropological") populations are considered contact populations under the
selective influence of a battery of novel pathogens. Disease stress early in life is
hypothesized to result in high selective mortality, eliminating those less resistant to
disease and producing hardy survivors who display reduced mortality as adults. In
contrast, many prehistoric populations were smaller and more isolated than historic
populations and, thus, not exposed to the almost constant threat of novel pathogens.
In this situation it is hypothesized that infant mortality was not as great as in contact
populations due to the lack of selection for the immunologically competent in infancy. This lack of early selection resulted in adult mortality higher than in historic
populations.

The archaeological and demographic analysis of the Pearson Village sample provided sources of information that were not available for the Late Archaic Duff
sample and allowed us to look more fully at potential sources of bias in this skeletal sample. Faunal and floral analyses have shown that Pearson Village was a late
spring and summer base camp and, thus, inhabited for only a portion of the year.
The most likely "ethnic" identity of the Pearson Village population (as well as the
Libben population) is ancestral Central Algonquian (Lovejoy et al., 1977; Stothers
and Abel, 1989). A characteristic feature of Central Algonquian populations is a
marked seasonal subsistence-settlement cycle in which following the autumn harvest of maize, village inhabitants moved to hunting grounds where they dispersed
into small, scattered camps of one or two families. With the onset of winter, inhabitants of many of the camps gathered into larger hamlets in sheltered areas to
pass the winter. In late winter–early spring, the inhabitants of the hamlets dispersed
to hunt, and only in April did the bands return to the spring-summer village to
plant. Thus, if the Pearson and Libben populations conformed even broadly to this
pattern, they were concentrated at their village (and cemetery) for only half the
year. The situation may have been even more extreme for the presumably more mobile, nonagricultural, Late Archaic Duff population. Sciulli et al. (1996) proposed
that a factor contributing to the low proportions of infants and older adults in the
Pearson sample was a culturally biased sample – the Pearson sample consists of a
seasonal subset of the dead: those dying in the late spring through early autumn.
Since winter mortality is greater among the very young, the old, and the sick and
disabled (Collins, 1993), we would expect that at least some of the deficiency in the
younger and older age groups are present in the hunting camps and winter hamlets
to which the Pearson population dispersed. Sciulli et al. (1996) present archaeological and age-at-death data, although limited, from camps and hamlets to support
this idea.

Since many populations in the Ohio Valley region were relatively mobile, and
since most samples from the middle and upper Ohio Valley have age-at-death
distributions similar to the above-mentioned samples, we are forced to accept the
possibility that these samples are not representative of their population. For this and

other reasons (Ubelaker, 1974; Wood et al., 1992), the frequencies of pathologies which we present in the sections below should be viewed only as broad estimates.

Dental Pathology

Tables 15.2 and 15.3 contain the results of a survey of caries, abscesses, and pre-mortem tooth loss for the permanent and deciduous teeth in middle and upper Ohio Valley populations. Caries frequency, which reflects the amount of carbohydrate in the diet, exhibits a relatively simple pattern among the populations. For individual samples in the Late Archaic through Late Woodland phases, caries frequency ranges from 0% to 8.6% while the totals for the phases range from 2.4% to 4.8%. These frequencies are in contrast to those from samples of the Late Prehistoric phase, which range from 5.6% to 43.8% and average 18.0%. This pattern is consistent with the archaeologically derived timing of the adoption of maize agriculture in this area, as well as with the pattern of carbon isotope values among populations over time. Table 15.2 contains the δC 12/13 ratios available for samples in the region. From the Late Archaic through the Middle Woodland, values range from -27.4 to -21.5, indicating no contribution to the diet from maize. Beginning with the Late Woodland, there is a slight increase in the ratio (-19.9 to -18.8), but in the Late Prehistoric phase, the ratio increases to -15.6 to -10.7, indicating the C_4 (maize) plants contributed up to 50% of the carbon in the diet. These results are summarized in Figure 15.2, which shows the increase of caries frequency over time and the concomitant increase in the carbon isotope ratio. The introduction of maize agriculture in the region thus resulted in a significant decrease in dental health as reflected in caries frequency.

The decline of dental health in the Late Prehistoric phase is also reflected in the other dental pathology indexes. For example, antemortem tooth loss averages 6.0% to 9.0% prior to the Late Prehistoric and then increases to 17.5%. Likewise, abscesses and the decayed–missing frequencies range, respectively, from 2.3% to 4.1% and from 8.8% to 12.1% before the Late Prehistoric to 5% and 29.5% during the Late Prehistoric phase.

The following hypothesis is proposed to explain these results. Prior to the Late Prehistoric period, the relatively low amount of simple carbohydrate in the diet resulted in a low frequency of caries. However, especially in aceramic Late Archaic populations, severe dental wear resulted in relatively high frequencies of antemortem tooth loss and abscesses (through pulp exposure from wear). With the introduction of ceramics, particularly the well-made varieties beginning in the Middle Woodland phase, food preparation was more extensive, resulting in reduced wear and, thus, lower frequencies of antemortem loss and abscesses. The introduction of maize in the Late Prehistoric period and the resulting higher carbohydrate diet resulted in higher frequencies of caries, the appearance of caries earlier in the life span of individuals, and, because caries are progressive, higher frequencies of tooth loss due to pulp exposure.

These results and the above hypothesis are based on the data for the permanent teeth in Table 15.2, but a brief review of the data for the deciduous teeth in Table 15.3 shows the same pattern of frequencies and leads to the same conclusion – the

Table 15.2: Dental Pathology in the Permanent Dentition of Late Archaic through Proto-historic Samples

| Site | Age (BP) | Culture | Location | δC12/13 | Caries | | | | | Totals | | Indexes | | | |
					No. caries	W2	W4	W6	W8	Teeth	Loci	Caries	Antemortem	Abscess	DM
Dupont	4485 ± 75	—	HLGD/SSS	−21.8	216	0	0	0	0	216	250	0.0	7.2	2.8	7.2
Scioto Co. Homes	4110	—	HLGD/SSS	—	383	0	1	2	3	389	591	1.5	14.6	10.5	15.6
Davis	3150 ± 120	—	HLGD	—	286	1	0	1	6	293	432	2.4	10.0	6.0	11.6
Duff	2950 ± 100	—	HLGD	—	1293	1	21	48	34	1397	1529	7.4	7.3	4.0	14.1
Boose	—	—	HLGD	—	428	0	0	8	11	447	562	4.2	9.1	5.7	12.4
Kirian Treglia	2850	Glacial Kame	HLGD	—	300	0	0	2	10	312	424	3.8	22.2	5.4	25.0
Clifford Williams	—	Glacial Kame	HLGD	—	271	0	0	1	1	273	448	0.7	11.8	2.7	12.3
Stratton Wallace	—	—	HLGD/LML	—	120	0	3	2	4	129	304	7.0	17.8	4.3	20.7
Muzzey Lake	—	—	HLGD	—	175	0	3	6	4	188	393	6.9	10.4	3.0	13.7
McKee	—	Glacial Kame	HLGD	—	387	0	5	11	6	409	693	5.4	3.2	2.5	5.5
Stech Shulte	—	—	HLGD	—	171	0	1	12	3	187	254	8.6	6.3	3.9	12.6
Berry Hill	2890	—	HLGD	−23.9	451	0	0	6	3	460	463	2.0	2.2	3.5	4.1
Williams Red Ocher	2680	Sandusky	HLGD	−21.5	883	2	4	3	1	893	1067	1.1	6.6	1.4	7.6
LATE ARCHAIC TOTALS					5364	3	38	102	86	5593	7410	4.1	9.0	4.1	12.1
Hickory Island	2500 ± 100	Sandusky	HLGD	—	163		0	0	0	163	154	0.0	3.9	3.2	3.9
Galbreath	2150	Adena	HLGD	—	357	0	1	4	6	368	439	3.0	1.4	1.6	3.9
McMurray	—	Adena	HLGD	—	253	0	0	5	4	262	332	3.4	8.1	3.0	10.8
Marblehead	1990 ± 70	Sandusky	HLGD	−27.4	132	0	0	0	0	132	197	0.0	17.3	6.1	17.3
Cowan Creek	—	Adena	GDI	—	76	1	1	4	2	81	112	6.2	15.2	3.6	19.6
EARLY WOODLAND TOTALS					1274	2	3	14	12	1307	1629	2.4	6.9	2.9	8.8
Turner	—	Hopewell	HLGD/GDI	−22.7*	978	23	31	5	3	1040	1572	6.0	5.9	3.5	9.9
Hopewell	—	Hopewell	HLGD	−22.1*	965	8	16	9	2	1000	1506	3.5	6.4	3.3	8.7
MIDDLE WOODLAND TOTALS					1943	31	47	14	5	2040	3078	4.8	6.0	3.4	9.2

Site	Date	Location	Soil	δ13C											
Gard Island	1280	W. Basin	HLGD	—	333	4	8	2	0	347	446	4.0	8.1	1.6	11.2
Scioto Trails	1185	Scioto	HLGD	−19.8	403	0	4	3	2	412	482	2.2	7.3	2.9	9.1
Baker I	1110 ± 80	Sandusky	HLGD	−18.8	72	3	7	10	0	92	137	21.7	31.4	2.2	46.0
LATE WOODLAND TOTALS					808	7	19	15	2	851	1065	5.0	10.7	2.3	14.7
												(3.0)**	(7.6)**	(2.3)**	(10.1)
Waterworks	930 ± 130	W. Basin	HLLD	−12.4	148	5	11	4	0	168	245	11.9	6.5	2.9	14.7
Reau	875	W. Basin	HLLD	—	102	0	7	3	1	113	180	9.7	13.3	3.3	19.4
Taylor	850	Sandusky	HLLD/LLLD	−10.7	180	7	16	7	7	217	453	17.0	14.6	5.5	22.7
SunWatch	800	Fort Ancient	HLGD	−11.6	1019	56	102	27	9	1213	1777	16.0	21.6	7.1	32.5
Pearson	725	Sandusky	HLLD	−13.2	2151	89	203	66	13	2522	3693	14.7	20.8	4.5	30.8
Anderson	700	Fort Ancient	GDI	—	944	35	55	19	14	1097	1475	11.2	16.7	4.8	25.0
Richards	680	Fort Ancient	SSS	—	268	28	61	20	2	379	674	29.3	12.0	6.1	28.5
Blacks Knoll	600 ± 80	Sandusky	HLLD	−11.7	170	4	1	1	4	180	254	5.6	17.3	5.9	21.2
La Salle	570 ± 100	Sandusky	HLLD	−11.4	396	21	25	21	2	465	489	14.8	8.4	4.3	22.5
Dodge	565	W. Basin	HLLD	−15.6	199	4	12	9	0	224	328	11.2	8.8	4.9	16.5
Monongahela	550	Mon.	SSS	−12.2	1758	121	245	59	14	2197	3221	20.0	18.3	5.1	32.0
Peterson	425	Sandusky	HLLD	—	68	6	29	15	3	121	—	43.8	—	—	—
Riker	390	Fort Ancient	SSS/LML	—	122	3	13	9	4	151	265	19.2	21.5	5.3	32.5
Buffalo	—	Fort Ancient	SSS	—	3089	316	542	96	20	4063	5855	24.0	22.1	5.6	38.7
Madisonville	—	Fort Ancient	HLGD/GDI	—	2180	130	204	53	5	2572	4588	15.2	11.6	4.2	20.1
Indian Hills	350	Sandusky	HLLD	−10.7	390	20	26	7	1	444	873	12.2	13.9	6.3	20.0
LATE PREHISTORIC TOTALS					13,214	845	1,552	416	99	16,126	24,370	18.0	17.5	5.0	29.5

Location refers to primary soil region. HLGD is high lime glacial drift; SSS is soil formed in sandstone, siltstone, and shale; LML is soils formed in low and medium lime glacial drift; GDI is glacial drift of Illinoisan Age; HLLD is high lime glacial lake sediments; LLLD is low lime glacial lake sediments. Caries number is recorded by wear score (Molnar, 1972); e.g., W2 is Wear Category 2. Indices are calculated per population totals.
* Data from Seip and Harnes sites.
** Total without Baker I.

Table 15.3: Dental Pathology of the Deciduous Dentition in Late Archaic through Proto-historic samples

Site	Caries						Indexes			
	No. caries	W2	W4	6	Teeth	Loci	Caries	Antemortem	Abscess	DM
Dupont	23	0	0	0	23	40	0.00	0.00	0.00	0.00
Scioto Co. Homes	8	0	0	0	8	14	0.00	0.00	0.00	0.00
Davis	61	0	0	0	61	78	0.00	0.00	0.00	0.00
Duff	280	0	0	0	280	298	0.00	0.00	0.00	0.00
Boose	122	0	1	0	123	142	0.81	0.00	0.00	0.70
Kirian Treglia	68	0	1	0	69	106	1.44	0.00	0.00	0.90
Clifford Williams										
Stratton Lake										
Muzzey Lake										
McKee	72	0	0	0	72	72	0.00	0.00	0.00	0.00
Williams Red Ocher	157	0	0	0	157	163	0.00	0.00	0.00	0.00
LATE ARCHAIC TOTALS	791	0	2	0	793	913	0.25	0.00	0.00	0.22
Hickory Island	25	0	0	0	25	—	0.00	—	—	—
Galbreath Sidner McMurray	90	0	2	0	92	119	2.17	0.00	0.00	1.68
EARLY WOODLAND TOTALS	115	0	2	0	117	119	1.71	0.00	0.00	1.68

Turner Hopwell	47	0	2	0	49	51	4.10	0.00	0.00	3.92
MIDDLE WOODLAND TOTALS	47	0	2	0	49	51	4.10	0.00	0.00	3.92
Scioto Trails	20	0	0	0	20	20	0.00	0.00	0.00	0.00
Baker I	40	1	1	0	42	90	4.76	0.00	0.00	2.22
LATE WOODLAND TOTALS	60	1	1	0	62	110	3.22	0.00	0.00	1.82
Waterworks	31	0	1	0	32	42	3.12	0.00	0.00	2.38
SunWatch	271	32	17	0	320	280	15.30	0.00	0.36	15.30
Pearson	383	4	28	3	418	434	8.37	0.00	0.00	8.06
Anderson	111	9	4	0	124	116	10.48	1.72	0.00	10.48
Richards	34	3	4	0	41	41	17.07	0.00	0.00	17.07
Blacks Knoll	38	0	0	0	38	50	0.00	0.00	0.00	0.00
Lasalle	41	3	5	0	49	64	16.33	0.00	0.00	12.50
Monongahela	377	26	71	2	476	427	20.80	0.94	0.94	24.12
Buffalo	333	31	78	0	442	283	24.66	0.00	0.00	24.66
Madisonville	163	11	14	0	188	355	13.30	0.00	0.00	7.04
Indian Hills	99	1	8	1	109	99	9.17	3.03	1.01	11.93
LATE PREHISTORIC TOTALS	1881	120	230	6	2237	2191	15.91	0.41	0.27	16.66

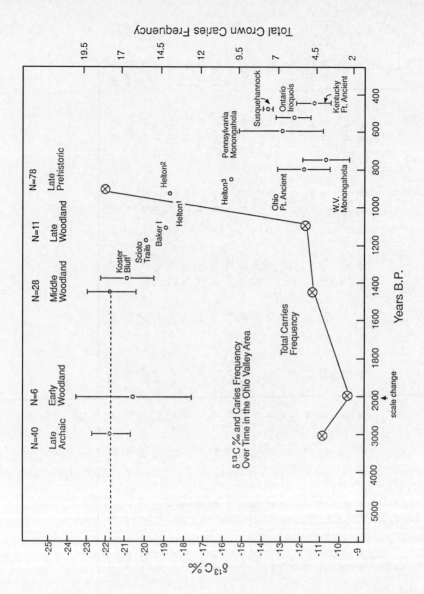

Figure 15.2. $\delta^{13}C\%$ and total caries index over time in populations from the Ohio Valley and adjacent regions. Koster Bluff, Early Late Woodland, and Helton 1, 2, 3, Early, Middle, and Late Emergent Mississippian, respectively, are sites in Illinois. Baker I and Scioto Trails are Ohio sites. Dashed line at approximately -22% indicates no maize (C_4 plants) in the diet. N above time period is the sample size for the carbon isotope data. Total caries frequencies are from Tables 15.2 and 15.3. Data from Bender et al. (1981); Broida (1984); Schwarcz et al. (1985); Stothers and Bechtel (1987); Buikstra et al. (1987).

Table 15.4: Stature Variation over Time in Ohio Valley Populations

Period	Soil	Males N	Males x	Males s	Females N	Females x	Females S	Dimorphism $(X_m - X_f / X_m)$
Late Archaic	LLS	9	163.8	6.2	9	152.2	6.1	7.1%
	HLS	63	169.3	5.6	59	154.8	5.4	8.6%
	TOTAL	72	168.6	5.9	68	154.5	5.5	8.4%
Early Woodland	LLS	5	164.8	3.2	2	146.7	—	(10.9%)
	HLS	32	167.1	3.7	25	149.9	5.3	10.7%
	TOTAL	37	166.8	3.7	27	149.7	5.3	10.2%
Middle Woodland	LLS	21	163.4	4.3	20	150.6	4.3	7.8%
	HLS	14	165.4	4.9	8	157.0	7.0	5.1%
	TOTAL	35	164.2	4.6	28	152.4	5.9	7.2%
Late Woodland	HLS	16	165.2	4.2	11	152.2	5.8	7.9%
Early Late Prehistoric	Pearson[a]	59	164.5	5.3	58	154.2	4.5	6.3%
	SunWatch[a]	30	166.4	4.3	26	153.3	4.2	7.9%
	Anderson[a]	15	165.3	6.8	14	154.5	4.5	6.5%
	TOTAL	94	165.2	5.5	9.8	154.0	4.5	6.8%
Mid Late Prehistoric	Monongahela[b]	37	162.4	5.4	38	151.7	6.9	6.6%
Proto-historic	Madisonville[b]	78	160.2	7.2	95	150.7	6.6	5.9%
	Indian Hills[b]	26	163.1	3.5	25	152.7	4.1	6.4%
	Buffalo[b]	98	164.9	6.4	108	153.9	6.0	6.7%
	TOTAL	202	162.9	7.0	228	152.4	6.5	6.4%
Historic	Iroquois	94	172.7		—	158.5	—	8.2%
	Delaware	48	171.5		—	158.6	—	7.5%
	Ottawa	98	169.9		—	158.8	—	6.5%
	Cherokee	104	167.7		—	154.9	—	7.6%
	TOTAL	344	170.2		—	157.5	—	7.3%

[a] High lime soil (HLS).
[b] Low lime soil (LLS).

introduction of maize to the diet in large quantities, whatever the other benefits or drawbacks to the populations, resulted in a significant reduction in dental health.

Stature

Table 15.4 and Figure 15.3 are summaries of stature data that have been collected for native populations of the middle and upper Ohio Valley (Sciulli et al., 1990; Sciulli et al., 1991; Sciulli and Giesen, 1993). The figures in Table 15.4 and Figure 15.3 are all calculated from femur lengths using sex-specific regression equations derived from the relationship between anatomical height and femur length in Ohio Valley natives (Sciulli et al., 1990; Sciulli and Giesen, 1993). In these investigations it was shown that body proportions throughout the prehistoric temporal phases were

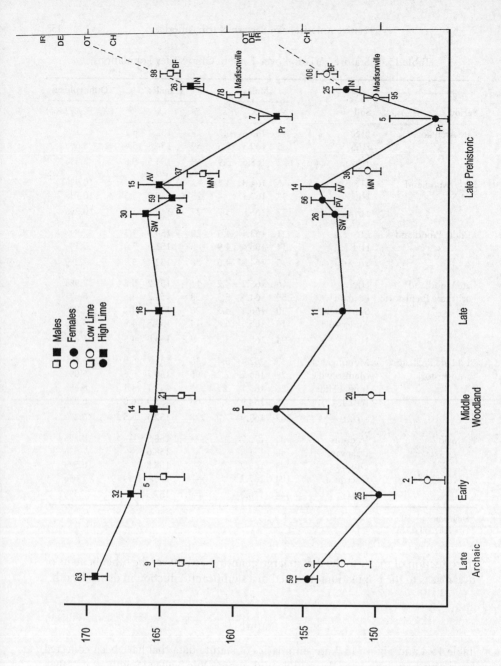

Figure 15.3. Temporal variation in stature in middle and upper Ohio Valley males and females. Data from Table 15.4. Historic samples on far right: IR, Iroquois; DE, Delaware; OT, Ottawa; CH, Cherokee. Historic males upper right, historic females lower right.

constant, as would be expected in populations derived from the same lineage, and so the sex-specific regression equations are applicable to all samples.

In Table 15.4 and Figure 15.3, samples are distinguished by temporal phase and the primary soil type at the location of the village or cemetery. As evident from Figure 15.3 at each time period, samples located on high-calcium (lime) soil exhibit greater stature than samples located on lower-calcium soils. In addition, particularly in the case of males, there appears to be a slight trend of decreasing stature over time.

While there is a modest decline in stature among males from high-calcium soils over time, in general, the differences between samples on different soils is greater than the differences through time. This indicates that ecological differences, possibly related to calcium availability, are primary factors affecting overall growth and development and that these factors may be at least as significant as changes in diet.

Figure 15.3 and Table 15.4 also contain, for comparison, average statures for historic Eastern Woodland groups (Boas, 1895). For all four groups (Iroquois, Delaware, Ottawa, and Cherokee), both males and females are taller than the Proto-historic groups (males 3–12cm taller and females 2–8cm taller) and are most similar in stature to the Late Archaic sample. If these historic groups are descendants of the Proto-historic groups, then there was a significant increase in stature among populations in this area subsequent to the mid-seventeenth century. Since contact with European populations was detrimental to the health of native populations, the increase in stature from Proto-historic to historic times may have been the result of selection wherein size and frailty were inversely related. Shorter, more frail individuals may have experienced greater mortality or a lower fertility due to increased frequencies of disease, reduced availability of food, and almost constant conflict. These data suggest that if selection operated, it need not have been dramatic (nor the relationship between stature and frailty perfect), as the increase in stature in males is on the order of 8cm in 300 years or 12 generations (AD 1600–1900) while in females, stature increase is on the order of 5cm in 12 generations, or about 5–7mm/generation.

SAMPLES AND PALEODEMOGRAPHY

From the approximately 40 samples available to us (Figure 15.1), we have chosen 7 for analysis of health status. The criteria for inclusion include size of sample, preservation, and completeness of individuals, and at least some representation of all age–sex classes. Our 7 samples are Duff, Boose, Kirian Treglia, Pearson Village, SunWatch, Monongahela, and Buffalo. The first three sites have been combined into a Late Archaic sample since the sites are geographically close and the samples are biologically (genetically) and culturally indistinguishable. Table 15.5 contains the age distribution for this total sample. From 175 Late Archaic individuals we included a sample of 134 of the most complete individuals proportional to the total age-at-death distribution.

Table 15.5 also contains the age distributions for the Late Prehistoric Pearson Village (Sandusky Tradition) and SunWatch (Fort Ancient) samples, and the Proto-historic Buffalo (Fort Ancient) sample. From each of these we chose a sample of the

Table 15.5: Age Distributions of the Ohio Valley Samples

Age	Archaic Number	f	Pearson Number	f	SunWatch Number	f	Buffalo Number	f	Monongahela Number	f
0	23	.131	67	.158	67	.411	111	.225	20	.164
1	7	.040	21	.050	10	.061	20	.041	3	.025
2	13	.074	14	.033	6	.037	12	.024	5	.041
3	6	.034	7	.017	1	.006	5	.010	3	.025
4	5	.029	10	.024	1	.006	4	.008	0	0
5	17	.097	40	.095	6	.037	45	.019	13	.107
10	10	.057	33	.078	4	.024	26	.053	9	.074
15	10	.057	32	.076	9	.055	25	.051	7	.057
20	11	.063	39	.092	4	.024	28	.057	7	.057
25	20	.114	26	.062	5	.031	45	.091	7	.057
30	17	.097	45	.106	15	.092	56	.114	17	.139
35	22	.126	55	.130	16	.098	60	.122	12	.098
40	10	.057	14	.033	13	.080	30	.061	9	.074
45+	4	.023	20	.047	6	.036	26	.052	10	.082
TOTAL	175		423		163		493		122	

most complete individuals proportional to the respective age-at-death distribution in each total sample. The final sizes for Pearson Village, SunWatch, and Buffalo are 96, 138, and 101 respectively.

The Monongahela group ($n = 122$) is comprised of individuals from 32 separate sites in western Pennsylvania and West Virginia. As such, this group does not represent a single sample, although its age-at-death distribution (Table 15.5) is very similar to that of Pearson Village and especially the Buffalo sample.

As noted above, the paleodemographic reconstructions of these groups yield implausible demographic features for a population. Because of these possible deficiencies in the demographic data, the frequencies of pathologies which we will present below should be viewed as only preliminary, broad estimates subject to significant error. In order to minimize the effects of age bias and underrepresentation of children, we will compare adults and children separately.

RESULTS

Postcranial Metrics

With respect to linear measures (humerus and femur length and thus stature), the Archaic sample exhibits, for both sexes, somewhat longer measures than the other samples (Table 15.6). However, with respect to area measures (humerus circumference, proximal femur cross section) there are few differences among the samples. Postcranial size and robustness vary somewhat in these samples but overall shape is virtually identical. Since bodily proportions are also the same, variation in size is most likely the result of minor environmental influences acting during growth and development.

Table 15.6: Metric Features on the Native American Samples of the Ohio Valley Area

Measure	Statistic	Archaic		Pearson		SunWatch		Monongahela		Buffalo	
		Male	Female	Male	Female	Male	Female	Male	Female	Male	Female
Femur length	N	26	37	22	23	31	23	32	32	26	29
	x̄	474.2	436.6	459	431.1	462.2	428	452.4	419.2	464.5	432.4
	SD	21.8	21	18.1	16.4	13.9	16.4	19.4	23.8	23.8	20.3
Humerus length	N	25	33	22	23	30	19	32	32	26	28
	x̄	338.7	210.3	330.5	302.7	330.3	305.4	325.3	301.3	329.5	311
	SD	16	17	17.4	12.2	13.4	13.3	14.6	16.8	15.5	15.4
Humerus circumference	N	26	38	21	21	31	21	34	29	26	29
	x̄	66.4	58.5	67.1	61.3	68.6	61.3	64.8	59.8	66.7	61.1
	SD	4.2	3.7	4.1	4.6	3.6	3.2	2.9	4.1	4.1	4
Femur midshaft A-P	N	25	28	21	18	31	22	31	29	26	29
	x̄	29.8	25.3	29.7	26.7	31.2	26.5	28.8	25.4	30.1	26.4
	SD	3.1	2.2	1.4	2	2.8	1.8	2.3	2.1	3.1	2
Femur midshaft M-L	N	25	29	21	18	31	22	31	29	26	29
	x̄	25.6	24.2	25.6	24.9	26.3	24.4	24.9	23.7	25.7	24.4
	SD	1.3	1.6	1.5	1.6	2	1.8	1.7	2	1.4	2.1
Stature	N	26	37	22	23	31	23	32	32	26	29
	x̄	169.1	155.1	165.2	153.8	165.8	152.6	163.4	150.1	166.7	153.6
	SD	6.2	6.1	4.7	4.6	3.7	4.7	4.9	6.9	6.3	6.2
Femur subperiosteal Area	N	24	26	21	18	31	31	31	29	26	29
	x̄	5.7	5.8	6.2	6.6	6.5	6.5	6.1	6.4	6.1	6.3
	SD	0.9	0.7	0.6	0.6	0.9	0.8	0.7	1	0.7	0.9
Femur AP/ML	N	25	28	21	18	31	21	31	29	26	29
	x̄	1.17	1.05	1.16	1.07	1.19	1.09	1.16	1.08	1.17	1.08
	SD	0.1	0.1	0.08	0.09	0.12	0.08	0.1	0.07	0.1	0.09

Metrically the Ohio Valley samples represent populations that were moderately large and robust. Over time there appears to have been a slight size decrease, but as noted previously, size difference by soil type during any temporal phase is as marked as the temporal differences. This suggests that ecological differences, possibly manifest as nutritional differences, contributed significantly to size variation among Ohio Valley populations.

Femur Growth

In the analysis of femur growth (Table 15.7), all subadults with a dental age estimate in the range 0–17.5 years and femur diaphysis length were included. Although the age range may be greater than that strictly applicable in the model of femur growth, the analysis indicates a good fit – the models explain 97% of the variation in femur length (Table 15.8).

The models for femur growth are very similar in all samples, suggesting little variation among the samples in the overall pattern of growth during the age range 0–17. As all of these individuals did not survive to adulthood, the differences in adult femur length (stature) in the samples may be the result of slightly different rates of growth between the survivors and nonsurvivors. However, among these nonsurvivors to adulthood, the pattern of growth as well as age-specific velocities are similar in all samples, suggesting that stressors, if present and most likely to be reflected in the growth of the femur (Sciulli, 1994), affected all populations in a broadly similar manner.

Dental Pathology

Table 15.9 contains the dental pathology data from the health status samples. The population indexes (at the bottom of the table) confirm that these samples represent the larger samples from which they were derived and that they reflect the general historical pattern exhibited by dental disease in the Ohio Valley area (e.g., Tables 15.2 and 15.3). The population caries index is 2 to 3 times greater in maize agriculturalist than in the primarily hunting-gathering Archaic group, and among the former, the caries index is greater in populations from areas with low-calcium soils. Among all samples except the Monongahela, the average caries index of males and females is virtually identical. The present Monongahela sample may not be representative in this case, however, as a larger sample showed no differences in caries frequencies among the sexes (Sciulli, 1996). All samples reflect the fact that each of the dental pathologies is age progressive. Table 15.9 shows that children (all individuals aged 16 or younger) in each sample exhibited much lower frequencies of each pathology. Although not included here, a previous analysis has shown that even among adults, the frequency of each of the pathologies is age dependent: older individuals have increased frequencies of each pathology (Sciulli, 1996).

The dental pathologies considered in this study appear to be a function of the normal aging process. However, diet and nutrient availability affected the frequency of occurrence of these pathologies during the aging process. In each sample,

Table 15.7: Femur Diaphysis Average Length (mm) per Age Class
in the Ohio Valley Samples

Age class	Denver	Archaic	Pearson	Sun-Watch	Monongahela	Buffalo
0.5	112	(4) 92	(10) 82	(41) 85	(16) 81	(19) 67
	0.23	0.20	0.19	0.19	0.19	0.15
1.5	154	(3) 135	(5)150	(6) 132	(5) 135	(4) 152
	0.31	0.30	0.34	0.30	0.31	0.34
2.5	185	(3) 171	(3) 187	(3) 161	(5) 174	—
	0.38	0.37	0.42	0.37	0.40	
3.5	214	(4) 190	(2) 206	—	(3) 197	(2) 191
	0.44	0.42	0.47		0.46	0.43
4.5	235	237	(4) 236	219	—	221
	0.48	0.52	(4) 0.54	0.50		0.50
5.5	258	265	(4) 236	206	247	(2) 244
	0.53	0.58	(4) 0.54	0.47	0.57	0.55
6.5	280	—	(5) 254	—	—	259
	0.57		(5) 0.58			0.59
7.5	31	(2) 246	(3) 269	(2) 246	(1) 250	(2) 273
	0.62	0.54	0.61	0.56	0.58	0.62
8.5	322	(1) 250	—	—	(7) 271	(1) 310
	0.66	0.55			0.63	0.70
9.5	340	(5) 282	(3) 305	—	(2) 300	(1) 356
	0.70	0.62	(3) 0.69		0.70	0.80
10.5	359	(1) 317	—	(1) 330	(1) 338	(1) 306
	0.73	0.69		0.75	0.75	0.69
11.5	378	(2) 350	(7) 345	(3) 302	(2) 331	(1) 351
	0.77	0.77	0.78	0.68	0.75	0.79
Adult femur length	489	457	441	441	431	442

Note: Under sample heading is the mean with sample size in parentheses. Below mean is the fraction of adult growth achieved. At bottom of each column is average adult femur length. The Denver data is from Maresh (1959).

older individuals have a greater average frequency of each pathology than younger individuals, and in the maize agricultural populations, the older individuals have a much greater incidence of dental disease than among the hunter-gatherers. In absolute terms, individuals in the oldest age class in the samples from maize agricultural populations have virtually every tooth affected by one or another of the pathologies.

Trauma

Traumas are relatively rare in the Ohio Valley samples (Table 15.10). Nasal, facial, and hand trauma as well as weapon wounds occur only in adults and have a frequency less than 1%. Healed fractures of the arm, leg, and cranial vault do reach appreciable frequencies, but never greater than about 6.0% in any sample.

Table 15.8: Equations for Femur Diaphysis Growth

Sample	A ± SE	B₁ ± SE	B₂ ± SE	R^2	N
Archaic	107.7 ± 5.4	15.5 ± 1.3	21.3 ± 4.9	0.97	37
P,B,S	115.0 ± 2.5	13.8 ± 0.6	27.1 ± 1.7	0.97	159
Monongahela	109.8 ± 4.6	14.5 ± 1.2	23.7 ± 3.2	0.97	53
Total	112.6 ± 2.0	14.2 ± 0.5	25.4 ± 1.4	0.97	249

	Velocity (mm/year)			
Age	Archaic	P,B,S	Monongahela	Total
1	36.8	40.9	38.2	39.6
3	22.6	22.8	22.4	22.7
5	19.8	19.2	19.2	19.3
7	18.5	17.7	17.9	17.8
9	17.9	16.8	17.1	17.0
11	17.4	16.3	16.6	16.5
13	17.1	15.9	16.3	16.1
15	16.9	15.6	16.1	15.9
17	16.8	15.4	15.9	15.7

Source: Age range 0 to 17.5 years. Equations are of the form FDL $= A + B_1(Age) + B_2(\ln age)$. P, B, S and M are sites Pearson, Buffalo, SunWatch, and Monongahela. Velocity is: $V = B_1 + B_2 \backslash Age$. Pearson, Buffalo, SunWatch are pooled because of similarity of adult femur lengths.

Table 15.11 contains the results of tests of independence between the sexes for arm, leg, and cranial vault trauma. In general, healed fractures are somewhat more frequent in males than in females. Exceptions are higher frequencies of healed arm fractures in Buffalo females and higher frequencies of vault fractures in Archaic females. However, in no cases are the sex differences significant (Table 15.11). As with dental pathology, trauma (arm, leg, and vault fractures) increase with age but the relationship is much weaker than dental pathology and age. For the total sample, arm, leg, and cranial vault trauma have a Spearman's correlation with age of $r = 0.18$ (P = 0.0001), $r = 0.11$ (P = 0.009), and $r = 0.12$ (P = 0.004), respectively; all low but significant. While dental pathology is a function of the normal aging process (due to constant use and lack of repair), the relationship of trauma and age is likely due to a greater time of exposure to accidents, and so on, by adults, as well as the greater liability of older individuals to fractures. Only in the latter sense are traumas a by-product of the normal aging process. Through time, the prevalence of trauma and the pattern of occurrence in the Ohio Valley samples were fairly stable (Table 15.12).

The frequency of trauma in Ohio Valley populations is very low, and for leg and arm trauma the vast majority are well healed. These populations likely had techniques to treat fractures, and this undoubtedly contributes to their low observed frequency since we see, for the most part, only those fractures which occurred relatively close to the time of death.

Table 15.9: Dental Pathology in the Native American samples from the Ohio Valley

	Archaic				Pearson Village				SunWatch Village				Monongahela				Buffalo Village			
	Male	Female	Child	Total	Male	Female	Child	Total	Male	Female	Child	Total	Male	Female	Child	Total	Male	Female	Child	Total
Summary numbers																				
# Teeth	745	1019	386	2150	397	422	455	1274	649	414	227	1290	504	590	380	1474	380	493	224	1027
# Caries	68	96	3	167	57	79	21	157	126	63	18	207	159	108	23	290	104	117	12	233
# Loci	930	1249	391	2570	670	600	506	1776	914	663	258	1835	858	832	417	2107	668	750	252	1670
# Ante	119	144	10	273	186	127	2	315	207	187	0	394	285	155	2	442	149	157	3	309
# Abscess	71	53	0	124	36	32	1	69	88	34	3	125	79	44	3	126	40	49	9	98
Indexes																				
Caries N	27	41	18	86	18	18	18	54	25	18	10	53	23	23	16	62	16	24	9	49
Caries o	0.10	0.10	0.00	0.08	0.15	0.19	0.04	0.13	.020	0.20	0.07	0.17	0.33	0.18	0.05	0.20	0.24	0.22	0.05	0.20
Caries SD	0.13	0.12	0.02	0.12	0.19	0.16	1.06	0.16	0.13	0.19	0.08	0.15	0.20	0.21	0.07	0.21	0.15	0.19	0.06	0.17
Ante N	31	42	18	91	23	22	20	65	30	23	10	63	33	31	19	83	25	29	12	66
Ante o	0.12	0.12	0.05	0.11	0.26	0.22	0.00	0.17	0.23	0.29	0.00	0.21	0.35	0.19	0.01	0.21	0.24	0.21	0.01	0.19
Ante SD	0.20	0.19	0.21	0.20	0.30	0.26	0.01	0.26	0.26	0.30	—	0.29	0.32	0.26	0.02	0.29	0.23	0.30	0.05	0.25
Abs. N	31	42	18	91	23	23	20	65	30	23	10	63	33	31	19	83	25	29	12	66
Abs. o	0.08	0.04	0.00	0.05	0.05	0.05	0.00	0.04	0.10	0.05	0.01	0.07	0.09	0.06	0.01	0.06	0.06	0.06	0.06	0.06
Abs. SD	0.08	0.06	—	0.07	0.06	0.06	0.01	0.06	0.10	0.05	0.01	0.06	0.08	0.07	0.02	0.07	0.05	0.06	0.06	0.06
Decay N	31	42	18	91	23	22	18	63	30	23	10	63	30	30	18	78	24	28	10	62
Decay o	0.22	0.21	0.03	0.18	0.42	0.38	0.05	0.30	0.41	0.43	0.07	0.36	0.56	0.36	0.06	0.37	0.48	0.41	0.10	0.38
Decay SD	0.22	0.22	0.11	0.22	0.36	0.29	0.06	0.32	0.29	0.33	0.08	0.31	0.31	0.34	0.07	0.35	0.28	0.32	0.12	0.30
Miss.																				

Population index

Index	Archaic	Pearson Village	SunWatch Village	Monongahela	Buffalo Village
Caries	7.8	12.3	16.0	19.7	21.2
Decay-Missing	24.1	29.7	35.7	38.2	37.8

461

Table 15.10: Frequency of Trauma among Native Americans of the Ohio Valley Area

		Archaic			Pearson Village			SunWatch Village			Monongahela			Buffalo Village		
		Male	Female	Child	Male	Female	Child	Male	Female	Child	Male	Female	Child	Male	Female	Child
Arm	N	30	39	52	22	21	39	29	23	76	34	32	53	26	29	46
	% Healed	13.3	2.6	0.0	13.6	9.5	0.0	0.34	0.0	0.0	14.7	3.1	0.0	0.0	6.9	0.0
	% Poor aligned	0.0	0.0	0.0	0.0	0.0	0.0	0.0	0.0	0.0	0.0	0.0	0.0	0.0	0.0	0.0
	% Fusion/joint	0.0	0.0	0.0	0.0	0.0	0.0	0.0	0.0	0.0	0.0	0.0	0.0	0.0	0.0	0.0
Leg	N	27	28	54	23	23	46	30	22	75	34	32	56	26	29	46
	% Healed	3.7	0.0	0.0	0.0	0.0	0.0	10.0	0.0	0.0	8.8	3.1	0.0	3.8	3.4	0.0
	% Poor aligned	0.0	0.0	0.0	0.0	0.0	0.0	0.0	0.0	0.0	0.0	0.0	0.0	0.0	0.0	0.0
	% Fusion/joint	0.0	0.0	0.0	0.0	0.0	0.0	0.0	0.0	0.0	0.0	0.0	0.0	0.0	0.0	0.0
Nasal	N	27	31	26	18	17	31	30	22	59	32	30	56	18	21	34
	% Present	0.0	0.0	0.0	0.0	0.0	0.0	3.3	0.0	0.0	3.1	0.0	0.0	0.0	0.0	0.0
Face	N	28	30	29	18	10	31	31	22	59	33	31	56	25	29	45
	% Present	0.0	0.0	0.0	0.0	0.0	0.0	0.0	0.0	0.0	3.0	3.2	3.2	0.0	0.0	0.0
Vault	N	31	42	48	23	23	42	31	22	66	34	32	46	25	29	46
	% Present	0.0	14.3	2.1	4.3	0.0	0.0	6.5	0.0	1.5	5.9	6.2	1.8	4.0	0.0	0.0
Hand	N	18	15	13	13	23	25	29	22	43	27	28	31	17	20	27
	% Present	5.6	6.7	0.0	0.0	0.0	0.0	0.0	0.0	0.0	0.0	0.0	0.0	0.0	0.0	0.0
Weapon wound	N	31	44	55	23	23	44	31	23	82	34	31	56	26	29	46
	% Present	0.0	0.0	0.0	0.0	0.0	0.0	3.2	0.0	0.0	0.0	3.2	0.0	0.0	0.0	0.0

Table 15.11: χ^2 Values for Tests of Independence between the Sexes for Trauma

Sample	Arm	Leg	Vault
Archaic	2.88	P = 0.83	P = 0.06
Pearson	0.18	—	P = 0.99
SunWatch	P = 0.61	P = 0.37	P = 0.58
Monongahela	2.67	0.90	0.004
Buffalo	P = 0.55	0.006	P = 0.93
TOTAL	G = 3.70, P $\sim$ 0.50	G = 3.66, P $\sim$ 0.05	G = 4.09, 0.05 > P > 0.10

Note: All tests have 1 degree of freedom. P = probabilities from two-tailed Fisher's Exact Tests. In no case is sexual dimorphism statistically significant.

Table 15.12: Ranking of Percent Trauma in the Ohio Valley Samples Tested from Earliest to Latest in Time

	Trauma			
Sample	Arm	Leg	Vault	Total
Archaic	3	4	1	8
Pearson	1	5	4	10
SunWatch	5	2	3	10
Monongahela	2	1	2	5
Buffalo	4	3	5	12

Note: Friedman's method (Sokal and Rohlf, 1981) indicates that time period/culture has no significant effect on trauma incidence. W is coefficient of concordance.
$\chi^2 = 3.73$.
P $\sim$ 0.50.
W = 0.31[NS].

Degenerative Joint Disease

Table 15.13 contains the frequencies of degenerative joint disease (DJD) among the Ohio Valley samples. Unlike trauma, DJD often reaches appreciable frequencies in samples: this is most notable for vertebral DJD. As a result, we have analyzed vertebral and other postcranial DJD (including temporomandibular joint) separately. Table 15.14 contains the sex-specific and total frequencies of the nonvertebral DJDs. Subadults are not included as in the entire sample; only one child aged 15 years from the Late Archaic Boose site exhibited DJD. Tests of association between sex and the presence of DJD revealed no cases of significant sexual dimorphism (Table 15.15). In addition, tests of association between DJD by anatomical site and samples ordered by time show no differences in males and females. However, for the pooled male–female samples, there is a significant association between DJD frequency and time period–culture: samples from later periods (especially Monongahela and the Proto-historic Buffalo sample) exhibit lower amounts of postcranial DJD than samples from earlier periods (Table 15.16). This finding is probably related to the greater mobility and less technological sophistication of the earlier populations.

Table 15.13: Frequencies of Degenerative Joint Disease among Native Americans of the Ohio Valley

Pathology	Expression	Archaic			Pearson Village			SunWatch Village			Monongahela			Buffalo Village		
		Male	Female	Child	Male	Female	Child	Male	Female	Child	Male	Female	Child	Male	Female	Child
DJD shoulder elbow	N	28	38	38	23	19	38	30	23	67	33	32	53	26	28	45
	% Initial	17.9	13.2	0.0	34.8	42.1	0.0	30.0	30.4	0.0	24.2	12.5	0.0	15.4	10.7	0.0
	% Major	3.6	2.3	0.0	0.0	5.3	0.0	3.3	0.0	0.0	6.1	0.0	0.0	0.0	0.0	0.0
	% Immobile	0.0	0.0	0.0	0.0	0.0	0.0	0.0	0.0	0.0	0.0	0.0	0.0	0.0	0.0	0.0
	% Systemat.	0.0	0.0	0.0	0.0	0.0	0.0	0.0	0.0	0.0	0.0	0.0	0.0	0.0	0.0	0.0
DJD hip knee	N	28	38	43	23	23	42	31	22	72	34	32	56	26	29	46
	% Initial	28.6	15.8	0.0	21.7	17.4	0.0	19.4	9.1	0.0	14.7	18.8	1.8	7.7	10.3	0.0
	% Major	0.0	7.9	0.0	4.3	13.0	0.0	6.5	4.5	1.4	0.0	0.0	0.0	0.0	0.0	0.
	% Immobile	0.0	0.0	0.0	0.0	0.0	0.0	0.0	0.0	0.0	0.0	0.0	0.0	0.0	3.4	0.0
	% Systemat.	0.0	0.0	0.0	0.0	0.0	0.0	0.0	0.0	0.0	0.0	0.0	0.0	0.0	0.0	0.0
DJD cervical vertebra	N	28	38	32	17	17	43	26	18	46	29	31	56	25	27	46
	% Initial	46.4	36.8	0.0	52.9	23.5	0.0	43.8	22.2	2.2	17.2	25.8	0.0	28.0	29.6	0.0
	% Extensive	7.1	10.5	0.0	0.0	0.0	0.0	3.8	5.6	0.0	20.7	6.4	0.0	0.0	0.0	0.0
	% Fusion	3.6	7.9	0.0	0.0	0.0	0.0	7.7	0.0	0.0	6.7	0.0	0.0	0.0	3.7	0.0
DJD thoracic vertebra	N	26	29	25	20	20	39	28	16	47	30	29	56	24	25	45
	% Initial	34.6	27.5	0.0	35.0	25.0	0.0	28.6	6.2	2.1	40.0	24.1	0.0	16.7	8.0	0.0
	% Extensive	0.0	6.9	0.0	0.0	0.0	0.0	7.1	12.5	2.1	10.0	3.4	0.0	.2	4.0	0.0
	% Fusion	3.8	0.0	0.0	0.0	0.0	0.0	3.6	0.0	0.0	3.3	3.4	0.0	0.0	0.0	0.0
DJD lumbar vertebra	N	26	33	31	19	22	40	30	19	48	29	30	56	25	26	46
	% Initial	46.1	21.2	0.0	36.8	54.5	0.0	30.0	26.3	0.0	24.1	13.3	0.0	36.0	42.3	0.0
	% Extensive	26.9	24.2	0.0	10.5	9.1	0.0	20.0	10.5	0.0	20.7	20.0	0.0	0.0	0.0	0.0
	% Fusion	3.8	3.1	0.0	0.0	0.0	0.0	3.3	5.3	0.0	10.3	0.0	0.0	0.0	0.0	0.0
DJD TMJ	N	30	38	37	20	19	39	30	22	47	32	32	56	26	28	46
	% Present	10.0	13.2	2.7	5.0	5.3	0.0	13.3	9.1	0.0	3.1	9.4	0.0	11.5	7.1	0.0
DJD wrist	N	29	32	27	19	19	34	29	23	62	32	32	55	26	28	46
	% Present	17.2	6.2	0.0	10.5	10.5	0.0	3.4	4.3	1.6	3.1	0.0	0.0	0.0	3.5	0.0
DJD hand	N	21	16	13	13	13	27	28	22	28	28	27	34	16	19	25
	% Present	23.8	0.0	0.0	7.6	15.4	0.0	7.1	9.1	0.0	10.7	0.0	0.0	6.2	5.6	0.0

Table 15.14: Frequency of Postcranial Degenerative Joint Disease in the Ohio Valley Samples

Site	Stat.	Archaic			Pearson Village			SunWatch			Monongahela			Buffalo		
		Male	Female	Total	Male	Female	Total	Male	Female	Total	Male	Female	Total	Male	Female	Total
Shoulder elbow	N	28	38	66	23	19	42	30	23	53	33	32	65	26	28	54
	%	21.5	15.8	18.1	34.8	42.1	38.1	33.3	30.4	32.1	30.3	12.5	21.5	15.4	10.7	13.0
Hip-knee	N	28	38	66	23	23	46	31	22	53	34	32	66	26	29	55
	%	28.6	23.7	25.8	26.0	30.4	28.3	25.9	13.6	20.8	14.7	18.8	16.7	7.7	13.7	10.9
Tempo-mandib	N	30	38	68	20	19	39	30	22	52	32	32	64	26	28	54
	%	10.0	13.2	11.7	5.0	5.3	5.1	13.3	9.1	11.5	3.1	9.4	6.2	11.5	7.1	9.2
Hand	N	21	16	37	13	13	26	28	22	50	28	27	55	16	19	35
	%	23.8	0.0	13.5	7.6	15.4	11.5	7.1	9.1	8.0	10.7	0.0	5.5	6.2	5.6	5.7
Wrist	N	29	32	61	19	19	38	29	23	52	32	32	64	26	28	54
	%	17.2	6.2	11.5	10.5	10.5	10.5	3.4	4.3	3.8	3.1	0.0	1.6	0.0	3.5	1.9

Table 15.15: χ^2 Values for Tests for Independence between the Sexes for DJD

Sample	Shoulder elbow	Hip-knee	TMJ	Hand	Wrist
Archaic	0.34	0.2	0.1	P = 0.09	1.81
Pearson	0.24	0.11	0	0.38	0
SunWatch	0.05	0.86	0.22	0.06	0.03
Monongahela	3.04	0.19	1.07	P = 0.5	P = 0.98
Buffalo	0.26	0.04	0.31	0.02	P = 0.98
TOTAL	G = 11.51	G = 6.84	G = 2.46	G = 2.46	G = 9.48
	G_{ADJ} = 11.35	—	—	—	G_{ADJ} = 9.35

Note: P = probabilities derived from a two-tailed Fisher's Exact Test. In no case is there significant sexual dimorphism.

Table 15.16: Rankings of Percent DJD by Anatomical Site in the Ohio Valley Samples

	Sample	Shoulder-elbow	Hip-knee	TMJ	Hand	Wrist	Total
Males							
χ^2 = 7.68	Archaic	4	1	3	1	1	10
p ~ 0.10	Pearson	1	2	4	3	2	12
W = 0.38[ns]	SunWatch	2	3	1	4	3	13
	Monongahela	3	4	5	2	4	18
	Buffalo	5	5	2	5	5	22
Females							
χ^2 = 6.36	Archaic	3	2	1	4.5	2	12.5
0.5 > P > 0.10	Pearson	1	1	5	1	1	9
W = 0.32[ns]	SunWatch	2	5	3	2	3	15
	Monongahela	4	3	2	4.5	5	18.5
	Buffalo	5	4	4	3	4	20
Total							
χ^2 = 10.24	Archaic	4	2	1	1	1	9
0.04 > P > 0.025	Pearson	1	1	5	2	2	11
W = 0.51	SunWatch	2	3	2	3	3	13
	Monongahela	3	4	4	5	5	21
	Buffalo	5	5	3	4	4	21

Note: Samples are listed from earliest to latest in time. Friedman's method (Sokal and Rohlf, 1981) indicates that the effects of time period/culture on DJD is significant only for the male–female sample. W is the coefficient of concordance.

Table 15.17 contains the results of the analyses of the average severity of hip-knee and shoulder-elbow DJD (the two most frequently observed classes of postcranial DJD) with age. Spearman's correlation between average severity and age is significant for all samples. Thus, like dental pathology, postcranial DJD seems to be a product of the normal aging process (constant use, no repair). Although all populations show this relationship, the strength of the relationship, and the frequency of postcranial DJD, is higher in the Archaic sample.

Table 15.17: Average Severity of DJD of the Shoulder-Elbow and Hip-Knee in the Ohio Valley Samples

Age class	Archaic N	x̄	Pearson N	x̄	SunWatch N	x̄	Monongahela N	x̄	Buffalo N	x̄	Total N	x̄
15–20	20	1.00	12	1.12	11	1.00	14	1.04	15	1.00	72	1.03
25	15	1.03	5	1.00	4	1.00	7	1.00	9	1.00	40	1.01
30	14	1.21	12	1.42	13	1.12	17	1.12	11	1.14	67	1.21
35	18	1.56	12	1.42	14	1.25	11	1.32	12	1.33	67	1.42
40–50	8	1.44	9	1.72	19	1.53	19	1.42	12	1.17	67	1.45
N	75		50		61		68		59		313	
r_s	0.57		0.43		0.48		0.44		0.34		0.45	
P	0.0001		0.0016		0.0001		0.0001		0.009		0.0001	

Note: r_s is Spearman's correlation.

Table 15.18 contains the frequencies of vertebral DJD in males, females, and the pooled sex samples. Tests of association between the presence of vertebral DJD and sex (Table 15.19) revealed only one significant association: lumbar vertebra DJD and males in the Archaic samples. Because the probability of association was borderline and because no other associations with sex were observed, this association is treated as a statistical anomaly, and sexual dimorphism is considered absent in vertebral DJD among these samples.

The analysis of associations between vertebral DJD and samples ordered by time showed in no cases, for males, females, and the total, a significant association (Table 15.20). The effect of time period–culture is insignificant on the rankings of vertebral DJD.

Table 15.21 contains the analysis of vertebral DJD by age in each sample. Spearman correlations between age and average severity of vertebral DJD is significant for cervical, thoracic, lumbar, and the combination (total) of all three. The correlations between the total severity and age is presented in Table 15.21 and serves to illustrate the overall relationship. As with postcranial DJD, vertebral DJD seems to be a product of the normal aging process which was similar, in this case, among all samples.

Hyperostosis, Infections, and LEH

Table 15.22 contains the frequencies of hyperostosis, infections, and hypoplasia among the samples. Tests of associations between sex and presence of these pathologies (Table 15.23) showed no significant sexual dimorphism, but tests of association among the ranked frequencies (samples ranked by time period) were significant, suggesting a somewhat higher frequency of pathologies in the more recent groups (Table 15.24). Tests of association indicate that cribra orbitalia, with especially high frequencies in the Monongahela sample; porotic hyperostosis, with high frequencies in the Pearson, SunWatch, and Monongahela samples; skeletal infection, with a low frequency in the Buffalo sample; and permanent canine LEH, with a high frequency in the Pearson sample, differed among the groups (Table 15.24).

Within some samples a number of the pathologies exhibited a significant association with age. Tibial infections and age are positively associated in the Pearson

Table 15.18: Frequency of Vertebral Degenerative Joint Disease in the Ohio Valley Samples

Site	Stat	Archaic			Pearson Village			SunWatch Village			Monongahela			Buffalo		
		Male	Female	Total	Male	Female	Total	Male	Female	Total	Male	Female	Total	Male	Female	Total
Cervical	N	28	38	66	17	17	34	26	18	44	29	31	60	25	27	52
	%	57.1	55.2	56.1	52.9	23.5	38.2	53.8	27.8	43.2	44.6	32.2	38.3	28.0	33.3	30.7
Thoracic	N	26	29	55	20	20	40	28	16	44	30	29	59	24	25	49
	%	38.4	34.5	36.4	35.0	25.0	30.0	39.3	18.7	31.8	53.3	30.9	42.4	20.9	12.0	16.3
Lumbar	N	26	33	59	19	22	41	30	19	49	29	30	59	25	26	51
	%	76.8	51.5	62.7	47.3	63.6	56.1	53.3	42.1	49.0	55.1	33.3	44.1	36.0	47.3	39.2

Table 15.19: χ^2 Values for Tests of Independence between the Sexes for Vertebral DJD

Sample	Cervical	Thoracic	Lumbar
Archaic	0.02	0.09	4.01
Pearson	3.11	0.48	1.10
SunWatch	2.95	1.98	0.58
Monongahela	1.00	3.00	1.40
Buffalo	0.17	0.70	0.21
	Cervical G = 8.60^{NS}	Thoracic G = 9.57 G_{ADJ} = 9.47^{NS}	Lumbar G = 7.70^{NS}

Notes: Only lumbar DJD in the Archaic samples shows a significant difference between the sexes. The degrees of freedom equal 1 for each test.

[a] G_{ADJ} = 4.06

($r_s = 0.34, P = 0.001$) and SunWatch ($r_s = 0.24, P = 0.006$) samples, while skeletal infections ($r_s = 0.25, P = 0.003$) are positively associated with age only in the latter. The remaining significant associations between pathologies and age are negative: skeletal infections ($r_s = -0.21, P = 0.02$), porotic hyperostosis ($r_s = -0.25, P = 0.006$), and cribra orbitalia ($r_s = -0.24, P = 0.016$) in the Monongahela sample;

Table 15.20: Rankings of Percent Vertebral DJD in the Ohio Valley Samples

	Sample	Cervical	Thoracic	Lumbar	Total
Males					
$\chi^2 = 6.97$	Archaic	1	3	1	5
$0.5 > P > 0.1$	Pearson	3	4	4	11
$W = 0.58^{ns}$	SunWatch	2	2	3	7
	Monongahela	4	1	2	7
	Buffalo	5	5	5	15
Females					
$\chi^2 = 3.33$	Archaic	1	1	2	4
$P \sim 0.5$	Pearson	5	3	1	9
$W = 0.28^{ns}$	SunWatch	4	4	4	12
	Monongahela	3	2	5	10
	Buffalo	2	5	3	10
Total					
$\chi^2 = 6.97$	Archaic	1	2	1	4
$0.5 > P > 0.01$	Pearson	4	4	2	10
$W = 0.58^{ns}$	SunWatch	2	3	3	8
	Monongahela	3	1	4	8
	Buffalo	5	5	5	15

Notes: Samples are listed from earliest to latest in time. Friedman's method (Sokal and Rohlf, 1981) indicates that the effects of time period/culture on DJD is significant only for the male–female sample. W is the coefficient of concordance.

Table 15.21: Vertebral DJD by Age in the Ohio Valley Samples

Age Class	Archaic N	Archaic x̄	Pearson N	Pearson x̄	SunWatch N	SunWatch x̄	Monongahela N	Monongahela x̄	Buffalo N	Buffalo x̄	Total N	Total x̄
Cervical vertebrae												
20	11	1.0	4	1.0	2	1.5	5	1.4	7	1.0	29	1.1
25	14	1.5	3	1.0	3	1.0	6	1.0	9	1.0	35	1.2
30	12	1.9	9	1.1	12	1.3	15	1.5	10	1.5	58	1.5
35	20	2.1	9	1.6	12	1.5	11	1.8	12	1.4	63	1.8
40–50	7	2.6	7	1.9	15	1.7	17	2.1	11	1.6	57	1.9
Thoracic vertebrae												
20	9	1.0	6	1.0	2	1.0	7	1.0	7	1.0	31	1.0
25	13	1.0	4	1.0	3	1.0	6	1.0	8	1.1	34	1.0
30	7	1.8	10	1.4	11	1.3	11	1.8	15	1.1	65	1.5
35	18	1.8	10	1.4	11	1.3	11	1.8	15	1.1	65	1.5
40–50	6	1.8	7	1.9	17	1.6	16	2.2	11	1.5	57	1.8
Lumbar vertebrae												
20	11	1.2	6	1.2	3	1.0	7	1.0	7	1.0	34	1.1
25	12	1.4	5	1.0	3	1.0	6	1.0	9	1.1	35	1.2
30	7	2.5	9	1.6	12	1.6	15	1.3	10	1.2	53	1.6
35	19	2.6	10	2.0	10	1.5	11	2.0	11	1.7	61	2.1
40–50	7	2.6	9	2.3	18	2.2	16	2.8	11	1.8	61	2.3
Total vertebrae												
20	11	1.08	6	1.08	3	1.11	7	1.14	7	1.00	34	1.08
25	14	1.31	5	1.00	3	1.00	6	1.00	9	1.07	37	1.14
30	12	2.04	12	1.36	12	1.54	15	1.38	10	1.30	31	1.52
35	20	2.18	11	1.64	14	1.45	11	1.88	12	1.39	68	1.75
40–50	8	2.31	9	2.06	18	1.88	18	2.30	11	1.70	64	2.04

	Archaic	Pearson	SunWatch	Monongahela	Buffalo	Total
N	65	43	50	57	49	264
r_s	0.68	0.75	0.40	0.66	0.71	0.59
P	0.0001	0.0001	0.0041	0.0001	0.0001	0.0001

Note: No individual under 20 years of age exhibits vertebral DJD.

permanent incisor hypoplasia ($r_s = -0.31$, P = 0.02) in the SunWatch sample; and permanent canine hypoplasia in the Archaic ($r_s = -0.23$, P = 0.04) and Monongahela ($r_s = -0.24$, P = 0.047) samples. As would be expected, the average age-at-death is lower in individuals with pathologies showing negative association with age (e.g., hyperostosis, hypoplasia), and average age-at-death is higher in individuals with pathologies showing a positive association with age (infections). However, because of demographic uncertainties in our samples, these findings must be considered preliminary and of uncertain significance.

In order to evaluate the pattern of association among these pathologies, as well as the associations of these pathologies with stature and dental disease, multiple correspondence analysis was employed. Correspondence analysis is a technique which uses contingency tables in order to determine whether or not the frequencies in the rows (individuals) are contingent upon the column (pathology) frequencies. In these analyses, we coded any expression of porotic hyperostosis or cribra orbitalia as reflecting anemia+, any expression of hypoplasia in the permanent teeth as LEH+,

Table 15.22: Frequencies of Hyperostosis, Infections, and Hypoplasias among Native Americans of the Ohio Valley Area

Pathology	Expression	Archaic			Pearson Village			SunWatch Village			Monongahela			Buffalo Village			Total		
		Male	Female	Child	Male	Female	Child	Male	Female	Child	Male	Female	Child	Male	Female	Child	Male	Female	Child
Cribria orbital.	N	30	42	51	21	19	29	30	21	64	30	27	42	24	28	39	135	137	225
	% Mild	3.3	2.4	7.8	0.0	0.0	0.0	0.0	4.8	14.1	6.7	7.4	28.6	0.0	3.6	2.6	2.2	3.6	11.6
	% Severe	0.0	0.0	0.0	0.0	0.0	0.0	0.0	0.0	0.0	0.0	0.0	0.0	0.0	0.0	0.0	0.0	0.0	0.0
Porotic hyper.	N	31	44	51	23	23	49	31	22	72	33	32	55	25	29	45	143	150	273
	% Mild	6.5	9.1	11.8	8.7	0.0	0.0	12.9	22.7	12.3	9.1	3.1	30.9	12.0	17.2	8.9	9.8	10.0	13.2
	% Severe	0.0	0.0	0.0	0.0	4.3	0.0	0.0	0.0	2.7	0.0	0.0	0.0	0.0	0.0	0.0	0.0	0.7	0.7
Tibial infect.	N	29	42	54	23	22	41	31	22	79	33	30	54	26	29	45	142	145	273
	% Mild	10.3	7.1	1.9	21.7	21.8	4.9	9.7	9.1	6.3	6.1	10.0	16.7	3.8	6.9	4.4	9.9	11.7	7.0
	% Moder.	0.0	0.0	0.0	0.0	0.0	0.0	3.2	4.5	1.3	0.0	0.0	0.0	3.8	0.0	0.0	1.4	0.7	0.4
	% Severe	0.0	0.0	0.0	0.0	0.0	0.0	0.0	3.2	18.1	1.3	0.0	0.0	0.0	0.0	0.0	0.7	2.8	0.4
Skelet. infect.	N	31	44	59	23	23	50	31	24	83	34	32	46	34	29	46	153	152	294
	% Present	32.2	20.4	11.9	21.7	26.1	18.0	38.7	16.7	16.9	8.9	12.5	14.3	8.8	10.3	10.9	22.9	17.1	14.3
	% Syste.	0.0	4.5	1.7	0.0	0.0	0.0	6.5	20.8	8.4	5.9	18.8	23.2	8.8	0.0	0.0	4.6	8.6	7.1
LEH upper incisor	N	21	22	26*	13	16	21*	22	14	46*	18	21	23*	10	20	22*	84	93	138*
	% 1	19.0	4.5	0.0	7.7	18.8	0.0	4.5	28.6	2.2	5.6	4.8	8.7	20.0	5.0	4.5	10.7	10.8	2.8
	% 2	0.0	0.0	0.0	0.0	0.0	0.0	4.5	0.0	0.0	0.0	0.0	0.0	0.0	0.0	0.0	1.2	0.0	0.0
LEH upper canine	N	25	30	33*	15	19	22*	26	18	57*	23	23	27*	20	22	18*	109	112	157*
	% 1	12.0	13.3	0.0	26.7	57.9	4.8	11.5	27.8	3.5	8.7	4.3	7.4	15.0	13.6	5.6	13.8	21.4	3.8
	% 2	0.0	6.7	0.0	6.7	0.0	0.0	3.8	0.0	0.0	0.0	4.3	0.0	0.0	4.5	0.0	1.8	3.6	0.0

* = deciduous teeth.

471

Table 15.23: χ^2 Values for Tests of Independence between the Sexes

Sample	Cribra orbitalia	Porotic hyperostosis	Tibial infection	Skeletal infection	LEH I	LEH C
Archaic	0.06	0.17	0.23	1.34	2.20	0.02
Pearson	0	0.31	0.01	0.12	0.74	3.32
SunWatch	P = 0.41	0.88	1.81	0.33	2.34	1.00
Monongahela	0.01	1.00	0.33	3.47	0	0.01
Buffalo	P = 0.56	0.29	0.01	0.68	1.67	0.08

Note: P = refers to probabilities derived from a two-tailed Fisher's Exact Test.

Table 15.24: Ranking of Percentage Pathology in Ohio Valley Samples

Sample	Cribra orbitalia	Porotic hyperostosis	Tibial infection	Skeletal infection	LGH I	LEH C	LEH di	LEH dc	Total
Archaic	3	4	5	4	5	4	4.5	5	34.5
Pearson	5	5	1	3	2	1	4.5	3	24.5
SunWatch	2	2	2	1	1	2	3	4	17
Monongahela	1	1	3	2	4	5	1	1	18
Buffalo	4	3	4	5	3	3	2	2	26

Notes: Friedman's method indicates that the effects of time period–culture on these pathologies is significant. W is the coefficient of concordance.
Observed: $\chi^2 = 9.98$.
Critical value: $\chi^2_{4[05]} = 9.49$.
W = 0.31.

at least one abscess as abscess+, and 3 or more caries (out of at least 10 teeth) as caries+. In addition, we considered sex, age (age > 30 as old, age < 30 young), and stature (femur length > mean for sample as tall, less than mean as short). Figures 15.4 to 15.6 contain the results of these analyses. Samples sizes are reduced as the analyses requires complete data for each individual.

Figure 15.4 is the result of the multiple correspondence analysis for the adults of the Archaic sample (17 males, 17 females). In this plot, axis 1 accounts for 27% and axis 2 accounts for 20% of the total variation. The total χ^2 for all dimensions is 363.3 with 225 d.f. This analysis suggests a number of associations. For example, LEH, anemia, and infections are located in the upper right quadrant along with the shorter individuals. This plot reflects the findings that short individuals exhibit LEH, anemia, and infections at 28.6%, 14.3%, and 52%, respectively, while tall individuals exhibit these conditions at the rates of 8.3%, 8.3%, and 31%. The other primary association is between age (young vs. old) and dental pathology (cavity and abscess). As would be expected from the previous analyses, older individuals are associated with the presence of pathologies.

A weaker but interesting association is between age and the presence of LEH, anemia, and infection. As the young category is located toward the right on axis 1, it is associated (on this axis) with infection and particularly LEH and anemia. Since the presence of LEH, infection, and anemia are associated with short and, to a

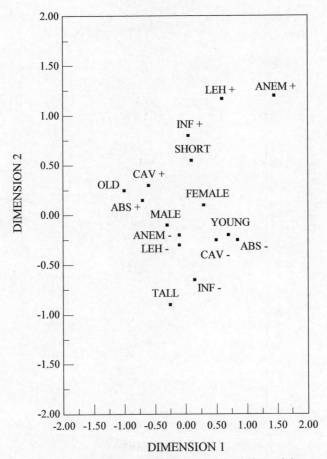

Figure 15.4. Multiple correspondence analysis Archaic adults.

lesser degree, young individuals, it may be possible to view these pathologies as effective stressors affecting growth and development, as well as limiting the life span.

Although there is some variation among the Late Prehistoric samples, a pooled sample (Pearson, SunWatch, Monongahela, and Buffalo) is used as it is consistent with individual samples and it is much larger ($n = 119$). Figure 15.5 is the plot of the multiple correspondence analysis of the total Late Prehistoric sample (male = 57, female = 62). Axes 1 and 2 account for 23% and 15% of the total variation, respectively; the total χ^2 for all dimensions is 1082.0 with 225 d.f.

The Late Prehistoric samples show a somewhat different pattern of associations compared to the Archaic sample. In the Late Prehistoric analysis, dental pathology is associated with older individuals, but LEH, anemia, and infection are not, and only LEH is associated with short size. This may indicate that in the 2,000 years that separated the Late Archaic and Late Prehistoric samples, populations had adapted or adjusted to conditions (e.g., moderate nutritional deficiencies, higher population density), yielding some of the consequences of these pathologies less disruptive

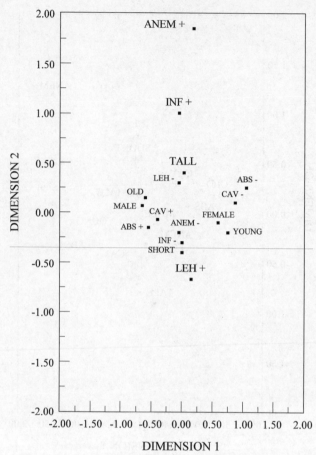

Figure 15.5. Multiple correspondence analysis Late Prehistoric adults.

to growth and viability. However, LEH, which indicates potent stress, apparently remained a severe consequence of stress and is associated both with growth deficiency (short size) and early mortality.

Figure 15.6 is a multiple correspondence analysis of all Late Archaic and Late Prehistoric individuals ($N = 153$, female $= 79$, male $= 74$), with each individual classified as to respective group (ARCH, LPRE). This plot summarizes well the separate analyses, showing the associations characteristic of each group (total $\chi^2 = 1605.2$, 289 d.f., axis 1 21.3%, and axis 2 14.7% of the total variation).

In the correspondence analysis of the adults, DJD and trauma were not included in the results presented as DJD was associated only with older adults, and trauma was rare and associated, but weakly, only with older adults. Their inclusion only cluttered the plots.

Correspondence analysis of subadults was done in a manner analogous to adults, except that size was not included (sample size reduced too greatly), sex could not be included, and permanent dental pathology was not included because many children

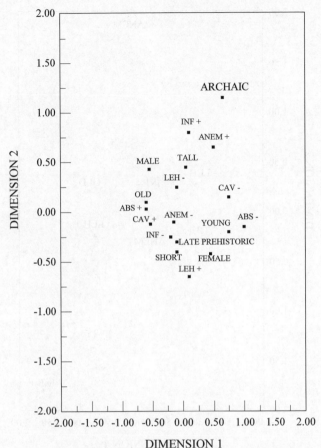

Figure 15.6. Multiple correspondence analysis total adults.

were under 5 years of age. Young and old were defined as less than 5 years and greater than 5 years, respectively. Figure 15.7 is a plot of the results for the Archaic children ($n = 11$). In this plot, anemia, LEH, and infection are associated with the older children but not with each other. In the Late Prehistoric sample ($n = 52$), Figure 15.8, LEH is also associated with older children, but anemia and infection are more common in younger children than is the case for the Archaic sample. These results may help explain to some extent the femur growth data. LEH is associated with shorter adults and with older (age > 5) children. Femur growth rate in all Ohio Valley samples is comparable to that in a modern healthy population in ages less than about 5 years, but growth rate is reduced for older children (Maresh 1955). Thus, the presence of LEH in both children and adults is associated with growth disturbance. Stress, which resulted in LEH, apparently also depressed the growth rate, and the children who survived this stress were shorter as adults. Figure 15.8 also shows that infection and anemia, which are not common in young Archaic children (as well as not associated), are more common in young Late Prehistoric children and

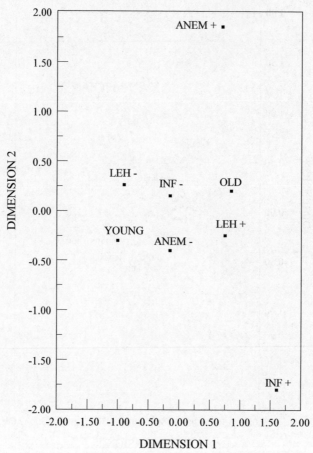

Figure 15.7. Multiple correspondence analysis Archaic children.

are associated. This suggests that the stressors resulting in anemia and infection are different in the Late Archaic and Late Prehistoric populations. Since diet is a primary difference between Late Archaic and Late Prehistoric populations, the association of infections and anemia with younger Late Prehistoric children may have been the result of the shift to a somewhat lower protein diet in the Late Prehistoric. This may be reflected by the overall increase in LEH in the Late Prehistoric samples as well.

Health Index

The overall health index (Steckel, Sciulli, and Rose, this volume) of the Ohio Valley Native American samples is relatively high (Table 3.2). All Ohio Valley samples, except SunWatch, are above the median for the percent of maximum quality-adjusted life-years (QALY) for the total Western Hemisphere sample. But even SunWatch is only slightly below the median. The principal reason for the high health index scores of the Ohio Valley samples is their comparatively large stature and low incidence of

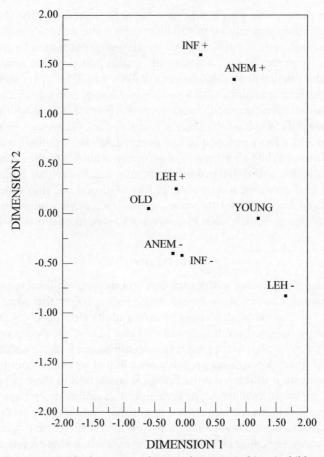

Figure 15.8. Multiple correspondence analysis Late Prehistoric children.

LEH. In addition, for all other attributes except dental pathologies, each sample is near or above the Western Hemisphere median. It is interesting to note that the two Ohio Valley samples which scored highest on the health index, in the top 25% of the total Western Hemisphere sample, are the Late Archaic and the Proto-historic Buffalo samples. The remaining Late Prehistoric samples show percent maximum QALY scores about 5% lower than the Late Archaic and Buffalo samples.

A possible explanation for these results is that the Late Archaic and Buffalo populations did not possess *developed* techniques, practices, and support for sick individuals. In the case of the Archaic population, in which groups were initially becoming less mobile and larger, this "infrastructure" was probably in the early stages of development. For the Buffalo population, almost certainly affected by European contact, the infrastructure was probably breaking down. In both cases, individuals with potentially life-threatening illnesses were probably somewhat more likely to die in a short time and thus leave a skeleton unmarked by the chronic effects of disease. This idea appears to be reflected in the results of the health index of the total Western

Hemisphere sample. The lowest 30% ($n = 20$) of the samples for the QALY scores are all samples from generally large, socially complex, and technologically advanced populations, each presumably with a well-developed infrastructure for treating sick individuals. In the top 20 samples, 30% are contact period Native Americans and 35% are older than 2000 BP (55% older than 1000 BP). Thus, there seems to be a general trend for populations with a presumably less-developed infrastructure to exhibit higher scores on the health index. Does this mean they were healthier? In the sense of quality of life, at least physically, it probably does. On average, individuals in populations with a less-developed infrastructure didn't linger as long with obvious effects of disease. While alive they were generally healthy. On the other hand, in populations with a well-developed infrastructure, sick individuals probably had a better chance of surviving at least acute phases of disease and thus generally lived longer, so that if chronic phases of diseases were to develop they would be manifested. Here it could be argued that while life was often longer, its quality was often lower.

SUMMARY

The patterns of occurrence and association among stress indicators in the Ohio Valley populations, as well as the overall health index, suggest that while stress was common it was not elevated. In most samples, adults were relatively tall and the frequency of pathological conditions relatively low. LEH in all samples is associated with growth depression, and the greater stress resulting in a higher frequency of LEH in Late Prehistoric populations probably contributed to their somewhat smaller stature. The greatest difference in pathological conditions in these populations is in acquired dental pathologies. Maize agriculturalists exhibit much higher frequencies of caries and increased frequencies of abscesses and missing teeth. While in all populations dental pathologies are a by-product of the normal aging process, among the maize agriculturalists, increased dietary carbohydrate resulted in earlier appearance and elevated frequencies of dental pathology. The increased reliance on carbohydrates is likely also associated with the appearance of anemia and infection earlier in childhood in the maize agricultural populations. Pathological conditions associated with normal wear and tear (DJD, trauma) are age associated and of similar frequency and severity in most populations. Thus, in the approximately 2,500-year time span from which these populations were sampled, the overall differences in health/pathology appear to be small. Aside from dental pathologies, other pathological conditions as well as growth rates and stature seem to show only relatively minor fluctuations. This may reflect the fact that during this time span, general life style did not significantly change until relatively late with the introduction of maize agriculture. Thus, it was only in the last 500 years of the time span that populations were experimenting with maize agriculture. However, even during this later period, heavy reliance continued to be placed on hunted and gathered foods. In the Ohio Valley, the experiment with maize agriculture and its associated ramifications for diet, health, social structure, and so on, which was introduced late into this area, may not have had time to become fully established, and thus, the transition from hunting and gathering was never fully achieved.

While the results presented here probably outline the broad trends in pathology experience among Ohio Valley populations, the results are preliminary. Much more work needs to be done in the area of paleodemography, and additional well-preserved large samples distributed in time and space are needed.

REFERENCES

Bender, M. M., D. A. Baerreis, and A. L. Steventon. 1981. Further light on carbon isotopes and Hopewell agriculture. *American Antiquity* 46:346–353.

Boas, F. 1985. Zur Anthropologie de nordamerikanischen Indianer. *Verhandlungen der Gesellschaft für Ethnologie* 27:366–411.

Box, G. E. P. 1949. A general distribution theory for a class of likelihood criteria. *Biometrika* 36:317–346.

Broida, M. 1984. An estimate of the percentage of maize in the diets of two Kentucky Fort Ancient villages. In *Late Prehistoric Research in Kentucky*, ed. D. L. Pollack, C. B. Hockensmith, and T. N. Sanders. Frankfort: Kentucky Heritage Chronicle, pp. 68–82.

Brose, D. S. 1979. A speculative model of the role of exchange in the prehistory of the Eastern Woodlands. In *Hopewell Archaeology*, ed. D. S. Brose and N. Greber. Kent, Ohio: Kent State University Press, pp. 3–8.

Buikstra, J. E., J. Bullinton, D. K. Charles, D. C. Cook, S. R. Frankenberg, L. W. Konigsberg, J. B. Lambert, and L. Xue. 1987. Diet, demography, and the development of horticulture. In *Emergent Horticulture Economics of the Eastern Woodlands*, ed. W. F. Keegan. Center for Archaeological Investigations, Occasional Paper 7. Carbondale: Southern Illinois University, pp. 67–85.

Coale, A. J., and P. Demeny. 1966. *Regional Model Life Tables and Stable Populations*. Princeton, N.J.: Princeton University Press.

1983. *Regional Model Life Tables and Stable Populations*, 2d ed. New York: Academic Press.

Collins, K. J. 1993. Seasonal mortality in the elderly. In *Seasonality and Human Ecology*, ed. S. J. Ulijaszek and S. S. Strickland. Cambridge: Cambridge University Press, pp. 114–131.

Drooker, P. B. 1997. *The View from Madisonville*. Memoirs of the Museum of Anthropology, No. 31. Ann Arbor: University of Michigan.

Giesen, M. J. 1992. *Late Prehistoric Populations in the Ohio Area: Biological Affinities and Stress Indicators*. Ph.D. diss., Ohio State University, Columbus, Ohio.

Griffin, J. B. 1983. The Midlands. In *Ancient North Americans*, ed. J. D. Jennings. San Francisco: W. H. Freeman, pp. 243–301.

Lovejoy, C. O., R. S. Meindal, T. R. Pryzbeck, T. S. Barton, K. G. Heiple, and D. Kotling. 1977. Paleodemography of the Libben site, Ottawa County, Ohio. *Science* 198:291–293.

Maresh, M. M. 1955. Linear growth in long bones of extremities from infancy through adolescence. *American Journal of Diseases of Children* 89:725–742.

Molnar, S. 1971. Human tooth wear, tooth function, and cultural variability. *American Journal of Physical Anthropology* 31:175–190.

Schwarcz, H. P., J. Melbye, M. A. Katzenberg, and M. Knyf. 1985. Stable isotopes in human skeletons of southern Ontario. *Journal of Archaeological Science* 12:187–206.

Sciulli, P. W. 1990. Cranial metric and non-metric trait variation and biological differentiation in terminal Late Archaic populations of Ohio: The Duff site. *American Journal of Physical Anthropology* 82:19–29.

Standardization of long bone growth in children. *International Journal of Osteoarchaeology* 4:257–259.

1996. Biological indicators of diet in Monongahela populations. *Pennsylvania Archaeologist* 65:1–18.

Sciulli, P. W. and B. W. Aument. 1987. Paleodemography of the Duff Site (33LO111), Logan County, Ohio. *Midcontinental Journal of Archaeology* 12:117–144.

Sciulli, P. W. and M. J. Giesen. 1993. An update on stature estimation in prehistoric Native Americans of Ohio. *American Journal of Physical Anthropology* 92:395–399.

Sciulli, P. W., M. J. Giensen, and R. R. Paine. 1996. Paleodemography of the Pearson Complex (33SA9) Eiden Phase Cemetery. *Archaeology of Eastern North America* 24:81–94.

Sciulli, P. W. and M. C. Mahaney. 1986. Evidence of local biological continuity for an Ohio Hopewell Complex population. *Midcontinental Journal of Archaeology* 11:181–199.

Sciulli, P. W., P. J. Pacheco, and C. A. Janini. 1991. Variation on limb bones of terminal Late Archaic populations of Ohio. *Midcontinental Journal of Archaeology* 16:247–271.

Sciulli, P. W. and K. N. Schneider. 1985. Cranial variation in the terminal Late Archaic of Ohio. *American Journal of Physical Anthropology* 66:429–443.

Sciulli, P. W., K. N. Schneider, and M. C. Mahaney. 1990. Stature estimation in prehistoric Ohio Native Americans. *American Journal of Physical Anthropology* 83:275–280.

Seeman, M. F. 1992. Woodland traditions in the Midcontinent: A comparison of three regional sequences. In *Research in Economic Anthropology*, ed. D. R. Cross, R. A. Hawkins, and B. L. Isaac. London: JAI Press, pp. 3–46.

Smith, B. D. 1989. Origins of agriculture in eastern North America. *Science* 246:1566–1571.

Sokal, R. R. and F. J. Rohlf. 1981. *Biometry*. New York, W. H. Freeman and Company.

Stewart, T. D. 1973. *The People of America*. New York: Charles Scribner's Sons.

Stothers, D. M. and T. J. Abel. 1989. The position of the Pearson Complex in the Late Prehistory of northern Ohio. *Archaeology of Eastern North America* 17:109–142.

Stothers, D. M., and S. K. Bechtel. 1987. Stable carbon isotope analysis: An inter-regional perspective. *Archaeology of Eastern North America* 15:137–154.

Ubelaker, D. H. 1974. *Reconstruction of Demographic Profiles from Ossuary Skeletal Samples: A Case Study from the Tidewater Potomac*. Smithsonian Contributions to Anthropology, No. 18. Washington, D.C.: Smithsonian Institution Press.

Wood, J. W., G. R. Milner, H. C. Harpending, and K. M. Weiss. 1992. The osteological paradox. *Current Anthropology* 33:242–270.

CHAPTER SIXTEEN

Cultural Longevity and Biological Stress in the American Southwest

Ann L. W. Stodder, Debra L. Martin,
Alan H. Goodman, and Daniel T. Reff

ABSTRACT

A wealth of data exists for the American Southwest on diet, health, settlement, and other aspects of life in the precolonial and colonial periods. The Western Hemisphere project provided a way to begin to synthesize these data on a regional and comparative scale. The health index, as the average of the quality-adjusted life-years lived by a group (that is, the combined effects of morbidity and mortality), demonstrates that individuals in the Southwest carried a morbidity burden higher than most of the other areas discussed in this volume. Mortality is high and morbidity is ubiquitous. The combination of these two related processes resulted in a health index score of 16.5/26.4 or 62.5%. The mean age at death of approximately 24 years suggests that Southwest groups were on the lower end of the mortality spectrum. Comparison of comparable data sets provides a dimension of analysis in the Southwest not previously possible, and as such, presents important additional information for the interpretation of health in the American Southwest.

INTRODUCTION

In pre-Columbian times, the Greater Southwest was a biogeographically, culturally, and politically complex area incorporating Arizona, New Mexico, and southern Utah and Colorado in the United States, as well as all the states of northern Mexico, including Chihuahua, Sonora, and Durango. It was then, and continues to be, a cultural, political, and economically diverse area where contact, trade, and boundary maintenance and dispute define local and regional interactions.

The Southwest is also a place where semiarid desert landscapes abound. Water is at a premium, and arable land is a limited resource. But from at least 100 BC in the American Southwest (and much earlier in Mexico), indigenous people have been horticulturalists focused on maize production (Leonard 1989:491). Archaeological, ethnohistoric, and linguistic studies suggest that regional groups had distinctive languages, architectural styles, and customs, yet they interacted with and shared many cultural attributes with adjacent and adjoining groups (e.g., Parezo 1996). Nor

481

were these communities isolated from people in more distant biogeographic and cultural regions. Local, regional, and interregional economic exchange networks are well documented for pre-Columbian (Cameron 1995; Fish and Fish 1994; McGuire 1986) and ethnohistoric peoples (Ferguson 1981; Hammond and Rey 1940; Riley 1975) of the Greater Southwest.

The long history of human occupation here is defined simultaneously by change and resiliency, and persistence and continuity. The theme of "persistence of ethnic identity in the face of constant change [including] . . . conquest, persecution, exile, and in some cases attempted genocide" is uniquely applicable (Sheridan and Perezo 1996:xxvi). The Yaqui, Rarámuri (Tarahumara), Seri, and Yuman, the Hopi, Zuni, Pueblo, O'odham, and Havasupai and other peoples of the Greater Southwest share strong ideological ties to the land and to their ancestors.

There is a striking degree of biological and cultural continuity among many indigenous groups still living in these regions. The Hopi people and their ancestors have lived on Black Mesa, Arizona, since AD 200 (Powell 1983). Hopi communities have very strong ties to their ancestral homelands, and they use information derived from archaeology, ethnohistory, and interviews with elders to identify ancestral sacred sites and locations (Dongoske et al. 1993). Huichol people living in Jalisco, Mexico, demonstrate continuity of at least a thousand years as documented through archaeological and ethnohistorical research at the site of La Quemada (circa AD 900) (Nelson et al. 1992). And intriguingly, these two indigenous groups (Hopi and Huichol) share some similar attributes of ceremony and architecture even though they are on the most northern and southern peripheries of the Greater Southwest and separated by thousands of miles (Shaefer and Furst 1996:59–60).

The indigenous people of the Greater Southwest have not become extinct, nor have they been assimilated into either Anglo or Hispanic mainstream culture. Both Anglo and Hispanic culture continue to be enriched by proximity to and involvement with native peoples. An understanding of their long in situ histories, particularly with respect to health, presents a unique opportunity to understand biological stress and its interplay with environmental and cultural variables over long periods of time and among regions within the Greater Southwest.

The Greater Southwest is represented in the Western Hemisphere project database by the skeletal series from Anasazi sites in the Dolores area of southwestern Colorado, protohistoric San Cristobal Pueblo in the Galisteo Basin of New Mexico, and the ancestral Zuni village of Hawikku in western New Mexico (Figure 16.1). These span the years from AD 600 to the time of Spanish contact (1539) and the first stage of European colonization of the Pueblo region, which ended in the Pueblo Revolt of 1680. These are the ancestors of the Hopi and Zuni tribes and 19 other Pueblo communities, such as those at Taos, Santa Clara, San Idelfonso, Santo Domingo, and Acoma.

Our earlier syntheses of bioarchaeological data from the Southwest have documented high levels of biological stress in the prehistoric and especially in later protohistoric populations (Martin 1995; Reff 1991, 1993; Stodder 1999; Stodder and Martin 1992). The health index and quality of life scores for these three skeletal series rank among the lowest in the Western Hemisphere project database. But the relative degree of morbidity is brought into much clearer relief when placed in the matrix of the data for the hemisphere. We are confronted with what seems to be a paradox: cultural longevity concomitant with high morbidity rates in the Southwest.

Given the marginal and risky nature of agriculture on the Colorado Plateau, and the evidence suggesting increases in population particularly during the twelfth century, we had hypothesized that Anasazi health would be comparable to that of other pre-Columbian agriculturists undergoing agricultural intensification and settlement aggregation. It is surprising to find that the Anasazi, whose history is characterized by resiliency and remarkable accomplishments (most evident being the architecture of Chaco Canyon and the Mesa Verde), scored lower than oppressed and traumatized groups (e.g., African slaves, Civil War soldiers). We believe that the "poor showing" by Pueblo peoples in the Western Hemisphere study reflects the difficulties of farming in the desert Southwest, and perhaps more importantly, the impact of European colonization and the introduction of Old World diseases.

The questions we attempt to address here revolve around understanding why the scores for these populations are so low, and which indicators of biological stress drove the scores downward. We first provide a description of the southwestern assemblages in the Western Hemisphere database, and provide contextual information on the region as a whole. We discuss the health status of these populations in the context of the larger regional picture of health in the Southwest, as documented in bioarchaeological studies of prehistoric (Anasazi) and protohistoric Pueblo people of the Colorado Plateau. Next we examine the relative ranking of the Southwest groups in the matrix of health index scores from the hemisphere, and the underlying morbidity patterns as demonstrated in the attribute scores contributed by the very high rates of anemia and hypoplasias in the Southwest assemblages. We explore the underlying factors that explain these trends and suggest ways that the Southwest fits into broader pan-hemispheric trends in health before and after European contact.

We propose that anthropologists, historians, and economists must consider the complex dynamics of social change and conflict and the relationship between ideology, resources, and health. We argue here that mortality and poor health are only a small part of the overall equation in understanding cultural viability. Although infinitely more difficult to quantify, the ideological framework within which stressed groups make sense of their health must be equally important.

SETTLEMENT AND ENVIRONMENT IN THE PREHISTORIC SOUTHWEST

There was sporadic habitation in the Southwest as early as 6000 BC, but excavated sites with associated skeletal remains are primarily from sites dated to the "Pueblo" periods. Archaeologists have divided the pottery-making phases into Pueblo I (AD 650–950), Pueblo II (AD 950–1150), Pueblo III (AD 1150–1350), and Pueblo IV (circa AD 1350 to Spanish contact circa 1540) (Adler 1996). In general, these major time periods mark increasing population, intensification of agricultural

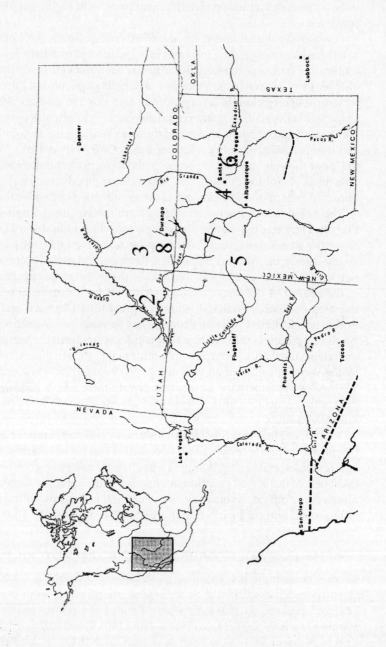

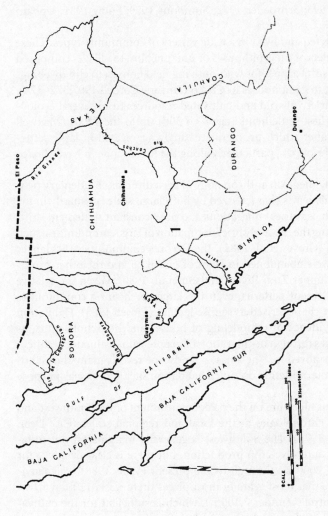

Figure 16.1. Map of the Greater Southwest showing where the major sites discussed in the text are located (1 = Tarahumara, 2 = Black Mesa, 3 = Dolores region, 4 = San Cristobal Pueblo, 5 = Hawikko (Zuni), 6 = Pecos Pueblo, 7 = Chaco Canyon, 8 = Mesa Verde region) (map reproduced from Cordell (1984) and modified by authors).

practices, greater emphasis on public architecture and trade, the appearance of large regional systems, increased morbidity, and rising rates of warfare and violence (Wilcox and Haas 1994). Spanish exploration and colonization of New Mexico led to profound disruptions, as Pueblo land, labor, and other resources were usurped and the Pueblo economy and culture were threatened by the invaders and their invisible allies – smallpox, measles, and other epidemic diseases (Kessell 1979; Reff 1991: 228–230, 1993; Riley 1995; Schroeder 1972; Simmons 1979; Snow 1981; Upham 1982; Wilcox 1981).

The Anasazi constructed and lived in a wide variety of community types. These ranged from small hamlets of a few pithouses or unit pueblos, to villages composed of multistory masonry surface pueblos with outlying field houses, to cliff dwellings in sequestered canyons, to great houses in Chaco Canyon (Cordell 1997:372–374). They utilized a wide variety of wild and cultivated resources from several ecological zones from the earliest settlements (circa AD 300) up to the 1400s (Maxwell and Anschuetz 1992), after which people increasingly aggregated in large settlements around riverine resources, particularly along the Rio Grande in New Mexico (Cameron 1995).

Despite the prevailing theme in anthropology of agriculturists as sedentary peoples, southwestern prehistory is characterized by both large-scale (primarily in the thirteenth and sixteenth centuries) migrations and near-constant settlement shifts at smaller scales, including the relatively brief occupation of large communities, such as Grasshopper Pueblo (Graves et al. 1982), the Dolores communities (Schlanger 1986), and those that were abandoned in favor of Hawikku and the other protohistoric pueblos of the upper Zuni River (Watson et al. 1980). Given the relative fluidity of Anasazi settlement patterns, even the larger prehistoric communities may be more accurately characterized as semisedentary (Powell 1983). Habitation sites show abundant evidence of remodeling of houses and household units, as additions to communities through in-migration of people with distinctive architectural styles and pottery moved in. The Anasazi landscape reveals many thousands of small, seasonally or intermittently occupied habitation sites and special-purpose sites.

There is a voluminous literature on the paleoenvironment of the Southwest and its relation to cultural chronologies at the local and regional scales (e.g., Dean et al. 1985; Euler et al. 1979). The Southwest is generally marginal, if not unfavorable, for large-scale, intensive crop production, but there is clear evidence for maize cultivation from 2000 BC through to the present (Wills 1988). Paleoenvironmental data indicate that most years in most places there was a 120-day frost-free period in lower altitudes (under 2,100m), which is sufficient for the cultivation of maize (Maxwell 1995). But high- and low-frequency variation in length of the growing season and in winter and summer precipitation patterns are well documented.

Archaeologists have long recognized the pattern of movement and relocation, and suggested environmental degradation and droughts as a force behind the decision to abandon one site and establish another (Cordell 1984:310–325). However, the physical environment was but one source of contingencies that are likely to have influenced migration. The possibility that the Anasazi – like their European contemporaries who participated in the Crusades – were "moved" by other than material forces has largely been ignored. As anthropologist and Zuni elder Edmund Ladd suggests, we seem not to appreciate that the Pueblo may have viewed the world entirely differently:

[T]here are a lot of Anasazi ruins. They're scattered all over the place because that's where our ancestors traveled. They weren't traveling because there were droughts or there was pestilence. They were traveling because they were looking, searching, for the center place. (1991:34)

Whatever the range of reasons for Anasazi migration, it is clear that Spanish colonization of New Mexico in 1598 added new and, in many ways, terrifying dimensions to the process of site abandonment. Before colonization in 1598 there were 75 to 90 occupied pueblo in the Rio Grande drainage; by 1643 only 43 remained (Schroeder 1972:48, 55). Even those pueblos that persisted (welcoming immigrants from elsewhere) experienced population losses. The population of Pecos declined by 40% between 1622 and 1641 (Kessell 1979:170). European exploration and, perhaps more importantly, Old World diseases were largely responsible for the demise of many pueblo settlements and their inhabitants.

Although it has been hypothesized that diseases like smallpox reached the Pueblo region before or shortly after European contact in 1539 (Dobyns 1983; Upham 1986), a stronger case can be made in the abstract, as well as empirically, for the introduction of disease following Oñate's founding of the first Spanish colony in New Mexico in 1598 (Reff 1991:102–103, 167). The spread of epidemic disease after this date over hundreds of miles via native populations is indicated in Jesuit missionary documents from northern and western Mexico (Reff 1987, 1991). One of the earliest explicit mentions of epidemic disease among the Pueblos was by a Franciscan superior, who noted in 1639 that smallpox and *cocoliztli* (a Nahuatl term thought to refer to fulminating smallpox) had claimed upwards of 20,000 lives in "recent years" (Hackett 1937:108). Epidemics are also noted in the missionaries' burial books, reports, and chronicles from the 1600s and 1700s (Kessell 1979:378; Reff: 1991:230–231; Stodder 1990; Stodder and Martin 1992).

THE STUDY POPULATIONS

In this section we briefly discuss the three southwestern assemblages and their paleoepidemiological and paleodemographic features. The localities and dates and sizes of the three assemblages are summarized in Table 16.1.

The Dolores Anasazi

The prehistoric Pueblos are represented in the Southwest database by the human remains recovered during the Dolores Archaeological Program (1978–1985) prior to the construction of the McPhee Dam and Reservoir about 20 miles north of

Table 16.1: Summary Information on the Southwest Skeletal Assemblages
in the Western Hemisphere Database

Site or locality	Dolores Archaeological Program	Hawikku	San Cristobal
Location	Southwest Colorado	Western New Mexico	Galisteo Basin, New Mexico
Dates	AD 600–980	1400–1680	1350–1680
Number of individuals in database	43	188	277
Bioarchaeology references	Stodder 1987	Stodder 1990, 1994, 1996	Stodder 1990, 1994, 1996
Archaeology references	Breternitz et al. 1986; Petersen and Orcutt 1987	Hodge 1937; Kintigh 1985; Smith et al. 1966	Lang 1977; Lycett 1995; Nelson 1914, 1916

Mesa Verde National Park in southwestern Colorado (Breternitz et al. 1986). An assemblage of human remains representing a minimum of 135 individuals was collected, but only 64 of these were represented by relatively complete skeletons from primary or secondary interments or other mortuary contexts (Stodder 1987). The assemblage is comprised mostly of young adults. For analytical purposes, the Dolores data were originally also analyzed as part of a larger regional sample of skeletal remains from contemporaneous sites on Mesa Verde, and in the Mancos, McElmo, and Yellow Jacket areas (Stodder 1984, 1987).

Dolores is located on the northeastern edge and at the elevational limit of Anasazi site distribution. The area is relatively cool, and this puts the horticulturalist at a higher threshold of vulnerability to late spring and early autumn frosts, which shorten the growing season. But there is also a higher precipitation rate, a microclimatic feature which favors dry farming. The fine-grained paleoclimatic data indicate that people moved to Dolores during a period of warm intervals with low precipitation (Petersen and Orcutt 1987). Regional population data indicate that people moved there from nearby Mockingbird Mesa and Woods Canyon during a specific climatic interlude, and then moved back to these other localities in the 900s (Schlanger 1986).

The Dolores Anasazi provide a snapshot of local behavior and population dynamics during the Pueblo I period. From AD 600 to 980, a series of settlements evolved, first as hamlets with four to five semisubterranean pit structures and later into larger communities like McPhee Village and Grass Mesa – each with several clusters of room blocks, pithouses, and kivas – thought to consist of corporate, possibly land-controlling, kin groups (Kohler 1992). Dolores population peaked at about 900 people in the mid-800s. Population density at that time is thought to have been as much as twice as high as for the historic Hopi Pueblos, suggesting that land suitable for cultivation may have been insufficient to support the population. There was rapid decline and nearly complete abandonment of the area by AD 950 (Schlanger 1986).

Demographically, the Dolores assemblage underrepresents younger and older individuals. The age distribution is as follows: 0–2 years: 3 individuals; 3–7 years: 6; 8–11 years: 0; 12–15 years: 2; 16–20 years: 11; 21–26 years: 18; 27–35 years: 5; 36–40 years: 6; 41 years and older: 2 individuals. Fifteen adult individuals were too fragmentary to be confidently assigned to an age interval. Females in the assemblage are younger than the males: 80% of females died between ages 16 and 26, compared to only 40% of the males.

The paleoepidemiological profile of the Dolores assemblage features cribra orbitalia in 78% (26 of 33 observable individuals) and porotic hyperostosis in 9% (2 of 22 individuals). Skeletal infections are present in 12.5% (8 of 64 individuals). These include 7 cases of nonspecific periostitis or osteitis, and 1 Brodie's abscess. Nine instances of traumatic injury were observed in the assemblage, affecting 14% of the individuals.

Average stature of the adult males ($n = 9$) from Dolores is 162.31cm – slightly taller than the 161.96 ($n = 17$) average for the Basketmaker III – Pueblo I (PI) males from the Mesa Verde regional sample. Females from Dolores averaged 155.95cm ($n = 12$), again just slightly higher than the regional average of 155.32 ($n = 12$) (Stodder 1984, 1987). Degenerative joint disease in the vertebral column and infracranial joints is present in most of the adults, including the younger individuals.

The rates of dental pathologies, including caries, abscesses, antemortem loss, calculus formation, and periodontal disease, is relatively low for an Anasazi population because these pathologies are progressive with age and this is a young sample. Antemortem tooth loss suggests one of the greatest threats to overall health for the Anasazi in general, and in the Dolores people attritional wear and antemortem tooth loss overtake the rate of caries and abscess formation. Enamel hypoplasias in the incisors and canines of the Dolores sample exhibit two peaks in developmental age of formation: at 2.5 to 3 years, and at 4 to 4.5 years, respectively. These are typical peaks in hypoplasia formation, representing temporary developmental arrest in enamel matrix formation, but as indicated below, this pattern changes over time in the Southwest.

The degree of local variability in adaptation in the Southwest, even among the Anasazi of the Colorado Plateau, suggests that no single assemblage of skeletal remains should be taken as archetypal. We would prefer that there were more prehistoric southwestern skeletal assemblages represented in the HEA database, but we are compelled to honor agreements made regarding the prohibition of publishing several osteology data sets collected in compliance with the Native American Graves Protection and Repatriation Act (NAGPRA).

However, when the Dolores data are contextualized in the larger data set for the Anasazi (below), it is apparent that this population is not unique in its paleoepidemiological status. The sequence of initial settlement in an era of local climatic favorability, followed by internal and migration-driven population growth, aggregation, agricultural intensification, degradation of local wood and wild resources, microclimatic shifts leading to unfavorable conditions for farming, and subsequent migration out of the Dolores Project Area, comprises a concise microcosm of patterns and processes in Anasazi prehistory.

Hawikku

Hawikku, founded in about 1425, was one of six or seven large, multistoried pueblos along the upper Zuni River that were occupied at the time of European contact in 1539. The six room blocks and nine midden deposits cover an area of about three acres on a mesa top near the Zuni River. The site was excavated by Frederick Webb Hodge and colleagues in the 1930s (Smith et al. 1966). Kintigh (1985) estimates that between 900 and 1,750 people lived at Hawikku, and that the total Zuni population at contact exceeded 4,000 people. In a letter to the king of Spain, Coronado indicated that the Zuni villages had between 2,000 and 3,000 "hearths" (Reff 1991a:643). If so, Kintigh's figure of 4,000 is a conservative estimate; others have estimated the Zuni population at more than 7,000 (Ellis 1974:256).

Archaeological and historical data suggest that Hawikku and the other Zuni Pueblos were enjoying a cultural florescence in 1539 (Ferguson 1981:336; Riley 1987:176–214). Coronado and his army of 2,000 Spaniards and Indian allies laid siege to Hawikku for several months in 1540 before finally being repelled. After nonconfrontational encounters with members of the Chamuscado and Rodriguez *entradas* in 1581 and 1583, the western Pueblos were left relatively alone until the establishment of the Franciscan mission at Hawikku in 1629 (Ferguson 1981). There were a number of uprisings and intermittent abandonments of Zuni villages in the years leading up to the Pueblo Revolt in 1680. The mission at Hawikku was burned in 1672 by Apaches, in a raid thought to have been orchestrated by the Zuni themselves (Hodge 1937). Eight years later when the Pueblo Revolt began, the Zuni abandoned all of their Pueblos and withdrew to Dowa Yallane Mesa. After the revolt, in 1596, the Zuni left the mesa and reoccupied only one of their former Pueblos (Halona:wa or Zuni Pueblo). Although the size of the Zuni population in 1596 is unknown, it is apparent that the population had declined to a fraction of what it had been at contact.

Before the fire in 1672, the declining Zuni population apparently congregated at Hawikku, as is suggested by the relatively large number of rooms occupied at the pueblo. Zuni population declined by about half during the 1500s, with continued decline in the seventeenth century (Kintigh 1985). But while Zuni population dropped, the number of occupied rooms at Hawikku did not decline substantially throughout this period (Kintigh 1985:63). The paleoepidemiological profile of the Hawikku skeletal assemblage reflects the enormous biological stress endured by the Zuni during this period of prolonged economic, political, and religious disruption.

The Hawikku assemblage has the highest reported rate of skeletal infection for any skeletal population from the Southwest: 36% (51% – 29 of 57 – in subadults, and 26% – 22 of 85 – in adults). Treponemal infection and tuberculosis are both present, and sometimes co-occur. We do not know whether the treponemal syndrome in this community was transmitted congenitally, but the high frequency of systemic infection in infants from Hawikku, and the presence of a notched incisor, suggests that this may have been the case (Stodder 1998).

Cranial indicators of anemia (orbital or postorbital lesions, either active or remodeling) are present in 84% of the Hawikku individuals. Half of the subadults have unremodeled lesions of cribra orbitalia or porotic hyperostosis (20 of 40 individuals aged 0–15.9 years).

Almost all (94%) of the individuals have at least one hypoplastic defect in a permanent incisor or canine, with peak ages of defect formation at ages 3–3.5 and 4.5–5 years. Caries and periapical abscesses are present in 53% and 58% of the Hawikku dentitions. Antemortem tooth loss progressed with age: overall, the average is 4.29 teeth lost per individual; the number peaks in those over age 45 who lost an average of 14.7 teeth.

Traumatic injury is evident in the remains of 15.9% of the skeletons from Hawikku (29 of 182). The rate of cranial trauma in adults is 17.5% in males (7/40), 7.5% in females (4/53). Life expectancy at birth is 21.48 years and 16 years at age 16 for the Hawikku assemblage.

San Cristobal

San Cristobal Pueblo is located on the eastern frontier of the Pueblo world. The site was first excavated by Nels Nelson in 1912, and later by Louis Sullivan, who collected a substantial number of burials from the middens. San Cristobal was founded in about 1350 and was one of 9 or 10 large Tano villages in the Galisteo Basin south of Pecos. The multistory site, situated on the north and south sides of San Cristobal Creek, is estimated to have had 2,000 ground-floor rooms (Nelson 1914) and a precontact population of about 3,200 people (Stodder 1990:62). Population peaked in the century prior to European contact, and both the number and size of the Galisteo Basin communities declined steadily thereafter (Lang 1977; Lycett 1995; Nelson 1914). Population of the historic component of the site is estimated at 1,300 people (Stodder 1990:63). The community was abandoned at the time of the Pueblo Revolt in 1680.

San Cristobal was visited by the Coronado expedition in 1540–1541, by the Chamuscado-Rodriquez party in 1581, by Espejo in 1582, and by Castaco de Sosa in 1590 (Hammond and Rey 1966). Food and other resources were extracted from the natives by these armed *entrada* parties, in a foreshadowing of the Spanish colony's extractive economic burden imposed after the establishment of Santa Fe and the civilian government in the first years of the 1600s. The residents of San Cristobal and other eastern Pueblos were undoubtedly affected by the economic burden imposed by the Spanish presence. The small colony was founded during a series of prolonged droughts, and a number of famines are recorded in the mission records. Additional droughts are recorded for the 1660s and 1670s – the decades preceding the Pueblo Revolt which temporarily drove the Spaniards out of New Mexico (Hackett 1937).

Based on Nelson's field notes, at least 70% of the San Cristobal burials date to the later occupation of the site, circa 1475–1680, a time of extreme stress, which followed several decades of local population decline in the Galisteo Basin.

The life table for San Cristobal yields a life expectancy of 22.2 years at birth, and 17.47 years at age 15. Rates of skeletal infection are 23% in the adults (32 of 143) and 22% in subadults (15 of 67). Several cases of treponemal infection are present, and one possible case of osteomyelitis variolosa. The most striking data from the San Cristobal skeletons is the suggestion of an epidemic wave of tuberculosis during the latter era of the occupation. One of the seven extramural middens contained 5 adults with tuberculosis. The presence of tuberculosis is not surprising given the context of biological, ecological, social, and political stress in the early historic Pueblos, and the opportunistic nature of the disease.

Cranial indicators of anemia (orbital or postorbital lesions, either active or re-modeling) are present in 90% of the San Cristobal individuals. Of the subadults, 42% (28 of 66) exhibit unremodeled lesions of cribra orbitalia or porotic hyperostosis.

Enamel hypoplasias are present on incisors or canines of 85% of the San Cristobal skeletons. Peak ages of hypoplasia formation in the incisors and canines are 3–4 years and 4–4.5 years, respectively. Caries and periapical abscesses are present in 57% and 46% of the San Cristobal dentitions. People at San Cristobal lost an average of 3.9 teeth during their lifetimes. In those who lived to age 45 or older, the average number of teeth lost antemortem is 12.6 per individual.

Evidence of traumatic injury is present in 22.7% (52 of 229 individuals) of the San Cristobal skeletons. The rates of cranial trauma in adults is among the highest recorded in the regional literature: 19.7% in males (13 of 66) and 10.8% in females (7 of 65). This is attributable to conflict with the invading and colonizing Spaniards, and as economic networks were altered by the Europeans, conflict with neighboring non-Pueblo peoples and eventually to conflict between Pueblo groups.

HEALTH AND DEMOGRAPHY IN THE PREHISTORIC SOUTHWEST

In this section we present data on the frequencies of skeletal pathologies that have been reported in the Anasazi/Pueblo bioarchaeological record. These are not detailed data and are not intended to support a fine-grained chronological analysis; they are included to provide a broader context for interpreting the Western Hemisphere data on these three assemblages from the Southwest. The scores and indexes generated by the Western Hemisphere project cast these early inhabitants of the Southwest as among the most unhealthy people in the history of the Western Hemisphere. While it is important to consider the factors and processes that created these rates of biological stress, it is also important to assess the extent to which these three skeletal assemblages are representative of the health status of the prehistoric and ethnohistoric eras of the northern Southwest.

The assemblages in Table 16.2 are listed in chronological order, but it is apparent that there is not a simple trend of increasing pathology over time. The health of Anasazi populations varied in time and space, as did the nature of their communities and settlement patterns, as well as the local resource mix utilized. Although a maize-based diet is low in iron, a simple model of increasing agricultural production and reliance on corn does not suffice to explain the variation in rates of anemia. The explanations are multifactorial and touch upon diet as well as community ecology and infectious and parasitic disease loads (Reinhard 1988, 1990; Stodder and Martin 1992; Walker 1985). It is apparent, however, that anemia reaches near ubiquity in skeletal samples from several localities, not only those included in the Western Hemisphere database.

Table 16.2: Percent Frequencies of Selected Pathologies Reported for Southwest Skeletal Samples

Location	Dates	Anemia* in 0–10-yr.-olds	Skeletal infection	Caries	Cranial trauma	Reference
Canyon de Chelley	300 BC–AD 700	72				El-Najjar et al. 1975
Dolores	600–980	78	12	71	1.5	Stodder 1987
Black Mesa	700–1100	85	23	26		Martin et al. 1990
Chaco Canyon	700–1100	68	17	85	1	Akins 1986
Pueblo Bonito	900–1100	45				Palkovich 1984
Mesa Verde Region	700–1300	79				Stodder 1987
Grasshopper	1245–1400	15	12	52		Hinkes 1983
Tijeras	1300–1425		3	23	2	Ferguson 1980
Paa'ko	1300–1600		4		3	Ferguson 1980
Arroyo Hondo	1300–1600	22	13		0	Palkovich 1987
Gran Quivira	1300–historic	18				El-Najjar et al. 1975
San Cristobal	1350–historic	87	23	57	15	Stodder 1990
Hawikku	1425–historic	74	36	53	12	Stodder 1990
Pecos	1425–1550			48	3	Hooton 1930
Pecos	1550–1600			61	8	Hooton 1930
Pecos	1600–1800				16	Hooton 1930

Note: Samples in the database are in italics.
* Includes porotic hyperostosis or cribra orbitalia, remodeled or active lesions.

Infection rates vary across time and space as well, but the high frequencies in the later communities stand out, particularly the greater number of cases of tuberculosis and treponematosis. Equivalent rates of infection are reported for San Cristobal and the much earlier Black Mesa assemblages, but the infections in the Black Mesa group are almost all cases of slight and moderate periosteal inflammation (Martin et al. 1990). This type of infection may be assumed to have had significantly less impact on community health and the functioning of afflicted persons than the cases of systemic infection and tuberculosis at San Cristobal and Hawikku. The lumping of all types of skeletal infection in the summary index scores for the Western Hemisphere project populations, without differential weighting, may in fact be quite misleading if the simple frequencies actually mask significant differences in the underlying conditions.

Dental health, represented by the percentage of individuals in each assemblage with one or more carious teeth, was poor in southwestern populations. However, the rate of caries actually declines with increasing cohort age in most dental assemblages from the region, because high rates of occlusal wear and attrition and frequent antemortem tooth loss overtake the rate of caries formation. This is exemplified by the contrast between the Dolores sample, which has a preponderance of young adults and a 71% caries prevalence, and the Black Mesa population, which has an equal imbalance in the opposite direction – more older individuals and a much lower caries rate.

The hypoplasia data in Table 16.3 do indicate a temporal trend in the patterns of developmental arrest and recovery experienced by Anasazi children.[1] Starting in Pueblo III times (AD 1100–1300), the Mesa Verde region people experienced a later incidence of the hypoplasia-forming stress. This suggests postweaning dietary stress, as well as other community health problems attendant to life in the cliff dwellings of the Mesa Verde canyons. While these are charming places to visit, the cliff dwellings represent a major increase in community population density compared to the earlier mesa top villages. A result may have been an overall decline in public health (Kunitz and Euler 1972).

Another paleoepidemiological transition is suggested by the earlier peak of arrest incidents recorded in the incisors of the protohistoric assemblages, and also by the later peak in the Hawikku hypoplasia formation patterns. The incidence of earlier-formed hypoplasias in the late populations reflects the higher rates of skeletal infection seen in very young children, and the unusual peak of physiological stress events in 4–5-year-olds documented in the late stage of canine formation in the Hawikku children appears to be related to treponemal disease (Stodder 1998). These trends are visible at a close level of inspection, probably reflecting localized economic and sociocultural factors as well.

---

[1] The enamel hypoplasia data are based on estimated ages at enamel formation, following the method of Swardstedt (1966) and of Goodman et al. (1980) and Goodman and Rose (1990). Recently, however, it has been shown that the first visible hypoplasia on incisors and canines occur nearly a year after previously assumed (Goodman and Song 1999; Fitzgerald and Rose 2000). This correction would push back the estimated ages of early enamel defects by as much as a year, but would have progressively less effect on the estimated ages for later-formed defects. The comparisons here remain valid as the pattern of defect formation is unchanged.

Table 16.3: Peaks in Enamel Hypoplasia Formation in Permanent Incisors and Canines

Locality and date stage	Developmental age in half year increments										
	.05–1	1–1.5	1.5–2	2–2.5	2.5–3	3–3.5	3.5–4	4–4.5	4.5–5	5–5.5	5.5–6
Black Mesa – BMIII					•		•	•			
Mesa Verde – BMIII-PII					•		•	•			
Late Mesa Verde – PIII						•	•	•			
San Cristobal – PIV-H		•				•		•			
Hawikku – PIV-H		•				•			•		

Sources: Black Mesa data from Martin et al. 1990; Mesa Verde: Stodder 1987; Hawikku, San Cristobal: Stodder 1990.

A substantial increase in cranial trauma rates over time, especially following Spanish contact, is indicated in Table 16.2. However, skeletal assemblages and architectural features from the Southwest tell stories of conflict and violence in the prehistoric past as well. A number of prehistoric human skeletal assemblages exhibit signs of dismemberment and disarticulation, perimortem damage, and thermal alteration. These assemblages (which include children and adults, males and females) have been variously interpreted to represent acts of cannibalism (Malville 1989; Nickens 1975; Turner and Turner 1999; White 1992), witchcraft killings (Darling 1999), warfare (Le Blanc 1999; Wilcox and Haas 1994), or ritualized dismemberment (Ogilvie and Hilton 1993). Whatever the motivations and social processes contributing to the formation of these assemblages – and we assume they were several – there is evidence of violence.

Intervillage conflict is suggested by strategically located sites, burned structures, and defensive architecture, including fortifications, towers, and palisades, the prevalence of which seems to have increased over time (Haas and Creamer 1993; Wilcox and Haas 1994). These architectural and mortuary features suggest fighting in the form of ambushes and raids by groups of aggressors, and these patterns of chronic warfare pushed previously egalitarian and loosely connected groups into larger, politically centralized units between AD 1100 and 1300. The relatively high incidence of cranial trauma following European contact is consistent with archaeological and historical evidence of warfare and violence, including increased warfare among the Pueblos themselves and with their Athapaskan and Plains neighbors (Riley 1995:185), all of whom found their lives transformed by epidemic diseases, guns, horses, and massive economic disruption.

Based on paleoepidemiological data, the health trends in southwestern populations may be summarized in the following ways. 1) Ubiquitous nutrition and health challenges led to arrest in dental enamel formation, anemia, antemortem tooth loss, and infectious disease. 2) In the later, larger pueblos, endemic diseases including treponematosis and tuberculosis were increasingly common, possibly reaching epidemic proportions in some postcontact settlements experiencing significant disruption. 3) During the protohistoric period, infectious diseases of European origin further, and probably dramatically, undermined Pueblo health. The arrival of Europeans likewise led to social conflict and internal strife, which, while present throughout prehistory, increased significantly during the protohistoric periods, as reflected in increased trauma and mortality.

Many of the challenges to health seen in the skeletal remains are endemic conditions today – in Native Americans and other human populations as well. Iron-deficiency anemia, apparently ubiquitous throughout the prehistoric occupation of the Southwest (Walker 1985), remains a significant health problem for Native Americans today (Kunitz 1994). Ancient Pueblo children experienced disruptions in their growth patterns due to ill health and poor nutrition, and those problems persist into the present (Moore et al. 1972). Tuberculosis, which is present in at least 11 southwestern skeletal series, including those from Black Mesa (Sumner 1985), Chavez Pass (El-Najjar 1979), Chaco Canyon (Akins 1986; Palkovich 1984), and San Cristobal and Hawikku (Stodder 1990; Stodder and Martin 1992), was also identified by Ales Hrdlicka as a major health problem facing the indigenous people of the Southwest in the early 1900s (Hrdlicka 1909), and this disease is a growing problem today (Becker et al. 1990).

SOUTHWESTERN PEOPLES IN THE HEMISPHERIC CONTEXT

As shown in Table 16.4, there is very little difference in mean age-at-death, quality of life scores, and health index scores for the three southwestern skeletal assemblages; scores for these three groups are very close in all dimensions. As a composite score, the health index incorporates the length of life experienced by members of the sample, and the quality of life as determined by the prevalence and age distribution of skeletal and dental pathologies. The higher health index for the prehistoric Dolores Anasazi, compared to the later protohistoric assemblages, illustrates the relatively lower rates of some pathologies in this group, especially infectious disease, and the broader trend of decline in health over time in the region – a trend observed in populations of the Georgia Coast (Larsen et al. this volume) and other diachronic studies of North American populations (Baker and Kealhofer 1996; Cohen and Armelagos 1984; Larsen and Milner 1994; Verano and Ubelaker 1992).

As we noted above, and as shown in Table 16.5, the health index scores for southwestern populations are at or near the bottom of the 65 populations represented in the Western Hemisphere project. The prehistoric and early historic natives of the

Table 16.4: Western Hemisphere Data Scores for the Southwestern Skeletal Assemblages

	Age-at-death	Quality score	Health index
Dolores	24.2	.69	16.4
Hawikku	23.5	.73	15.6
San Cristobal	24.6	.71	16.0

Table 16.5: Quality and Health Index Scores for Selected Western Hemisphere Project Assemblages

Assemblage	Quality score	Health index
Precontact Copan-Rural	0.67	32.4
Precontact Georgia	0.97	24.4
Tlatinga, Teotihuacan	0.77	24.3
Proto-historic Georgia	0.93	22.7
Historic plantation slaves	0.71	22.4
Precontact Copan-Urban	0.75	21.3
Historic African-American	0.74	17.3
Civil War soldiers		17.3
Precontact Dolores	0.69	16.4
Archaic Ohio		16.4
Protohistoric San Cristobal	0.71	16.0
Protohistoric Hawikku	0.73	15.6
Precontact Ohio	0.77	15.2

North American Southwest carried one of the highest morbidity burdens in the hemisphere. Based on chronic pathologies reflected in the skeleton, they rank lower in quality of life than soldiers who died in the Civil War, slaves on South Carolina plantations, residents of the Tlatilinga complex in prehistoric Teotihuacan, and a wide range of prehistoric and historic, agricultural and forager, urban and rural populations in North and South America. These data are provocative, precisely because the Pueblo Indians have, in fact, survived a history (and prehistory) marked by cycles of drought, food stress, warfare, disease, population growth and decline, multiple migrations, epidemics, and colonization over a period of 1,500 years.

Compared to the range of scores for the Western Hemisphere project as a whole (Table 16.6), Hawikku exhibits the greatest divergence from the Western Hemisphere mean. The score of 53.5% is more than two standard deviations below the mean for all the populations which generate an average composite attribute score of 72.6% of the maximum possible score. The Dolores and San Cristobal scores are only slightly higher. The attribute scores generated by age distribution and frequencies of specific pathologies suggest that enamel hypoplasia, anemia, and degenerative joint disease are the morbidity components which most strongly influence the low health ranking of the southwestern populations in the Western Hemisphere project composite analyses. Hypoplasia and anemia are especially powerful in tugging at the scores since these are childhood conditions with lifelong implications. As discussed above, these are ubiquitous in southwestern populations.

Table 16.6: Composite and Specific Attribute Scores for the Western Hemisphere Database and the Southwestern Assemblages

| Pathology | Western Hemisphere Project database | | | | Dolores | Hawikku | San Cristobal |
	Min.	Max.	Mean	s.d.			
% of maximum:	53.5	91.8	72.6	7.98	59.8	53.5*	57.3
all pathologies					−1.60	−2.39	−1.92
z-score							
Enamel hypoplasia	9.8	99.7	71.1	24.59	34.8	46.5	26.9
z-score					−1.47	−1.00	−1.79
Anemia	53.2	100.0	90.5	11.53	55.0	55.8	53.2
z-score					−3.08	−3.09	−3.23
Dental pathology	55.3	100.0	81.8	10.39	79.1	78.5	73.6
z-score					−0.26	−0.32	−0.79
Infection	44.1	98.7	75.1	16.97	91.0	80.0	88.1
z-score					−0.93	−0.29	−0.59
DJD	41.6	100.0	78.9	12.26	66.8	50.0	52.8
z-score					−0.98	−2.36	−2.13
Trauma	10.8	100.0	85.7	16.12	83.8	84.3	80.2
z-score					−0.15	−0.06	−0.34
Stature	0.4	67.8	20.7	16.86	7.9	4.0	1.7
z-score					−0.76	−0.99	−1.13

Note: Hawikku has the lowest of all combined scores in Hemisphere Project. Z-scores computed as the number of standard deviations an attribute value falls above or below the project mean.

Source: Data from Steckel et al. this volume.

CONCLUSION

The Southwest is a marginal environment for agriculture. Food production by prehistoric and historic peoples was vulnerable to climatic fluctuations, and the environment was sensitive to degradation by human impact, which affected the viability of agricultural soils and of important wild resources, such as pinyon nuts and wood for fires and construction (Kohler 1992, 1993). Layered onto this background of the Colorado Plateau environment are the parallel processes of agricultural intensification and population aggregation. Both of these impact human health in terms of diet, work load, and community ecology as they affect nutrition, physical stress, disease resistance, and transmission.

Yet the Spanish explorers and missionaries wrote about (and took advantage of) the relative wealth of the large villages like Hawikku and San Cristobal. In addition to the thousands of souls waiting to be saved in this new province, they enthused over the fields of corn and cotton and the impressive masonry pueblos they visited:

The land is so fertile that they need to cultivate only once a year. . . . In one year they harvest enough for seven years. . . . There were in these provinces large numbers of native hens and cocks. . . . The towns are free from filth. . . . The houses are well separated and extremely clean. (From Castaneda's account of the Coronado expedition, in Hammond and Rey 1940:355.)

While they often misunderstood and misrepresented the native peoples and their political and religious systems (Reff 1999), accounts by these early visitors are unanimous in their glowing commentary on the wealth and quality of life enjoyed by the Pueblos (Riley 1986:184, 232). They did not write about natives of the Greater Southwest as sickly, starving, and barely able to survive to adulthood, but rather they described strong, agile, and corpulent people who lived "to the age of decrepitude" (Perez de Ribas 1645:88). Some archaeologists call the late prehistoric a "classic period" or a "Golden Age" for the Pueblos (Riley 1995:93–118) – a time of great achievement in architecture, agriculture, trade, ceremonialism, and material culture. And considering the historical record, one could argue that warfare, famine, disease, and environmental degradation were more of a problem in sixteenth-century Europe than in the Pueblos (Sales 1991:28–36, 75–90, 134).

The indigenous peoples of the Southwest have always been in a state of growth, migration, decline, and movement. The themes of migration, movement, and hardship, tempered with a respect for the power of nature and climatic events in their everyday lives, are strongly entwined in their oral narratives. Hopi people living today on the mesas in northeastern Arizona know with certainty that their ancestors emerged from the Grand Canyon and that they made a pact with their god to travel about the landscape until they found their spiritual center (Dongoske et al. 1993). They lived in many places before arriving at their center place on Black Mesa. These migrating groups of people left many things behind in their wanderings, and it is these profane and sacred things (from potsherds to human burials) that archaeologists and physical anthropologists study in order to reconstruct the past.

Archaeologists account for "abandoned" sites in antiquity as the result of environmental degradation and droughts (Cordell 1997), but the Hopi explain movement and relocation in completely different terms (Dongoske et al. 1995). As their legend goes, the Indian people of the world were asked to choose different kinds of corn, and some choices signified long and prosperous lives. The Hopi chose the "short blue corn," which unfortunately meant a life filled with great hardship and many challenges (Courlander 1970). Their stories are filled with descriptions and prophecies that discuss the difficulties and struggles that are their destiny (Naquatewa 1967).

Life in the prehistoric Southwest posed challenges, but it is clear that Pueblo life became particularly challenging, short, and, for many, miserable following European colonization. The Pueblos were devastated by Old World diseases, especially smallpox and measles. These are not recorded in the skeletal remains, but it would be yet another injustice if we lost sight of these factors and focus only on the skeletal data as reduced to indexes and quality scores.

Long-term cultural longevity cannot be understood on the basis of data reduced to indexes of environmental productivity and counts of skeletal pathologies. The archaeological and historical records of the Southwest, and the native peoples' histories, document a persistent hold on traditional values and a commitment to "place" and land, along with a resiliency and flexibility in adapting to novel and challenging ecological, political, and cultural conditions. There are lessons to be learned from such groups as the Zuni and Hopi; although they have carried a morbidity burden that appears to be unparalleled in the Western Hemisphere, their cultures remain vibrant and viable. Demographically, their numbers have continued to rise and may currently be at sizes replicating those at contact (Sheridan and Parezo 1996).

REFERENCES

Adler, M. A., ed. 1996, *The Prehistoric Pueblo World AD 1150–1350*. Tucson: University of Arizona Press.

Akins, N. J. 1986 *A Biocultural Approach to Human Burials from Chaco Canyon, New Mexico*. Santa Fe, N. Mex.: National Park Service, Reports of the Chaco Center No. 9.

Baker, B. J. and L. K. Kealhofer, eds. 1996 *Disease and Biocultural Frontiers: Native American Adaptation in the Spanish Borderlands*. Gainesville: University of Florida Press.

Becker, T. M., C. Wiggins, and C. Peek. 1990. Mortality from infectious diseases among New Mexico's American Indians, Hispanic Whites and other Whites. *American Journal of Public Health* 80:320–323.

Breternitz, D. A., C. K. Robinson, and G. T. Gross, compilers. 1986. *Dolores Archaeological Program: Final Synthetic Report*. Denver, Colo.: Bureau of Reclamation Engineering and Research Center.

Cameron, C. 1995. Collaborative approaches to understanding the past. *Society for American Archaeology Bulletin* 12(1):11–12.

Cohen, M. N., and G Armelagos, eds. 1984. *Paleopathology at the Origins of Agriculture*. New York: Academic Press. Pp. 425–461.

Cordell, L. S. 1997. *Prehistory of the Southwest*, 2d ed. Orlando, Fl.: Academic Press.

Courlander, H. 1970. *The Fourth World of the Hopis: The Epic Story of the Hopi Indians as Preserved in their Legends and Traditions*. Albuquerque: University of New Mexico Press.

Darling, J. A. 1999. Mass inhumation and the execution of witches in the American Southwest. *American Anthropologist* 100:732–752.

Dean, J. S., R. C. Euler, G. J. Gumerman, F. Plog, R. H. Hevly, and T. Karlstrom. 1985. Human behavior, demography, and paleoenvironment on the Colorado Plateaus. *American Antiquity* 50:537–554.

Dobyns, H. F. 1983. *Their Number Become Thinned.* Knoxville: University of Tennessee Press.

Dongoske, K., T. J. Ferguson, M. Yeatts, and L. Jenkins. 1993. Hopi Oral History and Archaeology. Paper presented at the 1993 American Anthropology Association meetings, Washington, D. C., in Plenary Session, "Collaborative Approaches to Understanding the Past." On file (available) Hopi cultural Preservation Office, The Hopi Tribe, P.O. Box 123, Kykotsmovi, AZ 86039.

Dongoske, K., L. Jenkins, and T. J. Ferguson. 1995. Understanding the past through Hopi oral history. *Archaeology Magazine* July/August:24–31.

Ellis, F. H. 1974. *The Hopi: Their History and Use of Lands.* New York: Garland.

Euler, R. C., G. J. Gumerman, T. Karlstrom, J. Dean, and R. H. Hevly. 1979. The Colorado Plateaus: Cultural dynamics and paleoenvironment. *Science* 205:1089–1101.

Ferguson, C. 1980. Analysis of human remains. In *Tijeras Canyon: Analyses of the Past*, ed. L. Cordell. Albuquerque: University of New Mexico Press. Pp.121–148.

Ferguson, T. J. 1981. The emergence of modern Zuni culture and society: A summary of Zuni tribal history, AD 1450–1700. In *The Protohistoric Period in the North American Southwest, AD 1450–1700*, ed. D. R. Wilcox and W. B. Masse. Anthropological Research Paper No. 24. Tempe: Arizona State University Press. Pp. 336–353.

Fish, P. R., and S. K. Fish. 1994. Southwest and Northwest: Recent research at the juncture of the United States and Mexico. *Journal of Archaeological Research* 2(1):3–44.

Fitzgerald, C. M., and J. C. Rose. 2000. Reading between the lines: Dental development and subadult age assessment using microstructural growth markers of teeth. In *Biological Anthropology of the Human Skeleton*, ed. M. A. Katzenberg and S. R. Saunders. New York: Wiley-Liss. Pp. 163–186.

Goodman, A. H., G. J. Armelagos, and J. C. Rose. 1980. Enamel hypoplasias as indicators of stress in three prehistoric human populations from Illinois. *Human Biology* 52: 515–528.

Goodman, A. H., and J. C. Rose. 1990. The assessment of systemic physiological perturbations from developmental defects of enamel and histological structures. *Yearbook of Physical Anthropology* 33:59–110.

Goodman, A. H., and R. J. Song. 1999. Sources of variation in estimated ages at formation of linear enamel hypoplasias. In *Human Growth in the Past, Studies from Bones and Teeth*, ed. R. D. Hoppa and C. M. Fitzgerald. Cambridge: Cambridge University Press. Pp. 210–240.

Graves, M. W., S. J. Holbrook, and W. A. Longacre. 1982. Aggregation and abandonment at Grasshopper Pueblo: Evolutionary trends in the late prehistory of east-central Arizona. In *Multidisciplinary Research at Grasshopper Pueblo, Arizona*, ed. W. A. Longacre, S. J. Holbrook, and W. M. Graves. Anthropological Papers of the University of Arizona No. 40. Tucson: University of Arizona Press. Pp.110–121.

Haas, J., and W. Creamer. 1993. *Stress and Warfare Among the Kayenta Anasazi of the Thirteenth Century AD.* Chicago: Field Museum of Natural History Press.

Hackett, C. W. 1937. *Historical Documents Relating to New Mexico, Nueva Vizcaya, and Approaches Thereto, to 1773*, vol. 3. Washington, D. C.: Carnegie Institution of Washington.

Hammond, G., and A. Rey. 1940. *Narratives of the Coronado Expedition, 1540–1542.* Coronado Historical Series, vol.1. Albuquerque: University of New Mexico Press.

1966. *The Rediscovery of New Mexico, 1580–1594.* Albuquerque: University of New Mexico Press.

Hinkes, M. J. 1983. Skeletal Evidence of Stress in Subadults: Trying to Come of Age at Grasshopper Pueblo. Ph.D. thesis, Department of Anthropology, University of Arizona, Tucson.

Hodge, Frederick Webb. 1937. *History of Hawikuh.* Los Angeles: The Southwest Museum.

Hooton, E. A. 1930. *The Indians of Pecos Pueblo: A Study of Their Skeletal Remains.* Papers of the Southwestern Expedition 4. New Haven, Conn.: Yale University Press.

Hrdlicka, A. 1909. *Tuberculosis Among Certain Indian Tribes of the United States.* Washington D. C.: Bureau of American Ethnology Bulletin, No. 42.

Kintigh, K. 1985. *Settlement, Subsistence and Society in Late Zuni Prehistory.* Anthropological Papers of the University of Arizona, No. 44. Tucson: University of Arizona Press.

Kohler, T. A. 1992. Prehistoric human impact on the environment in the upland North American Southwest. *Population and Environment* 13(4):255–268.

——— 1993. News from the northern American Southwest: Prehistory on the edge of chaos. *Journal of Archaeological Research* 1(4):267–321.

Kunitz, S. J., 1994. *Disease and Social Diversity: The European Impact on the Health of Non-Europeans.* New York: Oxford University Press.

Kunitz, S. J., and R. C. Euler. 1972. *Aspects of Southwestern Paleoepidemiology.* Anthropological Reports, No. 2. Prescott, Ariz.: Prescott College Press.

Ladd, Edmund. 1991. Comments. In *The Anasazi: Where Did They Go?,* ed. J. Judge. Dolores, Colo.: Bureau of Land Management Series Press. Pp. 25–28.

Lang, R. 1977. *Archaeological Survey of the Upper San Cristobal Arroyo Drainage, Galisteo Basin, New Mexico.* Santa Fe: School of American Research Contract Archaeology Program Report No. 37.

Larsen, C. S., and G. R. Milner, eds. *In the Wake of Contact: Biological Responses to Conquest.* New York: Wiley-Liss.

LeBlanc, S. A. 1999. *Prehistoric Warfare in the American Southwest.* Salt Lake City: University of Utah Press.

Lycett, Mark. 1995. Archaeological Implications of European Contact: Demography, Settlement, and Land Use in the Middle Rio Grande Valley, New Mexico. Ph.D. thesis, Department of Anthropology, University of New Mexico, Albuquerque.

Malville, N. J. 1989. Two fragmented human bone assemblages from Yellow Jacket, southwestern Colorado. *The Kiva* 55(1):3–22.

Martin, D. L. 1995. Stress profiles for the prehistoric Southwest. In *Themes in Southwest Prehistory,* ed. G. Gumerman. Santa Fe, N. Mex.: School of American Research Press. Pp. 87–108.

Martin, D. L., A. H. Goodman, G. J. Armelagos, and A. L. Magennis. 1991. *Black Mesa Anasazi Health: Reconstructing Life from Patterns of Death and Disease.* Southern Illinois University at Carbondale, Center for Archaeological Investigations, Occasional Paper No. 14.

Maxwell, T. 1995. A comparative study of prehistoric farming strategies. In *Soil, Water, Biology and Belief in Prehistoric and Traditional Southwestern Agriculture,* ed. H. W. Toll. Albuquerque: New Mexico Archaeology Council Special Publication No. 2. Pp. 3–12.

Maxwell, T., and K. F. Anschuetz. 1992. The Southwestern ethnographic record and prehistoric agricultural diversity. In *Gardens in Prehistory: The Archaeology of Settlement Agriculture in Greater Mesoamerica,* ed. T. W. Killion. Tuscaloosa: University of Alabama Press. Pp. 35–68.

McGuire, R. H. 1986. Economies and modes of production in the prehistoric Southwestern periphery. In *Ripples in the Chichimec Sea,* ed. F. J. Mathien and R. H. McGuire. Carbondale: Southern Illinois University Press. Pp. 243–269.

Moore, W. M., M. M. Silverberg, and M. S. Read. 1972. *Nutrition, Growth and Development of North American Indian Children.* DHEW Publication No. 72–26 (NIH). Washington, D. C.: U. S. Government Printing Office.

Morris, E. H. 1939. *Archaeological Studies in the La Plata District.* Washington, D. C.: Carnegie Institute.

Nelson, N. C. 1914. Pueblo Ruins of the Galisteo Basin, New Mexico. *Anthropological Papers of the American Museum of Natural History* 15(1).

1916. Chronology of the Tano ruins, New Mexico. *American Anthropologist* 18:159–180.

Nelson, B. A., D. L. Martin, A. C. Swedlund, P. R. Fish, and G. J. Armelagos. 1992. Studies in disruption: Demography and health in the prehistoric American Southwest. In *Understanding Complexity in the Prehistoric Southwest*, ed. G. J. Gumerman and M. Gell-Mann. Chicago: Addison-Wesley. Pp. 59–112.

Naquatewa, E. 1967. *The Truth of a Hopi: Stories Relating to the Origin, Myths, and Clan Histories of the Hopi.* Flagstaff, Ariz.: Museum of Northern Arizona Press.

Nickens, P. R. 1975. Prehistoric cannibalism in the Mancos Canyon, southwestern Colorado. *Southwestern Lore* 41(3):13–26.

Ogilvie, M. D., and C. E. Hinton. 1993. Analysis of selected human skeletal material from Sites 423-124 and -131. In N. P. Hermann, M. D. Ogilvie, C. E. Hinton, and K. L. Brown, eds., *Across the Colorado Plateau: Anthropological Studies for the Transwestern Pipeline Expansion Project*, vol. 18. Albuquerque: Office of Contract Archaeology and Maxwell Museum of Anthropology. Pp. 97–128.

Palkovich, A. M. 1984. Agriculture, marginal environments, and nutritional stress in the prehistoric Southwest. In *Paleopathology at the Origins of Agriculture*, ed. M. N. Cohen and G. J. Armelagos. New York: Academic Press. Pp. 425–461.

1987. Endemic disease patterns on paleopathology: Porotic hyperostosis. *American Journal of Physical Anthropology* 74:527–538.

Pérez de Ribas, A. 1645 [1999]. *History of the Triumphs of Our Holy Faith Amongst the Most Fierce and Barbarous Peoples of the New World.* A critical, English-language edition by D. T. Reff, M. Ahern, and R. Danford. Tucson: University of Arizona Press.

Peterson, K. L., and J. D. Orcutt, compilers. 1987. *Dolores Archaeological Program Supporting Studies: Settlement and Environment.* Denver, Colo.: Bureau of Reclamation Engineering and Research Center.

Powell, S. 1983. *Mobility and Adaptation: The Anasazi of Black Mesa, Arizona.* Carbondale: Southern Illinois University Press.

Reff, D. T. 1987. The introduction of smallpox in the greater Southwest. *American Anthropologist* 91(1): 174–175.

1991. *Disease, Depopulation and Culture Change in Northwestern New Spain, 1520–1764.* Salt Lake City: University of Utah Press.

1991a. Anthropological analysis of exploration texts: Cultural discourse and the ethnological import of Fray Marcos de Niza's journey to Cibola. *American Anthropologist* 93: 636–655.

1993. An alternative explanation of subsistence change during the early historic period at Pecos Pueblo. *American Antiquity* 58(3):563–564.

1999. Critical introduction: The Historia and Jesuit discourse. In *History of the Triumphs of Our Holy Faith Amongst the Most Fierce and Barbarous Peoples of the New World*, trans. D. T. Reff, M. Ahern, and R. Danford. Tucson: University of Arizona Press. Pp. 11–46.

Reinhard, K. J. 1988. Cultural ecology of prehistoric parasitism on the Colorado Plateau as evidenced by coprology. *American Journal of Physical Anthropology* 77:355–366.

1990. Archaeoparasitology in North America. *American Journal of Physical Anthropology* 82: 145–163.

Riley, C. L. 1975. The road to Hawikuh: Trade and trade routes to Cibola-Zuni during late prehistoric and early historic times. *The Kiva* 41: 137–159.

1995. *Rio Del Norte*. Albuquerque: University of New Mexico Press.

Sale, K. 1991. *The Conquest of Paradise*. New York: Penguin Books.

Schlanger, S. H. 1987. Population studies. In *Dolores Archaeological Program Final Synthetic Report*, compiled by D. A. Breternitz, C. K. Robinson, and G. T. Gross. Denver, Colo.: Bureau of Reclamation Engineering and Research Center. Pp. 493–524.

Schroeder, A. 1972. Rio Grande enthnohistory. In *New Perspectives on the Pueblos*, ed. Alfonso Ortiz. Albuquerque: University of New Mexico Press. Pp. 41–70.

Shafer, S. B. and P. T. Furst. 1996. Introduction. In *People of the Peyote: Huichol Indian History, Religion and Survival*, ed. S. B. Shafer and P. T. Furst. Albuquerque: University of New Mexico Press. Pp.1–25.

Sheridan, T., and N. Parezo. 1996. *Paths of Life: American Indians of the Southwest and Northern Mexico*. Tucson: University of Arizona Press.

Simmons, M. 1979. History of Pueblo-Spanish relations to 1821. In *Handbook of North American Indians*, vol. 9, *Southwest*, ed. A. Ortiz. Washington D.C.: Smithsonian Institution Press. Pp. 236–255.

Smith, Watson C., Richard B. Woodbury, and Nathalie F. S. Woodbury. 1966. *The Excavation of Hawikuh by Frederick Webb Hodge. Report of the Hendricks-Hodge Expedition.* Contributions of the Museum of the American Indian, Heye Foundation, vol. 20. New York: Museum of the American Indian.

Snow, D. H. 1981. Protohistoric Rio Grande Pueblo economics: A review of trends. In *The Protohistoric Period in the North American Southwest, AD 1450–1700*, ed. D. R. Wilcox and W. B. Masse. Tempe: Arizona State University Anthropological Research Papers No. 24. Pp. 354–377.

Stodder, A. L. W. 1984. Paleoepidemiology of the Mesa Verde Region Anasazi. M. A. thesis, Department of Anthropology, University of Colorado, Boulder.

1987. The physical anthropology and mortuary behavior of the Dolores Anasazi: An early Pueblo population in local and regional context. In *Dolores Archaeological Program Supporting Studies: Settlement and Environment*. Compiled by K. L. Petersen and J. L. Orcutt. Denver, Colo.: U.S. Bureau of Reclamation Engineering and Research Center. Pp. 339–504.

1990. Paleoepidemiology of Eastern and Western Pueblo Communities in Protohistoric New Mexico. Ph.D. diss., Department of Anthropology, University of Colorado, Boulder.

1994. Bioarchaeological investigations of protohistoric Pueblo health and demography. In *In the Wake of Contact: Biological Responses to Conquest*, ed. C. S. Larsen and G. R. Milner. New York: Wiley-Liss. Pp. 97–107.

1996. Paleoepidemiology of eastern and western Pueblo communities in protohistoric and early contact period New Mexico. In *Disease and Biocultural Frontiers: Native American Adaptation in the Spanish Borderlands*, ed. B. J. Baker and L. Kealhofer. Gainesville: University of Florida Press. Pp.148–176.

1998. Bone by Bone, Pueblo by Pueblo: Reviewing the Evidence for Treponemal Infection in the Prehistoric Southwest. Presented at the 67th Annual Meeting of the American Association of Physical Anthropologists, Salt Lake City, Utah.

1999. Bioarchaeology of the Basin and Range Region. In *Bioarchaeology of the South Central United States*, ed. Jerome C. Rose. Fayetteville: Arkansas Archeological Survey Report No. 55. Pp. 184–220.

Stodder, A. L. W., and Debra L. Martin. 1992. Native health and disease in the prehistoric Southwest before and after Spanish contact. In *Disease and Demography in the Americas: Changing Patterns Before and After 1492*, ed. J. Verano and D. Ubelaker. Washington, D. C.: Smithsonian Institution Press. Pp. 55–73.

Sumner, D. R. 1985. A probable case of tuberculosis from northeastern Arizona. In *Health and Disease in the Prehistoric Southwest*, ed. C. F. Merbs and R. J. Miller. Anthropological Research Papers, No. 34. Tempe: Arizona State University Press. Pp. 340–346.

Swardstedt, T. 1966. *Odontological Aspects of a Medieval Swedish Population in the Province of Jamtland/Mid-Sweden.* Stockholm: Tiden-Barnangen AB.

Turner, C. G., and J. A. Turner. 1999. *Man Corn: Cannibalism and Violence in the Prehistoric American Southwest.* Salt Lake City: University of Utah Press.

Upham, S. 1982. *Polities and Power: An Economic and Political History of the Western Pueblo.* New York: Academic Press.

——— 1986. Smallpox and climate in the American Southwest. *American Anthropologist* 88: 115–128.

Verano, J. W., and D. H. Ubelaker, ed. 1992. *Disease and Demography in the Americas.* Washington, D. C.: Smithsonian Institution Press.

Walker, P. L. 1985. Anemia among prehistoric Indians of the American Southwest. In *Health and Disease in the Prehistoric Southwest*, ed. C. F. Merbs and R. J. Miller. Tempe: Arizona State University Anthropological Research Papers No. 34. Pp. 139–163.

Watson, P. J., S. A. LeBlanc, and C. B. Redman. 1980. Aspects of Zuni prehistory: Preliminary report on excavations in the El Morro Valley, New Mexico. *Journal of Field Archaeology* 7: 201–218.

Wilcox, D. 1981. Changing perspectives on the protohistoric Pueblos, A.D. 1450–1700. In *The Protohistoric Period in the North American Southwest, AD 1450–1700*, ed. D. R. Wilcox and W. B. Masse. Tempe: Arizona State University Anthropological Research Papers No. 24. Pp. 378–410.

Wilcox, D. R., and J. Haas. 1994. The scream of the butterfly: Competition and conflict in the prehistoric Southwest. In *Themes in Southwest Prehistory*, ed. G. J. Gumerman. Santa Fe, N. Mex.: School of American Research Press. Pp. 211–238.

CHAPTER SEVENTEEN

Health, Nutrition, and Demographic Change in Native California

Phillip L. Walker and Russell Thornton

ABSTRACT

Before the arrival of Europeans, California was inhabited by Native Americans with a diverse array of cultural adaptations that varied markedly through time and space. A few regional differences and weak temporal trends can be discerned in the health status of California's prehistoric inhabitants. However, the overall pattern suggested by the available bioarchaeological data is one in which health conditions greatly diverged through time within different geographical areas. Short-term declines in health status linked to fluctuations in local environmental productivity appear to have been common. Skeletal studies suggest a tendency during the prehistoric period toward declining health among the inhabitants of the densely populated Santa Barbara Channel and Sacramento Valley regions. In both areas, evidence of growth disruption and infectious disease increases significantly between the Early and Late Periods. Skeletal data and paleoenvironmental records suggested that in some areas, living conditions declined substantially around the end of the first millennium owing to climate-induced fluctuations in marine and terrestrial productivity. Although conditions improved significantly in some areas during the Late Period, the arrival of Europeans marked the beginning of a spectacular population decline. By the end of the nineteenth century, the combined effects of epidemics, genocide, and social disruption had reduced the once-thriving Californian Indian population to a few thousand individuals. During the last half of the twentieth century there has been a remarkable reversal of this trend toward population decline, owing to improved living conditions on reservations and the immigration of large numbers of Indians from other states to California's urban centers.

INTRODUCTION

The goal of this chapter is to provide a broad historical perspective on changes in the health, nutrition, and demography of California's population from the arrival of its earliest Paleo-Indian colonists until the present. Although some comparative data are available for nineteenth-century Euro-American skeletons, most of our bioarchaeological evidence derives from prehistoric Native American burials.

Owing to the widespread practice of cremation by California Indians, large skeletal collections are only available from a few areas. Consequently, our knowledge of spatial variations in health and nutrition is very incomplete. Skeletal collections large enough to allow a statistical analysis of temporal variation in health and nutrition are only available from the densely populated Santa Barbara Channel and Sacramento River Valley areas. Because high population densities contribute to the maintenance and spread of infectious disease, the health of Indians in these areas may differ from that of people who lived in more sparsely populated areas.

As will be clear from the data we present, health conditions varied markedly through time within the same geographical area. Although some trends can be discerned, short-term declines in health status linked to fluctuations in local environmental productivity appear to have been common. This spatial–temporal variation makes sweeping generalization about regional differences in health impossible. Since most of our data are from Santa Barbara Channel area sites, we will focus our discussion on the health and nutrition of the Indians who lived in this area of Southern California. When additional data are available, comparisons will be made with Euro-Americans and Native Californians from other areas of the state. Finally, data on the health status of the Native Californians in our sample will be compared with that of other populations included in the Health and Nutrition in the Western Hemisphere project.

For this overview, it is useful to divide the history of California into Paleo-Indian (pre–9000 BC), Early (9000–1000 BC), Middle (1000 BC–AD 1250), Late (AD 1250–AD 1782), and Historic Periods. These divisions of a continuous historical process are to some extent arbitrary, since the tempo of cultural change varied markedly in different areas of California. However, they do provide a useful framework for describing major socioeconomic changes that occurred throughout the state. Because some of the cemeteries we have studied were used for many generations, it is common for them to contain burials from more than one period. To accommodate these uncertainties, when necessary, we have grouped collections from different periods (Table 17.1). For example, many cemeteries were used throughout the Middle and Late Periods.

Table 17.1: Chronological Groupings and Numbers of Burials Examined

Period	Approximate dates	Native Americans		Euro-Americans
		Southern California	Northern California	
Historic Period	AD 1870–AD 1782	159		102
Late Period	AD 1782–AD 1250	1125	0	0
Late Middle Period	AD 1250–AD 500	417	233	0
Middle and Late	AD 1782–600 BC	354	217	0
Middle Period	AD 1250–600 BC	266	0	0
Early Period	1050 BC–5550 BC	491	0	0
Unknown	Prehistoric?	100	47	0

AN OVERVIEW OF CALIFORNIA PREHISTORY

Although a few researchers believe that people arrived in California more than 20,000 years ago (Orr 1968; Berger 1980), most archaeologists find the evidence of such an early occupation unconvincing (Glassow 1980:81; Moratto 1984). The earliest generally accepted evidence for the human occupation of California consists of a few sites containing large, fluted projectile points of a type that has been firmly dated elsewhere in North America to 10,000–9000 BC. Additional evidence for the presence of humans in California at this time comes from radiocarbon dates on human bone (Johnson et al. 1999) and deeply stratified cultural deposits (Erlandson et al. 1996). Most of these early sites are located in areas containing many large, shallow lakes during Paleo-Indian times. These lakes undoubtedly attracted migratory waterfowl and large game animals. The early Californians who exploited these resources probably lived in small, highly mobile groups with an economy that emphasized big-game hunting and the gathering of plant foods (Morotto 1984:29–70). The health status of people during this period is unknown, owing to the almost complete lack of skeletal material. However, because of their low population densities and the abundance of food in a recently colonized environment, it seems likely that living conditions were quite good.

During the Early Period, California Indians underwent a fundamental adaptive shift. An economic emphasis on big-game hunting was gradually replaced by economies that were heavily dependent on seed collecting (Wallace 1978:25). This economic transformation was, in part, a response to the environmental changes associated with the end of the Pleistocene. The lakes of Southern California gradually dried up because of reduced rainfall, and there was a concomitant decrease in the availability of big-game animals. This, along with other environmental changes, forced California Indians to diversify their subsistence strategies. The result was an economic emphasis on exploiting a broad range of plant and animal resources.

At the beginning of the Early Period, most of the state's population was concentrated in Southern California. During the next 5,000 years California Indians gradually evolved a broad spectrum of economic strategies that allowed them to occupy all but the most inhospitable areas of the state. Important advances were made in seed-processing technology during the Early Period. Sites begin to contain large numbers of loaf-shaped manos and flat milling stones that, based on ethnographic accounts, appear to have been used to grind hard seeds from chaparral and grassland plants. Between 4,000 and 5,000 years ago, mortars and pestles begin to appear in sites throughout the state. Ethnographic data suggest that these tools were primarily for acorn processing.

Studies of the frequency of different types of pathological conditions show that, in most respects, the health of people who lived during the Early Period was better than that of later populations. However, skeletal evidence does suggest that periods of seasonal starvation may have been more common than they were during the Late Period (McHenry 1968; Dickel et al. 1984).

By the beginning of the Middle Period, about 3,000 years ago, opportunities for continued population growth through territorial expansion had greatly diminished.

Instead, California Indians began to modify Early Period economic systems to allow more people to be supported within the areas they already occupied. New subsistence techniques were introduced and existing technologies refined. New forms of social organization that facilitated the exchange of food, manufactured goods, and raw materials were adopted. Instead of moving seasonally to exploit locally abundant resources, people increasingly began to focus their lives around permanent villages.

The way in which this economic intensification was accomplished varied according to the resources available in each area. For example, the Indians of the Santa Barbara Channel area became heavily dependent on marine resources, and people living in Central California intensified their use of acorns.

Settlement-pattern data show that California Indians became more sedentary during the Middle Period. As local population densities increased, the feasibility of moving over large areas on a seasonal round decreased. Gradually, people began to focus their activities around large, permanently occupied villages. This increased sedentism was made possible in part by the development of trade networks that facilitated the exchange of manufactured goods and locally abundant natural resources (Ericson 1977; C. King 1981). The diverse array of California Indian cultures described by early European explorers represented a continuation of these Middle Period trends toward increased economic specialization and trade.

The arrival of Europeans marked the beginning of a new phase of California Indian history. The process of cultural differentiation we have described was abruptly terminated by the death and cultural disruption of the contact period. These cataclysmic events posed a new set of adaptive challenges. What is now the State of California had a large, dense aboriginal native population. Although scholarly estimates vary widely, a contact population of 310,000 to 705,000 seems the best acceptable estimate we have today (Thornton 1980; Ubelaker 1988). Whatever the precise figure, demographers do agree that the California Indian population suffered a catastrophic decline following the arrival of Europeans and Euro-Americans (Figure 17.1). This demographic collapse occurred somewhat later in California than in most other regions of the United States, and the complex set of reasons for the population decline is unique. The primary causes of the decline of California's Native American population were: 1) the introduction of such epidemic diseases from Europe and Africa as smallpox, measles, malaria, cholera, typhus, and, syphilis; 2) the effects of the mission system; and 3) the Euro-American destruction of traditional patterns of subsistence, which not only produced starvation but was accompanied by warfare, raids, and outright genocide. These disruptive influences increased mortality rates and lowered fertility, and the population declined accordingly. The result was also a virtual collapse of Indian societies and cultures, a collapse preventing virtually any demographic recovery of California Indians until well into the twentieth century.

The decline in the California Indian population differs from that in most areas of the present-day United States for some basic reasons. First, the decline in California occurred relatively later, probably primarily during the nineteenth century; this was a result of the relative isolation of the area until the late 1700s and early

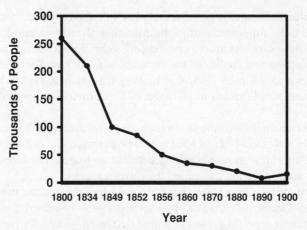

Figure 17.1. Decline of the American Indian population of California, between 1800–1900. *Sources*: Powers (1877: 416); Merriam (1905: 60); U.S. Bureau of the Census (1915: 10, 112); Mooney (1928: 19); Cook (1976: 69–71, 1978: 91); Stanley and Thomas (1978: 114); Thornton (1987: 109); Ubelaker (1988).

1800s. Second, epidemic diseases derived from Europe and Africa, while extremely important in California, were perhaps relatively less important than in many other regions of the United States; however, venereal diseases, especially syphilis, were probably relatively more important in California than elsewhere. Third, the mission system, introduced to control, colonize, and (theoretically) convert the inhabitants of an area, produced significant population decline (often in interaction with diseases, venereal and otherwise). Fourth, starvation among California Indians was most likely more widespread than in most areas of the United States, as traditional subsistence patterns were quickly destroyed. Fifth, vigilante raids and blatant genocide were surely more important in reducing native populations in California than elsewhere in North America. And, finally, sixth, the aftermath of population destruction was somewhat atypical, in that most California Indians were simply left "on their own" after their demographic, social, and cultural destruction. One result was that many became integrated as "wage laborers" at the very lowest rung of the of late-nineteenth-century California economic structure.

Depending on what one selects as the baseline population, the Indian population of California was still somewhat intact by the beginning of the nineteenth century, primarily because of its relative isolation. Dating from the first few decades of the nineteenth century, however, and extending to the latter decades of the century, the Indian population underwent a rapid decline. As also shown in Figure 17.1, the California Indian population reached its nadir around 1900: the Indian population totaled only slightly more than 15,000 at that time (with the non-Indian population of California being some 1.47 million). Since the beginning of the twentieth century, some population recovery has occurred (Figure 17.2): the 1980 U.S. census enumerated almost 200,000 American Indians in California (out of a total population of some 23.67 million). Perhaps only about one-fifth of this population, however, and surely no more than one-half of it, are the descendants of indigenous

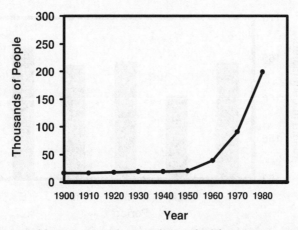

Figure 17.2. Recovery of the American Indian population of California, 1900 to 1980. The increase after 1960 in part reflects the migration of significant numbers of Indians to California. *Sources*: see Figure 17.1.

California Indians; the majority are Indians who migrated into the state from other areas, or their descendants.

California thus has a large, unique, and highly diverse American Indian population, the largest of any state. It is composed of both American Indians indigenous to the state and American Indians who have migrated there. A large proportion of this population are urban American Indians, but a significant proportion are rural and/or reservation and "rancheria" American Indians. A virtual one-third of all the tribes recognized by the U.S. government are located in California. This is remarkable in light of the tremendous demographic, social, and cultural destruction experienced by California Indians during the history of the state.

VARIATION IN HEALTH AND NUTRITION

Although systematic attempts to analyze spatial and temporal variation in health and nutrition based on California skeletal collections are in their infancy, a few patterns seem clear. We will first discuss the data we have on the population history of the Channel Island area, which is the source of our largest skeletal series. The Channel Island population will then be compared with contemporaneous Native Americans living in Northern California. Finally, the health and nutrition of Native Californians will be compared with that of the nineteenth-century Euro-American colonists who displaced them.

Body Size

In the Channel Islands area, there is a gradual decrease in body size during the Middle Period, with especially small statures during the Late Middle Period (Figure 17.3). There is little evidence of large-scale movement of people into the Santa Barbara

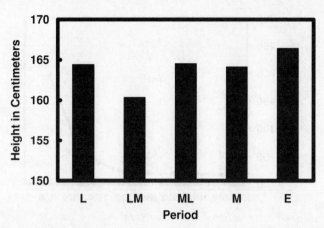

Figure 17.3. Temporal variation in height estimated from long bone lengths. Period abbreviations: L = Late Period, LM = Late Middle Period, ML = Middle and Late Period, M = Middle Period, E = Early Period. Chronological information on each period is provided in Table 17.1.

Channel area after its initial colonization. This temporal variation in stature, therefore, appears to be a result of in situ responses to the local environment instead of external influences. The Late Middle Period was a time of unstable environmental conditions and high levels of warfare and violence. It seems likely that the small stature of people during this period reflects stunting owing to these unfavorable environmental conditions (Walker and Lambert 1989). During the late prehistoric period, statures increase significantly, perhaps owing to improved living conditions. Although historic period collections are too small and poorly preserved to provide reliable stature estimates, comparisons of long bone diameters and tooth dimensions indicate that body size decreased significantly after the establishment of the mission system. Although a size reduction relative to precontact times is seen in collections from historic cemeteries (Walker et al. 1996), the largest size reduction appears to have occurred after the local Indians moved to the missions (Walker et al. 1989b).

These changes in body size are in some respects paralleled by changes in sexual dimorphism. Sex differences in stature decrease markedly during the Late Middle Period and then increase again during the Late Period (Figure 17.4). Data from the mission-period cemetery at Malibu suggest that sexual dimorphism in tooth size and some long bone dimensions decreased again when the local Indians began to interact more intensively with European colonists (Walker et al. 1996b).

Diet and Dental Health

Paleopathological and isotopic data suggest that the diets of California Indians varied regionally through time. For example, in the Santa Barbara Channel area, the shift from hunting and gathering to an economy based on intensive marine-resource exploitation is accompanied by a decrease in dental caries (Figure 17.5,

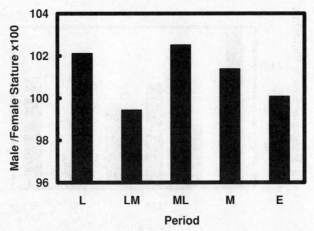

Figure 17.4. Temporal variation in sexual dimorphism. Stature estimates are based on long bone lengths. Period abbreviations: L = Late Period, LM = Late Middle Period, ML = Middle and Late Period, M = Middle Period, E = Early Period. Chronological information on each period is provided in Table 17.1.

Walker and Erlandson 1986) and tooth wear rates (Walker 1978). These changes are paralleled by a shift in the stable isotope concentrations in bone that suggest increasing dependence on protein derived from marine animals. On the Northern Channel Islands, these dietary changes appear to have affected men and women differently. Dental pathological and isotopic studies suggest that during the Early Period, the diets of women were more terrestrially oriented and less variable than those of men (Walker and DeNiro 1986; Walker et al. 1989a).

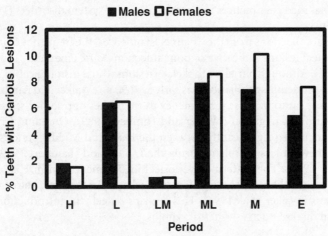

Figure 17.5. Temporal variation in dental caries rates in the Santa Barbara Channel area sites. Period abbreviations: H = Historic Period, L = Late Period, LM = Late Middle Period, ML = Middle and Late Period, M = Middle Period, E = Early Period.

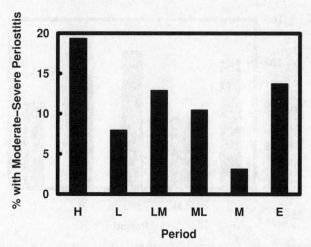

Figure 17.6. The percent of individuals with tibias affected by moderate to severe osteoperiostitis in Santa Barbara Channel area sites. Period abbreviations: H = Historic Period, L= Late Period, LM = Late Middle Period, ML = Middle and Late Period, M = Middle Period, E = Early Period.

Infectious Disease

Paleopathological studies show that bone lesions like those we now associate with streptococcal or staphylococcal infections were fairly common in some California Indian populations (cf. Roney 1959, 1966; Suchey et al. 1972). There is also evidence that tuberculosis, coccidioidomycosis, and treponematosis were present in prehistoric California (Roney 1959; Cybulski 1980; Hoffman 1987). Based on skeletal evidence for anemia, it seems likely that blood loss through gastrointestinal infections and water contamination were a health concern for some populations (Walker 1986). The prevalence of such problems is perhaps also suggested by elaboration of traditional medical practices for treating digestive system disorders (Walker and Hudson 1993).

In skeletal collections from the Channel Islands area, the frequency of individuals with periosteal lesions indicative of bone infections varies markedly through time (Figure 17.6). Although burials with skeletal lesions whose histological appearance is suggestive of endemic syphilis occur as early as 4600 BP (Walker and Lambert, 1998), such cases appear to increase in frequency during times of resource stress, warfare, and population aggregation (Walker and Lambert 1989). On Santa Cruz Island, periostitis increased significantly between the Early and Middle Periods and then became somewhat less prevalent during the Late Period (Lambert 1989; Lambert and Walker 1991). The pattern of periosteal involvement seen in Historic Period skeletons from Malibu appears to differ somewhat from that seen before the arrival of Europeans (Walker et al. 1996). This perhaps reflects the introduction of a new treponemal disease, such as venereal syphilis.

Warfare and Violence

Skeletal studies of the frequency of wounds inflicted by clubs, spears, and arrows clearly show that patterns of warfare and violence varied both regionally and through

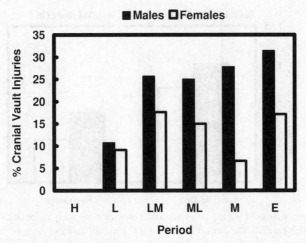

Figure 17.7. Percent of Santa Barbara Channel area crania with nonlethal depressed fractures of the cranial vault. Period abbreviations: H = Historic Period, L = Late Period, LM = Late Middle Period, ML = Middle and Late Period, M = Middle Period, E = Early Period.

time in prehistoric California. This is consistent with ethnographic evidence of marked intertribal variation in the prevalence of warfare and violence (Kroeber 1925; McCorkle 1978). Significant differences can be seen even within the territory of a single group. For example, in the Santa Barbara Channel area, nonlethal cranial injuries possibly associated with a local form of nonlethal dispute resolution are much more common than they are among members of the same tribe who lived on the mainland coast (Walker 1989, 1996).

Temporal variation in patterns of violence is also apparent. In the Santa Barbara Channel area, the frequency of nonlethal cranial injuries appears to decrease through time (Figure 17.7). This change in skeletal evidence for violence appears to be associated with the introduction of the bow and arrow. Beginning around AD 500, the bow and arrow started to be adopted by Native Californians, and it rapidly replaced clubs and spear throwers in warfare (Moratto 1984). This change in weapons technology coincided with the beginning of a period of fluctuating climatic conditions and increased violence (Moratto 1984:213–214; Walker et al. 1989b; Walker and Lambert 1989; Lambert 1994). In the Santa Barbara Channel area, the Late Middle Period was an especially violent time. For example, at the Calleguas Creek site, which dates from this time, more than 10 percent of the adult population shows evidence of arrow wounds (Walker and Lambert 1989).

Regional Comparisons

Although most of our skeletal data are from the Channel Islands area, information is also available on several Late Middle Period skeletal collections from the Sacramento Delta area of Northern California. Comparisons of these collections with roughly contemporaneous Late Middle Period collections from the Channel Islands area provide evidence for significant regional differences in health and nutrition.

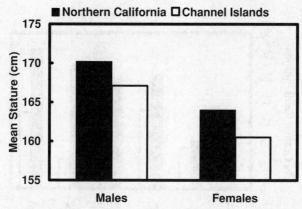

Figure 17.8. Comparison of stature estimates based on long bone lengths for Native Californians living during the Late Middle Period in northern California and the Channel Islands area of Southern California.

Long bone dimensions show that the stature of the Northern California population was significantly greater than that of their Southern California contemporaries (Figure 17.8). It seems unlikely that this regional variation in stature is entirely a product of environmental factors, such as diet or disease. Penutian-speaking people, who entered California later than the Hokan-speaking people of the Santa Barbara Channel area, occupied the Sacramento Delta. These stature differences may, therefore, reflect genetic as well as environmental differences between the two populations.

This interpretation is reinforced by an analysis of health indexes, such as the frequency of teeth with hypoplastic lesions (Figure 17.9). Based on these data, it

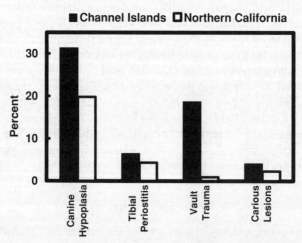

Figure 17.9. Comparison of health indexes for Native Californians living during the Late Middle Period in Northern California and the Channel Islands area of Southern California. Values for carious lesions are the percent of teeth with carious lesions. All other values are the percent of individuals affected. The values for tibial periostitis are for individuals with moderate to severe lesions.

appears that the health status of people living in Northern California was somewhat better than that of people living in Southern California during the Late Middle Period. This is the opposite of what would be predicted if the regional differences in stature were environmental in origin.

There is a striking difference between the Channel Island and Northern California collections in the frequency of healed cranial injuries (Figure 17.9). Such injuries are rare in the Northern Californians and exceptionally common among the Channel Islanders. The magnitude of this difference suggests that patterns of interpersonal violence sometimes varied markedly in contemporaneous California Indian groups.

Comparisons of Native Californians and Euro-Americans

Euro-Americans began moving into California in large numbers beginning in the mid-nineteenth century. Although our data on these immigrants is limited to observations of about 100 skeletons from mid-nineteenth-century cemeteries (Table 17.1), some striking differences between them and the Native Californians they displaced are nevertheless apparent.

First, the Euro-Americans who moved to California were much taller than Native Americans they encountered there (Figure 17.10). The average stature of male colonists was more than 174cm, which is nearly 8 centimeters greater than the male average for our California Indian sample. These heights are large in comparison to those of other nineteenth-century Euro-Americans (Steckel 1995). This suggests the possibility that the nineteenth-century Americans who moved to California were either unrepresentative of the American population as a whole or that the children of these immigrants experienced environmental conditions favorable to their growth and development.

Although the large body size of the colonists might be taken as an indication of good health, other indexes suggest that their health was poorer than that of

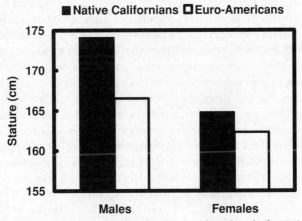

Figure 17.10. Comparison of stature estimates based on long bone lengths for Native Californians and nineteenth-century Euro-American immigrants to California.

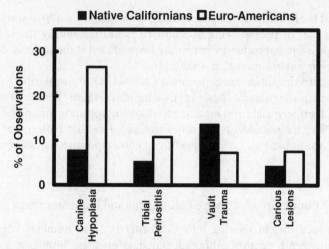

Figure 17.11. Comparison of health indexes for Native Californians and nineteenth-century Euro-American immigrants to California. Values for carious lesions are the percent of teeth with carious lesions. All other values are the percent of individuals affected. The values for tibial periostitis are for individuals with moderate to severe lesions.

Native Californians they displaced (Figure 17.11). The higher caries rate of the colonists undoubtedly reflects the access the settlers had to sugar and other refined carbohydrates. They also had more hypoplastic teeth and a higher frequency of moderate and severe periosteal lesions.

Western Hemisphere Comparisons

The Health and Nutrition in the Western Hemisphere database provides an unprecedented opportunity to compare the health status of ancient Native Californians with that of Native Americans living elsewhere in the New World. Such comparisons are of special interest because through hunting, gathering, and fishing, Native Californians were able to maintain population densities comparable to those of agriculturalists living elsewhere in the New World. Many bioarchaeological studies have shown a decline in health associated with the shift from hunting and gathering to agriculture. This is typically explained in terms of a decrease in the quality of the diet, owing to heavy dependence on a small number of cultigens and demographic changes that facilitated the spread of infectious disease, such as increases in sedentism, village size, population density, and level of intervillage interaction. Many of these same demographic changes occurred in the absence of agriculture in such areas of California as the Santa Barbara Channel region. Our California data, therefore, have the potential to give insights into the relative significance of dietary and demography variables as causes of the decline in health seen with the shift from hunting and gathering to a more sedentary village life.

The comparative value of the data from Native Californians is illustrated by the light they shed on skeletal evidence of iron-deficiency anemia (porotic hyperostosis and cribra orbitalia). An increased prevalence of anemia in American Indian populations with the shift from hunting and gathering to agriculture is often attributed to the nutritional deficiencies of a low-iron, low-protein, corn-based diet (Walker 1985). The health status of the agricultural populations sampled in the Health and Nutrition in the Western Hemisphere database lend credence to this hypothesis; the anemia index shows that those groups that depended heavily on maize as a dietary staple experienced more anemia than hunter-gatherers or people who practiced mixed agriculture. However, our comparative data from the Santa Barbara Channel area shows that heavy maize dependence per se is not a sufficient explanation of the variation in the prevalence of anemia seen in Native American populations. Skeletal evidence of anemia is just as common among some of the Indians of the Northern Channel Islands whose diet was composed mainly of fish and other iron-rich marine resources as it is among maize-dependent agriculturalists. This contrasts with the rarity of lesions associated with anemia among the Indians of the mainland, whose diet contained a larger proportion of iron-deficient plant foods (Walker 1985). These data suggest that the etiology of iron-deficiency anemia is complicated and that its prevalence depends upon multiple factors, with iron availability in the diet being only one. For example, the Northern Channel Island data suggest that iron loss associated with diarrheal disease and other infections may be just as important in the etiology of the condition as an iron-deficient diet.

Judging from the average summary health index score of 76.9 for the Native Californians in our sample, their health status was somewhat better than that of Native Americans who practiced intensive maize agriculture (average index = 68.9), but worse than that of other hunter-gatherers (average index = 82.1). This is not surprising in view of the unusual nature of the hunter-gatherer adaptations in the populations studied (intensive exploitation of acorns and riverine resources in Northern California, and intensive use of marine resources in the Santa Barbara Channel area). These subsistence strategies allowed for the maintenance of large, semisedentary village populations. Although village life produces many social and economic advantages that are unavailable to smaller groups, our data clearly show that it also has its health costs.

CONCLUSIONS

Skeletal studies show that overall, the health of people living in the densely populated Santa Barbara Channel and Sacramento Valley areas declined during the prehistoric period (Schulz 1981; Dickel et al. 1984; Walker 1986, 1989, 1990; Walker et al. 1989b; Lambert 1989). In both areas, evidence of growth disruption and infectious disease increases significantly between the Early and Late Periods. This decline in health appears to be largely a result of increased exposure to pathogens. As population densities and sedentism increased, so did the opportunities for the maintenance and spread of infectious disease. Concentrating people in one place not only creates sanitation problems, but it also provides an environment favorable to the spread of parasites and other pathogens.

In both areas, the socioeconomic changes of the Middle Period had significant health consequences. In Central California, there is evidence that the frequency of episodes of acute growth disruption decreased during the Middle Period (McHenry and Schulz 1978; Schulz 1981; Dickel et al. 1984). This has been interpreted as evidence that greater year-round economic security was one of the results of the heavy emphasis on acorn exploitation that evolved in this area during the Middle Period. In the Santa Barbara Channel area, the shift to more intensive use of marine resources may also have resulted in greater economic security. However, age-controlled studies of arthritis suggest that this was accomplished through an increase in workload, especially that of the men (Walker and Hollimon 1989).

Analysis of roughly contemporaneous Late Middle Period collections indicate that living conditions may have been somewhat better in the Sacramento Delta than in the Channel Islands area at this time. Without better temporal control, however, drawing firm conclusions about regional differences in health is impossible. This is because short-term environmental fluctuations can cause living conditions to vary markedly through time.

Our skeletal data show that living conditions declined strikingly at the end of the Middle Period in the Channel Island area. This appears to have been a time of increased warfare and violence throughout California (Moratto 1984:213–214; Walker and Lambert 1989). This increase in violence may in part be explained by drought-induced increases in competition over resources after AD 400 (Walker and Lambert 1989). There is considerable evidence for population movement and cultural disruption at the end of the Middle Period. Many parts of the Central Valley and Sierran foothills were abandoned at this time, and there was also a cessation of trans-Valley trade (Morotto 1984:564).

Although conditions improved significantly in some areas during the Late Period, the arrival of Europeans starting in 1542 marked the beginning of the demographic collapse of the California Indian population. During the last half of the eighteenth century, European colonization of California began in earnest, and this had catastrophic consequences for Native Californians. By the end of the nineteenth century, the combined effects of epidemics, genocide, and social collapse had reduced the once-thriving Californian Indian population to a few thousand individuals.

During the last half of the twentieth century, California's Indian population has experienced a remarkable demographic rebound (Figure 17.2). Although this can to some extent be attributed to improvements in the living conditions and health care available to Native Californians living in rural areas (Walker and Hudson 1993), most of the increase is a result of Indians from other states migrating into California's urban centers.

REFERENCES

Berger, Rainer. 1980. Early Man on Santa Rosa Island. In *The California Islands: Proceedings of a Multi-disciplinary Symposium*, ed. D. Power. Santa Barbara Museum of Natural History, Santa Barbara, Calif.

Cook, Sherburne F. 1976. *The Population of the California Indians, 1969–1970*. Berkeley: University of California Press.

1978. Historical Demography. In Robert F. Heizer, ed., *California*, vol. 8 of *Handbook of North American Indians*, pp. 91–98. Washington, D.C.: Smithsonian Institution.

Cybulski, J. S. 1980. Possible Pre-Columbian Treponematosis on Santa Rosa Island, California. *Canadian Review of Phys. Anthrop.* 2:19–25.

Dickel, David N., Peter D. Schulz, and Henry M. McHenry. 1984. Central California: Prehistoric Subsistence Changes and Health. In *Paleopathology at the Origins of Agriculture*, ed. M. N. Cohen and G. J. Armelagos, pp. 439–461. New York: Academic Press.

Ericson, J. E. 1977. Egalitarian exchange systems in California: A preliminary view. In T. K. Earle and J. E. Ericson, eds., *Exchange Systems in Prehistory*, pp. 109–126. New York: Academic Press.

Erlandson, Jon M., Douglas Kennett, B. Lynn Ingram, Daniel Guthrie, Don Morris, Mark Tveskov, G. James West, and Phillip L. Walker. 1996. An archaeological and paleontological chronology for Daisy Cave (CA-SMI-261), San Miguel Island. *California Radiocarbon* 38(2):355–373.

Glassow, Michael A. 1980. Early Man on Santa Rosa Island. In *The California Islands: Proceedings of a Multi-disciplinary Symposium*, ed. D. Power. Santa Barbara Museum of Natural History, Santa Barbara, Calif.

Hoffman, J. M. 1987. The Descriptive Physical Anthropology of the Cardinal Site, CA-SJO-154: A Late Middle Horizon–Early Phase I Site from Stockton, California. Colorado Springs, Colo.: *Colorado College Publications in Anthropology*, No. 12.

King, Chester. 1981. "The Evolution of Chumash Society: A Comparative Study of Artifacts Used in Social System Maintenance in the Santa Barbara Channel Region before AD 1804." Ph.D. diss., University of California, Davis.

Kroeber, Alfred. 1925. *Handbook of the Indians of California*. Bureau of American Ethnology of the Smithsonian Institution, Bulletin 78, Washington, D.C.

Kroeber, Theodora. 1961. *Ishi in Two Worlds*. Berkeley: University of California Press.

Lambert, Patricia. 1989. "Temporal Variation in the Health Status of the Prehistoric Population of Santa Cruz Island." M.A. thesis, Department of Anthropology, University of California, Santa Barbara.

1994. "War and Peace on the Western Front: A Study of Violent Conflict and its Correlates in Prehistoric Hunter-Gatherer Societies of Coastal Southern California." Unpublished Ph.D. diss., University of California, Santa Barbara.

Lambert, Patricia, and Phillip L. Walker. 1991. Physical Anthropological Evidence for the Evolution of Social Complexity in Coastal Southern California. *Antiquity* 65(249): 963–973.

McCorkle, Thomas. 1978. Intergroup Conflict. In Robert F. Heizer, ed., *Handbook of North American Indians*, vol. 8, *California*, pp. 694–700. Washington, D.C.: Smithsonian Institution.

McHenry, Henry. 1968. Transverse Lines in Long Bones of Prehistoric California Indians. *American Journal of Physical Anthropology* 29:1–18.

McHenry, Henry, and Peter Schulz. 1978. Harris Lines, Enamel Hypoplasia, and Subsistence Change in Prehistoric Central California. In D. R. Touhy, ed., *Selected Papers from the 14th Great Basin Anthropological Conference*, Ballena Press, Socorro Publications in Archaeology, Ethnology and History, No. 11, Menlo Park, Calif.

Merriam, C. Hart. 1905. The Indian Population of California. *American Anthropologist* 7: 594–606.

Mooney, James. 1928. The Aboriginal Population of America North of Mexico. In John R. Swanton, ed., *Smithsonian Miscellaneous Collections*, vol. 80, pp. 1–40. Washington, D.C.: U.S. Government Printing Office.

Moratto, Michael J. 1984. *California Archaeology*. Orlando, Fla.: Academic Press.

Orr, Phil. 1968. *Prehistory of Santa Rosa Island*. Santa Barbara Museum of Natural History, Santa Barbara, Calif.

Powers, Stephen. 1877. Tribes of California. *Contributions to North American Ethnology*, vol. 3. Reprint, Washington, D.C.: U.S. Government Printing Office.

Roney, J. G., Jr. 1959. Palaeopathology of a California Archaeological Site. *Bulletin of the History of Medicine* 33(2): 97–109.

1966. Paleoepidemiology: An Example from California. In *Human Paleopathology*, ed. S. Jarcho. New Haven, Conn.: Yale University Press.

Schulz, Peter. 1981. "Osteoarchaeology and Subsistence Change in Prehistoric Central California." Ph.D. diss., University of California, Davis.

Stanley, Sam, and Robert K. Thomas. 1978. Current Demographic and Social Trends among North American Indians. *Annals of the American Academy of Political and Social Science* 436:111–120.

Steckel, Richard. 1995. Stature and the Standard of Living. *Journal of Economic Literature* 33:1903–1940.

Suchey, J. M., W. J. Wood, and S. Shermis. 1972. Analysis of Human Skeletal Material from Malibu, California (LAn-264). *Report: Archaeological Survey, Department of Anthropology*, University of California, Los Angeles.

Thornton, Russell. 1980. Recent Estimates of the Prehistoric California Indian Population. *Current Anthropology* 21:702–704.

1987. *American Indian Holocaust and Survival: A Population History since 1492*. Normal: University of Oklahoma Press.

Ubelaker, Douglas H. 1988. North American Indian Population Size, AD 1500 to 1985. *American Journal of Physical Anthropology* 77:289–94.

U.S. Bureau of the Census. 1915. *Indian Population of the United States and Alaska, 1910*. Washington, D.C.: U.S. Government Printing Office.

Walker, Phillip L. 1978. A Quantitative Analysis of Dental Attrition Rates in the Santa Barbara Channel Area. *American Journal of Physical Anthropology* 48:101–106.

1986. Porotic Hyperostosis in a Marine Dependent California Indian Population. *American Journal of Physical Anthropology* 69:345–354.

1989. Cranial Injuries as Evidence of Violence in Prehistoric Southern California. *American Journal of Physical Anthropology* 80(3):313–323.

1996. Wife Beating, Boxing, and Broken Noses: Skeletal Evidence for the Cultural Patterning of Interpersonal Violence. In D. Martin and D. Frayer, eds., *Troubled Times: Osteological and Archaeological Evidence of Violence*, pp. 145–175. London: Gordon and Breach.

Walker, Phillip L., and M. J. DeNiro. 1986. Stable Nitrogen and Carbon Isotope Ratios in Bone Collagen as Indices of Prehistoric Dietary Dependence on Marine and Terrestrial Resources in Southern California. *American Journal of Physical Anthropology* 71(1):51–61.

Walker, Phillip L., Francine Drayer, and Susan Siefkin. 1996. *A Comparative Analysis of Skeletal Collections from Malibu (LAn-264)*. Report prepared for the California Department of Parks and Recreation, Sacramento, Calif.

Walker, Phillip L., and Jon Erlandson. 1986. Dental Evidence for Prehistoric Dietary Change on the Northern Channel Islands. *American Antiquity* 51(2):375–383.

Walker, Phillip L., Carol Goldberg, and Michael DeNiro. 1989a. Stable Isotopic Evidence of Prehistoric Diet and Culture Change in Southern California. *American Journal of Physical Anthropology* 78(2):229.

Walker, Phillip L., and Sandra Hollimon. 1989. Changes in Osteoarthritis Associated with the Development of a Maritime Economy Among Southern California Indians. *International Journal of Anthropology* 4(1):171–183.

Walker, Phillip L., and Travis D. Hudson. 1993. *Chumash Healing: Changing Health and Medical Practices in an American Indian Society.* Banning, Calif.: Malki Museum Press.

Walker, Phillip L., and Patricia Lambert. 1989. Skeletal Evidence for Stress during a Period of Cultural Change in Prehistoric California. In Luigi Capasso, ed., *Advances in Paleopathology, Journal of Paleopathology: Monographic Publication No. 1*, pp. 207–212. Chieti, Italy: Marino Solfanelli.

——— 1998. Prehistoric Treponematosis in the Western United States. *American Journal of Physical Anthropology*, Supp. 26:224.

Walker, Phillip L., P. Lambert, and M. DeNiro. 1989b. The Effects of European Contact on the Health of California Indians. In David H. Thomas, ed., *Columbian Consequences,* vol. I: *Archaeological and Historical Perspective on the Spanish Borderlands West,* pp. 349–364. Washington, D.C.: Smithsonian Institution Press.

Wallace, William. 1978. Post-Pleistocene Archaeology, 9000 to 2000 B.C. In Robert F. Heizer, ed., *Handbook of North American Indians,* vol. 8, *California,* pp. 25–36. Washington, D.C.: Smithsonian Institution.

CHAPTER EIGHTEEN

Welfare History on the Great Plains

Mortality and Skeletal Health, 1650 to 1900

S. Ryan Johansson and Douglas Owsley

ABSTRACT

The relationship between the longevity, health, and welfare of modern populations is difficult to assess, but all the complexities are multiplied when our evaluation must rely heavily on skeletal data from the remote past. This chapter uses skeletal data for several groups of Native American Indians who lived on the Great Plains of North America in the eighteenth and nineteenth centuries, to reconstruct their welfare history during the long process of contact with Europeans. The estimation of mortality involves putting the mean age-at-death for each group back into the relevant environmental, historical, and demographic contexts necessary to interpret that statistic as a true life expectancy. Subsequently, the growth-rate–sensitive life expectancy estimaters are integrated with various dimensions of skeletal health to compare the relative welfare of the settled horticultural groups with equestrian nomads.

WELFARE HISTORY AND MORTALITY

Welfare history involves comparing different groups living in different times and places, and how they fared with respect to each other and ourselves (Steckel, 1995). Hunter-gatherers have been described as leading lives that were nasty, brutish, and short compared to our own, or healthier and better, albeit simpler. The invention of agriculture can be seen as a defensive response to climatic change, one that meant having to do more work for less food, or, alternatively, a fortunate innovation that raised material standards of living and life expectancy for all subsequent generations (Cohen and Armelegos, 1984; Cohen, 1989). "Civilization" may have improved or reduced the health and welfare of women and so on (Coatsworth, 1996).

Data were collected at the University of Tennessee, the American Museum of Natural History, the Field Museum, the Nebraska State Historical Society, the University of Nebraska, and the Smithsonian Institution. Funding was provided by grants from the National Science Foundation and the Scholarly Studies Program of the Smithsonian Institution. Records transformation using the History of Health and Nutrition protocol was aided by Terri Newbill, Susanne Owsley, and Karen Bone. Malcolm Richardson assisted with the computer analysis, and the map was prepared by Dana Kollmann.

One exception to pervasive uncertainty about welfare history involves contact between Europeans and the Native peoples of the Americas. Most historians are convinced that contact initiated a sudden, massive loss of life among the peoples of the New World caused by the introduction of previously unknown infectious diseases (Stannard, 1992). An alternative research tradition stressed that contact was a more complicated and extended process with a wider range of welfare-related outcomes (Johansson, 1982), depending on the different geographical, social, and economic contexts in which previously isolated peoples first encountered one another (Crosby, 1986). Today highly contextualized research about the impact of contact is flourishing at the expense of sweeping generalizations (Reff, 1991; Guittierez, 1996; Axtell, 1997; Williams, 1997). Increasingly, research on specific groups favors the conclusion that "[f]actors other than disease were at least as significant as the introduction of new micro organisms into previously unexposed populations" (Kunitz, 1994: 5). By now, enough evidence has accumulated to raise serious doubts about the case for a generalized demographic holocaust (Hinige, 1998).

For one set of agrarian peoples (conventionally called "tribes") who lived along the Missouri River in the eighteenth century, archaeological evidence indicates that early contact with a handful of European traders improved their material welfare through trade, and temporarily encouraged population growth. It was not until intertribal conflict intensified, and local economies were seriously disrupted by warfare, that periodic epidemics caused irreversible population decline, well before Euro-Americans began to settle the area. In what has been called "the tribal zone," meaning the area of intensified intertribal conflict created by the expansion of European settlement (Ferguson and Whitehead, 1992), chronic warfare and economic distress prevented the demographic recovery that would have followed most epidemics.

The welfare history of various groups of Plains Indians can be told in narrative form, but since narration imposes relatively few constraints on the selection and interpretation of evidence, detailed histories do not lead to systematic comparisons. As a result, uncertainty remains high, and to most social science historians this seems like a form of continuing slavery to ignorance. Freedom comes from doing systematic research that transforms vague terms like "welfare" into more precise concepts that facilitate measurement and permit the systematic reconstruction of trends over time.

The social science drive for consensus on welfare history begins with identifying those components of "welfare" that are most universally valued *and* susceptible to measurement, among them "health" and "longevity." In theory, standardizing these concepts and devising robust methods of measurement should provide the basis for constructing semiformalized narrative histories based on systematic comparisons. But in practice, definition and measurement are not straightforward processes that automatically produce objective conclusions.

Just as the Great Plains of North America once contained different tribes competing for land and resources, modern universities contain experts competing to defend or take intellectual territory for their field. The more territory taken by a group of like-minded researchers, the greater the funding, the more graduates who can be supported, and the higher the relative status of particularly successful individuals within that field. Intense competition for research resources can and does interfere with producing knowledge for its own sake, instead of "knowledge" that promotes the individual's or group's self-interest.

To make a long story short: the conceptual and methodological foundations of any version of welfare history, even those that are most quantitative, must always be examined for distortions introduced by professional concerns, even if they involve nothing more than taking methodological shortcuts that are not empirically defensible. On the whole, mortality data has long been susceptible to distortion and manipulation because life expectancy estimates are directly related to welfare history and indirectly to present policy issues (Johansson, 1994). Although skeletal data is not deeply political, what it tells us about the health and longevity has sufficient resonance for modern debates about the welfare of surviving native peoples to make otherwise abstract methodological issues matter.

Section I of this chapter reviews the limitations of conventional methods of mortality estimation using skeletal data, and shows how their insensitivity to environmental and historical contexts causes serious distortions in evaluating the average length of human life before and after contact. Section II (A and B) applies multidimensional, context-sensitive methods to estimating life expectancy levels for several tribes of Indians once living on the Great Plains. Finally, Section III considers the general problem of linking skeletal longevity to skeletal health.

I. SKELETAL LONGEVITY IN THEORY AND PRACTICE

If we grant that most individuals and most groups would rather live long and healthy lives than sick and shorter ones, then, to the extent that skeletons preserve biological data about health and longevity, they contain fundamental data about human welfare history. For example, it was once commonly assumed that Native American populations lived in a disease-free paradise until the arrival of Europeans (Keenleside, 1998: 59); but continuing research has made that assumption seem more and more untenable. Instead there seems to have been a lot of site-specific variation in skeletal health among natives of the New World (Milner, 1992).

Chapter 3 by Steckel, Sciulli, and Rose (this volume) reveals how extensive the range of variability in terms of skeletal health could be between small populations before 1900 (see their Table 3.2). Out of a possible 100 points (the score associated with a set of skeletons in theoretically perfect health), the least healthy group scored 54, while the healthiest scored 92 points. It seems as if the skeletons from the most favored groups were almost twice as healthy as those from the most disadvantaged.

If the healthiest sets of skeletons come from the longest-lived populations, then those groups might have lived twice as long (on average) as the groups producing the least healthy skeletons. A review of expectancy-at-birth estimates for local populations living in premodern Europe shows that local life expectancy estimates ranged from circa 20 to circa 40+ years, at least before 1800 (Johansson, 2000). Local populations living 10 or 20 miles from one another could be found at both ends of this spectrum of values because survival prospects were once so sensitive to local disease environments (Dobson, 1997). It is hard to believe that environmental differences in the Americas would not have produced as much life expectancy variation in local populations as found elsewhere, at least before 1800–1900.

But thus far, life expectancy levels in the New World seem relatively homogeneous. Most of these premodern skeletal populations are estimated to have had a life expectancy at birth in the low 20s, whether or not the skeletons themselves are in poor, fair, or good skeletal health. For example, several sets of skeletons recovered from coastal South Carolina before and during contact score relatively high on the health index by site, but they have very low mean ages-at-death – 21–23 years (see Larsen et al. in this volume, Table 14.2). But most relatively unhealthy New World skeletal populations have similarly low mean ages-at-death. When life expectancy at birth values are higher, it is always because infant and child skeletons were poorly recovered, compared to adults. Missing infant skeletons always bias the mean age of death upward, but when they are added back, in the course of adjusting the raw data, the mean age-at-death falls back down to values in the low 20s.

The problem is that the mean age-at-death is not a good proxy for life expectancy at birth (Johansson and Horowitz, 1986). Treating the mean age-at-death as if it were equivalent to a life expectancy level is only legitimate when a population is/was stationary (i.e., it is not growing or declining) and it was closed to migration (no natives left the group and no strangers entered it) during the period under consideration (Coale, 1972). Under these very restricted conditions, the set of simple, mathematical relationships which comprise stable population theory does open a direct road back into the demographic past, uncomplicated by contextual/historical considerations.

But what if a set of archaeologically recovered skeletons came from a population that was growing or declining when their burial took place? Under such circumstances, stable population theory itself also proves that the mean age-at-death diverges from life expectancy at birth. How far apart the two can be is determined by the growth rate. Table 18.1 uses data from Coale and Demeny's model stable populations (the West set) to demonstrate that a number of model populations can share the same mean age-at-death (in this case, 20 years) while having a very wide

Table 18.1: Model Populations Sharing the Same Mean Age-at-Death (circa 20 years) but Experiencing Different Growth Rates and Doubling Times

Mean age-at-death	Growth rate	Life expectancy	Doubling time
20 years	−.5% per year	Circa 23 years	Decreases by half in 140 years
20 years	Zero	Circa 20 years	A stationary population
20 years	+.5% per year	Circa 23 years	Doubles in 140 years
20 years	+1.0%	Circa 27 years	Doubles in 70 years
20 years	+1.5%	Circa 32 years	Doubles in 51 years
20 years	+2.0%	Circa 38 years	Doubles in 32 years
20 years	+3.0%	Circa 45 years	Doubles in 23 years

Source: Coale and Demeny (1983).

range of life expectancy levels (extending from 20 to 45 years) conditional on their respective growth rates.

If faster-growing populations produce relatively healthy-looking skeletons,[1] then a particularly healthy population could well have had a mean age of death that was significantly below its true life expectancy at birth, even by as much as 10 to 20 years. To avoid being misled by low mean ages-at-death, it becomes essential to estimate a growth rate for the once-living populations now represented by a set of recovered skeletons. But estimating a growth rate can only be done by putting the recovered skeletal population back into a broad, real-world context that would be compatible with supplementary evidence for either growth, decline, or true stationarity (Swedlund, 1989).

The drawback is that context-sensitive mortality estimation requires extensive site-specific knowledge. A single expert is unlikely to have enough knowledge plus all the technical skills required to do everything necessary to put skeletal data into its proper context. Interdisciplinary cooperation is required; and the bottom line is that it takes more money, time, and effort to produce a single number (a life expectancy estimate). It is both cheaper and easier to assume that any skeletal group came from a stationary population closed to migration, without reviewing the archaeological and/or historical evidence for and against such an assumption. (For a recent example of this time-honored practice, see Alesan et al., 1999.)

At the global level, there are good reasons to suppose that the entire human population could not have grown rapidly through most of human history (Preston, 1995). But at the local level, there are equally good reasons to suppose that many small-scale populations were demographically dynamic, either growing or declining instead of remaining stationary (Harpending, 1997).

From an evolutionary perspective, the idea that all or most local populations were stationary most of the time is extremely puzzling. First of all, very small groups with fewer than 100 individual members (most hunting-gathering bands were in this size range) are inherently unstable demographic entities (Keckler, 1997). Had most small groups of hunter-gatherers living 100,000 to 30,000 years ago somehow managed to keep their numbers constant, human physical evolution would have proceeded at a much slower pace, and several subspecies of human beings would have survived until fairly recently.

At the very least, the last 30,000 years of human history must have involved considerable demographic dynamism favoring the expansion of "Cro-Magnon" groups at the expense of other forms of *Homo sapiens*. All living human populations are said to be of the Cro-Magnon type, which implies that their common ancestors must have had genetic and/or cultural advantages that permitted them to increase their numbers by extending their territory at the expense of other human groups. Even after the Cro-Magnon worldwide takeover, there is good evidence from the last few thousand years that some groups of Cro-Magnons continued expanding at the

---

[1] The alternative is to suppose that the health status of a group of recovered skeletons belonging to a single population of individuals is completely unrelated to their probability of dying; i,e., the risk of death is independent of sickness and disability. One could even assume that the risk of dying is reduced by poor health. In biological terms both assumptions are absurd.

expense of other groups (Diamond, 1998). From the invention of agriculture onward, food-growing groups grew relatively rapidly and successfully expanded at the expense of hunting-gathering groups, while in some regions, successful horticulturists fell prey to even faster-growing groups of nomadic peoples.

Daniel Scott Smith has enumerated the many reasons to suppose that we are all more likely to descend from individuals who once belonged to expanding populations, rather than to groups that remained stationary or declined to extinction (Smith, 2001). Whatever the shortcomings of "group selection" may be with respect to all or most animal populations,[2] human demographers have very good reasons for supposing that adult human females who lived in successful (growing) populations generally had a better chance of achieving individual reproductive success (i.e., being survived by more than one adult daughter) than those who lived in declining or stationary populations, particularly if those groups in decline were losing their control over essential material resources.[3]

IIA. PUTTING SKELETAL DATA INTO CONTEXT

Addressing the growth-rate problem in paleodemography means putting skeletal data back into context before using it to estimate life expectancy. This requires that explicit consideration be given to at least three distinct but related aspects of what Swedlund calls the "forest of context" (Swedlund, 1989).

1. *The first aspect of context involves general environmental influences on mortality-related welfare.* All New World groups coming into contact with Europeans after 1492 CE were intelligently adapted to the physical environments in which they lived, but that did not mean they lived in equally favorable environments. Some natural environments are more benign than others and, thus, more conducive to longevity, either because of climatic advantages, cleaner water, fewer insect vectors, and a more diverse, secure food supply, or all of the above. But there is no simple relationship between a local environment and a life expectancy level because human beings can use their intelligence to counter environmental disadvantages, just as they can create unnatural health hazards in the pursuit of pleasure or adventure.

Although it might be supposed that favorable material circumstances automatically resulted in relative health and longevity, even prehistoric prosperity had its

---

[2] From a demographic perspective (in contrast to a narrowly genetic perspective), accepting or rejecting the possibility of group selection would depend on whether or not individual animals or human beings lived in groups or were solitary. Solitary animals may live by depending on their own resources (genetic or otherwise), but for human beings, individual survival probabilities are raised or lowered according to the fortunes of the group to which they belong.

[3] Even if the most successful prehistoric populations could only expand by fission, creating daughter groups who would settle new territory, this branching process would have created large kin networks, which in turn would have had important welfare implications for individual survival and reproductive success. Kinship was once a form of insurance against local catastrophes. Anyone belonging to a large kinship network had the right to claim assistance in times of need, even from remote relatives they had not met. Individuals blessed with dispersed kinship networks had the most insurance against a temporary loss of material welfare, and thus a higher probability of surviving and reproducing in an environmentally uncertain world.

down side. A good environment was likely to promote population growth, local sanitation problems, and, thus, higher levels of exposure to pollution-related diseases, vector-borne diseases, and airborne infections. In some cases, wealthier groups may have even used their relative wealth to damage their health, which is what happens when trade goods were exchanged for toxic substances like alcohol or deadly weapons like guns.[4] The biggest disadvantage of local prosperity was that it attracted raiders out to steal what they themselves could not produce or obtain through trade. In the short run, group conflict always created some unnecessarily premature deaths through violence; and in the longer run, it carried the threat of economic disruption, lower standards of living, and the stress-related reduction of resistance to disease (Keckler, 1997). In other words, there were diminishing mortality returns to environmental advantages, which placed upper bounds on human life expectancy before the modern era, just as there were lower bounds on life expectancy below which the long-run viability of a group became impossible.

What these upper and lower bounds were remains uncertain, but very few human populations could expect to survive in the long run at a life expectancy at birth much below 20 years. At that level, about three-quarters of the ever born are dead by age 20, and the women survivors to age 45–50 would have had to produce an average of between seven and eight children to keep numbers stationary under difficult conditions. In contrast, at double that level of life expectancy, that is, 40 years, about three-quarters of the ever born survive to adulthood, and the women survivors to age 45–50 must produce only around three to four children on average to keep numbers stationary. In the absence of effective fertility control, twice as many would be born, and thus normal fertility combined with relatively high life expectancy would result in fairly rapid population growth as long as that combination persisted.

Before 1800, the average level of life expectancy at birth in Western Europe was somewhere between 27 and 33 years. In narrowly demographic terms, this is a comfortable level of life expectancy because a total fertility of six to seven births per woman leaves some margin for growth. Passing epidemics could temporarily reduce this normal level of life expectancy by 7 to 13 years without threatening long-run survival. For convenience, we can use a generic value of 30 years as the average level of premodern life expectancy for local communities living in normal environmental circumstances in Europe. Higher values were found under exceptionally favorable environmental circumstances, for example, among local populations living at least 100 feet above sea level, located off the main road (and thus protected from exposure to passing epidemics) with good access to clean water, and blessed with a fairly regular climate free of dangerous extremes which threatened the local food supply. In Europe, national and local governments also offered these small communities

---

[4] Populations that led materially privileged lives (by standards of their times) can show signs of skeletal disease that indicate the abuse of their privileges. One example of such a disease is diffuse idiopathic skeletal hyperostosis (DISH). In England the skeletal signs of DISH are most common among male skeletons recovered from monastic or ecclesiastic burial sites. Monks and clerics were very well fed populations, and some individuals became obese and even diabetic, thus predisposing themselves to DISH, without necessarily preventing them from reaching advanced middle age, and even old ages (Rogers, 1995).

protection from raiding by neighboring groups, and thus from high levels of vio-lence. Those European populations with life expectancy levels well below the average were comparatively rare and seem to be associated with urban poverty, malaria, or chronic warfare. Such communities could only maintain their numbers, let alone grow, through in-migration.

Was the normal level of human life expectancy at birth under normal environ-mental circumstances in Europe higher or lower than it was in the New World, especially before contact? We may never know. It is far more certain that in both worlds, local life expectancy levels varied from environment to environment. Groups living in difficult but still viable environments would survive at a life expectancy at birth of circa 20 years, while others would have a life expectancy twice as high. Those in the upper range of values (35+ years) were likely to be vigorous, growing popula-tions with a low mean age for both the living and the dead. It is only environmental considerations that could distinguish the groups that had a low mean age-at-death because they were growing, from groups that had an equally low mean age because they were not.

2. *The second aspect of contact-sensitive mortality estimation involves considering specific historical circumstances.* So long as environmental/social conditions are sta-ble, or they vary within predictable bounds, a normal (long-run) background level of life expectancy can be estimated. But few groups live outside history in unchanging environments. As New and Old World populations came into contact, their interac-tion was associated with particularly rapid environmental change for both native populations and invading Europeans.

The Europeans who left Great Britain to settle in New England benefited from rapid environmental change. After a brief period of high mortality involving adap-tation to specific local pathogens – contemporaries called it "seasoning" – and a few violent encounters with the native peoples, Euro-Americans from Britain who settled in New England began to live much longer than formerly. By 1700, normal levels of life expectancy in most New England communities seem to have risen to levels as high as 45–50 years, at least 15 years higher than average for Old England (Wells, 1992). Fertility levels rose as well, and population growth in New England was exceptionally rapid. Local populations grew by 3 percent a year and doubled every 23 years, unless out-migration helped keep numbers down.

In contrast, in the southern coastal colonies, where malaria was rampant, normal European life expectancy levels fell by 10 to 15 years. Given the local shortage of women, birthrates were low, and so high death rates would have caused overall numbers to fall were it not for continued in-migration from England, supplemented with forced migration from Africa (slavery).

If we had good skeletal data for a typical, high life expectancy, rapidly growing community in New England, it would have had a mean age-at-death of circa 18–20 years. But southern coastal populations (where life expectancy was as low as 20 years) would have had about the same low mean age-at-death. Thus, environmental dif-ferences encountered in the process of contact and settlement would have produced extreme differences in life expectancy levels, but similar mean ages-at-death. Given the demographic similarity, only environmental and historical circumstances would permit us to interpret the same mean age-at-death in different terms (Dumond, 1997).

In New England, rapid growth meant that every generation sent land-hungry sons out west in search of new land. It was this continuing expansion that led to conflict with most resident native populations, and thus to intensified warfare. Wherever warfare led to land loss and displacement, the losers were forced to move westward and adapt to new environments, often under very stressful circumstances over which they had little control. Depending on what their normal life expectancy level had been before contact, it would surely fall to lower levels. For groups already on the threshold of viability (i.e., with a life expectancy at birth of circa 20 years), recovery from a single epidemic might be impossible. But for more robust groups, whose initial life expectancy levels were moderate (30 years) or high (40 years), epidemics could cause life expectancy to fall substantially without leading to extinction, at least if the group itself was reasonably large to start with. (Small populations with less than a few hundred members are exceptionally vulnerable to any single shock.)

As European settlers increased the territory under their control, history worked for them to ensure that rapid population could be maintained. The process of social and economic development that was transforming Western Europe included the drive to bring epidemics of smallpox under greater control. The English developed inoculation by 1720, and vaccination after 1800 (Watts, 1997).[5] Wherever communities adopted these novel preventive measures, some children and adults were saved from premature death. Since smallpox was a leading cause of premature death, the existence of measures to counter it had important implications for mortality, even for some groups of Plains Indians after 1820.

In any case, what contact did to normal background levels of life expectancy depended on specific historical circumstances, and these must be taken into account in any mortality estimates based on the use of skeletal data.

3. *The last aspect of context-sensitive mortality estimation involves considering how the mean age-at-death is produced by the entire age-at-death distribution which it summarizes.* The mean age-at-death of a collection of skeletons collapses all deaths in that group into a single number, irrespective of how individual ages-at-death are distributed from birth to old age. As is well known, this single number often conceals a variety of problems, such as missing infant skeletons, or very poor age estimation resulting in age heaping. It is the entire distribution of deaths by age that reveals these problems, as well as whether or not the shape of the distribution is normal for the estimated life expectancy at birth, given the guidelines found in model stable populations. Because the entire distribution of deaths by age has so much to tell us, the mean age-at-death must be put back into its full demographic context.

In general, it takes a skeletal population with several hundred members to produce a meaningful distribution of deaths by age and, thus, a mean that is not inherently

---

[5] See Chapter 3. Watts suggests that information provided by an African slave led Cotton Mather, a Boston minister, to independently invent inoculation.

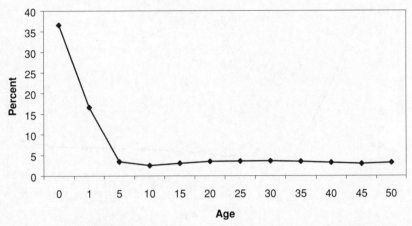

Figure 18.1. Model stable/stationary population with life expectancy at birth of 20 years. *Source:* Coale and Demeny (1983), Model West.

misleading because it is dominated by random variation instead of systematic demographic processes.[6]

When recovered skeletal populations start to have more than circa 100 members, random effects related to small numbers become less dominant, and model populations become more relevant to estimating life expectancy at birth. In the world of model populations, those falling within the normal premodern range of values for life expectancy at birth (i.e., 20 to 40 years) share a distinctive unimodal distribution of deaths-by-age. Deaths peak in infancy (0–1) or among the under 5s, fall off rapidly, and then flatten out for the rest of the distribution.

Figure 18.1 represents a normal distribution of deaths-by-age for a model population with a life expectancy at birth of close to 20 years. Model stationary populations with a real life expectancy at birth closer to 40 years show signs of developing a bimodal age-at-death distribution by starting a second and smaller peak for individuals who died after the age of circa 45 to 50 years.

Figures 18.1 and 18.2 remind us that in ideal (theoretical) circumstances, model populations with life expectancies at birth between 20 and 40 have distributions of deaths by age that look very similar to each other. The subtle differences between 20 and 40 may not be observable given that skeletal populations are fairly small, skeletal ages are so inexact, and age-specific recovery is imperfect. (Robert McCaa covers the same problem on a more graphically sophisticated level in this volume.) But the existence of relative flatness after age 10 provides us with some kind of reassurance that a recovered skeletal population is or is not of the normal premodern type.

---

[6] The smaller the skeletal sample, the less likely it is that stable population theory will apply to it. Simulations carried out by Rob Hoppa for this volume indicate that the skeletal mean age-at-death of a parish population can fluctuate markedly when samples contain fewer than 250 individuals. See S. Saunders et al., this volume.

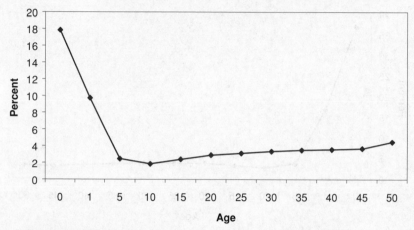

Figure 18.2. Model stable/stationary population with life expectancy at birth of 40 years. *Source:* Coale and Demeny (1983), Model West.

McCaa also points out that, compared to models based on European data, older people seem to be relatively scarce in Native American groups. The relative scarcity of older skeletons becomes particularly striking when we compare Native American data to technologically similar populations in Europe and Asia (Weiss, 1981).[7] This scarcity of older skeletons could be due to different methods of age estimation,[8] but it could also be a sign that Native American populations kept fewer old people alive for extended periods of time. Alternatively, it could mean that most Native American skeletons came from growing populations, since rapid growth itself can reduce the percentage of older skeletons in a distribution of deaths-by-age. At any rate, the scarcity of skeletons belonging to elderly people raises the possibility that under normal environmental conditions, adult life was shorter in the New World than it was in Europe even before contact began.

By putting a mean age-at-death in a simplified, three-dimensional context – environmental, historical, and demographic – we can begin to select a more specific life expectancy at birth level within the normal premodern range for any particular skeletal population. Assuming that a group of recovered skeletons came from a closed, stationary living population is only legitimate if there are no environmental and historical considerations that argue against it. As a final check on the plausibility of a life expectancy estimate, we can use the apparent level of skeletal health, as is done in Section III.

---

[7] Weiss gives the following values for "life expectancy estimates at age 50 years" (i.e., mean ages-at-death). For "average" hunter-gatherers the value is 13 years. For simple agricultural groups it is 18 years. But for "North-American Indians," the value given is 5 years. This reflects the comparative shortage of older skeletons. See pages 49–50.

[8] As individuals age it becomes more difficult for them to cope with climatic extremes and prolonged food shortages. In times of scarcity, older people in New World populations may have even chosen to sacrifice their lives for the good of the group. Alternatively, present aging techniques may not be good enough to distinguish between people over 60 years of age and those in their 40s and 50s. McCaa seems to favor this explanation, although it doesn't explain why more older individuals are found in premodern Eurasian skeletal populations.

IIB. ESTIMATING MORTALITY IN CONTEXT:
WELFARE HISTORY ON THE PLAINS

Recovering Skeletal Data. People have lived on North America's prairies and plains for at least 12,000 years, but scientific knowledge about them has only been produced since the nineteenth century. By now, professional archaeologists have accumulated a surprising amount of evidence about their material life, while recovering a comparatively large number of skeletons from once-living populations (Hofman, 1996).

All told, several thousand skeletons belonging to groups who once lived along the Missouri River have been exhumed and examined by bioarchaeologists, thanks largely to the River Basin Surveys Program sponsored by the federal government between 1945 and 1969. That program excavated cemeteries located near long-abandoned native villages because those sites were scheduled to be flooded and washed away as the result of dam building along the Missouri River. Salvage excavation was the only way to preserve their remains for scientific research or any other purpose (Owsley and Bruwelheide, 1996).

Fortunately for the evolving science of paleodemography, William Bass (a physical anthropologist at the Smithsonian Institution) and his associates were very systematic about the site-specific recovery of those individuals once buried by village populations in specific time periods.[9]

It is for that reason that the health and mortality history of a number of separate groups, such as the Arikara, Pawnee, and Omaha, can be studied during fairly specific phases of their contact history. Not only are the recovered skeletons relatively numerous, but those included in this study have all been individually aged by the same bioarchaeologist, in this case coauthor Douglas Owsley. Thus, one possible source of extraneous variation between groups is removed, that is, the one introduced by individually variable approaches to age assignment.

For this particular area, contact history is assigned the chronology shown in Table 18.2 based on archaeological data and early written sources. For different tribes, these "stages" came at different times, and for some they did not come at all. (For a list of specific sites see Table 18.3.)

The Arikara

The largest skeletal collection available for a single tribe that once lived along the Missouri River comes from a northern Caddoan-speaking, horticultural people known as the Arikara (see Figure 18.3). The particular collection of 273 Arikara skeletons in Figure 18.4 had a mean age-at-death of 19 years.[10] But can we assume that their life expectancy at birth was equally low?

---

[9] Owsley and Bruwelheide, 1996, p. 151. Since 1981, Bass's work has led to the production of over 29 M.A. theses and Ph.D. dissertations, most of which have explored the relationship between demography and the economic and social history of the peoples of the Great Plains.

[10] This set of Arikara skeletons does not include the 500 to 600 skeletons recovered from the Larson Site (deposition period 1679–1733). See Owsley and Bass, 1979.

Arikara skeletons from the Larson site included so many infants (254 out of 628) that the mean age-at-death was as low as 13.2 years! Far from indicating that the Arikara were in contact shock, it was the high representation of infant skeletons which was responsible for their very low mean age-at-death. If

Table 18.2: Contact History in the Plains Village: Conventional
Periodization, Two Traditions

(A) Coalescent Tradition

Extended variant. 1550–1675. (European trade goods but no traders.)
Postcontact variant. 1675–1780. (Numerous traders. Limited warfare/disease.)
Disorganized variant. 1780–1845. (Increasing warfare and disease.)

Alternatively, periodization can be based on the range of source materials used to
reconstruct the process of contact.

(B) Source Materials

Late Prehistoric. 1600–1650 (No written sources.)
Early Proto-historic. 1650–1740. (A few written sources.)
Late Proto-historic. 1740–1795. (More written sources.)
Historic Period. 1795–1832. (Good documentation.)

Source: Douglas Owsley, 1991. "Temporal Variation in Femoral Cortical Thickness of North American
Plains Indians." In *Human Paleopathology. Current Syntheses and Future Options*, ed. D. Ortner and
A. Aufderhelde. Washington D.C.: Smithsonian Institution Press. Pp. 105–109, p. 105.

Demographically, this distribution loosely approximates the flat, unimodel distribution consistent with a level of life expectancy in the normal premodern range
of 20 to 40 years, but it is somewhat less smooth than it "ought" to be. Infant
skeletons are well represented, but there is always the possibility that some are missing. (If so, the mean age-at-death should be even lower than the skeletal collection
indicates.) This group of skeletons also shows the usual "problematic" shortage of
older individuals (i.e., those who died above age 59) common to most New World
groups. If this collection of skeletons is age-representative of the once-living people
who buried them, we can use stable population theory to conclude that the low
mean age-at-death indicates that completed fertility was about 7 births per woman
(GRR 3.5) during the period these skeletons were buried.[11] (See Appendix.)

The slightly wavy character of the distribution of deaths by age, if taken seriously
as reflecting some past reality, suggests that instability dominated the period of
deposition, in response to climatic and/or disease-induced disturbances. There are
reports of epidemics in this period, but since fertility was high, demographic recovery would be fairly easy, provided the Arikara could retain control of their territory
and its resources while replenishing their numbers. Nothing in the overall shape
of the distribution of deaths-by-age suggests that the Arikara villages burying these
skeletons were already catastrophically disturbed populations plunging towards extinction as the result of contact with European traders and exposure to smallpox.

Although demographic considerations confirm that this group was highly likely
to have had a life expectancy at birth of between 20 years and 35 years, it can tell

anything, this indicates exceptionally high fertility. The average women surviving to age 45 probably
gave birth to between eight and nine infants instead of six to seven.

[11] If Arikara women completing fertility gave birth between the ages of 18 and 42 years, their average birth
intervals would be between three and four years long. This is a much longer birth interval than observed
in European women. It suggests extended breast-feeding with temporary sexual abstinence, a pattern of
behavior some Western observers thought existed among many native populations.

Table 18.3: Plain Indians Samples Grouped by Economy and Tribal Affiliation

Culture	Tribe	State/ province	Site name	Site number	Date (AD)	Number individuals
EN	Blackfoot	MT/Alberta	—	—	1870–1900	67
EN	Cheyenne	NE	—	—	1875–1885	42
EN	Crow	MT/Alberta	—	—	1870–1900	73
PV	Arikara	SD	Arzberger	39HU6	1250–1400	6
PV	Arikara	SD	Swan Creek	39WW7	1675–1725	149
PV	Arikara	SD	Four Bear	39DW2	1758–1774	72
PV	Arikara	SD	Leavitt	39ST215	1784–1792	24
PV	Arikara	SD	Buffalo Pasture	39ST216	1700–1750	22
PV	Pawnee	NE		25CX1	1650–1675 1770–1820	1
PV	Pawnee	NE	Linwood	25BU1	1850	72
PV	Pawnee	NE	Bellwood	25BU2	1795–1800	4
PV	Pawnee	NE	Barcal	25BU4	1750	20
PV	Pawnee	NE	Hill/Pike	25WT1	1750–1810	63
PV	Omaha	NE	Ryan	25DK2	1770–1820	39
PV	Omaha	NE	—	25DK10	1770–1820	67
PV	Ponca	NE	Ponca Fort	25KX1	1790–1800	59

EN: Equestrian nomad.
PV: Plains Village.

us nothing more precise. But the natural environment in which the Arirkara lived (i.e., the Northern Plains) had a number of distinct advantages that make relatively low life expectancy values seem unlikely. As horticulturists, the Arikara raised corn, beans, and squash in fields near their villages, and as hunters, they killed buffalo and deer who lived on wild grasses. Their environment also provided the Arikara with wild foods, such as sunflower seeds, prairie turnips, and berries (Lehmer and Wood, 1977). Altogether this tribe had an exceptionally diverse and healthy diet based on a mode of adaptation unique in northern America (Lehmer and Wood, 1977: 87).

But harsh winters had long tested the Arikara's ability to store enough food to last through the winter months. Although they developed an impressive range of food preservation and storage techniques, European traders, who described the Arikara as prosperous, also noted that they suffered through a few lean months every year. Moreover, like all agricultural peoples, the Arikara were vulnerable to periodic droughts and floods. Thus, seasonal and periodic scarcity may have repeatedly subjected the weakest and/or oldest Arikara to premature death once or twice a decade. This could be a possible explanation for the relative scarcity of older people in an otherwise materially rich environment.

If diet were all that mattered to longevity, the Arikara would have been relatively long-lived. But housing matters as well, and the Arikara lived in earth lodges containing 10 to 15 people, along with their horses and other animals. These lodges were well insulated, and they offered excellent protection from climatic extremes.

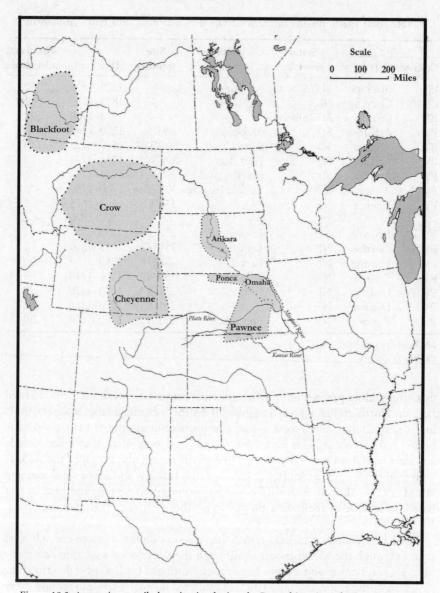

Figure 18.3. Approximate tribal territories during the Proto-historic and Historic Periods.

But dozens of lodges were crowded together into one fortified village for protection from hostile neighbors. In effect, the Arikara lived at a density sufficient to create pollution problems. As trade with Europeans increased, the river itself became a highway for both commerce and disease. In short, despite their healthy diets, and thus their potentially high level of resistance to disease, the Arikara were routinely exposed to pollution-related disease, and, as trade increased, to airborne diseases introduced by Europeans.

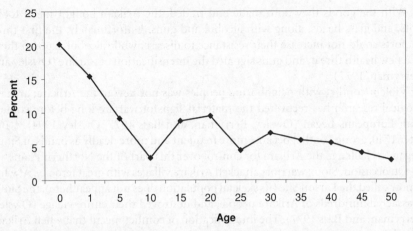

Figure 18.4. The Arikara: Age distribution of deaths. *Notes:* Mean age-at-death = 19. N = 273. The skeletons were buried between ca. 1675 and 1790. Adult males (44%), adult females (56%). Skeletons 59 years and older (ca. 2%).

Descriptions provided by traders indicate that the Arikara were hit by a few smallpox epidemics during the early eighteenth century (Palkovich, 1981). As an airborne disease, smallpox flourishes wherever people are crowded together, and since immunity is not boosted by superior nutritional status (for either Europeans or Native Americans), smallpox could quickly infect and kill these otherwise well-fed people. But in the period 1680 to circa 1740, there are no signs in the demographic or archaeological evidence that a few outbreaks initiated a rapid, unreversed population decline.

Quite the reverse, archaeological evidence indicates that by capitalizing on their role as middlemen in the fur trade, and increasing their domestic production of buffalo hides and surplus foodstuffs, the Arikara managed to improve their material welfare and increase the number of their villages (Owsley, 1994). Archaeological research for the period between 1680 and 1750 shows that at the village level, cache pit size (for food storage) was increasing, and so was the size of midden pits (refuse deposits) (Owsley, 1994). Average femoral cortical thickness was also increasing, which is an index of health particularly sensitive to the amount and regularity of the food supply. This is another indication that diets improved, or were more secure, during the five or six decades after 1675 when the number and size of Arikara villages increased. At their peak circa 1750, there may have been as many as 12,000 to 15,000 Arikara distributed over 18 or more villages.

Women contributed to this expansion through their hard physical labor, which was essential to the production of trade goods, as well as through their high fertility. But the combination of hard work and frequent childbearing could have easily undermined their health-related welfare in spite of good diets (see Section III). Arikara men, who specialized in trade and defense, were exposed to both more disease and, after circa 1740, to more violent conflict, and thus to an increased risk of violent death.

With the goods they both made and traded, the Arikara bought metal tools, pots, and glass beads, along with alcohol and guns. Unfortunately, the first three imports could not increase their resistance to disease, while alcohol exposed them to a new health threat, and guns signaled the intensification of warfare (Owsley and Berryman, 1977).

Violent conflict with neighboring peoples was not new to the Arikara; archaeological research has recovered the material signs of warfare long before contact with Europeans began (Owsley, Berryman, and Bass 1977; Owsley 1994).[12] But after 1740, group conflict became more frequent and more deadly as bands of Sioux began to challenge the Arikara for control over this part of the Northern Plains.

On occasion, Sioux warriors attacked Arikara villages with great ferocity. At what is now called the Larson Site (its skeletal population does not appear here), the Sioux massacred hundreds of Arikara people, and destroyed their entire village (Owsley, Berryman, and Bass 1977). The intensification of conflict meant that when Arikara men left a village to trade, hunt, or gather, those women, children, and older men remaining behind were no longer safe. If the adult men stayed home to defend the group, hunting was disrupted, the food supply deteriorated, and the flow of trade goods reduced. Either way, after 1750 the Arikara were losing control over the essential material resources which had paid for a burst of prosperity and driven a brief period of population growth.

The rise of the Sioux as a power on the Plains was a consequence of their own earlier displacement. Once pushed out of a woodland environment in the Great Lakes region (Ferguson and Whitehead, 1992), they had to adapt to an environment in which trees were scarce but buffalo abundant. By learning to ride horses and hunt buffalo on horseback, the Sioux reinvented themselves as equestrian nomads, who could hunt, trade, or raid, thus becoming competitors and enemies of the village-dwelling peoples of the Plains (Moore, 1987).[13]

By 1760–1780, definite signs of marked demographic contraction among the Arikara begin to appear in the archaeological record as conflict with the Sioux increased. Arikara villages became physically smaller (Trimbal, 1994). Around that time the Arikara were described in written sources as occupying only seven remaining villages, containing about 900 warriors (Owsley and Bass, 1979: 151). Using the usual multipliers, this translates to a total population of between 3,600 and 4,500 people. In the 1790s smallpox struck again, and this time its deadly effects were amplified by warfare and economic stress. The population collapsed. By 1830 only a few hundred Arikara had survived the potent combination of economic disruption, intensified warfare, and smallpox.

Most of the 273 Arikara skeletons included here were buried while times were still relatively good and numbers were increasing. Only part of the sample comes from the early period of gradual decline which preceded collapse. Since there are good archaeological reasons to believe that the Arikara were growing while most of the skeletons were buried, their life expectancy at birth must have been higher than

---

[12] Archaeological evidence for warfare on the Great Plains extends back for over a thousand years.

[13] The process whereby a previously existing population adapts to a new natural environment and creates a new identity is called *ethnogenesis*.

their low mean age-at-death of 19–20 years. Values as high as 30 years (an average level of life expectancy at birth) are not out of line, given the fact that they lived in a resource-rich environment. Higher values become unlikely because their high-density settlement patterns favored pollution-related disease and the rapid spread of airborne disease.

To have had a real life expectancy at birth near 30 years, the Arikara would have needed a growth rate of 1.5 percent a year from circa 1690 to 1740. With high fertility, this is not difficult to achieve. This combination of a fertility level and growth rate would produce a mean age-at-death of 19 years, given a GRR of approximately 3.3, or circa seven births per mature woman completing fertility. Since the skeletal health of Arikara was relatively good (see Section III), it seems very unlikely that the Arikara had a life expectancy at birth as low as their mean age-at-death.

The Pawnee

The Pawnee (Figure 18.3) were a group of Plains Indians whose ancestors had migrated northward to the Plains about 1,000 years earlier. Their adaptation to life on the Plains was very similar to the Arikara's, meaning that they too grew crops, hunted, and gathered wild foods. Their rich and diverse food supply would have given them a fairly high level of resistance to disease for most of the year, with the exception of the winter months. Like the Arikara, the Pawnee lived in crowded earth lodges and densely packed villages with all the standard implications for pollution-related disease.

Fortunately, Pawnee villages were located on a tributary of the Missouri River. Because they were situated off the main trade routes, their semi-isolation gave them a limited amount of geographical protection from exposure to epidemic diseases like smallpox, at least until circa 1800.

The Pawnee skeletons considered in Figure 18.5 come from a collection of five village cemeteries. They were buried between 1750 to 1820, which was a very benign historical period for the Pawnee, one relatively free of both epidemic disease and intensified group conflict. Nevertheless, the mean age-at-death is low – circa 21 years. Because overall skeletal preservation was not as good among the Pawnee as it was among the Arikara, the possibility exists that some infant skeletons may be missing. Once added back, the estimated missing infants would decrease the observed mean age-at-death still further, and reduce the percentage of older skeletons among the Pawnee, which is the highest for any Plains group.

The Pawnee also have the most balanced sex ratio among the Plains Indians, although adult Pawnee women buried near their villages still outnumber adult men (see Table 18.4). Both features of Pawnee skeletal demography could be plausibly interpreted as a sign of the group's relative security from attack at the time the recovered skeletons were buried. For example, adult Pawnee *males* had the highest mean age-at-death among the Plains Indians – a possible reflection of the absence of sustained conflict during this apparently benign period (Table 18.5).

The Arikara went into decline after 1740 just as the Pawnee were becoming more influential as farmers and traders on the Plains. Once again the historical evidence

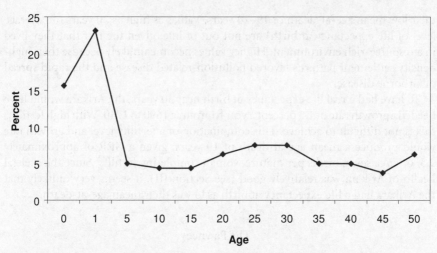

Figure 18.5. The Pawnee: Age distribution of deaths. *Notes:* Mean age-at-death = 21. N = 160. The skeletons were buried between ca. 1750 and 1820. Adult males (47%), adult females (53%). Skeletons 59 years and older (ca. 6%). If infant skeletons are underrepresented, the reported mean age-at-death is too high.

suggests that their numbers were increasing. When smallpox became a major threat to their survival after 1800, vaccination was just becoming available as a form of medical assistance delivered by the American government. Since Pawnee chiefs were receptive to this new means of controlling disease, this particular adaptation to historical novelty enabled the group to escape heavy population losses.

But the Sioux were expanding southward, and as they came into contact with the Pawnee, they began to raid their villages. Once again if Pawnee men left the village to hunt Buffalo, Pawnee women working in the fields could be abducted, molested, or killed. Fear of the Sioux began to limit group mobility, and thus its access to natural resources. Predictably, the Pawnee's supply of meat fell, and so did the number of buffalo robes they offered for trade (Wedel, 1977).

But this later period of increasing economic stress did not affect the Pawnee individuals whose skeletons are found in this collection. Most of them were buried when living standards were increasing but group conflict was minimal.

Table 18.4: Number of Adult Males and Females in Each Group

Group	Males		Females	
	N	%	N	%
Nomad	71	49	74	51
Arikara	62	44.3	78	55.7
Pawnee	38	46.9	43	53.1
Omaha	29	40.3	43	59.7
TOTAL	200	45.7	238	54.3

Table 18.5: Average Age-at-Death in Each Group and for Adult Females and Males

Group	All ages			Adults[1]			Males			Females		
	N	Mean	S.D.	N	Mean	S.D.	N	Mean	S.D.	N	Mean	S.D.
Nomad	182	32.5	20.5	145	39.1	17.66	71	38.7	14.8	74	39.4	20.11
Arikara	273	18.8	18.79	142	33.7	14.19	62	36.7	13.37	78	31.8	14.44
Pawnee	150	21.4	21.79	83	38.8	16.6	38	46.2	15.61	43	32.2	15.11
Omaha	165	16.2	18.51	72	33.9	14.78	29	35.4	12.02	43	32.8	16.44

[1] Adults aged older than 14 years.

543

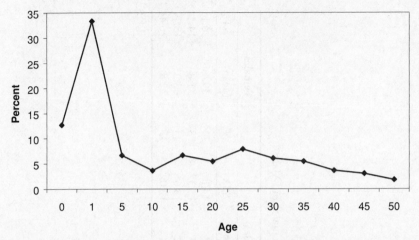

Figure 18.6. The Omaha and Ponca: Age distribution of deaths. *Notes:* Mean age-at-death = 16. *N* = 165. The skeletons were buried between ca. 1770 and 1820. Adult males (40%), adult females (60%). Skeletons 59 years and older (ca. 2%). Infant skeletons are underrepresented.

If the Pawnee had a growth rate of 1 percent a year in this prosperous period, their life expectancy at birth would have been 30 years, not 20 years. Higher growth rates (1.5 percent a year) would produce a life expectancy closer to 35 years, which seems quite a plausible value for a group blessed with environmental advantages, living in favorable historical circumstances.

As the Pawnee entered an increasingly stressful historical period, their life expectancy at birth would have surely fallen to lower values. But since vaccination prevented their demographic collapse, the Pawnee remained sufficiently numerous to be a power on the Plains as late as the 1840s. Afterward, as pioneer wagon trains began to stream through their territory, the Pawnee began to lose control over their land and resources, but without suffering extinction.

The Omaha and Ponca

The skeletons in this set come from two Omaha cemeteries and one Ponca cemetery. Since the groups were closely related, they have been combined to form the last population of Plain horticulturists considered here.

The group in Figure 18.6 has a particularly low skeletal mean age-at-death (16 years), which, if nothing else, gives us some confidence that most infant skeletons have been recovered. (Adding back any presumed "missing" infants would further reduce the mean age-at-death possibly to below 15 years.) Women who lived long enough to complete fertility in these villages probably had about eight children instead of seven. (The very low mean age-at-death suggests a GRR of 4.0.)[14]

---

[14] In the strict biological sense of "high," this level of fertility remains moderate. The highest biologically realistic level of fertility for an individual woman who is reproductively active between the ages of 15 and 45 is about 10 to 15 births over a reproductive lifespan of 30 years. Women who are more fecund than

Since the material environment of the Omaha and Ponca was similar to that of the Arikara and Pawnee, they probably had a resource base sufficient to support population growth. In the late seventeenth century, Europeans described them as a small group, but a century later their numbers were estimated in the 3,000 to 4,000 range. But the Omaha lived in the usual earth lodges crowded together in villages, which would have led to the standard disease problems. Since the Omaha were situated directly on the Missouri River itself, they were very quickly and frequently exposed to the diseases that spread along its banks as trade with Europeans increased.

During the period these bodies were buried, European observers described the Omaha as very prosperous (O'Shea and Ludwickson, 1992). Under the widely admired leadership of Chief Blackbird, the Omaha reached their zenith as a trading people around 1775–1800, and for that brief period, they were powerful enough to dictate terms of trade to the Spanish and English in the central Plains. The environmental and historical evidence favors the supposition that skeletons buried during this period came from a high-fertility, growing population with a life expectancy at birth higher than the "observed" mean age-at-death of 16 years. But it would have taken a growth rate of nearly 1.5 percent a year for these villages to have reached a real life expectancy at birth as high as 25 years. A value of 30 years would imply even more rapid growth.

By 1800, Comanche, Sioux, and even a few Pawnee groups had begun raiding the prosperous Omaha/Ponca, and in 1801 smallpox struck. This one epidemic is reported to have caused 400 deaths (O'Shea and Ludwickson, 1992). In 1837–1838, the Omaha lost about half their remaining population to another epidemic of smallpox, but this time the chiefs consented to the American offer of vaccination (Trimble, 1994). Once again, the adoption of this new method of disease control prevented the kind of catastrophic collapse which had affected the Arikara earlier on.

Although all the horticultural groups considered above had very low mean ages-at-death, in each case the totality of the contextual evidence – environmental, historical, and demographic – suggests that this is far more likely to reflect high fertility and population growth than exceptionally high mortality/low life expectancy. On the other hand, the weight of the evidence also suggests that life expectancy at birth was never as high as 40 years for any of the village-dwelling horticultural peoples.

Equestrian Nomads

The only native peoples living on the Plains with a relatively high "observed" mean age-at-death (meaning high by premodern standards) lived and died as equestrian nomads. Given that equestrian nomads also ate a diverse diet based on meat, wild foods, and grain obtained by trading or raiding, they had a good start on relative health. But they also lived at low densities and they rarely settled in one place for long, which minimized their exposure to both pollution-related and airborne diseases.

average (or who do not breast-feed) can have very short birth intervals and may give birth to many more than 10 to 15 live births. Seven to eight births per woman is less than half of the maximum possible biological fecundity.

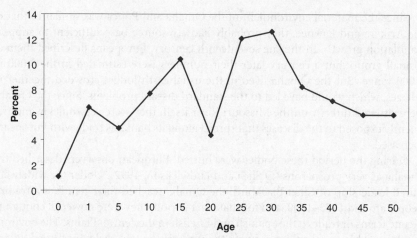

Figure 18.7. Equestrian Nomads: Age distribution of deaths. *Notes:* Mean age-at-death = 33. N = 182. The skeletons were buried between ca. 1870 and 1900. Adult males (49%), adult females (51%). Skeletons 59 years and older (ca. 10%).

At the first sign of an epidemic outbreak, a group of related families sharing a camp would disperse, and check its spread through isolation. Moreover, equestrian nomads usually benefited from raiding, since they were the attackers, not the victims. If any native populations reached the upper limits of premodern life expectancy (circa 40–50 years) it should be these groups.

But the last "group" of skeletons considered in Figure 18.7 does not represent a single population of equestrian nomads living in the traditional manner. Instead, they are a randomly assembled set of skeletons once belonging to several different no-madic populations, including the Blackfoot, Cheyenne, and Crow. (Unfortunately, no Sioux skeletons are included in this sample.) It is highly relevant that most of the older adults in this group were born and raised in the last few decades of nomadic freedom, while most of the younger skeletons were born during the reservation period, when conditions were much more environmentally stressful.

Although it is widely supposed that free-living nomadic groups had lower fertility than the settled horticultural peoples (five to six births per woman surviving to age 45 years instead of seven to eight births), even this disadvantage would not have prevented fairly rapid growth. With life expectancy levels toward the high end of the premodern spectrum (i.e., 35–40+ years), nomadic groups with relatively low fertility (a GRR of 2.5 instead of 3 or 4) would still have been able to expand at 1 to 2 percent a year until some disaster checked their growth. In the long run, that disaster came in the form of warfare with the United States Army, followed by consignment to reservations that brought their nomadic lifestyles to an end. But even as early as 1850, some equestrian nomads had begun fighting among themselves; for example, the Crow were already engaged in intensive warfare with the still expanding Sioux.

We will never know if pre-reservation life expectancy at birth levels were at the upper end of the normal premodern range, because nomads did not bury bodies under the ground. Instead, the dead were exposed to the open air, and thus few skeletons are recoverable for any specific group.

Far more certain is the fact that military defeat and reservation life caused a definite loss of welfare in the form of reduced control over territory and resources and in the adoption of unhealthy lifestyles. Reservation life imposed higher densities on former nomads. The food provided by government officials contained far too much flour and too little fresh meat to be healthful. As disease and malnutrition scarred the living, the bones of the dead recorded more and more signs of biological stress.

It might be considered reassuring that the mean age-at-death given for the 182 skeletons recovered is relatively high (32–33 years). But this particular mean age-at-death is as high as it is because so very few infant and child skeletons were included in the collection. (Given that equestrian nomads did not bury children or adults in the ground, we would expect the recovery of infant bones to be exceptionally poor.)

Nevertheless, adult survival still looks respectable in comparison to the other groups (Table 18.5). But even this cannot be taken at face value because during the early reservation periods, most groups began to decline in numbers, and after several decades of contraction, older skeletons would remain to represent the survivors of once-larger birth cohorts. Thus they would *seem* particularly abundant compared to younger adults who died earlier and came from smaller birth cohorts.

There are so many problems connected with this set of skeletons that taking age-at-death data out of their particularly complex historical context is bound to be misleading. But the possibility remains that by comparing their health status with other less advantaged populations, we can develop still another perspective on welfare history during this period of rapid change.

III. SKELETAL HEALTH, MORTALITY AND WELFARE HISTORY

In contemporary populations, "health" is a very complex concept with many different, culturally influenced definitions (Crimmins and Ingegneri, 1995). Its essential vagueness makes it very difficult to systematically compare living populations to each other, because there is no one way to measure "health" (Johansson, 1991). But, as Goodman and Martin point out in this volume, skeletal health is a different kind of health. Bones record forms of sustained biological stress, like those produced by slow-acting disease or hard work, as well as accidents and violence. Although not all the forms of skeletal stress recorded in bone would have produced perceived illness or disability among the living, they do indicate that the population was being subjected to biological stress in ways likely to compromise their resistance to disease. However, since paradoxical outcomes are possible, particularly in socially stratified groups (Wood et al., 1992), bad skeletal health for the young may not mean the same thing as bad skeletal health for older people.[15] As always, context matters.

---

[15] See note 13. Substantial but unobserved socioeconomic heterogeneity creates most of the potentially paradoxical outcomes discussed in this chapter. For example, if half the children in a group are poor, biologically stressed, and die young, then most young skeletons will show signs of that stress. The more

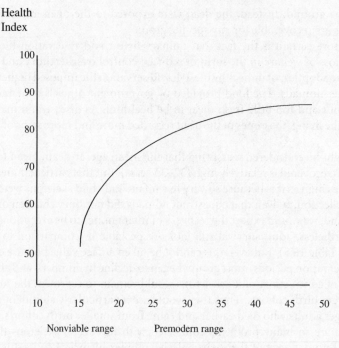

Health
Index

Life Expectancy at Birth in Years

Figure 18.8. Hypothetical relationship between life expectancy at birth and the health index by site. *Source:* See text.

The big problem with all skeletal data is that life-threatening, epidemic diseases do not leave traces in bone. Smallpox, for example, kills individuals so quickly that there are no skeletal traces of its eruption (Cohen, 1989). Nevertheless, it remains reasonable to suppose that far more often than not, the most biologically compromised sets of skeletons probably belonged to living populations that would have been least able to resist or recover from sudden biological shock in the form of periodic epidemics.

In general, the simplest assumption about skeletal health is that the healthier a set of skeletons appears to be, the more likely it was to have come from a relatively healthy living population. By extension, the healthier a living population was, the more likely it was to have had lower-than-average death rates. In premodern terms, that means its life expectancy at birth would have been closer to 40 years than 20 years. This simple hypothesis can be presented in graphic form (see Figure 18.8).

The exact shape or functional form of the relationship between skeletal health and life expectancy is uncertain, particularly before 1800, when nothing much in the way of medical care or welfare measures blocked the natural translation of poor

advantaged half of the population will survive, and look like relatively healthy adults. The combination of unhealthy children and healthy adults exists in the skeletal population, but not in the once-living population.

health into early death. The inmates in the Rochester poorhouse (see Chapter 6 in this volume) might be an exception to the relationship graphed above, but they may also be an example of the way that novel outcomes were becoming more common in the nineteenth century. In the case of Belleville (Chapter 5 in this volume), where real life expectancy at birth was about 36 years, DJD and poor dental health were also exceptionally prevalent. The possibility remains that after 1800, some aspects of health may have declined as life expectancy increased and medical/dental measures, combined with less strenuous lifestyles and increased support for the poor, began to blur what had once been a simple relationship. Clearly, more evidence is needed to explore the average shape of the relationship between skeletal health and longevity after 1800.

During the earlier period when traditional premodern conditions prevailed, as they did for the groups considered here, we would expect better skeletal health to be associated with higher life expectancies. If the observed mean age-at-death data violates this assumption, then we ought to suspect that growth rates may be complicating the picture, and that real life expectancy levels are higher.

The horticultural peoples of the Plains considered here all had low mean ages-at-death (high teens to low 20s); but in terms of their skeletal health (as measured by the score assigned to each group of Plains Indians by Steckel, Sciulli, and Rose), these groups appear to be moderately healthy. In the table titled "Health Index by Site" (Table 3.2 of Steckel, Sciulli, and Rose), the healthiest skeletal populations score 92 percent of the maximum value (100 percent), while the least healthy groups score 53 percent of the maximum possible. If we consider the Arikara sites, for example, they are given a middle ranking of 74–75 percent, roughly in the middle of the overall distribution. If skeletal health and life expectancy are positively related, then the Arikara ought to have been in the middle of the premodern range, having a life expectancy at birth level close to or above 30 years, which is what environmental and historical evidence also suggests.

Steckel, Sciulli, and Rose also break down their site-specific mean health index into individual attribute scores for each separate site (see their Table 3.3). With respect to relative height (as compared to all other groups in the project), Arikara groups also scored in the middle of the range. (The observed range goes from less than 1 percent of the theoretical maximum to 67.8 of the maximum, and the mean stature index for all groups is 20.7 percent of the maximum possible.) Separate Arikara sites score 16.8, 17.2, and 23.7, respectively, and the average for all three sites is 19, a value very close to overall mean. Although their dental health shows some variation between specific sites, no specific site is far from average. Degenerative joint disease also varies from site to site, but only one of the three separate Arikara sites is well above average. Compared to all the other groups in the project, however, the Arikara are relatively free of the signs of anemia.

The overall picture suggests that Arikara skeletal populations were in average health (for their chronological age) when burial occurred, at least according to the criteria created for this project. The existence of some site-specific variation is a possible sign that each site had its own specific environmental and historical characteristics, and that even minor environmental/historical differences between villages belonging to the same tribe may be preserved in bone.

Table 18.6: Frequencies of Cribra Orbitalia and Porotic Hyperostosis in Adult Males and Females

	Males				Females			
Group	N	#2	#3	%	N	#2	#3	%
C.O.								
Nomad	50	3	0	6.0	58	5	0	8.6
Arikara	48	4	0	8.3	50	1	0	2.0
Pawnee	20	0	0	0	28	0	0	0
Omaha	16	0	0	0	22	0	0	0
P.H.								
Nomad	52	1	0	1.9	57	1	0	1.8
Arikara	50	1	0	2.0	53	0	0	0
Pawnee	21	0	0	0	28	1	0	3.6
Omaha	16	0	0	0	22	0	0	0

N = Numbers of individuals.
#2 = Slight presence of lesions.
#3 = Moderate expansion of diploe.

Table 18.7: Frequencies of Cribra Orbitalia and Porotic Hyperostosis in Subadults Aged 1 to 10 Years

	Cribra orbitalia				Porotic hyperostosis			
Group	N	#2	#3	%	N	#2	#3	%
Nomad	20	4	1	25.0	20	0	0	0
Arikara	35	4	1	14.3	35	1	0	2.9
Pawnee	34	1	0	2.9	36	1	0	2.8
Omaha	45	1	0	2.2	45	1	0	2.2

N = Numbers of individuals.
#2 = Slight presence of lesions.
#3 = Moderate expansion of diploe.

In this chapter, separate Arikara sites were combined, and as one group they were compared to other groups of Plains Indians (sites combined) living similar lifestyles, but in different stages of contact. In the tables at the end of this chapter, the Arikara appear to be the only group of Plains horticulturists whose adults show signs of cribra orbitalia (Table 18.6); and their children display more of it than is found among the Pawnee and Omaha (see Table 18.7). If the signs of Arikara ill health come from those skeletons buried in the post-1750 period, rather than before, this makes historical sense. In Table 18.8, periosteal reactions in adult tibiae are slightly more frequent in the Arikara than in the other Plains Indians, particularly in males, which is probably an indication of their higher level of exposure to disease. Every form of wound and cranial bone fracture is also higher among Arikara adults than in the other two peoples (Table 18.9). Once again, these signs of trauma are consistent with the Arikara's relatively early historical exposure to warfare with the Sioux.

Table 18.8: Periosteal Reactions in Adult Tibiae by Sex and Group

Group	Males					Females					Adult %
	N	#2	#3	#4	%	N	#2	#3	#4	%	
Nomad	13	5	0	0	38.5	20	9	1	0	50.0	45.5
Arikara	28	6	0	0	21.4	31	3	0	0	9.7	15.3
Pawnee	24	2	0	1	12.5	18	1	1	1	16.7	14.3
Omaha	20	3	1	0	20.0	0	0	0	0	0	10.0

N = Number of individuals.
#2 = Slight periosteal reaction.
#3 = Moderate periosteal reaction.
#4 = Severe periosteal reaction including osteomyelitis.

Table 18.9: Weapon Wounds and Cranial Bone Fractures in Adult Males and Females by Group

Group	Males			Females			Adult %
	N	Trauma	%	N	Trauma	%	
Weapon Wound							
Nomad	71	13	18.3	74	3	4.1	11.0
Arikara	62	3	4.8	78	0	0	2.1
Pawnee	38	0	0	43	0	0	0
Omaha	28	1	3.6	43	0	0	1.4
Vault							
Nomad	53	15	28.3	57	7	12.3	20.0
Arikara	50	7	14.0	52	4	7.7	10.8
Pawnee	22	1	4.5	31	1	3.2	3.8
Omaha	17	0	0	22	0	0	0
Face							
Nomad	53	16	30.2	60	8	13.3	12.2
Arikara	52	9	17.3	56	3	5.4	11.1
Pawnee	24	0	0	35	1	2.9	1.7
Omaha	18	0	0	28	0	0	0
Nasal							
Nomad	49	4	8.2	54	5	9.3	8.7
Arikara	45	3	6.7	43	1	2.3	4.5
Omaha	18	0	0	21	0	0	0

Carious and abscessed teeth are also more frequent among the Arikara than the Pawnee and Omaha (Table 18.10). But, on the whole, caries rates for all the Plains horticulturists are very low, only slightly higher than the rate normally found among hunter-gatherers. This clearly reflects the continuing availability of meat in their diet.

Table 18.10: Dental Caries, Abscesses, and Antemortem Tooth Loss

Group	Number of teeth	Carious N	Carious %	Number of sockets	Abscesses N	Abscesses %	Premortem loss N	Premortem loss %
Nomad	1276	60	4.71	2571	63	2.5	242	9.4
Male	527	21	4.0	1077	24	2.2	108	10.0
Female	749	39	5.2	1494	39	2.6	134	9.0
Arikara	1609	102	6.3	1802	152	8.4	100	5.5
Male	821	46	5.6	1015	100	9.9	63	6.2
Female	788	56	7.1	787	52	6.6	37	4.7
Pawnee	921	40	4.3	1290	54	4.2	79	6.1
Male	410	9	2.2	542	27	5.0	38	7.0
Female	511	31	6.1	748	27	3.6	41	5.5
Omaha	697	31	4.4	1021	37	3.6	29	2.8
Male	334	3	0.9	585	11	1.9	8	1.4
Female	363	28	7.7	617	26	4.2	21	3.4

If we use femur length as an index of relative height, the Arikara males were the tallest Plains Indians considered here, although their women are the shortest. (This sex-linked difference reduces their apparent advantage in the column labeled "Stature" in Table 3.3: "Health Index as a Percent of Maximum.") Since both sexes shared the same disease environment, female babies could have been less well fed in early life, or worked much harder than male children from an early age, as some historical descriptions suggest. But females who married very young could have died in childbirth, even before reaching their full adult height, thus pulling the adult female average down (Table 18.11).

In any case, the division of labor between men and women may explain the surplus of adult female skeletons in Arikara village cemeteries (see Table 18.4). Males who died far from the village while hunting, fighting, or trading would not have been buried at home.

In terms of the overall health index devised by Steckel, Scuilli, and Rose (Chapter 3 in this volume), the Pawnees outrank the Arikara by about 5 points. But they also have a very low mean age-at-death. Taken literally, this would mean that an exceptionally healthy population (in skeletal terms) existed well below the margin of demographic viability.

In contrast, when their low mean age-at-death is put into the relevant environmental and historical circumstances, it is more likely than ever that the Pawnee were a vigorous, growing population with high fertility (see Appendix). As such, they probably had a life expectancy level that was higher than the Arikara's, just as they had a higher level of skeletal health. The recovered Pawnee skeletons come from a prosperous period in which this particular people were not yet under sustained attack by the Sioux. Their comparative freedom from violent conflict would

Table 18.11: Femur and Humerus Lengths and Midshaft Diameters

	Femur								Humerus		
	Length			Midshaft A-P			Midshaft M-L			Length		
Group	N	Mean	S.D.	N	Mean	S.D.	N	Mean	S.D.	N	Mean	S.D.
Male											
Nomad	9	460.9	15.42	10	32.7	2.21	10	28.4	1.35	6	337.0	8.00
Arikara	24	455.0	14.03	26	30.4	2.08	26	26.9	0.98	17	321.3	15.16
Pawnee	22	452.0	16.68	24	31.2	2.28	24	28.9	1.95	14	323.6	12.64
Omaha	13	446.8	20.71	13	29.3	2.98	13	25.9	2.19	13	313.3	9.34
Female											
Nomad	11	441.6	21.50	12	28.4	2.23	12	25.9	2.39	8	311.6	19.21
Arikara	25	417.2	17.89	26	25.9	2.17	26	24.1	1.60	18	297.7	12.91
Pawnee	11	430.6	16.74	16	26.8	1.76	16	24.9	2.39	11	308.4	13.49
Omaha	11	427.3	13.44	14	26.3	1.94	14	24.1	2.09	12	301.5	10.16

go far toward explaining the lower frequency of weapon wounds and bone fractures found among adult Pawnee males, as well as the apparent longevity advantages of mature males. (Table 18.9). On the whole, the Pawnee show fewer signs of disease than the Arikara, which is also consistent with their greater geographic isolation during the period the recovered skeletons were buried.

The fact that Pawnee women are relatively tall gives all Pawnee adults an overall, if slight, size advantage over the other Plains horticulturists. (Note, however, that this overall advantage is not reflected in male femur length. See Table 18.11.) On the whole, since the Pawnee had an above-average level of skeletal health (80.4 percent of the maximum possible), this score suggests that they had, at the very least, a life expectancy level above 30, possibly as high as 35 years.

The Omaha and Ponca results are more difficult to interpret. Both groups have an above-average health index by site. (See Steckel, Sciulli, and Rose, Table 3.2.) The Omaha and Ponca also display the fewest cases of cribra orbitalia and porotic hyperostosis among the settled peoples of the Plains (Table 18.6). In general, this is interpreted as a sign of good health reflecting the absence of anemia.[16] Together, the two groups have a very low mean age-at-death of 16 years. As a life expectancy at birth, this suggests that the Omaha/Ponca have fallen well below the margin of viability. But as a mean age-at-death, it can also be a sign of very high fertility and a growing population with a much higher, real life expectancy at birth. Historical evidence does suggest that the Omaha were growing rapidly at the time they buried

---

[16] Stuart-Macadam, 1991. Stuart-Macadam argues that porotic hyperostosis is not always a bad sign. When the environment imposes a high pathogenic load on the average individual (caused by a combination of chronic viral, bacterial, fungal, and parasitic infections), iron-deficiency anemia (the cause of porotic hyperostosis) can be a defense mechanism. It slows down the replication rate of iron-dependent bacterial and parasitic invaders. Even if this skeletal disease is a successful defense (rather than a sign of an iron-poor diet), it still indicates that the affected individuals are exposed to disease at a very high level.

these skeletons, but they would have had to be growing at over 2 percent a year to have had such a low mean age-at-death and a life expectancy at birth as high as 30 years.

In this case, good skeletal health may be deceptive. Perhaps their life expectancy at birth was reduced by a number of diseases that killed too quickly to leave its traces in bone. Given all the problems with skeletal data, it would be asking too much for every case to fit the model perfectly.

But it is reassuring to find that adult males are underrepresented in the Omaha-Ponca villages (Table 18.4). As riverine traders, some of the men would have died far from home and not been buried in their own village. Those who lived to die at home would have traveled more widely than women, and this could explain why four adult male skeletons show signs of disease (based on the number of periosteal reactions in Table 18.8), while no female skeletons do. Markers of traumatic death are normal for the Omaha (normal by Plains Indian standards), while the Ponca skeletons showed fewer signs of trauma than any other Plains Indian group.

Equestrian Nomads

The equestrian nomads, which were treated as one group in Section II B of this chapter, are actually a very mixed collection of skeletons buried by several different groups, none of which include the Sioux. Thus, it is not surprising that when data for the combined groups are disaggregated into site-specific data, they produce very different scores for their overall health in Steckel, Sciulli, and Rose's index (see Chapter 3). The Blackfoot skeletons are the healthiest group of equestrian nomads, but these skeletons are mostly skulls. The Cheyenne skeletons, in contrast, score well below the Arikara. While all equestrian nomads shared a basic lifestyle, they also had different histories of conflict with each other and the United States Army, as well as when and how they were eventually confined to reservations. We would expect these environmental and historical differences to have produced variations in skeletal health in the nineteenth century, and they did.

Recall that before 1800, most equestrian nomadic groups led healthy lifestyles with good diets and comparative freedom from pollution-related and epidemic diseases. The best evidence for their relative good health is that the complete skeletons recovered from nomadic populations are relatively tall by standards of the entire collection of populations. In Steckel, Sciulli, and Rose's Table 3.3, the Cheyenne and the Crow skeletons have a stature index that is twice that of the Plains Indians living in villages. (It is of interest that based on measurements made in the late nineteenth century, the adult males from Sioux groups remained exceptionally tall, even in the period of early captivity.) (Prince and Steckel, 1999.)

The fact that the skeletons from nomadic groups were taller than those from the settled, horticultural groups probably reflects life under pre-reservation conditions. But in the sample here, these tall adults also had the highest percentage of cribra orbitalia, indicating possible pre-death malnutrition, and/or increased exposure to parasites. This is not what we would expect to find in relatively tall adults living in comparatively healthy circumstances, and they may well be signs of increased exposure to disease in reservation environments, and/or the poor diets imposed on them there.

Almost all the subadult skeletons from equestrian nomad groups (see Table 18.7) came from children growing up under reservation conditions; and we would expect these children to have had high levels of anemia compared to children in the horticultural groups. It seems very doubtful that those children who survived bad diets and increased exposure to disease as a consequence of reservation life would have become as tall as their pre-reservation parents, but no evidence on this point is available.

Among all the equestrian nomad groups, the Cheyenne adults had the greatest frequency of weapon wounds and bone fractures (see Table 3.3 in Steckel, Sciulli, and Rose). This is very consistent with their reputation for being exceptionally active warriors (Moore, 1987). But even Cheyenne women were affected by signs of violence. This raises the possibility that female skeletal trauma is reflecting the domestic violence induced by despair and social disorganization after the confinement to reservations.[17] In contrast, the Crow Indians, as former equestrian nomads, show no more signs of trauma than the Plains horticulturalists.

Before their confinement to reservations, equestrian nomads were probably in above-average skeletal health, and thus longer lived than most village dwellers. Values at the high end of the premodern spectrum (40 years) are not improbable during the eighteenth century. Even if nomadic groups had lower natural fertility than the settled peoples (as is often supposed), it would have been easy for them to grow at well over 1 percent a year, so long as they could keep expanding the territory under their control. This they did for a century or longer until checked by the American Army after 1865.

IV. SOME CONCLUDING OBSERVATIONS

The arrival of Europeans in the New World is supposed to have initiated a rapid demographic collapse among all the native peoples. But this uniformity depends on the assumption that all of the groups involved were equally vulnerable to epidemic disease, irrespective of their initial levels of health and life expectancy (Milner, 1992). The assumed absence of variation between groups subsequently diminishes the value of detailed research on the welfare history of the native peoples either before or after contact in different environmental and historical circumstances.

A primary goal of the Western Hemisphere Project has been to use skeletal data from different groups of people living in different times and places in North, South, and Central America to look for significant variation in their health status. The evidence is overwhelming that such variation existed, and it now becomes imperative to reconsider oversimplified theories of contact shock.

Estimating the mortality of skeletal populations can be treated as a simple matter, or one that requires context-sensitive estimation methods. This chapter has argued against relying on the assumption that a group's mean age-at-death is the same

---

[17] Research suggests that some nomadic groups confined to reservations received a "less worse" settlement than others, and thus remained better nourished (see J. Prince, 1995).

as its life expectancy at birth. Instead, any mean age-at-death should be put back into its environmental, historical, and demographic context in order to estimate a plausible growth rate during the period of skeletal deposition. Subsequently, growth-rate estimates should be used to estimate life expectancy levels, if only because a relatively healthy/growing population can have the same low mean age-at-death as an unhealthy/declining one.

Finally, we can use skeletal health as an independent check on life expectancy estimates. If groups in average skeletal health (as defined by Steckel, Sciulli, and Rose for this project) normally had an average level of life expectancy at birth (using premodern standards for what is average), then only groups in below-average skeletal health are likely to have a genuinely low life expectancy, meaning one in the neighborhood of 20 years.[18] Since groups with a life expectancy at birth as low as 20 years are at the margin of demographic viability, even one epidemic might drive them over the edge to extinction. But groups with higher life expectancy levels, for example, those in the 30- to 40-year range, are sufficiently far enough from the margin of viability to absorb a few disease-related shocks, and continue to exist, albeit at a lower level of life expectancy. Thus, it should not surprise us that so many native peoples did survive contact shock, and continued to preserve a distinctive non-European ethnic and cultural heritage, even to this day.

The first Americans were more than just the tragic victims of epidemic diseases introduced by Europeans. Many survived a series of mortality shocks by using their intelligence to adapt to new circumstances. On the Great Plains, most of the native peoples who lived in villages were in reasonably good health by premodern standards when Europeans first appeared; and despite new epidemics, they were able to turn contact into an opportunity to improve their material welfare and increase their numbers. While they remained in control of their land and its resources they made American history as traders, producers, fighters and negotiators.[19] It was only when warfare with rival groups intensified, and their economies collapsed, that adverse circumstances, including epidemics, overwhelmed them. Thanks to this project, welfare historians can use skeletal data, along with other sources, to reconstruct the welfare history of the first Americans in ways that stress their intelligence, creativity, and resourcefulness, not just the diseases that Europeans introduced.

APPENDIX

Formal mathematical demonstrations can be used to prove that in stable population theory, the mean age-at-death can be converted into an index of fertility but not a mortality level.[20] Fertility can be measured in many ways, but the most relevant

---

[18] Given the excellent health of skeletons recovered from the Georgia Bight, it is unlikely that their real life expectancy at birth, both before contact and in its early phases, is as low as their mean age-at-death (22–23 years) indicates. Besides, it is very clear that infant skeletons are underrepresented in the skeletal samples, and that adjusting for that defect would further lower the mean age-at-death. Migration also appears to be disturbing the before-contact and early-contact sets of skeletons. See C. S. Larsen and A. W. Crosby in this volume.

[19] See, for example, Williams, 1997.

[20] Coale, 1972.

one in this case is the total fertility rate – the number of living children borne by the average woman who survives to menopause (circa 45 years of age).

Human populations in which fertility remains "natural" (meaning no attempt is made to deliberately restrict the flow of births) can have either high, medium, or low total fertility rates. In the case of high fertility, the average woman would have a first birth in her late teens and every 24 months thereafter: she would complete fertility with about 10 births. With a longer birth interval closer to three years (36 months), the average woman would complete fertility with about 7 births (moderate fertility). Long birth intervals (four years or more) will reduce completed fertility to 5 births per woman. This is low fertility by premodern standards. But at any level of fertility, when mortality falls (life expectancy rises), more women in a group will complete fertility. This will increase the annual flow of births to the group in the short run, even if gross reproduction rates remained the same.

When annual birthrates exceed annual death rates on a regular basis, the base of a group's age structure pyramid will broaden, and, as it does, the mean age-at-death for that group will fall, and so will the average age of the living population. In a declining stable population, the opposite happens. If mortality rises, fewer women will survive to the age of 45 years, and this will reduce the group's annual flow of births, even if birth intervals and total fertility rates remains unchanged. A sustained reduction in the annual flow of births to a premodern population will cause the base of its age structure pyramid (normally a triangle) to contract; as it does it becomes diamond shaped. The mean age of the living population will rise, and so will the mean age-at-death.

In animal populations under sustained environmental stress, those females who survive to the end of their reproductive life span can go on having babies at the same pace (twice a year, once a year, etc.). The same seems to be true of human populations unless they actively engage in preventing conception or inducing abortion until times improve.

REFERENCES

Alesan, A., M. Assumpcion, and C. Castellana. 1999. "Looking into the Demography of an Iron Age Population in the Western Mediterranean. 1. Mortality." *American Journal of Physical Anthropology.* 109: 285–301.

Axtell, J. 1997. *The Indians' New South: Cultural Change in the Colonial Southeast.* Baton Rouge: Louisiana State University Press.

Coale, A. 1972. *The Growth and Structure of Human Populations: A Mathematical Investigation.* Princeton, N.J.: Princeton University Press.

Coale, A., and P. Demeny. 1983. *Regional Model Life Tables and Stable Populations,* 2d ed. New York: Academic Press.

Coatsworth, J. 1996. "Welfare." *American Historical Review,* Feb.: 1–12.

Cohen, M. 1989a. "The Evidence of Prehistoric Skeletons." Chapter 7 in *Health and the Rise of Civilization.* New Haven, Conn.: Yale University Press.

Cohen, M. 1989b. "Conclusions." *Health & the Rise of Civilization.* New Haven, Conn.: Yale University Press. Pp 130–142.

Cohen, M., and G. Armelegos. 1984. "Paleopathology at the Origins of Agriculture: Editor's Summation." In *Paleopathology at the Origins of Agriculture,* ed. M. Cohen and G. Armelagos. Orlando, Fla.: Academic Press. Pp. 585–601.

Cook, N. 1998. *Born to Die: Disease and New World Conquest.* Cambridge: Cambridge University Press.

Crimmins, E., and Dominique G. Ingegneri. 1995. "Trends in Health of the US Population: 1957–89." In *The State of Humanity,* ed. Julian Simon. Oxford: Blackwell. Pp. 72–84.

Crosby, A. 1986. *Ecological Imperialism. The Biological Expansion of Europe, 900–1900.* Cambridge: Cambridge University Press.

Diamond, J. 1998. *Guns, Germs and Steel.* London: Vintage.

Dobson, M. 1997. *Contours of Death and Disease in Early Modern England.* Cambridge: Cambridge University Press.

Dumond, D. 1997. "Seeking Demographic Causes for Changes in Population Growth Rates." In *Integrating Archaeological Demography: Multidisciplinary Approaches to Prehistoric Population,* ed. R. Paine. Center for Archaeological Investigations, Southern Illinois, University of Carbondale, Occasional Paper No. 24. Pp. 175–190.

Ferguson, R., and N. Whitehead, eds. 1992. *War in the Tribal Zone, Expanding States and Indigenous Warfare.* Santa Fe, N. Mex.: School of American Research.

Gutierrez, R. 1997. *When Jesus Came the Corn Mothers Went Away.* Stanford, Calif.: Stanford University Press.

Harpending, H. 1997. "Living Records of Past Population Change." In *Integrating Archaeological Demography: Multidisciplinary Approaches to Prehistoric Population,* ed. R. Paine. Center for Archaeological Investigations, Southern Illinois, University of Carbondale, Occasional Paper No. 24. Pp. 89–100.

Henige, D. 1998. *Numbers from Nowhere: The American Indian Contact Population Debate.* Norman: University of Oklahoma Press.

Hofman, J. 1996. "Early Hunter-Gatherers of the Central Great Plains: Paleoindian and Mesoindian (Archaic) Cultures." In *Archeology and Paleoecology of the Central Great Plains,* ed. J. Hofman. Arkansas Archeological Survey Research Series, No. 48. Pp. 41–101.

Johansson, S. 1982. "The Demographic History of the Native Peoples of North America: A Selective Bibliography." *Yearbook of Physical Anthropology,* 25: 133–152.

——— 1991. "The Health Transition: The Cultural Inflation of Morbidity during the Decline of Mortality." *Health Transition Review* 1: 39–68.

——— 1994. "Food for Thought: Rhetoric and Reality in Mortality History." *Historical Methods,* 27: 101–125.

——— 1996. "The Politics of Discourse Synthesis in the Literature of Health Reserach." *Social Epistemology,* 10: 43–53.

——— 2000. "Macro and Micro Perspectives on Mortality History." *Historical Methods,* 33: 59–72.

Johansson, S., and S. Horowitz. 1986. "Estimating Mortality in Skeletal Populations: The Influence of the Growth Rate on the Interpretation of Levels and Trends During the Transition to Agriculture." *American Journal of Physicial Anthropology* 71: 233–250.

Johansson, S., and S. Preston. 1978. "Tribal Demography: The Hopi and Navaho Populations As Seen Through Manuscripts from the 1900 U.S. Census." *Social Science History,* 3: 1–33.

Keckler, Charles. 1997. "Catastrophic Mortality in Simulations of Forager Age-at-Death: Where Did All the Humans Go?" In *Integrating Archaeological Demography: Multidisciplinary Approaches to Prehistoric Population,* ed. R. Paine. Center for Archaeological Investigations, Southern Illinois, University of Carbondale, Occasional Paper No. 24. Pp. 205–228.

Keenleyside, A. 1998. "Skeletal Evidence of Health and Disease in Pre-Contact Alaskan Eskimos and Aleuts." *American Journal of Physical Anthropology,* 107: 51–70.

Kunitz, S. 1994. *Disease and Social Diversity: The European Impact on the Health of Non-Europeans.* New York: Oxford University Press.

Lehmer, D., and W. Wood. 1977. *Buffalo and Beans. Reprints in Anthropology,* 8: 85–89 (Lincoln, Neb.: J & L Reprint Company).

Milner, G. 1992. "Disease and Sociopolitical Systems in Late Prehistoric Illinois." In *Disease and Demography in the Americas,* ed. J. Verano and D. Ubelaker. Washington, D.C.: Smithsonian Institution Press. Pp. 103–116.

Moore, J. 1987. *The Cheyenne Nation.* Lincoln: The University of Nebraska Press.

O'Shea, J., and J. Ludwickson. 1992. *Archaeology and Ethnohistory of the Omaha Indians: The Big Village Site.* Lincoln: University of Nebraska Press. See pp. 20–26.

Owsley, D. 1994. "Warfare in Coalescent Tradition Populations of the Northern Plains." In *Skeletal Biology in the Great Plains,* ed. D. Owsley and R. Jantz. Washington, D.C.: Smithsonian Press. Pp. 333–344.

Owsley D., and W. Bass. 1979. "A Demographic Analysis of Skeletons from the Larson Site (39WW2) Walworth County, South Dakota: Vital Statistics." *American Journal of Physicial Anthropology,* 51: 145–154.

Owsley, D., H. Berryman, and W. Bass. 1977. "Demographic and Osteological Evidence for Warfare at the Larson Site (39WW2) Walworth County, South Dakota." *Plains Anthropologist Memoir* 13: 119–131.

Owsley, D., and K. Bruwelheide. 1996. "Bioarcheological Research in Northeastern Colorado, Northern Kansas, Nebraska, and South Dakota." In *Archeology and Paleoecology of the Central Great Plains,* ed. J. Hofman. Arkansas Archeological Survey Research Series, No. 48. Pp. 150–201.

Paine, Richard. 1997. "Uniformitarian Models in Osteological Paleodemography." In *Integrating Archaeological Demography: Multidisciplinary Approaches to Prehistoric Population,* ed. R. Paine. Center for Archaeological Investigations, Southern Illinois, University of Carbondale, Occasional Paper No. 24. Pp. 191–202.

Palkovich, A. 1981. "Demography and Disease Patterns in a Protohistoric Plains Group: A Study of the Mobridge Site (39WW1). *Plains Anthropologist Memoir,* 17: 71–84.

Preston, S. 1995. "Human Mortality Throughout History and Prehistory." In *The State of Humanity,* ed. Julian Simon. Oxford: Blackwell. Pp. 30–36.

Prince, J. 1995. "Intersection of Economics, History and Human Biology: Secular Trends in Stature in Nineteenth-Century Sioux Indians." *Human Biology,* 67: 387–406.

Prince, J., and R. Steckel. 1999. "Tallest in the World: Native Americans of the Great Plains in the 19th Century." Paper given at the Demographic Forum of the Norwegian Demographic Society, Oslo, June 10–13, 1999.

Reff, D. 1991. *Disease, Depopulation and Culture Change in Northwestern New Spain, 1518–1764.* Salt Lake City: University of Utah Press.

Rogers, J. 1995. "The Friar Tuck Syndrome." *Nonesuch. Bristol University Almanac Magazine,* Autumn: 51–52.

Smith, D. S. 2001. In conversation and correspondence.

Snooks, G. D. 1996. *The Dynamic Society: Exploring the Sources of Global Change.* London: Routledge.

Stannard, D. 1992. *American Holocaust: Columbus and the Conquest of the New World.* New York: Oxford University Press.

Steckel, R. 1995. "Stature and the Standard of Living." *Journal of Economic Literature,* 33: 1903–1940.

Stuart-Macadam, P. 1991. "Porotic Hyperostosis: Changing Interpretations." In *Human Paleopathology: Current Syntheses and Future Options,* ed. D. Ortner and A. Aufderheide. Washington, D.C.: Smithsonian Institution Press. Pp. 36–39.

Swedlund, A. 1989. "Issues in Demography and Health." In *Understanding Complexity in the Prehistoric Southwest*, ed. G. Guerman and M. Gell-Mann. SFI Studies in the Sciences of Complexity, Proc. Vol. XVI. Reading, Mass.: Addison Wesley. Pp. 39–58.

Trimble, M. 1994. "The 1837–1838 Smallpox Epidemic on the Upper Missouri." In *Skeletal Biology in the Great Plains*, ed. D. Owsley and R. Jantz. Washington D.C.: Smithsonian Institution Press.

Watts, S. 1997. *Epidemics and History: Disease, Power and Imperialism*. New Haven, Conn.: Yale University Press.

Wedel, W. 1977. "Plains Archeology." *Great Plains Journal* 17: 25–40.

Weiss, K. 1981. "Evolutionary Perspectives on Human Aging." In *Other Ways of Growing Old*, ed. P. Amos and S. Harrell. Stanford, Calif.: Stanford University Press. Pp. 30–60.

Wells, R. 1992. "The Population of England's Colonies in America: Old English or New Americans." *Population Studies*, 46: 85–102.

Williams, R. Jr. 1997. *Linking Arms Together: American Indian Treaty Visions of Law and Peace, 1600–1800*. Oxford: Oxford University Press.

Wood, J., G. Milner, H. Harpending, and K. Weiss. 1992. "The Osteological Paradox: Problems of Inferring Prehistoric Health from Skeletal Samples." *Current Anthropology*, 33: 34–70.

PART VII

## CHAPTER NINETEEN

Patterns of Health in the Western Hemisphere

Richard H. Steckel and Jerome C. Rose

ABSTRACT

This chapter discusses time trends and related patterns in the health index that emerge across sites arranged by categories, such as climate, settlement size, and topography. A substantial decline in the index occurred in the millennia before the arrival of Columbus. The good health of the least complex societies did not occur because the Western Hemisphere was a biological Garden of Eden, an epidemiological paradise substantially free of pathogens so detrimental to health in other parts of the world: pre-Columbian populations were among the healthiest and the least healthy in our sample. While pre-Columbian natives may have lived in a disease environment substantially different from that in other parts of the globe, the original inhabitants also brought with them, or evolved with, enough pathogens to create chronic conditions of ill health under conditions of systematic agriculture and urban living. Our research suggests that life *became* "nasty, brutish and short" for the typical person with the rise of agriculture, government, and urbanization. The transition may have been driven by several factors, including resource depletion, efforts by leaders to redistribute wealth and power, and a voluntary desire to live with material goods and lifestyle provided by urban areas.

This project reveals a rich and varied history of health in the Western Hemisphere, as indicated by substantial variation in the health index of those who lived during the past several millennia. Although none of these populations were healthy by standards of the middle or late twentieth century, they were widely arrayed on the health index and its components. Our tasks here are to describe and identify patterns in this variation, and to discuss possible explanations and their implications. Several interesting patterns emerge, including the pre-Columbian decline in health, the various environmental conditions that were important for health, and the rankings of Euro-Americans and African-Americans.

Table 19.1: Values of Health Index and Components for Major Groups Who Lived in the Western Hemisphere

Group	Statistic	Index	Stature	Hyp.	Anemia	Dental
Euro-Americans	Average ($N = 9$ sites)	71.4	26.6	79.3	96.6	72.0
	Std. Dev.	2.9	12.5	19.6	2.1	5.2
African-Americans	Average ($N = 5$ sites)	67.1	40.9	42.4	87.1	76.9
	Std. Dev.	5.7	23.6	21.1	17.4	7.9
Native Central	Average ($N = 8$ sites)	64.0	13.4	52.8	80.6	81.7
Americans	Std. Dev.	3.8	9.8	24.8	7.6	7.0
Native South	Average ($N = 15$ sites)	75.1	3.6	82.9	92.9	84.4
Americans	Std. Dev.	9.0	2.8	17.0	6.7	11.7
Native North	Average ($N = 10$)	78.1	32.2	86.7	94.7	81.7
Americans (East)	Std. Dev.	5.6	14.1	8.8	3.6	15.3
Native North	Average ($N = 18$)	73.7	21.3	66.1	83.8	85.5
Americans (West)	Std. Dev.	8.3	15.1	24.5	16.6	6.4
	Average, 65 sites	72.6	20.7	71.1	90.5	81.8
	Std. Dev, 65 sites	8.0	16.9	24.6	11.5	10.4
	Minimum, 65 sites	53.5	0.4	9.8	53.2	55.3
	Maximum, 65 sites	91.8	67.8	99.7	100.0	100.0

Source: Consolidated database.

GENERAL TENDENCIES ACROSS GROUPS

Table 19.1 shows that average values for the health index ranged from 64.0 for Native Central Americans to 78.1 for Native North Americans who lived in the East, a difference of 20 percent. All Native American groups except those from Central America exceeded the average for all sites (72.6). Euro-Americans, who are now the largest and healthiest group in the hemisphere, at one time occupied neither position.

Statistical analysis of components of the health index by site (see the methodology chapter by Steckel, Sciulli, and Rose in this volume) shows that correlations among the various elements of health were moderate to low. Thus, it is unsurprising to find diverse outcomes on components when aggregating results to the group level. European-Americans had above-average component scores for childhood indicators (stature, hypoplasias, and anemia – the last being the highest for any group) but had the worst dental health and the most trauma of any group. African-Americans were the tallest but had the highest level of hypoplasias, and they fell below average on other indicators with the exception of trauma. The Native Americans of Central America had the lowest scores of any group on anemia, infections, and degenerative joint disease, but the least trauma. Native South Americans were the shortest but had the fewest infections. Native North Americans in the East scored highest of any group on hypoplasias and degenerative joint disease, and fell slightly below average on only one component – dental health. Native North Americans of the West scored highest of any group on dental health, but fell below average on hypoplasias, anemia, and trauma.

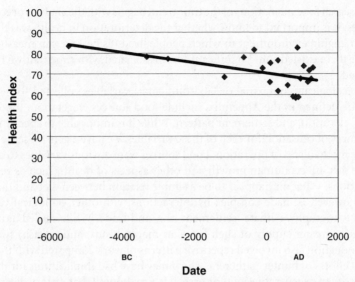

Figure 19.1. Average value of the health index by time period prior to AD 1500. *Note:* Deterioration in health is indicated by the downward trend of the linear regression line associated with these points ($R^2 = 0.53$; $p \leq 0.05$). The health index declined by an average of 2.5 points per millennium.

Pre-Columbian Time Trends

Figure 19.1 presents a scatter diagram of health index values by approximate year or date. The figure includes 23 precontact sites where all components of the health index are available. The downward trend over time is statistically significant according to the following estimated linear regression equation:

$$HI = 65.41 + 0.0025\,YBP,\ N = 23,\ R^2 = 0.53$$

$$(2.89)$$

where HI stands for the health index, and YBP represents years BP (before present, which is taken as 1950). *T*-values are shown in parentheses. The coefficient of the time variable indicates that the index fell, on average, by 0.0025 points per year from roughly 7,500 years BP to about 450 years BP, which amounts to 17.5 points over roughly 7 millennia. A decline of this magnitude represents a significant deterioration in health and is larger than the difference between the most and least healthy groups who lived in the Western Hemisphere (see Table 19.1).

For purposes of analysis and interpretation, it would be preferable if the data points were widely arrayed across the time axis. Unfortunately, the observations are concentrated in the two millennia before the arrival of Columbus, an era when there was clearly a great deal of diversity in health across sites. The highest value for the index did occur at the oldest site, but two sites in the later era also scored above 80. The least healthy sites (scores under 65), however, were all concentrated within 2,000 years of the present.

Our search for explanations of the time trend begins with the analysis of ecological variables. It is important to know whether the deterioration in health was the result of the changing environment in which people lived (as best we can measure it) or whether there existed some significant force associated with time that we have not measured.

The ecological (contextual or environmental) variables collected for each site, which are defined in the Appendix, include food sources, vegetation, topography, climate, elevation, and settlement pattern. While it is impossible to specify in detail the pathway of causation for each of these variables, we have a general sense of their possible mechanisms of operation. Food sources were obvious variables to consider because diet affects human growth and other aspects of health, such as resistance to infections. What may appear to be a simple relation between diet and the health index, however, is made complex by interactions with other ecological variables, such as topography, climate, settlement size, and trade. While settled agriculture provided a greater supply of such foods as maize, beans, and squash, systematic food production also involved repetitive patterns of work compared with the varied physical efforts of hunter-gatherers, which may have had implications for the onset and severity of degenerative joint disease. It is also thought that dietary diversity and quality may have suffered in the transition to settled agriculture. In addition, there is evidence that maize consumption led to dental decay. Thus, it is difficult to specify in advance the general magnitude and even the direction of effect that subsistence patterns may have had on the health index. In any event, all pre-Columbian sites lacked the dietary diversity that was later provided by the addition of plants and animals raised in Europe and the Mediterranean.

Vegetation surrounding the site may have affected health via the type and availability of resources for food and shelter. Forests, for example, provide materials for the diet, fuel and housing, and also sheltered animals that could have been used for food. Semideserts posed challenges for the food supply relative to more lush forests or grasslands, but the dry climate might have inhibited the transmission of some diseases.

Flood plains or coastal living provided easy access to aquatic sources of food and enabled trade compared with more remote, interior areas, but trade may have promoted the spread of disease. Uneven terrain found in hilly or mountainous areas may have provided advantages for defense, but could have led to more accidents and fractures.

Climate was relevant for health owing to its possible effects on the presence of pathogens. Insects and bacteria, for example, tend to thrive in warm, moist climates, while very cold climates often pose challenges for the food supply or for keeping warm. Climate also affects vegetation or biomass available for consumption and indirectly influences the type of settlement patterns that are feasible.

Elevation affects temperature, insect vectors, and vegetation, and often is associated with terrain, opportunities for trade, and settlement patterns. Low elevations, particularly coastal or flood plain areas, probably provided food and opportunities for trade, which were beneficial for health. But at most low elevations in our sample, the climate was tropical or subtropical, which could have increased exposure to disease. It is therefore difficult to predict the effect that elevation may have had on health.

A great deal is known about settlement patterns and health from historical records. Prior to the development of effective public health measures near the end of the nineteenth century, urban areas were notoriously unhealthy. Large, permanent concentrations of people led to the accumulation of waste that harbored parasites detrimental to health. Close contact, often in crowded places of living or work, readily spread many diseases. Cities usually had substantially unequal distributions of wealth and power – and therefore large differences in access to resources and in work effort, which were important for health. It seems likely that these same processes affecting health existed in the pre-Columbian world. Other things being equal, one would expect the more mobile, less densely settled populations to have been healthier than those living in paramount towns or urban areas.

We investigated the connection between ecological variables and the health index using a sequence of regressions that probed the statistical connection of one ecological category at a time. Mindful that the sample size was relatively small compared with the number of variables under investigation, we sought a parsimonious explanatory model by weeding out unimportant variables or distinctions. Using criteria of statistical significance and sizes of estimated regression coefficients, we found that many variables could be dropped from the regression analysis or that categories could be combined.[1] Specifically, in topography we created a coastal and a noncoastal variable, and elevation was collapsed into two categories: 0−300 meters and 300+ meters. In settlement patterns, dispersed and village were combined, as were paramount town and urban. With regard to plants, we aggregated the category of some domesticates and the category of maize (or potatoes), beans, and squash.

Somewhat to our surprise, climatic distinctions were completely irrelevant for the health index. The R^2 in a regression of the health index on climate categories was 0.002, and the largest t-value was only 0.18. This result does not mean that climate was everywhere irrelevant for health, but only that within the sample under study, our measure of health (the health index) was not affected by climatic distinctions we were able to make (tropical, subtropical, and temperate) for the pre-Columbian sites.[2] We therefore eliminated climate from further study, but plan to revisit this topic in later research.

[1] With regard to elevation, for example, the regression coefficients for 300 to 1,000 meters and 1,000+ meters were −8.4 and −12.8, respectively. Based on an F test, their difference was statistically significant at only 0.30, and the variables were combined. The coefficients are in similar value, which means that their effects on the index were about the same. The difference in the coefficients is 4.4, which amounts to 58 percent of the standard deviation in the health index. Therefore, even if these coefficients were significantly different, one might possibly argue that the categories could be combined because they do not delineate important differences in health. In contrast, the coefficients for the settlement categories shown in Table 19.2 were significantly different at 0.052, and their absolute difference is 6.2, which amounts to 82 percent of the standard deviation of the health index. Thus, on criteria of both statistical significance and practical significance, it is reasonable to retain the distinction between these categories.

[2] Rainfall is another climatic variable that we considered but regrettably did not include for study. While historical research on this variable has advanced significantly in the past decade, a refined geographic and temporal grid of results was not yet available when this project was initiated. Specifically, we suspect that

Table 19.2 presents a set of estimated regressions of the health index on categories of ecological variables. At least one of the categorical variables was statistically significant in each ecological category, and with the exception of the coastal variable, the regression coefficients were larger than the standard deviation of the health index (7.6). Therefore, most of the ecological categories were consequential (in a practical sense) for the health index. Most important in this respect was residence in a paramount town or urban area, where the health index was nearly 15 points (almost two standard deviations) below that of mobile groups.

While the regression coefficients of Table 19.2 measure the impact of environmental factors on health, additional work is required to determine which environmental changes were most important in explaining the pre-Columbian decline in health. For this purpose, we divided the sample into two roughly equal parts: early (pre-1500 BP) and late (post-1500 BP). Table 19.3 gives the sample means of the health index and of the important ecological variables in these two time periods. Between the early and the late period, the health index declined from 74.20 to 66.46, a difference of 7.74 points. Moreover, all ecological variables changed in a direction adverse to health; that is, people moved to higher elevations, out of mobile groups, and into open forest–grassland habitats; used more domestic plants; and left coastal areas. Column 4 of Table 19.3 shows that the largest move (a shift of 0.485) was into open forest–grassland areas, and by multiplying this shift by the regression coefficient (−8.39), we obtain a measure of the impact of this environmental change on the health index (−4.07 points). Column 6 of Table 19.3 presents similar calculations for other ecological variables. The calculations show that the rise of towns and urban areas (−2.25), the change in vegetation patterns (−4.07), and the use of domestic plants (−2.89) were the three most important factors in the decline of the health index in the pre-Columbian era.

The sum of all the ecological effects is −12.25, which is more than the decline in the health index (−7.74). Therefore, the accounting procedure given in Table 19.3 overexplains the deterioration in health. This is not surprising because many of the important changes occurred as a package; for example, domestic plants were more commonly used in urban areas and urban areas were more commonly located in open forest–grassland habitats. To the extent that change occurred as a package, the individual regression coefficients overstate the pure effect of an ecological category. The coefficient of town or urban (14.91) is large partly because it also incorporates the effect of subsistence and vegetation changes that accompanied urbanization. The correlations between the ecological variables, given in Table 19.4, help to identify the changes that occurred together.

Multiple regression analysis is designed to measure the pure effects of individual variables holding other variables constant. The multiple regression given in the last column of Table 19.2 in principle offers a solution to the problem of overexplanation.

some sites were influenced by micro-patterns and by seasonal phenomena that are not easily measurable. More problematic for our research is that we cannot pinpoint the exact dates of the burials for many sites, especially the older ones. Thus, we are unable to make solid links between changing rainfall patterns and our measures of health. As important new evidence accumulates on rainfall in the past, it would be a good idea to revisit this issue.

Table 19.2: Regressions of the Health Index on Ecological Variables

Variables	Regression 1		Regression 2		Regression 3		Regression 4		Regression 5		Regression 6	
	Coeff.	Sig. lev.	Coeff.	Sig. lev.	Coeff.	Sig. lev.	Coeff.	Sig. lev.	Coeff.	Sig. lev.	Coeff.	Sig. lev.
Elevation 300+ meters	−9.73	0.001									−7.17	0.027
Settlement pattern												
Dispersed or village			−8.71	0.021							−1.91	0.625
Town or urban			−14.91	0.001							−4.39	0.388
Vegetation												
Open forest-grassland					−8.39	0.006					−3.64	0.219
Subsistence plants												
Domesticates							−10.27	0.005			0.35	0.943
Topography												
Coastal									6.53	0.038	−1.66	0.622
Age BP (years before 1950)											0.0013	0.200
Constant	74.39	0.000	78.98	0.000	73.81	0.000	78.20	0.000	67.32	0.000	74.79	0.000
R^2	0.42		0.42		0.31		0.32		0.19		0.68	
Sample size	23		23		23		23		23		23	

Omitted classes: Elevation, 0–300 meters; settlement pattern, mobile; vegetation, forest or semidesert; subsistence plants, no domesticates; topography, noncoastal.

Table 19.3: Average Values of Ecological Variables in the Early and Late Pre-Columbian Periods, and Their Implications for Health Change

1 Variable	2 Early: before 1500 BP	3 Late: after 1500 BP	4 Col. 3 − Col. 2	5 Regression coeff.	6 Col. 4 × Col. 5
300+ meters	0.364	0.500	0.136	−9.73	−1.32
Dispersed or village	0.545	0.583	0.038	−8.71	−0.33
Town or urban	0.182	0.333	0.151	−14.91	−2.25
Open forest–grassland	0.182	0.667	0.485	−8.39	−4.07
Domesticates	0.636	0.917	0.281	−10.27	−2.89
Coastal	0.545	0.333	−0.212	6.53	−1.38
Health index	74.20	66.46	−7.74		Sum: −12.25
Sample size	11	12			

Source: Calculated from the consolidated database.

Table 19.4: Correlations between Ecological Variables, Pre-Columbian Sites Where All Components of the Health Index Were Measured

Variable	Dispersed or village	Town or urban	Open forest–grassland	Domesticates	Coastal
300+ meters	0.06	0.28	0.29	0.46	−0.59
Dispersed or village		−0.68	−0.12	0.18	−0.12
Town or urban			0.48	0.31	−0.12
Open forest–grassland				0.46	−0.42
Domesticates					−0.60

Source: Calculated from consolidated database.

The procedure, however, is contaminated by multicollinearity among the explanatory variables, which gives rise to high standard errors of the estimated regression coefficients. As a result, with the exception of elevation, none of the estimated coefficients is statistically significant despite a rather high R^2 of 0.68. The most effective solution to this problem is to obtain more data from sites that are diverse by ecological categories. That is, we need examples of sites where environmental change did not occur as a package. Thus, despite having the largest data set of its kind ever assembled, we are unable to measure the desired effects with precision. Even though the individual measures are imprecise, it is safe to conclude that changing environmental conditions led to a deterioration in health. In the multiple regression, the coefficient on the time trend (age BP) is much smaller (0.0013 versus 0.0025) than in the simple regression, and it is statistically insignificant when controlling for ecological factors.

Because the health index is an additive measure, it is readily possible to decompose or analyze its components. Keeping in mind that collinearity may cause the measured coefficients to overstate pure effects, Table 19.5 shows the regression

Table 19.5: Regression Coefficients of Ecological Variables on Components of the Health Index, Pre-Columbian Sites

Variable	Stature	Hypoplasias	Anemia	Dental	Infections	DJD	Trauma
300+ meters	−11.18**	−28.02***	−8.78**	0.019	−15.06***	−7.15*	1.58
Dispersed or village	−13.96**	−13.43	−3.54	−6.17	−9.10	−11.54***	3.13
Town or urban	−16.01**	−32.18**	−17.77***	−3.95	−33.66***	−12.64**	4.88*
Open forest–grassland	−2.44	−21.46**	−10.18***	−5.21	−14.70**	−0.91	0.59
Domesticates	−6.13	−20.41**	−6.97*	−7.33*	−17.35***	−12.41***	2.79
Coastal	−0.54	16.69**	6.14	7.13**	13.71**	7.99**	1.60
Age BP	−0.0014	0.0058**	0.0012	0.00039	0.0036**	0.0023**	−0.00095
Standard deviation	14.91	22.97	11.19	10.45	16.99	11.11	5.29
Sample size	33	28	35	36	34	36	34

Notes: Using two–ailed tests, * = significant at 0.10; ** = significant at 0.05; *** = significant at 0.01.

Omitted classes: Elevation, 0–300 meters; settlement pattern, mobile; vegetation, forest or semidesert; subsistence plants, no domesticates; topography, noncoastal.

Source: Calculated from the consolidated database.

coefficients of index components on ecological variables taken in categories. These coefficients are similar to those in the middle columns of Table 19.2, except that the dependent variables are components, rather than the health index. The column under stature shows, for example, the coefficients estimated in six different regressions, one for each category of independent variable.[3] The sizes of the coefficients and their statistical significance are guides to their importance in health change over time and across ecological zones. On these grounds, living in a paramount town or urban area was devastating for many aspects of health, particularly hypoplasias and infections, for which the regression coefficients were relatively large and statistically significant. Use of domestic plants was also bad for several aspects of health. Hypoplasias were particularly sensitive to ecological zones, where four out of six coefficients exceeded or nearly exceeded (in absolute value) the standard deviation of the component and all but one coefficient was statistically significant at 0.10 or less. Trauma showed virtually no systematic pattern by ecological category, indicating that this aspect of health may have had diverse and complex causes.

Three components of the health index – hypoplasias, infections, and degenerative joint disease – were systematically related to the time trend (age BP). Among these, hypoplasias were the most important for the time trend as determined by its large coefficient.

Native American Health in the Post-Columbian World

The health of Native Americans often deteriorated substantially after contact because Europeans brought conquest, new diseases, and social disruption. Some groups, however, benefited from new animals (for example, horses) and technology (such as metal tools) that diffused in varying degrees among natives. With the data at hand it is impossible for us to assess the impact of all these changes. However, we can ask whether pre-Columbian trends and determinants of health continued to prevail in the new era.

The small number of observations (15 sites) makes the task difficult. Although the data are inadequate to statistically analyze the index, we can study the effects of ecological variables on its components. Only 6 of the post-Columbian sites measured hypoplasias, but investigators measured other components for at least 14 sites.

Table 19.6 shows regression coefficients on ecological variables taken one category at a time, using a procedure parallel to that discussed for Table 19.5. The results reveal several important contrasts with the pre-Columbian period. First, several components actually improved over time; that is, the coefficient on Age BP was negative and statistically significant for stature, anemia, and dental (the latter at only 0.10). This trend, which was unlikely to have occurred in general, was caused by an unusually high concentration of healthy sites (mainly Great Plains equestrian nomads) that happened to be concentrated near the end of the post-Columbian

---

[3] Sample sizes vary because some investigators did not record all components of the index. Although settlement pattern is represented by two variables, it is treated as one category.

Table 19.6: Regression Coefficients of Ecological Variables on Components of the Health Index, Post-Columbian Sites

Variable	Stature	Hypoplasias	Anemia	Dental	Infections	DJD	Trauma
300+ meters	−6.49	−35.87	−2.67	−1.59	0.79	−12.16	−16.34
Dispersed or village	−31.82***	8.000	−4.00	−0.26	23.53**	−0.89	17.99*
Town or urban	−33.75***	a	−14.67	−19.80***	24.30**	−9.20	6.30
Open forest–grassland	−6.49	−35.87	−2.67	−1.59	0.79	−12.16	−16.34
Triad or New–Old Mix	−7.55	−20.76	−17.54**	−10.70**	4.95	−8.29	−1.75
Coastal	1.36	28.20	2.78	10.43*	−5.86	15.76	16.49
Age BP	−0.072**	−0.275	−0.076**	−0.031*	0.047	−0.023	0.014
Standard deviation	15.96	28.15	15.48	9.32	14.83	14.54	15.61
Sample size	14	6	14	15	14	15	14

Notes: Using two-tailed tests, * = significant at 0.10; ** = significant at 0.05; *** = significant at 0.01.

Omitted classes: Elevation, 0–300 meters; settlement pattern, mobile; vegetation, forest or semi-desert; subsistence plants, no domesticates; topography, noncoastal.

^a Insufficient observations for analysis.

Source: Consolidated database.

period. While the good health of the equestrian tribes was genuine (as measured by the health index and its components), the measured trend is an artifact of sample composition.

Fewer coefficients are statistically significant, which is attributable in part to the smaller sample sizes. This matter aside, the pattern of coefficients is also noteworthy. Inexplicably, infections were actually less prevalent (higher index value) in more densely settled areas. Domesticated plants continued to have adverse effects on anemia and dental health, while stature was systematically much lower in villages, towns, or urban areas. The ecological variables had little or no systematic impact on hypoplasias (note the very small sample size for this component), degenerative joint disease, and trauma. In sum, a few of the pre-Columbian patterns persisted, but ecological variables alone had less influence on health. As measured by the standard deviations, health varied considerably in the second era, but factors other than our measurable ecological categories were largely responsible for the variation.

The Health of Euro-Americans and African-Americans

It is impractical to use regression analysis to investigate systematic influences on the health of European-Americans and African-Americans using the data at hand. The number of sites is quite small (9 for European-Americans, 4 for free blacks, and 1 for slaves), and three of the Euro-American samples were atypical. The poorhouse was a small but very poor slice of the population, and the military had minimum health standards for entry but high rates of trauma. The soldiers also died and were buried at sites where they had lived and worked only temporarily; the accompanying ecological circumstances, such as elevation and topography, had little impact on measurable chronic health conditions. Therefore, the individual chapters in Part III of the book are the best source of information for generalizations about the health of these groups.

Whites fell below the average of all sites (69.9 vs. 72.6) for a variety of reasons. As a group, whites were relatively tall and tended to have good scores on childhood indicators, but each site scored very low on some attribute of health. The two military sites had by far the highest rates of trauma (index values of 24.8 and 10.8), and bestowing them with the average trauma score (85.7) would have increased their health index scores by nearly 10 points.[4] To the extent that violence was a part of the Euro-American way of life, however, trauma was a health cost that should be recognized.

The most affluent group, in terms of material conditions, lived in Belleville, Ontario. Their health index (69.3) was below average for all sites, but their wealth was insufficient to protect them from poor dental health and the highest rate of degenerative joint disease (index score of 41.6) among the 65 sites. Bestowing them with the average DJD score (78.9) and the average dental score (81.8) would have raised their overall health index score by 6.8 points. Yet, the European-American diet, with its emphasis on sugar and starch, was costly for dental health, and their ways of life involved stressful, repetitive motions that led to joint deterioration.

---

[4] Calculated as 1/7 of the difference between 85.7 and the average of 24.8 and 10.8.

Like whites, free blacks were also tall and generally scored well on anemia but suffered from high rates of hypoplasias and infections. Thus, the childhood experience was reasonably good, but similar to whites, the adults faced some adverse conditions. Slave health departed from the white and the free black pattern, registering very low on childhood indicators. Although trauma rates were low, like free blacks, the slaves also endured high rates of infections.

Implications

The transition to settled agriculture has been widely celebrated as a triumph leading to civilization. It has been argued that systematic production and storage of food improved diets, compared with the meager and unreliable supplies of hunting, fishing, and foraging. In this scenario, health improved and life was transformed from being "nasty, brutish, and short" to one where resources were available to support economic development and spawn the rise of government, learning, and architecture.

While not denying a connection between agriculture and political development, our research suggests that life *became* "nasty, brutish and short" for the typical person with the rise of agriculture, government, and urbanization. The hunter-gatherers and those living in dispersed settlements were the healthiest groups in our sample. They were taller and had fewer pathological lesions than residents of towns and cities who relied on the products of settled agriculture in a system administered by governments. Scholars have long recognized the adverse consequences of urbanization on health during industrialization, but our evidence establishes a very long trail of ill health that followed the collective efforts involved in creating modern civilization.

The good health of the least complex societies did not occur because the Western Hemisphere was a biological Garden of Eden, an epidemiological paradise substantially free of pathogens so detrimental to health in other parts of the world. Pre-Columbian populations were among the healthiest and the least healthy in our sample. While pre-Columbian natives may have lived in a disease environment substantially different from that in other parts of the globe, the original inhabitants also brought with them, or evolved with, enough pathogens to create chronic conditions of ill health under ecological conditions of systematic agriculture and urban living.

If the transition to settled agriculture and urban living led to a decline in health, why did it occur?[5] There are several possible explanations, but unfortunately we cannot adequately test them with the data at hand. First, the shift could have been a second choice forced on hunter-gathers by resource depletion. Farming might have been created in response to exhaustion of natural sources of subsistence. If correct, one would expect to observe a decline in health prior to the rise of settled

---

[5] From a global point of view, climatic change near the end of the Pleistocene was an important requisite (at least for the geographic areas in which agriculture first arose), creating environments and conditions necessary for domestication to occur. It is likely that no single cause was applicable to the world as a whole, and idiosyncratic local conditions were relevant.

agriculture. Our data are insufficiently rich and abundant to explore adequately this possibility.

Second, large-scale collective efforts may have given rise to redistribution that benefited some (dominant) groups at the expense of others. Leaders may have urged settled agriculture and urban living upon their followers as a way to gain political power and control over more resources. This objective might have been intertwined with strategies for military protection, whereby fortifications, warriors, and stores of weapons were important for survival. Unlike hunter-gatherer subsistence, where few stores of food existed, settled agriculture created inventories of food that could be taxed and distributed by the politically powerful. Similarly, the powerful expended less energy on work and were able to compel work, such as building monuments, which adversely affected health. Thus, some people gained while many lost in the transition. If redistribution was the primary motive, one might observe greater inequality in health in more complex, relative to less complex, societies. Consistent with this line of thought, inequality in wealth or income has been greater in urban versus rural areas in the historic period.

Third, the transition might have been largely voluntary if settled agriculture, trade, and urban living created material goods and ways of life that were preferable to those available in hunter-gatherer societies. This hypothesis recognizes that improved health may not have been the only important goal of early societies. Hunter-gatherers may have been tempted to switch by cloth and trade articles, such as shells, tools, metals, and other accoutrements of large, organized societies. In other words, settled agriculturalists may have been willing to trade consumer goods and the excitement of urban living for poorer health. We know that by the eighteenth century, urban living had a well-established reputation for poor health, yet populations of these areas continued to grow by in-migration. Many newcomers were apparently willing to risk their health for a job and the amenities of the city, and it is plausible to think that these priorities may have existed in earlier millennia.

Whatever the explanation for the transition to settled agriculture, the health costs of the change have not been recognized, at least not to the extent of the loss understood in the transformation from settled agriculture to industrial society in the past few centuries. Urban death rates approached those in rural areas in the early twentieth century, only after significant investments were made in waste removal, clean water supplies, and other aspects of public health and personal hygiene. Scholars must now recognize that significant health penalties have accompanied civilization and densely settled populations for the past several thousand years. Thus, the conquest of disease, along with improvements in food production and distribution during the twentieth century, rank as one of the greatest achievements of recent millennia. Even the poor countries of the world now have life expectancies in excess of 40 years, which likely exceeded that of hunter-gatherer populations in our sample.

Historians, economists, and other social scientists have long celebrated the contributions of industrialization and technological change to improvements in human welfare. But this study establishes the importance of drawing a distinction between material and health aspects of the quality of life. While we recognize the significance of these changes for the material standard of living – for the diversity and quality of products that were readily purchased – these goods were acquired at a significant price to human health prior to the twentieth century.

European-Americans and African-Americans tended to occupy the middle and lower portion of the distribution, an intriguing niche in the rankings of health. Comparisons of stature and mortality rates in the eighteenth and nineteenth centuries suggest that European-Americans were better off than Europeans. Therefore, skeletal data for the latter might place them very low in the rankings. One might suppose that Europeans in Europe, and especially in the Americas, would have done better, given their access to European and to Western Hemisphere animal and plant resources, notable technology, and their institutions of commerce, law, and politics that were placed in the service of global colonization. Whatever the nature of these advantages for health, they were offset by other aspects of their lives, notably dense settlement and the spread of communicable diseases associated with migration and trade.

It may be tempting to argue that most Europeans were victims of inequality. Perhaps their societies were rich and prosperous on average, but only a few lived well while the vast majority accumulated pathological lesions. While Europe in the eighteenth and nineteenth centuries is notable for its inequality, Euro-Americans had no such burden. Occupational differences in stature, for example, were virtually nil in America on the eve of the American Revolution, while class differences in average height exceeded 10 centimeters in England (Sokoloff and Villaflor, 1982; Floud, Wachter, and Gregory, 1990). It has been argued that inequality increased in nineteenth-century America, but it seems hard to believe that a major transformation could have occurred by the middle of the 1800s. The skeletons studied at the Belleville, Ontario, site represented middle- and upper-class Euro-Americans who were not oppressed by inequality, yet they attained only 65.5 on the health index – below the median for the Western Hemisphere sites as a whole.

Pre-Columbian Life in Long-Term Perspective

The Western Hemisphere population when Columbus first arrived might have been as high as 50 million to 100 million, and as many as 90 percent of the aboriginals may have died within the following two centuries.[6] This horrible devastation has been a major focus of historians who study the Native American experience. While the demographic disaster certainly is an important subject, the bulk of Native American health has been ignored in terms of chronological time. In order to tell the rest of the story, historians would be well served by embracing methodologies and sources of evidence that are provided by physical anthropology, human biology, and archaeology.

[6] For a brief discussion of these population issues, see Kiple and Beck (1997).

Our research shows that health was on a downward trajectory long before Columbus arrived. The healthiest Native Americans were those who lived several millennia ago. They had far fewer chronic conditions than Native Americans, European-Americans, or African-Americans who lived or appeared several millennia later. The earliest Americans lived in small bands, organized their lives in simple hunter-gatherer societies, and allocated (or wasted) no resources in building lasting monuments. Their diet was sufficiently rich and varied that they largely avoided the symptoms of childhood deprivation – stunting, hypoplasisas, and anemia. They lived with few material goods, their isolation protected them from infectious diseases, and their mobility prevented the accumulation of waste that harbored germs and parasites. Life was physically arduous for most adults; chronic diseases such as arthritis, skeletal infections, and dental deterioration eventually took a significant toll, and few individuals survived past age 50.

Over the millennia, societies became more densely settled and more complex for reasons not fully understood. Leaders who sought advantages may have encouraged this shift, or it could have been an adaptation to diminishing resources, defense needs, or perhaps a preference for some amenities of urban life. Whatever the reasons, this study shows that the health decline was precipitous with the changes in ecological environments where people lived. This idea is not new to the anthropological literature, but scholars in general have yet to absorb it.[7] Our approach provides the largest source of comparable evidence on the extent and nature of the decline. Moreover, this is the first study to allow urbanization and subsistence patterns to compete statistically as hypotheses, together with several other forces that have been deemed relevant to health, including climate, topography, and vegetation habitats. *Paleopathology at the Origins of Agriculture*, edited by Mark Cohen and George Armelagos, drew attention to the health costs of settled agriculture, primarily in Euro-Asia. When their work is considered with this study, it is clear that the adverse effect of agriculture on health was a very wide-ranging geographic phenomenon that extended well beyond the so-called Ancient World.

Health deteriorated in several dimensions as Native Americans increasingly lived in new ecological environments. Compared with less densely settled areas, urban places and higher elevations were harsh for infections and for childhood indicators – stature, hypoplasias, and anemia. The transition to domestic plants increased hypoplasias, anemia, infections, and degenerative joint disease.

Health has long been recognized as a strategic factor in the outcome of wars. While no one doubts the importance of germs, steel weapons, and horses in the ascent of Europeans in the Western Hemisphere, we argue that poor health was also a factor in the speed and ease of conquest. The populations most easily conquered were also the least healthy, who lived in upland urban areas and relied heavily on domesticated plants. Nomadic, hunter-gatherer societies, particularly those with horses, posed the greatest military challenges to colonizers.

---

[7] For a recent review of research on the health costs of settled agriculture, see Larsen (1995).

APPENDIX: DEFINITION OF ECOLOGICAL VARIABLES
COLLECTED FOR EACH SITE

SUBSISTENCE ANIMALS
1   No domesticates
2   New World
3   New and Old World mix

VEGETATION
1   Forest
2   Open forest
3   Grassland
4   Semidesert

CLIMATE
1   Tropical
2   Subtropical
3   Temperate

SETTLEMENT PATTERN
1   Mobile
2   Settled dispersed
3   Small/medium village
4   Paramount village/town
5   Urban

SUBSISTENCE PLANTS
1   No domesticates
2   Some domesticates
3   Maize (potatoes), beans, squash
4   New and Old World mix

TOPOGRAPHY
1   Major river flood plain
2   Coastal
3   Plains
4   Rolling (low hills)
5   Mountain

ELEVATION
1   Sea level to 100 meters
2   100 to 300 meters
3   300 to 1000 meters
4   1000 to 3000 meters
5   3000+ meters

REFERENCES

Floud, Roderick, Kenneth W. Wachter, and Annabel S. Gregory. *Height, Health, and History: Nutritional Status in the United Kingdom, 1750–1980.* Cambridge: Cambridge University Press, 1990.

Kiple, Kenneth F., and Stephen V. Beck. "Introduction." In Kenneth F. Kiple and Stephen V. Beck, eds., *Biological Consequences of the European Expansion, 1450–1800.* Brookfield, Vt.: Ashgate Publishing, 1997. Pp. xv–xxix.

Larsen, Clark Spencer. "Biological Changes in Human Populations with Agriculture." *Annual Review of Anthropology* 24 (1995): 185–213.

Sokoloff, Kenneth L., and Georgia C. Villaflor. "The Early Achievement of Modern Stature in America." *Social Science History* 6 (1982): 453–481.

PART VIII

CHAPTER TWENTY

Conclusions

Richard H. Steckel and Jerome C. Rose

This book began by extolling the benefits of studying very long-term trends in health using evidence from skeletal remains. To this end, we coordinated the preparation of the largest comparable database ever assembled in the field of bioarchaeology, which consists of observations on 12,520 individuals who lived over the past several millennia at 65 composite sites in the Western Hemisphere.[1] The database is available to the public and includes seven commonly measured, basic indicators of health: stature inferred from long bone lengths; evidence of anemia from porotic hyperostosis or cribra orbitalia; linear enamel hypoplasias; trauma; infectious lesions on bones; dental health; and degenerative joint disease. The first three indicators reflect the health quality of life in childhood, while the last two are connected with the degenerative processes of aging and hard work. Trauma and infectious lesions can occur at any age but are more common among older children and adults.

Our conclusions first highlight methodological contributions, beginning with a technique for measuring health based on two essential ingredients: health quality of life while living and length of life. The Mark I version of the health index, which roughly gauges chronic conditions of the first component, is based on the prevalence and severity of the basic health indicators. We tabulated separate indexes for each attribute and weighted them equally in calculating the overall index. Attributes for individual observations were scored from 0 (worst outcome) to 100 (no evidence of pathology), and the results at each site were converted to age-specific rates, which were weighted by the distribution of person-years lived by age in a reference population (Model West, level 4). The model distribution of deaths, rather than the actual distribution at the site, was used because unknown variations in fertility and migration may have influenced the age distributions of death.

Constructed in this way, the health index roughly measures only the health quality of life. But it could be modified to incorporate length of life simply by multiplying

---

[1] Commonly referred to as the Western Hemisphere database, the suggested citation is Richard H. Steckel, Paul W. Sciulli, and Jerome C. Rose, "A Health Index from Skeletal Remains," in this volume.

the index by the ratio of actual (or estimated) life expectancy at birth to the life expectancy in the reference population (26.4 years).

The second element of health (average length of life) is difficult if not impossible to estimate with useful precision using the age distribution of deaths alone, unless the population at the site was closed and approximately stationary, or existed under nearly unchanging conditions of fertility, mortality, and total population size. Chapters by Robert McCaa and by S. Ryan Johansson and Douglas Owsley show the importance of site-contextual information, such as clues to settlement growth, which shed light on likely rates of fertility or population growth. Fortified with "guesstimates" of likely population growth rates submitted by project members, McCaa estimated life expectancies by seeking the best fits between observed patterns of hazard rates and those from a menu of stable populations having the "guesstimated" growth rates. The results, presented in Table 4.2 of McCaa's chapter, should be regarded cautiously due to the slender basis for the population growth estimates.[2] Additional errors are introduced by the small sample sizes at numerous sites. An important conclusion, however, is the call for physical anthropologists to seek clues on population growth rates that would refine estimates of life expectancies. These clues include historical circumstances, such as wars, migration, and colonization; and also environmental factors, such as climate, the security of diverse food supplies, the availability of clean water, and likely disease vectors (see Johansson and Owsley, this volume).

Although heavily qualified, McCaa's life expectancy estimates deserve additional, tentative study. We put them and the health index to use investigating the "osteological paradox," which refers to the idea that skeletal pathologies result from selective mortality and unknown heterogeneity in frailty risks.[3] If correct, a high prevalence of skeletal lesions may merely indicate considerable longevity at a particular site, rather than heavy biological stress that adversely affected health in general. Advocates claim that the basic methodology of osteology might, at worst, be inverted and, at best, tell us nothing useful about health.

We test this hypothesis by regressing the health index on life expectancy. If better health (measured by longevity) makes for worse skeletons, then the coefficient on life expectancy should be negative and statistically significant; that is, a higher rate of pathological lesions (a lower health index) should be systematically associated with a longer average life span. On the other hand, if the environmental stress that caused a high prevalence of lesions also resulted in shorter lives, then the coefficient should be positive and statistically significant.

The data for the regression are taken from Table 3.3 of the health index chapter by Steckel, Sciulli, and Rose (this volume) and from McCaa's Table 4.2 (this volume), using the 50 sites where estimated life expectancies are available. In view of the large differences in sample sizes across sites, it is appropriate to use weighted least squares to estimate the regression; that is, sites with larger samples should be more influential in determining the regression coefficients. The weights are person-years

---

[2] The sites studied by Johansson and Owsley are an exception, in which contextual information has been considered in estimating population growth rates.

[3] For an exchange of views, see Wood et al. (1992) and Goodman (1993).

observed at each site, given in the last column of Table 3.3 in Steckel, Sciulli, and Rose. The estimated regression is:

$$\text{Index} = 59.95 + 0.37\,\text{LE}, \ N = 50, \ R^2 = 0.14$$

$$(14.38) \quad (2.81)$$

where Index refers to the value of the health index, LE refers to estimated life expectancy, and t-values are shown in parentheses. The estimated relationship is statistically significant [$F(1, 48) = 7.92$; $p = 0.007$], and for every increase in life expectancy of one year, the health index increased on average by 0.37 units. In other words, environmental stress tended to act in concert with the formation of pathological lesions and in reducing longevity. Populations with high life expectancies usually lived with fewer person-years of skeletal lesions, as measured by the health index.

The regression explains a low percent of the variance ($R^2 = 0.14$) in part because the sample sizes at most sites are rather small, leading to sampling errors in the prevalence of pathological lesions and in the observed age distribution of deaths. The Mark I version of the health index no doubt misrepresents some of the actual functional consequences of person-years lived with various chronic conditions (that impinged on life expectancy), which contributes to measurement error and reduces the R^2. Among these may be the practice of equally weighting the various attributes and the assumptions made about person-years lived with various lesions prior to death. It is important to note that most of the estimated life expectancies are based on "guesstimates" of population growth rates. To the extent that the guesses are in error, the estimated length of life will be incorrect and the share of the variance explained correspondingly reduced. These problems can be addressed by expanding the sample sizes, improving the health index, and by obtaining more contextual information that sheds light on population growth rates.

Even if the sample sizes were very large, an improved health index accurately reflected the functional consequences of pathological lesions, and the life expectancies were known with certainty, one could ask whether the correlation between the health index and life expectancy would be nearly perfect across a wide array of sites. The answer is probably "no" because life expectancy and pathological lesions measure somewhat different aspects of health that need not agree in detail. Even in modern populations where extensive records of health (broadly defined) are available for comparison, they may tell somewhat different stories. Moreover, it is possible to imagine circumstances that distort the comparisons. The Rochester poorhouse is a case in point, where the prevalence of the lesions alone suggests substantially better health than existed (as measured by length of life). Although we have not been able to estimate life expectancy at this site, it was undoubtedly very low because death rates were high (nearly 20 percent at Rochester and even higher – 20 to 30 percent – at almshouses in Massachusetts examined by Higgins et al. for comparison purposes); newcomers arrived in dire straits and lived in poor, crowded conditions. Yet the Rochester inmates died with relatively few lesions (the health index was actually somewhat above that at middle-class Belleville), probably because they lived so briefly under those poor conditions that few signs of chronic stress were able to accumulate on their skeletons. The poorhouse inmates also scored reasonably well on the childhood indicators (stature, anemia, and linear enamel hypoplasias), indicating favorable childhood circumstances before entering the poorhouse. Life expectancy at Belleville (estimated at 36 years) was no doubt considerably above that in the poorhouse, and once this is taken into account, health was significantly superior at Belleville.

Thus, we emphasize the importance of blending paleopathology with paleodemography in a research setting enriched by contextual information. If contextual information is totally lacking, such that nothing is known about population growth rates or lifeways at the site, then it is possible to be fooled by an osteological paradox. But the experience of this project also suggests that it is incorrect to think that substantial deception from the paradox is commonplace, literally hiding under every rock. We underscore the value of a large, diverse database combined with contextual information in depicting and analyzing health patterns using skeletal remains. But even at sites where contextual information is available and there is no evidence of a paradox, small differences in the health index may not be meaningful as general indicators of health; the Mark I version is a work in progress that should not be overinterpreted.

How many populations might have existed in which the health conditions were so oppressive that few pathological lesions had time to accumulate before most individuals died, such as the Rochester poorhouse? If regarded as a real (self-sufficient) population, the poorhouse was not self-sustaining simply because death rates greatly exceeded any plausible biological maximum for the birth rate (about 6 percent). Some populations in the past no doubt shrank and vanished due to a large and sudden reversal of environmental circumstances, creating a record of skeletal lesions that is considerably distorted about the state of health as measured by life expectancy. The evidence of the Western Hemisphere database suggests that deception is more likely when the reversals were large and sudden (as at the poorhouse), and which occurred without leaving contextual information. Major earthquakes and big volcanic eruptions qualify by creating large and sudden reversals in health, but ordinarily leave considerable evidence. The skeletons found at Pompeii, for example, present a situation in which bones mislead – life expectancy just prior to the eruption was very short, but the frequency of lesions would not reveal the actual impending state of health.

As a working hypothesis, we suggest that whenever time and resources were adequate to bury the dead with some ceremony, unassisted from the outside (unlike the poorhouse), then the possibility of substantial deception is unlikely when good contextual information is available. Even under the oppressive environmental conditions faced by the declining Maya and the Native American groups of the Southwest, the lesions were numerous, the health index was very low, and estimated life expectancy was short; that is, there is no paradox. It seems clear that a sudden change to even worse conditions was needed to create a significant deception – a situation so bad that the population vanished quickly without leaving evidence of the crisis.

The point of departure for this work was Cohen and Armelagos, *Paleopathology at the Origins of Agriculture,* a book emphasizing the adverse health consequences of the transition from hunting and gathering to settled agriculture. How do their conclusions square with those of our project, based on its large comparable database, new techniques of measuring health, and statistical analysis? In a nutshell, our results support their conclusions. The health index declined throughout the pre-Columbian era, as Western Hemisphere societies evolved from simple to complex and hierarchical. McCaa's demographic analysis also identifies the older pre-Columbian period as healthier in terms of life expectancy. In general, the healthiest populations were hunter-gatherers, and the least healthy lived in large settlements supported by systematic agriculture. Our statistical analysis of the health index identifies settlement size and use of domesticated plants as the two most important factors associated with the long-term decline in pre-Columbian health. Of course, other variables were relevant for skeletal health, including elevation, proximity to the coast, and topography. Thus, the long-term evolution of health is not simply a story that follows from the rise of settled agriculture and urbanization. While finding no systematic relationship between climate and health, we cautiously suggest that this might be the result of insufficient diversity in our sample and/or poor measures of climate.

RESEARCH NEEDS

We anticipate refinements in the health index, and hope these preliminary efforts inspire research to clarify the meaning and enhance the consistency of comparisons across populations. Several assumptions of the Mark I version, while reasonable and desirable in the name of simplicity, are not easily justified in the face of plausible alternatives. For example, the window of time on health provided by adult skeletons might be increased or reduced for dental, infections, degenerative joint disease and trauma. It may also be desirable to experiment with linear and with nonlinear declines in severity of pathological lesions over these windows of time prior to death. It is important to undertake studies that might reveal the length of time that individuals suffered from various skeletal lesions, so that a more refined longitudinal picture of functional impairment may be established. The severity of lesions may turn out to be an important guide to their length of time, and other markers of duration might also be discovered from skeletal materials.

Guided by some notions of functional implications (which themselves are functions of culture, lifestyle, and technology in use), we urge experimentation with alternative weights given to each category of defects. We will have greater confidence in our procedures if the results are highly correlated under alternative assumptions. Following a general public discussion of our methods and results, we look forward to the creation of Mark II and possibly other improved versions of the health index.

Inequality of health may be studied by using the index in the same way that inequality of income or wealth are studied for their insights into access to resources. We would like to know, for example, how women fared relative to men and the extent to which there were differences across classes and age groups within societies. The sample sizes are sufficiently large at some sites for this type of analysis.

There is a clear need for more reliable inferences on life expectancy derived from skeletal remains. In our view, this should be done by using contextual information that will shed light on probable population growth rates, as done by Johansson and Owsley (this volume). Such information may be difficult to acquire for many small sites, thus imposing limits on the possibilities for measuring this aspect of health. Yet, we feel that useful contextual data have not been adequately exploited at many sites.

Geographic Information Systems (GIS) data have been available only in the past few years, and historical versions of these data are in their infancy. Identification of sites by latitude and longitude has a huge potential for providing detailed information on vegetation, terrain, elevation, and so on that will inform us of likely access to resources within a day's walk, energy expenditure required for foraging patterns, the human energy required to engage in trade, and more. Experiments with GIS analysis are now under way using the consolidated database (see Steckel and Walker, 2000).

Despite the large size of our consolidated database, many questions remain about the temporal and geographic record of health. We see a great value in expanding the present database to include other continents and to include more information from the more distant past, particularly before the past two millennia. Frankly, our data are quite thin compared with the grand sweep of history over the past 10,000 years, and significant gaps remain in the historical record. We need sites that are more diverse with respect to ecological characteristics to resolve identification problems – the tendency of ecological conditions to change as a package. With the data currently available, we cannot easily identify or measure the pure effects of changes in one ecological dimension. Thus, we have developed a large project, for which we now seek funding, that would gather and analyze such data from around the globe (the Global History of Health project).

In consideration of the findings of the study, both in regard to its limitations and its strengths, we believe that it would be prudent to collect more information per individual skeleton, and more contextual information per site. For the present study, we deliberately chose quantity of individuals – literally, a cast of thousands – in order to depict the large picture of biological change. The study could be enriched by additional biocultural context, especially in regard to dietary reconstruction and nutritional inference. Diet for a number of regions in the present investigation is documented via stable isotope analysis (carbon and nitrogen), which allows more precise interpretation of health change, both at the individual and the population level. We do not have this rich context for many of the settings, but in principle it could be developed. Population history and biological relationships are also unclear at some of the sites. This could be alleviated by analysis of genetic similarity, using dental discrete traits for identifying biological relatedness, both in spatial and chronological context. New advances in extraction and amplification of ancient DNA from archaeological skeletons can inform the historical context of population relationships. We hope that this study lays the groundwork for future investigations that consider the broad, historical sweep of the human condition.

REFERENCES

Goodman, Alan H. "On the Interpretation of Health from Skeletal Remains." *Current Anthropology* 34, No. 3 (June 1993), 281–288.

Steckel, Richard H., and Phillip L. Walker. "A Geographic Information System Analysis of Variation in Health and Nutrition in the Western Hemisphere." Paper given at the meetings of the American Association of Physical Anthropologists, San Antonio, Texas, April 15, 2000.

Wood, James W., George R. Milner, Henry C. Harpending, and Kenneth M. Weiss. "The Osteological Paradox: Problems in Inferring Prehistoric Health from Skeletal Samples." *Current Anthropology* 33, No. 4 (Aug.–Sept. 1992), 343–370.

PART IX

EPILOGUE

## CHAPTER TWENTY-ONE

The Body as Evidence; The Body of Evidence

George J. Armelagos and Peter J. Brown

The Greek *skeletos*, meaning withered or dried up, is the source of the modern word skeleton. The skeletal remains of a once-dynamic living organism would appear to be shriveled or withered if that is all that remains of what was once a vital body and soul. The ancients would have been hard-pressed to use the bones to provide insights into the being of what was once that person. The early history of skeletal biology primarily consisted of descriptive inventories of the sex and age of skeletal remains found in archaeological excavations. The inventories were dry and lifeless, and their publications were forever buried as appendixes in archaeological reports. The analysis and insight in this early era of skeletal biology could easily be described as withered or dried up. Modern researchers now know that the bones of individuals long dead can provide information about the people themselves – their physical activities, their diet, and the diseases that afflicted them. The skeletons provide valuable clues as to how people lived and died.

Even after an influential article by S. L. Washburn (1953) heralding the era of the "new physical anthropology" nearly a half century ago, little changed. The new physical anthropology forecasted the replacement of typology and description with the study of process and hypothesis testing. Notwithstanding the promise of the new era of research with an emphasis on process, most skeletal biology remained typological and descriptive.

The development of physical anthropology was hampered by the role it played as the "handmaiden" to history, particularly versions of history that fit common cultural stereotypes (Lasker 1970). Geneticists manipulated the frequency of blood groups and other traits to reconstruct racial history. Archaeologists established population relationships by the typological analysis of crania. Thirty years after Washburn's appraisal, Armelagos and colleagues (Armelagos et al. 1982) still characterized skeletal biology as essentially a descriptive endeavor. The fundamental worldview that guided skeletal biology was methodologically sterile and theoretically impoverished. In the drive to reconstruct cultural history, racial models were still being determined by analyzing similarities in morphology. Similarities in morphology were defined racially and racial similarities explained cultural relation-ships. In paleopathology, the goal was the diagnosis of diseases and determining their chronology and geography. Fortunately, the last two decades have seen a transfor-mation of skeletal biology that negates its earlier "dried-up" character.

The Backbone of History: Health and Nutrition in the Western Hemisphere is an example of why the transformation has occurred and how an interdisciplinary effort can put "flesh" back on the bones of our ancestors. It is apt that this impressive collection incorporating knowledge from archaeology, skeletal biology, history, and economics uses the term "backbone" as a key word in its title. The contributions in *The Backbone of History* demonstrate the vitality of the field of bioarchaeology with contributions as solid as the bones they describe and analyze.

Three theoretical developments have set the stage for the production of the syn-thesis seen in *The Backbone of History*. First, the understanding of the disease process requires a consideration of its existence within the context of a population. Second is the realization that culture is a key environmental variable that affects the dis-ease process. From this perspective a group's technology, social organization, and ideology may play a major role in inhibiting or creating an environment for disease proliferation. This consideration of culture has led to a more thorough analysis of human/disease interaction. Third, instead of focusing on single pathological condi-tions, skeletal biologists began following the work of Jane Buikstra and Della Cook and my colleagues at the University of Massachusetts. Thereafter paleopathologists incorporated multiple stress indicators (the "signatures" that pathogens and other insults leave on bones) in their research.

In this volume, we see how effective the employment of this strategy is in addressing questions of vital interest. Alan H. Goodman and Debra Martin in "Reconstructing Health Profiles from Skeletal Remains" provide an excellent sum-mary of the skeletal indicators that are "the backbone" of these studies in the book. This chapter sets the standards essential for any successful comparative analysis that are fundamental for developing generalizations about disease and health. In a similar fashion, Robert McCaa, "Paleodemography of the Americas: From Ancient Times to Colonialism and Beyond," and S. Ryan Johansson and Douglas Owsley, "Welfare History on the Great Plains: Mortality and Skeletal Health, 1650 to 1900," not only provide a primer on demographic theory but also show how theoretical issues can be applied regionally to elucidate the adaptation of people to their environment.

Not everyone accepts the challenge of generating knowledge by hypothesis test-ing. Only a decade ago, two eminent skeletal biologists, Donald Ortner and Arthur Aufterheide (1991), lamented the state of paleopathology and claimed that the dis-cipline had reached a plateau. According to them, the lack of standardization in diagnosing pathology had brought paleopathology to a standstill. They suggested that paleopathologists halt any further hypothesis testing until scientists had an opportunity to develop methods and establish standards. Ortner and Aufterheide's assessment seems unduly harsh (Armelagos 1994) since paleopathology owes its vitality to researchers who work to develop standards *while at the same time* contin-uing to test hypotheses. In shepherding this volume, Richard H. Steckel and Jerome C. Rose demonstrate that it is possible to undertake this dual activity successfully.

They accepted the challenge and embraced the task of developing standards for researchers to score lesions in a similar manner by convening contributors who had a role in developing them and applying them in their studies.

The richness of the chapters in this volume would not have been possible had the contributors been comfortable with providing just descriptive compilations of the pathologies that they uncovered. The hypotheses generated in studies from many diverse cultures and varied environments make this an extremely interesting volume. The successful application of "strong inference" (Platt 1964) with its inductive approach has been effectively applied in many of the studies. Strong inference has transformed paleopathology, once described as the doctor's hobby (Eckert n.d.), into a science. Instead of relying on deductive abilities that are limited (Armelagos and Gerven 1993), the paleopathologist incorporates methods of induction that have the potential to falsify alternative hypotheses. There are four stages in the application of the strong inference: 1) devise alternative hypotheses; 2) devise experiments to exclude one or more of the hypotheses; 3) carry out experiments to get "clean results"; and 4) repeat the process.

Strong inference is very effective when applied to nonexperimental sciences, such as geology and paleopathology.[1] The application to paleopathology does require modification. Since they do not have the possibility of carrying out experiments to get "clean results," researchers must rely on comparative analysis from "natural experiments." The studies in this book provide examples of natural laboratories that can be used for hypothesis testing. Skeletal series from various regions in the Americas – inland and coastal environments, highland and lowland areas, and urban and rural settlements – have been used to provide the contrasts that will clarify health/disease relationships. These populations include economic groups as distinct as enslaved populations from North America, populations from poorhouses, and ancient people of the Mayan civilization.

The strong inference and the inductive methods require systematic application if they are to be successful. The model that Goodman and Martin propose in this volume is an effective tool for demonstrating the levels at which strong inference can be applied. The model provides a systematic framework for analysis of how insults, which can cause physiological disruption, potentially affect the individual, the population, and the region. This will make scientific testing amenable at all levels.

The methodology applied by researchers in this volume carries the use of multiple stress indicators to a new, higher level of analysis. We have alluded to the early studies in paleopathology when researchers were content with the diagnosis of a single pathological condition. The contributors in this volume have moved beyond simply applying multiple stress indicators to understanding disease ecology that is commonly practiced in paleopathology. Links between infection, nutritional deficiency, growth retardation, and growth interruptions and the relationships among these

---

[1] We acknowledge that the laboratory is an essential feature of bioarchaeology. The use of radiological, histological, and chemical analyses is an important part of most research protocols. The application of the most technologically advanced laboratory tool cannot substitute for a well-designed research protocol.

indicators should produce a synergy when applied effectively. They have become an important part of the contributions in this book.

The next research breakthrough, suggested by Steckel and Rose in "Conclusions," is likely to come with the use of multiple stress indicators that exist at different levels of analysis (ecosystem, population, individual, organ, tissue, cell, or chemical constituents of the cell, i.e., collagen, apatite crystals and DNA). For example, a dietary deficiency may cause a number of physiological disruptions, such as porotic hyperostosis, altered patterns of growth, and premature bone loss. In addition, the same dietary pattern may have different nutritional consequences within a population because population segments may be facing quite different risks. Women who are lactating may suffer a greater nutritional crisis from a shortage of calcium and iron than a healthy male of the same age.

Steckel and Rose acknowledge that *Paleopathology at the Origins of Agriculture* (Cohen and Armelagos 1984) was the stimulus for *The Backbone of History*. The empirical studies in that book examined the impact of change in health in populations undergoing subsistence transitions. The contributions in the book are best known for demonstrating the biological cost related to changes in sedentism and the intensification of primary food production. The increase in the pattern of infectious disease and the counterintuitive rise in nutritional disease that were seen in *Paleopathology at the Origins of Agriculture* and now in *The Backbone of History* was not the primary objective of the original research design. *Origins* grew out of a discussion that George Armelagos and Mark N. Cohen had after the publication *of The Food Crisis in Prehistory* (Cohen 1977) and the reports that showed a decline in health after the shift to an agricultural subsistence base at Dickson Mounds. Cohen had argued that the population increase during the Mesolithic stimulated the Neolithic revolution. If this were the case, evidence of nutritional deficiencies should be evident preceding the shift to agriculture. Cohen and Armelagos discussed a research design that would test these alternative hypotheses. The methodology that uses multiple stress indicators in a bioarchaeological context to test hypotheses is the most significant contribution of *Paleopathology at the Origins of Agriculture*.

The Backbone of History examines more than 12,500 individuals from 65 sites in the Western Hemisphere. For the studies reported in this volume, researchers developed and applied Mark I, a health index, in conjunction with the length of life to compare differences in adaptation. The index, which is an innovative measure of health, represents one of the first attempts to develop a tool for systematically and objectively comparing populations.

The index incorporates three important features: multiple indicators, age adjustment, and severity of the lesion. The lesions that are included in the index affect both children (linear enamel hypoplasia, stature, anemia) and adults (dental deficiencies, degenerative joint disease), and two affect all classes (trauma and infection). While the individual is the unit that is scored, the unit of analysis can be the individual or groups of individuals. Because of difficulties using the individual-level index, the comparisons reported in this volume include groups of Native Americans, European-Americans, and African-Americans.

The exciting aspect of the Mark I index is the ability to provide age-specific measures of each of its components. In addition, the researcher can compute estimated quality-adjusted life-years that provide a means to measure the impact of pathology in ways that have not been previously available.

There are a number of problems with computing the index that are inherent in the analysis of all skeletal populations. As with all measures of skeletal pathologies, the bones do not show evidence of acute diseases that quickly cause death. In addition, the incomplete skeletons are problematic when computing the Mark I index. Since the number of complete skeletons varies between sites (one-half of the 12,500 skeletons in the present study were incomplete), it was necessary to aggregate the data for each site.

While we do have some caveats about the use of the index, we are impressed with it as a work in progress and by the editors' commitment to refining the index. Our concern is that some researchers will see the computation of the Mark I index as an end in itself. Some researchers may compute the index and "quit early" by not doing what the editors describe as the "microanalysis." It is the microanalysis that will reveal what the index means by comparing it with the index in other populations. In addition, the index does not reveal the mortality cost of childhood lesions. Goodman and Armelagos (1988) showed that the occurrence of enamel hypoplasia in individuals may have as much as a nine-year reduction in mean age-at-death. Does the occurrence of enamel hypoplasias have such a dramatic effect in all populations?

If skeletal lesions are the first element in assessing health of the population, the second is the use of length of life. Life expectancy and issues related to the use of life tables go back a quarter of a century (Moore et al. 1975). Although there has been criticism of the methods in paleodemography that claims it as a "dead" topic (Bocquet-Appel and Masset 1982, 1985a, 1985b), the response (Greene, et al. 1986; Van Gerven and Armelagos 1983) suggests that it still is a useful research tool.

We are still refining the use of life tables and attempting to incorporate population growth and sample size in understanding difference in mortality. McCaa and Johansson and Owsley grapple with the theoretical issues and model ways to deal with these problems by using various measures of population growth in the context of bioarchaeology. We find the relationship between life expectancy and the Mark I health index in the material from the Western Hemisphere most interesting. While little of the variance is explained by the regression analysis, it does open up an innovative method for comparing these variables. The editors use these tools to test out the issues raised in the "osteological paradox" (Wood et al. 1992), which suggests that "better health" makes for "sicker" skeletons. The "paradox" claims that sicker individuals die earlier; the extra years lived by the healthier individuals give them more time to develop pathologies. Steckel and Rose show that the "osteological paradox" is not a general phenomenon, and they discuss the particular contexts in which the paradox will be evident.

The critical problem that remains to be resolved is the issue of sampling. In a sense, the large samples may "smooth" the problems of differences in the quality of excavation and curation, but questions are likely to remain in large comparative studies.

The Backbone of History will provide grist for the seminar mill for decades to come. It is interesting to see how the Mark I index enhances population comparisons from regions that were dealt with in *Paleopathology at the Origins of Agriculture*. Native American populations from Georgia, the Ohio River Valley, the American Southwest, and the Great Plains are represented in both volumes, and the regional summaries are a valuable addition to our knowledge. *The Backbone of History* provides more in-depth discussions of South and Central America. One of the most exciting contributions comes with the addition of European-American and African-American populations. We are now in a position to deal with such issues as inequality and its effect on health and disease (Goodman et al. 1995). This volume represents a "benchmark" for further studies and will forever remove any notion that the skeleton is a "dried-up" topic.

THE FUTURE

Steckel and Rose's proposal to expand the present study to include populations from throughout the world population offers an opportunity to examine issues in a broader context. For example, it provides an opportunity to examine epidemiological transition (Armelagos and Barnes 1999; Armelagos et al. 1996; Barnes et al. 1999; Barrett et al. 1998). A. R. Omran's (1971) concept of epidemiological transition refers to the shift from acute infectious diseases to chronic noninfectious, degenerative diseases. The increasing prevalence of these chronic diseases is related to the medical practices that lengthen life. Cultural and economic advances have resulted in a larger percentage of individuals reaching the oldest age segment of the population. Armelagos and co-workers (Armelagos and Barnes 1999) broaden the concept of epidemiological transition to include dramatic shifts in disease patterns in prehistory and contemporary society.

From the standpoint of health history, we can consider three epidemiological transitions. The first corresponded to a universally completed transition from food gathering to food production (the so-called Neolithic revolution). Although it occurred in multiple locations, and in slow, complex ways, this transition had revolutionary implications for subsequent human life on the planet. The Neolithic revolution both allowed and required population growth and increasing levels of social inequality.

It is a bit too simple to say that the Neolithic revolution was "*the worst mistake in the history of the human race*" (Diamond 1987). Certainly food production was a huge economic change that was associated with sedentary settlement patterns and population growth. The Neolithic revolution also marked the evolution of social stratification. It is difficult to overemphasize the importance of social stratification for health – either in prehistory or the present. The second epidemiological transition (the shift from infectious to chronic disease as the primary cause of mortality) has occurred only in certain developed societies. The second epidemiological transition was related to an overall decline in mortality that is a key aspect of the "demographic transition" (Caldwell 1982).

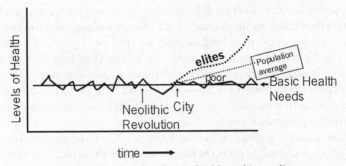

Figure 21.1. Cultural evolution, health, and inequality.

Human populations have recently moved into the third epidemiological transition, marked by the dawn of the end of the antibiotic era, in which there is a reemergence of infectious diseases that are often resistant to multiple antibiotics. Furthermore, the emergence of new diseases has a global impact. It is clear that infectious diseases remain an enormous problem for human populations. The World Health Organization (WHO) reports that of the 50 million deaths each year, 17.5 million are the result of infectious and parasitic disease. WHO states that 2 billion people in the world are infected with hepatitis B virus, 1.7 million have tuberculosis, and 30 million people are infected with HIV.

The Backbone of History provides the tools to examine the relationship between changing levels of socioeconomic inequality and health from an evolutionary perspective. The central question is what analysis of changing patterns of health/disease and social organization in the prehistoric past can tell us about processes and prospects of "struggling for health" in the contemporary world. There are important lessons to be learned, even if they are not very encouraging. Inequalities in health and wealth may have evolutionary roots, but such inequalities are not inevitable.

Inequalities that arose in post-Neolithic societies have accelerated with advances in technology (see Figure 21.1). The acceleration of social inequality between societies resulted in the improved health (for a minority of the world's population) of the second epidemiological transition. Ironically, the continued growth of inequality has also resulted in the acceleration of emerging and reemerging disease prevalences of the third epidemiological transition. The globalization of disease during a period that may see the end of the antibiotic era creates even greater danger. It is important to recognize that the economic gap between classes within society and differences in wealth among societies continue to widen and that these disparities have serious health implications. The prospects for closing the socioeconomic gaps within and between nations seem remote in the present world order.

An evolutionary perspective allows us to examine the relationship between health and wealth, disease and poverty, as part of continuing historical processes that have affected thousands of human generations. Social stratification originally evolved because it brought health benefits to emerging elites; in general, these benefits came at the expense of the poor.

When organisms utilize others as continuing sources of energy and food, we can characterize that relationship as parasitism. Disease organisms are microparasites that use the energy of the their host for their survival and reproduction; the "best" parasites live for a long time before ultimately killing their hosts. Similarly, social stratification, within societies and between them, is an evolutionary strategy that has been called "macroparasitism" (Brown 1987; McNeill 1976). Macroparasitism is a cultural process that institutionalizes and legitimizes the exploitation of the poor by powerful people in their own society.

With historical technological change has come an evolutionary tendency for the gap between the rich and the poor, the healthy and the sick, to increase. The widening gap occurs both within societies and between societies. In the twenty-first century, the gap between those on the top and the bottom of the social hierarchy is greater than ever before in human history, and it has serious health implications. While disease and death are inevitable parts of life, the major cause of unnecessary, premature, preventable disease and death is simple – it is the lack of access to adequate food, water, hygiene, and medical care, which is caused by an overall lack of resources.

The world's biggest killer and greatest cause of ill health and suffering is listed almost at the end of the International Classification of Disease (ICD). It is given in code Z59.5 – extreme poverty. Max Weber's definition of social class hinged on the notion of differential "life chances." Health indicators of morbidity, mortality, and life expectancy are therefore appropriate measures of "life chances" that vary inversely with wealth.

Of course, with this WHO ICD classification there is the question: what is *extreme* poverty? Extreme – compared to what? Certainly, basic human needs of food, water, adequate shelter, access to health care, and adequate social support might allow us to make a minimal definition. The World Bank estimates that 3 billion people in the world live on less than $2 a day. But is it appropriate or advantageous in considering health indicators to think of relative deprivation?

This is not a new idea. The downward spiral of disease and poverty ("poor are sicker, and they become sicker because they are poor") has been used as a rationale for investments in public health for the past 60 years. The implication is that a public health intervention (removing an environmental impediment to health) would reverse this into an upward spiral of health and wealth – an example is the "malaria blocks development model" (Brown 1997). Recently, Gallup and Sachs (http://www2.cid.harvard.edu/cidpapers/mal_wb.pdf) have demonstrated again, *on the level of cross-national data*, that such diseases as malaria carry a heavy economic burden that limits the possibility of economic growth in malaria-prone nations.

The positive correlation between health and per capita income is one of the most important indicators of modern development (Bloom and Canning 2000). Higher income provides better nutrition, safer water, and greater access to health care. Bloom and Canning suggest a converse in which development is linked to better health by increasing productivity, education, investment in physical capital, and a "demographic dividend." Improved health is seen as a key to third world development.

It is important not to romanticize the health conditions of food foragers – their diet was low in saturated fats and high in vitamin C, but life expectancy at birth was also quite low. They did not live in the "upper paleoterrific." Bioarchaeologists and paleopathologists in *Backbone* have shown that there was considerable variation in measures of nutritional stress in gatherer-hunters and agriculturalists. It is precisely this type of analysis that Cohen and Armelagos had hoped would be the outgrowth of *Paleopathology at the Origins of Agriculture*. Steckel and Rose have provided an innovative analysis that will continue to be discussed by even the next generation of anthropologists, historians, and economists.

We have already alluded to the use of backbone in the title of this book. Backbone literally and figuratively describes the contribution that the editors and contributors have made to the study of bioarchaeology in this volume and the potential it offers for the future. The sacrum forms the foundation of the backbone. The etymology of this word is from the Latin translation of the Greek word for sacred. The ancients literally believed that the sacrum played a role in resurrection since it survived after death. While we cannot attest to the success of the divine resurrections of the "cast of thousands" whose remains were studied in these pages, we can certainly vouch for the scientific "resurrection" that the bioarchaeologists have made in providing insights into the lives of these individuals long after their deaths. The contributors to this book have put "flesh" on their bones in a way even their gods might not have contemplated.

REFERENCES

Armelagos, George J. 1994. Review of *Human Paleopathology: Current Synthesis and Future Options*, ed. Donald J. Ortner and Arthur C. Aufderheide. *Journal of Field Archeaology* 21:239–243.

Armelagos, George J., and Kathleen Barnes. 1999. The Evolution of Human Disease and the Rise of Allergy: Epidemiological Transitions. *Medical Anthropology* 18(2): 187–213.

Armelagos, George J., Kathleen C. Barnes, and James Lin. 1996. Disease in Human Evolution: The Re-emergence of Infectious Disease in the Third Epidemiological Transition. *AnthroNotes* 18(3):1–7.

Armelagos, George J., David S. Carlson, and Dennis P. Van Gerven. 1982. The Theoretical Foundation of Development of Skeletal Biology. In *A History of Physical Anthropology, 1930–1980*, ed. F. Spencer, pp. 305–328. New York: Academic Press.

Armelagos, George J., and Dennis P. Van Gerven. 1993. "Paleopathologist as Detective: Disease and Death in Prehistory." In *Ela' Qua: Essays in Honor of Richard Woodbury*, ed. Dorothy Schlotthauer Krass, R. Brooke Thomas, and John W. Cole, pp. 269–282. Research Report 28, Anthropology Department, University of Massachusetts, Amherst

Barnes, Kathleen C., George J. Armelagos, and Steven C. Morreale. 1999. Darwinian Medicine and the Emergence of Allergy. In *Evolutionary Medicine*, ed. W. Trevethan, J. McKenna, and E. O. Smith. New York: Oxford University Press.

Barrett, R., C. Kuzawa, T. McDade, and G. J. Armelagos. 1998. Emerging Infectious Disease and the Third Epidemiological Transition. In *Annual Review of Anthropology*, ed. W. Durham. Palo Alto: Annual Reviews Inc.

Bloom, David E., and David Canning. 2000. The Health and Wealth of Nations. *Science* 287(5456):1207–1209.

Bocquet-Appel, J.P., and C. Masset. 1982. Farewell to Paleodemography. *Journal of Human Evolution* 11:321–333.

    1985a. Paleodemography: Resurrection or Ghost? *Journal of Human Evolution* 14:107–111.

    1985b. Small Populations: Demography and Paleoanthropological Inferences. *Journal of Human Evolution* 14:683–691.

Brown, P. J. 1987. Microparasites and Macroparasites. *Cultural Anthropology* 2:155–171.

    1997. Malaria *Miseria* and Underdevelopment in Sardinia: "Malaria Block Development" Cultural Models. *Medical Anthropology* 18:272–297.

Caldwell, John. 1982. *Theory of Fertility Decline.* San Francisco: Academic Press.

Cohen, M. N. 1977. *The Food Crisis in Prehistory.* New Haven, Conn.: Yale University Press.

Cohen, Mark N., and George J. Armelagos, eds. 1984. *Paleopathology at the Origins of Agriculture.* Orlando, Fla.: Academic Press.

Diamond, Jared. 1987. The Worst Mistake in the History of the Human Race. *Discover* 8(5):64–66.

Eckert, W. n.d. *International References on Paleopathology.* Wichita, Kans.: The International Reference Organization in Forensic Medicine.

Goodman, Alan H., and George J. Armelagos. 1988. Childhood Stress and Decreased Longevity in Prehistoric Populations. *American Anthropologist* 90(4):936–944.

Goodman, Alan H., Debra L. Martin, and George J. Armelagos. 1995. The Biological Consequences of Inequality in Prehistory. *Rivista di Anthropologia (Roma)* 73:123–131.

Greene, D. L., D. P. Van Gerven, and G. J. Armelagos. 1986. Life and Death in Ancient Populations: Bones of Contention in Paleodemography. *Human Evolution* 1(3): 193–207.

Lasker, Gabriel W. 1970. Physical Anthropology: Search for General Process and Principles. *American Anthropologist* 72(1–8).

McNeill, William H. 1976. *Plagues and Peoples.* New York: Anchor Books, Doubleday.

Moore, James A., Alan C. Swedlund, and George J. Armelagos. 1975. The Use of the Life Table in Paleodemography in Population Studies in Archaeology and Biological Anthropology, ed. Alan C. Swedlund. Society for American Archaeology, Memoir 30:57–70. *American Antiquity* 40(2): Part 2.

Omran, A. R. 1971. The Epidemiologic Transition: A Theory of the Epidemiology of Population Change. *Millbank Memorial Fund Quarterly* 49(4):509–537.

Ortner, Donald J., and Arthur C. Aufderheide. 1991. Introduction. In *Human Paleopathology: Current Syntheses and Future Options,* ed. Donald J. Ortner and A. C. Aufderheide, pp. 1–2. Washington, D.C.: Smithsonian Institution Press.

Platt, John R. 1964. Strong Inference. *Science* 146(3642):347–353.

Van Gerven, Dennis, and George J. Armelagos. 1983. Farewell to Paleodemography? Reports of Your Death Have Been Greatly Exaggerated. *Journal of Human Evolution* 12:353–360.

Washburn, Sherwood L. 1953. The Strategy of Physical Anthropology. In *Anthropology Today,* ed. A. L. Kroeber, pp. 714–727. Chicago: University of Chicago Press.

Wood, J. M., G. R. Milner, H. C. Harpending, and K. M. Weiss. 1992. The Osteological Paradox: Problems of Inferring Prehistoric Health from Skeletal Samples. *Current Anthropology* 33:343–370.

CHAPTER TWENTY-TWO

Overspecialization and Remedies

Philip D. Curtin

This volume represents a significant effort to solve one of the most pressing problems of intellectual life today. The explosion of knowledge, sometimes called the data revolution, has tended to force the individual into narrower and narrowed fields of specialization. This tendency is not merely the influence of the Internet or other electronic means of storing and distributing knowledge; it goes back a century and more. Electronic technology provides some relief in the form of easier access to what is known, but the problem is far from solved. Its most obvious manifestation over the past half century is the explosion of libraries trying to keep up with the flow of information.

At the same time, people are no more intelligent or able than they ever were. The dominant solution is to specialize, and increasingly, scholars in all fields are forced to limit the span of their knowledge in order to master some part of the vast assemblage available.

Much the same narrowing has occurred in the way fields of knowledge are defined within academic institutions. Two centuries ago, it was possible to be a "naturalist," taking an interest in almost anything that falls today under the category of biology and more. Today, such a span would be labeled dilettantism, and it is both rare and little respected. Clinical medicine became a separate professional category even earlier, and it has continued to separate into ever more numerous fields of subspecialization. Over the past century, nonclinical biological sciences have also subdivided, the widest gap being that between cellular and whole-animal biology, with ecology occupying another kind of niche in its effort to study the interaction of several species in one environment.

A similar development has taken place in anthropology. Beginning as a broad study of humankind, mostly humankind at a distance, it has subdivided into the present archaeology, linguistics, bioanthropology, and a variety of approaches to social and cultural anthropology. The same tendency toward overspecialization is present in history and economics.

This overspecialization is probably inevitable, given the expansion of knowledge and the limitations of the human intellect. It is also valuable as a route to even greater expansion of knowledge, but it carries severe limitations as well. It deprives scholars and scientists of the breadth of span they need in order to ask the most pertinent new questions, and the institutional definitions of fields of knowledge limit the individual's ability to cross over the boundaries in order to answer some of those important questions.

The project represented by this volume is, therefore, an important demonstration of what can be accomplished by asking questions and seeking answers that would be impossible either to ask or to answer within the framework of a single discipline. The editors represent two of the subdivisions within economics and anthropology, respectively – economic anthropology and economic history – and the project grew out of the interaction of recent developments within each of these fields.

On the side of economic history, recent decades have seen a marked movement away from institutional history and toward sophisticated quantification, sometimes called cliometrics. The chapter by Richard Steckel, Paul Sciulli, and Jerome Rose, "A Health Index from Skeletal Remains," represents an application of these new methods to a body of data drawn from the work of bioanthropologists.

From the side of anthropology, bioanthropology, beginning in the later 1960s, developed a whole array of new techniques for the analysis of the human condition from the study of skeletal remains. These new techniques are outlined by Alan H. Goodman and Debra Martin in their chapter on "Reconstructing Health Profiles from Skeletal Remains." The early work using these methods consisted of individual efforts with no common and recognized standard of measurement that could lead to comparative conclusions. This project added the important further step of reanalyzing the various collections of skeletal data so that each analysis meets such a standard.

The great strength of this project is that, of biological measures of the human condition, skeletal material is the best evidence available to indicate changes over the long run. A further strength is that it incorporates the best of the new methodology, both mathematical analysis from the side of economics and the new techniques applied by a distinguished group of bioanthropologists.

This said, the fact remains that the problem of assessing the quality of life over a period of a millennium and more, and in very different kinds of societies, is daunting. Although some of the authors occasionally appear to overstate the strength of the case they can make, they are also careful to indicate the limitations of the evidence. They recognize that skeletal material is the best comparative evidence we have for the human condition over such a long period of time, but it is not perfect.

All historical investigation is more imperfect than historians usually indicate; they imply without an overt claim that their accounts are the whole truth about the past – or at least the whole truth about what is important. One important by-product of overspecialization in historical studies is the confinement of the investigations of most historians to the questions they can answer with a particular kind of evidence.

Intellectual and cultural historians specialize in critical interpretation of texts, and they quarrel mightily about the meaning of texts – a tendency that adds fuel to the postmodern deconstruction borrowed from literary criticism. Political and military historians have another kind of reading of what is important that sometimes limits their accounts to a surface level of public life and leaves more fundamental changes in human society out of account. Economic historians have other limits to the evidence they are likely to consult, and they often have more faith in mathematical manipulation of their data than other historians are willing to credit.

These biases, if they really are biases, are part of the problem underlying all investigation. It is not possible to investigate everything at once, nor to tell the "whole truth" in history or any field of inquiry. This consideration applies to the present project as well. The authors are asking a limited question with the aid of an admittedly limited body of evidence, and their work can only be judged on that basis. Critics sometimes find fault with a work for not asking other questions than it seeks to answer. While it may be true that any body of investigators could better have spent their time doing something altogether different, that is not a legitimate criticism of the work at hand.

One can nevertheless seek to evaluate the way in which the evidence and conclusions of a project like this one fit into current thought about broader patterns of world history. There is emerging a tripartite division on human history into three periods – a preagricultural age, an agricultural age, and an industrial age. The precise chronological divisions will be different in different societies, but it is increasingly clear that the introduction of agriculture beginning about 10,000 years ago made an enormous difference in how humans conducted their affairs. Agriculture led in time to denser populations, literacy, and urban societies – with changes that are sometimes lumped together under the term "civilization."

The beginning of an industrial age in the most advanced regions of the world was clear by the nineteenth century. The industrial age was not created merely by the smokestack industries its name implies. It had many roots in differing technologies that made possible a marked and continuing upward trend in income per capita. Increasing crop yields meant that the majority of the people were no longer required for agricultural labor. Improving health conditions led to declines in mortality, which meant that the fertility rate necessary to sustain the population was reduced to a fraction of the preindustrial level. This, in turn, freed women to take up new roles in society, and the list of important changes that followed with the industrial age could be multiplied.

With each of these major transitions, the pace of technological change accelerated. It was faster in the agricultural age than it had been in the preagricultural, and it was faster still in the industrial period. What was sometimes known as the Industrial Revolution was not an acceleration followed by a new stability; it was a new pace of technological change that has continued to the present.

Each of these transitions is reflected in human skeletal changes. The physical deterioration of humans with the introduction of agriculture has been well known since the publication, in 1984, of Mark Cohen and George Armelagos's *Paleopathology at the Origins of Agriculture*,[1] and numerous bodies of data in these pages confirm their

---

[1] (New York: Academic Press).

findings. Yet although humans became physically worse-off in marked respects, they also began to be more numerous. The agricultural age made possible far denser populations, but less healthy ones than ever before. Historians, anthropologists, and others concerned with this apparent paradox are still exploring its implications in detail.

The next transition, to the industrial age, made far more difference in humans' physical well-being. The studies in this volume represent almost entirely the "before" aspect of the changes accompanying the industrial age. Even the nineteenth-century examples date from a period before the full benefits of modern medicine were realized. None of them show the "after" patterns, but common knowledge of present conditions can highlight the change. Many things we take for granted, such as modern dentistry, come into sharp focus when we read in these reports about the suffering of our ancestors. Recent life expectancy at birth in developed countries is more than 70 years, decades longer than the best recorded from this skeletal evidence – or any other evidence, for that matter. Perhaps the moral of this story is that skeletal evidence is the best we have for the human condition in the long run, but other kinds of evidence are a better guide to the recent past.

Still another aspect of world history illuminated by these studies is sometimes known as the "Columbus problem," which received special attention at the time of the quincentenary celebrations around 1992, centered on the disastrous epidemiological consequences of contact across the Atlantic. The fact of these epidemics is undoubted. The problem of interpretation often centered on a question of blame, as though the humans involved at the time had the slightest idea of what was going on biologically.

One by-product of these discussions, however, was a view that the New World before contact with the Old was virtually free of disease, and that this happy condition was only interrupted by the European and African diseases introduced by Columbus and his successors. Smallpox, yellow fever, and malaria, the most devastating of the newly introduced diseases, leave little or no trace on the skeleton of their victims. In spite of this weakness in skeletal evidence, other skeletal evidence of the physical well-being of the pre-Columbian Americas shows conclusively that however much it may have deteriorated on contact with the outer world, it was far from paradisiacal before the Europeans and Africans arrived.

The contribution of these studies to the Columbus problem highlights the strength and some of the weaknesses of this particular kind of interdisciplinary research. It also suggests other possible avenues of productive interdisciplinary effort. It is mainly a matter of what questions are asked. The valuable new question asked by this volume is implied by the title of the methodological essay (Chapter 2), "Reconstructing Health Profiles from Skeletal Remains." Broadening the question still further, to take in a greater variety of evidence, might make possible an even broader reconstruction of the physical environment in which humans were forced to operate in this long period of time.

Other scientists can contribute greatly to knowledge about the human condition by means of studies of the environmental and human ecology as it changed through time. The field broadly called paleoecology is concerned with these changes, studied by means of a number of techniques using evidence from the geological record, tree rings, core samples of pollen taken from sediment, or samples of glaciers or ice deposits like the Greenland icecap.

One of the most impressive changes in recent decades has come about through the study of core drillings under bodies of water that reveal strata of pollen deposits, annually over time,[2] which sometimes makes possible the tracing of vegetation changes in a region over a long period. Combined with other evidence from historical climatology, these core drillings make it possible for scientists to trace a broad pattern of the physical environment within which humans had to lead their lives. These studies are on a different time scale from those derived from skeletal remains, but they suggest an avenue that can be profitably explored to answer broad questions about the human condition.

Still another set of disciplinary approaches relevant to the human condition on a shorter time scale comes from nutritionists. Several of the studies in this volume pay appropriate attention to nutrition as a background circumstance, but it is rarely central to the inquiry. The recent and massive *Cambridge World History of Food*[3] illustrates the wealth of information available.

Historical epidemiology has an even closer relevance to the skeletal data. Epidemiology, of course, covers the whole range of health problems that are revealed in the skeletal evidence, including accidents. Historical epidemiologists, however, depend almost entirely on literary evidence, which is comparatively strong for diseases that leave no skeletal evidence, such as malaria, but weak for other conditions, such as dental problems, which, regardless of their importance, leave little written evidence, perhaps because they are less often fatal.

It would be a valuable test of the comparative value of the evidence from the bioanthropologists and from the written record if the two could be combined in examining the health of the same population. Few of the collections of skeletal evidence in this volume, however, are covered by equivalent written evidence, but the question asked could be rephrased, perhaps, to take fuller account of the rich resources of literary epidemiological evidence.

The most carefully recorded and valuable body of medical evidence from the United States in the nineteenth century is in the military records of the Surgeon General. They record the health only of males in the prime of life, but their data can be used for the comparative light they throw on other segments of the population. These records begin with Thomas Lawson, of the Surgeon General's Office, *Statistical Report on the Sickness and Mortality in the Army of the United States*,[4] which covers the period 1819 to 1839. The tradition continued with the Surgeon General's annual statistical reports on the health of the army from then onward.

---

[2] A series of articles published together under the heading "Paleoecology" in *Late-Quaternary Environments on the United States*. Volume 2. *The Holocene*, edited by H. E. Wright, Jr. (Minneapolis: University of Minnesota Press, 1983), pp. 109–268, illustrates the general conclusions reached by such studies up to that time. Major developments have followed since then, and they can be pursued through the technical literature in the several fields.

[3] Kenneth F. Kiple and Kreimhild Coneè Ornelas, eds., 2 vols. (New York: Cambridge University Press, 2000).

[4] 3 vols. (Washington, 1840–1860).

To be used properly, the data from paleoecology, the nutritionists, or the historical epidemiologists would require asking new questions, just as Steckel and Rose have asked new questions to combine the recent methodological achievements of economic history and bioanthropology. Perhaps the lesson to be drawn from this valuable combination is that even more is needed to cut across the tight and ever-narrowing disciplinary bounds that affect academic life at the beginning of the century.

Index